Native Americans

Volume II

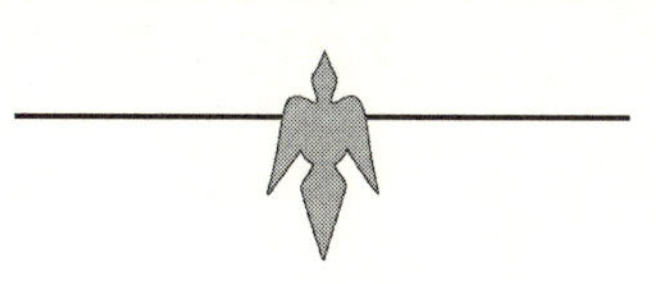

Native Americans

An Encyclopedia of History, Culture, and Peoples

Volume II

Barry M. Pritzker

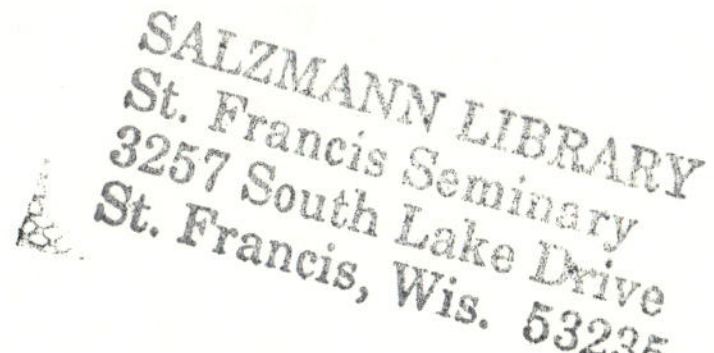

ABC-CLIO
Santa Barbara, California
Denver, Colorado
Oxford, England

Library of Congress Cataloging-in-Publication Data
Pritzker, Barry.
Native Americans : an encyclopedia of history, culture, and peoples / Barry M. Pritzker.
p. cm.
Includes bibliographical references and idex.
ISBN 0-87436-836-7 (alk. paper)
1. Indians of North America. I. Title.
E77.P89 1998
970.004'97—DC21 98-21718
CIP

05 04 03 02 01 00 99 10 9 8 7 6 5 4 3 2

ABC-CLIO, Inc.
130 Cremona Drive, P.O. Box 1911
Santa Barbara, California 93116-1911

Typesetting by Letra Libre

This book is printed on acid-free paper ♾.
Manufactured in the United States of America

Contents

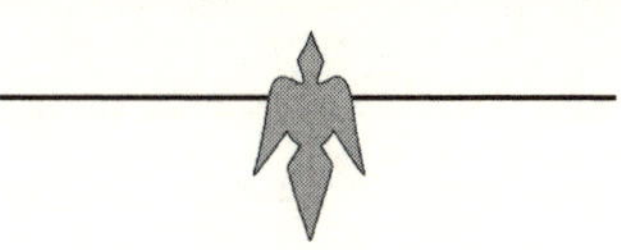

Chapter Six

The Great Plains

Right: A calumet and a beaded pouch for carrying it.
Far right: The medicine man Sitting Bull.

Above: Kea-Boat, a member of the Kiowas, holds a rattle and feather fan used in the Peyote ceremony.
Below: Religious activities among Dakota Indians included vision quests and ritual purification in the sweat lodge.

Great Plains

Indians living on the Great Plains shared both a physical environment and, to a large degree, a lifestyle. Their natural resources changed relatively little from thousands of years ago until the late nineteenth century, when the great buffalo herds were destroyed. Wanton elimination of the roughly 30 million buffalo, in addition to millions more deer, antelope, and other game, brought an end to the Plains lifestyle as well, centered as it was, particularly after the various bands and tribes acquired horses, around the great, shaggy beasts.

The Great Plains is generally defined as a region of about 1.5 million square miles between the Mississippi River and the Rocky Mountains and from central Alberta and Saskatchewan to central Texas. The region's greatest river is the Missouri, which is fed by tributary rivers and streams originating in the Rocky Mountains. The lower area between the Mississippi and roughly 100 degrees longitude constitutes prairie rather than true high plains, which in the west may range up to a mile or more in altitude. For comparative cultural purposes, however, the prairie region is usually discussed as part of the Great Plains.

Climatologically, the high plains is a relatively dry region—the average 15 inches of annual rainfall did not permit native agriculture as did the better-watered and more humid prairie. The plains' generally flat terrain allows frigid polar air to enter the region in winter, whereas summers are often stiflingly hot. Dramatic weather events, from tornadoes and severe thunderstorms to blizzards, are regular occurrences. Grasses covered the region, shorter in the west and longer and more lush in the prairie.

In addition to grasses, cactus and sage grow in the western plains. Stands of trees, often willow, oak, box elder, and cottonwood, are found mostly in the

Native Americans of the Great Plains

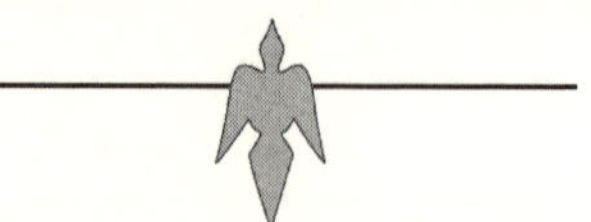

With the arrival of the horse in the late seventeenth to mid–eighteenth century, "classic" Plains Indian culture began to come into its own. This 1837 illustration shows a horseback hunt.

river valleys. Scrub cedar and juniper dot prominent features like mesas and cliffs, whereas deciduous and coniferous trees grow in the lower Rockies. A number of wild vegetable plants and fruits also grew in the region.

The horse, which came from the Spanish settlements in the south and west, represented a foreign influence on Indians of the Great Plains. Other influences, such as guns, soon followed, and non-native diseases, which rivaled and perhaps exceeded the horse in changing Indian circumstances, stalked the people from the sixteenth century on. Thus non-Indian influences were indispensable to the "classic" phase of Plains Indian culture, which lasted for about 100 to 250 years. Despite heroic resistance, however, by the late nineteenth century that culture—and more—was gone. Yet, like many other Indians, descendants of the prehistoric inhabitants of the Great Plains are determined to survive and prosper as Native Americans in twenty-first-century America.

The first bands of hunter-gatherers moved onto the Great Plains perhaps 40,000 years ago. About 10,000 years ago, as the last ice sheets melted and the Plains became drier, grass began to cover the region. Ancient species such as the horse, camel, mammoth, and bison disappeared and were gradually replaced by smaller bison from Mexico. Hunters found and killed these animals in accustomed watering places, but they were not yet able to pursue them freely across the vast expanse of the Plains.

Early prehistoric people stored wild fruits and vegetables in underground caches, and some people began to grow a few crops. Vast networks that focused on the exchange of goods and complex religious practices operated on the Plains during the first millennium, centered in the Ohio Valley Adena-Hopewell culture. But as the region became ever drier and less hospitable, the nomadic bands slowly followed the game and the water eastward until, by perhaps 1200, the Plains were virtually empty of human habitation.

Shortly after this period, however, a moderation in weather conditions combined with severe drought in the Southwest led to the gradual repopulation of the Plains. The people were drawn in part by the presence of buffalo and other game and, at least in the beginning, by the possibility of settlement without conquest. Caddoan tribes in east Texas, such as the Pawnee, may have been among the first to reenter the Plains. Shortly thereafter, Athapaskan bands from northern Canada began migrating southward along the eastern Rockies.

With the exception of the Kiowa and Comanche, the Shoshonean-speaking peoples remained on the western fringes of the Plains in the seventeenth century. Some of the agricultural Siouan peoples, motivated partly by aggressive Iroquois expansion and the dynamics of the French fur trade, migrated west from the Ohio Valley to the Mississippi and Missouri Valley regions, reaching the high plains in successive waves between the sixteenth and the nineteenth centuries. Late in the 1700s they composed about half of the total population of the Great Plains. Finally, Algonquian-speaking Indians such as the Cheyennes and Blackfeet arrived from the east between the sixteenth and eighteenth centuries.

Before the horse transformed life on the Plains, dogs pulled the travois. Buffalo were generally killed by driving them over cliffs or surrounding them on foot and shooting into the confused mass of animals. Even later, buffalo and other animals might be killed in this way or, especially in winter, by individual stalking.

With the arrival of the horse, generally in the late seventeenth to mid–eighteenth century, "classic" Plains Indian culture began to come into its own. Horses allowed the people to acquire more food by

traveling farther and faster after buffalo. Horse-drawn travois also increased overall mobility and thus people's ability to follow the herds. Plains Indians soon became among the most skilled horsemen the world has ever seen. At their best, using only a modified halter, they could ride low enough over a horse's flanks both to shield themselves while shooting their own arrows under the horse's neck and to pick up fallen comrades on the fly. They also rode expertly in the midst of thundering buffalo herds.

At that time, there were three types of Indian groups on the Plains. Those like the Blackfeet had no agricultural traditions. Those like the Teton Dakota (Lakota) traded a farming life for that of the nomad, and those like the Mandan and the southern Siouans continued to grow crops while also hunting buffalo and other game.

The nomadic tribes generally lived in conical tipis that were relatively lightweight, easily manufactured from products of the hunt, and portable. Women sewed together between 6 and 18 buffalo skins and stretched them over a frame of poles. Tipis were about 14 feet high and about 14 feet in diameter on the ground and held on average between five and eight people. An adjustable smoke hole at the top kept the tipi free of smoke and well ventilated. The unfastened, east-facing seam at the front was the door. The bottom could be staked or weighted down or rolled up for increased air circulation.

Sacred places that mirrored the cosmos, tipis contained an interior stone altar for burning incense during prayers. In winter, they were insulated with pelts added to the walls. Since the wind most often blew from the west, tipis were also slanted slightly to the east to decrease overall wind pressure. Decorations might represent war exploits or visions.

People living in permanent or semipermanent villages also used tipis on the hunt but otherwise lived in square or rectangular (later circular) earth lodges holding up to 40 or more people. They depended to a greater or lesser degree on corn, beans, squash, and sunflowers, and some also grew tobacco. Among these people, scattered settlements gave way in time to more consolidated villages, located on high bluffs overlooking river valleys. These villages were often

By 1900, non-Indians had deliberately and systematically destroyed the great buffalo herds. At this Dodge City, Kansas depot, 40,000 buffalo hides had been collected by one shipper alone (1885).

fortified by ditches and stockades. Both nomads and farmers ate large and small game such as buffalo, deer, elk, antelope, prairie chickens, and badgers, and most ate dogs, especially on special occasions. Some fished, and all gathered various wild nuts, fruits, and vegetables such as wild turnips and onions, gooseberries, and chokecherries.

Buffalo meat was eaten fresh or cut into strips, dried, and stored. Pemmican, consisting of cooked meat, fat, and berries, kept for months at least. Assuming that the buffalo herds were found during the autumn hunt, starvation was rarely a problem. Once the winter hit with its dangerous and unpredictable weather, the camp usually remained in a sheltered lowland location for up to five months. Horses could easily survive the winter on cottonwood bark.

Women made the clothing, generally from deer, mountain sheep, and/or buffalo skin. Tanning was an arduous process that consisted of stretching, scraping, treating (with a mixture of brains, fat, and other items), and soaking. Women wore a two-piece dress, with optional sleeves. For warmth, they also wore short leggings, moccasins, and buffalo robes. Men wore breechclouts and moccasins in warm weather, with a deerskin shirt, leggings, and a buffalo-hide robe in winter. Garments decorated with fringe and quillwork might reflect war honors. Plains Indians generally wore personal ornamentation such as necklaces and earrings made from bone, shell, hair, or feathers, as well as tattoos.

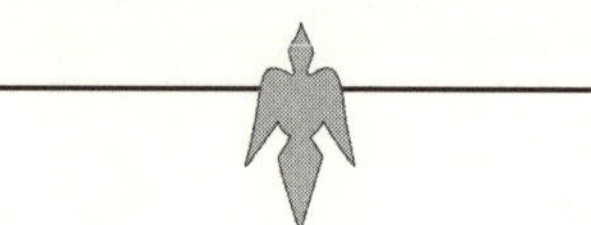

In addition to food, clothing, and shelter, the buffalo provided items such as bull-boats, parfleches, and other containers (hides and stomach); awls, hoes, and other tools (bones); rattles (hoof); bowstrings and thread (sinew); ropes and belts (hair); altars (skull); and spoons and cups (horn). The dried droppings even made excellent fuel. Other material items included saddles (although most people rode bareback) and riding gear, fish baskets and weirs, and elk antler or bone scrapers for tanning hides. Stone was also used as a raw material, particularly in earlier days. Plains Indians generally used two kinds of bow, a very fine one for buffalo hunting, and one for other purposes.

Plains Indians were noted for a wide-ranging artistic tradition. Ancient artifacts include birdstones and other items as early as 3000 B.C.E. and carved stone pipes as early as 700 C.E. More settled groups made pottery. Clothing and other items was decorated with porcupine-quill embroidery and, later, beadwork; both men and women painted leather goods such as tipis and parfleches.

For most Plains Indians, the circle was a sacred shape, the symbol of the interconnectedness of the universe. The sacred pipe, its bowl a circle, might be the property of one individual or the entire tribe. The use of a pipe in any kind of ceremony or agreement meant that an occasion was sacred and any associated vows or promises could not be broken. Sun and sky were foremost among a group of sacred natural beings and spirits known as *Wakan Tanka,* the Great Mystery.

Like many other Native Americans, Plains Indians also held vision quests, usually in a remote location and accompanied by personal deprivation. They took place only after purification in a sweat lodge and often at pivotal times, such as puberty or before war. Visions—also obtainable in dreams—were held to be direct communication with the world of sacred forces, which was considered ubiquitous. If successful, the vision quest resulted in the adoption of a guardian spirit.

Through their spirits, people received "medicine," or power, to be used in a variety of ways. Medicine often included certain behaviors, songs, and dances as well as the contents of a sacred bundle. Just as visions could benefit both individuals and the tribe as a whole, so also were medicine bundles the property of individuals or the entire tribe. Medicine bundles often conferred the power and the right to conduct a ceremony. They could be sold and the ceremonial rights transferred accordingly.

Although agricultural tribes conducted numerous ceremonies related to growing crops, the Sun Dance was the classic high plains Indian ceremony of the historic period. It originated during the early eighteenth century, although its antecedents predate that time. As the most important ceremony of the year, its purpose was to renew both nature and the well-being of the tribe. The dance was held in summer, when the various bands gathered for the communal buffalo hunt. During that period, the bands set up camp in a great circle, in which each band had a definite place and carefully proscribed behaviors. It was a time of socializing, courting, game playing, and generally reestablishing tribal unity.

Sponsored by a person seeking supernatural assistance, and led by a shaman, the Sun Dance itself lasted 12 days. Bands approached the Sun Dance circle over a four-day period. The four days following arrival of the bands was a time of ritual preparation. Marshals, children who would get their ears pierced, virginal female attendants, and people who obtained and prepared the Sacred Tree were all selected. This was a time of feasting and partying.

The ceremony itself took place over the following four days. It included mock battles with spirits, the "capture" and raising of the sacred tree and the mounting on it of a rawhide buffalo effigy, the erection of the sacred lodge, and sacred dancing and singing that included long periods of staring at the sun. As part of the ceremony, some tribes, such as the Teton Dakota, employed methods of self-torture, in which some participants implanted skewers in their chests or backs and danced until they ripped from the flesh. Other participants dragged buffalo skulls attached to skewers embedded in their chests around the field until the skewers ripped out. The purpose of the self-torture was to bring about visions for personal and tribal success.

Shamans, who were men and women possessing particularly powerful medicine, were intermediaries between the sacred and profane worlds. As such, they cured disease, helped people interpret their personal visions, and directed the hunt, since their powers were

believed to influence both the herds and the hunters' safety. In addition, some enjoyed varying degrees of political power. Shamanic priests, who received special training, played a key role in ceremonies.

With the necessities of life freely available, trade was not as well developed on the Plains as it was in some regions. Still, the development of a universal sign language greatly facilitated the exchange of goods, ideas, and information. Articles of the hunt were often exchanged for agricultural goods. Parfleches were a common item of trade, and even items from as far away as the Pacific Ocean (dentalium shells), the Great Lakes (copper), and the Gulf Coast (shells) were exchanged on the Plains. Two early trade centers were located at the Mandan and Arikara villages. After the seventeenth century, most trade items originated with non-natives. Chief among these (in addition to horses) were metal goods, guns, cloth, and beads.

Among the nomadic tribes especially, daring and bravery, particularly during the hunt and in raiding and war, were among the most important virtues. Military leadership was provided by a young man seeking glory. Plains Indian fighting was no less deadly than war ever is, yet warriors generally considered that the highest form of bravery was not killing an enemy but touching him, stealing his horse in a particularly daring way, or some other difficult and brave accomplishment. This custom was called counting coup, or war honors. Among most Plains tribes scalping, a custom that may have originated with the Spanish, did not merit a high war honor. Its importance lay primarily in representing the spiritual death of the victim.

War honors, which had to be publicly announced and accepted, were reflected in various articles of dress, such as feathers and types of shirt fringe. Eagle feathers symbolized the highest war honors. Warbonnets were worn only in parade, as a dress costume, with other highly decorated items. Shields, sacred by virtue of their designs, were normally kept covered.

The fundamental unit of Plains Indian society was the extended family. Bands or villages of variable constituency, composed of up to several hundred people of related families, formed the tribe. Some mostly semisedentary tribes also recognized clans and/or dual divisions. Bands only came together as a tribe in summer, when they united under a much more centralized political leadership to hunt, socialize, trade, raid, make war, and perform religious ceremonies. During these times, the camp police, composed of elite warrior societies, kept order and punished offenders, especially during the hunt. Among the nomadic peoples, bands often separated back into constituent families in winter.

Band and kin group chiefs, generally older men, had to have led lives characterized by generosity, bravery, proven ability in the hunt and in war, spiritual accomplishment, and honorable actions in every sphere. The position was honorific rather than authoritative. That is, the chief's authority stemmed from his stature and lasted only as long as he could command respect. Each band often contained more than one chief. Among some semisedentary tribes the chieftainship had hereditary elements. Bands were also led by a council of older men.

Men's, women's, and children's cultural or military societies had their own particular ceremonies, songs, insignias, dances, and medicine bundles. Open societies, generally age graded, could be entered by anyone of the proper age who could purchase admission. Closed societies could only be entered by invitation. Societies were associated with different levels of status. Outside of the societies, status, which was generally fairly fluid on the Plains, might also be obtained by being a shaman or a berdache. In the case of semisedentary groups, status also had a hereditary component.

Entry into womanhood was marked by isolation for several days while performing typical female work. A girl might acquire a vision during this time. If her parents could afford it, a feast and the distribution of gifts followed her seclusion. There were generally no formal puberty ceremonies for boys. A series of events, such as a boy's first successful buffalo hunt, first war party, and certainly first vision quest, marked his passage to manhood. Marriages could be arranged as a union between families, but many were romantic, and many stories attest to sweet flute serenades and secret rendezvous.

Certain near relatives, such as other-sex siblings and in-laws, were generally avoided out of respect. In Plains Indian society there was always an obligation to

provide for relatives; the extended family might number 30 people, each working to ensure the prosperity of the rest. Grandparents played a major role in culture transmittal and in day-to-day child rearing. Children were considered a blessing and were generally raised in what today might be considered a permissive manner. With the exception of the camp and hunt police, social order was generally maintained by peer pressure rather than any kind of systematic punishment. Early prehistoric traditions, particularly in the Ohio Valley, include mound burial. In later times, the dead were often buried in tree scaffolds or in the ground.

Even as the horse had transformed Plains Indian life, so disease epidemics—measles, influenza, and smallpox—decimated many Indian populations before the non-natives even arrived, thus setting up the "empty wilderness" that the latter came to covet. Beginning in the mid–nineteenth century, the presence of railroads and wagon trains disrupted the buffalo herds. Pioneers fought even friendly Indians. Their world under general attack, many of the warring tribes began to unite against the common enemy. Several major councils, particularly those at Fort Laramie in 1851 and 1868, produced treaties designed to strike a balance between Indian needs and non-native desires.

Later-nineteenth-century Plains Indian warfare retained its central role in ritual and status acquisition, but it also became a quest for survival and as such more brutal. Facing possible destruction and possessing superior horses and knowledge of the terrain, the Indians were successful at first. Ultimately, however, they were defeated by the sheer numbers of their opponents combined with their superior firepower.

The final "battle" took place on December 15, 1890, when U.S. soldiers wiped out up to 300 Indians, mostly women and children, at Wounded Knee, South Dakota. The massacre took place against the backdrop of the Ghost Dance, a new Indian religion that promised a return to a prewhite Indian paradise. The government had feared it could reignite widespread military resistance.

By 1900, non-Indians had deliberately and systematically destroyed the great buffalo herds. They had confined Plains Indians to reservations and taken most of their land. The 1877 Dawes Severalty Act was another major land-grab scheme as well as a frontal attack against the tribal way of life. The act allotted tribal land to individuals, the "surplus" (91 million acres total in the United States) to be opened to non-native purchase. Later, thousands of Indians lost their allotments through tax default.

Through missionaries, the government began a full-scale assault on Indian culture. Their means of subsistence gone and their traditional leaders killed or undermined, Plains Indians went into a long period of extreme transition. Their situation became characterized by dependence and poverty. In Canada, Plains Indians were forced to take up farming but were denied decent land, land ownership, credit, and even, without the permission of the government bureaucracy, the right to sell their produce.

Plains Indians in the United States were under similar pressures and faced similar difficulties. Furthermore, at least among the former nomads, agriculture was for a long time considered socially unacceptable. Plains Indians were individualists, but their ethic of generosity frustrated the efforts of government officials determined to make them more selfish. Toward this end, the government began removing Indian children, often by force, from the family environment and shipping them to violent, culture-killing boarding schools. Early in the twentieth century, the Peyote religion (Native American Church), with its origins in Mexico, became popular among several Plains Indian groups.

In the 1930s, the Dawes Act was superseded by the Wheeler-Howard Act, also known as the Indian Reorganization Act (IRA). Among other provisions, the IRA allowed Indians to set up constitutional governments. Although allowing Indians to deal government-to-government with the United States, the act also further undermined the traditional political structure. In the 1950s, the federal "termination" policy was designed to abrogate all treaties unilaterally. Also in the 1950s, the government again got into the business of forcibly relocating Indians, this time from reservations to urban centers. Ostensibly done in order to enhance economic opportunity, the result of this policy was the alienation of large numbers of Indians in urban

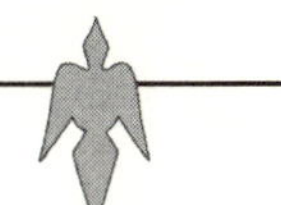

ghettos and their permanent loss to the reservation community.

Policies of the "self-determination" era of the 1960s and 1970s, combined with Great Society antipoverty programs, helped Plains Indians begin to pull away from chronic poverty. This era also saw renewed Indian activism. The American Indian Movement (AIM) encouraged Indians to throw off internal corruption while holding the federal government to its trust obligations. Several tribal colleges were begun. However, renewed funding cutbacks in the 1980s and 1990s negated some of these gains. Despite the rise of casino gambling on several reservations, poverty continues to stalk many Plains Indian communities. Most Indian reservations suffer from a lack of capital, and, with few exceptions, economic development remains an elusive goal.

Although Plains Indians have assimilated in varying degrees to mainstream society, many continue to lead lives deeply rooted in their cultural and spiritual traditions. Reservation life, although economically difficult, provides a vital focus for these activities. Many native Plains languages are in regular use. The Sun Dance, once banned with other "heathen" ceremonies, has reemerged in a modified version. Giveaways, traditional healing and other ceremonies, and art, craft, and aesthetic traditions remain very much alive and vital. The refusal of some tribes to sell the Black Hills for any price (the current offer is over $200 million) symbolizes the unyielding regard for and the enduring place of their heritage in the lives of Plains Indians today.

Alabama-Coushatta

See Alabama (Chapter 7)

Apache, Plains

Plains Apache (U `pa chē) have also been known to non-natives as Kiowa Apaches, Prairie Apaches, Plains Lipans, and possibly Catakas, Palomas, Wetapahatos, and Paducas. Their self-designation is *Na-i-shan Dine,* "Our People." *See also* Kiowa.

Location In the late eighteenth century the Plains Apache were located along the upper Missouri River. Today, most live near the towns of Apache and Fort Cobb, Oklahoma.

Population The 1780 population was about 400. That number had declined to about 150 in 1900. By the early 1990s, there were about 1,400 people calling themselves Plains Apaches.

Language Plains Apaches spoke an Athapaskan language.

Historical Information

History Tribal tradition notes a northern Plains origin. Ancestors of the historic Plains Apache may have lived in northeastern Wyoming and western South Dakota as early as the twelfth century. They may also have entered the Yellowstone Valley from Canada by 1600. The Kiowa, located just to their west, joined them in the early eighteenth century, having been displaced by the mounted Shoshone.

In the early eighteenth century, the Comanches on the west and the Pawnee on the east forced Apaches living on the central Plains south and southwest. Cut off from their fellow Apacheans around 1720, the people known as Plains Apaches may have joined the Kiowa for protection. Although they functioned effectively as a Kiowa band and were a Plains tribe in all senses, they maintained a separate language and never came under the jurisdiction of the Kiowa Tribal Council.

Kiowas and Kiowa Apaches, pressed by the Crow and the Wind River Shoshone, soon left Yellowstone Valley for the Black Hills, where they remained until about the end of the century. At the same time, some Kiowa moved south while others remained near the Black Hills with the Plains Apache. The northern group finally moved south, under pressure from the Teton Dakota, to join the larger group around 1805 in western Kansas.

Plains Apaches are probably the "Apaches del Norte" named in the historical record as that group of Apaches who arrived in New Mexico by the late eighteenth century. They moved back and forth between New Mexico and the upper Missouri area during the early nineteenth century, serving as trade intermediaries between New Mexico and upper Missouri tribes such as the Mandans and Arikaras.

With the Kiowa, Plains Apaches moved south to the Arkansas River area in the early nineteenth century. In the early 1850s, they were part of an unsuccessful effort of Arkansas River tribes to defeat a number of tribes encroaching from the east. By then they and the Kiowa were spending more time south rather than north of the Arkansas. They settled on the Kiowa-Comanche-Apache Reservation in 1868. In 1901, this reservation was allotted in 160-acre parcels to individual tribal members, with the "surplus" opened to non-native settlement.

Religion With their associated ceremonies, sacred bundles were a focus of Kiowa religious practice. Plains Apaches adopted the Sun Dance in the eighteenth century, although they did not incorporate elements of self-mutilation into the ceremony. Young men also fasted to produce guardian spirit visions.

Government From the early eighteenth century on, the Plains Apaches functioned as a band of the Kiowa. As such they had their own peace and war chiefs. They joined the Kiowa as part of their summer camp.

Customs From the nineteenth century on, there were four named categories of social rank. The highest was held by those who had attained war honors and were skilled horsemen, generous, and wealthy. Then came those men who met all the preceding criteria except war honors. The third group was people without property. At the bottom were men with neither property nor skills. War captives remained outside this ranking system. In general wealth remained in the family through inheritance.

Corpses were buried or left in a tipi on a hill. Former possessions were given away. Mourners cut their hair and mutilated themselves. A mourning family lived apart from the rest of the group.

Dwellings Women built and owned skin tipis.

Diet Before the people acquired horses, they hunted some nearby buffalo and ate local roots, berries, seeds, and bulbs. Buffalo became a staple after the mid–eighteenth century.

Men also hunted other large and small game. They did not eat bear or, usually, fish. Women gathered a variety of wild potatoes and other vegetables, fruits, nuts, and berries. Plains Apaches ate dried, pounded acorns and also made them into a drink. Cornmeal and dried fruit were acquired by trade.

Key Technology The buffalo and other animals provided the usual material items such as parfleches and other containers. Points for bird arrows came from prickly pear thorns. The cradle board was a bead-covered skin case attached to a V-shaped frame. Women made shallow coiled basketry gambling trays.

Trade During the eighteenth century, Plains Apaches traded extensively with the upper Missouri tribes (Mandans, Hidatsas, and Arikaras). There was also regular trade with New Mexico, where they exchanged meat, buffalo hides, and salt for cornmeal and dried fruit. During the nineteenth century they traded Comanche horses to the Osage and other tribes.

Notable Arts Calendric skins and beadwork were two important artistic traditions.

Transportation The people acquired horses by the early eighteenth century.

Dress Women dressed buffalo, elk, and deer hides to make robes, moccasins, leggings, shirts, breechclouts, skirts, and blouses.

War and Weapons Plains Apaches took part in the Plains war-and-raiding complex. There were numerous military societies. The tribe was allied with the Crow in the late seventeenth century and with the Comanche beginning around 1790. Enemies in the eighteenth and early nineteenth century included the Dakota, Cheyenne, and Osage.

Contemporary Information

Government/Reservations Because of their geographical location, contemporary Plains Apaches are sometimes referred to as the Cache Creek Apaches (located near Apache, Oklahoma) and the Washita

Apaches (near Fort Cobb, Oklahoma). They organized a tribal government in the 1970s. The tribal administrative center is in Anadarko, Oklahoma.

Economy Chronic high unemployment is a function of the lack of local economic opportunity.

Legal Status The Apache Tribe of Oklahoma is a federally recognized tribal entity.

Daily Life Plains Apaches intermarry at a high rate with Indians of other tribes. Language classes and other educational and social programs are held in the administrative complex; ceremonials are held near Fort Cobb in June and August. The people are known for their extensive collection of traditional music, and their singers, drummers, and dancers are in demand at many tribal powwows. They have produced many excellent artists and craftspeople who work especially in beads, silver, wood, paints, and feathers.

Arapaho

Arapaho (U `ra pu hō), probably from the Pawnee *tirapihu,* "trader," or the Kiowa and Spanish word for "tattered and dirty clothing." "Kanenavish" (various spellings), a term in use around 1800, was a corruption of the French *gens de vache* ("Buffalo People"). The Arapahos originally called themselves *Inuna-ina,* "Our People."

Location The Arapahos probably migrated in the early eighteenth century from the Red River region of present-day Minnesota and North Dakota to the upper Missouri River region. Then, as Northern and Southern Arapaho, they moved in the nineteenth century to Wyoming (along the North Platte River) and eastern Colorado and western Kansas (along the Arkansas River).

Population The total Arapaho population ranged between 3,000 and 5,000 people around 1800. There were about 6,500 Arapahos in 1993.

Language Arapaho is an Algonquian language.

Historical Information

History At least 3,000 years ago the Arapaho, possibly united with the future Gros Ventres and other peoples, probably lived in the western Great Lakes region, where they grew corn and lived in permanent villages. They migrated by the eighteenth century to the upper Missouri River region, acquiring horses about that time.

In the nineteenth century, the groups separated and divided into Northern and Southern Arapaho. The northern branch settled around the North Platte River in Wyoming and the southern branch in the area of Bent's Fort on the Arkansas River in Colorado. The two groups remained in close contact. By this time, the Arapaho had adopted the classic Great Plains culture: They were master horsemen, buffalo hunters, and raiders.

Early Anglo traders found the Arapahos very friendly and disposed to trade. Although fur traders entered the area in the 1730s, they merely observed intertribal trade of items of European manufacture, especially knives and guns but also metal tools and other items. Furs were not an important trade commodity until around the turn of the century. Traders also brought alcohol and disease into the region, both to devastating effect. Still, powerful chiefs like Bear Tooth, favorably disposed to non-Indians, kept the peace in the early nineteenth century.

In 1837 a major war broke out, with the Southern Arapaho and Southern Cheyenne fighting against the Comanche. Peace was established in 1840, largely on Arapaho-Cheyenne terms. However, the opening of the Oregon Trail brought more non-Indians to the Plains and encouraged growing conflict, based on ignorance of Indian customs, land hunger, and race hatred.

Arapahos played a major role in the nineteenth-century wars for the Plains. The northern branch fought along with the Lakota and the southern branch with the Southern Cheyennes and occasionally with the Comanches and Kiowas. Although Arapahos signed the 1851 Fort Laramie Treaty, major gold finds in 1858–1859 caused further frictions between Indians and non-natives. In the 1859 Fort Wise Treaty, Arapahos and Cheyennes agreed to live peacefully in a delineated section of land while retaining subsistence rights throughout their territory.

Despite the existence of the treaty, in 1864 a group of Southern Arapaho and Cheyennes, mostly women and children, were attacked, massacred, and mutilated by U.S. Army troops at Sand Creek, Colorado, as part of a successful campaign to drive all Indians out of Colorado. Cut off from the rich Colorado buffalo herds and under further pressure from the United States, the Cheyennes and Arapahos in 1867 signed the Medicine Lodge Treaty, under which they formally ceded their lands north of the Arkansas River and were placed on a reservation in the Indian Territory (Oklahoma). Little Raven, a skilled orator and diplomat, represented his people in these negotiations.

By the terms of the Fort Laramie Treaty (1868), the Northern Arapaho were supposed to settle with the Lakota on the Pine Ridge Reservation in South Dakota. Holding out for their own reservation, the Northern Arapaho remained in Wyoming, refusing also to settle with the Southern Arapaho in the Indian Territory. They finally (1878) agreed to become part of the Eastern Shoshones' Wind River Reservation.

The Arapaho, especially those on the Wind River Reservation, adopted the Ghost Dance religion in the late 1880s. By this time the enormous buffalo herds had been virtually wiped out. In 1890, Arapahos and Southern Cheyennes agreed to exchange their 3.5-million-acre reservation for allotments of 160 acres each. The group formally organized in 1937 as the Cheyenne-Arapaho Tribe.

Religion Medicine bundles, containing various sacred objects, were said to have magical powers. An individual knew which objects to obtain for the bundle through knowledge gained in dreams or the (adult) vision quest. Medicine men (shamans or priests) used their bundles in ceremonies; other bundles belonged to secret societies or to the whole tribe.

A flat pipe some two feet long, wrapped in a bundle, was the most sacred object for the tribe. Tobacco was smoked in it only as part of the most sacred ceremonies and occasions. The lead rider carried it during a move.

In the eighteenth century, the annual Sun Dance became the most important single ceremony. Its purpose was the renewal of nature and tribal prosperity. Although it was in part a test of endurance, the Arapaho, unlike other tribes, did not include extreme acts of self-torture. Some Arapahos adopted the Peyote religion in the 1890s.

Government Each of four bands had a chief, but there was no principal chief.

Customs Bands wintered separately, along streams, and came together in summer to hunt buffalo and celebrate ceremonies. Although menstruating women were avoided, and the subject was taboo, there was no formal girls' puberty ceremony or menstrual seclusion. Men could marry more than one woman. Marriage was generally matrilocal. Children were generally nursed for four years. Blood relative and in-law taboos were strict. Extended family members, such as uncles and aunts, had specific responsibilities concerning their nieces and nephews.

Arapahos played the hoop-and-pole game and the cup-and-ball game and held athletic contests. Curing techniques included sweating in the sweat lodge and fumigation with roots, twigs, or herbs. There was one women's society in addition to the series of men's societies (see "War and Weapons"). The dead lay in state in fine clothing before being removed by horse and buried in a nearby hill. A favorite horse was killed. Mourners cut their hair, wore old clothes, and cut their arms and legs.

Dwellings At least since the nineteenth century, women made buffalo-skin tipis. Willow-framed beds covered with skins lined the interior walls. There were no permanent villages, as the tribe migrated with the herds.

Diet Buffalo had become a staple by the nineteenth century. Men also hunted elk, antelope, deer, and small animals. Meat was boiled in a hole in the ground filled with water and hot rocks. To preserve it for winter, women dried it and sometimes mixed it with fat and chokecherries to make pemmican. They also gathered wild mountain fruits, roots, berries, and tobacco.

Key Technology Prehistoric Arapahos may have made ceramics. Most raw materials came from the buffalo or other animals. They carved items such as

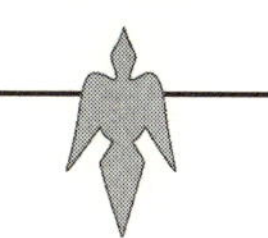

Since the nineteenth century, Arapaho women have made buffalo-skin tipis. In this 1913 photograph, the patches and heavy seams characteristic of buffalo-hide tipis are clearly visible.

bowls from wood, some of which had artistic and/or religious significance. They smoked black stone pipes and made shallow basketry trays.

Trade Mandan villages along the Knife River (North Dakota) were a primary regional trading center. By the early nineteenth century the Arapaho traded buffalo robes with Mexicans and Americans for items not provided by the buffalo. They also served as middlemen in trade between northern and southern Plains Indians.

Notable Arts Women decorated clothing, tipis, and other items with beautiful porcupine-quill embroidery and painting. Designs often included legends and spiritual beings. Designs, which often represented natural and celestial features, included diamonds with appendages such as forked trees (triangles atop a line).

Transportation The Arapaho probably acquired horses in the early eighteenth century. Babies were carried on the back in a U-shaped, wood-framed buckskin cradle board. The people used oval snowshoes in winter.

Dress Historic Arapaho dress was similar to that of other high plains tribes.

War and Weapons Eight military societies were graded according to age. One, the Crazy Dog Society, was noted for its extreme bravery and valor. Traditional enemies included the Shoshones, Utes,

Pawnees, Crows, Lakota, Comanche, and Kiowa. The latter three tribes had become allies, with the Southern Cheyenne, by the 1840s.

Counting coup, or touching the enemy with the hand or a stick, was highly prestigious, much more so than killing an enemy. Up to four people could count coup, in descending order of prestige, on the same enemy.

Contemporary Information

Government/Reservations The Wind River Reservation (1863; Shoshone and Arapaho tribes), Fremont and Hot Springs Counties, Wyoming, contains 2,268,008 acres. The 1990 Indian population was 5,674. Both tribes have business councils.

Roughly 3,000 (1993) Southern Arapahos live in western Oklahoma. They own no tribal land and live on the last of their allotments.

Economy Major economic activities at Wind River are ranching and crafts. There are some jobs in the school district and within the tribal government. There are also a number of small businesses. Some people regularly hunt and fish, and there is income from mineral leases. Un- and underemployment is chronically high (up to 80 percent).

The unemployment rate for Southern Arapahos and Southern Cheyennes in Oklahoma hovers around 70 percent (1993). They operate a smoke shop and a casino.

Legal Status The Arapaho Tribe of the Wind River Reservation and the Cheyenne-Arapaho Tribe of Oklahoma are federally recognized tribal entities.

Daily Life A Northern Arapaho family is keeper of the Scared Pipe, which remains the symbol of the tribe. Quasi-traditional religion remains important. The Sun Dance, held in July, has been explicitly Christianized and is now intertribal. Peyotism and sweat lodge ceremonies are popular. Giveaways, formerly related to public coup counting, are now associated with other occasions. Control of water rights has become an issue on the reservation.

High rates of substance abuse and suicide plague the reservation; related accidents have replaced disease as a primary killer. Outmigration remains a problem. Women have more freedom as well as political and social power, obtained in part through their participation in certain musical ceremonies. Wyoming Indian High School is Arapaho dominated; most Shoshone attend off-reservation public high schools. Traditional games such as the hand game, with its associated gambling, remain popular, especially at powwows.

Only a few people, mostly Southern Arapahos, still speak the language, despite the implementation of language programs at Wind River. There is still contact, particularly for ceremonies, between the northern and southern branches of the Arapaho tribe. Housing, most of which consists of modern "bungalows," is considered generally inadequate at Wind River. Canvas tipis are used for ceremonial purposes.

Arikara

Arikara (U `ri ku ru), "horn," referring to a traditional hairstyle. Their self-designation is *Tanish,* "Original People." In the historic period they were culturally similar to the Mandans.

Location Arikaras migrated from the central Plains into central South Dakota in the seventeenth and eighteenth centuries. Today most live in western North Dakota.

Population The late-eighteenth-century Arikara population was approximately 3,000–4,000. In the early 1990s, enrollment in the Three Affiliated Tribes was about 6,000 people.

Language Arikara is a Caddoan language.

Historical Information

History Around the beginning of the seventeenth century, the Arikara separated from the Skidi Pawnee in Nebraska and moved north along the Missouri River, spreading knowledge of agriculture along the way. They arrived in the Dakotas in the late eighteenth century.

Contact with French traders was established in the 1730s. During the early to mid–eighteenth

century they acquired horses and ranged even farther west, to eastern Montana, to hunt buffalo. In the 1780s the people suffered a smallpox epidemic but continued to live relatively well, despite harassment by Teton, Dakota, and other bands.

As a result of wars with the United States, the Arikara retreated south to join their Pawnee relatives on the Loup River in Nebraska from the early 1820s through about 1835. A devastating smallpox epidemic in 1837 brought them to the verge of extinction. About 1845, the weakened Arikara moved farther north and occupied land formerly under Mandan control (the latter having recently moved up the Missouri River with the Hidatsa).

In 1862, the Arikara also moved up the Missouri to the Mandan/Hidatsa village of Like-a-Fishhook and joined politically with those two tribes. Like-a-Fishhook Village was a center of trade and commerce at that time. The Fort Laramie Treaty of 1851 recognized tribal holdings of more than 12 million acres.

In 1870, the United States established the eight-million-acre Fort Berthold Reservation for the tribes. This land was reduced, mostly by allotment, to about one million acres during the 1880s. By this time, Like-a-Fishhook had been abandoned, the people scattering to form communities along the Missouri River. The Arikara lived in Nishu and Elbowwoods, on the east side of the river.

In the 1950s, against the tribes' vehement opposition, the United States built the Garrison Dam on the Missouri. The resulting Lake Sakakawea covered much of their land, farms, and homes. This event destroyed the tribes' economic base and permanently damaged their social structure.

Religion The Arikara believed in a supreme deity who shared power with four lesser gods. Most religious festivals were associated with corn, which they originally acquired from the south and southwest. Medicine men possessed particularly fine, generations-old ears of corn, within which resided the spirit of "mother corn."

Religious activity included fasting, acquiring visions, and the possession and use of personal sacred bundles. Certain religious positions, such as the priesthood and the keeper of the sacred tribal medicine bundles, were hereditary within families.

The Arikara men pictured here are members of the Medicine Fraternity. Most religious festivals were associated with corn, which the Arikara originally acquired from the south and southwest. Medicine men possessed particularly fine, generations-old ears of corn, within which resided the spirit of "mother corn."

Government Political centralization was weak among the Arikara. Villages combined in a loose confederation of named bands. Village chiefs made up the band council, which assisted the head chief.

Customs The Arikara were excellent swimmers; hauling trees out of the Missouri River provided them with firewood in an area short of trees. The game of shinny was particularly popular, as were feats of

A principal Arikara medicine man on his altar.

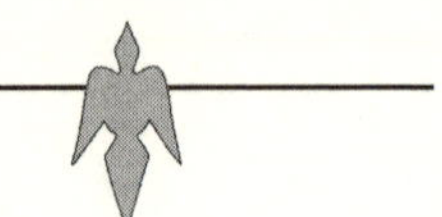

dexterity, skill, and magic. The people enjoyed building toys and whistles for and otherwise entertaining their children.

Families owned farms and dogs as well as dwellings. There were a number of mens' societies, focused on the hunt and on keeping order, as well as women's societies. Men hunted and provided protection; women were in charge of vegetable foods (garden plots), preparing hides for clothing as well as baskets and pottery, and caring for the lodge. Descent was matrilineal and residence was matrilocal. Social rank was hereditary to a significant degree. The dead were buried sitting, wrapped in skins, their faces painted red. A year of mourning followed a death.

Dwellings Arikaras located their villages on bluffs over the Missouri River. Later villages were strongly reinforced by wooden stockades and ditches. Partially excavated earth lodges measured about 40 feet in diameter and held two or more extended families. A wooden framework supported woven willow branches and grass covered with earth. A lodge might last up to 20 years. A larger structure, around which residential lodges were grouped, served as the medicine or ceremonial lodge. Skin tipis served as temporary field dwellings.

Diet Women grew corn (small, highly nutritious ears), squash, beans, and sunflowers, fertilizing their crops and rotating their fields. They also cultivated tobacco. Men hunted buffalo and other large and small game. They also fished and gathered berries and other plants.

Key Technology Material items included willow weirs (fish traps); farm equipment, weapons, and utensils from buffalo parts; stone mortars; pottery cooking vessels; a variety of baskets; and leather pouches and other containers.

Trade Women traded surplus crops to the Cheyenne, Kiowa, Lakota, and other groups for buffalo and other animal products. Later they traded with the French for European-made products. There was also some cultural and material exchange between the Arikara and the Mandan and the Hidatsa.

Notable Arts Pottery and basketry were traditional arts.

Transportation People used boats constructed of buffalo hide stretched over a willow frame (bull-boats) to cross the Missouri. They also wore snowshoes and used dogs and later (mid–eighteenth century) horses to pull travois.

Dress Women made blankets, robes, and moccasins of buffalo hide. They also made clothing of white weasel or ermine skin and made winter turbans of various animal skins.

War and Weapons The Arikara were alternately friendly and at war with the Mandans and Hidatsas. After about the late eighteenth century, the Lakota fought the Arikaras, cutting off both trading parties and buffalo hunters. Weapons included various flint projectiles and buffalo-hide shields.

Contemporary Information

Government/Reservations The Three Affiliated Tribes (Arikara, Hidatsa, Mandan) live on the Fort Berthold Reservation (roughly 900,000 acres in Dunn, McKenzie, McLean, Mercer, Mountrail, and Ward Counties, North Dakota). The 1990 reservation Indian population was 2,999. More than half of the reservation is owned by non-Indians.

Economy Tribal and federal governments are the largest employers. A few people have farms or ranches. The tribe opened a high-stakes casino in 1993. Unemployment remains very high.

Legal Status The Three Affiliated Tribes is a federally recognized tribal entity.

Daily Life Most Arikaras live on the east side of Lake Sakakawea, near the towns of White Shield and Parshall. Their lifestyle is similar to that of their non-Indian neighbors.

Although politically united, the three tribes continue to maintain separate identities. The annual powwow held by each reservation community has become a focus for tribal activities. War Bonnet dances help maintain an Indian identity. Crafts

include quilting and beadwork. Some Arikara practice sweat lodge ceremonies and are members of the Native American Church. Most consider themselves Christians.

Only elders speak the native language, despite attempts to institute regular language classes. The community operates several reservation schools, and it publishes the *Mandan, Hidatsa, and Arikara Times.* There is a museum at New Town.

Assiniboine

Assiniboine (U `sin u boin), "those who cook with stones" (Algonquian). Canadian Assiniboines are also known as Stoneys. Their traditional self-designation is unknown. *See also* Nakota.

Location The Siouan people probably originated in the lower Mississippi Valley and moved north through Ohio and into the Lake Superior region (northern Minnesota/southwestern Ontario). In the seventeenth century, the Assiniboine lived near Lake Winnipeg. From the eighteenth century on they have lived in present-day Montana and Saskatchewan.

Population The seventeenth-century population was roughly 10,000 people. In the 1990s about 8,000 Assiniboines, Gros Ventres, and Yanktonais lived on the two Montana reservations. There is also a Stoney population on Canadian reserves.

Language Assiniboines/Yanktonais speak the Nakota dialect of Dakota, a Siouan language.

Historical Information

History Assiniboines separated from the northern Yanktonai by perhaps the late sixteenth century, moving north from the Ohio Valley through Wisconsin and Minnesota, along the edge of the Woodlands into southern and southwestern Ontario. They became involved in the French fur trade in the early seventeenth century.

By later in that century they had made peace with the Plains Cree, joining them near Lake Winnipeg, and were trading with Hudson's Bay Company posts there. Assiniboines ranged over an extremely wide territory during that period, from near the Arctic Circle to the upper Missouri River and from James Bay to the Rocky Mountains. When trade with the Hudson's Bay Company declined, in the later eighteenth century, the Assiniboine became fully nomadic, continuing the westward migration and hunting around the Saskatchewan and Assiniboine Rivers and across much of the northern Plains.

Major smallpox epidemics struck the people in 1780 and 1836, and alcohol and venereal disease also took a heavy toll. During that period, the Assiniboine divided into a lower and an upper division. Decimation of the buffalo herds as well as their own sharp population decline forced them to sign the 1851 Fort Laramie Treaty, limiting Assiniboine lands to parcels in western Montana.

Some Assiniboines worked as scouts for U.S. and Canadian armies in their Indian wars. In 1887, upper division Assiniboines (and the Gros Ventres) were confined to the new Fort Belknap Reservation; Fort Peck, which they shared with the Yanktonai, was created in 1873. Several hundred Assiniboine died of starvation at Fort Peck in 1883–1884.

Meanwhile, in Canada, unregulated whiskey sales were taking a great toll on Indian people. In 1877, as a result of national police intervention in the whiskey trade, the Stoneys and some other tribes signed Treaty Number 7, exchanging their traditional territory for reserves in Alberta and Saskatchewan, although some groups attempted to maintain their autonomy. Much of the reserve land was alienated in the early twentieth century owing to allotting and permitting of non-Indian homesteads.

Religion Male and female specialists provided religious leadership. Ceremonial implements and techniques included rattles, chants, charms, and songs. In the eighteenth century, the annual Sun Dance became the people's most important religious ceremony, although the custom of self-torture was not generally present.

Wakonda was worshiped as a primary deity, although the Assiniboine also recognized natural phenomena such as sun and thunder. Sweat lodge purification was an important religious practice. Spirit visions could be obtained through quests or in dreams. Some ceremonies featured masked clowns.

Assiniboine and Gros Ventre chiefs adorned for the Grass Dance in Fort Belknap, Montana, circa 1906.

Government The Assiniboine were composed of up to 30 bands, each with its own chief. The chieftainship was based on leadership skills and personal contacts rather than heredity. Each band also had a council, whose decisions were enforced by the *akitcita,* or camp police.

Customs The people valued hospitality highly; they enjoyed visits with each other and with friendly tribes. There were a number of men's and women's dance societies with various social and ceremonial importance. There may have been clans.

The dead were placed on tree scaffolds with their feet to the west. When the scaffolds fell through age, the bones were buried and the skulls placed in a circle, facing inward. Cremation was also practiced. All burial areas were treated with great respect. Dead souls were said to inhabit a paradise to the south.

Dead warriors were dressed in their finest clothes. Their faces were painted red, their weapons placed beside them, and one of their horses was killed for use in the next life. Women's tools, such as those used for dressing skins, were placed beside them. Mourning practices included cutting hair, dressing in rags, and sometimes slashing limbs.

Pubescent girls were secluded for four days, during which time they observed dietary and behavioral restrictions. Brides were purchased. Marriage consisted of a simple gift-giving ceremony between parents. The people played lacrosse and games of skill and dexterity, such as shinny and the

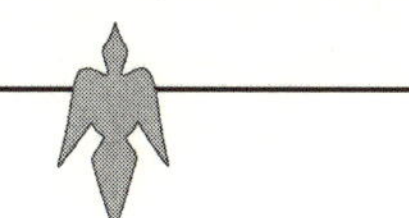

cup-and-ball game, and held athletic competitions. Most games were accompanied by gambling.

Dwellings A village might contain up to 200 skin lodges or tipis. The average, which held two to four families, had roughly a 30-foot circumference and was constructed of about 12 sewn buffalo hides. Assiniboine tipis had a three-pole foundation. A temporary brush field shelter was also used.

Diet Assiniboines on the high plains lived mainly on game such as buffalo, elk, and antelope. Women often accompanied hunters to butcher the animals and cut meat into strips to dry. Fresh meat was usually roasted on a spit, although it was sometimes boiled with hot rocks in a skin-lined hole. Other foods included wild berries, roots (turnip), fruits (grapes, plums), and nuts.

Key Technology The buffalo was the basis of all technology. Most items, such as clothing, tools, and utensils, were made of buffalo and other animal products. The flageolet, or flute, was used in part to convey surreptitious messages between young lovers. Assiniboines also played the rasp and the drum.

Trade The people were known as shrewd traders, especially in their role as middlemen with the Hudson's Bay Company. Before trade began with non-Indians, they generally traded pelts and meat with farming tribes for agricultural products.

Notable Arts Significant art included decorative beaded quillwork (nineteenth century) and designs on tree bark.

Transportation Dogs (later horses) carried saddle bags and travois. The people acquired horses in about the 1730s. They also used snowshoes.

Dress Dress on the high plains was similar to that of other tribes, particularly the Plains Cree. Men often wore their long hair coiled atop the head.

War and Weapons The Plains Cree were traditional allies, with whom the Assiniboine regularly fought the Dakota, Crow, Gros Ventre, and Blackfeet. The Assiniboine were recognized as highly capable warriors. Counting coup was more important than killing an enemy; four people might count coup on the same enemy, in descending order of prestige. Weapons included war clubs (a stone in a leather pouch attached to a stick), bow and arrow, and buffalo-hide shields.

Contemporary Information

Government/Reservations Fort Belknap (Blaine and Philips Counties, Montana), established in 1887, contains roughly 616,000 acres, about one-quarter of which are tribally owned. The 1990 Indian population was 2,332. The reservation is governed under an Indian Reorganization Act (IRA) constitution and by-laws.

Fort Peck (Daniels, Roosevelt, Sheridan, and Valley Counties, Montana), established in 1873, contains about 981,000 acres, about one-quarter of which are tribally owned. The 1990 Indian population was 5,782. Their 1927 constitution is not based on the IRA. The reservation adopted a representative government, the Tribal Executive Board, in 1960.

Canadian communities include Carry the Kettle, Pheasant Rump, and Ocean Man in Saskatchewan and Elexis, Paul, Wesley, Big Horn, and Eden Valley in Alberta.

Economy Both reservations lease land to non-Indian farmers and ranchers. Fort Peck owns and operates a profitable oil well. It also contains other mineral resources and has encouraged industrial development.

Legal Status The Assiniboine and Sioux Tribes of the Fort Peck Reservation is a federally recognized tribal entity. The Fort Belknap Indian Community (Gros Ventre and Assiniboine-Sioux) is a federally recognized tribal entity.

Daily Life Maintaining their cultural identity in a community shared with other tribes as well as non-Indians is a major challenge facing contemporary Assiniboines. The Bureau of Indian Affairs, which has long dominated the Fort Belknap Reservation, has traditionally viewed both Indian groups as one community, to the detriment of Indian cultural

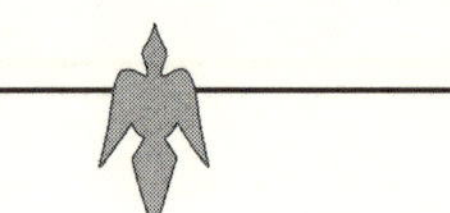

identity. Fort Peck has traditionally enjoyed stronger political leadership and consequently greater self-determination and economic opportunity.

Diabetes is an ongoing and serious health problem. Traditional religion is maintained in the form of the hand game and the Sun Dance. There are also a number of important ceremonies associated with funerals and sweat lodges. The sacred pipe remains central to Assiniboine religion. Some members of the tribe participate in the Native American Church as well as in Medicine Lodge (called Rain Dance in Canada) ceremonies. The Assiniboine language is spoken by young and old alike, although it is used primarily in ceremonies. Assiniboine women continue to make museum-quality star quilts for secular and religious purposes.

Atsina

See Gros Ventres

Blackfeet

The Blackfeet are a confederacy of three closely related Plains tribes. These include the *Pikuni* (Piegan, known as Peigan in Canada), meaning "small robes" or "poorly dressed robes"; the *Kainah,* "Blood" or "many chiefs"; and the *Siksika,* the Blackfeet proper. *Siksika,* a Cree word meaning "Blackfoot People," may have referred to their moccasins, blackened by dye or by the ashes of prairie fires. All three tribes were called the *Sakoyitapix,* "Prairie People," or the *Nitsitapix,* "Real People." The Piegan were further divided into northern and southern branches. The Blackfeet Confederacy also included the Sarcees and, until 1861, the Gros Ventres.

Location Around 1800, the Blackfeet proper and the Bloods lived around the Saskatchewan, Battle, and Bow Rivers (Alberta), and the Piegan claimed the area south of the Marais River (Rocky Mountain foothills of north-central Montana). Today, Blackfeet live in northwestern Montana as well as in southern Alberta.

Population The Blackfeet Confederacy in 1780 numbered around 15,000 people. In 1993 the tribe had over 13,000 members.

Language The Blackfeet groups spoke Algonquian languages.

Historical Information

History The Blackfeet people may have originated in the Great Lakes region but had migrated to between the Bow and North Saskatchewan Rivers well before the seventeenth century. During the eighteenth century they completed their move southward into Montana, displacing the Shoshones.

Like many peoples, the Blackfeet were transformed by the horse and the gun, both of which they acquired during the early to mid–eighteenth century. One result was that they had surplus buffalo products to offer for trade. Raiding, especially for horses, became an important activity. They joined in alliance with the Assiniboine, Arapaho, and Gros Ventre and were frequently at war during the historic period.

Blackfeet people first felt the influence of non-Indians in the seventeenth century. By the late eighteenth century they were engaged in the fur trade and were known as shrewd traders, playing American and British interests off against each other. The people experienced severe epidemics in 1781–1782, 1837, 1864, and 1869–1870. After one of their number was killed by a member of the Lewis and Clark expedition in 1804, the Blackfeet fought all Americans whenever possible until they began trading with them again in 1831.

The 1868 Fort Laramie Treaty gave the Blackfeet lands south of the Missouri River, although their traditional lands had all been north of the Missouri. Still, in various treaties between 1851 and 1878 they ceded land to the United States and Canada. Epidemics, the decline of the buffalo, and, later, whiskey hurt the Blackfeet more than anything, although in 1870 they were the victims of a U.S. Army massacre in which 173 peaceful Indians, mostly women and children, were killed.

The Blackfeet Reservation was established in 1855 in northern Montana. In exchange for the northern Montana plains, the Southern Piegan received fixed hunting grounds bordered by the Canadian, Missouri, and Musselshell Rivers and the Rocky Mountains; they also received promises of payments and annuities. Other Blackfeet groups

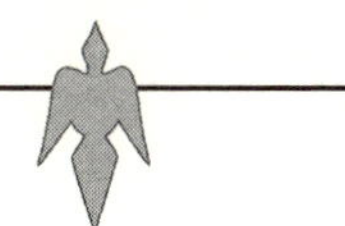

considered themselves to be British and did not treat with the Americans.

From the 1870s into the 1890s, the United States took away much of the huge Blackfeet Reservation. In Treaty Number 7 (1877), the Blackfeet (and others) ceded much of southern Alberta for a number of small reserves. Roughly 600 Blackfeet, mostly Southern Piegan, died of starvation in 1883 after the last great buffalo herd was destroyed.

After a farming experiment failed, Piegans began a program of stock raising around 1890, on land individually assigned by the Bureau of Indian Affairs. A few Indians became prosperous, but the majority leased their land to non-Indians, who often did not pay. A combination of events in 1919 left the people in dire poverty and dependent on government rations. During this period, over 200,000 acres of Indian land were lost through nonpayment of taxes and allotments that were sold to fend off starvation. Blackfeet on both sides of the border were also subject to having their children kidnapped and sent to missionary boarding schools. Log houses replaced tipis during this time. Most Canadian Blackfeet lost large portions of their reserves from 1907 to 1921.

Stock raising returned during the 1920s, accompanied by grain farming and some subsistence gardening. U.S. Blackfeet adopted an Indian Reorganization Act constitution in 1930s. Income rose, as the government provided credit for ranching enterprises. After World War II, up to one-third of the population was living off-reservation. Conditions on the reservations began to improve at that time, a trend that accelerated during the 1960s. Among most people, English replaced Blackfeet as the daily language in the 1970s. At the same time, many traditions severely declined.

Religion The Blackfeet envisioned a world inhabited by spirits, some good and some evil. Deities included sun and thunder as well as all animals. Religious feelings and practice were pervasive. Prayers were offered regularly throughout the day.

Some people had visions to benefit the tribe as a whole. They became holy men, or medicine pipe men, because their medicine bundle was particularly sacred. Such bundles, including scared pipes, were owned by individuals, societies, and bands. They were thought to ensure a long, happy, successful life and thus could be quite valuable if sold.

Ceremonies included the Sun Dance, probably acquired from the Arapaho or the Gros Ventres around the mid–eighteenth century. Unlike most Plains tribes, women participated in the Blackfeet Sun Dance. Religious societies were responsible for healing and curing. Individual religious activity focused on the acquisition of guardian spirits through prayerful vision quests in remote places. Guardian spirits would bring various forms of luck and/or skills.

Sweating was considered a religious activity as well as a preparation for ceremonials. Women were generally not permitted access to the sweat lodge. Sacred bundles were also smudged or smoked in the sweat lodge.

Government The constituent tribes of the confederacy were completely autonomous, although all were closely related and occasionally acted in concert. The tribes were in turn organized into autonomous bands of between 20 and 30 families (200 people) before the early eighteenth century.

Each band had a civil headman, or chief, chosen on the basis of acts of bravery and generosity. The chief had the most influence regarding the band's movements and also acted as judge. Each band also had a war chief, who exerted power only during military situations. All headmen constituted a tribal council, which in turn selected a temporary tribal chief when the bands came together. All decisions were taken by consensus.

Customs The bands lived separately in winter but came together in summer to hunt buffalo and observe their ceremonies. They generally followed the buffalo in all seasons save winter. Originally egalitarian, levels of social prestige based on horse ownership emerged after the mid–eighteenth century.

Men were members of one of seven age-graded military societies. In addition, men and women could belong to numerous other religious, dance, and social societies, each with its own symbols and ceremonies. There was also a society exclusively for women. Membership in all societies was drawn from all bands and functioned mainly when the tribe came together in summer.

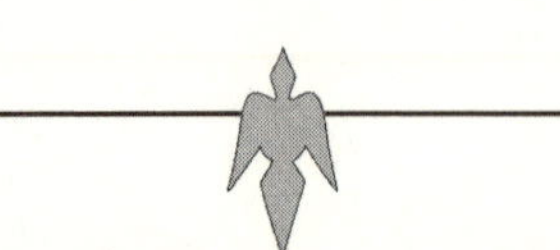

These Blackfeet blow eagle-bone whistles as part of a Sun Dance ritual to ensure good weather during the ceremony. Unlike most Plains tribes, women also participated in the Blackfeet Sun Dance.

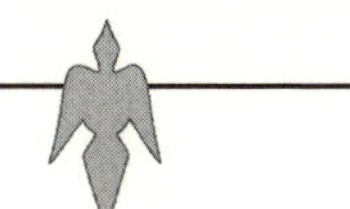

Virginity in women was held in high esteem. Depending on his wealth, a man might have more than one wife. Residence after marriage was generally patrilocal. Wedding formalities centered on gift giving. There was a mother-in-law taboo but none for a wife and her father-in-law. Divorce was possible on the grounds of laziness or infidelity (men) or cruelty or neglect (women).

Names were sometimes given by the mother but more often by a male family member based on his war experiences. Boys usually earned a new name around adolescence. Despite beliefs about the danger of contact with menstruating women, there was no particular ceremony when a girl reached puberty.

Public ridicule was generally an effective deterrent to socially unacceptable behavior. Winter nights might be filled with storytelling, gambling, or all-night smokes during which people sang their religious songs. Childrens' games included hide and seek, archery and other contests, throwing balls, playing with toys, or sledding.

The dead were placed on scaffolds in trees or in tipis if death took place there; horses were generally killed to help in the journey to the next world. Women mourners cut their hair, wailed ritualistically, and slashed their limbs. Men cut their hair and left the band for a while.

Dwellings Women constructed tipis from 12 to 14 buffalo skins over as many as 23 pine poles. There was a basic foundation of four poles upon which the others were laid. Tipis always faced east. Larger tipis, of up to 30 buffalo skins, were a sign of wealth. Tipis were smaller when dogs pulled the travois.

Diet Food was generally abundant, although droughts or blizzards could bring hunger or even starvation. Plains Blackfeet ate mostly buffalo but also other large as well as small game. Buffalo were driven over cliffs, surrounded on foot and shot, communally hunted with bow and arrow (most common after the Blackfeet acquired horses), and individually stalked. The Indians also ate waterfowl and their eggs. They did not eat fish or dog.

In addition to the usual wild fruits, nuts, and berries, Blackfeet women gathered camas roots, which they steamed in an underground oven. Some tobacco was grown for ceremonial purposes.

Key Technology Early, pre-Plains Blackfeet may have made pottery. The buffalo provided more than 60 material items. Various skin containers were often decorated with painted designs. Musical instruments included a rattle of skin around wood as well as a flageolet (flute). The people also used stone pounding mauls and war clubs attached to wooden handles, chipped stone knives, and brushes of porcupine bristles or horsehair bound with rawhide. They also made backrests of willow sticks tied with sinew and supported by a tripod.

Trade The Blackfeet traded as far south as Mexico in all seasons save winter.

Notable Arts Men painted tipis and other leather items with stars and designs such as battle events. Women made beaded quillwork, usually on clothing. In general, the people were known for the high quality of everyday items such as clothing, tools, tipis, and headdresses.

Transportation Dogs pulled the travois until horses arrived in the early to mid–eighteenth century. Temporary hide rafts, towed by swimmers, were used to cross deep streams.

Dress Women wore long, one-piece skin dresses, later fringed and beaded, and buffalo robes in winter. They wore their hair long and loose. Men dressed in skin shirts, leggings, and moccasins, as well as buffalo robes in winter. Men also wore their hair long down the back, with a lock of hair down their foreheads to their noses, and they plucked their faces. Young men might also paint their faces. Caps were made of bird or weasel skins.

War and Weapons All men were members of age-graded military societies known as All Comrades. Although they were generally allied with the Gros Ventre and Sarcee, the Blackfeet fought most other Plains and Plateau tribes, including Salish/Flathead, Nez Percé, Kootenai, Assiniboine (after the nineteenth century), Shoshone, Crow, and Cree. Blackfeet

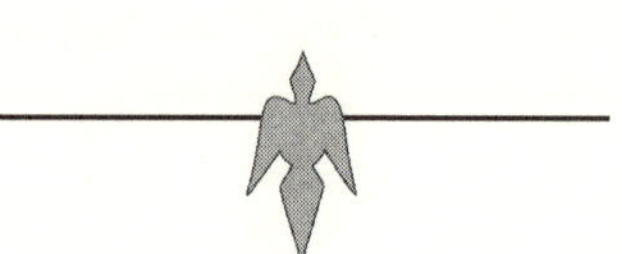

Blackfeet women constructed tipis from 12 to 14 buffalo skins over as many as 23 pine poles. Larger tipis, of up to 30 buffalo skins, were a sign of wealth.

Indians were considered among the best fighters, hunters, and raiders. Although the three divisions were politically autonomous, they acted in unison to fight their enemies.

Weapons included three-foot horn, sinew-backed bows, stone clubs, arrows (held in otter-skin quivers), and decorated buffalo-hide shields. Rather than counting coup with a stick, Blackfeet warriors gathered high war honors by wresting a gun or other weapon from an enemy. Taking a horse or a scalp merited honors but of relatively low caliber.

Contemporary Information

Government/Reservations The Blackfeet Reservation (Glacier and Pondera Counties, Montana), established in 1855, consists of roughly two million acres, of which the tribe owns about 70 percent individually or in common. The 1990 Indian population was 7,025. The reservation is governed by a tribal business council.

On all three Canadian reserves—Siksika, Blood, and Peigan—decisions of the tribal councils must be approved by the government, but this is considered a mere formality.

Economy The Blackfeet Tribe owns Blackfeet National Bank and a pencil and pen company as well as grazing and mineral leases. The tribe received a settlement of $29 million in 1982 as compensation for unsound federal accounting practices over the years. Their unemployment rate remains generally above 50 percent (nearer 80 percent in Canada). Most businesses and services are owned by non-Indians in the reservation town of Browning

In Canada, Indian-run businesses on the Siksika Reserve include a cafeteria, supermarket, video store, and furniture store. The Blood Reserve has a small mall and several service stations. There are several small stores and a crafts shop on the Peigan Reserve.

Legal Status The Blackfeet Tribe is a federally recognized tribal entity.

In Canada, the Blackfeet Tribe has changed its name to the Siksika Nation, and the Peigans are called both the Peigan Nation and the Pikuni Nation.

Daily Life Many Blackfeet have intermarried with non-Blackfeet or non-Indians, and many have adopted Christian religions. Still, the Sun Dance is maintained, as are medicine bundle, sweat lodge, and guardian spirit traditions. Language classes are in place to keep the language alive. Blackfeet Indians are better educated and have more and better jobs than ever before. Nevertheless, the unemployment rate remains high, with attendant social problems. The Museum of the Plains Indian as well as Blackfeet Community College (established 1976) is located on the reservation. There is an annual Medicine Lodge ceremony and Sun Dance in July.

Canadian Bloods operate Red Crow College, and a local college offers courses on the Siksika Reserve. The University of Lethbridge has a Native Studies program based mostly on Blackfeet culture.

Blood

See Blackfeet

Cheyenne

Cheyenne (Shī `an), a word of Lakota origin meaning "red talkers" or "foreign talkers." Their self-designation is *Tse-tsehese-staestse,* "People."

Location In the early nineteenth century, Cheyennes lived from the Yellowstone River to the upper Arkansas River. Today, most live in southeastern Montana and western Oklahoma as well as in cities throughout the West.

Population The late-eighteenth-century population was about 3,500 people. In the 1990s there are about 11,000 Cheyennes.

Language Cheyenne is an Algonquian language. There were at least two major dialects of Cheyenne in the early nineteenth century.

Historical Information

History The Algonquian people may have come north from the lower Mississippi Valley shortly after the last ice sheet receded. Late prehistoric (sixteenth and seventeenth century) Cheyennes lived in the

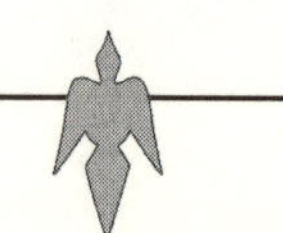

A Cheyenne dance before a crowd of whites in Miles City, Montana, circa 1891. Only 15 years after their defeat of General Custer, the Cheyenne were reduced to performing a powwow dance for tourists and local white settlers.

upper Mississippi Valley (northern and western Minnesota) in permanent villages and grew corn, beans, and squash. They also fished and hunted game, including buffalo.

Some bands encountered René-Robert La Salle in 1680, on the Illinois River. The French fur trade in the Great Lakes region was responsible for arming local Indian groups such as the Ojibwa with guns; these groups began attacking Cheyenne villages, eventually forcing them to abandon the region and undertake a slow migration westward throughout the eighteenth century. They lived near the Shyenne River (North Dakota), where they built a fortified town and continued their agricultural patterns. They also hunted buffalo and other game on a growing herd of horses but had not yet abandoned the agricultural life.

By the end of the eighteenth century, however, well-armed Ojibwas (Anishinabe) had destroyed a main Cheyenne village. Surviving Cheyennes moved farther west, to the upper Missouri River, joining some of their number who had gone there several years earlier. During that period they associated with the Mandan, Arikara, and Hidatsa. They continued to plant some crops but relied increasingly on the buffalo.

By the early nineteenth century, raids from Siouan tribes forced the Cheyenne out onto the Plains, where they gave up farming entirely, becoming nomadic buffalo hunters as well as fierce fighters. Allied with the Arapaho, they settled primarily near the Black Hills and then in the upper Platte–Powder River area, where they eventually became allied with

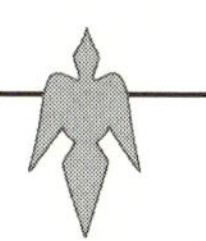

Pictured here is the September 1864 meeting in Camp Weld between Colonel John M. Chivington and the Cheyenne and Arapaho. In November 1864, Chivington spearheaded the massacre of several hundred of the Cheyenne and Arapaho people in Sand Creek, Colorado. The massacre forced the Southern Cheyenne to cede their lands in Colorado.

Lakota bands. It was also during that period that they absorbed another Algonquian group, the Sutaio tribe.

About 1832, some bands moved south, attracted by trade centered around Taos, New Mexico, as well as Bent's Fort on the Arkansas River in southern Colorado. The move precipitated a tribal split into Northern and Southern Cheyenne. In alliance with the Southern Arapaho, the Southern Cheyenne controlled most of the buffalo country between western Kansas and eastern Colorado and the Platte River.

In 1837 a major war broke out, with the Southern Arapaho and Southern Cheyenne fighting against the Comanche; peace was established in 1840, largely on Arapaho-Cheyenne terms. The Cheyenne signed the 1851 Fort Laramie Treaty, which reaffirmed their right to land between the North Platte and Arkansas Rivers. The treaty also formalized the separation of the Cheyenne groups. However, during the 1850s and 1860s they were regularly harassed by army troops and gold-seeking trespassers.

Meanwhile, non-Indian leaders of territorial Colorado had decided to force all Indians from that region. Pressure against the Southern Cheyenne was increased, especially after the Pike's Peak gold rush of 1859. Under Chief Black Kettle (Moketavato), the Southern Cheyenne repeatedly compromised in an effort to avoid war. However, the 1864 massacre and mutilation of several hundred of their people at Sand Creek, Colorado (where they had been told to camp under the protection of the U.S. Army and met the soldiers flying a white surrender and an American flag), forced the Southern Cheyenne to cede their lands in Colorado.

Black Kettle continued to seek peace but was shot down with his tribe, which offered no resistance, in the Washita Valley, Oklahoma, in 1868. At this point, the Cheyenne divided again. One group went north to the Powder River Country, and most of the rest settled on the Southern Cheyenne and Arapaho Reservation, established in 1869 in Indian Territory. This roughly four-million-acre reservation was eliminated through allotment and non-Indian settlement by 1902. Some Southern Cheyennes continued to fight with the Kiowa, Comanche, and Arapaho, until the few survivors were forced to surrender in 1875.

In the meantime, the Northern Cheyenne tried to resist the onslaught of the gold seekers and land grabbers who invaded their lands, ignoring the terms of the 1851 Fort Laramie Treaty. Formerly among the tribes who held out for peace, they turned to war following the Sand Creek massacre. Under chiefs like Roman Nose, some Northern Cheyennes fought with Red Cloud's Lakota in the successful effort to close the Bozeman Trail (1866–1868). The resulting Fort Laramie Treaty (1868) affirmed the exclusion of non-Indians from the Powder River region of Montana. In 1876, the Northern Cheyenne joined with other Plains Indians in defeating the United States in the Battle of the Little Bighorn.

Shortly thereafter, however, the U.S. Army caught and defeated the Northern Cheyennes, rounding up almost 1,000 and forcing them south to the Cheyenne-Arapaho Reservation in Indian Territory. Though exhausted after their forced march, sick and dying from malaria, and starving, roughly 300 desperate Northern Cheyennes under Dull Knife and Little Wolf escaped and headed toward home north of the North Platte River. Fighting valiantly for their freedom, they were pursued by soldiers and had to cross lands now inhabited by white farmers and ranchers. The people were recaptured with much loss of life and relocated to the Pine Ridge area of South Dakota in 1881. Three years later, the Tongue River Reservation in eastern Montana was established for this now-decimated people. Although this land was never opened to non-Indian purchase, allotments fragmented the reservation, causing long-term legal and cultural problems.

Christian missionaries, especially Mennonites, Catholics, and Southern Baptists, became active among the Cheyenne toward the end of the nineteenth century. Around the same time, the Peyote religion and the Ghost Dance became popular among the Northern Cheyennes. Following confinement to reservations, most Indians lived on government rations (often inadequate at best) and marginal gardening and wage labor. In 1911, the United States organized a 15-member Northern Cheyenne Business Council, largely under its control. The tribe adopted an Indian Reorganization Act (IRA) constitution in 1935. In 1918, Southern Cheyennes were among those who formally incorporated the Peyote religion into the Native American Church.

Religion The Cheyenne conceived of a universe divided into seven major levels, each with resident spiritual beings that were also associated with earthly plants and animals. They also believed in a creator of all life.

Through fasting and prayer, both men and women sought visions in remote places in order to acquire guardian spirit helpers. Spirit guides might appear during a vision quest or in a dream. They and their associated songs, prayers, and symbols would provide special skills or protection in times of crisis. Priests and doctors (shamans) used plants to cure disease.

Annual ceremonies included the Renewal of Sacred Arrows, the Sun Dance (New Life Lodge), and the annual, five-day Sacred Buffalo Hat ceremony. The first revolved around four scared arrows that were thought to have been given to the Cheyenne by their culture hero, Sweet Medicine, who had in turn received them from the Great Spirit. During the four-day ceremony, held at least every few years, the arrows were removed from the sacred bundle. They, and, by extension, the tribe, were restored to good condition and renewed.

Government On the Plains, traditional government consisted of the Council of Forty-Four: a group of 40 exceptionally wise, generous, brave, and able men, four from each of the 10 bands, plus four elders/religious authorities held over from the previous council. The latter four men, plus a tribal chief chosen by them, were known as the five sacred chiefs. Council terms were 10 years. Each band also had its own chief. Six military societies helped to carry out council directives and maintain strict internal discipline.

Customs Bands lived separately in winter so as to hunt more effectively in a wider space. In summer, the bands came together for the communal buffalo hunt and for sacred ceremonies. At these times, camp consisted of a large circle, within which each band had a designated position.

Murder was considered among the most reprehensible of crimes as well as a sin; murderers were ostracized for life or exiled. Bravery was highly valued, as was female chastity. Courtship was prolonged, with both families closely involved. Residence after marriage was generally matrilocal.

Games, generally accompanied by gambling, included lacrosse and the cup-and-ball game. In addition to the men's military societies, the highly prestigious buffalo society was open only to women who had embroidered at least 30 buffalo hides. Corpses were dressed in their best clothing, wrapped in robes, and placed on a scaffold, usually in a tree. Weapons and other items useful in the afterworld, including possibly a just-killed horse, were placed nearby.

Dwellings While still in the northern Mississippi Valley, Cheyennes lived in bark and, in North Dakota (Shyenne River area), earth lodges. By the late eighteenth century they had begun living in buffalo-hide tipis.

Diet Cheyennes grew corn, beans, and squash; gathered wild rice; fished; and hunted in the northern Mississippi and Shyenne valleys. From the late eighteenth century on, as the tribe became nomadic hunters, their diet depended largely on the buffalo. Women participated in all hunts, helping to drive the herds within range of the hunters. Women also cut the meat into strips to dry and dressed the skins. Cheyennes also ate other large game as well as dog. The Plains diet was supplemented by wild turnips, berries, and prickly pear cactus.

Key Technology The Cheyenne made pottery prior to their move to the Plains. Once there, the buffalo provided most of their clothing, dwellings, tools, containers, and utensils. They also made small, shallow basketry trays, primarily used for gambling.

Trade Cheyennes traded at both precontact trade centers of the northern Plains: Mandan villages on the Knife River and Arikara villages in present-day South Dakota. In the early nineteenth century, for instance, they were trading buffalo products for agricultural ones. They also traded for tobacco after they ceased growing it around 1800. Both divisions, especially the Southern Cheyenne, were highly skilled traders.

Notable Arts Traditional artists worked with leather, wood, quills, and feathers. They also carved pipes. Slender figures to divide space into five parts, especially on parfleches and other such items, was a regular artistic motif.

Transportation Cheyennes acquired horses by the mid–eighteenth century.

Dress Women dressed the skins for clothing. They made moccasins, leggings, breechclouts, shirts, and robes for men, and for themselves they made two-piece dresses and moccasins with leggings and robes in winter. Clothing was usually decorated with beaded quillwork.

War and Weapons During the late eighteenth through the mid–nineteenth century, the Cheyennes were great warriors and raiders, plundering the Spanish and other Plains tribes as well. Six interband military societies, such as the prestigious Dog Soldiers, selected a war chief. Four members of each society also constituted a 24-member war council. Each society had its own rituals, objects, and symbols.

The Siouan tribes were enemies until they and the Northern Cheyennes joined forces in the mid–nineteenth century. The Southern Cheyennes fought many regional tribes, particularly the Kiowa

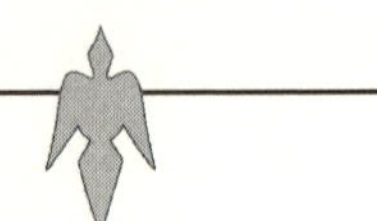

Three Cheyenne Indians, White Antelope, Alights on a Cloud, and Little Chief, from a daguerreotype taken during their delegation trip to Washington, D.C., in 1851–1852. They are wearing traditional moccasins, leggings, breechclouts, and shirts. Cheyenne clothing was usually decorated with beaded quillwork.

and the Comanches, until they joined with these two tribes in about 1840 to fight the Crows, Pawnees, Shoshones, Utes, and Apaches. Cheyennes also fought alongside the Arapaho.

As Plains dwellers, counting coup in battle by touching an enemy counted for more prestige than killing him. Weapons included the horn bow, arrows, clubs, shields, and spears.

Contemporary Information

Government/Reservations The Northern Cheyenne Reservation (Big Horn and Rosebud Counties, Montana), established in 1884, consists of 436,948 acres. There are also Northern Cheyenne Trust Lands in Rosebud County, Montana, and Meade County, South Dakota. According to the 1935 IRA constitution, amended in 1960, the tribe is governed by a council in which the president is popularly elected. The 1990 Indian population was 3,542.

A 28-member elected business council governs the Cheyenne-Arapaho Tribe, formed in 1937. Most Southern Cheyennes live in cities and towns of western Oklahoma. Their estimated population in 1990 was about 5,000.

A modified Council of Forty-Four, composed of chiefs, religious leaders, and military society members, continues its authority over Northern and Southern Cheyennes. Their decisions do not always accord with those of the official tribal governments.

Economy On the Northern Cheyenne Reservation, most jobs are provided by the tribal and federal governments, several power companies, a financial company, a construction company, and the Forest Service (seasonal fire fighting). Unemployment commonly ranges between about 50 and 90 percent. Additional tribal income comes from land use fees and leases.

Although the reservation contains a large coal reserve, many tribal members resist mining out of respect to traditional cultural values. Kerr-McGee strip mined coal, devastating vast stretches of the Northern Cheyenne Reservation, until the tribe canceled all leases in 1973.

Among the Southern Cheyenne, wheat, oil, ranching, and government-sponsored projects provide most individual income. The Southern Cheyenne also suffer from chronically high unemployment and very low average annual incomes.

Legal Status The Cheyenne-Arapaho Tribe of Oklahoma and the Northern Cheyenne Tribe of Montana are federally recognized tribal entities.

Daily Life Both tribes are focused primarily on ensuring their cultural survival. In addition, they are working on providing economic opportunities and social services. Land reacquisition is another important goal. Most Northern Cheyennes live in almost 1,000 mobile homes or government housing, much of which is of substandard quality.

All reservation schools include Cheyenne language and culture courses. Southern Cheyenne children attend public schools. Northern Cheyenne youth, in particular, are plagued with social problems such as high drop-out rates, substance abuse, and violence. Dull Knife Memorial College was chartered in 1976 "to promote academic excellence and the Cheyenne way of life."

Many Cheyenne continue to employ traditional healing practices to restore spiritual as well as physical health. Many Cheyennes continue traditional religious beliefs and practices. The Sacred Buffalo Hat is kept among the Northern

Cheyenne and the Sacred Arrow generally in Oklahoma. Many see ecological destruction, resulting from improper religious veneration, as heralding the end of the universe. Many Cheyennes are also Christians and members of the Native American Church. Cheyenne remains a living language, although few young people can speak it fluently.

A number of cooperative organizations, based on the old societies, include the military societies as well as women's groups such as Quillwork Society and War Mothers' Association. Cheyenne artists continue to work in traditional media, making items for ceremonial as well as tourist consumption. The Northern Cheyennes, with other signatories of the 1868 Fort Laramie Treaty, have refused any financial compensation for the Black Hills offered by the U.S. government. They insist on a return of the land. A congressional bill to this effect (financial compensation plus some land return) was filed in 1985. It was opposed by the South Dakota delegation and withdrawn in 1990.

Comanche

Comanche (Ku `man shē), a name derived from either the Ute *Komantcia,* "People Who Fight Us All the Time," or the Spanish *camino ancho,* "broad trail." Their self-designation was *Numinu,* "People." *See also* Shoshone, Eastern or Wind River (Chapter 4).

Location The Comanche lived in the Rocky Mountain regions of Wyoming and northern Colorado until the mid– to late seventeenth century, when the people moved into the central and southern Great Plains. Today, most Comanches live in Oklahoma.

Population In the late eighteenth century there were between 7,000 and 12,000 Comanches. Their population in the 1990s is about 8,500.

Language Comanche is part of the Uto-Aztecan language. During the eighteenth and early nineteenth centuries, variations of Comanche were used as a common trade language throughout the southwestern Great Plains.

Historical Information

History The Comanche were originally part of the Eastern Shoshone, who had lived along Arizona's Gila River from about 3000 B.C.E. to about 500 B.C.E. At that time, a group of them began migrating north toward Utah, growing a high-altitude variety of corn that had been developed in Mexico. This group, who grew corn, beans, and squash and also hunted and gathered food, is known as the Sevier Complex.

In time, Sevier people moved north of the Great Salt Lake. When a drought struck the Great Basin in the thirteenth century, the Sevier people spread out north of the Great Salt Lake. Known then as Shoshones, they lived by hunting and gathering throughout much of the Great Basin.

By about the late seventeenth century, some Shoshone bands, from the mountainous regions of Wyoming and northern Colorado, later known as

A Comanche warrior with a peyote rattle (1908). War Chief Quanah Parker played a major role in bringing the Peyote religion to the Comanche and many other Indian tribes after 1890.

Comanche, had acquired horses. The bands began migrating into New Mexico and toward the Arkansas River on the central Plains. They adopted the cycle of buffalo hunting, raiding, and fighting characteristic of Plains life.

By about 1750 they had acquired vast horse herds and dominated the central high plains. Their population had increased considerably, in part owing to the capture and adoption of young women and the abundance of buffalo meat to feed the growing numbers of children. They were also trading directly with the French by this time, from whom they acquired a steady supply of guns.

In 1780–1781 the Comanche (as well as most other Plains tribes) lost a large number of their people, perhaps as many as half, to a smallpox epidemic. In about 1790, several thousand northern Comanches and Kiowas joined together in a lasting alliance. There was a brief period of peace between the Spanish and the Comanche, roughly from 1787 to 1810, during which these two peoples were allied against the Apaches.

The Comanche continued southward throughout the eighteenth and into the early nineteenth century, pressured from the north by the Dakota/Lakota and other tribes and drawn by trade and raiding opportunities in the Southwest into New Spain/Mexico. During this period they continued to drive Apachean groups from the Plains. They also prevented the Spanish from colonizing Texas extensively, and they acted as a brake to French trade expansion into the Southwest.

By the mid–nineteenth century, Comanches were roughly separated into three divisions. The southern group lived between the Red and Colorado Rivers in Texas. The middle group wintered in Texas but followed the buffalo in summer north toward the Arkansas River. The northern group wintered on the Red River and wandered widely during the summer. In 1840, northern Comanches made peace with the Southern Cheyennes and Arapahos, after the latter had staged several successful raids against them. As part of this agreement, the Comanche gave up land in western Kansas north of the Arkansas River.

A cholera epidemic in 1849–1850 took a heavier toll on Comanche population than had all battles to date. During the 1840s and 1850s, the Comanche fought bitter wars with the Texans, the latter bent on exterminating all Indian groups. In 1853, the Comanche joined with some Apaches in a failed bid to destroy the Indians who had been settled since the 1830s on "their" lands in the Indian Territory.

The Comanche defeated Kit Carson in 1864, but they and the Kiowa signed a treaty in 1865 that reserved much of western Indian Territory (Oklahoma) for them and their allies. When the U.S. government failed to keep non-Indians out of these lands, the Indians rebelled. In the ensuing 1867 Medicine Lodge Treaty, some Comanche bands agreed to accept a reservation in southwestern Indian Territory with the Kiowa and Kiowa Apaches. Hostilities over non-Indian squatters and the difficulties of life in captivity continued for another eight years. However, by the late 1860s the Comanche were in serious trouble. The great buffalo herds had been hunted to near extinction and the U.S. Army was pursuing Indians relentlessly.

After the 1868 Battle of the Washita, in which the United States massacred a group of Cheyenne Indians, a few Comanche leaders surrendered their bands at Fort Cobb, Oklahoma; these roughly 2,500 people were later moved to Fort Sill, Oklahoma, and began farming corn. Several bands, however, remained on the Plains, holding on to the free life for several more years. The Comanche adopted a modified version of the Sun Dance in 1874. At about the same time, a short-lived religious movement led to an unsuccessful battle against the United States at Adobe Walls.

In 1874, War Chief Quanah Parker led the last free Comanche bands, along with some Kiowa and Cheyenne refugees from Fort Sill, into Palo Duro Canyon, Texas, site of the last great buffalo range. There they lived traditionally until the army found and destroyed their camp and horses. In 1875, Parker surrendered to mark the end of Comanche resistance.

Parker continued as an important leader on the reservation, overseeing favorable land leases and playing a major role in bringing the Peyote religion to the Comanche and many other Indian tribes after 1890. Reservation lands were allotted beginning in 1892. Nonallotted lands were sold to non-Indians, and nothing remained of the reservation by 1908.

Religion Comanche deities included numerous celestial objects such as the sun and moon. The Eagle Dance and Beaver ceremony were important, but they did not adopt the Sun Dance until 1874. Shamans interceded with the spirit world to cure the sick.

Young men undertook vision quests in remote places, hoping to attract a guardian spirit helper. When they returned, shamans helped them to interpret their visions, which included associated songs and taboos, and to prepare their personal medicine bundles.

Government Membership was fluid in each of the roughly 13 bands, including 4 major ones. Each band had a chief or headman, who was assisted by a council of the leading men of the band. Bands cooperated with each other, but there was no overall tribal organization or leadership, a fact that limited their nevertheless great effectiveness on the Plains.

Customs In contrast to most other Plains Indians, the fiercely independent Comanche maintained virtually no police to keep order in the camp. Leaders for buffalo hunts maintained authority for that hunt only. Men might have more than one wife. Corpses were dressed in their best clothing, face painted red and red clay on eyes, and buried in flexed position in a cave or shallow grave. Mourners cut their hair, arms, and legs; gave away their possessions; and burned the dead person's tipi, never mentioning his or her name again. After the move to the Plains, the custom of killing all of a man's horses when he died was replaced by that of killing only the best one, with the rest to be distributed among other people.

Dwellings Women made Plains-style buffalo-skin tipis.

Diet Buffalo was the main staple on the Plains. They were driven over cliffs, stalked individually, or, most popular after the people acquired horses, surrounded on horseback. Men also hunted other large and small game. Women gathered wild potatoes, fruit (plums, grapes, and currants), nuts, and berries.

Key Technology Babies were cradled in beaded skin pockets attached to V-shaped frames. Comanches also made shallow basketry gambling trays.

Trade Comanches frequented both northern Plains aboriginal trade centers. One was located in southern North Dakota, centered on the Knife River Mandan villages. The other was located north of the mouth of the Grand River, in present-day South Dakota, and centered on the Arikara villages there.

By the early eighteenth century, Comanches were also trading at Taos and Santa Fe, New Mexico, although they also raided these areas mercilessly. Other important eighteenth- and nineteenth-century trading partners included the Wichita and Osage, with whom the Comanche traded horses for guns, and Mexicans, from whom the Comanche obtained tobacco. Because of their wide range, the Comanche helped to spread the use of horses throughout the Plains.

Notable Arts Comanches were known for their silver and copper ornaments.

Transportation Having acquired horses during the late sixteenth century, probably from the Utes, the Comanche became among the most highly skilled horsemen on the Plains. They were excellent breeders and trainers as well as raiders and maintained some of the largest horse herds on the Plains. Both boys and girls began riding around age five. During the eighteenth century they began using pack horses to pull travois.

Dress Women made moccasins, leggings, breechclouts, shirts, and robes for men, and for themselves they made two-piece dresses and moccasins with leggings and robes in winter. Clothing was often decorated with beaded quillwork.

War and Weapons Comanches used red paint for battle on their horses' heads and tails as well as themselves. Other battle gear included buffalo horn headdresses, high buffalo-hide boots, and horsehair extensions to their already long hair. Weapons included feathered lances, buffalo-hide shields, and bows, mainly of Osage orange wood. The people

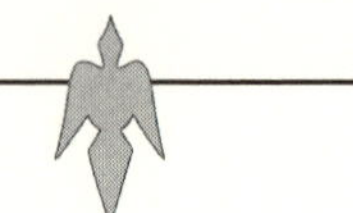

adopted military societies beginning in the eighteenth century as well as many other features of Plains warrior culture.

Traditional enemies of the Kiowa, the two groups made peace about 1790 and became raiding partners. Apaches became a favorite raiding target beginning in the late eighteenth century, as did groups such as the Ute (allies before about 1750), Navajo, Pawnee, Osage, and eastern Pueblos as well as non-Indians in the Southwest. Allies included Caddo-speaking tribes such as the Pawnee. About 1840 the Comanche joined in a loose confederacy with the Southern Cheyennes and Southern Arapahos.

Contemporary Information

Government/Reservations The Comanche Indian Tribe of Oklahoma is governed by a business committee under a 1967 constitution. The chair and other officials are popularly elected. They have no reservation or tribally owned land. Roughly 5,000 Comanches live near the tribal headquarters north of Lawton.

Economy Craft sales and government programs represent the only alternative to the local economy.

Legal Status The Comanche Indian Tribe is a federally recognized tribal entity.

Daily Life Many Comanches have intermarried with other Indian and non-Indian people. Perhaps 250 elderly Comanches spoke their language in 1993. Efforts, undertaken by tribal members as well as the University of Oklahoma, are under way to preserve the language from demise.

Since the Indian Self-Determination Act of 1975, Comanches have administered many of their own programs, such as education scholarships and assistance for the elderly. Continuing crafts include elaborate dance costumes characterized by fine feather and beadwork. The hand game, with its associated singing and gambling, is still widely played. Comanches participate in numerous local powwows, especially the Comanche Homecoming Powwow, held in July at Walters, Oklahoma. Most Comanches are Christians, although some are also members of the Native American Church.

Cree, Plains

Plains Cree (Krē), a division of the Cree Indians of central Canada. The name comes from the French *Kristenaux,* a corruption of a Cree self-designations. *See also* Cree (Chapter 9).

Location Early in the seventeenth century, Crees inhabited the forests between Lake Superior and Hudson Bay. By the eighteenth and nineteenth centuries, groups of Crees had moved into western Saskatchewan and eastern Alberta and south to northern Montana. These were the northernmost of the Plains Indians.

Population From an early-seventeenth-century total Cree population of about 15,000, there were roughly 4,000 Plains Cree in 1780. There are some 60,000 Cree today, mostly in Canada.

Language All nine Cree dialects belong to the central division of the Algonquian language family.

Historical Information

History The earliest Algonquians may have come north from the lower Mississippi Valley shortly after the last ice sheet retreated from the Great Lakes and St. Lawrence River regions. Their population grew until a large number of them lived north and west of the Great Lakes. Crees probably originated in central and northern Manitoba around 1100. By 1500 they were located at the forest's edge along and south of the Saskatchewan River. Cree bands began acquiring guns and other goods from the French in the mid–seventeenth century, trading furs, especially beaver, for them. Hudson's Bay Company opened a post in Cree territory in 1667.

During the period of the French fur trade, many Cree and French intermarried. Many *voyageurs* and *coureurs de bois* were mixed French and Cree, as were the mixed-blood Métis. During the later seventeenth century, the quest for furs, as well as their own growing population, pushed the Cree on toward the west until they stretched from near Labrador in the east to the Great Slave Lake and south to Alberta, northern Montana, and North Dakota in the west. During these migrations they displaced their ancient

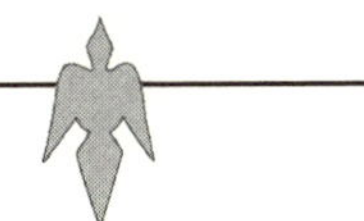

enemies to the west, the Athapaskans, and pushed Dakota bands westward as well.

Crees formed a close alliance with the Assiniboine in the late seventeenth century. They experienced severe smallpox epidemics in 1737 and 1781, particularly in the Lake Winnipeg area. By the early eighteenth century, the Cree were roughly divided into Woodland (eastern and western) and Plains divisions, having reached Lake Winnipeg and beyond. During this period they still retained much of their old Woodland culture.

Plains Crees acquired horses in the mid– to late eighteenth century and adopted much of classic nomadic Plains Indian culture, including warring, raiding, and using the buffalo for food, clothing, shelter, tools, equipment, and fuel. Some also intermarried with Mohawk Indians who were serving as guides for non-Indian fur trading companies, which the Cree were provisioning with buffalo meat. By the early nineteenth century, Plains Crees controlled the area north of the Missouri River and were pressuring the Blackfeet to the west and south.

A sharp decline set in during the 1850s, however, owing primarily to smallpox epidemics and warfare with the Blackfeet. Canadian officials created Cree reserves in the 1870s, on which Crees were theoretically encouraged to turn to the agricultural life. In fact, the Indians themselves were aware that the buffalo life was soon to end and wanted help in making the change to agriculture. Though they might well have adapted to this change, most were denied access to key resources, such as implements and livestock (both promised in treaties). Such items, if they were issued at all, were generally inappropriate and/or of poor quality.

From the Indian point of view, they had given up their land for empty promises. Privation and even starvation stalked Indian communities. Government officials tended to blame Indian farming failures on their presumed idleness. Of course, non-Indians also had problems farming the Plains during these years, but they were free to move at will and were not subject to discrimination or undue restrictions in marketing their yield or obtaining loans, credit, and basic supplies.

Despite these obstacles, some bands did make a relative success of farming, to the extent that non-Indian farmers were complaining toward the end of the 1880s about unfair competition from Native Americans. In 1890, the Canadian government turned to a policy of peasant farming, in which the reserves were subdivided. Land was allotted in severalty, "surplus" land was sold to non-Indians, and mechanized farm equipment was taken away. With this policy, Canadian officials succeeded in dramatically reducing total land under Indian cultivation as well as the number of Indian farmers and in maintaining the reserves in poverty. Indian protests were routinely ignored or repressed.

In 1885, Poundmaker and Big Bear led the Cree in the Second Riel Rebellion (Louis Riel was a Métis nationalist leader). They and the Métis joined forces to try to stem the flow of non-Indian settlers to the vicinity of the Canadian Pacific Railway line in Saskatchewan and to create a native state. The Cree were not defeated but surrendered shortly after their Métis allies did. One group of Cree became associated at that time with Little Shell's band of Chippewas in Montana. Big Bear, a leader of the rebellion, escaped with 200 Cree to the United States, where they wandered for three decades in Montana until joining with a band of Chippewa under the leadership of Stone Child, or Rocky Boy. In 1916, the U.S. government created the Rocky Boy Reservation in the Bearpaw Mountains of Montana for these people. Little Shell's band eventually settled in nearby towns and reservations.

Religion Adolescent boys undertook vision quests. Shamans used their spirit powers to cure illness. In midsummer, bands (either individually or collectively) celebrated the Sun Dance.

Government There were from 8 to 12 bands of fluid composition among the Plains Cree, each with a headman and a loosely defined hunting territory. The leadership position required excellent hunting and speaking skills as well as the traits of bravery and generosity and could be hereditary. Each band also had a warrior society.

Customs Newborn infants were dried with moss or soft wood and, after a few days, placed in a hide sack stuffed with moss. A baby later wore a small pouch containing the umbilical cord around the neck. Babies were named at a feast soon after birth by a same-sex relative. The child's name was associated with the name-givers' spirit vision. Most people also had nicknames. Names associated with supernatural power and with the dead were not commonly spoken.

Children were nursed for up to five years. Girls were secluded for four nights at the onset of puberty. During this time they performed various tasks, ate little, and scratched their heads with a stick. They also often acquired their spirit visions. A feast followed this initial period of seclusion. Married women also withdrew when menstruating. There were no male puberty ceremonies, except that boys were encouraged to fast and undertake a vision quest.

For marriage gifts, the bride's family gave the couple a fully equipped tipi. The groom received a horse from his father-in-law as well as moccasins from his new wife. Plains Crees observed the mother-in-law taboo.

Corpses were dressed in their best clothing, and their faces were painted. They were taken out the side of the tipi, not the door, and buried in the ground, in log chambers, or in tree scaffolds. Some eastern bands built gabled-roof grave houses. A filled pipe and a container of grease were buried with the body. Close relatives sliced their limbs and wore their hair loose until the mourning period ended. Bundles containing ancestral locks of hair were considered extremely important and were carried by the women when the camp moved. The possessions of the dead were given away.

The early Cree practiced tattooing with needles and leather threads. Shinny was widely played. Both men and women used tobacco, obtained from traders and mixed with dried bearberry leaves, for ceremonial purposes.

Dwellings Plains Crees lived in buffalo-hide tipis with three-pole foundations.

Diet Buffalo was the staple food. Men hunted in small groups during the winter and communally in summer. Buffalo were driven into brush impoundments or, in winter, into marshes or deep snow. Men also hunted other large game.

Women snared a variety of small game, fished, and caught birds (and gathered their eggs). They also gathered roots (such as prairie turnip), berries (such as Saskatoon berries), fruits, and tubers. Most of these were dried and stored for winter. At least as early as the early nineteenth century, some Plains Crees maintained gardens and even kept cattle to help ensure a constant food supply.

Key Technology Plains Crees periodically burned the grasslands in autumn to encourage higher yield and earlier growth, thus helping to maintain the buffalo herd. They also used fire to drive a herd toward a particular area and to keep them away from key trade sites. In addition to the usual buffalo-based technology, Plains Crees fished using weirs, platforms, and spears.

Trade Crees acted as intermediaries between non-Indian traders and Indian tribes such as the Blackfeet in the late seventeenth century.

Notable Arts Like many Plains Indians, the Cree made beaded quillwork and painted hides.

Transportation Dogs carried extra goods with the help of a strap across the chest before the advent of the travois. Later, dog-drawn and, after about 1770, horse-drawn travois were used to transport goods. The Cree also used snowshoes and canoes, which they abandoned during the seventeenth and eighteenth centuries in favor of crude, temporary buffalo-hide rafts.

Dress In general, the upper body remained bare except for a robe or ceremonial garments. The people also wore one-piece moccasins as well as rawhide visors against the sun.

War and Weapons Each band had a warrior society. Early enemies included the Iroquois and Dakotas to the south as well as Athapaskan and Inuit tribes to the north. Later, they fought with the Blackfeet. Allies included the Ojibwa and the Assiniboine.

Unlike many Plains tribes, the Cree placed a high value on scalping. One customarily gave away

much of the booty captured in a raid. Weapons included sinew-backed bows and war clubs consisting of a stone in a bag on the end of a stick.

Contemporary Information

Government/Reservations The Rocky Boy Chippewa-Cree Reservation (1,485 Indians in 1990) and Trust Lands (397 Indians in 1990) is located in Chouteau and Hill Counties, Montana. It was established in 1916 and contains 108,015 acres. The tribe is governed by the Chippewa-Cree Business Committee. Roughly half of the population lives off-reservation.

The Little Shell people, some of whom are of Cree descent, had a 1990 population of 3,300.

There are Cree reserves in Alberta, Saskatchewan, Manitoba, Ontario, and Quebec.

Economy Activities in Montana include cattle grazing, wheat and barley farming, some logging and mining, and recreation and tourism. Unemployment regularly approaches 75 percent.

Legal Status The Chippewa-Cree Indians of the Rocky Boy Reservation, Montana, are a federally recognized tribal entity.

The Little Shell people have been seeking federal recognition since the 1920s. Other Montana Cree, such as the people of Hill 57, also remain landless and unrecognized.

Daily Life The Chippewa-Crees opened Stone Child Community College in 1978. Crees along Lubicon Lake in Alberta, Canada, have had to contend with serious pollution caused by non-Indian oil drilling companies. Most children of landless Cree attend public schools. Many Chippewa-Crees are Christians. Many also participate in the Sun Dance, sweat lodge ceremonies, and the Native American Church. Cree is still spoken on the reservation and by some older people living off-reservation.

Crow

The Crow (Krō) self-designation was *Absaroke,* after a bird once native to the region. *See also* Hidatsa.

Location The Crow traditional homeland was south of Lake Winnipeg. By the late eighteenth century they inhabited southwestern Montana and northern Wyoming. Today, most Crows live in Bighorn and Yellowstone Counties, Montana.

Population There were about 4,000 Crows in the late eighteenth century. There were 8,491 enrolled members of the tribe in 1991.

Language Crow/Hidatsa is a Siouan language.

Historical Information

History The Hidatsa-Crow lived originally in the Ohio country. From there, they moved to northern Illinois, through western Minnesota and into the Red River Valley, south of Lake Winnipeg. There they remained for at least several hundred years, beginning around the twelfth or thirteenth century, growing gardens and hunting buffalo.

Pressured by newly armed bands of Ojibwas and Crees, the group moved southwest to Devil's Lake in the mid–sixteenth century and then again toward the upper Missouri River, north of the Mandans, where they continued to hunt and grow corn. In the late seventeenth century, the Crow struck out on their own toward southwestern Montana and northern Wyoming and the vicinity of the Yellowstone, Powder, and Mussellshell Rivers. During this period, they separated into mountain (southern Montana and northern Wyoming) and river (lower Yellowstone region) divisions.

The Crow acquired horses, probably from the Shoshone, and became full-fledged nomadic Plains Indians during the mid–eighteenth century. In addition to the Crows' warring and raiding activities, they also traded with the Shoshone and other Great Basin and Plateau groups for horses that they then exchanged with easterly tribes. Whenever possibly they avoided non-Indians. During that period they were considered a wealthy tribe with many horses. Their land between the Yellowstone River and Big Horn Mountains contained plenty of pasture as well as excellent natural defenses.

Major smallpox epidemics struck the people in 1781 and 1833. Crow boundaries under the 1851 Fort Laramie Treaty included about 38.5 million

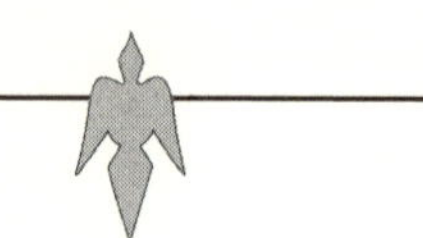

American Indians on horseback at Buffalo Run, Yellowstone, circa 1924.

acres, mostly in the Yellowstone region. The Powder River country remained in dispute between them and the Lakota. However, their lands were drastically reduced in 1868 and again in subsequent years. During that period the Crows became seminomadic, building winter camps that included a few log cabins. In much of the 1860s and 1870s, Crows served the United States as scouts in the Indian wars, especially against the Lakota and the Nez Percé.

Despite their help to the United States, the U.S. government treated the Crow no differently than it did any other Indians. By the late 1880s the Crow had been forced to cede most of their remaining land. Catholic missionaries and boarding schools had made inroads into the reservation and into Crow culture. Many aspects of traditional Crow culture, such as giveaways and the Sun Dance, had been outlawed in 1884. It was also illegal to leave the reservation without permission and to sell a horse to another Indian. In the seven years from 1914 to 1921, Crow horse herds declined from roughly 35,000 to less than 1,000. Some leaders, like Chief Plenty Coups, urged accommodation, especially in the area of education.

Meanwhile, the Crow developed a tribal council that managed to keep the Bureau of Indian Affairs staff at arm's length and provide them with a semi-independent decision-making body. In the 1950s, the government coerced the Crow into selling their rights to the Bighorn Canyon, where it built the Yellowtail Dam, ironically named for one of its chief opponents. In 1981, legal ownership of the Bighorn River passed to the state of Montana.

Religion Like other Plains Indians, the Crow placed great importance in supernatural guardian helpers acquired in dreams or during vision quests. Their main ceremonies included the Sun Dance, the Medicine Lodge, and the triennial Tobacco Society

American Indians near lodges at Buffalo Run, Yellowstone, circa 1924.

ceremony, performed by both men and women in honor of the tribe's sacred plant.

The existence of the Tobacco Society conferred benefits on both planters and the tribe as a whole. Payment of a high fee entitled one to membership in the society and the right to learn and perform the associated songs and dances. The proper place for planting tobacco was determined by consultation over ranking members' dreams. Seed preparation and planting were highly ritualized, although the area was always burned over first.

Planting was followed by a dance and then a feast. In a subsequent ceremony, new members were adopted into the society; this ceremony was also highly ritualized and included fees paid for various honors, painting, dancing, singing, and sweating as well as the acquisition of medicine bundles. Members observed various behavior restrictions during the year. The harvest was also accompanied by ritual.

Government Each of about 13 matrilineal clans was led by a headman selected on the basis of his war record. A council of chiefs governed the tribe; one member of the council was head of the camp. Each spring, one of the men's military societies was appointed camp police force, which was charged with maintaining internal order, supervising the buffalo hunt, and regulating war parties.

Customs Generosity was highly valued among the Crow, as with most Plains tribes. For instance, the leader of a successful raid was entitled to all its plunder but was socially obligated to give it away.

Unlike most Plains nomads they were organized into matrilineal clans. Most girls married before puberty to men outside the clan, and most men purchased their wives. Pre- or extramarital sex was not punished, but female chastity was valued. Wives were also gained by inheritance and capture.

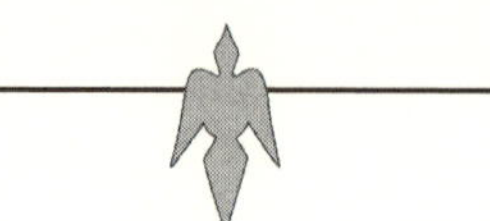

Mother-in-law and father-in-law taboos were observed.

Parents spent a great deal of time nurturing, teaching, and encouraging their children to prepare for life as adults. There were no orphans, as orphans were immediately adopted by aunts or uncles. Children rarely, if ever, received corporal punishment. Instead, "joking relatives" used pointed humor to keep people in line.

Corpses were removed from the tipi through the side, dressed in their best clothes, painted, and placed on a scaffold. The bones were later buried among rocks or in a cave, except that tipis were erected over the scaffolds of great chiefs. Mourners cut their hair, gashed their limbs (or sometimes cut off their fingers), and gave away their property.

Games included the hand game, dice games, shinny, contests, and hoop and pole. Most games included gambling. Relatively high prices were commanded for various ceremonial privileges.

Dwellings When Crows lived near Lake Winnipeg and with the Hidatsa along the Missouri River, they built earth lodges. Later, women made four-pole, 25-foot-high (or higher) skin tipis of between 7 and 20 buffalo skins. The larger tipis could house as many as 40 people, but the average was about 12. The tipi owner or a special guest slept at the rear (opposite the door). A draft screen around the lower inside was painted with pictures of the owner's war feats.

Diet Pre-Plains Crows raised corn and other crops. Buffalo were hunted by driving them into impoundments or over cliffs or by means of the mounted surround. Men also hunted deer, antelope, and other large game, sometimes by wearing the skin of such an animal and stalking it. Meat was roasted over a fire, cooked in the ashes, or stone boiled in a skin-lined pit. It was also cut into strips, dried, and stored for the winter. Women dug roots and gathered berries, fruit, and other wild foods. The Crow grew their ceremonial tobacco but traded for the everyday variety.

Key Technology Pottery predated the move to the Plains. Material goods included, in addition to the usual buffalo-based items, fire drills; bows from hickory, ash, or even elk antler; and stone scrapers and other tools. The cradle board, mostly a means of transportation, was U-shaped at the top and tapered at the bottom. Backrests for use within the tipi were made of willow sticks bound with sinew and hung from a tripod.

Trade The Crow played the role of intermediary between the Mandans and Hidatsas to the east and Great Basin and Plateau tribes such as the Shoshone, Salish (Flathead), Nez Percé, and Ute. The Crow-Mandan trade continued until the early nineteenth century.

Notable Arts Weapons were extremely finely made, as were clothing, blankets, and leather items such as decorated parfleches. There were also various ceremonial carvings.

Transportation Dogs carried movable goods and pulled travois. After the people acquired horses in the mid–eighteenth century, they became highly skilled horsemen and perhaps the best horse thieves on the Plains. They used skin rafts to cross rivers.

Dress Typical Plains clothing included, for men, a shirt, hip-high leggings, moccasins, and a buffalo robe. Women wore a long dress, knee-high leggings, and moccasins. Both used rawhide visors against the sun. Before braiding became customary, the Crow parted their hair in the middle and wore it, sometimes with additions of horse hair, as low as ground level. In the later period, women's dresses were decorated with elks' teeth and fur trim.

War and Weapons The various men's societies were voluntary and not age-graded, although some were more important than others. Most or all had military, hunt, or police-related functions. The Crazy Dogs were dedicated to unusual bravery in combat. Dog Soldiers were the camp police. Some societies occasionally engaged in annual wife capturing.

Traditional enemies included the Shoshone, Lakota (after circa 1800), and Blackfeet. Allies included the Mandan, Salish (Flathead), and Nez Percé. Crows preferred to count coup rather than to scalp. Four people could count coup against the same enemy, with diminishing honor. Four war activities worthy of formal honors were, in descending order: leading a successful party, touching an enemy, stealing a picketed horse, and taking a weapon in a hand-to-hand encounter. Weapons included wooden or horn bows and arrows, stone-headed war clubs, knives, and painted, feather-decorated shields.

Contemporary Information

Government/Reservations The Crow Reservation (Big Horn and Yellowstone Counties, Montana), established in 1868, is composed of over 1,500,000 acres, of which about 400,000 are tribally owned. The 1990 resident Indian population was 4,724. The constitution dates from 1948. All adults are members of the general council, which elects four tribal officers and various governing committees. The council governs the tribe, along with the tribal court. Almost half the land base is owned by non-Indians.

Economy The reservation is rich in natural resources, such as coal, although the Crow for years had been unable to profit greatly from it. However, in 1993 the tribe concluded a settlement with the United States that called for the creation of a trust fund of up to $85 million in compensation for mismanaged mineral resource development. There are jobs with the tribal government, Little Bighorn College, and mining companies. Most agricultural land is leased to large corporations. There is also a visitor center and motel complex. Unemployment regularly tops 50 percent

An interior of a Crow Indian home in Montana, circa 1910.

Legal Status The Crow Tribe is a federally recognized tribal entity.

Daily Life Most Crow people speak the native language. A matrilineal clan system and regular giveaways help maintain a semitraditional family structure. Other customs, such as traditional healing ceremonies, the giving of Indian names, and the use of medicine bundles in traditional prayers, are also maintained.

The annual fair in August, featuring feasting, rodeos, giveaways, and other traditional and semitraditional activities, is a time to renew social and family ties. Crows adorn their costumes and riding gear with expertly made beadwork, although they do not generally sell it to tourists.

Tribally controlled Little Bighorn College represents a continuing focus on educational achievement. Some Crows are Christians. Many also practice sweat lodge, Sun Dance, and Native American Church ceremonies. People still undertake vision quests, and the Tobacco Society remains active. The Crow continue to battle high unemployment and its associated social problems, such as substance abuse, as well as continuing racial discrimination.

Dakota

Dakota (Dä `kō tä), a Siouan dialect spoken by the Eastern group of the tribe commonly referred to as Sioux. The divisions of the Eastern group include Sisseton ("swamp village," "lake village," or "fishscale village"), Wahpeton ("dwellers among the leaves"), Wahpekute ("shooters among the leaves"), and Mdewakanton ("People of the Mystic Lake"). The latter two divisions are also known as Santee (from *Isanati,* "knife.") and shared a closely related culture.

The Dakota refer to themselves as Dakota ("ally"), Dakotah Oyate ("Dakota People"), or *Ikce Wicasa* ("Natural" or "Free People"). The word "Sioux" is derived originally from an Ojibwa word, *Nadowe-is-iw,* meaning "lesser adder" ("enemy" is the implication), which was corrupted by French voyageurs to *Nadoussioux* and then shortened to *Sioux.* Today, many people use the term "Dakota" or, less commonly, "Lakota" to refer to all Sioux people.

All 13 subdivisions of Dakota-Lakota-Nakota speakers (Sioux) were known as *Oceti Sakowin,* or Seven Council Fires, a term referring to their seven political divisions: Teton (the Western group, speakers of Lakota); Sisseton, Wahpeton, Wahpekute, and Mdewakanton (the Eastern group, speakers of Dakota); and Yankton and Yanktonai (the Central, or Wiciyela, group, speakers of Dakota and Nakota). *See also* Lakota and Nakota.

Location In the late seventeenth century, the Dakotas lived in Wisconsin and north-central Minnesota, around Mille Lacs. By the nineteenth century they had migrated to the prairies and eastern plains of Minnesota, Iowa, Nebraska, and eastern South Dakota. Today, most Dakotas live on reservations in the Dakotas, Nebraska, and Minnesota and in regional cities and towns.

Population Dakota, Lakota, and Nakota speakers numbered about 25,000 in the late seventeenth century. At that time there were approximately 5,000 Dakota speakers. There were about 12,000–15,000 Dakota and Nakota speakers in the late eighteenth century. Today there are at least 6,000 Dakotas living in the United States and Canada.

Language The Eastern group speaks the Dakota dialect of Dakota, a Siouan language.

Historical Information

History The Siouan linguistic family may have originated along the lower Mississippi River or in eastern Texas. Siouan speakers moved to, or may in fact have originated in, the Ohio Valley, where they lived in large agricultural settlements. They may have been related to the Mound Builder culture of the ninth through twelfth centuries. They may also have originated in the upper Mississippi Valley or even the Atlantic seaboard.

Siouan tribes still lived in the southeast, between Florida and Virginia, around the late sixteenth and early seventeenth century. All were destroyed either by attacks from Algonquian-speaking Indians or a

A government agent distributes food rations to Dakota Indians.

combination of attacks from non-Indians and non-Indian diseases. Some fled and were absorbed by other tribes. Some were also sent as slaves to the West Indies.

Dakota-Lakota-Nakota speakers ranged throughout more than 100 million acres of the upper Mississippi region, including Minnesota and parts of Wisconsin, Iowa, and the Dakotas, from the sixteenth to the early seventeenth century. Some of these people encountered French explorers around Mille Lacs, Minnesota, in the late seventeenth century, and Santees were directly involved in the great British-French political and economic struggle. Around that time, conflict with the Cree and Anishinabe, who were well armed with French rifles, plus the lure of great buffalo herds to feed their expanding population, induced bands to begin moving west into the Plains. The people acquired horses around the mid–eighteenth century.

Dakotas were the last to leave, with most bands remaining in prairies of western Minnesota and eastern South Dakota. They also retained many eastern Woodland/western Great Lakes characteristics. Around 1800, the Wahpeton established villages above the mouth of the Minnesota River. Fifty years later they had moved farther upriver and broken into an upper and a lower division. The Mdewakanton and Wahpekute tribes (Santee) established villages around the Mississippi and lower Minnesota Rivers and began hunting buffalo communally, competing with the Sauk, Fox, and other tribes.

Dakotas ceded all land in Minnesota and Iowa in 1837 and 1851 (Mendota and Traverse des Sioux Treaties), except for a reservation along the Minnesota River. Santees were served by a lower agency, near Morton, and Sissetons and Wahpetons by an upper agency, near Granite Falls. At the mercy of dishonest agents and government officials, who cheated them out of food and money, and all but overrun by squatters, the Santees rebelled in 1862. Under the leadership of Ta-oya-te-duta (Little Crow), they killed hundreds of non-Indians.

Since many Wahpetons and Sissetons remained neutral (or, as in the case of Chief Wabasha, betrayed their people), and support for the rebellion was not deep, it shortly collapsed. In reprisal, the government hanged 38 Dakotas after President Lincoln pardoned over 250 others and confiscated all Dakota land and property in Minnesota. All previous treaties were unilaterally abrogated. Little Crow himself was killed by bounty hunters in 1863. His scalp and skull were placed on exhibition in St. Paul.

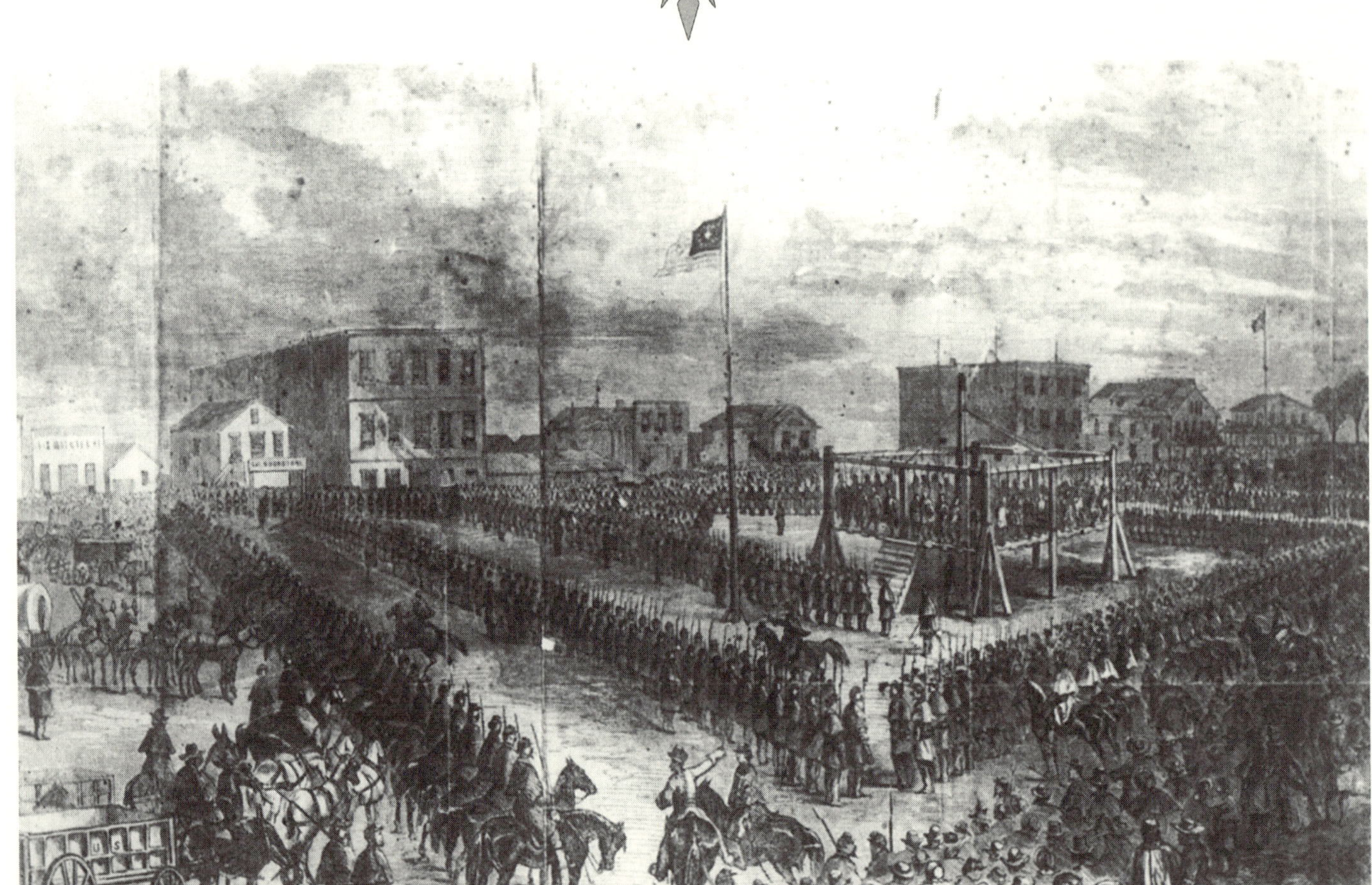

At the mercy of dishonest agents and government officials who cheated them out of food and money, the Santees rebelled in 1862. This drawing by W. C. Childs depicts the mass hanging of 32 Santee Dakota Indians at Mankato, Minnesota, on December 2, 1862, for their participation in the revolt.

Many Santees fled to Canada and to the West, to join relatives at Fort Peck and elsewhere. Many more died of starvation and illness during this period. Mdewakanton and Wahpekute survivors were rounded up and finally settled at Crow Creek, South Dakota, a place of poor soil and little game, where hundreds of removed Dakotas died within one year. Thus ended the long Santee occupation of the eastern Woodlands/prairie region.

In 1866, Santees at Crow Creek were removed to the Santee Reservation, Nebraska, where living conditions were extremely poor. Most of the land was allotted in 1885. Missionaries, especially Congregationalists and Episcopalians, were influential well into the twentieth century. Most people lived by subsistence farming, hunting, fishing, and gathering.

Two reservations were established for Wahpetons and Sissetons around 1867: the Sisseton-Wahpeton Reservation, near Lake Traverse, South Dakota, and the Fort Totten Reservation, at Devil's Lake. By 1892, two-thirds of the Lake Traverse Reservation had been opened to non-Indians, with the remaining one-third, about 300,000 acres, allotted to individuals. In order not to starve, many sold their allotted land, so that more than half of the latter acreage was subsequently lost. For much of the early twentieth century, people eked out a living through subsistence farming combined with other subsistence activities as well as wages and trust-fund payments.

Several hundred Dakotas left the Santee Reservation in 1869 to settle on the Big Sioux River near Flandreau, South Dakota, renouncing tribal membership at that time. Some federal aid was

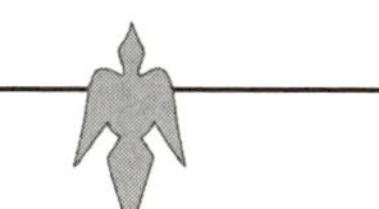

arranged by a Presbyterian minister, but by and large these people lived without even the meager benefits provided to most Indians. Some Flandreau Indians eventually drifted back to form communities in Minnesota. The official status of these communities was uncertain well into the twentieth century.

Religion Male and female shamans provided religious leadership. Depending on the tribe, their duties might include leading hunting and war parties; curing the sick; foretelling the future, including the weather; and interpreting visions and dreams. Wahpeton shamans also divined the whereabouts of the enemy and lost objects. They performed feats of skill and magic in front of large audiences to impress the public with their powers.

Sissetons and Wahpetons believed in Wakan Tanka, the Great Spirit and creator of the universe, as well as other gods and spirits. The secret Wahpeton Medicine Lodge Society performed the Medicine Dance several times a year. Participants used drums, deer hoof rattles, whistles, and sacred pipes carved of pipestone. Other religious activities included vision quests and ritual purification in the sweat lodge. The Sisseton later adopted some Plains ceremonies, such as the Sun Dance.

Government All but the Wahpekute were divided into seven bands, each usually led by a chief. In more recent times that position was often hereditary. For the same three bands, the *akitcita* was an elite warrior group that maintained discipline at camp and on the hunt. This police society was distinctive of Siouans and may have originated with them. The Seven Council Fires met approximately annually to socialize and discuss matters of national importance.

Religious activities among Dakota Indians included vision quests and ritual purification in the sweat lodge. These men are seated in a sweat lodge with its covering partially raised. Before the advent of tin buckets, water was carried in buffalo bladders into which hot stones were dropped.

Customs Mdewakantons wrapped their dead in skins or blankets and placed them on scaffolds. Remains were taken to a tribal burial grounds after a few months or years and buried in mounds with tools and weapons. Burial mounds were at least several feet high and up to 60 feet in diameter.

Sissetons treated their dead similarly but included tools, weapons, and utensils. Bodies with heads facing south were placed in scaffolds or trees. A horse might be killed for a dead warrior to use in the next life. Murder victims were placed face down in the ground. Mourners cut their hair and slashed their limbs.

Wahpetons buried their dead early on but changed to scaffolds, probably as a result of Sisseton influence. The Dakota bands may once have been clans. Favorite games, usually accompanied by gambling, included lacrosse and shinny. Descent was patrilineal.

Dwellings Dakotas built small, occasionally palisaded villages near lakes and rice swamps when they lived in the Wisconsin-Minnesota area. At that time they lived in large, heavily timbered bark houses with pitched roofs. In winter, some groups lived in small conical houses covered with skins. Both men and women helped build the houses. The Sisseton sometimes used tipis after their move to the prairies.

Diet Siouan people in the Ohio Valley farmed corn, beans, and squash. While still in the Great Lakes region, women grew corn, beans, and squash. People ate turtles, fish, dogs, and large and small game and gathered wild rice. Buffalo, which roamed the area in small herds, was also an important food source. People burned grass around the range and forced the buffalo toward an ambush. The Sisseton, especially, turned more toward buffalo with their westward migration.

Key Technology Bows and arrows were the main hunting weapons. The Sisseton carved pipestone (catlinite) ceremonial pipes and wove rushes into mats. The Wahpeton wove rushes into mats and also wove cedar and basswood fiber bags. All groups made pottery. Fish were either speared or shot with a bow and arrow. Iron-containing clays were pulverized in stone mortars and mixed with gluey material to make paint. Brushes were made of bone, horn, wood, or a tuft of antelope hair mounted on a stick. The flageolet was a common musical instrument.

Trade Depending on time and location, Dakota tribes traded various woodland/prairie/plains goods. Items included wild rice, pottery, and skins and other animal products.

Notable Arts The Dakota made fine painted rawhide trunks. They incised and painted parfleches, pipe pouches, robes, and other items. Women tended to make geometric designs, whereas men made more realistic forms. Clothing was embroidered and, later, beaded.

Transportation The Sisseton made dugout canoes, and the Wahpeton made birch-bark canoes. Most groups obtained horses beginning around 1760, but the eastern groups never had as many as did the western groups.

Dress Most clothing was made from buckskin. In the Woodlands, the people wore breechclouts, dresses, leggings, and moccasins, with fur robes for extra warmth. On the Plains, they decorated their clothing with beads and quillwork in geometric and animal designs.

War and Weapons The idea that the purpose of war was to bring glory to an individual rather than to acquire territory or destroy an enemy people was distinctive to the Siouan people and may have originated with them. Dakotas did not generally fight other Dakotas. The *akitcita,* known particularly among the Mdewakanton, was an elite warrior group that maintained discipline at camp and on the hunt. The Ojibwa were traditional enemies, at least around the seventeenth and eighteenth centuries.

Contemporary Information

Government/Reservations The Fort Peck Reservation, Roosevelt, Sheridan, and Valley Counties, Montana (Assiniboine-Sioux [Upper Yanktonai and Sisseton-Wahpeton]), established in 1873, consists of about one million acres, about one-quarter of which is

Sam Kills Two, a Brulé Dakota, paints a winter count in 1926. The death of Turning Bear, killed by a locomotive in 1920, is shown in the second row just above Kills Two's left foot. Some Plains tribes kept records of events by means of symbolic figures or pictographs.

tribally owned. Their 1927 constitution is not based on the Indian Reorganization Act (IRA). Their representative government, the Tribal Executive Board, dates from 1960. Enrollment in 1992 was 10,500, with 6,700 residents.

The Devil's Lake (formerly Fort Totten) Reservation, Benson, Eddy, Nelson and Ramsey Counties, North Dakota (Sisseton, Wahpeton, and Cuthead Yanktonai), established in 1867, consists of 53,239 acres, most of which have been allotted. There were 4,420 enrolled members in 1992, with about 2,900 in residence. The IRA constitution adopted in 1944 calls for elections to a tribal council.

The Lake Traverse Reservation, Richland and Sargent Counties, North Dakota, and Cadington, Day, Grant, Marshall, and Roberts Counties, South Dakota (Sisseton and Wahpeton), established in 1867, consists of about 105,000 acres. Under a 1934 constitution and by-laws, the people elect district representatives to a tribal council. Tribal enrollment was 10,073 in 1992, with a resident population of 5,306.

The Santee Sioux Reservation, Knox County, Nebraska (Santee), established in 1863, consists of about 3,600 acres. Enrollment in 1992 was about 2,000. In the same year there were 748 residents. A tribal council governs the reservation.

The Flandreau Santee Sioux Reservation, Moody County, South Dakota (Santee), established in 1935, consists of about 2,180 acres. The constitution and by-laws were approved in 1931 and then amended in 1936 to conform to the IRA. Enrolled membership in 1992 was 611 with about 230 residents. An executive committee governs the reservation.

The Lower Sioux Community, Redwood County, Minnesota (Santee), established in 1887, owns 1,742.93 acres. The 1992 enrollment was 750 with about 300 residents. The people elect a community council.

The Prairie Island Community, Goodhue County, Minnesota (Santee), established in 1887, consists of about 534 acres. Enrollment in 1992 was 440, with 56 residents in 1990. A community council is popularly elected.

The Upper Sioux Community, Yellow Medicine County, Minnesota (Sisseton, Wahpeton, Flandreau Santee, Santee, Yankton), established in 1938, consists of 743.57 acres. There were 43 residents in 1990. Political power is exercised by a board of trustees.

The Prior Lake (Shakopee) Community, Scott County, Minnesota (Santee), established in 1969, consists of about 293 acres. Enrollment in 1992 was 227, with 174 residents. A community council governs the community.

The Wabasha Community (Minnesota) consists of 110.24 acres. There are no residents. It was purchased in 1944 as part of the Upper Mississippi Fish and Wildlife Refuge.

Some Wahpetons and other Dakotas also live on Canadian reserves, such as Portage la Prairie, Sioux Valley, Pipestone, and Bird Tail in Manitoba and Fort Qu'appelle, Moose Wood, and Round Plain in Saskatchewan.

Economy The Devil's Lake Sioux have a plant that makes nonviolent armaments such as camouflage nets. There are also a bingo hall and a casino. Lake Traverse has a bingo hall and casino as well as a plastic bag factory. With an inadequate land base and little industry, many residents of the Santee Sioux Reservation must seek employment in nearby cities and towns. A pharmaceutical company provides a small number of jobs.

The Flandreau Reservation opened the Royal River Casino in 1990. Fort Peck has a bingo hall, and land is leased to non-Indian farmers and ranchers. Fort Peck owns and operates a profitable oil well. They also have other mineral resources and have encouraged industrial development.

The Lower Sioux own a casino, as do Prairie Island (casino and bingo hall), Upper Sioux (casino), and Prior Lake (casino and bingo hall).

Legal Status The Assiniboine and Sioux Tribes of the Fort Peck Reservation, the Devils Lake Sioux Tribe, the Flandreau Santee Sioux Tribe, the Lower Sioux Indian Community of Minnesota Mdewakanton Sioux Indians, the Prairie Island Indian Community of Minnesota Mdewakanton Sioux Indians, the Santee Sioux Tribe, the Shakopee Mdewakanton Sioux Community (Prior Lake), the Sisseton-Wahpeton Sioux Tribe (Lake Traverse), and the Upper Sioux Indian Community are federally recognized tribal entities.

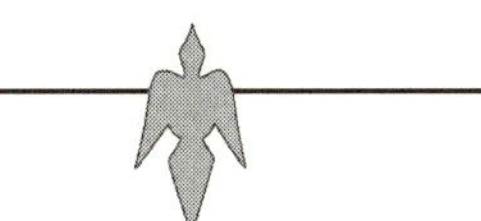

Daily Life The Wahpeton and Sisseton people are closely related, in part through much intermarriage. At Lake Traverse, Sisseton-Wahpeton Community College opened in 1979, and Tiospa Zina High School emphasizes tribal values. Many people speak Dakota at Devil's Lake, which is a relatively traditional community. They sponsor a powwow in July. The Native American Church and Sacred Pipe ceremony, among other religious practices, remain active. People on the Santee Reservation resisted a casino in favor of cultural revival. Flandreau received new homes, irrigation, and health care facilities in the 1960s.

Gros Ventres

Gros Ventres (Grō vant) is French for "big belly," after a mistranslation of the sign language for their name. They were once known to non-Indians as Gros Ventres of the Prairie as opposed to the Gros Ventres of the Missouri (Hidatsa). The Blackfeet gave these people another of their common names, Atsina; their self-designation is *Haaninin,* "Lime People" or "White Clay People."

Location In the late eighteenth century, Gros Ventres lived from north-central Montana to southern Saskatchewan. Today, most live in north-central Montana.

Population The Gros Ventre population was about 3,000 in the late eighteenth century. It was approximately 2,900 in 1992.

Language Gros Ventre is an Algonquian language.

Historical Information

History At least 3,000 years ago the Arapaho, possibly united with the future Gros Ventres and other peoples, probably lived in the western Great Lakes region to the Red River Valley, where they grew corn and lived in permanent villages. Under pressure from the Ojibwa (Anishinabe), they migrated to the upper Missouri River region in the early eighteenth century.

During the migration, perhaps around Devil's Lake, the Gros Ventre separated from the Arapaho. They acquired horses in the early to mid–eighteenth century. Shortly thereafter they became a Plains tribe and joined the Blackfeet Confederacy.

The people signed the 1851 Fort Laramie Treaty after spending a brief period of time with the Arapaho. Another treaty in 1855 led to further land cessions. In the early 1860s the Gros Ventres joined with their Crow enemies to fight their traditional friends, the Blackfeet, but were soundly defeated in 1867. Following a further decline caused mostly by disease, in 1888 survivors were placed on the Fort Belknap Reservation, which they shared with the Assiniboine, also former enemies.

The Gros Ventres filed a lawsuit in 1897 to gain compensation for lands seized under the 1855 treaty; during the twentieth century the tribe has received several land claims awards. Also around the turn of the century, members of the tribe sold under extreme duress a 28-square-mile strip of reservation land. Tuberculosis was a severe problem in the early twentieth century, affecting more than 90 percent of the tribal population.

Religion Two sacred pipes figured prominently in traditional Gros Ventre religion. Gros Ventres also observed other Plains religious customs such as vision quests, medicine bundles, and the Sun Dance.

Government There were 12 autonomous bands in historic times, each with its own chief.

Customs Bands camped separately in winter, coming together in summer for communal buffalo hunt and celebrations, including the Sun Dance. At this time they camped in a circle, with each band having a designated place.

Descent was patrilineal. People generally found marriage partners outside of the parents' band. Girls were often married by age 12, usually to men around 20. Polygamy and divorce were common. The mother-in-law taboo was in force.

Age-graded male societies had their own costumes, dances, and paraphernalia. Men moved through the various rankings with their peers, each group purchasing the regalia of the next-higher group, until the men at the top sold out and retired with a large amount of wealth. Healing, through medicines

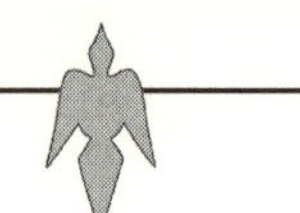

and ritual, was a job that one might attain by fasting and attaining special powers. Corpses were wrapped in robes and placed on a scaffold, in a cave, or on a high rock.

Dwellings On the Plains, groups of women made skin tipis with three-pole foundations.

Diet Buffalo were hunted by driving them into chutes; after about 1730, they were hunted on horseback. Women cut meat into strips and dried it or made pemmican. Fresh meat was roasted over the fire or boiled, using red-hot rocks in a water-filled hole. People also ate deer, elk, and puppies and gathered foods such as rhubarb, berries, and eggs. They did not eat fish.

Key Technology Women dressed skins with brains and liver. Men made bows of ash or cherry wood and also of horn. Horn bows were covered with rattlesnake skin. Sewing equipment included buffalo sinew thread and bone awls.

Trade Gros Ventres participated in the regional trade complex, trading horses and animal products for agricultural items and, later, non-Indian items.

Notable Arts Gros Ventres made fine painted leather items and tanned and embroidered clothing.

Transportation Horses arrived around 1730. Both dogs and horses pulled the travois. People made makeshift rafts of tipi covers and poles.

Dress Women made the clothing, usually of elk skin or deerskin. They wore dresses; men wore leggings, breechclouts, shirts, and moccasins. Both sexes wore buffalo-skin caps and mittens in winter.

War and Weapons Weapons included buffalo-hide shields and bows and arrows. In the mid–nineteenth century, Gros Ventres fought Crows with the Blackfeet and then fought the Blackfeet in alliance with the Crow. Other enemies included the Shoshone, Salish (Flathead), and Assiniboine. Traditional allies included the Arapaho, Cheyenne, and Cree.

Contemporary Information

Government/Reservations The Fort Belknap Reservation (Blaine and Philips Counties, Montana), established in 1887, contains roughly 616,000 acres, about one-quarter of which are tribally owned. The 1990 Indian population was 2,332. A constitution and by-laws based on the Indian Reorganization Act were approved in 1935. The community council has 12 elected members, 6 Gros Ventres and 6 Assiniboines, as well as 3 appointed officers.

Economy Income is generated through land leases to non-Indian farmers and ranchers. There is also some reservation farming and ranching. The federal government is a major employer. Un- and underemployment is chronic.

Stores and a bingo hall provide more money, although some gambling money comes from tribal members who can least afford it. Interest from land claims payments is used for burial assistance as well as for annual direct family payments.

Legal Status The Fort Belknap Indian Community (Gros Ventre and Assiniboine-Sioux) is a federally recognized tribal entity.

Daily Life The Bureau of Indian Affairs, which has long dominated the Fort Belknap Reservation, has traditionally viewed both native groups as one community, to the detriment of Indian self-determination and cultural identity. The strip of land sold in 1897 is now, still under protest, being mined for gold. The mines have severely contaminated the regional environment and are associated with health problems on the reservation.

As of 1993, the Gros Ventres were considering officially changing their name to Ah-ah-nee-nin, as well as instituting a confederation form of government, in the interests of preserving individual tribal identity. Most children attend reservation public schools. There is also a mission school, and some attend off-reservation boarding schools. Fort Belknap Community College, containing a library and tribal archives, opened in 1984. A museum is proposed.

Hardly anyone in the early 1990s spoke the language fluently, although it is taught at the elementary and community college levels, and

language and cultural retention are a major priority. Traditional religion is still practiced. Many Gros Ventres are also Christians, especially Catholics. The reservation hosts annual powwows.

Hidatsa

Hidatsa (Hē `dät sä), possibly taken from the name of a former village. Called Gros Ventres of the Missouri by French traders, they have also been known as the *Minitaris* (Mandan for "they crossed the water").

Location Most Hidatsas lived along the upper Missouri River in western North Dakota in the late eighteenth century. Today, most live in western North Dakota.

Population The late-eighteenth-century Hidatsa population was about 2,500. In the early 1990s, there were about 6,000 enrolled members of the Three Affiliated Tribes.

Language Hidatsa is a Siouan dialect.

Historical Information

History Siouan people may have lived originally along the lower Mississippi River, slowly migrating north through Tennessee and Kentucky and into Ohio. Some then went east across the Appalachian Mountains, but most continued northwest. Originally one people, the Hidatsa-Crow were perhaps the first Siouan group to leave the Ohio country. They moved to northern Illinois, through western Minnesota, and into the Red River Valley.

For at least 400 years, beginning around the twelfth or thirteenth century, they grew gardens and hunted buffalo south of Lake Winnipeg. Finally, pressured by newly armed bands of Ojibwas and Crees, the group moved southwest to Devil's Lake in the mid–sixteenth century. They then moved again toward the upper Missouri River, where they continued to hunt and grow corn, encouraged by receiving seeds and acquiring new techniques from the Mandans.

In the late seventeenth century, the Crow struck out on their own, leaving the Hidatsa behind. At this time, the latter associated with other agricultural tribes such as the Mandans and Arikaras. Non-Indians also traded regularly at Hidatsa villages, exchanging items of non-native manufacture for furs. Early non-Indian explorers, such as Meriwether Lewis and William Clark, also lived among the Hidatsa. The people lost significant population in the late eighteenth century through warfare, primarily with the Dakota, as well as smallpox epidemics. By about 1800 they had been reduced to a few villages along the Knife River.

The smallpox epidemic of 1837 devastated the tribe; surviving Hidatsas and Mandans regrouped by 1845 into a single village called Like-a-Fishhook, located near Fort Berthold, North Dakota. They were joined there by the Arikara in 1862. The Fort Berthold Reservation was created in 1871 for Hidatsas, Mandans, and Arikaras. Although the 1851 Fort Laramie Treaty recognized the tribes' claims to 12 million acres, the original reservation consisted of 8 million acres; by 1886 it had been reduced to about 1 million acres.

Like-a-Fishhook was an important regional commercial center until the 1880s, when most people left it to establish communities along the Missouri River. The Hidatsa lived on both sides of the river, in Lucky Mound, Shell Creek, and Independence. During the 1950s, against the tribes' vehement opposition, the United States built the Garrison Dam on the Missouri. The resulting Lake Sakakawea covered much of their land, farms, and homes. This event destroyed the tribes' economic base and severely damaged its social structure.

Religion The Corn Dance Feast of the Women was based on mythological concepts and offered as thanks for their crops. Elderly women hung dried meat on poles and then performed a dance. Younger women fed them meat and received grains of corn to eat in return. The dried meat would be left on the poles until harvest time. The Hidatsa also learned the Sun Dance.

There were a number of religious societies. The right to perform ceremonies was either inherited or purchased. The associated bundles were purchased, even from parents. Hidatsas undertook vision quests from an early age.

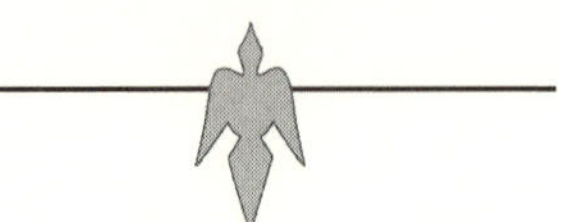

Government The tribe contained several bands, including the Hidatsa proper, the Awatixa, and the Awaxawi. Villages were ruled by a council, a chief, and a war chief. The chieftainship had a hereditary component.

Customs Descent was matrilineal, and the extended family was the primary economic unit. Land was held by groups of related families known as lineages, which were in turn organized into larger groups, with formal leadership usually provided by older men. Lineages remained within one village, but the larger groups crossed villages. Within villages, each larger group was divided into two divisions; this organization played a key role in village leadership as well as games and other competition. The Hidatsa also recognized about seven clans.

Women controlled the gardens and were in charge of harvest distribution to their families. The White Buffalo Society, which featured dancing to lure buffalo to the hunters, was open only to women. Age-graded men's societies had mainly military functions. Each group had its own dances, songs, and regalia, which were acquired by the youngest group and purchased en masse from the next-higher group, the buyers displacing the sellers as the latter also "moved up."

Social rank was hereditary to some degree. Most adults were excellent swimmers. "Joking relatives," whose fathers were in the same clan, teased or upbraided each other for deviating from normative conduct. This mechanism was very effective for maintaining social customs and proper behavior. Food, weapons, and personal items were placed on scaffolds along with corpses. Mourners cut their hair. When chiefs died, all lodge fires were extinguished.

Dwellings From around 1700 on, the people lived in permanent villages on bluffs overlooking the upper Missouri River. Groups of people erected circular, dome-shaped earth lodges about 40 feet in diameter. Each housed two to three families or up to about 40 people. A wooden framework supported interwoven willow branches and grass, covered with mud or clay. Posts, beams, and rafters were skillfully fitted together. Entrance was via a covered passageway. Floors may have been partially excavated. The lodges lasted from seven to ten years.

Cooking took place inside in winter and outside in summer. Cook kettles were suspended on poles over central fires. People slept on rawhide platform beds. Furniture also included willow back rests and buffalo-robe couches. Interior floors contained deep storage pits, with more storage behind beds and against walls. People also used smaller earth lodges in winter, when they took refuge in forests. Skin tipis were used while traveling or hunting.

Diet Women cooperated in growing corn, beans, squash, pumpkins, and sunflowers. Gardens were located in river bottoms below the villages. They stored corn in earth caches, lined with logs and grass and covered with grass. Corn was boiled and eaten fresh or shelled and dried for the winter, when it was pounded and eaten as meal with other vegetables and meat. Squash was cut into strips and sun dried. Crops were harvested in midsummer and especially in early fall.

Old men grew a small tobacco crop. Tobacco was sacred and some ritual surrounded its cultivation, harvesting, and use. Only elderly men generally smoked, in pipes and for ceremonial purposes.

Buffalo and other meat was acquired primarily through trade, although men did hunt buffalo and other animals. After the people acquired horses they tracked the buffalo farther onto the plains, into present-day South Dakota and Montana. Women also gathered berries, most of which were dried. Sugar came from box elder sap. Other foods included fish and dogs.

Key Technology Many material items, such as agricultural implements (bone hoes and rakes) and horn utensils and tools were made of buffalo and elk parts. Mortars, pestles, and digging sticks were made of wood. Women made twilled plaited baskets and pottery. Especially before they acquired horses, people used tumplines and chest straps for carrying burdens on their backs.

People felled and burned trees in order to enrich the soil for growing. Garden plots were left fallow after about three years of cultivation. Cache pits (for crop storage) were about 8 feet deep, 2 or 3 feet wide at the top, and perhaps twice as wide at the bottom. Women placed ears of corn around the outside and shelled corn

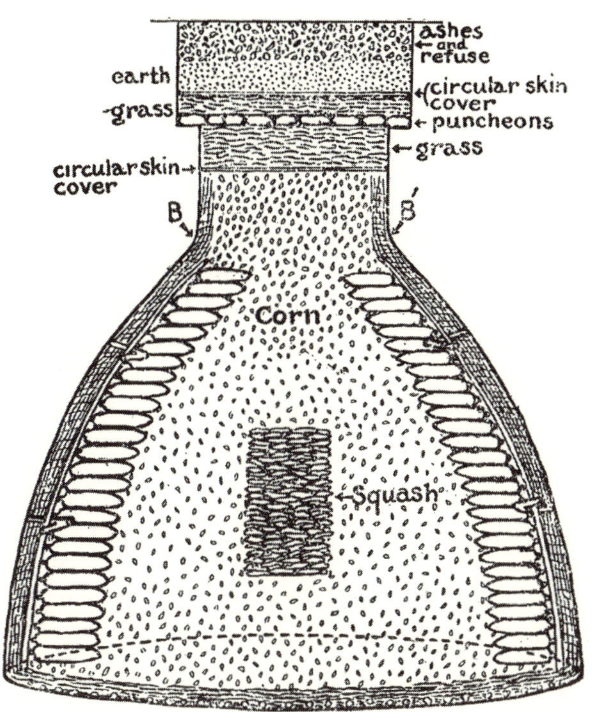

A cache pit for crops. Cache pits were about eight feet deep, two or three feet wide at the top, and perhaps twice as wide at the bottom. Women placed ears of corn around the outside and shelled corn and squash in the center. They covered the pits with ashes, dirt, and grass. Entrance was via a ladder.

and squash in the center. They covered the pits with ashes, dirt, and grass. Entrance was via a ladder.

Painted rawhide trunks or boxes, more typical of Woodland tribes, were about 15 inches square and 10 inches high. The people also painted parfleches and built seven-hole flageolets from box elder wood with the pith removed. They also made music with rattles, rasps (notched wood), hand drums, or tambourines and by singing.

Trade Village people traded agricultural products with nomads for meat and other animal products. Trade occupied an important position in Hidatsas' lives.

Notable Arts Artistic expression was particularly manifest in painted skins, baskets, and pottery.

Transportation Serviceable boats were made of buffalo hides stretched over circular willow frames. Hidatsas tended to rely more on dogs than horses to pull their travois.

Dress Women made clothing from skins and furs, particularly white weasel and ermine. Buffalo-hide blankets were the main cold-weather item. Tattoos were common.

War and Weapons Traditional enemies included the Dakota and Shoshone, whereas the Hidatsa were often allied with the Mandan. The men's groups included Dog Soldiers, a military-police society.

Contemporary Information

Government/Reservations The Three Affiliated Tribes (Arikara, Hidatsa, Mandan) live on the Fort Berthold Reservation (roughly 900,000 acres in Dunn, McKenzie, McLean, Mercer, Mountrail, and Ward Counties, North Dakota). The 1990 reservation Indian population was 2,999. More than half of the reservation is owned by non-Indians. The governing structure was established during the 1930s.

Economy The tribal and federal governments are the largest employers. A few people have farms or ranches. Although the tribe opened a high-stakes casino in

George Gillette, left, chairman of the Fort Berthold Indian Tribal Business Council, covers his face as he weeps in the office of Secretary of Interior J. A. Krug in Washington, D.C., May 20, 1948. Krug is signing a contract whereby the tribe sold 155,000 acres of its reservation in North Dakota for the Garrison Dam and Reservoir Project.

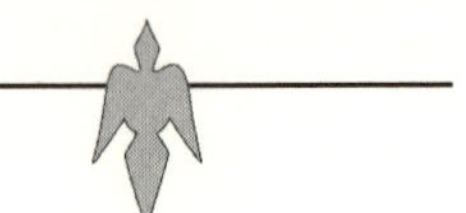

1993, unemployment remains very high. There is some tourism along Lake Sakakawea.

Legal Status The Three Affiliated Tribes is a federally recognized tribal entity.

Daily Life Most Hidatsas live in the town of Mandaree. Their lifestyle is similar to that of their non-Indian neighbors. Only elders speak the native language, despite the attempt to institute regular language classes.

Some Indians practice sweat lodge ceremonies and are members of the Native American Church. Most consider themselves Christians.

Ceremonies called Warbonnet Dances also help maintain an Indian identity. Ongoing crafts include quilt making and beadwork. The annual powwow held by each reservation community has become a focus for tribal activities.

Although the three tribes continue to maintain separate identities, they operate several reservation schools and publish the *Mandan, Hidatsa, and Arikara Times.* There is a tribal museum at New Town.

Hunkpapa

See Lakota

Hunkpatina

See Nakota

Ioway

Ioway (`Ī ō ā), from *ayuhwa,* "sleepy ones." Their self-designation is *Pahoja,* "dusty noses." Along with tribes such as Otoes, Missourias, and Winnebagos, they had elements of both Plains and Woodland cultures.

Location In the seventeenth century, most Ioways lived in northern Iowa and southern Minnesota. Today, most live in extreme northeast Kansas and in central Oklahoma.

Population There were about 1,100 Ioways in 1760. In the early 1990s, tribal enrollment was roughly 2,000 in Kansas-Nebraska and about 350 in Oklahoma.

Language Iowa-Otoe-Missouria is a member of the Chiwere division of the Siouan language.

Historical Information

History According to tradition, the Ioway, Winnebago, Missouria, and Otoe once lived together north of the Great Lakes. Migration toward their historic areas began in the sixteenth century. Moving south through Wisconsin, the Ioway crossed the Mississippi River in the late sixteenth and early seventeenth centuries and began building villages in northeastern Iowa, just south of Minnesota.

Shortly thereafter, they continued west to the Des Moines River area of northwestern Iowa and southwestern Minnesota. In the mid–seventeenth century, the Ioway, constantly on the move and under pressure from the Dakota, moved west again into northern Nebraska. By the late seventeenth century they had crossed the Missouri eastward back into Iowa.

After they acquired horses in the early to mid–eighteenth century, they began to range farther west and take on more characteristics of Plains Indians. They were heavily engaged in the fur trade in the eighteenth and early nineteenth centuries, when some bands were living as far west as the Platte River. Around 1800 they were engaged in territorial wars with the Sauk, Fox, and Dakota tribes. They also suffered a major smallpox epidemic in 1803.

The tribe signed treaties with the United States in 1824, 1825, 1830, 1836, and 1837, eventually ceding all of their lands. In 1836, they were assigned a reservation along the Great Nemaha River (southeastern Nebraska and northeastern Kansas) that was subsequently reduced in size. In the 1870s, the tribe divided into two independent groups, the Southern Ioway, in Oklahoma, and the Northern Ioway, in Kansas and Nebraska. The former group preferred to live in the traditional way, on lands held in common, whereas the latter group accepted individual allotments of land. The Southern Ioways were assigned a reservation in the Indian Territory in

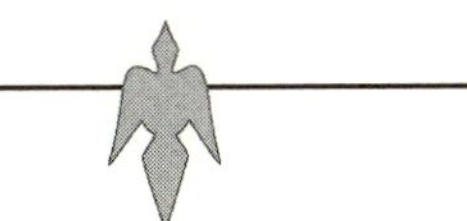

1883, but it was opened to non-Indian settlement several years later.

Religion The Ioway practiced a ceremony similar to the Grand Medicine Dance of the Woodland tribes. A candidate for admission to the secret Ojibwa medicine society, for example, was "shot" with a shell and then "revived" by members. The Ioway offered the first puff of tobacco smoke to the sky spirit. In the late nineteenth century, the people adopted a semi-Christianized Peyote religion.

Government Hereditary clan and war chiefs held positions of authority.

Customs The people played lacrosse and the moccasin (guessing) game, games customarily played by Woodlands tribes. There was a dual tribal division. Patrilineal clans were divided into subclans.

Dwellings Semipermanent villages contained earth lodges. When hunting and traveling, people used bark-covered pole-frame lodges as well as skin tipis.

Diet The major crops were corn, beans, squash, melons, sunflowers, and pumpkins. Buffalo were taken, using the surround method, in two communal buffalo hunts a year. Men also hunted other animals such as deer, beaver, raccoon, otter, and bear. Women gathered plant foods such as nuts, berries, and roots. The Ioway also fished.

Key Technology Fishing equipment included spears and possibly weirs and basketry traps. Men made a combination quiver and bow case. After the eighteenth century, women dressed skins with elk-horn scrapers. They also wove reed floor mats over a bark-cord foundation. Like Woodland tribes, Iowas made soft-twilled buffalo-hair wallets and rawhide box containers or trunks.

Trade During the early eighteenth century, Ioways were selling Indian slaves, probably Pawnees, to French traders for resale to Gulf Coast plantation owners. They were actively involved in the fur trade at that time. They also traded pipes to other tribes.

Notable Arts Ioways were particularly adept at weaving and wood working.

Transportation The Ioway acquired horses about 1730.

Dress Women made clothing of tanned animal skins.

War and Weapons After their adoption of many Plains traits in the eighteenth century, the people gave highest war honors to those who led several successful raids. In descending order, other honors included killing an enemy, touching an enemy, and scalping. They also created rival military clubs.

Contemporary Information

Government/Reservations The Iowa Reservation, Brown and Doniphan Counties, Kansas, and Richardson County, Missouri, established in 1836, contains about 1,500 acres of mixed Indian and non-Indian ownership. The 1990 Indian population was 83. Governing structures included a tribal council and an executive committee.

There are also about 1,300 acres of individually owned land in Oklahoma, mostly in Lincoln, Payne, and Logan Counties, plus about 200 acres held in trust. The Oklahoma tribe ratified an Indian Reorganization Act constitution and is administered by a business committee.

Economy The Iowa Tribe of Kansas and Nebraska owns a dairy farm, gas station, bingo parlor, and grain processing operation. The Oklahoma tribe owns a bingo operation and leases most of its land to non-Indians for grazing or farming operations. Most wage work is in nearby towns. There is also some individual income from oil and gas leases. Both groups of Ioway received almost $8 million in land claims settlements in the 1970s.

Legal Status The Iowa Tribe of Kansas and Nebraska and the Iowa Tribe of Oklahoma are federally recognized tribal entities. The latter is a member of the United Indian Nations of Oklahoma.

Daily Life Although both groups are largely assimilated, extended kinship groups still form a basis

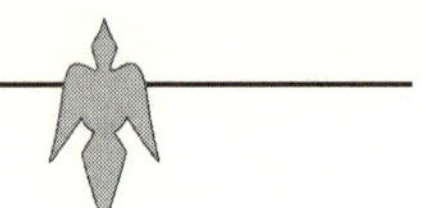

of community life, and a modified clan system persists in Oklahoma. Despite the existence of primers and a lexicon, few people speak the native language. Most Ioways consider themselves Christian, although some attend some traditional ceremonies such as sweats, funerals, and namings and are also members of the Native American Church. Some also participate in intertribal dances.

Among the northern group, reacquisition of the land base is a prime goal, as is economic self-reliance. The Oklahoma tribe contracts with the Potawatomis for food and health programs. They are fighting the development of a toxic waste dump, proposed by a subsidiary of Amoco, on the site of a burial ground. Each tribe sponsors an annual powwow, in part because factionalism prevents extensive contacts between the two groups. The Kansas Ioway also present a rodeo.

Itazipco (Sans Arcs)

See Lakota

Kansa

See Kaw

Kaw

Kaw (Kä), also known as the Kansa (or Konza) tribe. Their self-designation is *Hutanga,* "by the edge of the shore," referring to a mythical residence on the Atlantic Ocean.

Location The Kaw migrated from the Ohio Valley in the fifteenth century to the Kaw Valley in the sixteenth century. Today, most Kaws live near Kaw City, Oklahoma.

Population About 5,000 people in 1700, the 1993 enrollment was 1,678, including five full-bloods.

Language With the Osage, Omaha, Ponca, and Quapaw, the Kaw spoke a dialect of the Dhegiha branch of the Siouan language family.

Historical Information

History Perhaps once one people with other southern Siouans such as the Quapaw, Omaha, Ponca, and Osage, the Kaw remained in the Wabash Valley until driven out, possibly by the Iroquois, with the others in the early sixteenth century. They traveled down the Ohio River to the Mississippi and then north to near present-day St. Louis.

Finding the lower Missouri Valley open, the Kaw moved north on that river to the Kaw Valley, where they stopped and built lodges. The Spanish explorer Juan de Oñate saw them there in 1601. They lived peacefully, at least for a while, with their Pawnee and Apache neighbors. The other tribes continued in various directions.

Direct trade with the French out of New Orleans began at least as early as 1719. During the eighteenth and nineteenth centuries, the Kaw were frequently at war with both Indians and non-Indians. In 1724, at the request of French officials but also out of their own self-interest, over 1,000 Kaw traveled to Apache villages on a successful peace mission. The Kaw acquired their first horses at that time, and a brief peace was also established between the Apache and the French, the latter hitherto actively engaged in the trade in Apache slaves.

Shortly after that summer, however, French traders resumed their purchase of Apache slaves from, among others, the Kaw, the latter preferring good trade relations with the French to peace with the declining Apaches. A French trading post was built near their territory during the period, and the Kaw soon took over some land in western Kansas vacated by the departing Apaches. The Kaw acquired horses at that time and began to adopt the characteristics of Plains Indians.

By the late eighteenth century, the well-armed Kaw, along with other tribes such as the Osage, Pawnees, and Wichitas, represented the eastern boundary of the huge Comanche country. The Kaw ceded all of their Missouri land in 1825 in exchange for a two-million-acre reservation in Kansas. That land in turn was ceded in 1846, and they were removed to a 265,000-acre reservation farther west, at Council Grove, on the Neosho River. The United States took those lands in 1873, and the remaining Kaw were removed to the Indian Territory. Their remaining lands were allotted in 1902, and the tribe was legally dissolved. A significant number of the full-bloods, such as Chief Al-le-go-wa-ho, had opposed allotment, a situation that exacerbated factionalism and the legal struggles that followed tribal dissolution. An example of the "progressive" faction was congressman and later vice president Charles Curtis, who was largely responsible for the Kaw Allotment Act of 1902 that stripped the Kaw people of their tribal lands.

The tribe reconstituted itself in 1959 under the auspices of the Department of the Interior. Tribal holdings at that time included 260 acres near the mouth of Beaver Creek. In the mid-1960s, the U.S. Army built the Kaw Reservoir, flooding most of these lands. The cemetery and council house were moved, the latter to a 15-acre tract that was subsequently enlarged by Congress to 135.5 acres.

Religion Traditional religious belief held that spirits dwelt in aspects of nature, such as celestial objects. The sun was a deity to which prayers were offered and donations made, as were the wind and a sacred salt spring in northern Kansas. Pubescent boys were taken by their fathers to a remote spot for at least three days, where they sought visions via fasting and self-deprivation.

Government Each village was ruled by a council-elected chief; a head chief ruled over all the villages. War chiefs led military operations.

Customs Sixteen patrilineal clans, each including several families, combined into seven larger organizational units. There were also two tribal divisions, *Nata* and *Ictunga.*

Men were mostly concerned with war and hunting while women did most of the work around the village. Kaws placed an extremely high value on morality and also on the chastity of women. Dog Soldiers served as camp police and administered public punishments as needed. After being painted and covered with bark, corpses were buried in a sitting position facing west. Food and possessions were buried with them. The mourning lasted a year.

Dwellings Circular or oval lodges were framed in wood and covered with mats woven of reed, grass, or bark and then a layer of earth. They ranged up to 60 feet in diameter and housed five or six families. Smoke holes were placed in the center. Skin-covered wood platforms around sides served as beds. The people also used skin tipis on hunting trips.

Diet Buffalo, and other animals as well, were the most important food source. There were two large, communal buffalo hunts a year. Women grew corn, beans, squash, and sunflowers in valley bottomlands. There were generally two harvests, one in midsummer and another in early fall. Women also gathered prairie potatoes and other foods.

Key Technology Farm implements included hoes, digging sticks, and rakes. Most items came from the buffalo, including utensils and the raw material for various woven items.

Trade The Kaw traded in buffalo skins and products. They also supplied the French with slaves in exchange for guns and other items.

Notable Arts Weaving, skin tanning, and painting were the most important arts.

Transportation Dogs carried burdens before horses, which were acquired from the Apache in 1724.

Dress Kaws dressed in typical Plains skin clothing. The men plucked or shaved all of their hair except for a single lock at the back.

War and Weapons Weapons included bows, arrows, and buffalo-hide shields. The people chose war chiefs as needed. Enemies, beginning in the eighteenth century, included the Sauk, Fox, Omaha, Osage, Ioway, Otoe, Pawnee, and Cheyenne.

Contemporary Information

Government/Reservations The Kaw Nation administers 135.5 acres as trust lands. Tribal headquarters is at Kaw City, Oklahoma. The present constitution was adopted in 1990. The tribe is governed by an elected seven-member executive committee.

Economy The Kaw Nation owns and operates a bingo enterprise, a nursery, a truck stop, and discount tobacco shops. With the Pawnee, Tonkawa, Ponca,

and Otoe-Missouria, the Kaw are members of the Chilocco Development Authority. The Kaw Enterprise Authority seeks to increase the Kaw land base in and develop the tribal economy on former tribal land in Kansas City, Kansas.

Legal Status The Kaw Nation of Oklahoma is a federally recognized tribal entity.

Daily Life Fewer than a dozen Kaws are fluent in their native language (1993); language preservation programs are under way. The tribe provides academic scholarships for tribal members as well as social service programs. Kaw Nation district and supreme courts were dedicated in 1992. There is a tribal powwow in August.

Kiowa

Kiowa (`Kī u wu), "Principal People," is a derivation of *Ka'i gwu,* their self-designation.

Location The Kiowa migrated in the seventeenth century from the Gallatin-Madison Valleys in southwestern Montana to the Black Hills. By the early nineteenth century, their territory included southeast Colorado, extreme northeast New Mexico, southwest Kansas, northwest Oklahoma, and extreme north Texas.

Population In the late eighteenth century there were around 2,000 Kiowas. Roughly 10,000 people were enrolled Kiowas in the early 1990s.

Language Kiowa is considered a linguistic isolate that might be related to Tanoan, a Pueblo language, as well as Shoshonean.

Historical Information

History The Kiowa may have originated in Arizona or in the mountains of western Montana. They began drifting southeast from western Montana in the late seventeenth century, settling near the Crow. In the early eighteenth century, the Kiowa Apaches became cut off from their fellow Apacheans, at which time (if not a generation before) they joined the Kiowa for protection. Although they maintained a separate language and identity they functioned effectively as a Kiowa band.

Meanwhile, the Kiowa had acquired horses, probably through trade with upper Missouri tribes, and were living in the Black Hills as highly successful buffalo hunters, warriors, and horsemen. Individual Kiowas and Kiowa Apaches also lived in northern New Mexico, probably brought there originally by Comanches and others as prisoners or slaves. Later in the century, the Kiowa, still in the Black Hills, acted as trade intermediaries between Spanish (New Mexican) traders and the upper Missouri tribes.

The people suffered a smallpox epidemic in 1781, from which they gradually recovered. A large group of Kiowa and Kiowa Apache migrated south during that period, to be followed by the rest around the turn of the century. At that time, the Kiowa were pushed south to the Arkansas River area by Dakotas,

Kea-Boat, a member of the Kiowas, holds a rattle and feather fan used in the Peyote ceremony.

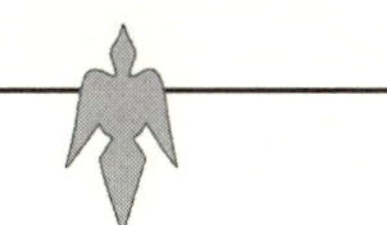

Arapahos, and Cheyennes (southeastern Colorado), where they ran into the Comanche barrier. They were also drawn south by raiding opportunities provided by Spanish and Pueblo settlements in New Mexico and Mexico. In the early nineteenth century they ranged between New Mexico and the upper Missouri River area.

In 1814 they concluded a treaty with the Dakota defining the boundary between the two groups. Making peace also with the Comanche, these two groups raided for horses, guns, and food as far south as Durango, Mexico. They were known as fierce, effective, and wide-ranging raiders, fighting other Indian groups as well as Spanish, Mexicans, and Anglos. By the mid–nineteenth century, the Kiowa spent more time south of the Arkansas than north of it. In the 1830s they made peace with longtime Cheyenne, Osage, and Arapaho enemies.

In the early 1860s, the Kiowa strongly resisted non-native intruders, land thieves, and immigrants. In 1865 they agreed to a reservation south of the Arkansas River. In the 1867 Medicine Lodge Treaty, they ceded tribal lands and, in exchange for a shared reservation in the Indian Territory, agreed to hunt buffalo only south of the Arkansas and withdrew opposition to a railroad. After the U.S. massacre of Cheyennes called the Battle of the Washita (December 1868), Kiowas and others were ordered to Fort Cobb, Oklahoma. Kiowas, citing provisions in the Medicine Lodge Treaty that allowed then to continue to live and hunt south of the Arkansas, refused. During a peace meeting in 1869, the Kiowa negotiators, Satanta (White Bear) and Lone Wolf, were taken prisoner and placed under a death sentence unless the Kiowa surrendered, which they did.

Two thousand Kiowas and 2,500 Comanches were placed on a reservation at Fort Sill, Indian Territory (Oklahoma). The United States encouraged them to farm, but the Kiowa were not farmers. With starvation looming, the United States permitted them to hunt buffalo. In 1870 and 1871, the Kiowa went on a buffalo hunt and continued their old raiding practices to the south. Some argued for remaining free while others spoke for cooperating with the United States. In 1871, soldiers arrested Kiowa leaders Satanta, Satank, and Big Tree for murders committed during the raids. Satank was killed on the way to his trial in Texas. The other two were convicted and sentenced to life imprisonment. During a meeting in Washington the following year, Lone Wolf won their release as a condition for keeping the Kiowas peaceful.

In 1873, a party of Kiowas and Comanches raided in Mexico for horses. The following year, a group of Indians including Kiowas fought a losing battle against whites at Adobe Walls. By this time, most of the great buffalo herds, almost four million buffalo, had been killed by non-Indians. That summer, a large group of Kiowas and Comanches left Fort Sill for the last great buffalo range at Palo Duro Canyon, Texas, to live as traditional Indians once again. In the fall, U.S. soldiers hunted them down and killed 1,000 of their horses. Fleeing, scattered groups of Indians were hunted down in turn.

The last of these people surrendered in February 1875. They were kept in corrals. Satanta was returned to prison in Texas, and 26 others were exiled to Florida. Kicking Bird died mysteriously two days after the exiles he selected had departed, possibly poisoned by those who resented his friendship with the whites. Within a few years, the great leaders were all gone, and the power of the Kiowa was broken.

The late 1870s saw a major measles epidemic and the end of the Plains buffalo; more epidemics followed in 1895 and 1902. Many Kiowas took up the Ghost Dance in the late 1880s and early 1890s. In 1894, Kiowas offered to share their reservation with their old Apache enemies who were exiles in Florida; Geronimo and other Chiricahua Apaches lived out their lives there.

Almost 450,000 acres of the reservation were allotted to individuals in 1901, with the remaining more than two million acres then sold and opened for settlement to non-natives. Kiowas were among the group of Indians who organized the Native American Church in 1918, having adopted ritual peyote use around 1885. Thanks to the legacy of Kicking Bird and others, Kiowas in the twentieth century have concentrated on education, sending their children to boarding schools (including Riverside, still active in the 1990s) and several nearby mission schools.

Religion Kiowas gained religious status through shield society membership and/or guardianship of sacred tribal items, such as the Ten Grandmother

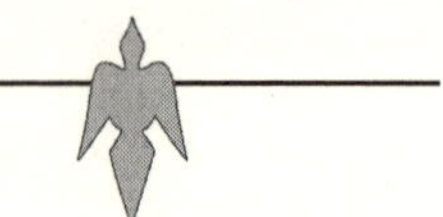

Bundles. According to legend, the bundles originated with Sun Boy, the culture hero. With their associated ceremonies, they were a focus of Kiowa religious practice.

Kiowas adopted the Sun Dance in the eighteenth century, although they did not incorporate elements of self-mutilation into the ceremony. Young men also fasted to produce guardian spirit visions.

Government There were traditionally between 10 and 27 autonomous bands, including the Kiowa Apache, each with its own peace and war chiefs. Occasionally, especially later in their history, a tribal chief presided over all the bands.

Customs Beginning in the nineteenth century the Kiowa adopted a social system wherein rank was based especially on military exploits and also on wealth and religious power. There were four named categories of social rank. The highest was held by those who had attained war honors and were skilled horsemen, generous, and wealthy. Then came those men who met all the preceding criteria except war honors. The third group included people without property. At the bottom were men with neither property nor skills. War captives remained outside this ranking system.

Generosity was valued, and wealthy men regularly helped the less fortunate, but in general wealth remained in the family through inheritance. Sons from wealthy families could begin their military training earlier and thus, through military success, gain even more wealth. There were numerous specialized men's and women's societies.

Bands lived apart in winter but came together in summer to celebrate the Sun Dance. Corpses were buried or left in a tipi on a hill. Former possessions were given away. Mourners cut their hair and gashed themselves, even occasionally cutting off fingers. A mourning family lived apart during the appropriate period of time.

Dwellings Women built and owned skin tipis.

Diet Buffalo supplied most of the food, shelter, and clothing for Kiowas on the Plains. Buffalo hunts were highly organized and ritualized affairs. After the hunt, women cut the meat into strips to dry. Later, they mixed it with dried chokecherries and fat to make pemmican, which remained edible in skin bags for up to a year or more.

Men also hunted other large and small game. They did not eat bear or, usually, fish. Women gathered a variety of wild potatoes and other vegetables, fruits, nuts, and berries. Kiowas ate dried, pounded acorns and also made them into a drink. Cornmeal and dried fruit were acquired by trade.

Key Technology Kiowas made pictographs on buffalo skins to record events of tribal history. They used the buffalo and other animals to provide the usual material items such as parfleches and other containers. Points for bird arrows came from prickly pear thorns. The cradle board was a bead-covered skin case attached to a V-shaped frame. Women made shallow coiled basketry gambling trays.

Trade During the eighteenth century, Kiowas traded extensively with the upper Missouri tribes (Mandans, Hidatsas, and Arikaras). They exchanged meat, buffalo hides, and salt with Pueblo Indians for cornmeal and dried fruit. During the nineteenth century they traded Comanche horses to the Osage and other tribes.

Notable Arts Calendric skins and beadwork were two Kiowa artistic traditions.

Transportation The people acquired horses by 1730.

Dress Women dressed buffalo, elk, and deer hides to make robes, moccasins, leggings, shirts, breechclouts, skirts, and blouses.

War and Weapons The highest status for men was achieved through warfare. Counting coup and leading a successful raid or fight were the most prestigious military activities. Raiding groups were usually drawn from kin groups, whereas revenge war parties were larger (up to 200 men) and formally organized following a Sun Dance. War honors were recounted

The beadwork in this young Kiowa girl's finery (1921) exemplifies a long-standing Kiowa artistic tradition.

following the fight and at any future event at which the recipients spoke formally.

The numerous military societies included the Principal Dogs (or Ten Bravest), a group of ten extremely brave and tested fighters. During battle, one of these warriors would drive a spear through his sash into the ground and fight from that spot, not moving until another Principal Dog removed the spear. Satank (Sitting Bear) was the leader of the Principal Dogs during the last phase of Kiowa resistance.

Kiowas beginning a raid sometimes appealed to a group of women for their prayers, feasting them upon their return. The tribe was allied with the Crow in the late seventeenth century, and the Comanche beginning around 1790. Enemies in the eighteenth and early nineteenth century included the Dakota, Cheyenne, and Osage.

Contemporary Information

Government/Reservations The Kiowa organized a tribal council in 1968. A 1970 constitution and by-laws divided power between the Kiowa Indian Council (all tribal members) and the eight-member elected Kiowa Business Committee. Tribal headquarters are located in Carnegie, Oklahoma.

The Kiowa land base is 208,396 acres in Caddo, Kiowa, Comanche, Tillman and Cotton Counties, Oklahoma. This land was first designated to them in 1867. Just over 7,000 acres are tribally owned.

Economy Important sources of income include farming, raising livestock, and leasing oil rights.

Legal Status The Kiowa Tribe of Oklahoma is a federally recognized tribal entity.

Daily Life Many prominent Kiowa artists have played an important part in the twentieth-century revival of Indian arts, beginning in 1927 with the introduction of the "Kiowa Five"—Spencer Asah, Jack Hokeah, Stephan Mopope, Monroe Tsatoke, and James Auchiah. In addition to painting, contemporary Kiowa artists are involved in media such as buckskin, beads, and silver. N. Scott Momaday, a distinguished novelist and professor, won the 1969 Pulitzer for his novel *House Made of Dawn.*

Most Kiowas are Christians, predominantly Baptists and Methodists. Many also belong to the Native American Church. As of the early 1990s, fewer than 400 spoke the native language, and almost all of these were over 50. Still, many elements of traditional culture have been preserved. Even the children's Rabbit Society, with its special songs and dances, endures. The tribe publishes the *Kiowa Indian News.*

Kiowa Apache

See Apache, Plains

Lakota

Lakota (Lä `kō tä), a Siouan dialect spoken by the Western or Teton *(Titunwan,* "prairie dwellers") group of the tribe commonly referred to as Sioux. The subdivisions of the Western group include Oglala

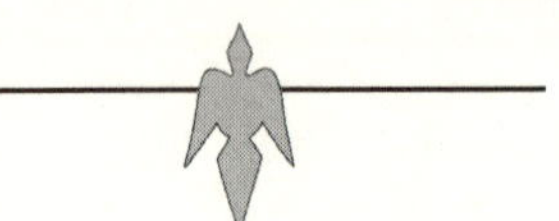

("they scatter their own"), Sicangu ("burned thighs"; also known by the French name *Brulé*), Hunkpapa ("end village"), Minneconjou ("plant beside the stream"), Itazipco ("no bows"; also known by the French name *Sans Arcs*), Sihasapa ("black feet"), and O'ohenonpa ("two kettles").

The Lakota refer to themselves as Lakota ("ally"), as Lakotah Oyate ("Lakota People"), or as *Ikce Wicasa* ("Natural" or "Free People"). The word "Sioux" is derived originally from an Ojibwa word, *Nadowe-is-iw,* meaning "lesser adder" ("enemy" is the implication) that was corrupted by French voyageurs to *Nadousssioux* and then shortened to *Sioux.* Today, many people use the term "Dakota" or, less commonly, "Lakota" to refer to all Sioux people.

All 13 subdivisions of Dakota-Lakota-Nakota speakers ("Sioux") were known as *Oceti Sakowin,* or Seven Council Fires, a term referring to their seven political divisions: Teton (the Western group, speakers of Lakota); Sisseton, Wahpeton, Wahpukute, and Mdewakanton (the Eastern group, speakers of Dakota); and Yankton and Yanktonai (the Central, or Wiciyela, group, speakers of Dakota and Nakota). *See also* Dakota; Nakota.

Location In the late seventeenth century, the Lakota lived in north-central Minnesota, around Mille Lacs, and parts of Wisconsin. By the mid–nineteenth century they had migrated to the western Dakotas, northwestern Nebraska, northeastern Wyoming, and southeastern Montana. Today, most Lakotas live on reservations in South Dakota as well in as regional and national cities. Many Lakotas leave the reservation to find work but return for summer visits and, often, to retire.

Population Dakota, Lakota, and Nakota speakers numbered approximately 25,000 in the late eighteenth century; almost half of these were probably Lakotas. In the mid-1990s there were roughly 55,000 Lakotas living on U.S. reservations, mostly Oglalas at Pine Ridge and Sicangus at Rosebud. There were 103,255 "Sioux" people in the United States, according to the 1990 census.

Language The Western group speaks the Lakota dialect of Dakota, a Siouan language.

Historical Information

History The Siouan language family may have originated along the lower Mississippi River or in eastern Texas. They migrated to, or may have originated in, the Ohio Valley, where they lived in large agricultural settlements. They may have been related to the Mound Builder culture of the ninth through twelfth centuries. The Siouans may also have originated in the upper Mississippi Valley or even the Atlantic seaboard.

Siouan tribes still lived in the southeast, between Florida and Virginia, around the late sixteenth and early seventeenth century. All were destroyed either by attacks from Algonquian-speaking Indians and/or a combination of attacks from non-Indians and non-Indian diseases. Some fled and were absorbed by other tribes. Some were sent as slaves to the West Indies.

Dakota-Lakota-Nakota speakers inhabited over 100 million acres, mostly prairie, in the upper Mississippi region, including Minnesota and parts of Wisconsin, Iowa and the Dakotas, in the sixteenth to early seventeenth century. They largely kept clear of the British-French struggles. Conflict with the Cree and Anishinabe, who were well armed with French rifles, plus the lure of great buffalo herds to feed their expanding population, induced bands to begin moving west onto the Plains in the mid–seventeenth century. The Teton migration may have begun in the late seventeenth century, in the form of extended hunting parties into the James River basin.

Lakotas acquired horses around 1740; shortly after that time the first Teton bands crossed the Missouri River. They entered the Black Hills region around 1775, ultimately displacing the Cheyenne and Kiowa, and made it their spiritual center. As more and more Teton bands became Plains dwellers (almost all by 1830), they helped establish the classic Plains culture, which featured highly organized bands, almost complete dependence on the buffalo, and a central role for raiding and fighting. The Teton subdivided into their seven bands during that time.

In 1792 the Lakota defeated the Arikara Confederacy, allowing the Lakota to expand into the Missouri Valley and western South Dakota. In 1814 they concluded a treaty with the Kiowa marking boundaries between the two peoples, including

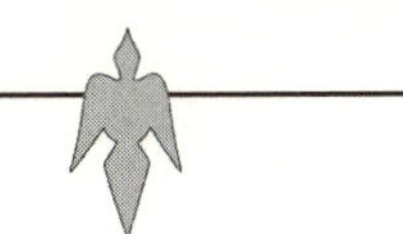

recognition that the Lakota now controlled the Black Hills (known to them as *Paha Sapa*). By that time, at the latest, the Lakota were well armed with rifles.

Around 1822, the Lakota joined with the Cheyenne to drive the Crow out of eastern Wyoming north of the Platte. During that period, Tetons were engaged in supplying furs for non-Indians, although contacts were usually limited to trading posts, particularly Fort Laramie after 1834 and the Oglala move to the Upper Platte region. In the 1840s, wagon trains passing through Teton territory began disrupting the buffalo herds, and the Indians began attacking the wagons. In the 1851 Fort Laramie Treaty, the Indians agreed to give the wagons free access in exchange for official recognition of Indian territory.

In the early to mid-1860s, the Oglala chief Red Cloud (Makhpiya-luta), pictured on the right in 1891, led and ultimately won a brutal and protracted fight to force the U.S. government to close the Bozeman Road through the Powder River country, the last great hunting ground of the Lakota.

Conflict continued throughout the 1850s. In one series of incidents, in which a group of Sicangu ate and offered to pay for a stray Mormon cow, the U.S. Army attacked Sicangu villages and killed over 100 people. In the early to mid-1860s, the Oglala chief Red Cloud (Makhpiya-luta) led and ultimately won a brutal and protracted fight to force the United States to close the Bozeman Road through the Powder River country, the last great hunting ground of the Lakota. The road through it had been opened illegally as a route to newly discovered gold fields in Montana; it crossed Teton territory without their permission, in violation of the 1851 Fort Laramie Treaty. Fighting with the Tetons were Northern Cheyennes under their leader, Dull Knife, as well as Northern Arapahos.

The 1868 Fort Laramie Treaty was an admission by the United States of the Indian victory in the so-called Red Cloud's war. The government agreed to close the Bozeman Road and stay out of Teton territory. In exchange, the Indians agreed to stop their raids and remain on a "Great Sioux Reservation." Both Red Cloud and the Sicangu leader Spotted Tail remained committed to peace, although they often spoke against easy accommodation to U.S. terms.

In 1874, gold was discovered in the Black Hills during an illegal military expedition. This event brought swarms of miners and other non-Indians, in direct violation of the treaty. With Red Cloud and Spotted Tail settled on reservations, it fell to new leaders, young and free, such as the medicine man Sitting Bull (Tatanka Yotanka) and Crazy Horse (Tashunka Witco), to protect the sacred and legally recognized Teton lands against invasion. The United States rebuffed all Indian protests, and the Indians rejected U.S. efforts to purchase the Black Hills.

In 1876, army units ceased protecting the Black Hills against non-Indian interlopers and went after Teton bands who refused to settle (which they were under no obligation to do under the terms of the Fort Laramie Treaty). In March, Tetons under Crazy Horse repelled an attack led by Colonel Joseph Reynolds. At Rosebud Creek the following June, Crazy Horse and his people routed a large force of soldiers as well as Crow and Shoshone scouts under the command of General George Crook. Later that month, Teton and Cheyenne Indians led by Oglalas under Crazy Horse

With Red Cloud and Spotted Tail settled on reservations, it fell to new leaders such as the medicine man Sitting Bull (pictured here) to protect the sacred and legally recognized Teton lands against invasion.

and Hunkpapas under Sitting Bull and Gaul wiped out the U.S. Seventh Cavalry, under General George Custer, at the Little Bighorn River.

Here the Indian victories came to an end. The army defeated a large force of Cheyennes in July, and in September General Crook's soldiers captured a combined force of Oglalas and Minneconjous under American Horse. Two months later, Dull Knife and his Northern Cheyennes lost an important battle, and Crazy Horse himself was defeated in January 1877 by General Nelson Miles. Finally, Miles defeated Lame Deer's Minneconjou band in May 1877. Meanwhile, Sitting Bull, tired of the military harassment, had taken his people north to Canada. With his people tired and starving, Crazy Horse surrendered in April 1877. In August he was placed under arrest and was assassinated on September 5. He is still regarded as a symbol of the Lakotas' heroic resistance and as their greatest leader.

Defeated militarily and under threat of mass removal to the Indian Territory, Red Cloud, Spotted Tail, and the other Lakota and Santee chiefs signed the treaty ceding the Black Hills and the Powder River country. Shortly thereafter, the army confiscated all Lakota weapons and horses and then drove the people into exile to reservations along the Missouri River.

After unilateral "cessions" in 1877, the Great Sioux Reservation consisted of 35,000 square miles of land, but a coalition of non-Indians, including railroad promoters and land speculators, maneuvered to break up this parcel. Meanwhile, Canada proved completely inhospitable to the exiled Lakota, and gradually they began drifting back to the United States. Sitting Bull returned to formal surrender in 1881.

The giant land grab came in 1888, when the United States proposed to carve the great reservation up into six smaller ones, leaving about nine million acres open for non-Indian settlement. The government unsuccessfully offered the Lakota $.50 an acre for the land. They then offered $1.50 an acre and prepared to move unilaterally if this offer were to be rejected. The government needed three-quarters of the adult male votes for approval. Despite the opposition of Red Cloud, about half of the Oglalas signed the treaty. With Spotted Tail dead (he had been assassinated in 1881), most of the Sicangu signed. Sitting Bull was the loudest voice opposed, but he was physically restrained from attending a meeting presided over by accommodationist chiefs, and the signatures were collected. The Great Sioux Reservation was no more.

Deprived of their livelihood, Lakotas quickly became dependent on inadequate and irregular U.S. rations. The United States also undermined traditional leadership and created their own subservient power structure. A crisis ensued in 1889 when the government cut off all rations. The general confusion provided fertile ground for the Ghost Dance.

In 1888, a Northern Paiute named Wovoka, building on previous traditions, popularized a new

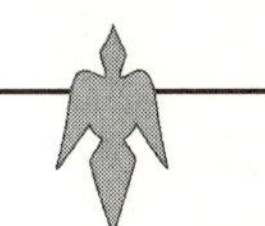

religion that came to be called the Ghost Dance (*see* Paiute, Northern [Chapter 4]). Wovoka foretold the return of an Indian paradise if people would pray, dance, and abandon the ways of non-Indians. The new religion gave hope to many Native Americans whose societies by this time had reached a crisis point, and it quickly spread over much of the West. Many Indians also thought special Ghost Shirts could stop bullets.

Fearing that the Ghost Dance would encourage a new Indian militancy and solidarity, white officials banned the practice. In defiance, Oglala leaders in 1890 planned a large gathering on the Pine Ridge Reservation. To keep Sitting Bull, the last strong Lakota leader, from attending, the Indian police arrested him in December. During the arrest he was shot and killed.

The Minneconjou leader Big Foot once supported the dance, and for this reason General Miles ordered his arrest. Big Foot led his band of about 350 people to Pine Ridge to join Red Cloud and others who advocated peace with the United States. The army intercepted him along the way and ordered him to stop at Wounded Knee Creek. The next morning (December 29) the soldiers moved in to disarm the Indians. When a rifle accidentally fired into the air, the soldiers opened fire with the four Hotchkiss cannon on the bluffs overlooking the camp, killing between 260 and 300 Indians, mostly women

Dead Indians are frozen in the ice the morning after the Battle of Wounded Knee, 1890. The Wounded Knee massacre remains very much in the hearts and minds of Lakotas, with many annual remembrance ceremonies and pilgrimages to the site. The Wounded Knee massacre marked the symbolic end of large-scale Native American armed resistance in the United States.

Indians stand guard outside the Sacred Heart Catholic Church in Wounded Knee, March 3, 1973. This was the scene of a violent confrontation between the American Indian Movement (AIM), called in to protect the people against abuses, and tribal forces supported by U.S. military power.

and children. The Wounded Knee massacre marked the symbolic end of large-scale Native American armed resistance in the United States.

From the 1880s into the 1950s, most Lakota children were forced to attend mission or Bureau of Indian Affairs (BIA) schools, There the children were taught menial skills, and their culture was violently repressed. During the twentieth century, tipis slowly gave way to government-issue tents and then log cabins. Many Lakotas became Catholics or Episcopalians, although traditional customs and religious practices also continued, including the officially banned Sun Dance.

Bands were broken up, in part by the allotment process. As the United States worked to replace traditional leadership, education, religion, and other cultural and political structures, Lakota society underwent a profound demoralization. Most Lakota were fed government-issue beef, which they had trouble eating after a steady diet of buffalo. In general, government rations were of low quality and quantity.

Lakotas were ordered to begin raising cattle. Despite some success in the early twentieth century, U.S. agents encouraged them in 1917 to sell their herds and lease their lands to non-Indians. When the lessees defaulted in 1921, the government urged Indians to sell their allotments for cash. By the

1930s, devoid of cattle and land, general destitution had set in.

Lakotas adopted the Indian Reorganization Act in 1934, after which reservations were governed by an elected tribal council, although the traditional system of chief-led *tiyospayes* (subbands) was still in place. A tribal court system handled minor problems; more serious offenses fell under the control of the U.S. court system.

Native Americans were part of the ethnic pride movement of the 1960s. The Red Power movement had its origins in the formation of the National Congress of American Indians (NCAI) in 1944. In 1972, many Lakotas participated in a march to Washington, D.C., called the Trail of Broken Treaties, during which they took over the BIA.

The following January, under the leadership of the American Indian Movement (AIM), several hundred Pine Ridge Lakotas attempted to end and reverse U.S.-sponsored corruption on Pine Ridge, particularly the strong-arm tactics of the tribal chair at that time. The context was decades of poverty and frustration on the reservation. The government responded with a massive show of force. During the 71-day siege, known as Wounded Knee II, two Indians were killed by federal agents. The event forged a new solidarity among Lakotas and other Indians but also left deep scars among the reservation population.

Religion According to legend, White Buffalo Calf Pipe Woman brought the people seven ceremonies: the Sweat Lodge *(Inipi),* Making of Relatives *(Hunka),* Vision Quest *(Hanbleceya),* Girls' Puberty Ritual *(Isnati alowanpi),* Throwing of the Ball *(Tapa wankayeyapi),* Keeping of the Soul ceremony *(Wakicagapi),* and the Sun Dance *(Wiwanyang wacipi).*

Given originally by a legendary personage, the Sacred Pipe is a symbol of the vitality of the nation and its relationship with the creative forces of the universe. It was removed from its pouch only on the most important occasions, such as famine or pledging peace. Pipes, carried by members of a special society, were used in peace ceremonies and to "sacredize" decisions and agreements. Members of the society also had special responsibilities such as organizing camp moves, camping locations, and large hunts.

Shamans, or medicine people (men or women), were healers and curers as well as interpreters of visions. Curing ceremonies generally involved burning sage, sweet grass, and tobacco. Shamans danced and sang power songs. They could also cause illness. They also found lost objects, divined the future, and provided important leadership during war or hunts. They received their powers from especially powerful guardian spirits and had a particularly close relationship with all of the deities. They were especially familiar with all legends, symbols, rituals, ceremonies, and cosmology. Common ailments were generally cured with the use of herbs. Women generally had the greater knowledge of curing herbs.

A guardian spirit, usually in the guise of an animal, appeared to people on a vision quest, which was a period of self-deprivation in a remote place, or perhaps in a dream. Spirits were associated with particular songs, prayers, and symbols that, properly used, could bring the individual luck, skills, and/or protection from evil or danger. Women as well as men sought visions. Shamans assisted in preparing for and interpreting such visions. Not all visions were of equal potency, and not everyone received a vision, although people who did not generally kept trying. Women could receive visions but generally did not seek them. Personal medicine bundles were made up of objects dictated by the guardian spirit during the vision quest. They were kept on the person and provided special protection.

Shamans also led the Sun Dance, the most important of Plains ceremonies after about the mid–eighteenth century, when the horse transformed Plains dwellers into full-time nomadic buffalo hunters. Among the Lakota the Sun Dance brought together their most important beliefs about themselves and the universe. *Wakan Tanka,* or the Great Spirit, as the supreme creator of the universe, or the sacred hoop, was first among 16 gods representing forces of nature. The number four was particularly sacred to the Lakota, representing the four cardinal directions, the pantheon of gods (four groups of four), and the four stages of life. The highly symbolic, 12-day-long Sun Dance brought benefits both to the participants and the nation as a whole. Individually sponsored as the result of a vow taken the previous

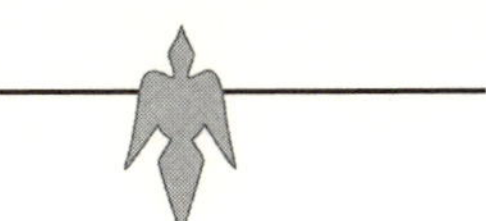

winter, the dance itself contained elements of dancing, feasting, praying, fasting, and self-torture.

Government Elected chiefs in the Woodlands gave way to leadership by warriors. The subdivisions became more autonomous, and themselves divided into bands and their basic units. These were known as *tiyospaye,* a group of fluid composition composed of relatives and led by a warrior-chief. Each had its own recognized hunting area.

Chiefs were older men who had distinguished themselves in hunting and battle and were noted for their wisdom, well-spokenness, and generosity. Each band also had a council of such men, who governed without any force to back them up except the respect engendered by their position and a consensus-style of decision making.

In the later historical period, the Oglala had a society composed of older men, which elected seven lifelong chiefs. In practice, authority was delegated to four highly respected "shirt-wearers," who also served for life. There were also four *wakikun,* or camp police, who were temporary officials assisted by the members of the *akitcita.*

The seven Teton divisions met regularly, ideally annually in summer, from at least the late eighteenth century to about 1850. At these times there was a Sun Dance, and people socialized and generally renewed acquaintances. A supreme council of four chiefs met to discuss national policies. Still, the nation was very decentralized, with no overall political or military coordination, and the supreme council's power was largely symbolic.

Customs On the Plains, patrilineal clans gave way to bilaterally descended extended families. The band, Oglala, for example, came together only for the summer activities. Otherwise it was divided into independent subbands, which themselves broke into even smaller groups during winter.

Generosity was highly valued, as were bravery, fortitude, wisdom, and fidelity. In the "giveaway" custom, people shared generously, especially with the less able or fortunate and during important times in their lives. Thus did people achieve prestige while actually reducing individual suffering and want.

In winter, people repaired their tools and weapons and made crafts and clothing. Social control was effected mostly by peer pressure and ridicule, although serious crimes were punished by revenge and/or adjudication by the council. Various voluntary societies included those for men (mostly war related); feast and dance societies, which included social groups of both sexes and groups for women only; dream cult societies (such as the Heyoka, or clown, society); and craft societies. Games included various guessing games, cup-and-ball, and competitions. Adult games were usually accompanied by gambling. Toys included conical tops and sleds. In general, storytelling was a favorite pastime.

Work was generally divided by gender but not by profession, except for medicine men and berdaches. Prestige was based less on wealth than on bravery, generosity, oratorical ability, supernatural powers, and other factors. Wealth and kin connections did, however, play a part, and status ultimately rested on a combination of individual and family qualities.

Although premarital sex was frowned upon, the extent to which it occurred may be inferred by the fact that some Lakotas kept their young daughters in chastity belts at night. Polygamy was practiced, although it was expensive. Each wife might or might not have a separate tipi. Marriage was mainly a matter of parental agreement, often based on the couple's choice, and divorce was common and easy to obtain. Fidelity in marriage was an ideal, and disloyal women might have the end of their noses cut off.

Children, especially boys, were always welcomed. Infants spent their first few months swaddled in a cradleboard. They were allowed to nurse on demand. Children were treated with love and affection and were rarely struck. They were generally weaned after about four years, after which time their ears were pierced. Boys and girls (except for brothers and sisters) generally played together until puberty. Games revolved around future adult activities.

During menstruation, girls and women were secluded for a few days, as men considered them dangerous. Girls having their first period were seen only by women and instructed on proper womanly behavior. Several weeks later, fathers who were able gave a ceremony, presided over by a shaman, for their daughters. The relative lavishness of the ceremony reflected on the whole family. Girls who had reached puberty were considered marriageable.

Boys did not have a specific puberty ceremony. Their vision quests, first successful buffalo hunt, first war party, and so forth might be marked by feasts and gifts and were considered rites of passage. Men generally married slightly older than did women, having first to prove their manhood and perhaps acquire enough goods to distribute.

As a matter of respect there was no verbal communication between a man and his mother-in-law. Aged people were generally accorded a great deal of respect. When people reached what they considered to be the end of their functional lives, they might elect to remain behind the migrating band, although sometimes this action was taken involuntarily.

The dead were buried with their effects on high hills or in scaffolds in trees. In the prehistoric period remains were buried in an earth mound. In the late historical period a chief's favorite horse might be killed.

Dwellings Winter camps on the plains were places containing wood and water, such as valley cottonwood groves. People also needed forage for horses and some natural protection against weather and enemies. Winter camps were small, generally consisting of between 5 and 50 related families

In the Woodlands, Lakotas lived in pole-frame lodges covered with woven mats or bark. Once on the Plains, they shifted to conical buffalo-skin tipis in both summer and winter. The average tipi was made of about 12 buffalo skins, dressed and sewn together by women and placed over a pole framework. A tipi held one family. The interior fire was slightly off center. Two skin flaps at the top, attached to long poles, regulated the smoke hole. A small, elevated doorway was covered by a rawhide door.

Skin liners helped insulate against the cold and wind. Tanned buffalo robes served as beds and blankets and buffalo robes as carpeting. Women also erected and took down the tipis, which could be moved quickly and easily. Tipis were often painted with special symbols and war exploits and were also decorated with feathers, quills, or other items.

Diet Large and small game, wild rice, maple sugar, and fish constituted the bulk of the Woodland diet. On the Plains, people mostly ate buffalo. No part of the animal went to waste. The communal hunt, which was often but not always very successful, was accomplished by fire surrounds, shooting with bow and arrow, clubbing, or driving the animals off cliffs. Men also hunted individually or in family groups. Following the main hunt, which took place in summer, women butchered the meat and carried it back to camp. Meat was roasted on a spit, stone boiled in a buffalo stomach with dried berries and tubers, or cut into strips and dried. Pemmican (buffalo meat pounded with fat and dried chokecherries) was eaten on the hunt and in some ceremonies.

Lakotas also ate antelope, deer, and other large and small game as well as birds, eggs, turtles, tortoises, and fish. Young dog, considered a delicacy, was often eaten at feast times. Women gathered foods such as wild potatoes and turnips, berries, chokecherries, cactus, acorns, and wild onions. Some Teton women occasionally planted a little maize. There were also many medicinal herbs and plants.

Key Technology On the Plains, most manufactured items came from the buffalo. Many tools were also made of stone, until iron became available from non-Indian traders. Bone fishhooks were fastened onto sinew lines attached to willow poles.

Women tanned the skins using elk antler scrapers with an attached stone (or iron) blade; the hair was either left on or soaked and scraped off. Rawhide was often used to attach items to each other, such as clubs and mauls. People made willow back rests for use in tipis.

Trade Lakotas traded at Arikara villages, north of the mouth of the Grand River, in present-day South Dakota, until about 1800, when they completely subjugated the Arikara. They acted as intermediaries for the catlinite (red pipestone) trade between the Yankton and most northern Plains tribes. Part of an extensive trade complex stretching throughout the West, the Tetons traded buffalo products to the eastern Dakota for non-Indian goods the latter had obtained through the fur trade.

Notable Arts Art was integral to all Lakota materialism. Winter counts were pictographs on hides that recorded annual events. Clothing and bags were decorated with painting and porcupine quillwork, later beadwork. Bags, robes, and tipis were also painted.

Designs were either realistic (generally painting, often made by men) or geometrical (generally quillwork and beadwork, often made by women). Musical instruments included flageolets, rattles, rasps, and drums.

Transportation Lakotas used birch-bark and dugout canoes and snowshoes in the Woodlands. On the Plains, dogs served as the first beast of burden; the original migrations of the seventeenth and early eighteenth centuries were accomplished with the aid of dogs pulling travois. They still played a role in transportation even after the Lakota acquired horses during the mid–eighteenth century, probably from the Arikaras. Tetons became extremely skilled riders. Horse travois carried tipis and other goods. Poles, carried along because wood was often hard to find on the plains, facilitated the travois structure.

Dress Men wore deerskin or elk-skin breechclouts, leggings, and soft-sole moccasins. They braided their hair, and they often wore face and body paint. Some wore their hair in a roach. In winter, women wore long elk-skin dresses, knee-length leggings, and moccasins. They braided and parted their hair in the middle. They also wore face paint and earrings. Both sexes wore buffalo-hide robes. Some of the above clothing was discarded in summer.

Plains clothing often was fringed and decorated with colorful beadwork, especially in the later historical period and for ceremonial purposes. People made ornaments of bone, dentalium shell, elk and grizzly bear teeth, beads, copper and obsidian, and perhaps turquoise.

From about the mid–nineteenth century on, certain war leaders wore long eagle-feathered war bonnets for ceremonial purposes, although even before that period young men wore eagle feathers in their hair to signify achievements in battle. Chiefs and other people of authority also often wore special clothing and other paraphernalia at official occasions.

War and Weapons Tetons were feared fighters but did not fight each other. By 1800 they subjugated the Arikara, mostly by harassing the Kiowa and other important Arikara trade partners. They raided Mandans, Hidatsas, and most everyone else on the northern Plains, Indian or not.

The *akitcita* was an elite warrior society that kept order in camp and especially on the hunt. Severe penalties were meted out to those who disrupted the summer hunt.

Warfare and raiding were the primary means to gain prestige. Weapons included bows and arrows, buffalo-hide shields, war clubs, and lances. Military societies had their own songs, paraphernalia (such as feathered headgear), and ceremonies. War leaders, generally young men, had absolute authority but only over the war party while on a sortie. War and raiding parties were completely voluntary, motivated mainly by the desire to attain prestige. Men generally engaged in ritual purification in the sweat lodge before battle. Large battles involving hundreds of warriors occurred only in the late historical period

As practiced in the early nineteenth century, counting coup meant achieving bravery in a hand-to-hand encounter with the enemy or some other feat of daring such as stealing a horse within a village. Killing and scalping generally merited less honor than did counting coup, although, in the nineteenth century, scalping was important to the Lakota for ritualistic purposes. There were several levels of coup, each with accompanying symbols, such as feathers, and corresponding levels of prestige. Lakotas were often allied with Cheyennes and Arapahos in the nineteenth century.

Contemporary Information

Government/Reservations Standing Rock Reservation, Sioux County, North Dakota, and Carson County, South Dakota (Hunkpapa, Sihasapa, Minneconjou, O'ohenonpa, and Yanktonai), established in 1868, contains 847,799 acres, almost 300,000 of which are tribally owned. In 1990 there were 4,866 Indian residents. Government is by tribal council.

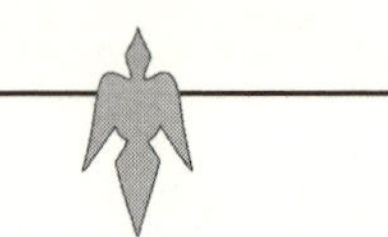

Lakota Sioux Indians at a slaughterhouse on the Rosebud Reservation, circa 1893.

Cheyenne River Reservation, Dewey and Ziebach Counties, South Dakota (Itazipco and Sihasapa), established in 1889, contains 1,419,499 acres, 911,000 of which are tribally owned. The 1990 Indian population was 5,100. Government is by tribal council.

Lower Brulé Reservation, Lyman and Stanley Counties, South Dakota (Sicangu and others), established in 1868, contains 114,219 acres, about 66,600 of which are tribally owned. The 1990 Indian population was 994. Government is by tribal council.

Crow Creek Reservation, Buffalo, Hughes, and Hyde Counties, South Dakota (Hunkpatina and others), established in 1863, contains 125,483 acres. The 1990 Indian population was 1,531. Government is by tribal council.

Pine Ridge Reservation and Trust Lands, Jackson, Shannon, and Bennett Counties, South Dakota, and Sheridan County, Nebraska (Oglala), established in 1868, contains 2,778,000 acres, more than 372,000 of which are tribally owned. The 1990 Indian population was 11,180; 23,000 people (both Indians and non-Indians lived there in 1992. Government is by tribal council.

Rosebud Reservation and Trust Lands, Todd, Gregory, Lyman, Mellette, and Tripp Counties, South Dakota (Sicangu and O'ohenonpa), established in 1868, contains almost 1 million acres, about 409,000 of which are tribally owned. The 1990 Indian population was 1,160; 18,000 Indians and non-Indians lived there in 1992. Government is by tribal council.

Some Lakotas also live on the Standing Buffalo and the Wood Mountain Reserves in Saskatchewan, Canada.

Economy Moccasins are manufactured at Pine Ridge. The Standing Rock Reservation leases land to

Girls in the sewing room of the Lower Cut Meat Creek Camp Indian School on the Rosebud Reservation.

Texas ranching firms. Pine Ridge has plans to open a casino.

Except for a few gas stations, convenience stores, and arts and crafts stores, most retail businesses on the reservations are owned by non-Indians. In general, land leasing is the most important economic activity. Unemployment on all Lakota reservations is commonly over 50 percent and has reached 80 percent. Federal commodities support continues.

Legal Status The Cheyenne River Sioux Tribe, the Crow Creek Sioux Tribe, the Lower Brulé Sioux Tribe, the Oglala Sioux Tribe, the Rosebud Sioux Tribe, and the Standing Rock Sioux Tribe are federally recognized tribal entities.

Lakotas continue to press for legal possession of the Black Hills. Modifications to the 1868 Fort Laramie Treaty required the signatures of a minimum of three-quarters of adult males. Although it did not have nearly enough signatures, the United States simply appropriated 7.7 million acres that included the Black Hills, the Lakota's holiest land. The Lakota began a series of legal actions to recover the land in 1920, as soon as it had legal standing to do so. After a number of complicated rulings from various courts, the U.S. Supreme Court ruled in 1980 that the Lakotas' treaty rights had been violated and that they were entitled to compensation of $17.5 million plus interest.

All eight tribes (the South Dakota Lakotas plus the Santees in Nebraska and the Fort Peck Sioux of Montana) have refused a cash award, holding out for congressional action that would return the land to them. A bill to that effect, opposed by the South Dakota delegation, died in the Senate in 1990. The Lakota succeeded in defeating a plan by the Honeywell Corporation to build a munitions testing facility in the Black Hills. In 1981, a group of Lakotas established Camp Yellow Thunder as an initial step toward reoccupying the Black Hills.

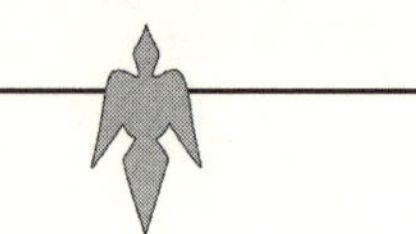

Taking a census at Standing Rock Reservation in the Dakota territory in 1921.

Daily Life Such seminal mid- to late-nineteenth-century events as the Battle of the Greasy Grass (also known as Custer's Last Stand) and the Wounded Knee massacre remain very much in the hearts and minds of Lakotas, with many observing annual remembrance ceremonies and pilgrimages to sites.

There is ongoing tension between the tribal councils, dating from the 1930s, and traditional *tiyospaye* governing structure. According to Lakota custom, the latter voice is the stronger, but the U.S. government supports the former. Today, most *tiyospaye* are organized around Christian churches, which have also become associated with many traditional ceremonies.

Although many Lakotas consider themselves Christian, they continue to follow many traditional ceremonies and customs. Summer remains a time of traditional ceremonies and feasting, including the Sun Dance, which today lasts for four days, not including preparation time. Giveaways, which have their origin in the Keeping of the Soul ceremony, continue to act as expressions of traditional culture and family life. The original sacred pipe of the Lakota Nation is kept at the Cheyenne River Reservation.

In general, the Lakota reservations face problems associated with poverty, including relatively poor health related in part to substance abuse. Most reservations have hospitals and clinics. Schools feature classes in many aspects of Lakota culture and history. Lakota institutions of higher education include two-year colleges at Cheyenne River and Standing Rock in addition to the four-year Oglala Lakota College (Pine Ridge) and Sinte Gleska University (Rosebud). Lakotas rank among the best contemporary Native American artists.

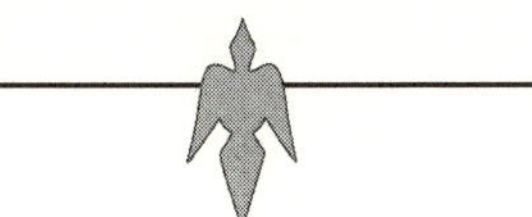

In 1975, a Lakota and two Federal Bureau of Investigation (FBI) agents were killed during a confrontation near Wounded Knee, South Dakota. The incident stemmed from continuing unrest in the area following the battles between AIM and the corrupt Pine Ridge Tribal Council; these battles themselves grew out of the appalling level of violence directed against local Indians, in part by council-controlled thugs. In an extremely controversial trial, Leonard Peltier, an Anishinabe/Dakota Indian, was found guilty of killing the FBI agents and sentenced to two consecutive life sentences in federal prison. For many Lakotas and others, his case remains emblematic of the continuing mistreatment of Indians by the U.S. government.

Mandan

Mandan (`Man dan) is a Dakota word. Their self-designation was *Numakiki,* "People."

Location For centuries before the coming of non-Indians, Mandans lived along the upper Missouri River and near the mouth of the Heart River, in central North Dakota. Today, most Mandans live in Dunn, McKenzie, McLean, Mercer, Mountrail, and Ward Counties, North Dakota.

Population The early-eighteenth-century Mandan population was around 3,600. In the mid-1990s, enrollment in the Three Affiliated Tribes was about 6,000.

Language Mandan, related to but unintelligible with Hidatsa, is a Siouan language.

Historical Information

History The Mandan arrived in the Missouri River region from the southeast (Ohio Valley) between about 1000 and the thirteenth century, perhaps as early as the seventh century. They gradually moved upriver and away from other Siouan-speaking people.

The first smallpox epidemics arrived in the early sixteenth century. The acquisition of horses in the early to mid–eighteenth century allowed the Mandan to expand their buffalo hunting, but they did not give up their sedentary lifestyle. During the mid–eighteenth century, the Mandan became intermediaries between French and Indian traders, dealing in furs, horses, guns, crops, and buffalo products.

The Mandan suffered a gradual decline beginning in the late eighteenth century, owing primarily to smallpox and warfare with the Dakota and other tribes. In the early nineteenth century, Mandans were friendly to non-Indians, even allowing visitors to study their religious ceremonies. In 1837, a major smallpox epidemic dropped the Mandan population by over 90 percent, to just about 125 people. In 1845, surviving Mandans joined the Hidatsa people to establish Like-a-Fishhook village on the Missouri. They were joined by the Arikara in 1862. Like-a-Fishhook was a significant commercial center at this time.

Although the 1851 Fort Laramie Treaty recognized native holdings of more than 12 million acres, the 1870 Fort Berthold Reservation, created for the Three Affiliated Tribes (Mandan, Hidatsa, and Arikara) consisted only of eight million acres, which was reduced, mostly by allotment, to about one million during the 1880s. By that time, the people had abandoned Like-a-Fishhook to form communities along the Missouri River.

In 1910, the United States unilaterally removed a large section of land from the reservation. During the 1950s, the United States built the Garrison Dam on the Missouri, against the tribes' vehement opposition. The resulting Lake Sakakawea covered much of their land, farms, and homes. This event destroyed the tribe's economic base and severely damaged its social structure as well as its infrastructure.

Religion Sacred or medicine bundles (called "Mother") symbolized fertility and crop productivity. They were owned by individual men who passed them down to their descendants or sold them. All bundles had a mythological component and were considered so sacred that the welfare of the entire village depended on their safety and proper care. They were associated with specific ceremonies, songs, and activities

The four-day Okipa ceremony, similar to and a likely precursor of the Sun Dance, was a ritual enactment of their worldview. Its dual purpose was

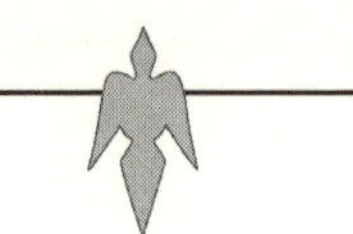

The men's Buffalo Dance, depicted in this early-nineteenth-century engraving, was one of several agricultural and hunting festivals. The acquisition of horses in the early to mid–eighteenth century allowed the Mandans to expand their buffalo hunting.

tribal renewal and bringing the buffalo. Prompted by their vision, individuals pledged to offer the summer ceremony, which included periods of fasting and ritual self-torture. The preparation period lasted several months at least. The ceremony contained masked performers representing animals, and required a special lodge fronting the village plaza. Creation legends were told during this time but in an unintelligible language; the uninformed could pay for a translation. Participants hoped to receive a vision afterward.

People accepted as Okipa Makers (those entitled to sponsor the Okipa ceremony) were required to give feasts and to possess a certain quantity of material goods. In acquiring these goods they were assisted by members of their kin group, because individual honor reflected on the group.

Other agricultural and hunting festivals included the women's Corn Dance and the men's Buffalo Dance. Clan chiefs were in charge of ceremonial activities, aspects of which were overseen by dual (summer and winter) divisions. The Mandans also had secret religious societies.

Government There were nine villages in the early nineteenth century. Villages had two hereditary chiefs, one from each division, roughly the same as a war and a peace chief. The people were also governed by a council of older males who made decisions by consensus. In the eighteenth century there were about five bands, each speaking slightly different dialects. There was also a police group called the Black Mouth Society.

Customs Women grew the crops and processed animal skins into clothing. Descent was matrilineal, and residence was matrilocal. Households controlled the garden plots, but the land was actually held by lineages composed of several extended families. About 13 matrilineal clans, composed of extended family lineages, were loosely ranked by status, depending on their ritual importance. The tribe was also divided into two groups, each producing a village leader, which competed against each other in games and contests.

Social class determined status to a far greater degree than did war deeds. High individual rank was affirmed through lavish giveaways and brave personal acts, but a high inherited status did not always need this sort of affirmation. Similarly, a commoner could not rise to be a chief despite the most extensive gift giving and remarkable personal exploits.

Age-graded societies and ranked social clubs united nonrelatives. Organized around hunting, dancing, or curing, membership was purchased from existing members, who then purchased their way up to the next level. Only a few reached the highest level, which in any case was open by invitation only.

Grandparents largely brought up the children. Marriage, which consisted of an exchange of gifts between the two families, took place outside of the division and clan. Corpses were buried in the earth, although the people adopted scaffold burial in later times. After a four-day mourning period, and when the bones had dried, people placed skulls in circles around the village.

Dwellings People lived where there was arable land and a supply of wood. Permanent villages, composed of between a dozen to as many as 150 earth lodges, were on high bluffs overlooking the river, often where tributary streams joining the Missouri were protected on two sides by the steep riverbanks. Heavily fortified with wooden stockades and barrier ditches, they were fairly impervious to attack. The central plaza was the focus of the village, the place where games were played and ceremonies took place. In the depth of winter, people sought shelter in more protected, wooded areas, where they built smaller, cruder earth lodges. They also used skin tipis for hunting and traveling.

The main lodges were semiexcavated. A heavy wooden frame was overlaid with willow branches and overlapping strips of sod and covered with an outer layer of earth. These lodges sheltered as many as 50 people but usually about 20–40 extended family members. The lodges were about 40 feet or more in diameter. A set of planks in front of the rawhide door further protected against cold winds. Animals occasionally stayed in the lodges as well.

Rawhide beds on raised platforms were placed next to the outer wall. The fire was in the center. Roofs were strong enough so that people regularly congregated on them and used them for storing and drying maize. Deep pits, wider at the base, were dug into the earth for crop storage. An altar and weapons storage area was located on the righthand side of the lodge. Furniture included willow back rests and buffalo-robe couches.

Diet Men hunted elk, deer, and smaller mammals. Buffalo were hunted communally in summer as well as individually. Before the people acquired horses, they hunted buffalo by driving the herd into a channel made of wood and stone that led to the edge of a cliff or an enclosure.

Women grew maize, sunflowers, beans, squash, and tobacco. Burned trees provided additional soil fertilizer to the already rich bottomlands. Mandan maize was a variety adapted by the people to their short growing season. Women parched sunflower seeds and then ground them into meal used for thickening boiled dishes. Men also ate balls of this meal as travel food.

Green corn was eaten freshly boiled and dried for the winter. Squash was sliced and sun dried. The people also ate fish and gathered a variety of wild foods. Dogs were eaten in times of want, although puppy stew was considered a delicacy. Tobacco was considered sacred and grown only by the older men.

Key Technology Material items included willow fish weirs, buffalo horn and bone utensils, pointed digging sticks, antler or willow rakes, hoes made from the shoulder blade of a buffalo or elk, and clay and stone pipes. Women made baskets (twilled plaited carrying and coiled gambling) and pottery.

Trade Mandan villages on the Knife River were a major center of aboriginal trade. They traded surplus agricultural products to the Assiniboine and other

nomadic tribes for hides and meat. As early as 1738, the Mandan had obtained guns from the Assiniboine as well as horses, which they used mostly for trade. They traded with the Kiowa from the late eighteenth into the first years of the nineteenth century.

Notable Arts Mandans were famous for their painted buffalo robes. They also made fine baskets. Painted skins depicted battles and other significant events.

Transportation Horses began pulling sleds or travois toboggans around 1745. Bull-boats were made of hide stretched over a wooden framework. They were paddled across rivers laden with a cargo of people, meat, and/or hides.

Dress Women made the clothing, such as blankets, robes, and moccasins. In addition to buffalo, deer, and elk, they also used white weasel or ermine skin. The Mandan wore animal skin head wraps in winter.

War and Weapons Traditional allies were the Hidatsa and the Crow. Enemies included Dakota tribes from the eighteenth century on. Weapons included bows and arrows, clubs, and buffalo-hide shields.

Contemporary Information

Government/Reservations The Three Affiliated Tribes (Arikara, Hidatsa, Mandan) live on the Fort Berthold Reservation (roughly 900,000 acres in Dunn, McKenzie, McLean, Mercer, Mountrail, and Ward Counties, North Dakota). The 1990 reservation Indian population was 2,999. More than half of the reservation is owned by non-Indians. The Indian Reorganization Act constitution provides for government by a business council.

Economy Tribal government and the federal government are the largest employers. A few people own farms or ranches. The tribe opened a high-stakes casino in 1993. Unemployment remains very high.

In 1992, the tribe received $143 million in additional compensation (on top of $12 million previously awarded) for damages caused by the Garrison Dam.

Legal Status The Three Affiliated Tribes is a federally recognized tribal entity.

Daily Life Most Mandans live on the west side of the reservoir, near the town of Twin Buttes. Their lives are similar to those of their non-Indian neighbors.

The annual powwow held by each reservation community has become a focus for tribal activities. Ceremonies called Warbonnet Dances help maintain an Indian identity. Some Indians practice sweat lodge ceremonies and are members of the Native American Church. Most consider themselves Christians.

Only elders speak the native language well, despite the attempt to institute regular language classes. The tribes operate several reservation schools and publish the *Mandan, Hidatsa and Arikara Times.* Craft workers make quilts and beadwork. There is a museum at New Town.

Mdewkanton

See Dakota

Métis

See Ojibwa, Plains

Minneconjou

See Lakota

Missouria

Missouria (Mi `zor ä) or Missouri, an Algonquian term probably meaning "People with Dugout Canoes." Their self-designation was *Niutachi,* or "People of the River Mouth." They were closely related to Poncas, Ioways, Otoes, and Winnebagos. All Southern Siouans had elements of both Plains and Woodland cultures.

Location Located near the Missouri and Grand Rivers in the late eighteenth century, today most Missourias live in the Red Rock region of Oklahoma and in regional cities and towns.

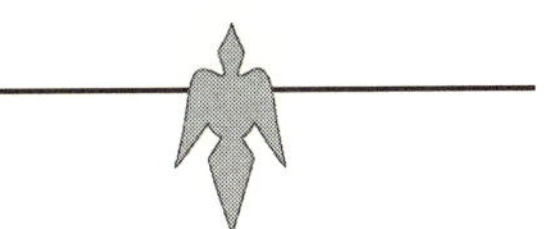

Population There were about 1,000 Missourias in the late eighteenth century. Enrolled membership as of the mid-1990s was about 1,500.

Language Iowa-Otoe-Missouria was a member of the Chiwere division of the Siouan language family.

Historical Information

History According to tradition, the Winnebago, Ioway, Missouria, and Otoe once lived together north of the Great Lakes. In the sixteenth century, the groups began migrating south toward their historic areas. The Otoe and Missouria continued past the Ioway and especially the Winnebago until they reached the junction of the Missouri and Grand Rivers around 1600. There the tribes had a falling out ascribed to a love affair between the two chiefs' children.

After the split, the Missouria were under constant attack from such tribes as the Sauk and Fox. They were also regularly struck by smallpox and other diseases. Jacques Marquette encountered the Missouria in 1673 by the Missouri and Grand Rivers. Trade with the French soon developed and continued for about a century.

In 1730, after the Sauk killed several hundred of their people, the Missouria moved across the Missouri River and settled near the Osage. After they acquired horses in the early to mid–eighteenth century, their lives became much more focused on hunting buffalo. The Missouria were nearly all killed in a 1798 Fox ambush on the Missouri River. Many rejoined the Otoe at that time. Some also went to live with the Osage and the Kaw. Several years later, the rest of the tribe, including the fewer than 100 survivors of the devastating 1829 smallpox epidemic, joined the Otoes.

Several difficult decades followed, during which the people continued to battle disease as well as Indians and non-Indians. By treaties in the 1830s and 1854, the Otoe-Missouria ceded all land and moved to a 162,000-acre reservation on the Kansas-Nebraska border, along the Big Blue River. Additional land cessions in occurred in 1876 and 1881.

Two factions developed in 1880 over the issue of acculturation. The Coyote, or traditional faction, moved to the Indian Territory (Oklahoma). The Quakers ceded their land for a 129,000-acre reservation near Red Rock in north-central Oklahoma. Most Coyotes joined them by 1890, having lived for a time in a separate village on the Iowa Reservation. The reservation was allotted by 1907.

The tribe established a court system for both civil and criminal cases by 1900. Many people lived by growing grains and potatoes. After oil was discovered on their land in 1912, the United States forced many Otoe-Missourias to give up their allotments. During the early to mid–twentieth century, intermarriage truly created one tribe. Many Indians left the region during the 1930s. The tribe received a $1.5 million land claim settlement in 1955 and another payment in 1964. Both were divided on a per capita basis.

Religion Wakonda was recognized as a universal spirit, to which the people could draw closer through fasting and vision seeking. There were secret curing and dance societies and a hereditary priesthood. As part of a Woodland ceremony related to the Ojibwa Midewiwin, members of a particular religious society "shot" a prospective member with a magic shell. The candidate was later restored by older shamans.

Government Political authority was vested in hereditary clan and war chiefs.

Customs Each of about ten patrilineal clans had specific social and religious responsibilities. The people played lacrosse, a Woodland game. Corpses were placed in a tree or buried in the ground. A four-day mourning period followed funerals, and a horse was sometimes killed so that the dead person's spirit might have transportation to the spirit world.

Dwellings Missourias lived in small farming villages of between 40 and 70 semiexcavated earth lodges. Each lodge measured about 40 feet in diameter and was constructed of interwoven brush and grass over a heavy wooden framework, with an outer earthen layer. From the eighteenth century on, the people used skin tipis on hunting trips.

Diet Women grew corn, beans, and squash in river bottomlands. Men assisted with the crops but mainly hunted buffalo (twice a year from the eighteenth century on), deer, and small game. Hunting, in fact, was a major occupation, and once on the Plains the Missouria gradually came to rely more on buffalo than on crops. The people also gathered plant foods such as nuts, berries, and roots, and they ate fish.

Key Technology Crops were stored in underground bell-shaped caches. People speared fish or caught them in weirs and basketry traps. Women dressed skins with elk antler scrapers.

Material items included buffalo wool bags; reed floor mats woven over a bark-cord foundation; twined rectangular storage bags; rawhide trunks or containers, bent and sewn into place; and buffalo-hair wallets. The latter two items were more typical of Woodland tribes such as the Sauk and Fox.

Trade During the late seventeenth and early eighteenth centuries, Missourias traded heavily with the French, supplying Indian slaves, among other items.

Notable Arts Woodworking was particularly well developed among the Missouria.

Transportation The Missouria acquired horses during the early eighteenth century.

Dress On the Plains, Missourias dressed similarly to other local Indians. Skins tanned by women formed the basis of most clothing. Men wore leggings and a breechclout; women wore a one-piece dress. Both wore moccasins. Cold-weather gear included shirts, robes, and fur caps.

War and Weapons Missourias and Otoes were usually military allies. Traditional enemies included the Sauk, Fox, Pawnee, Omaha, and Dakota.

Contemporary Information

Government/Reservations About 800 Otoe-Missourias lived in Oklahoma's Red Rock region in the mid-1990s. The tribe is governed by a tribal council under a 1984 constitution.

Economy Jobs are available in the local economy as well as through the various tribal enterprises, such as elderly and community health programs. There is also a tribal bingo parlor.

Legal Status The Otoe-Missouria tribe is a federally recognized tribal entity.

Daily Life Traditional kinship and family ties remain alive and important. The tribe hosts a powwow in July. Other gatherings and ceremonies take place regularly, often in the cultural center. Children study the native language in school, assisted by a Chiwere grammar published in 1975.

The people began buying land and adding to their land base in the 1970s. At that time they received a series of federal grants to reconstruct tribal facilities and institute services. Religious affiliations include Protestant, Catholic, and the Native American Church.

Nakota

Nakota (Nä `kō tä), a Siouan dialect spoken by the Central group—whose divisions include Yankton ("end village") and Yanktonai ("little end village")—of the tribe commonly referred to as Sioux. Yanktonai was divided into Upper Yanktonai and Lower Yanktonai (Hunkpatina), from which Assiniboine/Stoney was derived.

The Nakota refer to themselves as Nakota ("ally") or as *Ikce Wicasa* ("Natural" or "Free People"). The word "Sioux" is derived originally from an Ojibwa word, *Nadowe-is-iw,* meaning "lesser adder" ("enemy" is the implication) that was corrupted by French voyageurs to *Nadousssioux* and then shortened to *Sioux.* Today, many people use the term "Dakota" or, less commonly, "Lakota" to refer to all Sioux people.

All 13 subdivisions of Dakota-Lakota-Nakota speakers ("Sioux") were known as *Oceti Sakowin,* or Seven Council Fires, a term referring to their seven political divisions: Teton (the Western group, speakers of Lakota); Sisseton, Wahpeton, Wahpukute, and Mdewakanton (the Eastern group, speakers of Dakota); and Yankton and Yanktonai (the Central, or Wiciyela, group, speakers of Dakota and Nakota). *See also* Assiniboine; Dakota; Lakota.

Location Nakota speakers migrated from north-central Minnesota, around Mille Lacs, in the early seventeenth century, to near the Missouri River in present-day eastern North and South Dakota, southwestern Minnesota, and southwestern Iowa in the nineteenth century. Today, Yanktons and Yanktonais live on reservations in the Dakotas and Montana as well as in regional cities and towns.

Population Dakota, Lakota, and Nakota speakers numbered approximately 25,000 in the late seventeenth century. At that time there were approximately 5,000 Nakota speakers. In the mid–nineteenth century there were about 3,000 Yanktons and 6,000 Yanktonais. Today there are roughly 10,000 Yanktons and Yanktonais.

Language Nakota is a dialect of Dakota, a Siouan language.

Historical Information

History The Siouan family may have originated along the lower Mississippi River or in eastern Texas. Siouan speakers moved to, or may have originated in, the Ohio Valley, where they lived in large agricultural settlements. They may have been related to the Mound Builder culture of the ninth through twelfth centuries. They may also have originated in the upper Mississippi Valley or even the Atlantic seaboard.

Siouan tribes still lived in the southeast, between Florida and Virginia, around the late sixteenth and early seventeenth century. All were destroyed either by attacks from Algonquian-speaking Indians or a combination of attacks from non-Indians and non-Indian diseases. Some fled and were absorbed by other tribes. Some were sent as slaves to the West Indies.

Dakota-Lakota-Nakota speakers ranged throughout more than 100 million acres in the upper Mississippi region, including Minnesota and parts of Wisconsin, Iowa, and the Dakotas, in the sixteenth to early seventeenth century. At this time the Yankton and Yanktonai were one tribe, the Assiniboine having separated from the Yankton/Yanktonai, probably by the mid–sixteenth century.

French explorers encountered Eastern group tribes around Mille Lacs, Minnesota, in the late seventeenth century. Shortly afterward, the latter probably became directly involved in the fur trade. But conflict with the Cree and Ojibwa, who were well armed with French rifles, plus the lure of great buffalo herds to feed their expanding population, induced bands to begin moving west onto the Plains.

Struck by the Ree was born in Yankton, South Dakota, on August 30, 1804, while the explorers Lewis and Clark were encamped there. On learning that a male child had been born in the camp, Captain Lewis sent for him, wrapped him in an American flag, and declared him "an American." This photo was taken during a delegation visit to Washington. D.C., between February 17 and April 8, 1867.

The Yankton and Yanktonai separated near Leech Lake in the late seventeenth century. The Yankton had moved out of the northern Woodlands and onto the southern prairies (near the pipestone quarries of southwest Minnesota and then west of the Missouri in northwest Iowa) by the early eighteenth century. A hundred years later, Yanktons ranged

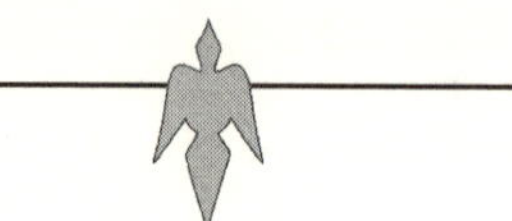

north and northwest into Minnesota and South Dakota.

Meanwhile, the Yanktonai left their homes in Mille Lacs by the early eighteenth century to follow Teton tribes west, making winter villages on the James River (South Dakota) at least as early as 1725. They acquired horses in the mid– to late eighteenth century. By the early nineteenth century they were hunting buffalo between the Red and the Missouri Rivers and north to Devil's Lake.

A general Yankton decline set in during the 1830s. Its causes were smallpox, the growing scarcity of game, and war, particularly with the Pawnee, Otoe, and Omaha. Yanktons ceded their Iowa lands (2.2 million acres) to the United States in 1830 and 1837 treaties and ceded over 11 million acres in 1858. They did retain a 430,000-acre reservation near Fort Randall, South Dakota. They also claimed the 650-acre Pipestone Reservation in Minnesota.

By 1860, Yanktons had ceded all of their remaining lands. Most moved to the Yankton Reservation in South Dakota; others went to the Crow Creek and Lower Brulé Reservations in South Dakota and to the Fort Totten (now Devil's Lake) Reservation in North Dakota. The Yanktonai ceded their remaining lands in 1865. They were removed to a number of reservations, including Standing Rock (South Dakota), Devil's Lake (North Dakota), Crow Creek (South Dakota), and Fort Peck (Montana). In 1866 they replaced the Santee at Crow Creek when the latter were moved to Nebraska. Yanktons sold the Pipestone Reservation in 1929 for almost $330,000 plus guarantees of Indian access.

Religion Wakan Tanka was known as the great spirit and creator of the universe. There were other deities as well; Nakotas were a very prayerful people. Access to the supernatural world was provided in part by guardian spirits obtained through quests and in dreams. From the eighteenth century on, Nakotas performed the Sun Dance.

Government The Yankton were organized into eight bands. The upper division Yanktonai consisted of six bands, and the Hunkpatina had seven bands. The governing band council was composed of band chiefs and clan leaders. The Seven Council Fires met approximately annually to socialize and discuss matters of national importance.

Customs Nakota bands were composed of patrilineal clans. Around the mid–eighteenth century, Nakotas adopted many Plains customs. They wrapped their dead in skins and placed them on high scaffolds with their belongings. Belowground interment took place occasionally. Mourners cut their hair, wore white clay on their faces, and affected an unkempt appearance.

Dwellings Small villages were located near lakes and rice swamps when the people lived in the Wisconsin-Minnesota area. In summer they lived in large houses of timbered frames with pitched roofs and bark-covered sides, whereas in winter they lived in small mat-covered houses. From the mid– to late eighteenth century, the Yanktonai lived in earth lodges like the Arikara, as well as in tipis.

Diet While still in the Great Lakes region, women grew corn, beans, and squash. People also gathered wild rice and ate turtles, fish, and dogs. Large and small game, especially buffalo, which roamed the area in small herds, were also an important food source. Buffalo were hunted in part by burning grass around the range and forcing the animals toward an ambush. With the westward migration, buffalo became increasingly important, although men still hunted deer, elk, and antelope. Women also grew some corn, beans, and squash along river bottomlands and gathered fruits and berries.

Key Technology In addition to the usual tools and other items made of animal parts, Nakotas caught fish with weirs and basket traps and wove mats and various containers. They also made pottery and pipes.

Trade As the Missouri River trade developed, the Yankton controlled the catlinite, or red pipestone, quarry in southwest Minnesota, supplying its clay to most of the northern Plains groups. During the early nineteenth century, the Yanktonai traded along the Jones River, acting as intermediaries for British goods between the Sisseton and Wahpeton Dakota and the Tetons farther west.

Notable Arts Pottery, pipe carving, and skin tanning were well-developed arts.

Transportation Nakotas plied the northern Woodlands in birch-bark and dugout canoes. On the Plains, horses replaced dogs as travois carriers around 1760. They also used round bull-boats when crossing water.

Dress Most clothing was made from buckskin. In the Woodlands, the people wore breechclouts, dresses, leggings, and moccasins, with fur robes for extra warmth. On the Plains, they decorated their clothing with beads and quillwork in geometric and animal designs.

War and Weapons The Plains warrior ideal—that the purpose of war was to bring glory to an individual rather than to acquire territory or destroy an enemy people—was distinctive to and may have originated with the Siouan people. Dakota people did not generally fight other Dakotas. The *akitcita* was an elite warrior group that maintained discipline at camp and on the communal hunt. Nakota enemies included the Ojibwa (seventeenth and eighteenth centuries).

Contemporary Information

Government/Reservations The Yankton Reservation, Charles Mix County, South Dakota (Yankton), established in 1853, contains roughly 36,000 acres. Enrollment in 1992 was about 6,000, with about 3,400 in residence. The original constitution was adopted in 1891; as of the late 1990s, the constitution does not conform to the Indian Reorganization Act (IRA). The reservation is governed by a business committee.

The Upper Sioux Community, Yellow Medicine County, Minnesota (Sisseton, Wahpeton, Flandreau Santee, Santee, Yankton), established in 1938, contains 743.57 acres. There were 43 residents in 1990. Political authority resides in a board of trustees.

The Fort Peck Reservation, Daniels, Roosevelt, Sheridan, and Valley Counties, Montana (Assiniboine-Sioux [Assiniboine, Upper Yanktonai, and Sisseton-Wahpeton]), established in 1873, contains about 1,000,000 acres, roughly one-quarter of which are tribally owned. Although their 1927 constitution is not based on the IRA, they adopted a representative government, the Tribal Executive Board, in 1960. Enrollment in 1992 was 10,500, with 6,700 residents.

The Devil's Lake Reservation (formerly Fort Totten), Benson, Eddy, Nelson, and Ramsey Counties, North Dakota (Sisseton, Wahpeton, and Cuthead Yanktonai), established in 1867, contains 53,239 acres, most of which are allotted. There were 4,420 people enrolled in 1992, with about 2,900 in residence. The IRA constitution adopted in 1944 calls for elections to a tribal council.

The Standing Rock Reservation, Sioux County, North Dakota, and Carson County, South Dakota (Hunkpapa, Blackfoot Lakota, Yanktonai), established in 1868, contains 847,799 acres, almost 300,000 of which are tribally owned. There were 4,866 Indian residents in 1990. Political authority is vested in a tribal council.

The Crow Creek Reservation, Buffalo, Hughes, and Hyde Counties, South Dakota (Hunkpatina), established in 1863, contains 125,483 acres. There were 3,521 enrolled members in 1992, with about 1,200 in residence. A 1923 constitution and by-laws, since revised, call for an elected tribal council.

Economy The Devil's Lake people have a bingo hall and casino as well as a plant that makes nonviolent armaments such as camouflage nets. Income at Fort Peck is provided by a bingo hall and land leases to non-Indian farmers and ranchers. Fort Peck owns and operates a profitable oil well. The Indians also have other mineral resources and have encouraged industrial development.

At Crow Creek there is a tribal farm and the Lode Star Casino. Other sources of employment include a muffler plant, a boarding school, federal and tribal jobs, and off-reservation jobs. The people have received more than $5 million for land taken for dam projects. The Fort Randall Casino on the Yankton Reservation provides full employment for that community. Important economic activities at Standing Rock include cattle ranching and leasing land to Texas ranching firms.

Legal Status The Assiniboine and Sioux Tribes of the Fort Peck Reservation is a federally recognized tribal entity. The Devils Lake Sioux Tribe, the Standing Rock

Sioux Tribe, the Crow Creek Sioux Tribe, the Yankton Sioux Tribe, and the Upper Sioux Indian Community are federally recognized tribal entities.

Daily Life The Devil's Lake community remains relatively traditional. People perform sacred pipe ceremonies, and many speak Dakota. There is an active Native American Church. The powwow is held in July. At Crow Creek, religious observances include sacred pipe ceremonies as well as the Native American Church.

Standing Rock Community College was chartered in 1973. The reservation has a history of maintaining cultural integrity through relative isolation by resisting full federal funding as well as IRA compliance. Members of the Deloria family—including Philip J., Vine, Sr., Vine, Jr., and Ella Cara—of the Standing Rock community have achieved national and international prominence as writers, teachers, activists, and leaders.

There is also a community college at Fort Peck. That reservation has bucked the gambling tide, refusing to turn their bingo hall into a casino. They have enjoyed relatively effective political leadership. Many Yanktons and Yanktonais have achieved success as artists.

Oglala

See Lakota

Ojibwa, Plains

Plains Ojibwa (Ō `jib wə), "puckered up," refers to a distinctive style of moccasin seam. They were also known as "Bungi." Their self-designation is *Anishinabe,* "First People." People of Ojibwa/Cree/French ancestry are known as Métis, or Mitchif. The Plains Ojibwa are the westernmost branch of the large Ojibwa people, also known variously as Ojibwe, Ojibway, Chippewa, and Anishinabe. *See also* Anishinabe (Chapter 8).

Location Located along the northern Lake Superior shore in the late seventeenth century, the proto–Plains Ojibwa migrated to the Red River Valley (Lake Winnipeg to the North Dakota–Minnesota border) in the eighteenth century. In the nineteenth century, the Plains Ojibwa were located in north-central Montana (vicinity of Milk and Judith Rivers). Today, most live on a reservation in Chouteau and Hill Counties, Montana; in nearby towns such as Havre, Great Falls, and Helena; and in eastern Montana and western North Dakota.

Population There were roughly 35,000 Ojibwa in the mid–seventeenth century and about 3,000 Plains Ojibwa in the late eighteenth century. In the early 1990s there were roughly 3,100 enrolled members of the Rocky Boy Reservation, about 1,000 residents of the Montana Allotment Community, and about 25,000 enrolled members of the Turtle Mountain Reservation.

Language Ojibwa is an Algonquian language.

Historical Information

History The Plains Ojibwa originated in the eastern Great Lakes region. The so-called Salteaux Anishinabe bands had their origin in the vicinity of Sault Sainte Marie. During the late sixteenth century, the people came into friendly, trade-based contact with Dakota bands west and south of Lake Superior. The first French traders and missionaries arrived in the early seventeenth century. Later in that century, the Anishinabe became heavily involved in the fur trade.

The Anishinabe also began to expand their territory during the seventeenth century, an event caused in part by pressure from the Iroquois as well as the overtrapping of food and pelts. One migration route was westward into northern Wisconsin and Minnesota (upper Mississippi basin)—displacing Dakotas, Sauks, Foxes, and Kickapoos along the way—where these people became influenced by the Cree. Wild rice became an important part of their diet during this time. This group emerged from the forest about 1690.

Anishinabe groups that continued into the Red River area (northwest Minnesota, northeast North Dakota, and Canada) during the eighteenth century, such as the Pembina band of Chippewa, were armed with French guns and thus able to displace Hidatsa, Arikara, and Cheyenne bands. From this base there were four separate migrations to Montana.

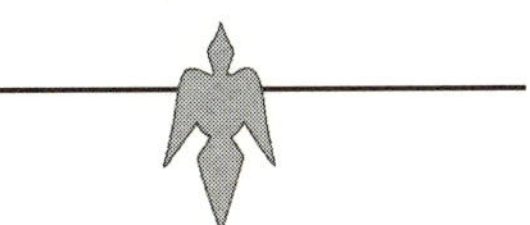

During the eighteenth century, Red River Valley Ojibwa, Cree, and Métis traveled west in response to the continued overtrapping of small game. They acquired horses in the late eighteenth century and became buffalo hunters, fully adapting to life on the Plains by the early nineteenth century. After a failed effort to establish a native state in Manitoba, Canada, in 1868, about 4,000 Chippewa-Cree from the Pembina Band moved into present-day Montana. During the 1880s, the United States forced many Cree out of the United States into Canada. Many Chippewa and Métis were also forced out; their homes were burned behind them.

In 1885, the Chippewa, Cree, and Métis, now back in Canada, again attempted to create a native state in Manitoba under the leadership of the Métis Louis Riel. When this effort failed, the Chippewa chief Stone Child, or Rocky Boy, led a group of people back into Montana. In the late 1870s another group of Chippewa-Cree followed the buffalo into Montana from the Turtle Mountain area in North Dakota. They generally moved between Montana and North Dakota Chippewa-Cree communities.

In 1882, the United States recognized the Turtle Mountain Band's claim to 20 townships in north-central North Dakota. Two years later, however, it decided that the reservation was too large. The Little Shell Band, away hunting buffalo in Montana, was excluded from a government census, as were all Métis, who were declared to be Canadian. Despite the existence of these roughly 5,000 people, the North Dakota Reservation was reduced by about 10 million acres, or about 90 percent.

Little Shell's people sought refuge and a reservation near their relatives at Fort Belknap, Montana. Some remained on that reservation, with others settling in towns such as Havre, Great Falls, and Helena. Little Shell himself worked from the 1880s to his death in 1900 to establish a reservation for his people in Montana. He also worked to restore the size of the Turtle Mountain Reservation and to reenroll the Métis.

In the early twentieth century, following the negotiations over the Turtle Mountain Reservation, many of those people were forced to accept allotments on the public domain in North and South Dakota and eastern Montana. In 1904 the United States paid the Turtle Mountain band $1 million for their land cession, or about 10 cents an acre, but they refused to reenroll the Métis. Cree Chief Little Bear's people joined the Indians already in the Rocky Boy community in 1910. The Rocky Boy Reservation was established in 1916.

By 1920, many of the exiled Turtle Mountain and Pembina Chippewas, having lost their allotments through tax foreclosure, returned to the North Dakota community. During the next several decades the situation became, if anything, worse, with the poverty-stricken people squeezed on an inadequate land base. Many left the reservation during those years in search of work, never to return. The Turtle Mountain people were saved from termination in the 1950s only by the deplorable example of the Menominee termination fiasco (*see* Menominee [Chapter 8]).

Religion Gitchi Manito, the Great Spirit, and other spirits pervaded all nature. Children were encouraged to attract guardian spirit helpers by fasting in remote places. The people adopted the Sun Dance in the nineteenth century.

The Midewiwin, or Medicine Lodge Society, included both men and women. Candidates, who usually had to have experienced dream spirit visions, were initiated in a dance ceremony lasting several days. The main event included being "shot" by a member with a white shell that, taken from the medicine bag, carried supernatural power into the initiate. Upon being "revived" by older members, the initiate would spit out the shell. Members "shot" at one another as well to demonstrate their magical power. The meeting events were recorded on birch-bark scrolls with bone awls dipped in red paint. Members wore special medicine bags, usually of otter skin.

Government While still living around Lake Superior, people lived in small hunting bands of about ten people, each with its own hunting area. On the Plains, government conformed largely to the Plains model, including the presence of soldier societies.

Customs On the Plains, patrilineal clans gave way to bilaterally descended extended families. Generosity

was highly valued, as were bravery, fortitude, wisdom, and fidelity. People shared regularly, especially with the less able or fortunate. Thus did people achieve prestige while actually reducing individual suffering and want. Wealth and kin connections also played a part, however, and status ultimately rested on a combination of individual and family qualities.

Winter was generally a time for repairing tools and weapons and making crafts and clothing. Social control was effected mostly by peer pressure and ridicule, although serious crimes were punished by revenge and/or council action. Among the various social and religious groups were men's dance societies. Games included various guessing games, cup-and-ball, and competitions. Adult games were usually accompanied by gambling. Toys included conical tops and sleds. In general, storytelling was a favorite pastime.

Polygamy was practiced, although it was expensive. Each wife might or might not have a separate tipi. Marriage was mainly a matter of parental agreement, often based on the couple's choice, and divorce was common and easy to obtain. Infants spent their first few months swaddled in a cradle board. Children were treated permissively. Boys and girls (except for brothers and sisters) generally played together until puberty. Games revolved around future adult activities.

During menstruation, girls and women were secluded for a few days, as men considered them dangerous. Several weeks later, fathers who were able gave a ceremony, presided over by a shaman, for their daughters. Girls who had reached puberty were considered marriageable. Boys did not have a specific puberty ceremony. Their vision quests, first successful buffalo hunt, first war party, and so forth might be marked by feasts and gifts and were considered rites of passage. Men generally married slightly older than did women, having first to prove their manhood and perhaps acquire enough goods to distribute.

As a matter of respect there was no verbal communication between a man and his mother-in-law. Aged people were generally accorded a great deal of respect. The dead were buried with their effects on high hills or in scaffolds in trees. In the prehistoric period remains were buried in an earth mound.

Dwellings Winter camps on the Plains were places containing wood and water, such as valley cottonwood groves. People also needed forage for horses and some natural protection against weather and enemies.

On the Plains, the people lived in conical buffalo-skin tipis in both summer and winter. The skins were dressed and sewn together by women and placed over a pole framework. A tipi held one family. Two skin flaps at the top, attached to long poles, regulated the smoke hole. A small, elevated doorway was covered by a rawhide door.

Skin liners helped insulate against the cold and wind. Tanned buffalo robes served as beds and blankets and buffalo robes as carpeting. Women erected and took down the tipis, which could be moved quickly and easily. Tipis were often painted with special symbols and war exploits and also decorated with feathers, quills, or other items.

Diet While in the vicinity of Lake Superior, rabbits and wild rice were staples. On the Plains, buffalo, hunted communally, became the main food. Men also hunted other large and small game. Women gathered local roots, berries, and nuts. Sugar syrup came from box elder or maple trees.

Key Technology Bone fishhooks were fastened onto sinew lines attached to willow poles. Many tools were also made of stone, until iron became available from non-Indian traders. On the Plains, most manufactured items came from the buffalo.

Women tanned the skins using elk antler scrapers with an attached stone (or iron) blade; the hair was either left on or soaked and scraped off. Rawhide was often used to attach items to each other, such as two-piece clubs and mauls. People made willow back rests.

Trade Plains Ojibwas exchanged sugar syrup with tribes that had no such traditions. Among the products they imported were pipes. Part of an extensive trade complex stretching throughout the West, Plains tribes traded buffalo products to eastern groups for non-Indian goods the latter had obtained through the fur trade.

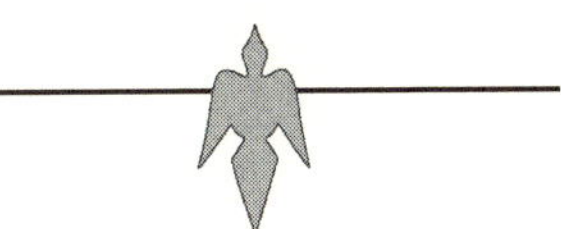

Notable Arts Some people used a pointed tool (or, occasionally, pieces of wood) to cut into the inner layer of birch bark to produce line drawings; most such drawings related to the Midewiwin society. Such pictograms also combined to illustrate song texts. People occasionally used incised drawings to decorate prayer sticks and weapons. Some groups also used a different style of decoration, consisting of zigzags and bands of triangles combined with symbolic shapes. On the Plains, the people decorated clothing and hides with paint, beads, and quillwork. Nineteenth-century quillwork consisted mainly of floral designs. Carved pipes were also a notable Plains Ojibwa art form.

Transportation Canoes were common in the Woodlands. The Plains Ojibwa acquired horses in the later eighteenth century.

Dress On the Plains, women made tailored skin clothing and buffalo robes. They decorated the clothing with geometric designs and floral patterned beadwork. Both sexes wore hard-soled moccasins.

War and Weapons The Ojibwa historically were fierce warriors. They adopted Plains-style soldier societies in the nineteenth century. Weapons included bows and arrows, clubs, and shields.

Contemporary Information

Government/Reservations Modern communities of Plains Ojibwa groups are as follows:

The Rocky Boy Chippewa-Cree Reservation (1,485 resident Indians in 1990) and Trust Lands (397 resident Indians in 1990), Chouteau and Hill Counties, Montana, established in 1916, contains 108,015 acres. The tribe is governed by a written constitution delegating authority to the Chippewa-Cree Business Committee. There is also a tribal court. Roughly half of the population lives off-reservation.

The Little Shell people, some of whom are of Cree descent, had a 1990 population of 3,300. They are governed by a tribal council under a constitution. Their main offices are in Havre and Helena, Montana.

There is also a community of Chippewa, established during the process of allotting the Turtle Mountain Reservation, living in eastern Montana. The seat of their government is in Trenton, North Dakota.

The Turtle Mountain Reservation and Trust Lands, Rolette, Burke, Cavalier, Divide, McLean, Mountrail, and Williams Counties, North Dakota, and Perkins County, South Dakota, established in 1882, contains over 45,000 acres, of which about 30 percent is controlled by non-Indians. The 1990 resident Indian population was 6,770. The reservation is governed by an elected nine-member Tribal Council under a 1959 constitution and by-laws.

Economy The Rocky Boy Chippewa-Cree Development Company manages that tribe's economic resources. The tribe's beadwork is in high demand. The company organized a propane business and owns a casino as well as recreational facilities. The largest employers on the reservation are the tribal government, Stone Child Community College, and industry. Other activities include cattle grazing, wheat and barley farming, some logging and mining, and recreation/tourism. Unemployment regularly approaches 75 percent.

People in the Montana Allotment Community are integrated into the local economy. Turtle Mountain operates a casino.

Legal Status The Chippewa-Cree Indians of the Rocky Boy Reservation, Montana, are a federally recognized tribal entity.

The Turtle Mountain Band of Chippewa Indians is a federally recognized tribal entity.

The Saginaw Cippewa Tribe (Swan Creek and Black River Chippewa) is a federally recognized tribal entity.

The Little Shell Tribe of Chippewa Indians, as well as some of the "landless Chippewa," have been seeking federal recognition since the 1920s.

Daily Life People from all four Montana Chippewa communities (Rocky Boy, Little Shell, Allotment Community, and "landless community") are generally related and often visit and move freely between locations. A renaissance of Montana Chippewa communities has taken place in the 1990s. The people look toward to a future well grounded in the past.

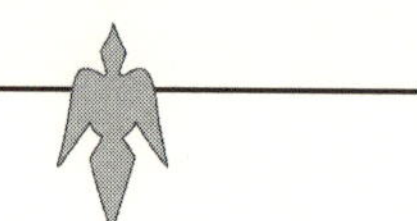

The Chippewa-Crees opened Stone Child Community College in 1978. Many Chippewa/Crees/Métis are Christians. Many also participate in the Sun Dance, sweat lodge ceremonies, and the Native American Church. Most Chippewa/Crees/Métis consider themselves one people and commonly intermarry. Indians living on the Rocky Boy Reservation speak English, Cree, and Métis.

Turtle Mountain Community College is located in Belcourt, North Dakota. At Turtle Mountain, the Chippewa and Métis languages are still spoken. Most people are Catholic. Some tribal members have received payments as part of a settlement regarding the unfairness of the original land claims payment. Turtle Mountain author Louise Erdrich has set many of her stories in the Turtle Mountain area. The Midewiwin Society remains active but has incorporated elements of Christianity.

Omaha

Omaha (ˋŌ mə hä) comes from *Umon'hon,* "those going against the current," a reference to the people's migration down the Ohio River and then north on the Mississippi. They were closely related to the Ponca.

Location The Omaha inhabited the Ohio and Wabash Valleys in the fifteenth century. In the late eighteenth century they had migrated to northeast Nebraska. Today, most Omahas live along the Iowa-Nebraska border.

Population The late-eighteenth-century Omaha population was about 2,800 people. In the early 1990s, about 6,000 people were enrolled in the tribe.

Language Omaha is a member of the Dhegiha division of the Siouan language family.

Historical Information

History The group of Siouan people known as Omaha left the Wabash and Ohio River regions in the early sixteenth century. Shortly thereafter, they reached the Mississippi River and split into five separate tribes. The initial exodus was prompted in part by pressure from the Iroquois. Those who continued north along the Mississippi became known as Osage, Kaw, Ponca, and Omaha; the people who headed south were known as Quapaw.

The Omaha and Ponca, accompanied by the Skidi Pawnee, followed the Des Moines River to its headwaters and then traveled overland toward the Minnesota catlinite (pipestone) quarries, where they lived until the early to mid–seventeenth century. Then, driven west by the Dakota, they moved to near Lake Andes, South Dakota, where the Omaha and Ponca briefly separated.

Reunited, the two tribes traveled south along the Missouri to Nebraska, where they separated once again, probably along the Niobrara River, in the late seventeenth century. The Omaha settled on Bow Creek, in northeast Nebraska. After acquiring horses about 1730, the people began to assume many characteristics of typical Plains Indians.

During the eighteenth century, the Omaha visited French posts as far north as Lake Winnipeg. Well supplied with horses (from the Pawnee) and guns (from French traders), the Omaha were able to resist Dakota attacks, even acting as trade intermediaries with their enemies. In 1791–1792, the two warring groups signed a peace treaty.

By the early nineteenth century, heavy involvement in the non-native trade had altered Omaha material culture. A severe smallpox epidemic in 1802 reduced the population to around 300. In 1854 they were forced to cede their land and, the following year, to take up residence on a reservation. In 1865 the government created the Winnebago Reservation from the northern Omaha Reservation. In 1882 the reservation was allotted.

By 1900 most Omahas knew English, and many spoke it well. All lived in houses, and nearly all wore nontraditional clothing. Most children attended school, and a significant number of adults were succeeding as farmers or in other occupations in the nontraditional economy. Still, throughout the twentieth century, the Omaha fought further encroachments on the reservation and tribal sovereignty. Well-known twentieth-century Omahas include Francis La Flesche, who

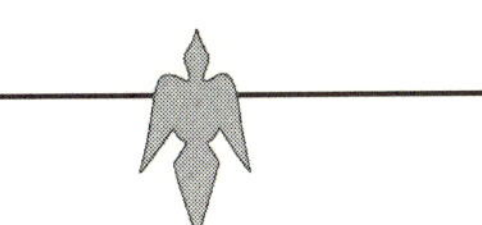

An Omaha group representing the North American Indians at the Colonial Exposition in Amsterdam in 1883. In the late eighteenth century the Omaha migrated to northeast Nebraska. Today, most Omahas live along the Iowa-Nebraska border.

coauthored the classic ethnographic study *The Omaha Tribe* (1911); Susan La Flesche Picotte, the first Native American woman to earn a medical degree; and Thomas L. Sloane, mayor of Pender, Nebraska, and president of the Society of American Indians in the 1920s.

Religion Wakonda was the supreme life force, through which all things were related. People sought connection to the supernatural world through visions, which were usually requisite for membership in a secret society.

Two pipes featuring mallard heads attached to the stems were the tribe's sacred objects. There were two religious organizations, the Shell and Pebble societies, which enacted a classic Woodlands ceremony of "shooting" a candidate with a shell and having him revived by the older members.

Government Each of the two tribal divisions, sky people and earth people, were represented by a head chief and a sacred pipe, symbolized by a sacred pole. A tribal council of seven chiefs acted as arbitrators of disputes, with the ability to pronounce sentences that included banishment and the death penalty, and as representatives to other tribes. They also chose the buffalo hunt leader and a group of camp and hunt police.

Customs The two divisions were each composed of five patrilineal clans. There were numerous social and secret societies. Marriage took place outside the

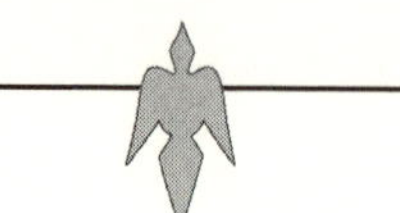

division. A man might have as many as three wives. The dead were placed in trees or scaffolds or were buried in a sitting position facing east. In the latter case, mounds of earth covered the grave.

Homicide was considered a crime against the wronged family; murderers were generally banished but allowed to return when the aggrieved family relented. The people played shinny and other games, including guessing/gambling games. During the communal buffalo hunt, tipis were arranged by clan in a circle. People gained status both in war and through their generosity.

Dwellings In villages located along streams, men and women built earth lodges similar to those of (and probably adopted from) the Arikara. About 40 feet in diameter, they were built of willow branches tied together with cords around a heavy wooden frame. The whole was covered with grass and sod. Skin curtains covered either side of the 6-to-10-foot entranceway. The fireplace was located in the middle, with an opening at the top for smoke.

In the nineteenth century, the Omaha built embankments around four feet high around their villages when they learned of an impending attack. Women also built skin tipis, which were mostly used during hunting trips—including the tribal spring and late-summer buffalo hunt—or in sheltered winter camps.

Diet Women grew corn, beans, and squash. Dried produce was stored in underground caches. After planting their crops, people abandoned the villages to hunt buffalo. The spring and summer buffalo hunts provided meat as well as hides for robes and tipis and many other material items. Men also hunted deer and small game. The people ate fish.

Key Technology Especially after the mid–eighteenth century, most material items were derived from buffalo parts. Hoes, for instance, came from buffalo shoulder blades. The Omaha made pottery until metal containers became available from non-Indian traders. They speared fish or shot them with tipless arrows. Nettle fibers were made into ropes. Bowls, mortars and pestles, and utensils were fashioned occasionally from horn but usually from wood. Hairbrushes were made of stiff grass.

Trade In the eighteenth and nineteenth century, the Omaha traded regularly and often with French, British, and U.S. traders as well as local Indians.

Notable Arts Omaha artists made items using quills, paints, and beads. Black, red, and yellow were the traditional colors.

Transportation Horses were acquired about 1730. The people used hide bull-boats to cross bodies of water.

Dress Women dressed the skins for and made all clothing. They wore fringed tunics that left the arms free. Men wore leggings and breechclouts. Tattoos were used, especially ceremonially (such as a sun on the forehead and a star on the chest). Both sexes wore smoked skin moccasins as well as cold-weather gear such as robes, hats, and mittens.

War and Weapons Men's warrior societies existed, although they were not as important as other religious and social organizations. Men fought with bow and arrow, clubs, spears, and hide shields. Enemies included the Dakota, at least from the eighteenth century on. The Skidi Pawnee were early (seventeenth-century) allies.

Contemporary Information

Government/Reservations The Omaha Reservation (Monona County, Iowa, and Burt, Cuming, and Thurston Counties, Nebraska), established in 1854, contains 26,792 acres, about 8,500 of which are tribally owned. There were 1,908 resident Indians in 1990. Authority is vested in an elected council of seven members plus a tribal chair.

Economy The Omaha tribal farm raises livestock. There is also income from the Chief Big Elk Park recreation area.

Legal Status The Omaha Tribe is a federally recognized tribal entity. The tribe gained civil and

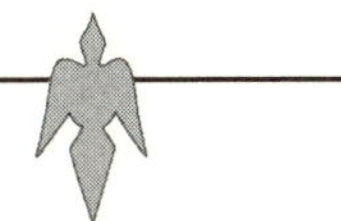

criminal jurisdiction over the reservation from Nebraska in 1970.

Daily Life Omaha children learn Omaha in schools, and roughly half of the people speak the language. Many former ceremonies have been lost. Some people are active in the Native American Church. Omahas also participate in traditional activities such as the hand game and the Gourd Dance. Traditional gift giving forms an important part of the annual tribal powwow. Omaha traditional music, especially warrior songs, has influenced the contemporary music of other Plains tribes.

In 1989, the tribe obtained the return of its sacred pole from Harvard's Peabody Museum. Two years later the people effected the return, from the Museum of the American Indian in New York, of their sacred White Buffalo Hide. Plans for an interpretive center to house these and other items and exhibits are under way. Omahas have also worked for the return from museums and schools of human remains.

O'ohenonpa (Two Kettles)

See Lakota

Osage

Osage (`Ō sāj) is the French version of *Wazhazhe,* one of their three historical bands (Great Osage, Little Osage, and Arkansas Osage). Their self-designation was *Ni-U-Ko'n-Ska,* or "Children of the Middle Waters."

Location In the late seventeenth century, Osage Indians lived along the Osage River in western Missouri. Today, most live in Osage County, Oklahoma.

Population The early-eighteenth-century Osage population was about 1,000. The people had grown to over 6,000 within the century. In 1993, the Osage tribe had about 11,000 enrolled members.

Language Osage is a member of the Dhegiha division of the Siouan language family.

Historical Information

History A group of Siouan people, known as Omaha, split into five separate tribes after they reached the Mississippi in the late sixteenth century from the Wabash and Ohio River regions. The initial exodus was prompted in part by pressure from the Iroquois. Those who continued north along the Mississippi and Missouri Rivers became known as Osage, Kaw, Ponca, and Omaha; the people who headed south were known as Quapaw.

The French explorers Jacques Marquette and Louis Joliet encountered the Osage in 1673, when the Indians were living in two villages along and nearby the south fork of the Osage River. Around 1700, the Osage acquired horses and began hunting buffalo. They organized a smaller hunt in June for about four weeks and a larger hunt in October and November. Nearly the whole tribe was involved in the fall hunt; only the very young and old stayed behind to guard the crops against birds and animals. Soon half of their food came from the buffalo, and they relied on that animal for material needs as well.

In the early eighteenth century, the Osage formed a strong alliance with the French, who gave them special trade treatment in exchange for pelts and slaves. The Osage captured the slaves from raids on Ponca and Pawnee villages. Osage warriors helped the French fight Fox Indians, the English, and various other enemies. During the mid–eighteenth century, the Osage were well armed and powerful, able both to defend their farming villages and to hunt buffalo on the western plains. The Spanish, a presence in the later eighteenth century, also tried to stay on good terms with the Osage, despite Osage raids on their outlying settlements.

In 1802, half of the Great Osage Band, under Chief Big Track, moved to the Arkansas River in Oklahoma to be near a trading post opened by the friendly Chouteau family. Thereafter they were known to non-Indians as the Arkansas Osages. In 1808, however, following the large-scale arrival of non-Indians in the region, the Osage ceded most of Missouri and northern Arkansas to the United States. The Little and Great Bands then moved to the Neosho River in Kansas.

By treaties in 1818 and 1825, the Osage ceded all of their lands except for a reservation in extreme

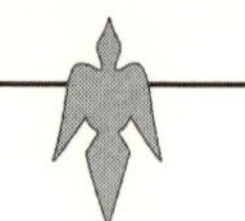

southern Kansas, to which all bands had relocated by 1836. In the 1850s, in alliance with Plains tribes such as the Cheyenne, Kiowa, and Comanche, they fought and lost a battle to stem the tide of eastern bands, such as the Cherokee, Choctaw, and Chickasaw, who had been moved to their lands by the United States. The Osage fought for both the United States and the Confederacy during the Civil War. Following that war, Osage men scouted for the United States in its wars against the Cheyenne in 1868–1869.

By 1870, the Osage had sold their Kansas lands and bought roughly one million acres of land from the Cherokee in northeastern Indian Territory (Oklahoma). There, they settled in five villages and retained a structure of 24 clans and two divisions. Many Osage embraced the Native American Church in the 1890s.

Large oil deposits were discovered on the reservation in 1897, and the Osage became very wealthy during the 1920s. In 1906, influenced by the prospect of oil wealth, the Osage created and implemented a voluntary allotment plan, dividing the tribal land individually, with the tribe retaining mineral rights. By the 1960s, however, half of the allotted parcels were lost. Although the oil wealth conferred many benefits, it also brought a large measure of corruption, through which people were cheated out of land and money, as well as greatly increased substance abuse. There was a general decline in revenues during the Depression and a resurgence during the Arab oil embargo of the early 1970s.

Religion Wakonda was the supreme life force, with which people might connect through the acquisition of supernatural visions. Shamans provided religious leadership. There was a secret religious society to which both men and women belonged. Ceremonies revolved around planting, peace, and war. The oral history of the tribe was recounted in the Rite of Chiefs.

Government Each of two divisions (see "Customs") had a peace and a war chief. In certain cases, clan leadership was hereditary. There was also a council of older men to make laws and arbitrate disputes. From the nineteenth century on, the tribe was divided into three political divisions (bands): Great Osage, Little Osage, and Arkansas Osage. Discipline during the hunt was provided by the hunt/camp police, who could publicly whip offenders in order to maintain order.

Customs Two divisions, Sky/Peace *(Tzi-sho)* and Land/War *(Hunkah)* people, encompassed a total of 21 patrilineal clans, each of which held distinctive ceremonial and political functions. Marriage was exogamous. Men who married older sisters were entitled to marry the younger ones as well. At death, chiefs and other important people were placed in a sitting position, surrounded by rocks and logs, and covered with earth. Others were buried in the ground with food, water, and various possessions. From the eighteenth century on, mourning ceremonies required the promise of an enemy scalp.

Dwellings The Osage located their villages along wooded river valleys. They built oval or rectangular pole-frame houses, 36–100 feet long, 15–20 feet wide, and 10 feet high, covered with woven rush mats or bark. The arched poles were tied together on top and then interlaced with saplings. People lived in tipis while on buffalo hunts.

Diet Women grew corn, squash, pumpkins, and beans and gathered foods such as persimmons, wild fruits and berries, and acorns and other nuts. In addition to buffalo, men hunted deer, wild fowl, beaver, and wildcat. Before they acquired horses, men hunted buffalo by using fire and costumes to stampede them over cliffs.

Key Technology Osage orange was considered the best wood for bows. The people also built carved wooden cradleboards, cattail and rush mats, and buffalo-hair bags.

Trade By around 1700, the Osage were supplying the French with Indian (mainly Pawnee and then Apache) slaves in exchange for guns, among other items. In the later eighteenth and into the nineteenth century, Osages had a surplus of horses to trade, in part because they did not require as many as did the truly nomadic Plains buffalo hunters. Being short on winter pastureland, they generally traded most of their horses in the fall, restocking again in the spring. Osages acted as middlemen in the horse trade, moving Comanche horses to the Midwest markets. They also traded with Wichita and Comanche Indians, generally horses for guns.

Notable Arts Osages were particularly skilled at woodcarving and skin tanning.

Transportation The people acquired horses around the late seventeenth century, probably from the Apache.

Dress Most clothing was made of deerskin. Women wore a shirt and a cape; men wore leggings and a breechclout. They wore their hair in a roach. Men also wore body paint, jewelry, and scalp locks. Through acts of bravery, a warrior gained the privilege to tattoo himself and his wife and daughter(s).

War and Weapons On the Plains, war was a way of life, and the Osage fought with most tribes on both sides of the Mississippi, especially nearby Plains and Caddoan-speaking peoples.

Contemporary Information

Government/Reservations Most Osage live in Osage County, Oklahoma. The administrative center is in Pawhuska. Only those people who have inherited land from the original (1906) allottees may vote in tribal elections.

Economy Oil dollars have made the Osage tribe rich, although revenues have slipped in the 1990s, and the future of the oil fields is uncertain. Individual Osages work in the local economy. Some work in tribal administration or for the tribal bingo parlor; others farm or ranch.

Legal Status The Osage Tribe is a federally recognized tribal entity.

Daily Life In the mid-1990s only about one-third of the parcels allotted in 1906 were still owned by Osage Indians. There are also three 160-acre community-held village sites (Pawhuska, Hominy, and Grayhorse) and a larger site for tribal administration and facilities. Any Osage can live free of charge in one of the villages.

By law, the oil wealth (and thus political power) must remain among inheritors of the original (1906) allottees. In the mid-1990s, the group of Osage Indians who did not meet these criteria constituted a majority of enrolled members. The effective disenfranchisement of these people is one reason that the concern over oil leases and payments still dominates the business of the tribal council.

Most Osages are Catholic, some are Protestant, and some are also members of the Native American Church. Fewer than 300 people spoke Osage fluently in 1993. Traditional dances are held in June, and Osage people attend many pan-Indian powwows across the country.

Otoe

Otoe (`Ō tō), or Oto, from *Wahtohtata,* "lovers" or "lechers," referring to an alleged incident between the children of an Otoe and a Missouria chief. An earlier self-designation may have been *Che-wae-rae.* Otoes are closely related to Poncas, Ioways, Missourias, and Winnebagos. All Southern Siouans had elements of both Plains and Woodland cultures.

Location Late-eighteenth-century Otoes lived along the Platte River in eastern Nebraska. In the 1990s, most lived in the Red Rock region of Oklahoma.

Population Otoe population in 1780 was about 900. There were about 1,550 enrolled tribal members in the mid-1990s.

Language Otoe-Iowa-Missouria is a member of the Chiwere division of the Siouan language family.

Historical Information

History According to tradition, the Winnebago, Ioway, Missouria, and Otoe once lived together north of the Great Lakes. In the sixteenth century, groups began migrating toward their historic areas. The Otoe and Missouria continued past the Ioway and especially the Winnebago until they reached the junction of the Missouri and Grand Rivers, in the late sixteenth to early seventeenth century.

There the two tribes had a falling out, traditionally ascribed to a love affair between the two chiefs' children. After the split, the Otoe moved west along the Missouri. Trade with the French began soon after Jacques Marquette and Louis Joliet encountered the Otoe in 1673 and continued for about a century. Between 1680 and 1717, the Otoe lived along the upper Iowa River and then the Blue Earth River. From 1717 to 1854 they lived along the Platte in various locations, including its mouth at the Missouri River. The people acquired horses early in that period and became much more involved in hunting buffalo.

The Otoe people absorbed the smallpox-decimated Missouria, with whom they had been fighting the Sauk and Foxes for years, in 1829. Several difficult decades followed, during which the people battled disease as well as Indians and non-Indians. By treaties in the 1830s and 1854, the Otoe-Missouria ceded all land and moved to a 162,000-acre reservation on the Kansas-Nebraska border, along the Big Blue River. Two more land cessions occurred in 1876 and 1881.

Two factions developed in 1880 over the issue of acculturation. The Coyote, or traditional faction, moved to the Indian Territory (Oklahoma). The Quakers ceded their land for a 129,000-acre reservation near Red Rock in north-central Oklahoma. Most Coyotes joined them by 1890, having lived for a time in a separate village on the Iowa Reservation. The reservation was allotted by 1907.

By 1900, the tribe had established a court system for both civil and criminal cases, Many individuals grew crops of grains and potatoes at that time. After oil was discovered on their land in 1912, the United States forced many Otoe-Missourias to give up their allotments. During the early to mid–twentieth century, intermarriage truly created one tribe. Many Indians left the region during the 1930s. The tribe received a $1.5 million land claim settlement in 1955 and another payment in 1964. Both were divided on a per capita basis.

Religion Wakonda was the universal spirit, to which people could draw closer by fasting and acquiring visions. There were a number of secret curing and dance (religious) societies as well as a hereditary priesthood. In a ceremony related to the Ojibwa (Woodland) Midewiwin, members of a religious society "shot" an initiate with a magic shell. He was later "restored" by older shamans.

Government Political and military leadership was provided by hereditary clan and war chiefs.

Customs There were about ten patrilineal clans, each with particular responsibilities. The people played lacrosse, among other games. Corpses were placed in a tree or buried in ground. A four-day mourning period followed funerals, during which a horse was occasionally killed to provide transportation to the spirit world.

Dwellings Otoe villages were composed of from 40 to 70 semiexcavated earth lodges. Each lodge was about 40 feet in diameter. People caked clay or earth over a wooden framework interwoven with brush and grass. Skin tipis were used on hunting trips.

Diet Women grew corn, beans, and squash in river bottomlands. Men assisted in this work but mainly hunted buffalo (twice a year), deer, and small game. Hunting, in fact, was a major occupation, and once on the Plains the people gradually shifted to rely more on buffalo than on crops. Women gathered plant foods such as nuts, berries, and roots. The people also ate fish.

Key Technology Crops were stored in underground, bell-shaped caches. Material items included buffalo wool bags; a combination quiver and bow case; twined rectangular storage bags; rawhide trunks or containers, bent and sewn into place; and soft-twilled buffalo-hair wallets. The latter two were items more typical of Woodland tribes such as the Sauk or Fox.

Fish were caught using spears and possibly weirs and basketry traps. Women used elkhorn scrapers (post–eighteenth century) in the tanning process. They also wove reed floor mats over a bark-cord foundation.

Trade During the late seventeenth and early eighteenth centuries, Otoes traded heavily with the

French, supplying Indian slaves, among other commodities.

Notable Arts Artistic endeavors including weaving and woodworking.

Transportation Otoes acquired horses in the early eighteenth century.

Dress On the Plains, Otoes dressed similarly to other local Indians. Skins tanned by women formed the basis of most clothing. Men wore leggings and breechclout, and women wore a one-piece dress. Both wore moccasins. Cold weather gear included shirts, robes, and fur caps.

War and Weapons Traditional enemies included the Pawnee, Sauk, Fox, Omaha, and Dakota. Otoes often joined forced with the Missouria.

Contemporary Information

Government/Reservations About 800 Otoe-Missourias lived in Oklahoma's Red Rock region in the mid-1990s. The tribe is governed by a tribal council under a 1984 constitution.

Economy Some jobs are provided by federal and tribal governmental projects. Most Otoes work within the local economy.

Legal Status The Otoe-Missouria tribe is a federally recognized tribal entity.

Daily Life Children study the native language in school, assisted by a Chiwere grammar published in 1975. In the late 1970s, the people began buying land and adding to their land base. At that time they received a number of federal grants to reconstruct tribal facilities and institute certain services. Religious affiliations include Protestant, Catholic, and the Native American Church. Traditional kinship and family ties remain important. In addition to the annual powwow held in July, other ceremonies and gatherings take place regularly, often in the tribe's cultural center.

Pawnee

Pawnee (Pä `nē) comes from the Caddoan *pariki,* or "horn," referring to the distinctive male hairstyle, or from *parisu,* "hunter." Their self-designation was *Chahiksichahiks,* "Men of Men." By about 1700, if not sooner, the Pawnee had divided into four independent subtribes: the Panimaha (Skidi), the Kitkehaki (Republican), the Chaui (Grand), and the Pitahauerat (Tappage). All but the Skidi spoke a similar dialect and were sometimes known as the Southern Pawnees. The Skidi were also known as Loups (French), Lobos (Spanish), and Wolves (English). The Pawnee were closely related to the Wichita and the Arikara and maintained attributes characteristic of southwestern and Mesoamerican cultures.

Location In the sixteenth century, Pawnees were located along the Arkansas, Platte, and Loup Rivers and on the Republican Fork of the Kansas River (Skidi) in east-central Nebraska. Most Pawnees inhabited the Platte River Valley in the late eighteenth century. In the 1990s, Pawnees lived in Oklahoma and in other states.

Population The late-eighteenth-century Pawnee population was about 10,000. The figure stood at about 2,500 in the early 1990s.

Language Panian (Skidi Pawnee, Southern Pawnee, and Arikara) is a Caddoan language.

Historical Information

History Pawnee tradition has the people originating in the Southwest, but they may have their origin in the southeast, perhaps in the Gulf region of southern Texas, and may have been associated very early on with Iroquoian people. Caddoan people occupied the Plains, from Texas to the Arkansas River region of Oklahoma and Kansas, inconsistently for perhaps several thousand years. Caddoans had major ceremonial centers by 500, including large temple mounds.

Upon leaving east Texas (thirteenth century), the Skidi Pawnee separated from the other bands and traveled east across the Mississippi, following the trail of the Iroquois to the northeast and settling in the

Ohio Valley. In the sixteenth century, pressured by the initial stages of Iroquois expansion, the Skidis headed down the Ohio. They were joined along the way by the Omaha. Together, the two people traveled to the Des Moines River, where the Skidi left the Omaha, continuing west to join their cousins and settling on the Loup fork of the Platte River.

Despite a separation of several hundred years, the Skidis reintegrated smoothly among the other Pawnee groups and soon became the largest and most powerful Pawnee tribe. They encountered the Spanish during the sixteenth century. Residents of western Pawnee villages were victims of Apache raiders from the mid–seventeenth century into the eighteenth century. The men were killed, and the women and children were sold as slaves. Thus occurred a gradual abandonment of Pawnee villages in western Nebraska and northeastern Colorado. The Illinois and other tribes also raided them for slaves in the eighteenth century.

Pawnees acquired a few horses around 1700, and within a generation they became great raiders and buffalo hunters, slowly relying less on crops and more on the buffalo for their food. Direct contact with French traders began in the early eighteenth century and expanded rapidly. By the 1750s, the French switched from buying Pawnees to buying Apaches, which the Pawnee, among other tribes, gladly provided. The guns they received in trade helped protect them against Apache attacks, which soon ended against them.

From about 1770 to 1800, the Skidi Pawnee, reduced from eight villages to only one, lived with the Taovayas Band of Wichita Indians on the Red River in northeastern Texas. Pawnees first met Anglo-Americans, including Meriwether Lewis, William Clark, and Zebulon Pike, in the early nineteenth century. After the Louisiana Purchase, more and more Americans entered Pawnee land. Most generally received a friendly and peaceful welcome.

By the terms of the 1805 Treaty of Table Rock, all Pawnee were relocated to a reservation in Genoa, Nebraska. During the 1830s and 1840s, they often fought and raided in the vicinity of the Arkansas River in southeastern Colorado and southwestern Kansas. Many also served as scouts for the U.S. Army during that period and later. Presbyterian missionaries arrived in 1834. Three years later, the Pawnee suffered a major smallpox epidemic.

By 1850, cholera and warfare with the Dakota tribes had greatly reduced the Pawnee population. They held their last tribal hunt in 1873. Pressured in 1876 to cede their reservation, the tribe moved to a new one, of over 200,000 acres, in north-central Indian Territory (Oklahoma). Part of this reservation was allotted in 1892, with more than half then opened for non-Indian settlement. In 1906, the tribal population had declined 94 percent, to about 600 from about 10,000 just a century before. In 1966, the tribe won a land claims award of over $7 million, and in the 1970s they forced the return of tribal lands given by the United States to the city of Pawnee.

Religion *Tirawa,* the sun, was the great spirit or creator and ruler of lesser deities. Among the Skidi, the morning and evening stars represented the masculine and feminine elements respectively. The celestial bodies formed the basis of a complex mythology.

Much of the rich ceremonial life revolved around the heavenly bodies as well as planting, cultivating, and harvesting corn and hunting buffalo. In the Morning Star ceremony, a young girl, usually a captive, was ritually sacrificed (shot with arrows while tied to a wooden frame) to the morning star at the time of the summer solstice to ensure the success of their crops. Petalesharo (Man-Chief) was responsible in 1816 for forcing the priests to stop holding this ceremony.

Hereditary priests were a large and powerful class of people. They conducted the rituals, knew sacred songs and rituals, and were associated with the sacred bundles. Shamans obtained powers from supernatural beings. They performed a large ceremony in late summer or early fall at which they impressed people with feats such as handling live coals and plunging their hands in boiling water. Shamans were also priests insofar as they were trained to lead ceremonies.

Sacred bundles, connected with various rituals and associated with specific villages, dominated Pawnee life. Wrapped in buffalo skin, many bundles contained smoking materials, paints, feathers, and corn. Chiefs kept the bundles, but priests used them. There were also many secret societies, each with its own paraphernalia and rituals. Sacred animal lodges were associated with the Southern people.

Government The chieftaincy was inherited through the female line. Villages were political units, each of which had chiefs, priests, bundles, and a council. The four independent subtribes were united in a confederation.

Councils made all final civil and military decisions. They were established at the different levels of societal organization (village, tribe, confederacy). Each successive level of council was composed of members of the preceding level.

All but two of the Skidi villages were joined in a political and religious confederation before they were forced to consolidate into one village following the smallpox epidemic of 1780–1781. The Chaui had but one village.

Customs A dual division, winter and summer people, came into play during games and ceremonies. Descent was matrilineal. Most people married from within the village. Corpses were wrapped in matting and buried in a sitting position, usually on high ground away from the village. The grave was covered with mounds of dirt.

People owned the right to perform dances and ceremonies. A society of single and elderly women effected shabby dress and tortured prisoners of war. There were various men's societies as well, generally revolving around military and religious themes. Pawnees played various games, including contests, dice (women) and shinny, and hoop-and-pole (men). Only a few old female doctors were allowed to smoke.

Dwellings By 1500, some Pawnees were living in permanent villages of between 5 and 15 earth lodges. The lodges were round, semiexcavated, and about 40–60 feet in diameter. They featured a pole framework interwoven with brush and grass, covered with a thick layer of soil and clay. Some had separate sleeping areas partitioned by mats or wickerwork. Such lodges were designed to last eight to ten years. Religious ceremonies accompanied lodge construction.

By the early nineteenth century, most Pawnees used temporary semicircular summer tents that differed from standard tipis. After driving small, arched poles into the ground along the circumference, people placed four larger posts vertically across the front. They also used standard skin tipis on buffalo hunting trips.

Diet Unlike their neighbors who lived at similar longitudes, Pawnee women grew corn, beans, pumpkins, and sunflowers in small gardens. There were generally two harvests, one in midsummer, of green corn (boiled or roasted, shelled, dried, and stored in bags), and the main one in late summer to early fall.

The people also hunted buffalo in early summer and in winter. They preferred two or three small drives to one massive slaughter. Meat was quickly butchered and dried. Those less able stayed at the villages to protect the crops. Before they acquired horses, Pawnee men stampeded buffalo over cliffs or into swamps.

There was also at least one antelope drive each year, during which the animals were surrounded and clubbed or lanced. The people depended about equally on corn and buffalo, although more on buffalo in the nineteenth century. Men also hunted antelope, elk, deer, and small game, including fowl and birds. Women gathered roots, berries, plums, grapes, chokecherries, and nuts.

Key Technology Women wove twilled, plaited baskets and shallow gambling trays as well as mats used for floor coverings and bedding. People used both pottery and buffalo-hide containers. Babies were wrapped in fur or fleece and tied with buckskin lacing onto decorated flat wooden cradle boards. Garden tools included hoes from buffalo or elk shoulders, digging sticks, and antler rakes.

Trade Pre–seventeenth century Skidis traded with the Omaha and other related Siouan tribes. In the early to mid–eighteenth century, they exchanged Apache slaves, buffalo robes, and animal pelts with the New Orleans French for French guns, tools, and other items. By later in the century they were trading guns for Comanche horses, which they traded in turn to the Omaha, Ponca, and other tribes.

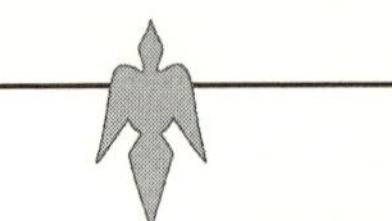

Notable Arts Pawnee art included basketry and incised pottery. They occasionally smoked their fine tanned hides. Tipis, robes, and shields were painted with heraldic designs.

Transportation Dogs pulled the travois until they were slowly replaced by horses during the seventeenth century.

Dress Women made most clothing of antelope or elk rather than buffalo hide. Men wore breechclouts and moccasins, plus leggings and a robe in the cold or on special occasions. They also tied a scarflike turban around their heads and plucked their facial hair. Women wore moccasins, a skirt and cape, and leggings and a robe in winter. Both sexes painted their faces. Warriors stiffened a lock of hair with paint and fat, making it curve like a horn (a style known as a roach).

War and Weapons Enemies included the Apache (mid–seventeenth to eighteenth century), Dakota, Cheyenne, Arapaho, and Kiowa. The Pawnee raided a huge area, more or less the entire Plains. Allies included the Comanche and, later, the United States. On the Plains, the Pawnee adhered to the system of war honors known as counting coup. Weapons included the bow and arrow, club, and buffalo-hide shield.

Contemporary Information

Government/Reservations The Pawnee tribe still owns several hundred acres of land in Pawnee and Payne Counties, Oklahoma. The present tribal government was established in 1934. The tribe is governed by two eight-member bodies, the Nasharo (chiefs) Council, chosen by band, and an elected Business Council.

Economy An annual annuity (from the 1857 treaty) and funds obtained from mineral (oil and gas) leases and agriculture are disbursed on a per capita basis. The tribe also sponsors bingo games. There is chronic high unemployment around Pawnee.

Legal Status The Pawnee Indian Tribe is a federally recognized tribal entity.

Daily Life Administrative offices, ceremonial roundhouse, recreation room, community building, and campground are located on the tribal land. The tribe administers various social programs with the help of federal grants. Traditional activities surviving at least in modified form include various dances (war, ghost, round) and the hand game. However, the Pawnee language is approaching the point where complete decline may be irreversible. Most people are Christians; some are also members of the Native American Church. The many social clubs sponsor various activities. There is a four-day Pawnee homecoming in July.

Pawnee warriors stiffened a lock of hair with paint and fat, making it curve like a horn (a style known as a roach). Made in 1910, this roach, made of porcupine and deer guard hairs, is over 11 inches long and 8 inches high. The roach was tied to the wearer's scalplock by means of a thong and a carved comblike roach spreader.

Peigan

See Blackfeet

Piegan

See Blackfeet

Ponca

Ponca (`Pon ku) is a word possibly meaning "sacred head." The Ponca are linguistic and cultural relatives of the Omaha.

Ponca Indians skinning a buffalo.

Location Poncas inhabited present-day northeast Nebraska in the late seventeenth century. Today, Northern Poncas live mostly in Nebraska, South Dakota, and Iowa, and most Southern Poncas live in north-central Oklahoma.

Population The late-seventeenth-century Ponca population was about 800. In 1993 there were about 2,360 Southern Poncas and perhaps 900 Northern Poncas.

Language Ponca, with Kaw, Omaha, Osage, and Quapaw, is part of the Dhegiha division of the Siouan language family.

Historical Information

History Dhegiha speakers probably originated in the southeast and entered the Plains from the Ohio Valley. After arriving at the Mississippi in the mid–sixteenth century, the Ponca traveled upriver with the Kaw, Omaha, and Osage. Continuing north with the Omaha into Iowa and Minnesota, the groups settled on the Big Sioux River near the pipestone quarries.

Pressure from the Dakota forced them to the Lake Andres area of South Dakota, where they separated from the Omaha in the early to mid–seventeenth century. From there they traveled west to the Black Hills and then east again, rejoining the Omaha and moving south along the Missouri River to Nebraska. They settled on the mouth of the Niobrara River around 1763. The Omaha left them soon after to settle on Bow Creek.

Epidemics had reduced the Ponca population by over 90 percent by the time they encountered the Lewis and Clark expedition in 1804. Poncas were generally friendly with Americans and eager to trade. Treaties with the United States, beginning in 1817, cost them over two million acres of land. In 1858, the people accepted a reservation of about 100,000 acres and promises of protection against Lakota tribes. However, ten years later the Lakota successfully claimed most of this land in the 1868 Fort Laramie

Treaty. Lakota attacks were worse then ever, since they now controlled the disputed land by treaty.

In contravention of the treaties and in the face of active resistance of the chiefs, the United States forced the Poncas to remove to the Indian Territory (Oklahoma). There the Indians received a reservation of just over 100,000 acres near the Arkansas and Salt Fork Rivers. Within a year, about a quarter of the tribe died in those new lands from hunger and disease.

In 1877, Chief Standing Bear and others led their people on a 500-mile walk back to the Niobrara River to bury their dead. They were arrested and detained, but a precedent-setting trial established their rights both to legal standing and to their Nebraska land, to which they soon returned. Fearing for the very survival of the reservation system, however, not to mention the corrupt system of supplying reservation Indians with substandard food and materials, the United States refused permission for the rest of the Poncas to return to Nebraska. From then on, Poncas living in Nebraska were known as Northern Ponca, and the Southern Ponca remained in Oklahoma.

The Oklahoma land was allotted 1908. Most people later sold their allotments or leased them to non-Indians. Among the Southern Ponca, strong antiallotment sentiment led to factionalism within the tribe. Two Poncas were among those who established the Native American Church in the 1910s; the church's first president was a Ponca.

The Northern Ponca were formally "terminated" in the 1950s. By the mid-1960s, over 400 Poncas had lost all of their remaining 834 acres of land. The Ponca Clyde Warrior and a Paiute, Mel Thom, formed the National Indian Youth Council, a group dedicated to advancing Indian rights, in 1961.

Religion Wakanda was the Great Spirit or universal creator. All things had supernatural power, which could be accessed through guardian spirits obtained in vision quests. The original tribal Sacred Pipe was carved of catlinite when the Ponca lived in Minnesota. It was used in the Pipe Dance and on other occasions, as were its later replacements. Other important events included the Medicine Lodge ceremony, Sun Dance, and War Dance. The Ponca Sun Dance included self-torture. Shinny, a ball game, also had religious import.

Government Hereditary chiefs governed the clans. On the Plains, buffalo police kept order during the hunt.

Customs Two divisions, Chighu and Wazhazha, were each subdivided into four patrilineal clans. The people wrapped corpses in buffalo robes with food and other articles and buried them in graves. The people adopted scaffold burial with other aspects of Plains life. The mourning period lasted up to a year. The Ponca envisioned two afterworlds, a happy one for the worthy dead and an unhappy one for unworthy spirits.

Dwellings The Ponca built permanent villages on bluffs over rivers and fortified them with log and earth stockades. They lived in east-facing earth or hide-covered lodges. There was also a ceremonial earth lodge. Skin tipis were used on buffalo hunts.

Diet Women grew corn, beans, squash, pumpkins, and tobacco in gardens located on river bottomlands. There were two annual communal buffalo hunts. Before the people acquired horses, buffalo were often stampeded over cliffs. Men also hunted other large and small game. The people ate fish as well as a variety of wild foods.

Key Technology Material goods included pottery, mats, baskets woven from willow and bullrush stems, and trunks and boxes of cut, folded, and sewn rawhide.

Trade Poncas were involved in the early-eighteenth-century slave trade, selling mainly Pawnees to the French, from whom they received guns, among other items.

Notable Arts Notable art items included carved wooden goods, blue clay pottery, woven mats and baskets, and work in quills and beads in floral and geometric designs.

Transportation Around 1730 the people acquired horses, which then began pulling the travois. They used rawhide bull-boats for crossing rivers.

Dress Women tanned the skins and made the clothing. They wore a one-piece dress and moccasins. Men wore leggings and breechclout as well as moccasins. Cold weather gear included shirts, mittens, robes, and caps. On the Plains men wore their hair long, a custom they probably adopted from the Dakota.

War and Weapons Weapons included the bow and arrow, buffalo-hide shield, and wooden war club. The Omaha were alternately allies and enemies. The Dakota were generally enemies. On the Plains, the Ponca acquired the institution of rival military clubs, probably from the Tetons.

Contemporary Information

Government/Reservations Since 1990, the Northern Ponca tribe has reacquired 413 acres of its former reservation and is continuing to add to its land base. The people are also involved in reestablishing a tribal government and constitution.

The Southern Ponca are located in north-central Oklahoma. They adopted a constitution and by-laws in 1950. The tribe is governed by a seven-member Tribal Business Committee.

Economy High unemployment is endemic among the Northern Ponca. An economic development plan remained to be implemented in the late 1990s. The Southern Ponca run a bingo facility and a smoke shop.

Legal Status The Ponca Tribe of Nebraska (Northern Ponca) was federally rerecognized in 1990. The Ponca Tribe of Oklahoma (Southern Ponca) is a federally recognized tribal entity.

Daily Life Termination cost the Northern Ponca a great deal in the way of cultural survival. Among these people, the War Dance Society survives. Annual powwows feature traditional singing and dancing. Members participate in Sun Dances held by other tribes. Few speak the native language, but it is closely related to Omaha, which is more widely spoken. The people, who suffer especially from diabetes and hypertension, are generally less healthy than are those of the nearby non-Indian community. The Northern Ponca would like formally to reestablish their reservation.

The Southern Ponca built many facilities in the 1970s, including a clinic, headquarters, cultural center, and gymnasium. The factionalism that beset these people in the 1970s and 1980s eased in the 1990s. The annual Southern Ponca powwow is intertribal in nature. The Ponca Indian War Dance Society, formed in the 1950s from old traditions, sponsors semiannual dances. The people also perform a scalp dance and various other dances. There are regular games of shinny, especially in the spring. A regional tribal center and museum are planned. Many Poncas are Christians and/or members of the Native American Church.

Quapaw

Quapaw (Kwu `pä) comes from *Ugakhpa,* "Downstream People," referring to their migration south along the Mississippi. The Quapaw were also known as Arkansas Indians.

Location These people lived along the Ohio River, near the mouth of the Wabash, in the sixteenth century. By the late seventeenth century they had migrated to near the mouth of the Arkansas River. Today, most Quapaws live in northeast Oklahoma.

Population The late-seventeenth-century population was about 15,000. In the mid-1980s, approximately 3,000 Indians called themselves Quapaws.

Language Quapaw is a member of the Dhegiha division of the Siouan language family.

Historical Information

History Quapaw ancestors may have been the Indian Knoll people of Kentucky and vicinity, of about 500 C.E., who lived along rivers and ate mainly shellfish. In the sixteenth century, with the Omaha and other Siouan groups, the Quapaw migrated through the Ohio Valley to the Mississippi River. When the others continued north along the Mississippi, the Quapaw struck out toward the south.

Shortly after the people met Jacques Marquette and Louis Joliet in 1673, they were decimated by smallpox and ongoing warfare. They acquired horses in the early eighteenth century and adopted much of

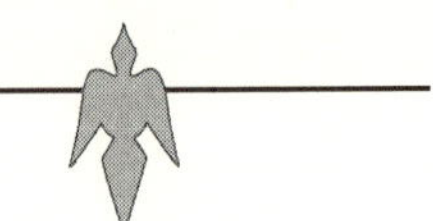

Plains buffalo culture. Although in general the Quapaw avoided taking sides in the regional European colonial struggles, they fought the Chickasaw in the eighteenth century as French allies as well as to avenge raids made against them.

In 1818 the Quapaw ceded their claims to southern Arkansas, southern Oklahoma, and northern Louisiana. They did reserve about one million acres of land in Arkansas but were forced to give that up by 1824. Landless now, they went to live with the Caddo south of the Red River, but following several crop failures as a result of floods they drifted back to Arkansas.

The Quapaw were forced to relocate to a reservation in the Indian Territory (Oklahoma and Kansas) in 1833. In 1867 they lost their Kansas lands when that territory became a state. The tribe voted in 1893 to liquidate the reservation by allotting 240 acres each to 230 tribal members. About this time, a variant of the Peyote religion was introduced to the people.

Rich mineral deposits (zinc and lead) were found on Quapaw land in 1905. For a few years non-Indians defrauded the Quapaw out of land and money. After the government finally stepped in and exercised its trust responsibility, considerable monetary benefits began to accrue, despite the fact that royalties were paid to the federal government and not to the tribe. Many individuals who managed to share in the wealth spent most or all of their money in the 1920s. The tribe received a land claims payment in the early 1960s of roughly $1 million.

Religion Wakonda was the great universal spirit who encompassed any number of other spirits or deities. Pipes featured prominently in their ceremonies, and the Green Corn Dance celebrated the beginning of the harvest. There were also numerous other agriculture-related ceremonies.

Government A hereditary chief and a council of elders governed each village. Beginning in the eighteenth century, the people created an overall tribal chief.

Customs Two divisions were subdivided into 22 patriarchal clans. People were buried with tools, weapons, and other items, both in and above the ground. If above, the graves were covered with rocks and dirt.

Dwellings Some villages were protected with palisades. Women built rectangular houses with domed roofs covered with cypress bark, grass, woven mats, and hides. Several families lived in each house.

Diet Women grew three crops of corn a year, plus beans, squash, and tobacco. They also gathered foods, including persimmons, walnuts, berries, and plums. Men hunted buffalo, fowl, and other large and small game. The people also ate fish.

Key Technology Fish were captured in weirs. The people carved stone pipes, made pottery, wove mats, and stored corn in gourds or cane baskets.

Trade Quapaws traded pottery and other items primarily to the Chickasaw, the Tunica, and, later, the French.

Notable Arts Painted and incised pottery was a Quapaw specialty.

Transportation Before the onset of Plains culture, Quapaws made walnut and cypress dugout canoes. They acquired horses in the early eighteenth century.

Dress Prior to the eighteenth century, men generally went naked, pierced their nose and ears, and wore their hair short. On the Plains, men and women adopted the typical dress, including breechclouts, leggings, shirts, dresses, and robes.

War and Weapons Quapaws fought the Chickasaw in the eighteenth century. Their best bows were made of Osage orange wood.

Contemporary Information

Government/Reservations The new tribal headquarters is located near Quapaw, Oklahoma. The people elect a business committee. There were about 1,500 local Indian residents in the early 1990s.

Economy Many Quapaws farm or work in local businesses. There are also a tribal bingo parlor and a gas station.

Legal Status The Quapaw Tribe is a federally recognized tribal entity.

Daily Life Little traditional culture survives. A few people speak the native language. Most Quapaws are Christians. The Native American Church is a minor presence among the people. Their annual powwow, at which the people perform tribal dances, is nationally noted.

Santee

See Dakota

Saulteaux

See Ojibwa, Plains

Sicangu (Brulé)

See Lakota

Sihasapa (Blackfeet Teton)

See Lakota

Sioux

See Dakota; Lakota; Nakota

Sisseton

See Dakota

Stoney

See Assiniboine

Teton

See Lakota

Tonkawa

Tonkawa (ˋTon kə wä) is a Waco word possibly meaning "they all stay together." Their self-designation was *Titska Watitch,* possibly meaning "Most Human People."

Location Tonkawas traditionally lived in east-central Texas. In the late twentieth century, most lived in and around Kay County, Oklahoma.

Population From a fifteenth-century population of perhaps 5,000 people, their numbers declined to about 1,600 people in the late seventeenth century and 34 people in 1921. The 1993 Tonkawa population was 186 people.

Language Tonkawan is considered a language isolate but may relate to the Hokan-Coahuiltecan group of languages.

Historical Information

History The Tonkawa may be descended from Indians who lived in southern Texas and northern Mexico. They had contact with the Spanish in the 1530s. Beginning in the late seventeenth century, the people were caught up in the colonial struggle between Spain and France for control of Texas. The Tonkawa lived around Mission San Gabriel in east Texas for a time before it was abandoned in 1758. They acquired horses in the late seventeenth or early eighteenth century.

El Mocho was a captured Apache who became a Tonkawa chief in the late eighteenth century. His dream was to unite the Apaches and the Tonkawas against the Spanish. At a council attended by over 4,000 Indians, the two peoples failed to resolve their differences. El Mocho was captured and killed by the Spanish.

After Mexican independence in 1821, the Tonkawa became allied with Anglo-Texans against the Comanche and Waco Indians. Along with other Texas tribes, the Tonkawa were assigned two small reservations on the Brazos River in 1855. Despite their past alliance with non-native Texans, in 1859 the Tonkawa were deported from Texas and relocated to Fort Cobb on the Washita River, Indian Territory (Oklahoma). From there some fought for the

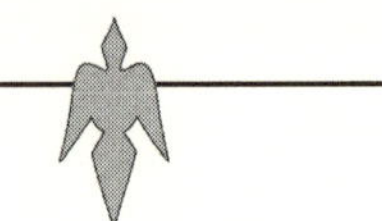

Confederacy during the Civil War, and in 1862 more than half of the tribe were killed in a raid by Unionist Caddo, Shawnee, and Delaware people.

Survivors returned to Texas, where they remained until 1884, when they were assigned to the former Nez Percé Reservation in the Indian Territory. This reservation was allotted in 1896. Some Tonkawas participated in the Pawnee Ghost Dance in the early twentieth century.

Religion The people recognized numerous deities. They may have engaged in cannibalism, possibly for religious reasons. Psychotropic plants also played a part in their religious practice.

Government There were at least 20 autonomous bands with loose, decentralized governing structures.

Customs The Tonkawa were excellent runners. For most of their existence they were nomadic hunters. Infants were tied in cradle boards, resulting in some possibly inadvertent head flattening.

Dwellings On the Plains, the people lived in skin tipis.

Diet Men hunted large and small game, especially buffalo and deer. Women gathered roots, seeds, nuts, prickly pear, and other wild foods. The people also ate fish, shellfish, and rattlesnake meat but neither wolf nor coyote.

Key Technology Like all Plains tribes, most of their material goods came from the buffalo and other animals.

Trade Tonkawas traded buffalo-derived materials for feathers and other items. They were also well-known horse traders. Pueblo groups were among their trade partners. They imported copper from the north.

Notable Arts Painting—of shields, tipis, and their own bodies—was a major part of Tonkawa art.

Transportation The people acquired horses in the late seventeenth or early eighteenth century and soon became expert riders.

Dress Women made all clothing from animal skins. They wore short wraparound skirts and either let their hair hang long or made one braid. Men wore long breechclouts and long, braided hair. Men also plucked their beards and eyebrows. Moccasins or fiber sandals were rarely worn. Both sexes wore buffalo robes, and both tattooed and painted their bodies and wore many personal ornaments.

War and Weapons Tonkawa men had a reputation as fierce raiders, with many enemies, especially the Apache and Comanche. Their weapons included the bow and arrow, hide vests, feathered helmets, and hide shields. They were considered excellent shots. They painted for war in red, yellow, green, and black. Warriors may have cut their hair on the left side, leaving the long hair on the right to be tied with a thong.

Contemporary Information

Government/Reservations In the mid-1990s, the Tonkawa owned 398.74 acres, most of which were allotted, in Kay County, Oklahoma. They were governed by a 1938 constitution calling for elected officers. The tribal council meets monthly.

Economy All jobs are provided by local small businesses.

Legal Status The Tonkawa Tribe, a federally recognized tribal entity, includes some members of a former Texas coast tribe known as Karankawas.

Daily Life The native language is extinct, and most traditional culture has been lost. Some people are members of the Native American Church. The people hold an annual powwow.

Wahpekute

See Dakota

Wahpeton

See Dakota

Wichita

Wichita (`Wi chi tä) is the name of one band of a loose confederacy of several tribes living in separate villages. The Spanish called them *Jumanos.* They have also been called Black Pawnee as well as by the names of related tribes such as Waco, Tawakoni, Tawehash, and Akwits. Their self-designation was *Kitikiti'sh,* meaning "Men."

Location Wichitas lived in central and southeast Kansas, along the Great Bend of the Arkansas River, in the mid–sixteenth century. They migrated to the Kansas-Oklahoma border area in the early eighteenth century and to the Red River region of southeastern Oklahoma in the late eighteenth century. By the mid–nineteenth century they had moved to southwestern Oklahoma. Today, most live in Caddo County, Oklahoma.

Population The Wichita population (including associated tribes) was at least 15,000 in the mid–sixteenth century. That number had dwindled to about 3,200 in the late eighteenth century. In the 1890s there were 153 Wichitas. There were 1,764 enrolled tribal members in 1993.

Language Wichita is a Caddoan language.

Historical Information

History The people who were to become the historic Wichita split apart from the proto-Pawnee about 1,500 years ago. These people may have lived near the Washita River of western Oklahoma about 1,000 years ago. They probably moved north from eastern Texas in the fourteenth century to the Great Bend of the Arkansas River. There they were visited by Francisco Vasquez de Coronado in 1541, when he referred to their villages as Quivira. The people acquired horses by 1700.

During the eighteenth century, under pressure from the well-armed Osage, the Wichita began moving south toward Oklahoma and Texas. Trade with the French began after 1720; with the southern Pawnee, the Wichita dominated the gun trade out of New Orleans. However, in the mid– to late eighteenth century the French trade was suspended while the Wichita were engaged in periodic wars with the Spanish.

A severe smallpox epidemic crippled the people in 1801. Osage and non-Indian raids depleted their population even further in subsequent years. An 1835 treaty between the United States and the Wichita, Comanche, and several eastern tribes marked the first time that the Wichita were officially referred to by that name.

In 1854, several Wichita bands settled with the Shawnees and Delawares on a reservation on the Brazos River, although the non-native Texans soon forced them out. The United States established a Wichita reservation in Indian Territory (Oklahoma), south of the Canadian River, in 1859. Wichitas left the Indian Territory for Kansas (near present-day Wichita) during the Civil War but returned in 1867. They formally ceded all their nonreservation land in 1872 in exchange for a 743,000-acre reservation along the Washita River. However, the agreement was never ratified by Congress. Tribal lands were allotted in 1901. The government paid them $1.25 an acre for the "excess" and then opened that land to non-Indian settlement.

Religion Kinnikasus was the great creator. Other deities were recognized, too, particularly those related to the celestial bodies. The people held a deer dance three times a year. They also performed a calumet (pipe) ceremony. There were many secret societies, for both men and women, each with its own ceremonies and dances.

Government The Wichita were traditionally a loose confederation of several bands or tribes occupying independent villages. A chief and a subchief, chosen by a council of warriors, presided over each village.

Customs The smallest economic unit was the family. Descent was matriarchal. Corpses were buried in a nearby hill with various goods associated with their earthly activities. Mourners cut their hair and gave away some of their possessions.

Dwellings The various Wichita bands lived in separate villages near rivers. In the sixteenth century,

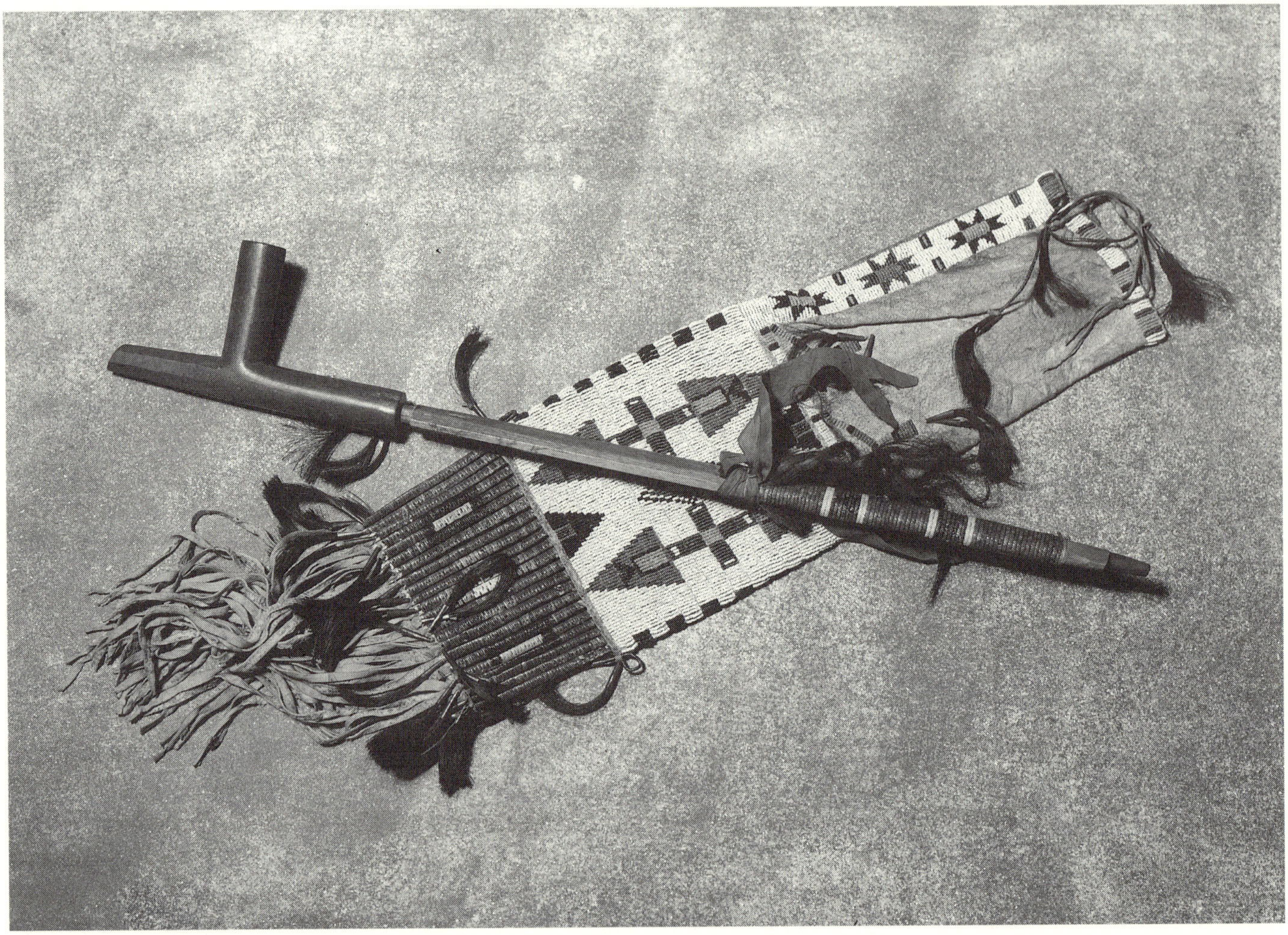

A calumet and a beaded pouch for carrying it. These pipes were important in Plains ceremonials.

settlements consisted of up to 1,000 round houses, each 15–30 feet in diameter and built of a pole framework tied with branches or reeds and thatched with grass. The houses had two doors, a smoke hole in the center, and sleeping platforms along the walls. The people also used ramadas in summer and for some occasions as well as skin tipis during the fall buffalo hunts.

Diet Women grew corn, beans, squash, and tobacco. Crops were stored in underground caches. Pumpkins were cut, dried, and woven into mats for storage. Women also gathered foods such as plums, grapes, and nuts. Men hunted buffalo, usually twice a year—in June and following the harvest—after they obtained horses. They also hunted deer, elk, rabbit, antelope, and bear.

Key Technology Wichitas made items typical of agricultural societies, such as pottery, manos, and metates.

Trade They traded agricultural goods to nomadic tribes in exchange for animal goods. Although the two societies did communicate, there was little trade with the New Mexico pueblos. After 1720, the Wichita acted as intermediaries between the French (tools, guns) and the western nomadic tribes (hides, furs). Following a 1746 friendship treaty, they traded guns to the Comanche for horses, which went eventually to the plantations on the lower Mississippi or southeastern states.

Notable Arts Native artists focused on making pottery and clothing as well as some items of personal ornamentation.

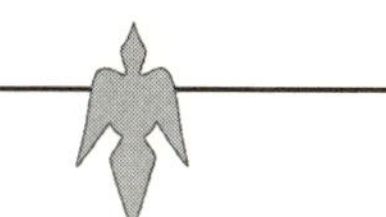

Three kinds of Wichita shelters are depicted in this 1898 photograph: a thatched structure for cooking, a grass house for sleeping, and a frame for a tipi used on buffalo hunts.

Transportation The people acquired horses by 1700.

Dress Women made all clothing of animal skins. Both sexes practiced extensive body and facial tattooing.

War and Weapons War horses wore leather armor. Although the Wichita were generally a peaceful people, they did fight the Osage and the Apache. After 1746 they were allied with the Comanche.

Contemporary Information

Government/Reservations The Wichita tribe owns 10 acres of land and holds another 2,400 acres in joint trust with Caddos and Delawares in Caddo, Canadian, and Gray Counties, Oklahoma. They elect seven tribal officers. Tribal headquarters is located near Anadarko, Oklahoma.

Economy The tribal government and the local clinic are major employers. The tribe also collects license and vendor fees.

Legal Status The Wichita Tribe is a federally recognized tribal entity.

Daily Life The native language is almost extinct, although there are programs designed to save it. Most Wichitas are Baptists; some are members of the Native American Church. The Caddo-speaking tribes of Texas have a long history of ritual peyote use. There is an annual dance in August and an annual large-scale visit with the Pawnee, each tribe taking turns hosting the event.

Yankton

See Nakota

Yanktonai

See Nakota

Chapter Seven

The Southeast

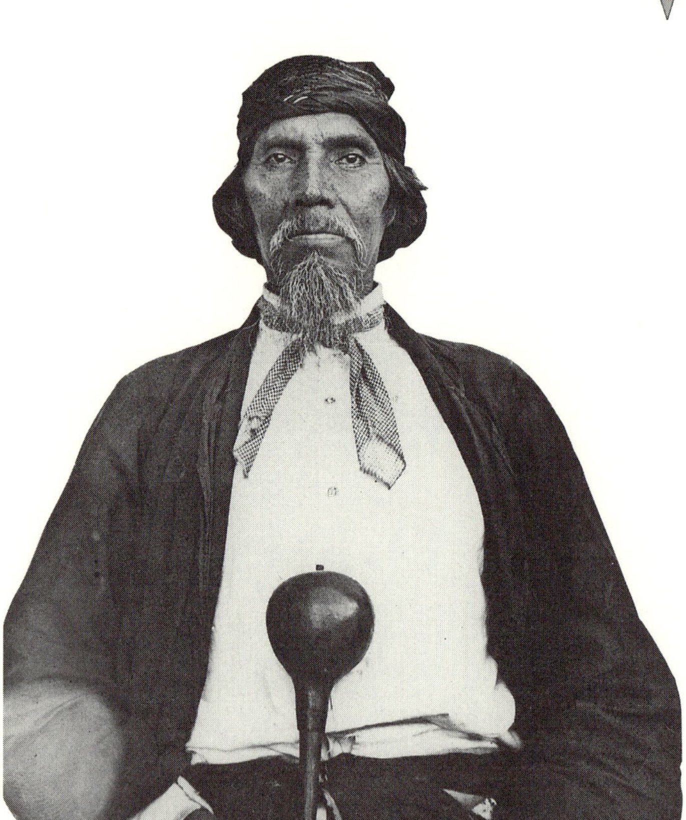

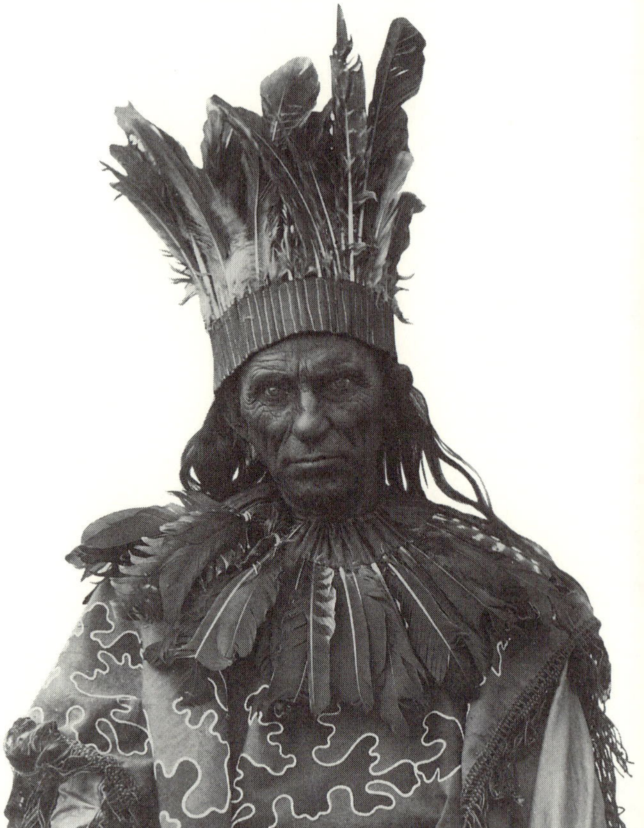

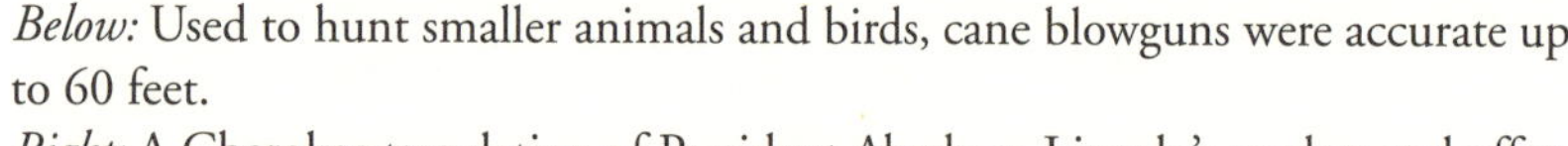

Below: Used to hunt smaller animals and birds, cane blowguns were accurate up to 60 feet.
Right: A Cherokee translation of President Abraham Lincoln's pardon and offer of amnesty to the Indians who fought with the Confederate army during the Civil War.

THE

PRESIDENT'S PROCLAMATION

OF PARDON AND AMNESTY

IN THE CHEROKEE LANGUAGE.

TRANSLATED AND PRINTED AT FORT GIBSON, C. N.

BY ORDER OF COLONEL WM. A. PHILLIPS,

COMMANDING FIRST BRIGADE, ARMY OF THE FRONTIER.

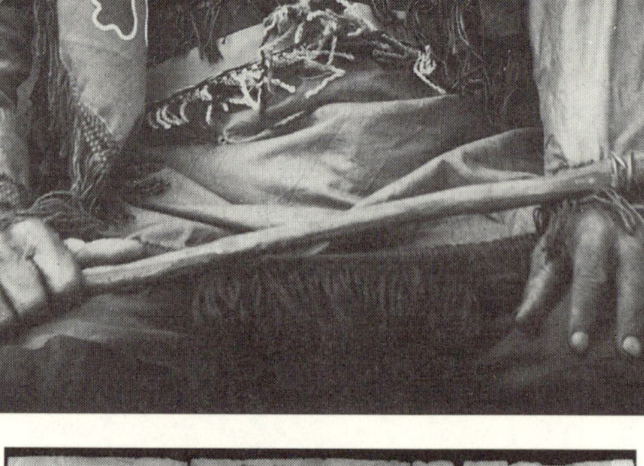

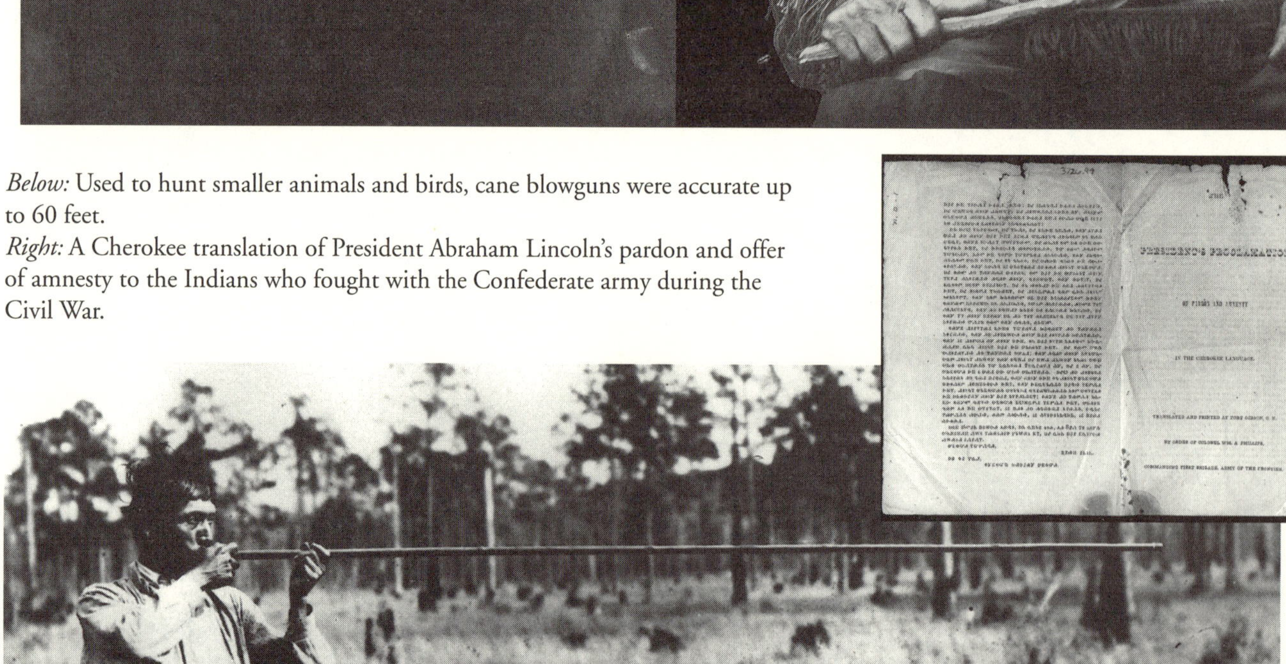

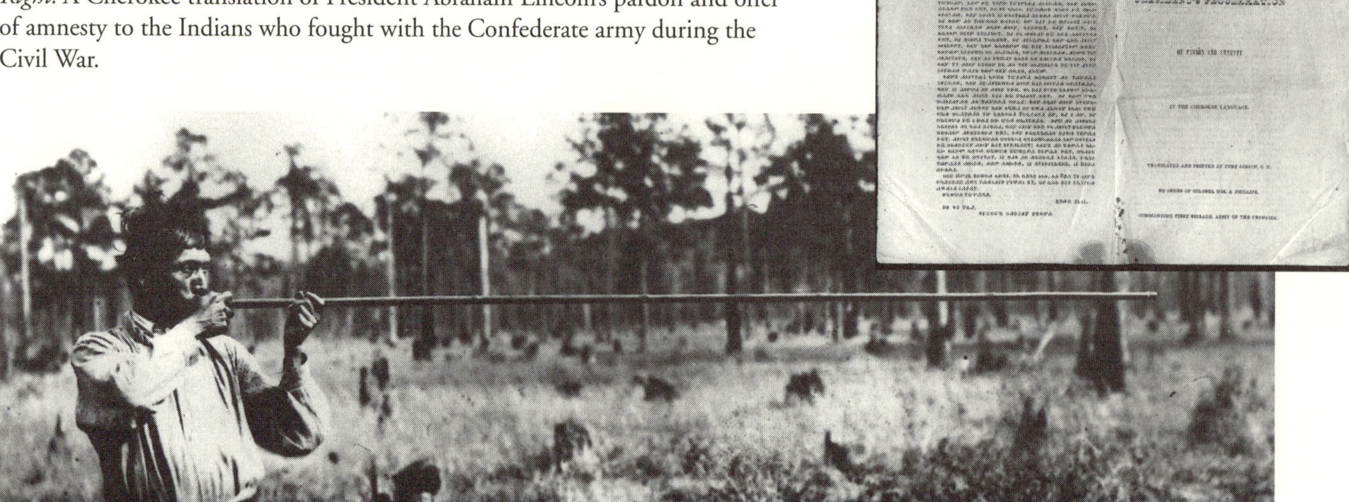

Southeast

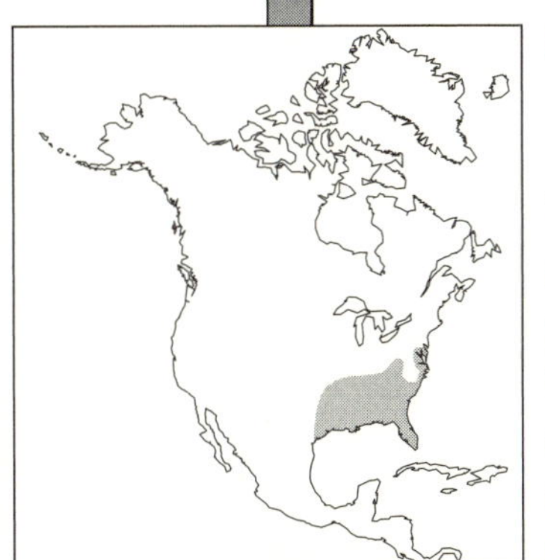

The Southeast cultural area may be thought of as comprising several distinct environmental zones. The Appalachian Mountains run northeast to southwest; their highest point is a 6,684-foot peak in North Carolina. Here such southern hardwoods as chestnut and hickory meet more northerly species, such as birch, sugar maple, and hemlock. The mountain region includes numerous well-watered plateaus and valleys, such as the Cumberland Plateau, the Appalachian Plateau, and, to the west, the Great Valley. Well west of the mountains is the great Mississippi River. Preeminent southeastern rivers include the Shenandoah, the James, the Savannah, the Roanoke, the Coosa, and the Tennessee.

East of the mountains, the Piedmont Plateau is located between the mountains and the coastal plain. Its heavy forests, mainly of oak, pine, sassafras, sycamore, and gum, contained a great quantity and diversity of animal life. Descending still lower, below the fall line, the mild, wet coastal plain itself extends inland for between 100 and 300 miles. Salt marsh, lagoons, and swamps characterize the coastal regions from the Atlantic to the Gulf of Mexico. Cypress, cane, and palmetto grow in the southern part of the plain, and cypress and red gum in the river valleys; conifers and scrub oak dominate the somewhat higher interior.

At least in the early historic period, the four major languages of southeastern Indians were Muskogean, spoken by, among others, Chickasaws, Choctaws, and Creeks; Algonquian, spoken mainly by coastal Indians of Virginia and North Carolina as well as the interior Shawnee; Iroquoian, spoken by the Cherokee and other tribes in the north and northeast of the region; and Siouan, spoken by people living in South Carolina and on the Louisiana and Mississippi coasts. There were several linguistic isolates as well.

Far left: Ayyuini (Swimmer), a Cherokee medicine man.
Left: William Terrill Bradby, a Pamunkey Indian.
Above: The Cherokee Ballplayers' Dance on Qualla Reservation in North Carolina.

Native Americans of the Southeast

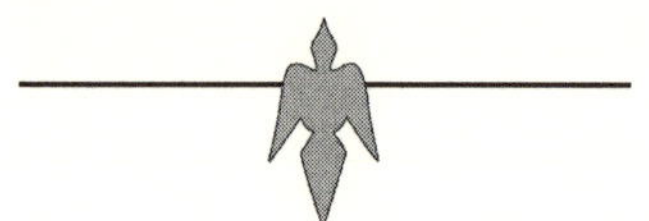

At least 150,000 people, and perhaps ten times that number, probably lived in this region of over 400,000 square miles in the fifteenth century. In general, the area was hospitable to humans, providing a variety of large and small animals, fish, marine life, wild fruits, vegetables, and nuts. Most southeastern Indian tribes adopted large-scale agriculture after about 900, and some also developed large towns and highly centralized social and political structures.

Contact with non-natives began in the early sixteenth century. By the eighteenth century, extensive involvement with non-native traders, combined with population loss from disease and slave raiding, had fundamentally altered Native American societies. Radical dispossession occurred in the 1830s, after which most southeastern Indians rebuilt their lives in Indian Territory (Oklahoma). A relative few remained in the southeast, to continue living as Indians as best they could, but many of the old tribes simply disappeared.

The first people appeared in the southeast at least 11,000 years ago, perhaps from the north but more likely from the west. Early people hunted and then fished for and gathered their food. Initial game included species that have since become extinct. People constructed material items from stone, bone, and wood. Pottery appeared well into the onset of this period, around 2000 B.C.E.

The two definitive technological innovations of the period were the spear thrower, or atlatl, and the grinding stone. The former consisted of a wooden shaft used to provide extra force and range for a wooden spear tipped with a stone point. Armed with this implement, early hunters had little trouble bringing down white-tailed deer and other game. Grinding stones, made of stone or wood, along with stone pestles, were used to pulverize seeds and nuts prior to processing and cooking.

Depending on location and time of year, bands lived either in their constituent nuclear families or occasionally, after about 6000 B.C.E., together as a group. Tribal organization was unknown until the natural abundance of certain places was great enough to produce early civilizations such as Adena (circa 800 B.C.E. to 200 C.E.) and Hopewell (circa 300 B.C.E. to 700 C.E.). Both cultures peaked around the beginning of the present era. Although centered in the Ohio Valley (Adena) and Mississippi-Ohio Valleys (Hopewell), their influences were felt strongly in much of the southeast.

Adena and Hopewell people tended to live in permanent villages. Adena people built earthworks and burial mounds, some up to a quarter of a mile long and shaped like animals, over their dead, to whom much ritual attention was paid. These people enlisted the assistance of shamans to mediate between the human and nonhuman worlds. Copper ornaments and "stamped," or imprinted, pottery were produced. Society may have been hierarchically ordered. Hopewell was also characterized by mound building, advanced art, and, later, by extensive agriculture.

As early as 2500 B.C.E., but especially during the Adena and Hopewell periods, southeastern Indians participated in a number of interregional trade networks. Items such as Gulf Coast conch and other shells, mica and other stone, and clay items moved north into the Midwest, Northeast, and even the Far West. In exchange, obsidian, copper, iron, quartz crystals, and other goods moved back into the south. Most exchange took place between groups of related families rather than among professional, long-distance traders.

Corn was introduced into the southeast from the Midwest in the early part of the first millennium, although large-scale agriculture and its often-related societal centralization did not truly begin until about 900. The bow and arrow was also introduced into the region, probably from the eastern woodlands, around this time. By about 1200 many people were growing the famous triad of corn, beans, and squash.

Concurrent with the rise of large-scale agriculture, most southeast tribes had developed matrilineal clans, which were often grouped into two opposing divisions—red and white—to counter the tendency to overcentralize power. The tribes themselves, in fact, were loose aggregations of clans. Descent was reckoned through the mother's line, and her brothers were often more important to a child than was his or her biological father. Clan membership generally established one's role or position in rituals and in society in general.

Late in the first millennium, some tribes had built on technological advances such as the bow and arrow, flint hoes, and a hardier type of corn to

construct highly centralized, hierarchically ranked societies (chiefdoms) led by powerful, even absolute, chiefs. Members of the elite classes received tribute in the form of goods and services from the common people. Palisaded urban centers of up to tens of thousands of people contained a ceremonial plaza with mounds on which the temple and chief's and priests' houses stood. The people built temples on mounds of up to 300 acres in size, grew fields of crops up to several square miles in area, and had a rich artistic and ceremonial life. These "Mississippian" cultures, which peaked between the eleventh and thirteenth centuries, were likely influenced by people from Mesoamerica.

Among the chiefdoms, religion was characterized by the existence of three cults, or modes of religious expression. One featured large, flat-topped temple mounds located in the ceremonial grounds. The Mound Builders expressed their core idea—the primacy of purity over pollution—by placing layers of white (purity) sand over red (disorder) clay. A second cult revolved around warfare and the glorification of the warrior; a third featured stone, wood, and clay figurines used to represent ancestral spirits.

By the dawn of the historical period, Mississippian culture was in general decline, although burial customs were still often elaborate. Most religious activity in the region was centered around the idea of the sun as life-giver and chief deity. A priesthood conducted rituals in which the sacred fire, as a representative of the sun, figured prominently, as did corn. Shamans, or conjurers, interceded with the spirit world to cure disease, divine the future, and control the weather. The ceremonial round began generally in the spring and culminated with the Green Corn Ceremony (described under the discussion of the nineteenth century), although various other dances might continue into the fall. Leaders conducted business and rituals in the ceremonial plaza, or Square Ground.

Most late prehistoric southeastern Indians lived in permanent villages, built in river valleys wherever possible. Towns, consisting of houses or groups of houses, with a social and ceremonial center, were often strung out for miles. The classic dwelling was made of pole frames covered with branches and vines and then a layer of mud or clay. Summer houses were generally rectangular, with gabled, thatched roofs. Circular winter "town" houses were plastered inside and out. Materials such as animal hides, grasses, bamboo, bark, woven mats, and palm leaves might also be used in their outer construction. Many people also built houselike storage structures in addition to the dwelling unit. Large towns contained huge town houses, with up to several hundred seats, for conducting business and rituals. Sweat houses were also common.

Most southeastern Indians were farmers of corn, beans, squash, and sometimes sunflowers. Surplus grain was often stored in special granaries. Men hunted large (deer, bear, buffalo) and small (beaver, otter, squirrel) game. As in most native cultures, animal products such as sinew, oil, and horn were used extensively for various purposes in addition to food and clothing. Hunting took place between planting and harvest and especially in winter, when the people often left the villages in small hunting parties.

Important wild plant foods included hickory and other nuts, acorns, persimmons and other fruits, berries, wild rice, and mushrooms. Shellfish was an important staple in certain areas. Birds, especially the turkey, played an important role in diet as well as decoration. Depending on location, southeastern Indians used different techniques for capturing fish, including weirs, spears, and poison. Most cultures utilized tobacco.

Stone and bone remained important raw materials into the historical period; they were used to make mortars, clubs, scrapers, adzes, axes, and various other tools as well as arrowheads. People made wooden stools with legs. Cane was a widely employed raw material, used in making baskets and mats, houses, arrows and darts, containers, musical instruments, and many other items. Men and boys used blowguns and darts to bring down birds or small animals, and women manufactured pottery, twilled baskets, and wove mats. Cypress was the favored wood for canoe manufacture, although pine, poplar, and other woods were also suitable, and bark canoes were also used in the interior.

Although most clothing was made from skins, mainly deer, women also used the inner bark of the mulberry tree to make items such as hair nets and

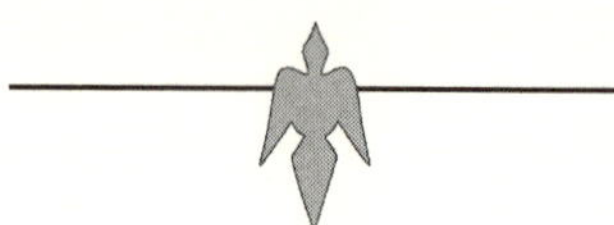

some textiles. Bear or buffalo robes were important winter garments. Some people also made ornate feather mantles or cloaks from turkeys and other birds. Men generally wore breechclouts and perhaps shirts, shawls, or cloaks. Leggings were more common around the Gulf region. Women generally wore a short skirt as well as a mantle or tunic, although there were considerable regional variations. Moccasins were used mainly for travel. Personal ornamentation, especially in the form of shell beads, pearls, and copper, was common. Body paint was generally reserved for special occasions, although elaborate tattooing was widespread.

Intercourse between the tribes included regular trade fairs. Items of the hunt—primarily hides, meat, and animal products—were exchanged for manufactured items such as pipes, bowls, dishes, and spoons. Also, coastal tribes offered shells, fish products, and "black drink" leaves to peoples of the interior, who provided red pigment, pottery, and feather cloaks. Salt, copper, wood, and mica were other important items of exchange. Even catlinite pipes from Minnesota were seen at some trade fairs, which were also occasions to feast and visit. The Choctaws created a language that was used as a lingua franca in regional intertribal trade.

Clan vengeance was a primary motivation for war. Weapons included the bow and arrow and assorted clubs, spears, knives, and hatchets. Hide shields were also used. The practice of warfare varied from place to place, but there was often a great deal of ritual preparation, and warriors often left distinguishing signs to show who had committed the violent deeds. Some carried along a sacred war ark filled with various medicines. Prisoners, if there were any, were often taken home and tortured or sold into slavery. Scalping was common, at least in the early historic period; it constituted, along with other practices, war honors. War parties were often led by war chiefs.

A form of modern-day lacrosse was the most common game played by southeastern Indians. Indeed, more than a game, it had considerable significance in the realms of social custom and ceremony. Two sticks were generally used, as was a deer-hide ball. The sides consisted of different divisions or towns. Among some tribes, a great deal of ceremonial preparation took place for up to a week or more before a game, and medicine men played an important role before and during play. Gambling was extensive. Play was very rough, and severe injuries, sometimes leading to death, were not unusual. Most, although not all, such games were all male. There were separate games for women, and people of both sexes played many games besides stickball. In particular, chunkey, a variety of the hoop-and-pole game, was widely played.

By around 1600, the power of the chiefs, still mainly band leaders, ranged from advisory—with power, such as it was, being held mainly by a representative council—to absolute. Some tribes associated in confederacies, such as the Powhatan, Natchez, Calusa, Cofitachiqui, and Creek. Among the Creek, up to 50 or more towns spoke different Muskogean and even non-Muskogean languages. Professional interpreters were employed to maintain effective communication between the constituent elements. Towns assumed an identity characterized by war (red) or peace (white).

The arrival of Columbus in 1492 inaugurated the contact period in southeastern history. News of the effects of this event on the offshore native people—massive death, mistreatment, and enslavement—may have reached Florida well before the actual arrival of Europeans. By the time of the 1519 Juan Ponce de León expedition and other Spanish explorations well into the interior soon after, many Indians knew enough to fear the intruders. Despite efforts to protect themselves, many Indians suffered violence and death from non-native depredations and disease.

As contact between Indians and Europeans became more regular after the mid– to late sixteenth century, Indian culture itself began to change. Indian societies were drawn into increased trade with French and British adventurers, who arrived in the seventeenth century to join Spanish traders, missionaries, and colonists. At the same time, the Indians continued to die in large numbers from disease and were increasingly forced to deal with other problems, such as factionalism, fraud, land grabbing, and the introduction of alcohol. Several aspects of traditional culture, such as clan and political structure, began to break down, and overall conflict increased.

By the mid–eighteenth century there was a thriving regional trade in deerskin and other products. Hundreds of thousands of pounds of skins went to Europe every year. The effects of this trade completed an essential transformation in southeast native life. Native manufacture of certain items ceased, since they were more readily obtained through trade. As the deer disappeared, many Indians began to raise cattle for meat and skins. Also part of regional trade was the traffic in slaves, in which Indians participated as buyers and sellers as well as victims. Some southeastern tribes, but especially the Seminole, welcomed African Americans into the ranks of tribal membership. Populations moved or were moved to suit trade and political exigencies.

In some respects, however, native culture remained solidly rooted in its traditions. The classic Green Corn ceremony (or Busk), for example, which flourished in the nineteenth century, had its origins deep in Mound Builder culture. Held when the new late corn crop ripened, the four-day ceremony was a thanksgiving for the crop, a time for purifying or renewal, and a new year's festival. There were many variations on the ceremony, but, in general, the precise starting day was ascertained first of all. Housing was found or made for all visitors, followed by a great feast.

Men then repaired and cleaned the public places and women the homes. Men separated from women and children and began a fast while religious leaders prepared an emetic, high-caffeine black drink. All fires were extinguished. Then the priest and his assistants, dressed in special clothing, kindled a new sacred fire, from which all home fires were lit. The ceremony concluded with a sermon by the chief, the green corn dance itself, a ritual immersion in water, and a feast that included the new corn. Most past wrongs were forgiven, and most exiles could return.

Meanwhile, loss of native land accelerated, especially after the Indian defeat in the pivotal Battle of Horseshoe Creek in 1814. Despite the fact that at least the larger, so-called civilized tribes had adopted a lifestyle very similar to that of their non-native neighbors—including slave-based agriculture, literacy, Anglo-style government and laws, and, to some extent, Christianity—they were almost completely dispossessed in the 1830s. The Trail of Tears, a term originally depicting the removal of the Cherokee to Indian Territory (Oklahoma), is now applied to the removal of the Creek, Chickasaw, Choctaw, and Seminole as well (from their hideouts in Florida's Everglades, some Seminoles were able to resist removal). Tens of thousands of Indians were forcibly uprooted, and significant numbers of them died in transit or shortly after their arrival.

Indians rebuilt their lives out west, reestablishing their villages, towns, fields, and institutions. They fared poorly during and following the Civil War, in which many supported the Confederacy. Indian casualties were relatively high, and further dispossession and forcible removal followed the fighting. Missionaries redoubled their efforts. Toward the end of the century, the government decided to break up the reservations and terminate tribal governments. Oklahoma became a state in 1907. By the 1950s, much of the Indian-held land had been lost to non-natives, mostly through fraud and tax default. Oklahoma Indians became increasingly polarized. Wealthier people gravitated toward Anglo society, whereas poorer Indians continued to resist allotment and hold tenaciously to a more traditional Indian identity.

Today, most "southeast" Indians live in Oklahoma. Traditional culture is preserved in varying ways and to different degrees. Although most Indians are Christians, many tribes celebrate traditional rituals, such as the Green Corn ceremony, as well as pan-Indian ones. There are also tens of thousands of Indians in most southern states, notably Florida, North Carolina, and Mississippi. Even many contemporary southeastern tribes that are not federally recognized retain their Indian identities to varying degrees.

Alabama

Alabama (A li `ba mu) or Alibamu, "plant" or "medicine gatherers" or "thicket clearers." Alabamas were culturally related to the neighboring Creeks and Choctaws.

Location Most fifteenth-century Alabamas lived along the upper Alabama River. By the seventeenth century they had moved to the lower course of that

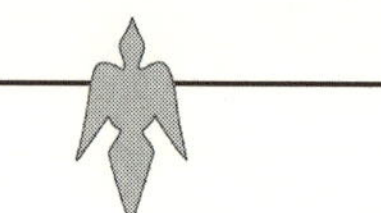

river. Today, most Alabamas live in Polk County, Texas; Allen Parish, Louisiana; and eastern Oklahoma.

Population Alabamas numbered between 700 and 1,000 in the eighteenth century. In the 1990s there were about 400 living in Louisiana, about 800 enrolled in Texas, and 900 enrolled as part of the Creek Nation.

Language Alabamas spoke a Muskogean language.

Historical Information

History Alabamas probably descended from Mound Builder cultures and may have originated north and west of the Mississippi. They encountered a hostile Spanish party under Hernando de Soto in 1540. By the early eighteenth century they had become allies of the French, who built Fort Toulouse in Alabama country in 1713.

Many Alabamas left their homeland following the French defeat in 1763. Some joined the Seminoles in Florida. Some resettled north of New Orleans, and later some of that group moved on to western Louisiana and Texas. Land given them in recognition of their contribution in the 1836 fight against Mexico was promptly stolen by non-natives. In 1842, the Alabamas and the Coushatta Indians were given a 1,280-acre reservation along the Trinity River. The United States added 3,081 acres to that reservation in 1928. In 1954 the tribe voluntarily terminated its relationship with the federal government, at which time the state took over control of the reservation. The tribe reverted to federal status in 1986.

Those who remained in Alabama fought unsuccessfully with the Creeks against non-natives in the 1813–1814 Creek war. Survivors of that conflict settled in the Alabama town of Tawasa. Most were resettled in Indian Territory (Oklahoma) with the Creeks in the 1830s. Part of the Creek Nation until 1938, the Alabama-Quassartes at that time received a federal charter, several hundred acres of land, and political, but not administrative, independence.

Louisiana Alabamas maintained a subsistence economy during the early twentieth century, gradually entering the labor market. Tourism and tourist-related sales of cane baskets and wood crafts began to grow in midcentury.

Religion The sun (fire) was worshiped, as were a host of lesser deities and beings. Alabamas celebrated the Green Corn ceremony as well as other ceremonies throughout the spring, summer, and fall. Dances might be social or ceremonial in nature. Most councils and ceremonies began with an emetic tea (black drink). Priests, doctors, and conjurers underwent a rigorous training period that included healing techniques, songs, and formulas.

Government Alabamas were part of the Creek Confederacy, although each village was politically sovereign. In most towns of the confederacy, a chief *(miko),* usually from a white clan, was chosen largely by merit. He was head of a democratic council that had ceremonial and diplomatic responsibilities. The nature of his power was to influence and to carry out certain duties, not to command. Decisions were taken by consensus. There were also a subchief and a war chief. A town crier announced the governmental decisions to the people.

Customs Chunkey was a popular game. One threw a pole after a rolling stone disc, scoring points by hitting the disc and coming closest to where it finally fell. There were also many other games, most of which involved gambling. The dead were buried with their heads to the east and sometimes a knife in the hand for fighting eagles on the way to the afterworld. Alabamas had over 50 clans in the eighteenth century, although probably fewer before contact. Infidelity in marriage was an offense punishable by public whipping and exile.

Dwellings Towns were laid out in a square and enclosed by walls up to several hundred feet long. By design, entrance and egress were difficult: On one side the gate was too low for a horse to enter, and another side might open onto a steep embankment. Many towns were surrounded by mud-covered wooden stockades. Their ceremonial centers included bark-covered, circular structures, a plaza, and a game field.

Dwellings were pole-frame structures with plastered walls and bark-covered or shingled, gabled roofs. The outer covering was of mud and grass or mats. Many families had a winter house and a summer house. They also had a two-story granary,

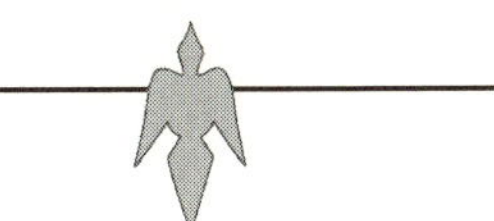

one end of which was used for storing grain and roots (lower) and for meetings (upper). The other end, with open sides, was a general storage area (lower) and a reception area (upper). A fourth building, if one could afford it, was a storehouse for skins. The four buildings were placed to form a square, in the manner of the ceremonial Square Ground. Fires stood on the bare floor or on a stone hearth; there was usually a smoke hole in the roof.

Diet Alabamas ate fish, squirrels and other small game, deer and other large game, and their crops. The winter hunt, during which men traveled up to 250 miles or more, lasted from after the harvest until the spring planting. The less able remained behind in the villages.

Key Technology Fish were taken with spears, bows and arrows, and poison. Women wove cane or palmetto baskets. Many points and knives were made of flint, although mortars and pestles were generally wooden. Bows were also made of wood (cedar was considered the best), with hide (perhaps bark in earlier times) strings. Men also hunted with blowguns and possibly spears. Other notable items included hide wrist guards, drums, and pottery.

Trade Alabamas exported flint and animal products and imported pipes and shells. They participated in the general interior-coastal trade.

Notable Arts Women made pottery and wove geometric designs into their baskets. Artisans worked silver ornaments from the sixteenth century on.

Transportation Most precontact transportation was via dugout pirogues.

Dress Personal adornment included ornaments in pierced ears and noses, body paint, and various armbands, bracelets, and necklaces. In the late eighteenth century, women wore cloth skirts, as well as shawls, or capes, that covered one breast and were fastened over the left shoulder, made of the skin of buffalo calves. They parted their hair down the middle and tied each section off. Men generally had four braids, two behind and two in front. They wore breechclouts, cloaks or shirts, and bear or buffalo robes in winter.

War and Weapons Alabamas often joined forces with the Coushatta people against the Tohome, among others. Men decorated their hair for war with buffalo horns. They fought with the war club and bow and arrow. The war chief carried along the sacred war ark or medicine bundle. Life (of one's own people) was considered precious, and warriors were extremely careful not to risk inopportune or imprudent fighting or capture.

Contemporary Information

Government/Reservations The Alabama-Coushatta Reservation, established in 1854, is located in Polk County, Texas. It consists of 4,400 acres and is governed by a tribal council. There were 477 Indian residents in 1990.

The 154-acre Coushatta Reservation is located in Allen Parish, Louisiana. About 400 people lived there in the early 1990s. Indian residents are often referred to as Koasati Indians. They are governed by a tribal council.

The Alabamas and Quassartes of Oklahoma live mostly near Weleetka, in Okfuskee County. Tribal headquarters is in Henryetta. They are still administered together with the Creek Nation.

Economy Some Alabamas continue to make traditional arts and crafts. There is income from tourism, including camping and recreation, in Texas. The Coushatta in Louisiana own a Christmas tree farm and a bingo establishment.

Legal Status The Coushatta Tribe of Louisiana, the Alabama-Coushatta Tribe, and the Alabama-Quassarte Tribal Town of the Creek Nation are federally recognized tribal entities.

Daily Life Most Alabamas are Protestants. The Alabama-Coushattas operate a tribal museum; they also host various dances as well as a June powwow. Both the Alabama and the Coushatta languages are still spoken in Texas. In Louisiana, federal money has helped the people improve sanitation and build schools, a health clinic, and a tribal center. Residents of Oklahoma often visit and intermarry with members of the other communities. A few older people in Oklahoma speak both languages.

Biloxi

See Tunica

Caddo

Caddo (`Ca dō), "true chiefs," from Kadohadacho, a principal tribe. The Caddo Indians included people of the Natchitoches Confederacy (Louisiana), the Hasinai (Tejas or Texas) Confederacy (Texas), the Kadohadacho Confederacy (Texas and Arkansas), and the Adai and Eyish people. There were about 25 Caddo tribes in the eighteenth century.

Location Traditionally, Caddos lived in a wide area from the Red River Valley (Louisiana and Arkansas) to the Brazos Valley in Texas. Today, the highest concentration of Caddo Indians is found in Caddo County, Oklahoma.

Population Numbering around 8,000 people in the late seventeenth century, there were 3,371 enrolled Caddos in the early 1990s.

Language Caddos spoke a Caddoan language.

Historical Information

History Caddoans are thought to have originated in the Southwest. They reached the Great Plains in the mid–twelfth century and the fringes of the Southeast cultural area shortly thereafter. They gave the Spanish under Hernando de Soto a mixed reception in 1541. Few of the Spanish missions in their country had any success.

Trade with the French began in the early seventeenth century. The Indians traded their crops for animal pelts, which they then traded to the French for guns and other items of non-native origin. During the eighteenth century, Caddo villages suffered from Spanish-French colonial battles. Many tribes were wiped out by disease during that period.

In 1835, the Caddos ceded their Louisiana land and moved to Texas. In the 1850s, however, non-native Texans drove all Indians out of Texas, and the Caddos fled from their brutality to the Indian Territory (Oklahoma). In 1859, the United States confined them to a reservation along the Washita River, which the Wichitas and Delawares later joined.

Rather than support the Confederacy, most Caddos fled to Kansas during the Civil War, returning in 1868. Some scouted for the U.S. Army during the Plains wars, in part as a strategy of supporting farmers against nomads. The boundaries of their reservation were secured in 1872, but despite Caddo objections, most of the reservation was allotted around 1900. After extensive litigation and appeals, the tribe won over $1.5 million in land claim settlements in the 1980s.

Religion Their supreme deity was known as Ayanat Caddi. There were also other deities and spirits, including the sun. Most annual ceremonies revolved around the agricultural cycle.

Government Each Caddo tribe was headed by a powerful chief, who was assisted by other people of authority. Among the Hasinai (at least), a high priest had supreme authority.

Customs Clans were more hierarchical and social classes more pronounced among the western Caddo than in the east. Guests were greeted by ritual wailing and ceremonially washed. Shell beads were used as a medium of exchange. The people practiced frontal head deformation. Chiefs were carried on the shoulders of the people. Popular games included hoop and pole and also foot races. Men placed fowl down on their heads in preparation for feasts.

Premarital sexual liaisons were condoned. In some tribes, men were allowed to have more than one wife, although in others a woman might not allow it. Divorce was easily obtained and occurred regularly. The dead were buried with food and water as well as appropriate items (weapons for men, utensils for women). War dead were cremated. Six days after death, all spirits went southward to a pleasant house of the dead. Some tribes may have engaged in ritual murder.

Dwellings At least one seventeenth-century town had over 100 houses. Some villages may have been

reinforced with towered stockades. Houses in the east were round, about 15 feet high and between 20 and 60 feet in diameter. They were constructed of a pole frame covered with grass thatch, through which smoke from the cooking fires exited; roofs came all the way to the ground. Western Caddos built earth lodges, with wooden frames and brush, grass, and mud walls reaching to the top. There were also outside arbors. Sacred fires always burned in circular temples.

Houses were generally grouped around an open plaza or game/ceremonial area. Cane beds, separated by mats, were raised about three feet off the ground. Doors usually faced east, although sometimes southeast or south. There were also indoor compartments near the entrance and outdoor areas to store dried corn and other items.

Diet Women grew two corn crops a year, as well as beans, pumpkins, sunflowers, and tobacco. They also gathered wild foods such as nuts, acorns, mulberries, strawberries, blackberries, plums, pomegranates, persimmons, and grapes. Agricultural products were most important in the diet, although buffalo grew in importance as the group moved westward. Men hunted deer, bear, raccoon, turkey, fowl, and snakes. They stalked deer using deer disguises. Dogs may have assisted them in the hunt. Fish were caught where possible.

Key Technology Bows were made of Osage orange whenever possible. Most fish were taken in traps. Caddos made a variety of baskets and mats. Other important items included wood and horn dishes; wooden mortars, chests, and cradles; drums; rattles; and flutes (flageolets). Deer sinew was generally used as thread.

Trade Caddos exported Osage orange wood and salt, which they obtained from local mines (licks) and boiled in earthen (later iron) kettles. They imported Quapaw wooden platters, among other items. The Texas Caddos traded with Chichimecs from Mexico.

Notable Arts Fine arts included basketry, pottery, and carved shells.

Transportation Single-log dugout canoes and cane rafts were used to navigate bodies of water. The people acquired horses in the late seventeenth century.

Dress Most clothing was made of deerskin. Men wore breechclouts, untailored shirts, and cloaks, Women wore skirts and a poncho-style upper garment and painted their bodies. They parted their hair in front and fastened it behind. Both wore blankets or buffalo robes and tattooed their faces and bodies, especially in floral and animal patterns. Girls wore grass or hay breechclouts from birth.

War and Weapons Weapons included the bow and arrow and lances. Warriors underwent special ceremonies in a war house prior to battle; the house was burned down when the war party departed. Enemies included the Osage and Choctaw, whereas in the later period the people were often allied with the Delaware.

Contemporary Information

Government/Reservations Tribal facilities are located on 42.5 acres near Binger, Oklahoma. A constitution and by-laws were adopted in 1938 and revised in 1976. An elected eight-member tribal council with a chair governs the tribe. The people also claim almost 2,400 acres of land held in trust in Oklahoma with the Wichita and Delaware.

Economy Unemployment often reaches 40 percent among Indians in Caddo County. Caddos participate in the local economy as professionals, ranchers, farmers, and workers of many kinds. The tribal economy relies heavily on oil, gas, and land leasing. With the other two tribes, the Caddo operate a smoke shop, a factory, and a bingo parlor.

Legal Status The Caddo Tribe of Oklahoma is a federally recognized tribal entity. The people are considering changing their name to the Caddo Nation in Oklahoma.

Daily Life Tribal facilities include administrative offices, dance grounds, and several community centers. The tribe improved its housing in the 1990s and is seeking to build new program and activity

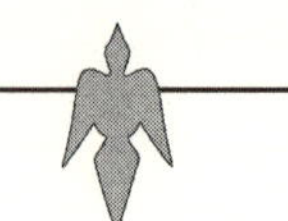

buildings. The people have retained a significant amount of traditional culture, especially songs and dances, and there are many programs designed to revitalize Caddo traditions. There is an active Native American Church.

Catawba

The Catawba (Cə `täw bä) people were also known as Issa or Esaw, "People of the River."

Location Catawbas traditionally lived along the North Carolina–South Carolina border, especially along the Catawba River. Today, most live near Rock Hill, South Carolina. Some live in Oklahoma, in Colorado, and in other states.

Population The Catawba were the largest of the eastern Siouan tribes in the early seventeenth century, with a population of about 6,000. There were roughly 1,400 people enrolled in the tribe in the mid-1990s.

Language Catawba is probably a Siouan language.

Historical Information

History Catawbas may have come to the Carolinas from the northwest. They first encountered non-natives—Spanish explorers—in the mid–sixteenth century. Extensive contact with British traders in the late seventeenth and early eighteenth centuries transformed their lives. A dependence on non-native goods caused them to hunt ever farther afield for pelts with which to purchase such goods. Encroachment on other peoples' hunting grounds combined with the heavy volume of goods carried along the trade routes encouraged increased attacks by enemy Indians. Catawbas also underwent severe depopulation from disease.

In order to maintain trade relations with the colonists, the Catawba took their side in a 1711–1713 war with the Tuscarora Indians. By 1715, however, some Catawbas had taken the Indian side in the Yamasee war, rebelling against unfair trade practices, forced labor, and slave raids. The non-native victory in this conflict broke the power of the local Indians.

In the mid–eighteenth century smallpox epidemics almost wiped the tribe out: Their precontact population of about 6,000 had declined by over 90 percent to 500 or fewer. Alcohol sold and aggressively promoted by Anglo traders took many more lives. Catawbas tended to absorb local tribes who suffered the same fate, such as the Cheraw, Sugaree, Waxhaw, Congaree, Santee, Pedee, and Wateree.

In 1760–1761 the Catawbas were forced by their dependence on the state of South Carolina to fight against the powerful Cherokee in the French and Indian War. By 1763 they were confined within a 15-square-mile (144,000-acre) reservation, as non-natives continued to take their former lands. Part of the agreement creating the reservation stipulated that non-Indians would be evicted from it (which never happened) and that the Catawba continued to enjoy hunting rights outside the area. Their last great chief, Haigler, or Arataswa, died at that time.

The declining tribe took the patriot side in the American Revolution and began a long process of intermarriage with the Pamunkey of Virginia at that time. After the war, they granted many long-term renewable leases to non-natives. They also established two towns, Newtown and Turkeyhead, on both sides of the Catawba River.

Some of the few remaining, poverty-stricken Catawbas went to live with the Cherokee in western Carolina in the 1830s. In 1840 they signed a treaty with the state of South Carolina, agreeing to cede lands in that state and move to North Carolina. Unable to buy land there, however, most dispersed among the Cherokee and Pamunkey, although a very few remained in South Carolina.

In the 1850s, most Catawbas who had gone to live with the Cherokee returned to South Carolina. A few families moved to Arkansas, the Indian Territory, Colorado, Utah, or elsewhere. Those in South Carolina acquired a reservation of 630 (of the original 144,000) poor-quality acres. They also obtained the promise of annual payments from the state.

Many South Carolina Catawbas began sharecropping at that time but returned occasionally to live on the reservation. They also continued to speak their language and to make their traditional crafts. The Catawba Indian School opened in 1896 and ran until 1962. Mormons also played a large role

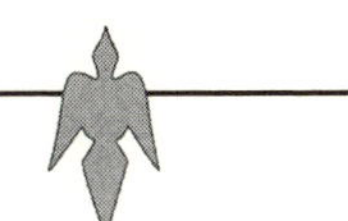

in educating Catawba children beginning in the 1880s.

Many Catawbas worked in textile mills beginning after World War I. The Indians added to their reservation by purchasing land in the mid–twentieth century. By that time, however, traditional Catawba culture had all but expired. Although the federal trust relationship was formally begun only in 1943, as a result of Catawba legal pressure, in 1962 the tribe voluntarily ended its relationship with the federal government, at which time individuals took over possession of the recently purchased tribal lands.

Religion The people made use of wooden images in their ceremonies, which were relatively unconnected to the harvest. Enemies were killed to accompany the dead to an afterworld.

Government There were two bands in the early eighteenth century. Some of their chiefs—men and women—were quite powerful.

Customs Catawbas may have practiced frontal head deformation. The chunkey game was a variety of hoop and pole, played with a stone roller. They also played stickball, or lacrosse. At puberty, young women learned how properly to wear decorative feathers. Doctors and conjurers cured and detected thieves by consorting with spirits. Men alone were punished in cases of adultery. Divorce was easy to obtain, and widows could remarry at once. Corpses were buried under bark and earth; later, the bones of chiefs were dug up, cleaned, wrapped in deerskins, and redeposited in a crypt. Personal enemies may have been poisoned.

Dwellings Six early villages were located in river valleys. People lived in bark-covered pole-frame houses. The town houses were circular, as were the temples. Open arbors were used in summer.

Diet Women grew corn, beans, squash, and gourds. Men hunted widely for large and small game, including buffalo, deer, and bear. The people also ate fish, pigeons, acorns, and various other wild plant foods.

Key Technology Blowguns with an average length of 5–6 feet and with an effective range of no more than 30 feet were used to bring down birds. Darts, about 8–10 inches long, were made of wood slivers. Scratchers, similar to combs, were made of a split reed with rattlesnake teeth. A number of clay items were made, including pipes.

Trade The main regional aboriginal trade routes ran right through Catawba territory. The Catawba became heavily involved with British traders, especially in the mid–eighteenth century but beginning at least in 1673.

Notable Arts Pottery was an ancient and highly developed art. It was often stamped with a carved piece of wood before firing. Baskets were constructed of rushes, roots, or grasses.

Transportation Rivers were navigated on dugout and possibly birch bark canoes.

Dress Chiefs wore headdresses of wild turkey feathers. Women may have worn leggings as well as, when mourning, clothing made from tree moss.

War and Weapons Traditional enemies included the Cherokee, Shawnee, and Iroquois, with whom they fought often. They also fought the Delaware in historic times. Catawba raiding parties traveled long distances, even to the Great Lakes.

Contemporary Information

Government/Reservations The Catawba State Reservation (650 acres) is located near Rock Hill (eastern York County), South Carolina. The tribe gained nonprofit corporate status in 1973 and elected an eight-member tribal council and executive committee at that time. The 1990 Indian population was 124.

Economy The tribe is known for its pottery, which, unlike any other eastern tribe, they continue to make approximately in the ancient way. There is also individual and tribal income from the 1993 settlement (see "Legal Status"). The people are relatively well educated and enjoy a range of economic opportunities.

Legal Status The Catawba Indian Nation is a federally recognized tribal entity. The tribe claimed possession of its 144,000-acre colonial reservation, holding that the lands were never legally transferred. An agreement with the United States was effected in 1993, by the terms of which federal tribal status was reinstated and the tribe was paid $50 million.

Daily Life Catawbas in Colorado and other western states, though not formally enrolled, communicate regularly with the Carolina people. Pottery making and training are still important activities. Other crafts include hide tanning, blowgun making, and beadwork. Most Catawbas are Mormons. The tribe sponsors an annual cultural festival and is involved with numerous local and regional museums. Efforts are under way to revive the native language. The old knowledge and ceremonies have long since disappeared.

Cherokee

Cherokee (`Cher ə kē), probably from the Creek *tciloki,* "People Who Speak Differently." Their self-designation was *Ani-yun-wiya,* "Real People." With the Creek, Choctaw, Chickasaw, and Seminole, the Cherokee were one of the so-called Five Civilized Tribes; this non-native appellation arose because by the early nineteenth century these Indians dressed, farmed, and governed themselves so nearly like white Americans. At the time of contact the Cherokee were the largest tribe in the southeast. Cherokees were formerly known as Kituhwas.

Location Between about 70 and 100 precontact villages were located in roughly 40,000 square miles of the southern Appalachian region, including parts of the present-day states of North Carolina, Kentucky, Tennessee, Virginia, South Carolina, Georgia, and Alabama. There were towns in the lower region (headwaters of the Savannah River), the middle region (headwaters of the Little Tennessee River), and the upper region (lower Little Tennessee River and the headwaters of the Hiwassee River). Today, most Cherokees live in northeastern Oklahoma. A sizable minority lives in western North Carolina.

Population There were roughly 29,000 Cherokees in the mid–sixteenth century and perhaps 22,000 in 1650. In 1990, 308,132 people identified themselves as Cherokees, although fewer than half belong to federally recognized groups.

Language Cherokee is an Iroquoian language. The lower towns spoke the Elati dialect; the middle towns spoke the Kituhwa dialect; the upper (overhill and valley) towns spoke the Atali dialect. The dialects were mutually intelligible with difficulty.

Historical Information

History The Cherokee probably originated in the upper Ohio Valley, the Great Lakes region, or someplace else in the north. They may also have been related to the Mound Builders. The town of Echota, on the Little Tennessee River, may have been the ancient capital of the Cherokee Nation.

They encountered Hernando de Soto about 1540, probably not long after they arrived in their historic homeland. Spanish attacks against the Indians commenced shortly thereafter, although new diseases probably weakened the people even before Spanish soldiers began killing them. There were also contacts with the French and especially the British in the early seventeenth century. Traders brought guns around 1700, along with debilitating alcohol.

The Cherokee fought a series of wars with Tuscarora, Shawnee, Catawba, Creek, and Chickasaw Indians early in the eighteenth century. In 1760 the Cherokee, led by Chief Oconostota, fought the British as a protest against unfair trade practices and violence practiced against them as a group. Cherokees raided settlements and captured a British fort but were defeated after two years of fighting by the British scorched-earth policy. The peace treaty cost the Indians much of their eastern land, and, in fact, they never fully recovered their prominence after that time

Significant depopulation resulted from several mid–eighteenth century epidemics. Cherokee support for Britain during the American Revolution encouraged attacks by North Carolina militia. Finally, some Cherokees who lived near Chattanooga relocated in 1794 to Arkansas and Texas and in 1831 to Indian Territory (Oklahoma). These people eventually became known as the Western Cherokee.

After the American Revolution, Cherokees adopted British-style farming, cattle ranching, business, and government, becoming relatively cohesive and prosperous. They also owned slaves. They sided with the United States in the 1813 Creek war, during which a Cherokee saved Andrew Jackson's life. The tribe enjoyed a cultural renaissance between about 1800 and 1830, although they were under constant pressure for land cession and riven by internal political factionalism.

The Cherokee Nation was founded in 1827 with "western" democratic institutions and a written constitution (which specifically disenfranchised African Americans and women). By then, Cherokees were intermarrying regularly with non-natives and were receiving increased missionary activity, especially in education. Sequoyah (also known as George Gist) is credited with devising a Cherokee syllabary in 1821 and thus providing his people with a written language. During the late 1820s, the people began publishing a newspaper, the *Cherokee Phoenix.*

The discovery of gold in their territory led in part to the 1830 Indian Removal Act, requiring the Cherokee (among other tribes) to relocate west of the Mississippi River. Despite significant public pressure to let them remain, and despite a victory in the U.S. Supreme Court, President Andrew Jackson forced the Indians out. When a small minority of Cherokees signed the Treaty of New Echota, ceding the tribe's last remaining eastern lands, local non-natives immediately began appropriating the Indians' land and plundering their homes and possessions. Indians were forced into internment camps, where many died, although over 1,000 escaped to the mountains of North Carolina, where they became the progenitors of what came to be called the Eastern Band of Cherokees.

Sequoyah is credited with devising a Cherokee syllabary in 1821 and thus providing his people with a written language.

The removal, known as the Trail of Tears, began in 1838. The Indians were forced to walk 1,000 miles through severe weather without adequate food and clothing. About 4,000 Cherokees, almost a quarter of the total, died during the removal, and more died once the people reached the Indian Territory, where they joined—and largely absorbed—the group already there. Following their arrival in Indian Territory, the Cherokees quickly adopted another constitution and reestablished their institutions and facilities, including newspapers and schools. Under Chief John Ross, most Cherokees supported slavery and also supported the Confederate cause in the Civil War.

The huge "permanent" Indian territory was often reduced in size. When the northern region was removed to create the states of Kansas and Nebraska, Indians living there were again forcibly resettled. One result of the Dawes Act (late 1880s) was the "sale" (virtual appropriation) of roughly two million acres of Indian land in Oklahoma. Oklahoma became a territory in 1890 and a state in 1907. Although the Cherokees and other tribes resisted allotment, Congress forced them to acquiesce in 1898. Their land was individually allotted in 1902, at about the same time their native governments were officially "terminated."

Ten years after the Cherokee removal, the U.S. Congress ceased efforts to round up the Eastern Cherokee. The Indians received state (North Carolina) citizenship in 1866 and incorporated as the Eastern Band of Cherokee Indians in 1889. In the early twentieth century, many Eastern Cherokees were engaged in subsistence farming and in the local

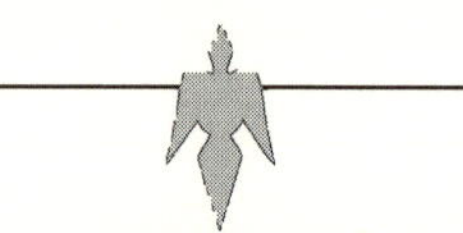

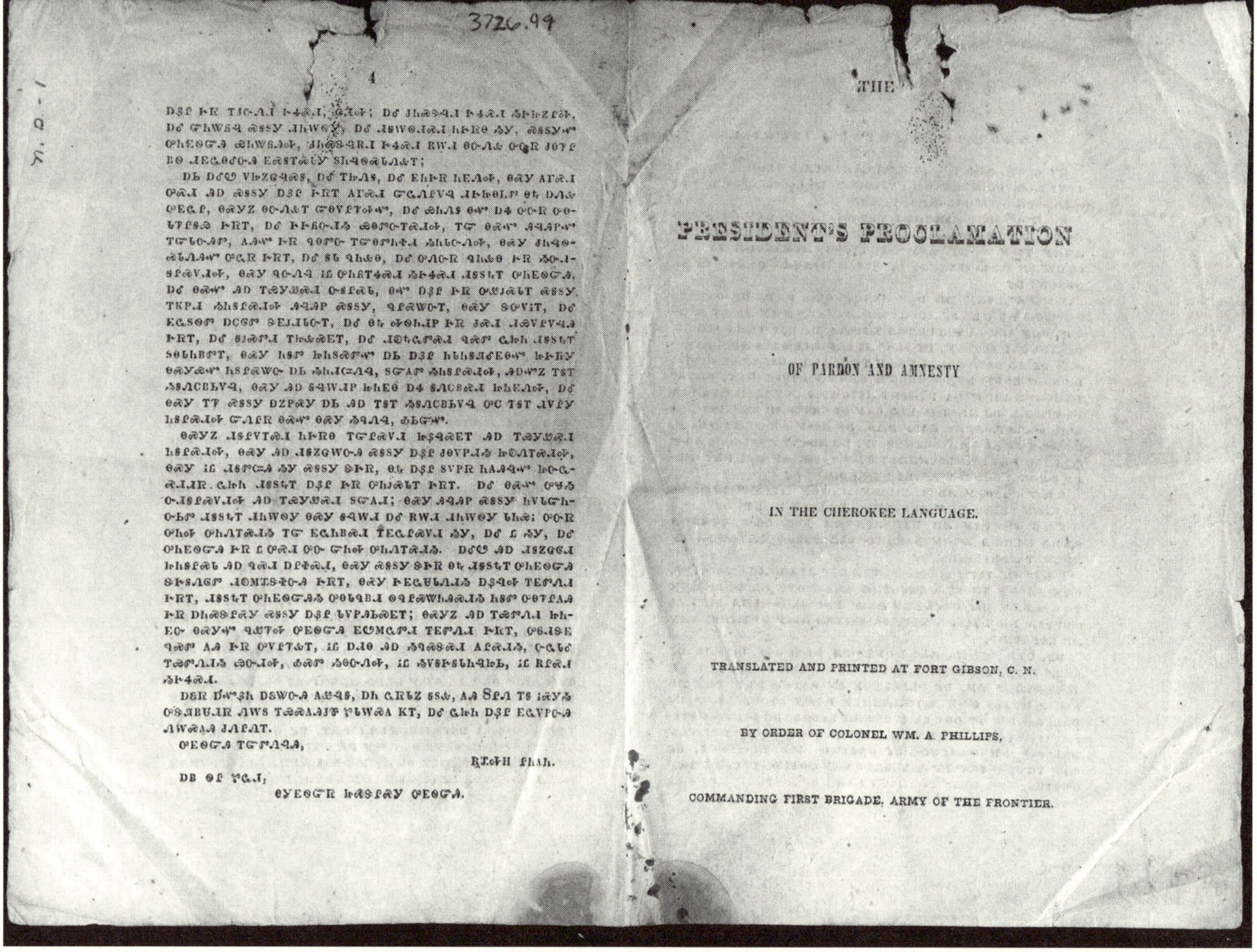

THE

PRESIDENT'S PROCLAMATION

OF PARDON AND AMNESTY

IN THE CHEROKEE LANGUAGE.

TRANSLATED AND PRINTED AT FORT GIBSON, C. N.

BY ORDER OF COLONEL WM. A. PHILLIPS,

COMMANDING FIRST BRIGADE, ARMY OF THE FRONTIER.

Most Cherokees supported slavery as well as the Confederate cause in the Civil War. This is a Cherokee translation of President Abraham Lincoln's pardon and offer of amnesty to the Indians who fought with the Confederate army during the Civil War.

timber industry. Having resisted allotment, the tribe took steps to ensure that it would always own its land. Although the Cherokee suffered greatly during the Depression, the Great Smoky Mountain National Park (1930s) served as the center of a growing tourist industry.

In the 1930s, the United Keetoowah Band (UKB), a group of full-bloods opposed to assimilation, formally separated from the Oklahoma Cherokees. The group originated in the antiallotment battles at the end of the nineteenth century. In the early twentieth century the UKB reconstructed several traditional political structures, such as the seven clans and white towns, as well as some ancient cultural practices that did not survive the move west. The name Keetoowah derives from an ancient town in western North Carolina. They received federal recognition in 1946.

Religion The tribe's chief deity was the sun, which may have had a feminine identity. The people conceived of the cosmos as being divided into an upper world, this world, and a lower world. Each contained numerous spiritual beings that resided in specific places. The four cardinal directions were replete with social significance. Tribal mythology, symbols, and beliefs were complex, and there were also various associated taboos, customs, and social and personal rules.

Many ceremonies revolved around subsistence activities as well as healing. The primary one was the

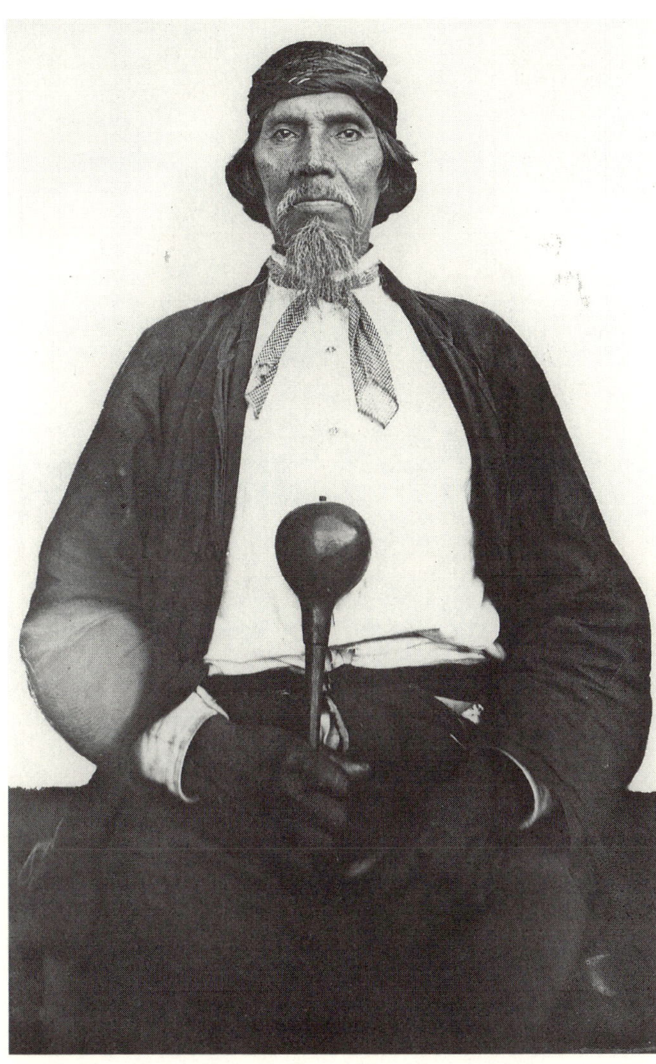

Ayyuini (Swimmer), a Cherokee medicine man (1902). Medicine people were curers, conjurers, diviners, wizards, and witches. They could, by magical means, influence events and the lives and fortunes of people.

annual Green Corn ceremony (Busk), observed when the last corn crop ripened. Shamans were religious leaders and curers. The people thought of disease as being caused by dreams or animals, real or mythical. Cures consisted of herbal treatments, sweats, changes in diet, deep scratching, rubbing, and spiritual remedies.

Medicine people (men and women) were curers, conjurers, diviners, wizards, and witches. They could, by magical means, influence events and the lives and fortunes of people. Witches, when discovered, were summarily killed. Learning sorcery took a lifetime. Medicine powers could be used for good or evil, and the associated beads, crystals, and formulas were a regular part of many people's lives.

Government The various Cherokee villages formed a loose confederacy. There were two chiefs per village: a red, or war, chief, and a white chief (Most Beloved Man or Woman), who was associated with civil, economic, religious, and juridical functions. The red chief was also in charge of lacrosse games. Chiefs could be male or female, and there was little or no hereditary component. There was also a village council, in which women sat, although usually only as observers. Its powers were fairly limited. The Cherokee were not a cohesive political entity until the late eighteenth century at the earliest.

Customs Men played intraclan lacrosse and chunkey. They also held athletic races and competitions. Lacrosse had serious ceremonial aspects and accompanying rituals, including dances and certain taboos. There were seven matrilineal clans in the early historic period. Cherokees regularly engaged in ceremonial purification, and they paid careful attention to their dreams.

Both men and women, married and single, enjoyed a high degree of sexual freedom. Divorce was possible; men who were thrown out returned to their mothers. Pregnant women were expected to pray and bathe every new moon for several months prior to delivery. Babies were bathed every morning, and young children bathed every morning for at least the first two years. Twins were accorded special treatment and were often raised to be wizards. Children were treated gently, and they behaved with decorum. In general, Cherokees, valuing harmony as well as generosity, tried to avoid conflict.

Intraclan, but not interclan, murder was a capital offense. Names were changed or added to frequently. As with chiefs, towns may also have been considered red and white. Women owned the houses and their contents; this custom, along with matrilineal descent and the clan system, weakened with increasing exposure to non-native society. Kinsmen avenged the death of their kinsmen, according to the law of retaliation.

People did not address each other directly. In place of public sanctions, Cherokees used ostracism and public scorn to enforce social norms. Burial with possessions took place in the earth or under piles of stone.

For the Cherokee, lacrosse had serious ceremonial aspects and accompanying rituals, including dances and certain taboos. Pictured in this 1889 photograph is the Cherokee Ballplayers' Dance on Qualla Reservation in North Carolina. In the ceremony before the game, the women's dance leader (left) beats a drum and the men's dance leader (right) shakes a gourd rattle. The ballplayers, carrying ball sticks, circle counterclockwise around the fire.

Dwellings Towns were located along rivers and streams. They contained a central ceremonial place and in the early historic period were often surrounded by palisades. People built rectangular summer houses of pole frames and wattle, walls of cane matting and clay plaster, and gabled bark or thatch roofs. The houses, about 60 or 70 feet by 15 feet, were often divided into three parts: a kitchen, a dining area, and bedrooms. Some were two stories high, with the upper walls open for ventilation. There was probably one door. Beds were made of rush mats over wood splints, and animal skins served as bedding.

Smaller, circular winter houses (which also served as sweat houses) were simply 20-foot-high pole-and-earth cones placed over pits. Cherokees also built domed town/council/ceremonial houses and seven-sided temples, the latter located on raised mounds in the village plaza, of earth over a post-and-beam frame. Some were large enough to hold 500 people. Tiered interior seats surrounded a center fire.

Diet Cherokees were primarily farmers. Women grew corn (three kinds), beans, squash, sunflowers, and tobacco, the latter used ceremonially. Corn was roasted, boiled, and ground into flour and then baked into bread.

Wild foods included roots, crab apples, persimmons, plums, cherries, grapes, hickory nuts, walnuts, chestnuts, and berries. Men hunted various animals, including deer, bear, raccoon, rabbit, squirrel, turkey, and rattlesnake. They stalked deer using entire deerskins and deer calls. Hunting was preceded by the proper prayers and songs. Meat was broiled or boiled.

They fished occasionally, and they collected maple syrup in earthen pots and boiled it into syrup.

Key Technology Fish were caught using spears, weirs, poison, and the hook-and-line. Hunting gear included the bow and arrow, stone hatchet, and flint knife. Smaller animals and birds were shot with darts blown out of hollow 9- to 10-foot-long cane stems; these blowguns were accurate up to 60 feet.

Other material items included cane and root baskets; stone pipes on wooden stems; pottery of various sizes and shapes, often "stamped" with carved wooden designs; wooden medicine boxes; reed arrows with bone or fish-scale points attached with deer sinew; and drums, flutes, and gourd rattles. Ovens were a hot, flat stone covered with an inverted dish.

Trade Cherokee pipes were widely admired and easily exported. The people also traded maple sugar and syrup. They imported shell wampum that was used as money.

Notable Arts Plaited cane baskets, pottery, and masks carved of wood and gourds were especially fine. Pipes and moccasins may have been decorated with porcupine quills.

Transportation Men built 30- to 40-foot-long canoes of fire-hollowed pine or poplar logs. Each canoe could hold between 15 and 20 people. The people may also have used bark canoes.

Dress Women made most clothing of buckskin and other skins and furs as well as of mulberry bark fibers. Men wore breechclouts; women wore skirts. In winter, both wore bear or buffalo robes. Men also wore shirts and leggings, and women wore capes. Both sexes wore moccasins as well as nose ornaments, bracelets, and body paint. Men wore their hair in a roach; women wore it long. There were also ceremonial turkey and eagle feather headdresses and capes. Men slit their ears and stretched them with the use of copper wires.

War and Weapons Each village had a red (war) chief as well as a War Woman, who accompanied war parties. She fed the men, gave advice, and determined the fate of prisoners. Women also distinguished themselves in combat and often tortured prisoners of war. Cherokee enemies over time included the Catawba, Shawnee, Congaree, Tuscarora, Creek, and Iroquois. They were often allied with the Chickasaw. Weapons included the bow and arrow, knife, tomahawk, and darts, or short lances. The people often painted themselves, as well as their canoes and paddles, for war. The party carried an ark or medicine chest to war, and it left a war club engraved with its exploits in enemy territory.

Contemporary Information

Government/Reservations Cherokee Tribal Headquarters is located in Tahlequah, Oklahoma. As of the early 1990s there were more than 122,000 enrolled members of the Cherokee Nation. The 61,000-plus acres of tribal land is not a reservation but an administrative entity. Governmental leaders have been popularly elected since the 1970s. The tribe adopted a new constitution in 1975 that mandates a tripartite form of government.

The Qualla Boundary Cherokee Reservation, established in 1874, is located in western North Carolina. The enrolled population in 1990 was almost 10,000, nearly two-thirds of whom lived on tribal lands. The group owns more than 56,000 acres of land in North Carolina, mostly in Jackson and Swain Counties, and more than 76 acres in eastern Tennessee. Individuals hold title to most of this land, but they may transfer it only to other tribal members. Tribal government is composed of executive (three offices, two of which are elected), legislative (popularly elected tribal council), and judicial branches. As part of its responsibilities as a trustee for tribal lands, the U.S. government manages schools, lands, and public health.

The United Keetoowah Band is located in northeastern Oklahoma. It is governed by a tribal council. There were 7,450 members in the early 1990s. As they are legally unable to obtain a land base within the Cherokee Nation, they are currently seeking one elsewhere.

Economy Important economic activities include oil and gas sales and leases, arts and crafts, bingo, a utility company, and ranching, poultry, and woodcutting operations. In the early 1990s, the tribe

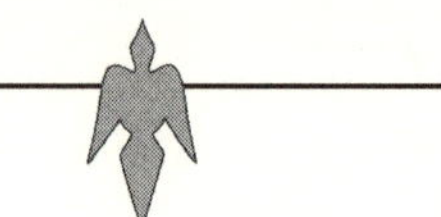

was generating about half of its annual operating budget of over $65 million. It also anticipated payments from the settlement of disputed control of resources under the Arkansas riverbed, but this situation is still being argued, and no settlement has been achieved.

In North Carolina there are a craft factory, a lumber business, tourist enterprises, and numerous other businesses. People work seasonally in non-native tourist enterprises.

Legal Status The Eastern Band of Cherokee Indians, the Cherokee Nation of Oklahoma, and the United Keetoowah Band are federally recognized tribal entities. More than 50 other groups in 12 states also claim Cherokee identity.

Daily Life Oklahoma and North Carolina Cherokees stage an annual presentation for tourists. Since the 1970s, two people, Ross Swimmer and Wilma Mankiller, have dominated Cherokee tribal politics. In Oklahoma, there is some division between rural "conservatives" and "progressives," who tend to be wealthier and more urban. Most people are Christians. Many live in fairly isolated hill communities. Of the three Cherokee dialects, the Atali (Overhill) is still spoken in Oklahoma by about 13,000 people and another (the Middle, or Kituhwa) in North Carolina by about 1,000 people, primarily in religious services. In the 1990s, the Cherokee Nation adopted its own tax code as well as various self-governance mechanisms. Its major celebrations are held over Labor Day weekend. The Keetoowah Society (or the Nighthawk Keetoowas) closely adheres to traditional religious practice.

Eastern Cherokees have created a vibrant, economically stable community secure in its Indian identity. Most of their high school students attend college. There are various celebrations in the fall that feature traditional games and dancing. Facilities include a reproduced ancient village and a museum. The people still speak the language and still practice traditional medicine. The Eastern Band and the Cherokee Nation meet in joint council every two years. The UKB continues to resist reintegration into the Cherokee Nation. They conduct their own cultural activities.

Chickasaw

Chickasaw (`Chi kə sä), a Muskogean name referring to the act of sitting down. The Chickasaw were culturally similar to the Choctaw. Along with the Cherokee, Choctaw, Creek and Seminole, the Chickasaw were one of the so-called Five Civilized Tribes.

Location Chickasaws traditionally lived in northeastern Mississippi as well as northern Alabama, eastern Arkansas, western Kentucky, western Tennessee, and throughout the Mississippi Valley. Many Chickasaws now live in southern Oklahoma.

Population There were about 5,000 Chickasaws in 1600. In the mid-1990s, roughly 26,000 people identified themselves as Chickasaw.

Language Chickasaw is a Muskogean language.

Historical Information

History The Chickasaw may once have been united with the Choctaw. The people encountered Hernando de Soto in 1541. At first welcoming, as their customs dictated, they ultimately attacked the Spanish when the latter tortured some of them and tried to enslave others.

In the late seventeenth and early eighteenth centuries, warfare increased with neighboring tribes as the Chickasaw expanded their already large hunting grounds to obtain more pelts and skins for the British trade. Increasingly dependent on this trade, they did not shrink from capturing other Indians, such as the Choctaws, and selling them to the British as slaves. In general, the Chickasaws' alliance with the British during the colonial period acted as a hindrance to French trade on the Mississippi.

Constant warfare with the French and their Choctaw allies during the eighteenth century sapped the people's vitality. In part to compensate, they began absorbing other peoples, such as several hundred Natchez as well as British traders. A pattern began to emerge in which descendants of British men and Chickasaw women (such as the Colbert family) became powerful tribal leaders. Missionaries began making significant numbers of converts during that time.

Tribal allegiance was divided during the American Revolution, with some members supporting one side, some the other, and some neither. The overall goal was to preserve traditional lands. The tribe did not rally behind Tecumseh in 1809 (*see* Shawnee entry in Chapter 8). With game growing scarce, many Chickasaws became exclusively farmers during the early to mid–nineteenth century. Some also began cotton plantations, and the tribe owned up to 1,000 African American slaves during that period. By 1830 they had a written code of laws (which banned whiskey) and a police force.

As non-native settlement of their lands increased during the 1820s, many Chickasaws migrated west, ceding land in several treaties (1805, 1816, 1818) during the period. Finally they ceded all lands east of the Mississippi in 1832. Roughly 3,000 Chickasaws were forcibly removed to Indian Territory (Oklahoma) after 1837, where many died of disease, hunger, and attacks by Plains Indians who resented the intrusion. The Chickasaw fared somewhat better than did the Cherokee, being able to purchase many supply items, including riverboat transportation, with tribal funds. Most settled in the western part of Choctaw lands.

Survivors of the ordeal resumed farming and soon, with the help of their slaves, grew a surplus of crops. However, as a tribe the people had lost most of their aboriginal culture. Their own reservation and government were formally established in 1855 and lasted until Oklahoma statehood in 1907. In the years before the Civil War, the people operated schools, mills, and blacksmith shops, and they had started a newspaper. Chickasaws fought for the Confederacy in the Civil War. Unlike some other Oklahoma tribes of southeast origin, the Chickasaw never adopted their freed slaves.

Their lands were allotted around 1900. All tribal governments in Oklahoma were dissolved by Congress in 1906. By 1920, of the roughly 4.7 million acres of preallotment Chickasaw land, only about 300 remained in tribal control, a situation that severely hampered tribal political and economic development well into the century. Many prominent twentieth-century Oklahoma politicians were mixed-blood Chickasaws. From the 1940s on, individuals received payments from the sale of land containing coal and asphalt deposits.

Religion The supreme deity was *Ababinili,* an aggregation of four celestial beings: Sun, Clouds, Clear Sky, and He That Lives in the Clear Sky. Fire, especially the sacred fire, was a manifestation of the supreme being. Rattlesnakes were also greatly revered, and the people recognized many other lesser gods as well as evil spirits.

Two head priests, or *hopaye,* presided over ceremonies and interpreted spiritual matters. They wore special clothing at such times. Healers *(aliktce),* who combated evil spirits by using various natural substances, and witches were two types of spiritual people. Men painted their faces for ceremonies. People used charms and observed various food taboos.

Government Political leadership was chosen in part according to hereditary claim but also according to merit. The head chief, chosen from the Minko clan, was known as the High Minko. Each clan also had a chief. There was also a council of advisers, which included clan leaders and tribal elders. The fundamental units were local groups.

Customs Key Chickasaw values included hospitality and generosity, especially to those in need. Two divisions were in turn divided into many ranked matrilineal clans. The people played lacrosse, chunkey, and other games, most of which included gambling and had important ritual components. Tobacco was used ritually and medicinally. Murder was subject to retaliation. Chickasaws liked to dance, both on social and religious occasions.

Boys were toughened by winter plunges and special herbs. Women were secluded in special huts during their menstrual periods. There was some childhood betrothal. Marriage involved various gift exchanges, mainly food or clothing. A man might have more than one wife. Men avoided their mothers-in-law out of respect. In cases of adultery only the woman was punished, often by a beating or an ear or nose cropping. Chickasaws practiced frontal head deformation.

The dead were buried in graves under houses, along with their possessions, after an elaborate funeral rite. They were placed in a sitting position facing west, with their faces painted red. After death they were only vaguely alluded to and never directly by name.

All social activities ceased for three days following a death in the village. Chickasaws maintained the concept of a heaven generally in the west, the direction of witchcraft and uneasy spirits.

Dwellings Chickasaws built their villages on high ground near stands of hardwood trees. They were often palisaded and more compact during periods of warfare.

Rectangular summer houses were of pole-frame construction, notched and lashed, and clapboard sides, with gabled roofs covered with cypress or pine-bark shingles. They were whitewashed in and out with powdered oyster shell or white clay. Outside materials included grass or cane thatch, bark, and hide. A small doorway, usually facing east, offered protection against insects. The people also built several outbuildings for fowl, corn, sweating, and other purposes.

Winter houses were semiexcavated and circular, about 25 feet in diameter, with a narrow, 4-foot-high door. They were plastered with at least 6 inches of clay and dried grass. Bark shingles or thatch covered conical roofs with no smoke holes. Furniture included couches and raised wood-frame beds, under which food was stored. Town houses or temples were of similar construction.

Diet Crops—corn, beans, squash, and sunflowers—were the staple foods. Corn was made into a variety of foods, including an unfermented drink. Men also hunted buffalo, deer, bear, and numerous kinds of small game, including rabbits but probably not beaver or opossum. Hunting techniques included shooting, trapping, and using animal calls and decoys. Birds and their eggs were included in the diet.

Women gathered nuts, acorns, honey, onions, persimmons, strawberries, grapes, and plums. Tea was made from sassafras root. Chickasaws ate a variety of fish, including the huge (up to 200 pounds) Mississippi catfish.

Key Technology Earthen pots of various sizes and shapes served a number of purposes. Men stunned fish with buckeye or green walnut poison. Women wove mulberry bark in a frame and used the resulting textile in floor and table coverings. Other material items included stone axes, fire drills, wooden mortars, and various cane baskets, some of which could hold water. Musical instruments included drums (wet skins over clay pots), gourd rattles, and flutes.

Trade Chickasaws traded as far away as Texas and perhaps even Mexico. Among other items, they traded deerskins for conch shell to use as wampum. Vermilion may have been counted as a basis of wealth.

Notable Arts Cloth items (from woven mulberry inner bark) were decorated with colorful animal and human figures and other designs. The people also made exceptional dyed and decorated cane baskets.

Transportation Men hollowed dugout canoes out of hardwood trees. Caddo Indians brought horses in from the Red River region; some were also stolen from the early Spanish. Eventually, the Chickasaw developed a horse breed of their own. Some chiefs may have been carried in litters.

Dress Most clothing was made of deerskin, although other hides, including beaver, were also used. Wild mulberry bark formed material for items of "cloth." Men wore breechclouts, with deerskin shirts and bearskin robes in cold weather. Most kept their hair in a roach soaked in bear grease. There were also high boots for hunting. Women wore long dresses and added buffalo robes or capes in winter. They tended to tie up their hair.

People generally went barefoot, although they did make moccasins of bear hide and occasionally elk skin. Women made turkey feather blankets. Some young men slit their ears and expanded them with the use of copper wire. Other personal ornamentation included nose rings, head bracelets, and body paint.

War and Weapons Chickasaws were known as fierce, enthusiastic, and successful warriors. Their enemies included the Choctaw and the Caddo. In the early eighteenth century, the Chickasaws joined with the Cherokee to drive the Shawnees from the Cumberland Valley, but they often fought the Cherokee as well.

Raiding parties usually consisted of between 20 and 40 men, their faces painted for war. They engaged

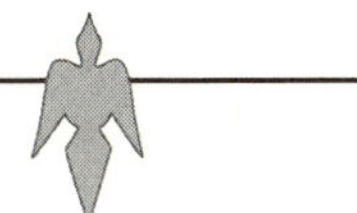

in ritual preparation before they departed as well as ritual celebration, which might include the bestowal of new war names, upon their return. Weapons included bows and (sometimes flaming) arrows, knives, clubs, spears, tomahawks, and shields. The party carried along a sacred war ark, or medicine bundle. Particularly respected warriors were tattooed, usually with the picture of an animal.

Contemporary Information

Government/Reservations Over 9,000 Chickasaws (mid-1990s) lived in a 13-county area in southern Oklahoma. Their headquarters is located in Ada, Oklahoma. Congress granted the right in 1970 to elect their own leadership. A 1983 constitution provides for a tripartite government, including a 13-member legislature. The Chickasaw Nation's land base, held in trust, is about 77,600 acres.

Economy With a $15 million annual budget (1990), the Chickasaw Nation itself provides many employment opportunities. It owns recreational parks, tobacco shops, and bingo parlors. There is some industrial development. Payments are anticipated from the settlement of disputed control of resources under the Arkansas riverbed, but this situation is still being argued, and no settlement has been achieved. In the early 1990s, roughly 20 percent of Chickasaw families in Oklahoma were living below the poverty line.

Legal Status The Chickasaw Nation is a federally recognized tribal entity.

Daily Life Most Chickasaws are Methodists or Baptists. About 500 mostly older people still speak the language, which is taught with the aid of a dictionary. Tribal celebrations, especially the annual festival in September/October, feature traditional foods such as cracked corn and pork, corn grits, and poke greens. There is a tribal museum and library, as well as a tribal newspaper, the *Chickasaw Times*. The Nation controls its own schools.

Chitimacha

Chitimacha (Chi ti `mä chä or Shi ti `mä shä) may have meant "those living on Grand River," "those who have pots," or "men altogether red." They may have comprised three or four separate tribes in the early sixteenth century.

Location The Chitimacha traditionally lived along the lower Louisiana coast, especially around Grand Lake, Grand River, and Bayou Teche. Today, most live in St. Mary Parish, Louisiana.

Population From about 3,000 people in 1700, the population dropped to 51 in the 1930 census. There were 720 enrolled members in the early 1990s.

Language Chitimacha may be an isolate, or it may be related to Tunican.

Historical Information

History Resident in their historic area for at least 2,500 years, the Chitimacha may have migrated south from the region of Natchez at some early time and east from Texas still earlier. Their decline began with the French arrival in the late seventeenth century. French slaving among the Indians created a generally hostile climate between the two peoples, especially in the early eighteenth century. Peace was established in 1718, but by then the Chitimacha population had suffered great losses through warfare and disease. Survivors were forcibly relocated north or taken away as slaves.

The influx of French Acadians in the late eighteenth century led to intermarriage (with Acadians as well as with other surviving local Indian groups), further land thefts, and the increased influence of Catholicism. In 1917, the Indians' remaining land base was privately purchased and sold to the United States. Throughout the twentieth century, chiefs have continued to govern the people and struggle to retain tribal land and sovereignty.

Religion Chitimachas recognized a sky god, possibly feminine in nature. Boys and girls sought and obtained guardian spirits through solitary quests. Priests oversaw religious life. A 12-foot-square temple on Grand Lake served as a center of religious activity, especially for the annual six-day midsummer festival. The main event here was the male adult initiation

ceremony, during which the young men fasted and danced until exhausted.

Government There was a chief in each town and a subchief in each village; leadership was largely hereditary. Head chiefs possessed a large measure of authority and power and were fed, at least in part, by others.

Customs Among the different social classes, priests, headmen, and curers constituted a nobility. There may also have been clans. Women might obtain any religious or political position. The dead may have been laid on scaffolds, where special people (Buzzard Men) disposed of flesh and returned cleaned bones to families, where they were eventually buried under mounds of earth. The Buzzard Men may instead have burned the bones and buried the ashes in a basket under a mound. A special ceremony was conducted at the reburial of war chiefs' bones. The people played chunkey and other games. They practiced frontal head deformation. A man became known by his child's name as soon as the latter was born.

Dwellings Village populations reached up to 500 in the early historic period. Pole-frame houses were covered with palmetto thatch. Smoke escaped through a hole in the roof. Walls were occasionally plastered with mud.

Diet The people ate bear, alligators, turtles (and their eggs), and deer, among other animals. They were highly dependent on fish and shellfish. Women grew sweet potatoes as well as beans, squash, sunflowers, and possibly four varieties of corn. They also gathered water lily seeds, palmetto seeds, nuts, and various wild fruits and berries.

Key Technology Men used blowguns as well as bows and arrows for hunting. They caught fish with nets, basket traps, and hooks and lines. Cane baskets with fitted tops were used, among other things, for food storage. Women wove cane matting with various colors (red, yellow, and black) and designs, and they made pottery. The people also used the fire drill, dried alligator skin rasps, and gourd rattles.

Trade Exports included fish and salt; imports, mainly from inland tribes, included flint, stone beads, and arrow points. They traded often with the Atakapa and the Avoyel Indians.

Notable Arts Patterned black-and-yellow cane baskets, made with a unique double weaving technique, were especially fine. Pottery was also of generally high quality.

Transportation Extensive canoe transportation was made easier by the natural harbor provided by Grand Lake.

Dress Nose ornaments, bracelets, and earrings were common personal adornments. Both sexes kept their fingernails long. Men wore their hair in roaches, or perhaps long, and decorated with feathers and lead weights.

War and Weapons The people may have poisoned their enemies. Warriors also used the bow and arrow. There were four or five war chiefs per village.

Contemporary Information

Government/Reservations The Chitimacha Reservation (1830) consists of roughly 250 acres in St. Mary Parish, Louisiana. There were 212 resident Indians in 1990. The tribe operates its own housing program and is governed by a council.

Economy Tribal enterprises include a processing plant, a store, and a recreation/museum complex. They also lease land to oil companies. Most people work in the oil or fishing industries. Some people make cane baskets as well as traditional and generic "Indian" jewelry for the tourist trade.

Legal Status The Chitimacha Tribe is a federally recognized tribal entity.

Daily Life The language no longer survives. There is a Bureau of Indian Affairs school in the reservation. Efforts continue to obtain compensation for land expropriations. The tribe supports ongoing training in traditional craft techniques. There is a tribal fair over the Fourth of July weekend.

Choctaw

Choctaw (`Chok tä or `Shok tä), originally Chahta. An early name for the tribe might have been *Pafallaya,* or "long hair." They were culturally related to the Chickasaws and Creeks. With the Cherokee, Chickasaw, Creek, and Seminole, they were regarded by whites as one of the Five Civilized Tribes.

Location In the sixteenth century, most Choctaws lived in southern and central Mississippi, as well as parts of Alabama, Georgia, and Louisiana. Today, most live in southeastern Oklahoma and east-central Mississippi.

Population There were probably between 15,000 and 20,000 Choctaws in the mid–sixteenth century. In 1984 almost 20,000 Choctaws lived in Oklahoma, and roughly 4,000 lived in Mississippi in 1990.

Language Choctaw is a Muskogean language.

Sam Folsom, a Choctaw. With the Cherokee, Chickasaw, Creek, and Seminole, the Choctaw were regarded by whites as one of the Five Civilized Tribes.

Historical Information

History Choctaws probably descended from Mississippian Temple Mound Builders. They may once have been united with the Chickasaw. Early encounters with the Spanish, starting with Hernando de Soto about 1540, were not peaceful, as de Soto generally burned Choctaw villages as he passed through the region.

The French established a presence in Choctaw territory in the late seventeenth century, and the two groups soon became important allies, although there was always a faction of Choctaws friendly to the British. Fighting along with the French and other Indian tribes, the Choctaws helped defeat the Natchez revolt of 1729. Bitter internal fighting around 1750 between French and British supporters was resolved generally in favor of the former.

Intertribal war continued with the Chickasaw and the Creek until in 1763 the French ceded all lands east of the Mississippi to Britain. Choctaws fought the Creeks even after that, until the United States took "possession" of greater "Louisiana" in the early nineteenth century. Small bands of Choctaws began settling in Louisiana in the late eighteenth century. At the same time, alcohol, supplied mainly by British traders, was taking a great toll on the people.

Largely under the influence of their leader, Pushmataha, the Choctaw refused to join the pan-Indian Tecumseh confederacy (*see* Shawnee [Chapter 8]). However, non-natives continued pushing into the Choctaws' territory. One strategy that non-natives used to gain Indian land was to encourage trade debt by offering unlimited credit. Under relentless pressure and threats, the Choctaw began ceding land in 1801. Although treaties usually called for an exchange of land, in practice the Indians seldom received the western land they were promised, in part because the United States traded land that was not the government's to give or that it had no intention of allowing the Indians to have.

By the 1820s, the Choctaw had adopted so many lifeways of the whites that the latter regarded them as a "civilized tribe." Nevertheless, and although the Choctaws had never fought the United States, President Andrew Jackson signed the Indian Removal Act of 1830, requiring the Choctaw and other southeast tribes to leave their homelands and relocate west of the Mississippi. A small minority of unrepresentative Choctaws signed the Treaty of

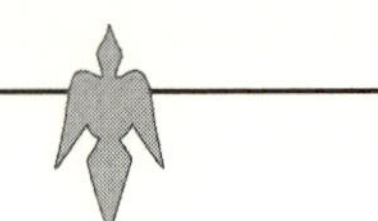

Dancing Rabbit Creek, ceding all of their land in Mississippi, over 10 million acres. Articles in the treaty providing for Choctaws to remain in Mississippi were so full of loopholes that most of those who did so were ultimately dispossessed. At the same time, the state of Mississippi formally made the Indians subject to state laws, thus criminalizing tribal governments.

Removal of roughly 12,000 Choctaws took place between 1831 and 1834. Terrible conditions on this forced march of several hundred miles caused about a quarter of the Choctaws to die of fatigue, heartbreak, exposure, disease, and starvation. Many more died once they reached the Indian Territory (Oklahoma). Roughly 3,000–5,000 Choctaws escaped to the back country rather than join the removal. Many of these people were removed in the 1840s, but some remained. Although they continued living as squatters in a semitraditional manner, their condition declined. Officially illegal, they were plied with alcohol and relentlessly cheated, and they became disheartened.

The bulk of the people reestablished themselves out west and prospered in the years before the Civil War, with successful farms, missionary schools, and a constitutional government. Most Choctaws fought for the Confederacy; the war was a disaster for them and the other tribes. A relatively high percentage of Indians died in the war, and further relocations and dispossessions followed the fighting. After the war, the Choctaw paid for the removal of African Americans living on their territory, although most were eventually adopted into the tribe.

In the last two decades of the nineteenth century, the General Allotment Act and the Curtis Act were passed over the opposition of the tribes. These laws deprived Oklahoma Indians, including the Choctaw, of most of their land. The "permanent" Indian Territory became the state of Oklahoma in 1907 (the name "Oklahoma," a Muskogean word for "Red People," was introduced by a Choctaw Indian), at which time the independent Choctaw Nation became subject to U.S. control. The tribe spent decades attempting to reassert control over its institutions.

After the Reconstruction period, the Mississippi and Louisiana Choctaws lived by sharecropping, subsistence hunting, some wage labor, and selling or bartering herbs and handicrafts. Their community and traditions were kept alive in part by the retention of their language and their rural isolation, both from Euro-Americans, who branded them nonwhite, and African Americans, with whom the Choctaw refused to identify.

The government finally recognized the Mississippi Choctaw in the early twentieth century, and the Bureau of Indian Affairs began providing services, such as schools and a hospital, during the 1920s and 1930s. It began purchasing land for them as well. Reservations were created in 1944, and the tribe adopted a constitution and by-laws in 1945. Educational and employment opportunities remained severely limited until the 1960s owing to the Mississippi's Jim Crow policies.

Religion Choctaws worshipped the sun and fire as well as a host of lesser deities and beings. They celebrated the Green Corn ceremony and other festivals, mainly in late summer and fall.

Government Three or four districts were each headed by a chief and a council. Also, each town had a lesser chief and a war chief. The power of these chiefs was relatively limited, and the Choctaw were among the most democratic of all southeastern Indians. Although there was no overall head chief, a national council did meet on occasion.

Customs The people placed a high priority on peace and harmony. Lacrosse, played with deerskin balls and raccoon-skin-thong stick nets, was a huge spectator sport as well as a means for settling disputes. Rituals and ceremonies began days before a game. There was always gambling; sometimes the stakes included a person's net worth. Players were assisted by shamans who tried to use spiritual power in the service of their team. Games could be quite dangerous, as they were played with few rules regarding physical contact. There were both male and female teams. The people also played chunkey and other games of chance.

Women adulterers were severely punished; some contributed to a class of prostitutes. Both men and women observed food taboos when a child was born. Infants' heads were generally shaped at birth. Maternal uncles taught and disciplined boys. At puberty, boys were tattooed, and some wore bear

claws through their noses. Homosexuality was accepted.

Corpses were wrapped in skins and placed on a scaffold along with items the deceased might need, including food and drink, on the way to the land of the dead. Their skulls were painted red. A dog or, later, a pony might be killed to accompany the person in the afterlife. A ritual mourning or crying time took place at designated periods throughout the day. Paid mourners were also used. A person's house was burned and the possessions sold. After some one to six months, special bone pickers scraped the bones clean with long fingernails, disposed of any remaining flesh, and then placed the bones in a coffin that they returned to the family. Periodically, the people of each village buried their people's bones under mounds.

The tribe was organized into two divisions. Many people wrote music and poetry; new songs were often introduced at festivals. Names often referred to the weather. Healing techniques included bleeding and cupping. Both men and women used herbal and plant remedies to cure illness, many of which were quite effective. Doctors also chanted, danced, and used magical formulas.

Dwellings Perhaps 100 or more Choctaw villages (summer and winter) existed in the seventeenth century. Border towns, especially in the northeast, were generally fortified, whereas interior towns were more spread out. Towns, which were groups of villages and houses surrounded by farms, usually contained a public game/ceremonial area.

Men built pole-frame houses roofed with grass or cane-reed thatch and walled with a number of materials, including crushed shell, hide, bark (often pine or cypress), and matting. Doors may have faced south. Summer houses were oblong or oval with two smoke holes. The winter houses were circular and insulated with clay. Water poured over hot rocks provided steam for internal moisture.

Diet Choctaws farmed bottomland fields along the lower Mississippi. They often realized food surpluses. Women, with the assistance of men, grew corn, beans, squash, sunflowers, tobacco, and later potatoes and melon. Also, in the eighteenth century they grew leeks, garlic, cabbage, and other garden produce, the latter strictly for trade. Corn was also made into bread, as was sweet potato seed.

Large game, such as buffalo, deer, and bear (killed mainly for their fat), were particularly important when the harvest was poor. Men hunted deer with decoys and costumes. Small game included squirrel, turkey, beaver, otter, raccoon, opossum, and rabbit. Other foods included birds' eggs, fish, and wild fruits, nuts, seeds, and roots. Sassafras root was used for tea and as a thickener.

Key Technology Fields were cleared using slash-and-burn technology. People fished using spears, nets, stunning poison, and buffalo-hide traps. They carved bows, mortars, and stools of wood; made skin-covered gourd and horn pouches; and wove bags from twisted tree bark. Women wove and dyed baskets. Spun buffalo wool was also used as a fabric. Cane, another important raw material, was used for such items as knives, blowguns, darts, and baskets. Musical instruments included drums of skins stretched over hollowed logs, rattles, and rasps.

Trade Traders developed a regional trade language mixed with sign language for wide communication. They traded food, especially to the Chickasaw. In the eighteenth century this food included garden produce such as garlic, leeks, and cabbage; after the mid–eighteenth century it also included fowl and hogs. They imported soapstone pipes from the Minnesota quarries.

Notable Arts There were fine carvings on mortuary houses. Some of the dyed cane baskets were woven tight enough to hold water.

Transportation The people used carved dugout canoes sparingly. Horses arrived as early as the sixteenth century. In time, the Choctaw and other tribes developed their own breeds.

Dress Choctaws followed the general southeastern dress of deerskin breechclouts, skirts, and tunics and buffalo or bear robes and turkey-feather blankets for warmth. Some women made their skirts of spun buffalo wool plus a plant fiber. Both men and women

A widely employed raw material, cane was used to make baskets and mats, arrows and darts, musical instruments, and many other items. This man is using a cane blowgun (1912). Used to hunt smaller animals and birds, these blowguns were accurate up to 60 feet. Animals were shot with darts blown out of long, hollow cane stems.

wore long hair except, for men, in time of mourning. Both also tattooed their bodies.

War and Weapons The Choctaw partook less of war than did many of their neighbors, although they did not shirk from defensive fighting. Above all, they did not value victory bought with many of their own dead. Weapons included bow and arrow, knives, clubs, hatchets, and shields. They fought the Chickasaw in the early historical period. Any captured property was divided completely among families who had lost warriors in that battle. Adult captives were regularly burned; others were enslaved. Men tattooed records of war feats on their bodies. Warriors celebrated pre- and postwar rituals.

Contemporary Information

Government/Reservations The Choctaw Nation is located in ten counties in Oklahoma. Their headquarters is in Durant, and their capital in Tuskahoma. The land base is roughly 145,000 acres.

The Mississippi Choctaw Reservation (17,819 acres, almost all tribally owned) was established in 1830. The Mississippi Band of Choctaw communities include Bogue Chitto, Bogue Homa, Conehatta, Pearl River, Redwater, Standing Pine, and Tucker, Mississippi. The reservation and trust lands are located in Attala, Jackson, Jones, Kemper, Leake, Neshoba, Newton, Scott, and Winston Counties. The band manages over 500 housing units. The 1990 Indian population was roughly 4,000 of an enrolled

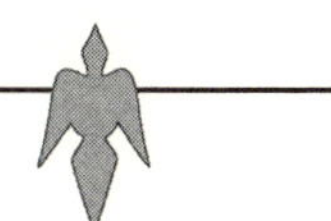

membership of roughly 8,000. The tribal government consists of an elected chief and council.

The Mowa Band of Choctaw Indians lives on roughly 300 acres in Mt. Vernon, Alabama. This community is governed by a tribal council.

Economy Oklahoma Choctaws will share with the Cherokee a settlement regarding riverbed resources of the Arkansas River, but this situation is still being argued, and no settlement has been achieved. Other resources include bingo, a finishing company, a factory (Texas Instruments), a travel center, and a cattle ranch.

The Mississippi Band organized a private stock company in 1969 to oversee economic development. The main natural resource is timber. Its projects have included several construction projects and an industrial park. Profits are reinvested in new projects. Other businesses include wire harness, electronics, and several other companies as well as a resort and casino.

Legal Status The Choctaw Nation of Oklahoma, the Jena Band of Choctaw (Louisiana), and the Mississippi Band of Choctaws are federally recognized tribal entities.

The Choctaw-Apache Community of Ebard, Louisiana, has petitioned for federal recognition. It is governed by a tribal council and maintains an officially recognized Indian school. The Clifton Choctaw Indians in Louisiana and the Mowa Band of Choctaws in Alabama have also petitioned for federal recognition. The Washington City Band of Choctaw Indians of Southern Alabama was denied federal recognition in 1998.

Daily Life In Oklahoma, most Choctaw children attend public school, although some attend Jones Academy, an Indian school. Most Oklahoma Choctaws are Baptists. The language survives, although mainly in hymns and dictionaries. The annual Labor Day festival features traditional foods, games, and dance. There is also a museum and a monthly newspaper, *Bishinik.*

The Mississippi Choctaws still play lacrosse. They also hold an annual fair. Many are Baptists. The language remains current, especially among older people. The tribe operates several schools, a small hospital, a radio station, and a monthly newspaper.

The Mowa Band of Choctaw Indians holds powwows and operates two schools.

Coushatta

See Alabama

Creek

Creek (Crēk), taken from Ochesee Creek, the British name for the Ocmulgee River. The so-called Creeks were actually composed of many tribes, each with a different name, the most powerful of which was called the Muskogee (or Mvskoke), itself a collection of tribes who probably migrated from the Northwest. With the Cherokee, Choctaw, Chickasaw, and Seminole, the Creeks became known by non-natives in the early nineteenth century as the Five Civilized Tribes.

The Creek Confederacy was a loose organization that united many Creek and non-Creek villages. Muskogee-speaking towns and tribes formed the core of the confederacy, although other groups joined as well. It was founded some time before 1540 but strengthened significantly in the seventeenth and eighteenth centuries. Tribes of the Creek Confederacy included the Alabama, Mikasuki, Yuchi, Shawnee, Natchez, Koasati, Tuskegee, Apalachicola, Okmulgee, Hitchiti, and Timucua, as well as many others. Through intermarriage or adoption, some of these people ultimately became part of Muskogee towns, whereas others, including escaped slaves and whites, lived among them as ethnic minorities.

Location Traditionally, Upper Creeks lived along the Coosa and Tallapoosa Rivers, in Alabama. Their two main towns were Tukabahchee and Abihkba. The Lower Creeks lived along the Flint and Chattahoochee Rivers in eastern Georgia and along the coast. Their main towns were Coweta and Kashita. Today, most Creeks live in east-central Oklahoma, with much smaller groups in Alabama and Florida.

Population There were perhaps 22,000 people in the Creek Confederacy in the mid–sixteenth century,

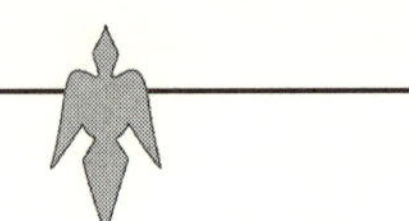

of whom roughly 80 percent were Muskogeans. In 1990 there were about 30,000 enrolled Creeks, over half of whom lived in Oklahoma.

Language Creeks spoke two principal Muskogean languages.

Historical Information

History Creek people probably descended from Mississippian Temple Mound Builders, entering their historic area from the west. Hernando de Soto passed through the region in 1540. In the colonial wars, Creeks were traditional allies of the British, although they were often successful in playing the European nations off against one another. Early on, the Creeks were grouped very informally into a "lower" section, located in eastern Georgia and more accommodating to Anglo society, and an "upper" section, more traditional and resistant to assimilation.

As British allies in the late seventeenth and early eighteenth centuries, the Creek fought the Spanish as well as other Indian tribes, such as the Apalachee, the Timucua, the Choctaw, and the Cherokee. They also absorbed some of the tribes they defeated in battle, such as part of the Apalachicola and the Apalachee about 1704. Creeks took part in the 1715 Yamasee war, as years of British abuse, including slaving, rape, and cheating, temporarily disrupted the Creek-British alliance. Following the Yamasee defeat, the bulk of the Creeks moved inland to the Chattahoochee River.

Creeks were more cautious about choosing sides in the French and Indian War and the American Revolution. Few favored the colonists, however, which was reason enough for the victors to demand land cessions after the fighting. In the late eighteenth century, the Creek leader Alexander McGillivray dominated the confederacy's diplomatic maneuvering and attempted to reorganize its political structure to his advantage. In 1790 he signed a treaty, later repudiated by the leaders of the confederacy, accepting U.S. protection and involvement in the people's internal affairs.

Many Creeks resisted joining Tecumseh's plan for a united Indian attack against the Americans, but in 1813 and 1814 they mounted their own military challenge. This was actually a civil war resulting from continuing diplomatic pressures and relentless encroachments from the Georgians as well as their own political and economic decline. The White Stick faction (mainly Lower Creeks) supported the United States and the Red Sticks the British. Despite early successes, the war was put down. As punishment, the Creeks, both Red and White, were made to sign the Treaty of Horseshoe Bend, ceding 23 million acres of land. Many Creeks migrated to Florida around that time to become part of the newly formed Seminole people.

In 1825, 13 chiefs ceded all remaining Creek lands to the state of Georgia. These chiefs were later condemned by their people for high treason, and two were shot. Although the treaty was illegal, the state of Georgia proceeded to act as if it owned the land, and the United States soon backed the state, calling for complete Indian removal. President Andrew Jackson signed the Indian Removal Act in 1830. Non-natives obtained the remaining Indian lands in the usual way: fraud, intimidation, and outright theft.

In 1832, Creeks signed the Treaty of Washington, ceding five million acres of land. Farcically, the treaty offered the Creeks a choice to remain or move and stated that white usurpers would be removed if the Indians chose to stay. In the mid-1830s, more Creeks joined the Seminoles in Florida while others made a last-ditch military stand. Forced relocation began in 1836. The Indians were taken to a place between the Canadian and the Arkansas Rivers. Of the roughly 14,000 who were relocated, almost 4,000 died of starvation, disease, exposure, and heartbreak during the march and shortly after their arrival in Indian Territory.

Once there, the people began to rebuild, accepting missionary schools and reestablishing towns, fields, and government. Christianization proceeded rapidly after removal. In 1856 the Creek lost over two million acres along the Canadian River to the Seminoles. Although the Creeks split in their allegiance during the Civil War, they suffered with the other Five Civilized Tribes, which had largely supported the South, and lost land, goods, crops, and political power.

The 1867 constitution of the Muskogee Nation reaffirmed the sovereignty of tribal towns and provided for a democratic governmental structure. Following the war, a full-blood, pronorthern,

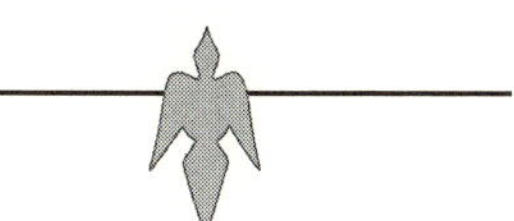

traditional faction that took a hard line on land cessions emerged, as did a moderate Muskogee Party and a number of other parties. Creeks also pressed for intertribal cooperation among Oklahoma tribes. Their land base was gradually whittled away until they lost all of it in 1907, as well as their political independence, when Oklahoma became a state.

From 1907 until 1970, the federal government recognized only the Creek Nation, an entity of the accommodationist Lower Creeks. Its principal chiefs were appointed by the U.S. government. Around 1900, an Upper Creek named Chitto Harjo (Crazy Snake) led a rebellion against allotment, the process that gave tribal holdings to individuals and made the "surplus" available for non-native purchase. In 1917, the Upper Creeks again took up arms as part of the Green Corn Rebellion, a movement of African Americans, Indians, and whites dedicated to obtaining federal help for the rural poor.

In the 1930s, three tribal towns, including the Alabama-Quassartes, opted out of the Creek Confederacy to accept charters under the Indian Reorganization Act. Many people left the Creek communities for cities during and after World War II. By 1970, 95 percent of preallotment tribal land was owned by non-natives, and non-natives held petroleum leases worth $50 billion. In 1970, a new law allowing for the democratic election of the principal chief gave rise to the Creek Nation of Oklahoma.

Religion The Green Corn ceremony, also called the Busk, marked the new year. It was both a thanksgiving ceremony and one of renewal. Some participants drank a black drink that was mainly caffeine and that induced vomiting when consumed in quantity; it was designed to purify the body. The ceremony also included dancing, fasting, feasting, games, and contests. It ended with a communal bath and an address from the head chief. Most crimes were forgiven at that time. Other ceremonies in spring and early summer included "stomp dances." Another group of feasts culminated in the late fall Dance of the Ancient People. Most dances were both social and ceremonial, and most councils and ceremonies began with the black drink (or "white drink," as they called it, reflecting its role in purification).

The supreme being, "master of breath," presided over the Land of the Blessed Dead. It received an offering of the first buck killed each season and also a morsel of flesh at each meal. Its representative on earth was the Busk fire. There were also many spiritual beings, particularly dwarfs, fairies, and giants. Priests and doctors underwent a rigorous training period that included healing techniques, songs, and formulas. Numerous diviners, weather control experts, and religious advisers claimed religious identity as well.

Government Tribal towns *(talwas)* were the main political unit. Each contained about 100 to over 1,000 people, and each was politically sovereign, the alliance among them determining the nature of the confederacy. Towns chiefs *(mikos)* were largely chosen by merit, although membership in a white clan was an advantage. The power of the chiefs was to influence (and to carry out certain duties), not to command. They were head of the democratic council, which had ceremonial and diplomatic responsibilities. Decisions were taken by consensus. There was also a subchief and a war chief. A town crier announced governmental decisions to the people.

The council met daily in the square ground or the town house. The people drank "black drink" and smoked tobacco before each important council meeting. Part of the council was a group of elders known as the Beloved Men. There were also Beloved Women, although women generally did not have formal power. Another council, composed of white clan members, oversaw internal public works affairs.

Customs A dual division within most tribes manifested itself in the existence of red towns and white towns. Red was associated with war, and white with peace. There were also about 40 matrilineal clans, unequal in prestige, with animal names. Clans were the fundamental social unit.

Lacrosse games were played between towns of different divisions, in part to relieve tensions. The many pregame ceremonies included preparations administered by medicine men. The goals were up to a quarter-mile apart; 60 or so people played on a side. Games were quite wide open and rough. They also had significant political and ritualistic significance. A great deal of personal wealth was often bet on games.

In addition to games, people participated in archery and other contests.

Unmarried women had considerable sexual freedom. There was also a class of prostitutes. Men could marry more than one wife. Marriage was formalized by gift giving, repeatedly in the case of multiple wives. Divorce was unusual, especially if there were children. Both parties were killed or punished in cases of adultery, unless they could escape punishment until the next Busk. Rape, incest, and witchcraft were capital offenses, as was nonseclusion during a woman's periods. Infanticide was permitted within the first month of life. Widows or divorcées were obligated to remain single for four years, but a widower could remarry in four months. Men generally avoided their mothers-in-law out of deference.

People bathed before eating. Women made pottery, baskets, mats, and other such items; prepared food and skins; made clothing; helped with the communal fields; and grew all the garden crops. Men also helped with the communal fields, and they hunted, fished, fought, played ball games, led ceremonies, built houses and other structures, and made tools. Men also carried skin pouches containing medicines, tobacco, and knives that hung by their sides. The dead were buried with their possessions beneath houses, in a sitting position and with reddened hair. Only the worthy could made it to the land of the dead, located beyond the Milky Way. Strict mourning rites were observed.

Dwellings Fifty towns, each with between 30 and 100 houses and located on river or creek banks, formed the original core of the confederacy. Each town was organized around a central square or plaza, which contained several features: a circular town (or hot) house at least 200 feet around, with 12-foot walls, a 12-foot roof, no windows, a small smoke hole, and beds around the walls; a game field; and a summer ceremonial house, or square ground.

The square ground was actually four sheds around a square of one-half acre or so, in the center of which was the sacred fire. The single-story buildings were about 30 feet long and roughly 25 feet high; they had clay walls and a gabled bark roof. Walls came within about 2 feet of the roof, for circulation, and the front was left open. Some of the sheds were divided into compartments, and they also had tiered benches or beds. Supporting timbers were often painted or carved with human and animal designs.

In cold or bad weather, the council met in the hot house, around a spiral-shaped or circular fire, and ceremonies were also celebrated here. In summer the square ground served these purposes. Both the hot house and the square ground were built atop mounds prior to the eighteenth century.

Private homes were clustered in groups of up to four. They were pole framed with plastered walls and grass or mats on the outside. Gabled roofs were covered with bark or shingles. Each reasonably prosperous family had a winter house and a summer house, both generally rectangular. A third structure was a two-story granary, one end of which was used for storing grain and roots (lower) and for meetings (upper). The other end, with open sides, was a general storage area (lower) and a reception area (upper). A fourth building, if one could afford it, was a storehouse for skins. The four buildings were placed to form a square, after the ceremonial square ground design.

Diet Crops—corn, beans, and squash—were the staples. Corn was consumed in many, perhaps over 40, different ways. The people had both private gardens and communal fields. Women gathered persimmons, nuts, sweet potatoes, wild rice, acorns, and grapes, among other foods. Nut oil was used in food preparation. Hunting was important for meat and skins. Most men left the villages during winter to hunt. Women often accompanied the hunting parties, mostly to attend to the meat and skins along the way. The people also ate fish.

Key Technology Hoes and digging sticks were the most important agricultural tools. Animals were shot, trapped, and snared. People fished with hook and lines, spears, bow and arrows, weirs, hand nets, baskets, and narcotic roots. Women made coiled pottery, wove mats, and spun material for clothing.

Other important technologies included the fire drill, steatite (soapstone) pipes and pots, flint points, and wooden and horn utensils. Bows were generally made of hickory, and arrows were pointed with fish

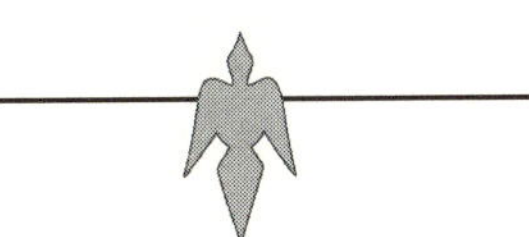

bones and flint. Blowguns, 8–10 feet long, were used mostly for shooting small animals and birds. Musical instruments included drums, flutes, and tortoise-shell ankle rattles. Bead belts may have served as records of events. Baskets and other items were made of cane.

Trade Creeks utilized the Choctaw trade language. Some groups exported flint and salt. Their pipes came from the Cherokee and Natchez, and/or they traded for catlinite pipes from the early eighteenth century on. In the early contact period, Creeks traded horses (obtained from Apalachee Indians) to British Carolinians for guns and other goods.

Notable Arts People in some towns carved figures of a nonreligious significance, perhaps to honor a dead warrior. A pictographic system represented historical events. Women made pottery, glazed with smoky pitch, and cane and hickory splint baskets.

Transportation Men made large cypress dugout canoes. Some early chiefs may have been carried on litters. Creek horses came from Mexico and the Spanish southeast; Lower Creeks had no horses until the eighteenth century.

Dress Creeks generally made a greater use of leggings than did many nearby peoples. Except on the Georgia coast, where they used tree moss, women made their clothes largely from skins and textiles. They also roached their hair. Only prostitutes painted their faces. Women sewed clothing with a bone awl and sinew thread. Skirts that reached below the knee were tied around the waist.

Men wore breechclouts and often leggings. Some young men wore nose ornaments and enlarged their ears with copper wire. Many men shaved their heads, except for two thin strips of hair running from temple to temple and straight down the top of the head. The hair at the ends was allowed to grow long. Some men wore moustaches. There were turkey feather cloaks for ceremonial purposes.

Both sexes wore buffalo- and deer-hide moccasins as well as extensive tattoos. Boys often went naked until puberty. Rank was reflected in clothing and adornment.

War and Weapons There were three levels of warriors: war chiefs, big warriors, and little warriors, depending on their level of accomplishment. Most fighting took place in spring. The purpose was generally honor and revenge. Men painted their bodies black and red for war. In addition to their weapons, they brought blankets, cordage, leather for moccasin repair, corn, and the sacred ark with them. Weapons included bow and arrow, knife, tomahawk, war club, spear, and shield. There were a number of pre- and postwar rituals.

A successful war party left signs to indicate who had done the deeds. Parties that resulted in the loss of many men, no matter how successful otherwise (captured horses, war honors, and so on) were considered failures. Enemies were often scalped and dismembered; those remaining alive might be enslaved or whipped and otherwise tortured by the women, unless they could escape. Enemies in the historic period included the Apalachee, Cherokee, and Choctaw.

Contemporary Information

Government/Reservations Headquarters for the Creek Nation of Oklahoma is in Okmulgee, Oklahoma. The land base encompasses roughly 143,384 acres, all held in trust, in eight counties of northeast Oklahoma.

The Kialegee Creek Tribal Town is located in Wetumka, Oklahoma.

The Thlopthlocco Creek Tribal Town is located in Okemah, Oklahoma.

The Alabama-Quassarte Tribal Town is located in Henryetta, Oklahoma.

The Poarch Band Reservation is located near Atmore, in Elmore and Escambia Counties, Alabama. Established in 1984, it consists of 213 acres. Its total population was roughly 1,875 people in the early 1990s, although the 1990 Indian population was just 149.

Economy Individuals may apply for funds for various emergencies and pressing needs. Most jobs are with the tribal government, farms, and bingo halls.

Legal Status The Creek Nation of Oklahoma, the Poarch Band, the Kialegee Tribal Town of the Creek

Nation, the Thlopthlocco Tribal Town of the Creek Nation, and the Alabama-Quassarte Tribal Town (*see* Alabama) are federally recognized tribal entities.

Unrecognized Creek communities include the Principal Creek Indian Nation East of the Mississippi, in Florala, Alabama; the Lower Muskogee Creek Tribe East of the Mississippi, Inc., in Cairo, Georgia; the Creeks East of the Mississippi, in Molino, Florida; the MaChis Lower Alabama Creek Indian Tribe, in New Brockton, Alabama; the North Bay Clan of Lower Creek Muskogee Tribe, in Lynn Haven, Florida; the Star Clan of Muskogee Creek Tribe of Pike County, in Goshen, Alabama; and the Florida Tribe of East Creek Indians, in Bruce, Florida.

Daily Life Several former tribal towns *(talwas),* now rural communities, retain some centuries-old traditions. The annual cycle of native activities revolves around a traditional stomp ground. Other activities include a rodeo and an annual festival. Facilities include an excellent health care complex, over a thousand new homes, a museum, and a library.

From his 1971 election as principal chief into the 1990s, Claude Cox, a Methodist church leader, created a political party with a base of Lower Creeks that has dominated the Creek Nation and led it into a quasi-alliance with the Republican Party. The mainly Upper Creek opposition held that the Creek Nation was illegal under the 1867 constitution, but the dominant faction simply rewrote the constitution; the new document was adopted in 1979. Members of both groups sit in the National Council.

There is little trace of aboriginal culture among the Poarch Band. They receive federal grants for education, health care, and economic development. Their Thanksgiving powwow is based mainly on Plains Indian traditions.

Houma

Houma (`Ū mä), or Ouma. The word means "red" in Choctaw and Chickasaw, but it may have been a shortened form of Chakchiuma, a tribe from whom they probably descended. It may also be an abbreviation of their tribal symbol, *sakti homma,* or "red crawfish." Many Houma prefer simply the word "Indian" as a self-designation.

Location In the late seventeenth century, Houmas lived on the east side of the Mississippi River, opposite the mouth of the Red River. Today, most live in the southeastern Louisiana marshes.

Population There were perhaps 1,000 Houmas in 1650 and between 600 and 700 around 1700. There were about 11,000 enrolled members in the early 1990s.

Language Houma is a Muskogean language.

Historical Information

History Shortly after they made their initial alliance with the French, in 1686, more than half the tribe was killed by disease. Catholic missionaries began operating among the Indians after 1700. The Tunica Indians, to whom the Houma had given permission to settle in the area in 1706, soon killed more than half of their hosts. The survivors moved south after the massacre.

In 1718, shortly after the conclusion of the Chitimacha war, the Houma joined some Chitimachas and members of other tribes and migrated south again, to the vicinity of New Orleans, and then north again to present-day Ascension parish. After the Natchez defeat at the hands of the French, Houmas, who aided the Indian refugees, were in their turn attacked by French forces; hundreds were captured and sold as slaves in New Orleans.

By the early eighteenth century the Houma had begun a process of absorbing some smaller, neighboring tribes, such as the Acolapissa, Bayogoula, Biloxi, and Chitimacha. Beginning some time in the early nineteenth century, the people still in Ascension parish moved south and settled on the Gulf Coast (present-day Lafourche and Terrebonne parishes). Other portions of the tribe intermarried with the Atakapa and moved to their territory or migrated to Oklahoma or to the north, toward their original homeland, and became lost to history.

The Houma remained generally isolated well into the twentieth century. In the 1930s, oil speculators began taking advantage of the Indians' illiteracy and lack of understanding in order to obtain their land. In response, local Indian leaders pushed their people to learn English. Still, most Houmas did

not attend school until after World War II. Schools in the area were desegregated in the 1960s. Centuries of intermarriage thoroughly integrated Catholicism and the French language into Houma identity.

Religion Temples were fronted with carved wooden figures. There may also have been earthen images of deities inside. The people probably worshiped a number of gods, in particular the sun, thunder, and fire. Young people may have sought guardian spirits through quests.

Government Houma head chiefs, if they existed at all, were less powerful than the Natchez Suns. Women were known to have served as war chiefs.

Customs Corpses were placed on scaffolds. After a certain period of time, special workers cleaned the bones and placed them in a chest, in which they were subsequently buried. The people played chunkey and other games. They practiced head flattening, which they probably learned from the Natchez when the Houma migrated south.

Dwellings Each town may have had over 100 cabins, possibly arrayed in a circle. Houses were square, pole-frame structures, from 15 to more than 30 feet on a side, and with walls of adobe and Spanish moss. They were covered with cane matting inside and out and then by grass thatch without. Doors were less than 4 feet high. There were no smoke holes.

Diet Traditionally horticulturists, the Houma grew corn and other crops. They also collected shrimp and other marine food as well as a variety of wild plant food, and they ate muskrat and other small game.

Key Technology Palmetto was used in the manufacture of baskets, mats, and other items. Hunters used a two-piece blowgun. Musical instruments included clay-pot drums with skins stretched over the top.

Trade The Caddo were significant trade partners. Marine food was an important export. The people probably imported flint and bow wood. They may also have traded in salt and bird feathers.

Notable Arts Houmas carved wooden satyrs and animals, some in relief, and painted in black, white, red, and yellow on their temple vestibules.

Transportation The primary method of transportation was by pirogue, or hollowed-out canoe.

Dress Men wore deerskin cloaks or went naked. Some men and women wore turkey-feather or woven muskrat-skin mantles. They may also have worn skin leggings and moccasins and possibly bearskin blankets in winter. Girls, from about eight to ten years of age until marriage or the loss of their virginity, may have worn a waist-to-ankle–length mulberry thread netting garment, fringed and ornamented. Their clothing may have been colored red and/or yellow and/or white. Most men wore their hair long.

War and Weapons Allies included the Okelousa, and enemies included the Bayogoula, at least in the late seventeenth century. The Houma fought with bows and arrows, knives, and clubs.

Contemporary Information

Government/Reservations Most Houmas live in Terrebonne and Lafourche parishes, Louisiana, and particularly in the Dulac–Grand Caillou and Golden Meadow communities. They are governed through an elected tribal council. There is no tribal land base.

Economy Fishing, trapping, and hunting are still important. People also work in nearby oil fields. The people have been unable legally to substantiate their claims to oil-rich land.

Legal Status The United Houma Nation, Inc. (1979), was denied federal recognition in 1998.

Daily Life Few Houma Indians interacted with their non-native neighbors until after the 1960s. Around that time, traditional shrimping and muskrat trapping were being undermined, by technologically advanced competition in the former case and by competition and ecological problems in the latter. Despite intermarriage with both whites and African Americans, and although the three races live and work in close proximity, there remains some racially based tension among them and within the Indian community.

Ongoing traditional palmetto crafts include baskets, mats, dolls, and fans. Kinship patterns also remain as do healing and other cultural traditions. Healers often use native methods combined with Christian prayers. French is the first language, with English second. Only a few words still exist of Houma, which was probably in sharp decline in the middle of the last century. The lack of a land base, among other things, has worked against community cohesion.

Lumbee

Lumbee (`Lum bē), a historical Indian tribe whose ancestors were Indians of indeterminate tribal affiliations, Anglos, and African Americans. The name is taken from the Lumber (formerly Lumbee) River.

Location From colonial times to the present, Lumbee Indians have lived in and near Robeson County, in southeastern North Carolina, and also in several counties in northeastern South Carolina. This region was formerly characterized by extensive marshland. There are also Lumbee communities in Baltimore, Philadelphia, and Detroit.

Population In the mid-1990s there were about 48,000 members of the Lumbee Indian tribe.

Language The Lumbee have always spoken English.

Historical Information

History Lumbee Indians have lived in North Carolina since at least the mid–eighteenth century. Their origins are obscure. They are probably descended from Cheraw Indians and other local Siouan speakers. Their ancestors may also include British settlers from the "lost" colony of Roanoke, Virginia (1587), who may have joined Hatteras Indians living on Croatoan Sound. There are at least 20 surnames of Roanoke colonists among contemporary Lumbees. Their ancestors may also include Cherokee, Tuscarora, and Croatoan Indians.

The marshy character of the Lumber and Pee Dee River area made it a likely haven for refugees of all sorts. Lumbee Indians, free frontier farmers, were first encountered by British and Scots settlers in the early eighteenth century. At that time they had no Indian traditions or customs, although their skin color was suggestive of an Indian origin. They maintained little contact with Anglo settlers, most of whom were more interested in the better and more accessible land farther west.

In the 1760s, the Lumbee experienced increasing competition with Highland Scots settlers. Land incursions were resisted where possible, but Lumbees soon lost much land to the Scots and to the tidewater planters, often by fraudulent means. The state of North Carolina formally disenfranchised them, along with other "persons of color," in 1835.

During the Civil War, Lumbees were conscripted into service as forced labor; when they resisted they were attacked by soldiers. Lumbee resistance to this oppression was led by Henry Berry Lowry (or Lowerie), who led raids on plantations to feed the poor of all races. Lowry kept up his campaign for justice even after the war, taking on as well the Republican (Reconstruction) Party, which sided with the Democrats and branded Lowry's organization as bandits. He eluded capture at least until his disappearance in 1872.

The Lumbees pressed their claim for state and federal recognition after war's end, but with the defeat of the multicultural Lowry movement, their identity turned more inward. They accepted a status as a third racial caste, with more rights than African Americans but not as many as whites. In 1885 the North Carolina General Assembly recognized them as "Croatoan Indians" and allowed them to operate their own schools, segregated from whites but apart from African Americans. A normal (teacher training) school was also opened, which later became a college and, around 1970, Pembroke State University. In 1911 the North Carolina legislature dubbed them "Robeson County Indians." This was changed to "Cherokee Indians of Robeson County" until protests by the Cherokees forced a withdrawal of that name. The people filed an unsuccessful request for federal recognition as the Siouan Tribes of the Lumber River.

Most Lumbees continued farming until after World War II. They were recognized by the state of North Carolina as Lumbee Indians in 1953. Partial

In 1958, thousands of Lumbees stood up to the Ku Klux Klan and drove it from Robeson County. Charlie Warriax (left) and Simeone Oxendine (right) proudly display the Ku Klux Klan banner they confiscated when the Lumbees broke up a KKK rally near Maxton, North Carolina. Oxendine, a Veterans of Foreign Wars district commander, is wearing a VFW hat.

federal recognition came in 1956, although the tribe was prohibited from receiving federal benefits. In 1958, thousands of Lumbees stood up to the Ku Klux Klan and drove them from Robeson County. They lost control of their school system in the 1960s. The tribe formed the Lumbee River Regional Development Association, a nonprofit corporation, in 1968.

Contemporary Information

Government/Reservations The Lumbee River Regional Development Association is located in Robeson County, North Carolina. Fourteen elected directors represent nine county districts. The directors elect their officers.

Economy Lumbees are integrated into the local economy at all levels.

Legal Status Lumbees have been federally acknowledged since 1956, but they are not fully recognized by the Bureau of Indian Affairs (BIA) and do not receive most federal services. The Lumbee Regional Development Association, Inc., has been determined to be ineligible to petition for official BIA recognition. The Lumbee Indians have been recognized by the state of North Carolina since 1953.

Daily Life Lumbees have held important political offices, including that of mayor, in Pembroke. Kinship networks help the people maintain a Native American identity. Most Robeson County Lumbees belong to all-Indian Protestant churches. The annual homecoming and parade in July bring thousands of people together from all over the country. Local schools (students and teachers) are mostly Lumbee. There is a community newspaper. As members of the Eastern Seaboard Coalition of Native Americans, the Lumbees (and other un- or incompletely recognized tribes) attempt to obtain some BIA benefits.

Miccosukee

See Seminole

Muskogee

See Creek

Natchez

Natchez (`Nat ches), an extinct tribe that had a marked similarity to Mississippian Mound Builder culture in the early historic period. They were the largest, most powerful tribe on the Mississippi in the mid–sixteenth century.

Location The early historic location of the Natchez was along St. Catherine's Creek, near present-day Natchez, Mississippi. Their lands were fertile but protected against chronic flooding.

Population The Natchez population was about 4,000 to 4,500 in 1650 and 300 in 1731.

Language Natchezean languages may have been related to the Muskogean language family, with possible Tunican influences.

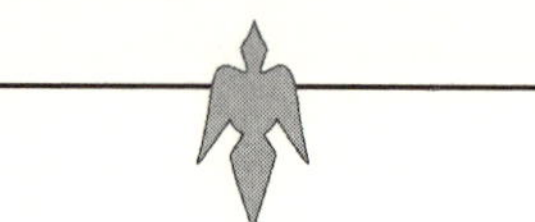

Historical Information

History With other Muskogean people, the Natchez may have come to their historical territory from the northwest. The Natchez had clear cultural ties to the Mississippian Mound Builder civilization, which may in turn have been influenced by Mesoamerican Indian cultures.

Contact with the Hernando de Soto party in 1542 was likely casual and not particularly friendly. French explorers entered the region in the later seventeenth century, and Catholic missionaries soon followed. The little nation soon divided its loyalties between France and Britain. By 1715 it was raiding nearby Indians such as the Chawasha in the service of British slave traders.

The Natchez population was greatly reduced by wars with the French beginning in 1716. The final conflict began when a governor of Louisiana moved to take over the site of the Natchez Great Village. In late 1729, partly at British instigation, Natchez warriors sacked Fort Rosalie and other French settlements, killing and capturing hundreds of people. The Yazoo Indians soon joined in, but the Choctaw sided with the French. In 1731 the French achieved a decisive victory. They killed many people and sold even more (including the last Great Sun) into slavery. Some people managed to escape to local tribes, especially to the Chickasaw and also to the Creek and Cherokee.

Three to five Natchez towns continued among the Creek into the nineteenth century. After removal to Oklahoma, Natchez descendants formed communities in the eastern part of the reservation. By about 1900, intermarriage had ended a distinct Natchez identity. The Natchez held their last formal ceremony in 1976; the last native speaker died in 1965. Some traces of Natchez ceremony and culture remain among various groups, such as the Muskogee Creeks of the Arbeka Stomp Grounds and the Cherokee Red Bird Smith Ceremonial Ground.

Religion The sun was the supreme deity. Its son was said to be responsible for Natchez culture, and its authority was continued in the sun caste. The people also recognized many minor servant spirits. Natchez society was a theocracy. An absolute monarch called the Great Sun wore a crown of red-tasseled swan feathers. Sitting on a throne of goose feathers and furs high on a mound, he directed some ceremonies and guided the sun every morning.

A ceremonial center in the main village included a partitioned, rectangular sun temple and the house of the Great Sun, each built on mounds of adobe and covered with woven mats. A fire, tended by a select group of eight people, always burned within the temple, and the roof was decorated with three carved and painted birds. The door faced east. Other villages had smaller ceremonial centers as well.

The Natchez also offered human sacrifices, especially upon the death of a chief. They observed the Great Corn ceremony, which corresponded to the Creek Busk, in mid to late summer. Most ceremonies were led by the Great Sun and/or other suns. There was also a priesthood, whose members shaved their heads. Doctors acquired supernatural powers by fasting for nine days in a cabin while shaking a gourd rattle. Failure to cure or to correctly foretell the weather might be met with death. Curing consisted of sweating, bleeding, dancing, singing, and evoking spirits of plants or animals. There were also many plant medicines. Curers were usually old men, but women might be herbalists.

Government The Great Sun was a hereditary monarch. Although his power was absolute, it was tempered in part by his personal abilities as well as by his respect for the opinions of the council.

Customs The Natchez recognized two social classes, nobles and commoners. The former included the king, or Great Sun; the king's brothers and uncles (little suns), from whom were chosen the war chief and head priest; hereditary nobles; and honored men and women, a status obtainable by merit. Commoners (or Stinkards) farmed, built the mounds, and did most of the manual labor. They gave food and other presents to the suns, and the Great Sun redistributed some of it.

There were elaborate deferential codes of behavior and speech between the classes. Members of the higher classes, even the Great Sun, were required to marry commoners. The offspring of a male of high rank and a commoner were a step below the man's rank, but the offspring of a highly ranked woman and a male commoner kept the mother's rank.

When a person of high rank died, his or her commoner spouse, if there was one, and several servants were killed for companions in the afterlife. Much ritual attended the deaths of nobility. Dead suns were placed in the temple, their bones preserved and later buried nearby. Dead nobles were dried on platforms; commoners were buried in the earth or placed on a scaffold and enclosed in a plaster vault, to which food and water were periodically brought. Houses of the dead were burned. The afterlife destination was based on earthly conduct: There was a paradise of equality and freedom from want and a hell full of mosquitoes.

Women enjoyed a high degree of sexual license before marriage, although fidelity after marriage was the norm, and divorce was rare. Men occasionally lent their wives to other men. Women generally married around age 25. The Natchez practiced infant head flattening. Babies nursed until they stopped voluntarily or the mother became pregnant. Children's bodies were rubbed with bear oil, in part to keep off flies. Older male relatives were responsible for boys' discipline and education. People older than three bathed at least daily.

Men engaged in generally cooperative work, such as hunting, fishing, cultivating the sacred fields, fighting, playing games, dressing skins, building houses, and making canoes and weapons. They were fed before women and generally enjoyed a higher status. Women prepared food; kept the fires going; made pottery, baskets, mats, clothing, and beadwork; and tended crops. Much of their work was performed alone. Berdaches assumed women's economic as well as sexual roles.

As part of the Great Corn ceremony, men played a hand ball game with as many as 1,000 or more players, the object of which was to keep the ball from touching the ground. They also played chunkey and staged an occasional deer surround for sporting or diversionary purposes. Women played dice or split cane games. There were also contests and many games of chance.

Dwellings Nine villages were scattered among woods and fields. Low, windowless square adobe houses with domed, thatched roofs over cane matting were built in rows around a central plaza. Platform beds stood along the walls. There were no smoke holes.

Diet Diet was agriculture based. Men and women grew corn as well as pumpkins and beans and also melons and peaches in the historic period. They made corn into at least 42 different dishes, including gruel (hominy) and bread. Sowing and harvesting were highly ritualistic activities. The people also grew a particular grain-bearing grass as well as tobacco.

Women gathered wild rice, nuts, berries, grapes, mushrooms, and persimmons; the latter were made into bread. Men hunted deer, turkey, and buffalo as well as a host of other game. They stalked deer with deer head disguises and went on communal buffalo hunts in the fall. Hibernating bears were routed with fire shot into their hollows. Bear fat oil was an important seasoning. The people also ate duck, other fowl, fish, and shellfish. Fish and meat were preserved by smoking and cooking. The people may have eaten dog on ceremonial occasions.

Key Technology Wooden items, carved and/or hollowed by fire, included mortars, stools, and bowls. Bows were fashioned of black locust wood, their strings of sinew and tree bark. Arrow tips were fire hardened or made of bone. Men used cane spears, perhaps with flint tips, for hunting large game. Many other items were made of cane as well. Fish were netted or harpooned. Women made pottery, mats, and baskets. Curved hickory sticks as well as buffalo shoulder blades became hoes. Bead belts recorded certain significant information, such as the line of Great Suns. Food was stored in pottery or gourd containers.

Trade Natchez Indians participated in local trading. Among other items, they obtained salt from Caddo tribes to the northwest.

Notable Arts Women made incised pottery, dyed cane baskets and mats, and white fabric from the inner bark of mulberry trees. They also wove baskets and nets. Men carved and painted religious figures, such as birds and rattlesnakes. They also made pipes from a black stone, especially in the later eighteenth century.

Transportation Men burned logs to fashion dugout canoes, some up to 40 feet long. Travelers used cane

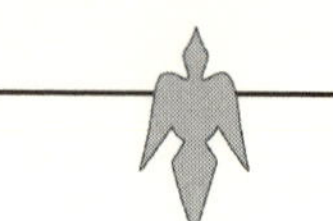

rafts to cross bodies of water. Women transported goods using bearskin shoulder straps or tumplines. Chiefs and high nobles were carried on litters.

Dress Clothing and personal adornment indicated differences in rank. Most clothing was made of mulberry tree inner bark fabric and/or deerskin. Women wore a knee-length skirt. Men wore a deerskin breechclout. Both wore high, laced moccasins, a long deerskin shirt, and leggings in colder weather. Other winter wear included buffalo robes and feather mantles. Girls remained naked until about age 10, when they wore a two-piece tasseled mulberry net apron. When they were no longer virgins, the garment was replaced with the standard skirt. Boys remained naked until puberty, when they donned the buckskin breechclout.

Both sexes painted and tattooed faces and bodies. Women also blackened their teeth with tobacco and ash and wore spike-shaped earrings. Warriors were tattooed from head to foot; they slit the lower part of their ears and decorated them with wire. Some men roached their hair and some wore it long, at least on one side. Women wore their hair long, tied in a queue with mulberry netting and tassels. Belts and garters were made of spun and woven buffalo and opossum hair. The Great Sun wore a crown of feathers in a beaded cap. Children, depending on their social rank, wore shell and pearl ornaments.

War and Weapons The Natchez recognized three classes of warriors, and war was seen a means of social advancement. Most war parties were led by the head war chief. Warriors wore breechclouts, belts, and ear pendants and carried rattles. Weapons included war clubs, bows and arrows with garfish points, axes, and sometimes shields. There were various prewar rituals, including drinking an emetic, feasting on dog meat, dancing and relating war stories, and planting the war post. Warriors carried fetishes of war spirits with them. Male captives were generally scalped and burned alive, whereas women were kept as slaves.

Pamunkey

See Powhatan

Powhatan

Powhatan (`Pow u `tan or Pow `ha tən), "falls in a current of water," part of a group of Algonquian speakers from North Carolina to New Jersey known as Renápe ("human beings") or Lenápe in the L dialect. The Powhatan tribes (Renápe of Virginia) were culturally intermediate between the southeast and northeast regions.

Powhatan was also the main tribe and village of the roughly 30-tribe Powhatan Confederacy. Other prominent tribes included the Pamunkey, Chickahominy, and Mattaponi.

Location Powhatans traditionally lived in the Chesapeake Bay region of present-day Virginia. Today, most live in the Delaware Valley of Pennsylvania and New Jersey as well as in Oklahoma and Canada.

Population The confederacy numbered between 9,000 and 14,000 people in the early seventeenth century. That number had declined to about 500 in 1705. Today, about 600 people claim membership in the Powhatan-Renápe Nation. There were roughly 450 Pamunkeys in the early 1990s.

Language Powhatan Indians spoke an Algonquian language.

Historical Information

History Aside from a short-lived Spanish mission in 1570, the British were the first European power in the region. By 1607, Chief Wahunsonacock (known to early British colonists as Powhatan) had expanded the confederacy by conquest from 6 or 8 tribes to more than 30. Shortly after the establishment of the Jamestown colony in 1607, the settlers began wide-scale cultivation of tobacco to sell in Europe. Because tobacco rapidly depletes the soil, the British constantly needed more land and did not shrink from obtaining it by fraud and trickery from the Indians.

According to legend, Pocahontas, daughter of Chief Wahunsonacock, intervened with her father to save the life of the leader of the Jamestown colonists, Captain John Smith. Smith was among a group captured in part because of Wahunsonacock's anger at the colonists' land grabbing and released after Wahunsonacock was crowned king in a British-style

In this nineteenth-century sketch, Pocahontas, the daughter of Chief Wahunsonacock, intervenes to save the life of the leader of the Jamestown colonists, Captain John Smith. Smith was among a group captured in part because of Wahunsonacock's anger at the colonists' land grabbing and released after the chief was crowned king in an English-style ceremony.

ceremony. Meanwhile, the colonists had captured Pocahontas and held her as surety against the other prisoners' release. During her captivity she converted to Christianity and married a settler, inaugurating a period of peace between the two groups. Pocahontas traveled to Britain and died there in 1617, and Wahunsonacock died shortly thereafter.

In 1622, the Powhatans determined to break the cycle of land thefts. Now led by Opechancanough, Wahunsonacock's brother, they organized a revolt that killed almost 350 colonists and destroyed all settlements except Jamestown. In response, the colonial militia began a push to sweep the Indians farther inland. At one point, the British attacked a group of Indians who had come to attend a peace council. After years of bitter fighting, during which the Powhatans lost many people, peace was restored in 1636, but Opechancanough organized another revolt in 1644, at which time he may have been over 100 years old. Over 500 colonists died during this campaign. After Opechancanough was captured and shot in 1644, his people were forced out of Virginia or placed on reservations, and the confederacy came to an end.

Powhatan people were attacked by whites in 1675 after being falsely accused of depredations; the following year the whites massacred a large number of Powhatan men, women, and children living at a fort near Richmond. By this time, most Powhatan people and towns had disappeared. The people lost several of their reservations in the early eighteenth century. In 1722, Iroquois Indians agreed to stop attacking the Powhatans. Beginning in the 1770s, surviving Powhatans began migrating north to New Jersey, a movement that accelerated during and after the Civil War.

Pamunkey and Mattaponi reservations of about 800 and 1,000 acres, respectively, remained in 1800. The reservations existed as a result of treaties signed with colonial governments. In 1831, most surviving Powhatans, many of whom had intermarried with African Americans, were chased away by whites in the aftermath of the Nat Turner slave rebellion. Few Powhatan Indians fought in the Civil War; those that did mainly did so on the Union side.

Following the Civil War, Virginia's Indians fought successfully for a social—and legal—status higher than that of African Americans; the result was a three-way segregation system. This negotiation affected their legal identity as Indians. For instance, during World War I, Pamunkey and Mattaponi Indians protested the fact that they were drafted, since they were not citizens. The courts ruled in their favor. Having made their legal point, many proceeded to enlist.

Prior to World War II, many Pamunkeys continued to live by fishing, hunting, and trapping. Also during that time, attention paid to Virginia Indians by anthropologists stimulated a renewal of their ethnic identity and political organization, although this soon provoked a fierce white backlash. Powhatans began a community in the Philadelphia-Camden area, maintaining their native identity in part through a close network of families. They frequently intermarried with Nanticokes of Delaware and members of other tribes. Formal organization began in the 1930s, culminating in the emergence of the Powhatan Indians of the Delaware Valley in the 1960s and the Powhatan-Renápe Nation in the 1970s.

Religion The chief deity was known as Okee. There were carved images of various kings and deities in the temples, as well as carved idols, dressed in various clothing and ornaments. There were at least one priest and temple in every village. Priests as well as conjurers were considered holy men. Chiefs had their own, private temples. Constructed like the houses, and partitioned with mats, these were used for worship as well as for burials of kings and for storehouses.

Priests made sacrifices of meat and tobacco at outdoor stone altars. Two or three children may have been sacrificed annually to propitiate the gods. There were regular communal ceremonies, including singing and dance, especially in times of triumph or crisis and at the harvest. Common people were thought to have no afterlife, but chiefs and priests were said to inhabit a western paradise until they were born again.

Government Each town, or kingdom, was led by a chief, or king. Sometimes, when kings controlled more than one town, a regent did the king's bidding in his absence and paid him tribute. Chiefly descent was mainly matrilineal. Chiefs regularly poisoned their rivals.

The Powhatan Confederacy was an alliance of about 30 tribes (200 villages) at its peak in the early seventeenth century. Wahunsonacock, at least, was an absolute authority and inflicted torture or death at will. He also took a high tribute or tax from the people and was well guarded around the clock.

Customs Children were bathed daily in cold water for strengthening. Also for this purpose, various concoctions were rubbed into their skin. Furthermore, male children may have been beaten as part of a general toughening ceremony. Some of these young men may have been killed, perhaps as a sacrifice to the gods, while others were cast out into the wilderness for nine months, afterward to become priests or conjurers.

Men provided animal food, conducted ceremonies, fought, and probably made tools and weapons as well as houses and canoes. Women (except upper-class women) prepared food; grew and harvested crops; dressed skins; made mats, baskets, pots, and (perhaps) mortars; and carried burdens. As a rule, men and women did not eat together. Murder, certain thefts, and adultery were capital crimes. Goods and food were stored in holes in the ground. Doctors could cure certain wounds quite well. Sweating cured some sicknesses.

Corpses of commoners were wrapped in mats and buried in the ground, following which women wailed for a full day. Dead chiefs were ornamented with necklaces of beads and pearls. Baskets containing their valuables were placed at their feet. They were then wrapped in mats and placed on a scaffold. There was a period of public mourning, followed by a feast. Later, their bones were collected, hung from their houses, and buried with the remains of the houses when the latter fell apart or were destroyed.

Men had many wives; Wahunsonacock is said to have had over 100. Men announced their intentions by bringing the women a quantity of fresh food. After her family received presents and promises of more to come, the women was brought to the man for a small wedding ceremony, followed by a feast. Once she had a baby, the king's wife was given a quantity of goods and dismissed, after which she was free to marry someone else; the child was taken from her and raised in the king's household.

Dwellings Villages, often palisaded in the early seventeenth century, were usually located along a river. There were between 2 and about 100 houses and between 50 and 500 families per village/kingdom. Houses were constructed by bending and tying off saplings and then covering them with bark or woven mats. Roofs were rounded, with a smoke hole over the central fire. There were generally two mat doors that may have faced east. Beds, with skin covers, were placed along the walls.

Houses were generally built under trees. They may have had windows. Some elongated houses may have reached more than 100 feet in length, but most were much smaller. Several families lived in each house. There may also have been a combination raised storage/drying area under which men congregated.

Diet Fish and shellfish constituted a major part of the diet. Agriculture was somewhat less intensive than in other parts of the southeast. Women grew corn (three varieties), beans, and squash in fields of up to 200 acres. Corn was roasted or boiled and eaten fresh or pounded into cornmeal cakes. The people also gathered acorns and other nuts, fruits, and berries.

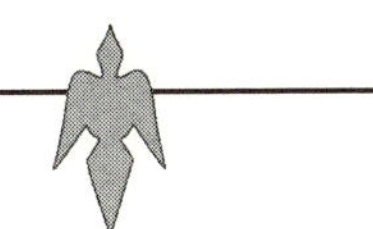

Some nuts and fruits were dried and stored for winter. A milky drink was made from walnuts. Men hunted deer, beaver, opossums, otters, squirrels, and turkeys, among other animals. Meat was broiled on a spit or boiled. The people also ate birds' eggs.

Key Technology Men hunted using bows and arrows, spears, clubs, snares, and rings of fire. They speared and netted fish from their canoes; nets came from tree bark or grass woven with sinew. Digging sticks and hoes were the main farming tools. Women pounded grain in wooden mortars. Pottery, baskets, and mats were used for many purposes. Reeds and shells were fashioned into razors. Men carved pots and platters from wood. Musical instruments included rattles, drums, and reed flutes. Pipes were of both clay and stone. The people also built wooden bridges over creeks.

Trade Powhatans traded dried oysters for various furs and skins, deer fat cakes, vegetables, and possibly buffalo-horn spoons.

Notable Arts The main arts were basketry, beadwork, and pottery as well as ceremonial clothing woven from turkey feathers. Men carved religious images from wood.

Transportation Dugout canoes were up to 50 feet long.

Dress Women made the clothing, mostly from skins. Married women wore hairstyles that were different—longer in front—than those of unmarried women. They may have worn flowers and feathers in their hair. Men wore their hair long on the left side. They also wore earrings of bone and pearl as well as animal parts. Both sexes painted their bodies, particularly black, yellow, and red. The chief priests wore turkey feather cloaks and snake and weasel skin headdresses. Priests, but not common men, may have worn beards.

War and Weapons Weapons included tomahawks, bows and arrows, clubs, and shields. Priests had the final say about making war. The war chief and soldiers were generally appointed. The purpose of warfare was generally for revenge and to capture women and children; men were killed, often after torture. Women prepared the warriors' hair with bear grease and special ornamentation, and they painted their faces. War parties left signs marking their presence and deeds.

Contemporary Information

Government/Reservations The Pamunkey State Reservation, located in King William County, Virginia, was established in 1658. It consists of about 1,200 acres and was home to about 30 families in the mid-1990s. The 1990 Indian population was 35. Other Pamunkeys live in nearby cities and towns and in New York, New Jersey, and Pennsylvania. Government consists of an all-male seven-member tribal council, six non-Indian appointed trustees, and several committees. There is also a Pamunkey Indian Baptist Church governing board.

William Terrill Bradby, a Pamunkey Indian, at Pamunkey Reservation in 1899. The Pamunkey State Reservation, located in King William County, Virginia, was established in 1658. It consists of about 1,200 acres and was home to about 30 families in the mid-1990s.

A turn-of-the-century Powhatan family from Virginia poses for a portrait in non-Indian dress. Prior to World War II, Powhatans began a community in the Philadelphia-Camden area, maintaining their native identity in part through a close network of families. They frequently intermarried with Nanticokes of Delaware and members of other tribes.

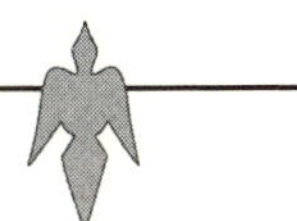

The Mattaponi State Reservation, King William County, Virginia, was established in 1658 and consists of 150 acres. There were 65 Indian residents in 1990.

A group of Chickahominy Indians lives along the Chickahominy River in New Kent and Charles Counties, Virginia.

The Powhatan-Renápe Nation is a group of about 600 Chickahominys, Eastern Chickahominys, Mattaponis, Pamunkeys, Nansemonds, Nanticokes, Upper Mattaponis, and Rappahannocks living in the Delaware Valley of New Jersey and Pennsylvania. The Nation acquired a 350-acre reservation (the Rankokus Reservation) in 1981 from the state of New Jersey.

Economy Pamunkeys and Powhatan-Renápes are fully integrated into the regional economy.

Legal Status The Powhatan-Renápe Nation is a state-recognized, nonprofit tribal entity. The Pamunkey Nation is recognized by the state of Virginia. The Eastern Chickahominy Indian Tribe, the Chickahominy Indian Tribe, and the Nansemond Indian Tribal Association are state-recognized tribal entities. The Upper Mattaponi Indian Tribe is recognized by the state of Virginia and has petitioned for federal recognition. The United Rappahannock Tribe and the Nanticoke Lenni-Lenápe Indians of New Jersey are state recognized and have petitioned for federal recognition.

Daily Life Facilities on the Powhatan-Renápe Nation Reservation include an education center, conference center, art gallery, nature center, museum, and reconstructed traditional village. The people hold various crafts, language, and traditional culture classes. There is also an annual arts festival.

As mandated in the 1677 treaty on which their reservation is based, the Pamunkey continue every fall to deliver a quantity of fresh game to the Virginia legislature. This tribe won a land claim settlement in 1979; other cases are pending. The Pamunkey Indian museum, completed in 1979, forms the core of the people's efforts to preserve their traditions. The Pamunkey Pottery Guild has helped revitalize pottery traditions and market the product.

Although many or most Powhatans resemble their non-native neighbors in looks and lifestyle, there is still an awareness of the key role of their Indian identity. The nature of this identity remains for many a matter of very personal negotiation. The Chickahominy hold a fall festival in September.

Renápe

See Powhatan

Seminole

Seminole (`Se mi nōl) means "pioneer," or "runaway," possibly from the Spanish *cimarrón,* "wild." The Seminoles, known as such by 1775, formed in the eighteenth century from members of other Indian peoples, mainly Creeks, but also Oconee, Yamasee, and others. Their traditional culture was similar to that of the Creeks. The Creek, Choctaw, Chickasaw, and Cherokee, and Seminole were known by non-natives in the nineteenth century as the Five Civilized Tribes.

Until 1962, the Miccosukee Indians were part of the Seminoles. According to their traditions, they were descended from Chiaha Indians. The name Miccosukee means "Red Person."

Location Located in north Florida in the early eighteenth century, the Seminole and Miccosukee were forced southward into the swamps, and west to Oklahoma, from the mid–nineteenth century on.

Population From a population of perhaps 1,500 in 1800, the tribe grew to about 5,000 in 1821. Roughly 400 Miccosukees and 2,000 Florida Seminoles were enrolled in the early 1990s. There were also roughly 10,500 Oklahoma Seminoles in 1991.

Language Seminoles spoke two mutually unintelligible Muskogean languages: Hitchiti, spoken by Oconee Indians and today mostly by Miccosukees, and Muskogee.

Historical Information

History Apalachee and Timucua Indians were the original inhabitants of north Florida. By about 1700, most had been killed by disease and raids by more northerly tribes. Non-Muskogee Oconee Indians from south Georgia, who moved south during the early eighteenth century, formed the kernel of the Seminole people. They were joined by Yamasee refugees from the Carolina Yamasee war, 1715–1716, as well as by some Apalachicola, Calusa, Hitchiti, and Chiaha Indians, and escaped slaves. The Chiaha were known by the late eighteenth century as Miccosukee. Several small Muskogean groups joined the nascent Seminoles in the late eighteenth century.

Seminoles considered themselves Creek; they supported Creeks in war and often attended their councils. They experienced considerable population growth after the 1814 Creek war, mainly from Muskogeans from Upper Creek towns. From this time on the dominant language among the Seminoles was Muskogee, or Creek. However, Seminole settlements, mainly between the Apalachicola and the Suwannee Rivers, were too scattered to permit the reestablishment of Creek towns and clan structures.

Prior to the Civil War some Seminoles owned slaves, but the slaves' obligations were minimal, and Seminoles welcomed escaped slaves into their communities. Until 1821, U.S. slaves might flee across an international boundary to Florida. Even after that year, the region remained a haven for escaped slaves because of the presence of free African American and mixed African American and Seminole communities.

Seminoles first organized to fight the United States in 1817–1818. The conflict was begun by state militias chasing runaway slaves and resulted in the Spanish cession of Florida. Southern whites feared the possibility of an African American–Indian military alliance, and they were aware of the numbers of escaped slaves living in the area. Despite the best U.S. efforts, which included burning villages and other such tactics, the Seminole did not fall.

In the Treaty of Moultrie Creek (1823), the Seminole traded their north Florida land for a reservation in central Florida. The 1832 Treaty of Payne's Landing, which was signed by unrepresentative chiefs and was not supported by most Seminoles, called for the tribe to relocate west to Indian Territory. By 1838, up to 1,500 Seminoles had been rounded up and penned in concentration camps. These people were forcibly marched west, during which time as many as 1,000 died from disease, starvation, fatigue, heartbreak, and attacks from whites. Although under pressure to do so, the Seminole consistently refused to give up the considerable number of African Americans among them. In 1856, the western Seminole were given a strip of land of about two million acres west of the Creeks.

Resistance to relocation and to white slave-capturing raids led to the second Seminole war of 1835–1842. Under Osceola, Jumper, and other leaders, the Seminole waged a guerrilla war against the United States, retreating deep into the southern

In the Second Seminole War of 1835–1842, the Seminoles, under Chief Osceola (pictured here in a painting by George Catlin), waged a guerrilla war against the U.S. government. Although Osceola was captured and died in captivity, and although at the war's end most Seminoles were forced into Indian Territory, the Seminole were not militarily defeated.

swamps. Although Osceola was captured (at a peace conference) and soon died in captivity, and although at war's end most Seminoles, about 4,500 people, were forced into Indian Territory, the Seminole were not militarily defeated. The war ended because the United States decided not to spend more than the $30 million it had already spent or to lose more than the 1,500 soldiers that had already been killed.

Most of the several hundred remaining Seminoles were either Cow Creek Indians (Muskogees) or Big Cypress Indians (Miccosukees).

A third Seminole war took place from 1855 to 1858. From their redoubt in the Everglades, the Indians attacked non-native surveyors and settlers. The army, through its own attacks and by bringing in some Oklahoma Seminoles, succeeded in persuading another 100 or so Seminoles to relocate, but about 300 remained, undefeated, in Florida. There was never a formal peace treaty.

In the 1870s, as the first non-natives began moving south of Lake Okeechobee, there was another call for Seminole removal, but the government decided against an attempt. In the late nineteenth century, a great demand for Seminole trade items led to close relationships being formed between Florida Indians and non-native traders.

Western Seminoles settled in present-day Seminole County, Oklahoma, in 1866. By the 1890s the people had formed 14 bands, including two composed of freedmen, or Black Seminoles. Each band was self-governing and had representation on the tribal council. Most of the western Seminole reservation, almost 350,000 acres, was allotted in the early twentieth century. Through fraud and other questionable and illegal means, non-natives by 1920 had acquired about 80 percent of the land originally deeded to Indians. Tribal governments were unilaterally dissolved when Oklahoma became a state in 1907. An oil field opened on Seminole land in 1923, but few Indians benefited. Many Oklahoma Seminoles moved away from the community during and after World War II in search of jobs.

Indian Baptists from Oklahoma achieved the first large-scale successes in Christianizing Florida Seminoles in the early twentieth century. Most Florida Seminoles lived by subsistence hunting, trapping, and fishing, as well as by trading, until non-natives overhunted and out-trapped the region. Around the time of World War I, the subsistence economy disintegrated even further as Florida began to drain the swamps and promote agriculture. By the 1920s, the new land boom, in conjunction with the drainage projects, led to significant Indian impoverishment and displacement.

Most Seminoles relocated to reservations during the 1930s and 1940s. There they quickly acculturated, adopting cattle herding, wage labor, schools, and Christianity. With the help of Florida's congressional delegation, the tribe avoided termination in the 1950s. At that time they adopted an Indian Reorganization Act–style corporate charter. Formal federal recognition came in 1957. By the 1950s, a group of more traditional Mikasuki-speaking Indians, mostly living deep in the Everglades, moved to separate themselves from the Seminole, whom they regarded as having largely renounced their Indian traditions. After a great deal of struggle, the Miccosukees were given official permission by the federal government to form their own government, the Miccosukee Tribe, which they did in 1962.

Religion The Seminoles considered themselves children of the sun. They observed the Green Corn ceremony as early as May or June. This ritual helped to unify the tribe after the wars. It began with the presentation of buckskin-wrapped medicine bundles, which contained items such as crystals, ginseng, horn, and white deer hair, all individually wrapped in buckskin. Medicine bundles were considered central to the identity of the people.

Seminoles believed that a person's soul exited the body when he or she slept. Illness occurred when the soul failed to return, in which case a priest was called to coax the soul back.

Government Before the wars, Seminole towns had chiefs and councils of elders. Afterward, there were three bands, based on language (two Miccosukee and one Creek). Each had its own chief and council of elders.

Customs Matrilineal clans helped provide cultural continuity among widely scattered bands after the wars. There was also a dual division among the

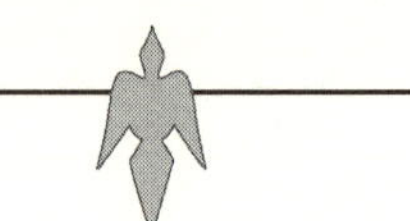

people. Particularly after 1817, the Seminole lived in small extended families. Oklahoma Seminoles retained more of traditional Creek social and religious structures, such as the *talwas,* or band/towns, than did the Florida people. Lacrosse and other Creek games played a similar social and ceremonial role. Snakes were not killed out of fear of their spirits. Bloodletting through scratching was thought to alleviate illness or troublesome behavior.

Dwellings Owing to a fairly mobile and decentralized existence, early towns were much less organized than were those of the Creeks. For example, there were no chunkey yards and only a vague public square. People living in these towns generally owned a longhouse, divided by mats into a kitchen, dining area, and sleeping area, and another, smaller house of two stories, similar to the Creek granary.

People in south Florida built their villages on hammocks and near rivers. Houses, or chickees, had pole foundations of palmetto trunks and palmetto-thatched roofs, platforms raised about three feet off the ground, and open walls. The thatch was watertight and could resist very strong winds. A small attic provided storage space. Cotton cloths were occasionally suspended around sleeping areas for privacy and insect protection. Utensils hung from the poles or from stakes driven in the ground. One cook hut sufficed for the village; fires burned in it continuously, and women cooked for everyone.

Diet Women grew corn, beans, squash, and also tobacco. They made hominy and flour from corn and "coontie" from certain roots. They also grew such non-native crops as sweet potatoes, bananas, peanuts, lemons, melons, and oranges. The fields often were on different hammocks, up to a day's journey distant from their homes. They also gathered wild rice; cabbage palmetto; various roots and wild foods, such as persimmon, plum, honey, and sugarcane; and nuts, such as hickory and acorns.

Men hunted alligator, bear, opossum, rabbit, squirrel, wild fowl, manatee, and turkeys (using calls for the turkeys). The people ate fish, turtles, and shellfish. Turtles were often roasted alive over a fire. Favorite dishes included *sofkee* (corn soup) and boiled hominy with wood ash (for flavor). From the beginning they traded with non-natives for coffee and other items.

Key Technology Spears were used to kill fish and alligators. Baskets, such as winnowing baskets, were fashioned of palmetto and cane. Many items were made from the palmetto tree, such as house frames and platforms from the trunk and roof thatch and beds from the leaves. Arrows of cane and wood were tipped with iron, 4- to 6-foot bows were made from mulberry or other woods, and deer rawhide was used for bowstrings. Before matches, fire was kindled with flint and steel on a bit of gunpowder and tinder. The people also had drums, flutes, and rattles.

Trade Traditional trade items included alligator hides, otter pelts, bird plumes, and foods. Bird plumes and alligator hides in particular were very much in demand in the late nineteenth century. The people imported firearms, canned foods, clothing, cloth, and hand-operated sewing machines.

Notable Arts Seminoles were known for their patchwork clothing and baskets. Their geometric designs were often in the pattern of a snake. Ribbon appliqué, previously consisting mainly of bands of triangles along borders, became much more elaborate during the later nineteenth century.

Transportation Men built fire-hollowed cypress dugout canoes, often poled from a stern platform. Canoes were relatively flat to accommodate the shallow, still water of the swamps. Some had sails, for journeys on Lake Okeechobee and even to the Bahamas. Their horses may have been of Mexican origin. The Seminoles eventually developed their own breed.

Dress Women made patchwork clothing beginning around 1900. It consisted of colorful pieces of material sewed into strips that were in turn sewn into garments. Some clothing was made of tanned deerskin as well. Women wore short shirts and long skirts, both generally of cloth. In cool weather they added a cotton shawl. They also wore as many as 200 bead necklaces around the neck.

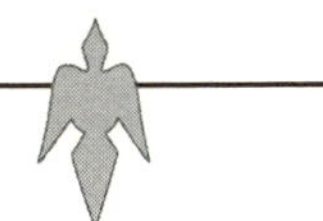

A Seminole family poses for a photographer. The women wear long skirts and many necklaces of beads and coins. The man wears a vest, a long shirt, and a tall turban fashionable among the nineteenth-century Seminole.

Men, especially among the Miccosukee, wore turbans made of wrapped shawls. Some had silver bands with bird feathers in them. Other clothing included shirts, neckerchiefs, breechclouts, and, occasionally, buckskin moccasins. Belts held up pockets containing hunting items and supported a long knife. Young children generally went naked, with older children wearing shirts (boys) and skirts (girls). Both sexes wore ornaments of silver and other metals and painted their faces and upper bodies.

War and Weapons There was no intertribal warfare: Seminoles fought only with the U.S. Army and local non-native settlers. Quartz crystals were thought to ward off bullets and to bring success in warfare, hunting, and other pursuits.

Contemporary Information

Government/Reservations The Seminole Tribe of Florida elects a tribal council with representation from all reservations. It also elects a board of directors to supervise business affairs.

Big Cypress Reservation (Seminole) is located in Broward and Hendry Counties, Florida. It consists of 42,700 acres. The 1990 Indian population was 447.

Brighton Reservation (Seminole) is located in Glades County, Florida. It consists of 35,805 acres. The 1990 Indian population was 402.

Hollywood (formerly Dania) Reservation (Seminole) is located in Broward County, Florida. It consists of 480 acres. The 1990 Indian population was 481.

Miccosukee Reservation (Miccosukee) is located in Broward and Dade Counties, Florida. It consists of 333 acres. The 1990 Indian population was 94. Leadership is elected but is traditionally dominated by certain families and clans.

The Florida State Reservation (Miccosukee and Seminole) is located in Broward County, Florida. It consists of 104,000 acres; there are no residents.

There is also a Seminole community in Tampa, Florida.

Most Oklahoma Seminoles live in Seminole County, Oklahoma. Tribal headquarters is located near Wewoka. Other tribal buildings are south of Seminole, Oklahoma. Roughly 35,000 acres remain in Seminole hands. A new 1970 constitution calls for an elected chief, an assistant chief, and a tribal council that represents all 14 bands.

Economy The large Florida reservations, Big Cypress and Brighton, are home to large cattle and farming (citrus) enterprises. Other important economic activities include tourism (sales of patchwork clothing, baskets, and other crafts), small business, and forestry. The Florida Seminole also have hunting and fishing rights on the Florida State Reservation.

The Seminole Tribe of Florida, Inc., oversees tribal business activity, such as tax-free cigarette sales and high-stakes bingo. These two activities provide the bulk of tribal income and fund various services as well as a per capita dividend. Miccosukee enterprises include a restaurant/service station, cultural center, and bingo hall and casino.

In Oklahoma, unemployment is chronically high. There are some jobs in the oil industry, retail, small business, and agriculture.

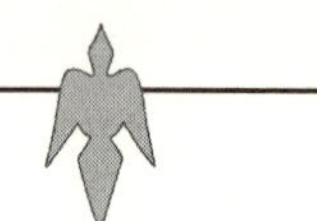

Legal Status The Seminole Tribe of Florida, including each of the four constituent reservations, and the Seminole Nation of Oklahoma are federally recognized tribal entities. The Oklewaha Band of Seminole Indians (Florida) has petitioned for federal recognition.

Daily Life Most Florida Seminoles continue to speak Mikasuki and Muskogee, or Creek, whereas most Miccosukees speak Mikasuki. The Miccosukees live in modern housing about 40 miles west of Miami or in suburban Miami. They offer classes, provide health and recreation services, and have their own police and court system. The tribe controls about 200,000 acres of wetlands. It also holds an annual arts festival. The people were relatively traditional as late as the 1950s, but today's Miccosukees wonder if the allure of Miami and modern society will destroy the old ways forever. The severe pollution and reduction in area of the Everglades has significantly impacted the Miccosukees' and Seminoles' traditional life.

Seminole reservations feature recreation facilities and community centers. Almost all Seminoles live in modern housing. The Hollywood Reservation contains a re-created traditional village, and ceremonials are held there in mid-July. Most children attend public school; there is also a tribal elementary school at Big Cypress. Clan and kinship structures remain in place, although traditional knowledge is in danger of being lost.

After years of internal disputes regarding the allocation of a $16 million land claims victory in 1976, the Oklahoma Seminole decided on a compromise in 1990. Hitchiti is no longer spoken in Oklahoma, but many Oklahoma Seminoles speak Muskogee. Although most Oklahoma Seminoles are Christians, most also retain many traditional cultural and religious practices and, except for jobs and schools, remain apart from non-native life. There are three stomp grounds; these, plus several located among the Creek, serve as the focus of traditional religious activities, especially the Green Corn Dance. The clan structure has been severely weakened, although band descent remains matrilineal.

Tunica

Tunica (`Tū ni kä), "Those Who Are the People." They were culturally similar to the Yazoo.

Location The people lived anciently in northwestern Mississippi and Arkansas as far as the Washita River. By the later seventeenth century they had migrated to the Lower Yazoo River in present-day Mississippi. Today, most live in Avoyelles Parish, Louisiana.

Population From about 2,000 in the late seventeenth century, their population declined to no more than 30 in 1800. There were 430 members of the Tunica-Biloxi tribe in the early 1990s.

Language Tunica was one of several Tunican languages.

Historical Information

History Tunicas had ancient links to southern Hopewell culture. Hernando de Soto came through their territory in 1541. Around 1700, the French claimed the lower Mississippi area, at which time Jesuit missionaries established a presence. The Tunica became loyal French allies, in part to counter pro-British Chickasaw slave traders.

Out of fear of the Chickasaw and other tribes, the Tunica moved south to a Houma town, opposite the mouth of the Red River, around 1705. Despite being given a friendly reception, after several years they killed most of their hosts and forced the others to move away. The Tunica were important French allies in the 1729 Natchez war and fought the Yazoo and several other tribes in 1731.

The Tunica fought the British as part of the Pontiac uprising when the French lost political control of the region in 1763. For years after that event, the Tunicas attempted to maintain a delicate diplomatic balance between the European powers. They sided with Spain and the colonies in the American Revolution. Their existence and their rights ignored, at best, by the U.S. government, the Tunicas dispersed in the later eighteenth century, moving up the Red River to the Avoyelles prairie. Others joined the Atakapa, and still others joined the Choctaws in Indian Territory.

The tribe hired a lawyer to protect its interests in the early nineteenth century. Still, ignoring federal law, the United States denied the Tunicas long-established title to their land. The Indians lived in

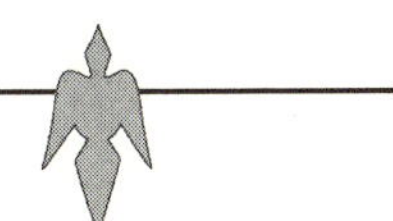

relative harmony with their neighbors, however, until their chief was murdered in 1841 for resisting the theft of tribal land. In a state trial, centering on the land dispute, the Indians were formally awarded some of their own land, which became the basis of their reservation.

The Tunica continued to hunt, farm, fish, and practice traditional healing and religion into the twentieth century. They merged with the Biloxi, a small Siouan tribe, in the 1920s. Participation in several court cases in the early twentieth century underscored the need for literacy and formal recognition. Faced with a severely diminished population, one chief proposed in the 1940s to sell all tribal lands and move the people to Texas, for which he was removed from office. The last chief died in 1976.

The Tunicas were important French allies in the 1729 Natchez War and fought the Yazoo and several other tribes in 1731. In this 1732 French sketch, the chief of the Tunicas is shown with the widow and child of the former chief, who was killed by the Natchez. The living chief carries three Natchez scalps on his staff.

Religion Tunicas worshiped the sun, among other deities. They celebrated the Green Corn feast. Clay figures stood inside thatched temples built atop mounds. They may have engaged in sacrificial killing.

Government Chiefs were relatively authoritarian, although not at the level of the Natchez.

Customs Men planted, harvested, and dressed skins. Women made pottery, clothing, and mulberry tree–bark fabric. The people buried their dead in the ground with their heads facing east. A four-day fasting and mourning period followed the funeral, after which participants bathed in the river. Cemeteries were located on hills and were guarded. The custom of infant head deformation was probably acquired in the late prehistoric period. If personally witnessed, adultery was severely punished. The Tunica played stickball and enjoyed various dances.

Dwellings Villages were located on the Mississippi floodplain in the mid–sixteenth century but on the bluffs overlooking the floodplain in the late seventeenth century. At least in the early eighteenth century, towns were laid out in a circle. Thatched houses were partly square and partly round and contained no smoke holes. Granaries, possibly square, were built on posts. A square chief's cabin was decorated with carved wooden images.

Diet The Tunica economy was based on agriculture. Men and women grew corn as well as pumpkins and beans. They integrated crops such as melons and peaches after contact with non-natives. Corn was made into at least 42 different dishes, including gruel (hominy) and bread. The people also grew a particular grain-bearing grass.

Women gathered wild rice, berries, fruits, grapes, mushrooms, and nuts. In season, persimmon bread was a staple food item for at least a month. Deer, turkey, and buffalo were the most important animal foods. Men stalked deer with deer head disguises and went on communal buffalo hunts in fall. They used fire to rout hibernating bears out of their hollows.

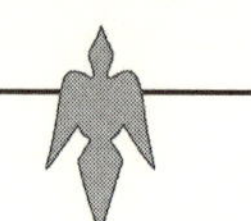

Bear fat oil was an important seasoning. Other foods included ducks and other fowl, fish, and possibly dogs.

Key Technology Cloth fabric woven from mulberry bark was used in a number of items. Women also made pottery and pine straw baskets. Men hollowed logs for mortars and cut saplings for pestles.

Trade Tunicas mined and boiled down salt from licks to trade with other tribes, particularly the Quapaw and Taensa.

Notable Arts The people made very fine pottery as well as well-dressed skins.

Transportation Carved dugout canoes enabled the people to move around the many rivers and lakes.

Dress Most clothing was made from deerskins. Men wore breechclouts, and women wore a wrapped waist-to-knee skirt made from deerskin or mulberry cloth. Mantles or cloaks were made from turkey feathers or muskrat skins. Girls wore a two-piece tasseled mulberry-net apron, like those of the Natchez. Most men wore their hair long. Women blackened their teeth. Both sexes tattooed their bodies.

War and Weapons Traditional enemies included the Chickasaw, Alabama, and Houma. War parties visited the temple before they departed and after they returned. Weapons included the bow and arrow, club, and knife.

Contemporary Information

Government/Reservations The Tunica-Biloxi Reservation is located in Avoyelles Parish, near Marksville, Louisiana. It consists of 130 acres and had 16 resident Indians in 1990. There is an elected tribal council.

Economy The tribe operates a housing authority and owns a cattle herd and a pecan-processing plant. It is developing a program to facilitate crafts training and marketing.

Legal Status Since the 1980s, the Tunica-Biloxi tribe has been a federally recognized tribal entity.

Daily Life The Tunica language is no longer spoken. The people continue to celebrate the New Corn ceremony. They also hold a parallel, secular festival around the same time, which features craft sales, dancing, and ball play. Tribal leaders are active in local and national Indian affairs. There is a tribal museum.

Tuscarora

Tuscarora (Tu sku `rōr ə), from *Skaroo'ren,* "hemp gatherers," their self-designation and possibly the name of one of the constituent tribes or villages. *See also* Oneida (Chapter 8).

Location In the sixteenth century, the Tuscarora were living near Cape Hattaras on the Roanoake, Neuse, Tar, and Pamlico Rivers, in North Carolina. The people migrated to New York in the early eighteenth century.

Population There were about 5,000 Tuscaroras in 1500. In the early 1990s there were roughly 1,400 enrolled members living in New York, of a total of around 3,000 in the United States, as well as an additional 1,200 living in Canada.

Language Tuscaroras spoke an Iroquoian language that changed markedly following the northward migration.

Historical Information

History The Tuscarora people came originally from the north, perhaps around the St. Lawrence Valley–Great Lakes region. They may have moved southward as late as around 1400. In the sixteenth century, and for some time thereafter, they were the dominant tribe in eastern North Carolina, despite losing upward of 80 percent of their population to European diseases during the seventeenth and early eighteenth centuries. Their somewhat inland location kept them from extensive contact with non-native settlers until the mid–seventeenth century.

Tuscaroras were traditionally friendly to the British settlers, even to the point of helping them fight other Indians. Active involvement in the deerskin, rum, and slave trade led to a growing factionalism within the tribe, which was most intense

in villages closest to trade centers. Involvement with rum also contributed significantly to a general decline of the people. Throughout the seventeenth and into the eighteenth century, non-natives regularly took advantage of Indian generosity, taking their best lands, cheating them in trade, and stealing their children for slaves.

War between the two groups broke out in 1711. It was largely a reaction to years of British abuse and to continuing population loss due to disease. Led by Chief Hancock, the Indians raided settlements and killed perhaps 200 British, who took their revenge as they could. Some Tuscarora villages remained neutral because of especially pro-British contact and sympathies; the "neutral" and "hostile" camps each had their Indian allies from other tribes. Freed African Americans played a significant role in construction of European-style forts among the Indians.

The conflict soon became a general war, with some tribes, such as the Coree and Pamlico, fighting with the Tuscaroras and others, mainly Algonquians, fighting with the Carolina militias. In 1713, as a result of a betrayal by Tuscarora leader Tom Blount, Carolina soldiers killed or captured almost 1,000 Tuscaroras. Many of the captives were sold into slavery. Most survivors migrated to New York to live among their Iroquoian-speaking relatives. Those who did not join the initial exodus lived for some additional years on the Susquehannah and Juniata Rivers, and some neutrals continued to live for a time in North Carolina. Virtually all Tuscaroras had left by 1802.

In 1722 or 1723, under the sponsorship of the Oneida, the Tuscarora were formally admitted into the Iroquois League, although their chiefs were not made official sachem chiefs. The former southerners soon adopted much of northern Iroquois culture. With the Oneidas, most Tuscaroras remained neutral or sided with the colonists in the American Revolution, although the rest of the league supported the British. The Seneca and a non-native land company donated land to the Tuscarora consisting of three square miles near Niagara Falls. The tribe purchased over 4,000 acres in 1804. It also received over $3,000 from the North Carolina legislature from the sale of Tuscarora land in that state.

Most Tuscaroras had become farmers and Christians by the end of the nineteenth century. Meanwhile, those loyal to Britain in the war settled in Oshweken, Ontario, on the Six Nations Reserve. The Tuscarora rejected the Indian Reorganization Act in the 1930s. In the 1950s, the government proposed that a massive reservoir be built on their land. The Indians' refusal to sell led to many protests and a court battle. Although they ultimately lost, and the reservoir was constructed, the process contributed significantly to their own, as well as other tribes', sense of empowerment and national identity.

Religion Tuscaroras believed that after death the immortal soul traveled to a western paradise. They buried their dead on scaffolds; bones were later placed in a village repository. Eventually the people adopted the practice of ground burial in bark, cane, or woven rush coffins. There were a number of planting and harvest festivals. Priests addressed every large gathering of any purpose.

Government The "tribe" was a collection of autonomous villages, each with its own chief, or headman, and council. The office of chief may or may not have been hereditary. Women served in some political capacity. Ultimate political authority was vested in the people and the council. The Tuscaroras were at first represented by the Oneida in the Iroquois League's annual council.

Customs Clan descent was matrilineal. There were eight clans in New York. Women nominated the clan chiefs. For five or six weeks, once in their lives, older children were secluded in a cabin and tortured with hunger and emetic plants. Some died from this treatment, which was ostensibly done to toughen them. The people may have played a mathematical reed game, in which high-stakes gambling figured prominently. At least in the historical period, villagers moved to hunting locations in late fall; such quarters were often within a day's walk of their permanent villages.

A great deal of ceremony was associated with the burial of men, the degree of ritual and expense being related to a person's social standing. The corpse lay in state for a day or so, in a cane hut, in which relatives cried, mourned, and painted their faces black. Then the bodies were wrapped in blankets, covered with

mats, and placed within a woven reed or cane shroud. One or more shamans conducted the funeral, at which they delivered lengthy eulogies. A small house was raised over the grave, which was then covered with earth. Chiefs were later disinterred. Their bones were cleaned and reassembled, and, dressed in white deerskins, they were buried in a crypt or house with other past chiefs.

Curing methods included shaking gourd rattles, sucking blood and fluids, and using snakes. Curers also used many herbal and plant medicines. The cures were often quite effective, and early non-native observers noted that these Indians were generally much healthier than were the colonists and other Europeans.

Dwellings Some villages were palisaded, at least in the early historical period. A village might have hundreds of houses; the average early-eighteenth-century village population was around 400. A village consisted of several "hamlets," or cabins near an open ceremonial area surrounded by fields. People who lived in "the country" had more distant neighbors.

Houses were ridged-roof pole lodges covered with cypress, cedar, or pine bark. There was a center fire and no smoke hole. Mats or deerskins served as bedding. In the north, multifamily longhouses were divided into compartments, each with its own fire, beds, and storage.

Diet Corn was the staple food, north and south. People also grew beans and squash. Women gathered wild fruits, nuts, berries, and roots. Men hunted game, including deer, bear, beaver, otter, rabbit, cougar, opossum, raccoon, partridge, pheasant, geese, and ducks. Seafood also played an important dietary role.

Key Technology Bows were carved from black locust wood whenever possible. Animal bones were used as hoes. Men made bowls, dishes, spoons, and utensils from tulip, gum, and other wood. Women made pottery and wove baskets of bark and hemp as well as mats of rush and cane. In the north, the people acquired many of their material goods by trade.

Trade Tuscaroras were very active traders, at least in the early to mid–seventeenth century. Intertribal trade included wooden bowls and utensils, and possibly white clay tobacco pipes, for raw skins. They also imported copper from the west.

Notable Arts Tuscarora arts included carved wooden items, woven mats and baskets, and pottery.

Transportation The people navigated rivers and marshes in cypress log canoes. They acquired horses in the mid– to late seventeenth century.

Dress Men wore hand-tanned breechclouts; women wore a wraparound skirt and a tunic. Both were made from Spanish moss or softened tree bark. Outerwear consisted of turkey feather, fur, or deerskin mantles. Men, especially among the wealthy, wore copper bracelets and other ornaments. Both men and women painted their bodies extensively.

War and Weapons The people celebrated both war and peace. Traditional enemies included the Catawba, Creek, and Cherokee (the latter may also have been allies). Allies included the Coree, Pamlico, and Machapunga. During the Tuscarora war, the people built and lived in forts about a mile apart.

Contemporary Information

Government/Reservations The Tuscarora Reservation is located in Niagara County, New York. Established in 1784, it contains roughly 5,700 acres and had a 1990 resident population of 310 Indians (of an enrolled population of about 1,200). Each clan is represented on the council of chiefs. Titles are conferred by Iroquois Confederacy sachems.

Tuscaroras (about 200 in the mid-1990s) also live on the Six Nations Reserve, Ontario, Canada.

Economy There is little or no employment specific to Indians. Most jobs are located in the Buffalo and Niagara Falls areas, especially in construction and heavy industry but also in business and the professions.

Legal Status The Tuscarora Nation is a federally recognized tribal entity.

Daily Life Most Tuscaroras are Christian, and most of these are Protestant. The Longhouse religion is also

In 1958, the New York State Power Authority planned a reservoir that would flood the Tuscarora Reservation in Niagara County, New York. As part of a public and legal protest, William Rickard (left) and Wallace "Mad Bear" Anderson (right) warn officials to leave their land alone.

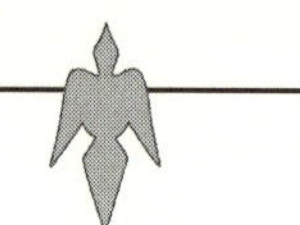

active. Local issues include the status of non-natives living on the reservation as well as individual efforts to sell tax-free cigarettes and gasoline and to open gambling establishments. Language classes are held at the Tuscarora Indian School. The people join in pan-Iroquois festivals. A field day in July and a community fair in October are both open to non-natives.

Yuchi

Yuchi (`Yū chē), possibly "from far away" or possibly Hitchiti for "People of Another Language." The tribe consisted of several distinct, named bands, one of which may have been called Chisca. They were culturally similar to the Catawba Indians. *See also* Creek.

Location Yuchis lived in the eastern Tennessee hills in the mid–sixteenth century. In the seventeenth century they built towns on the Ohio River and in Illinois. By later in that century they had expanded into the Savannah River region and into parts of Tennessee, North and South Carolina, Georgia, and Florida. Today, most Yuchis live in Oklahoma.

Population There were at least 2,500 Yuchis in the mid–seventeenth century and around 1,500 in the early 1990s.

Language Yuchean was an linguistic isolate, possibly related to the Siouan language family.

Historical Information

History Yuchis may have descended from Siouan peoples. They may have encountered Hernando de Soto around 1540 but were certainly attacked by the Spanish in 1566. In the 1630s, Yuchi bands began a process of leaving the Appalachian highlands to raid Spanish settlements in Florida. Some of these bands remained in the south, settling in west Florida among the Upper Creeks. The people encountered British settlers in Tennessee and North Carolina in the 1670s.

In the mid– to late seventeenth century, under pressure by the Shawnee, many Yuchi bands left the high country and followed the Savannah River toward coastal Georgia. They joined Yuchis who had migrated there earlier. With the Creek, both groups became British allies, conducting slave raids for them on Spanish settlements and among other tribes, such as the Apalachee, Timucua, Calusa, Guale, and Cusabo. This wave was soon driven away from the Savannah, however, and moved west toward the Chattahoochee River in central Alabama. A final wave of Yuchis migrated south in the early eighteenth century. By the late 1700s, most Yuchis were living near the Coosa and Tallapoosa Rivers, although some remained in southeast Georgia.

By the nineteenth century, the Yuchi no longer existed as a tribe, having combined with other peoples. Yuchis in Tennessee and North Carolina merged with the Cherokee. Georgia Yuchis joined the Creeks, and Florida Yuchis joined the Seminoles. As many as 900 Yuchis were removed with the Creeks to Indian Territory in 1836. They formed 11 communities in present-day Creek County, Oklahoma.

In the early twentieth century, the Yuchis remained legally united with the Creeks but maintained their own stomp grounds and churches. They refused their own charter in 1938, fearing the motives of the federal government. They maintained their own language and customs, as well as ties to religious sites in Georgia, through the 1950s.

Religion The sun was recognized as the chief deity and power. The three-day corn harvest festival included dancing, a new fire ceremony, and male deep scarring. The Green Corn festival included a stickball game as well as the formal initiation of boys into manhood. Disease was said to be caused by offended animal spirits; shamans cured with herbs, chants, and dancing. One of the four souls possessed by each person could pass to another life.

Government Each band had its own chief and leadership structure.

Customs Yuchis belonged to one of two societies, chief and warrior. Membership was determined by patrilineal descent. Babies were named on the fourth day of life. Matrilineal clans may or may not antedate their associations with the Creeks.

Dwellings Yuchis built their villages—stockaded in the mid–seventeenth century—near streams. They grouped their houses around a central square used for ceremonial and social purposes. Houses were wood-frame structures covered with clay or woven mats and roofed with cypress bark or shingles.

Diet Corn, beans, and squash were planted in river valleys. Corn was the staple food. It was served in many ways and often mixed with other foods, including powdered hickory nuts and meat. Wood ash was added for flavor. Men hunted buffalo, bear, elk, deer, turkey, and birds. They used calls to attract deer and turkey and possibly fire to drive deer. Game might be roasted on a cottonwood stick over an open fire. Women gathered a number of wild foods, including fruits, nuts, and berries. Hickory nut oil was preserved and used in cooking or as a beverage.

Key Technology Men hunted using bows and arrows and blowguns (for birds and small game). Bows were made of Osage orange, sassafras, hickory, or other woods, with squirrel skin, deer sinew, or rawhide strings. Arrows were wooden or cane, pointed with stone and feathered with hawk and turkey tail feathers. Dogs assisted on the hunt. Fish were taken with willow and hickory traps, cane harpoons, various hook devices, wooden spears, and poisons.

Most men owned two large leather pouches decorated with beads and slung over the shoulder on straps. Turkey-feather fans were used mostly by men to keep insects away and as a sign of leadership. Log mortars and wooden pestles may also have had religious significance. Sewing awls were made of deer antler with bone points. The people also made pottery, baskets, and assorted wooden utensils and tools.

Trade The Yuchi may have been a link in moving copper south from the Great Lakes. Some groups, using the Choctaw trade language, traded in flint or salt. Their pipes came from the Cherokee and Natchez, and they also traded for catlinite pipes from the early eighteenth century on. In the early contact period they also traded horses for other non-native goods.

Notable Arts Especially fine pottery included pipes and decorated bowls. Women also made fine cane and split hickory baskets. Turtles and snakes were a common design. Other design motifs included geometric diamonds made of *V*s and *W*s.

Transportation Canoes were hollowed out of logs and may also have been made of bark.

Dress Men wore deerskin leggings, sashes, and moccasins, although they frequently went barefoot. In the later eighteenth century they wore bright-colored cloth shirts and jackets, modified breechclouts, leggings tied to a belt, cloth turbans, and various ornaments. Women wore cloth dresses, short leggings, belts, moccasins, and personal ornaments.

Men wore their hair in a roach with a fringe of hair along the forehead. Only unmarried women painted their faces, although the practice later became widespread. A male's face paint pattern was related to his particular society. It was worn on ceremonial occasions, including ball games, and at death.

War and Weapons Little is known about aboriginal Yuchi war practices. Weapons probably included the bow and arrow as well as knives, clubs, hatchets, and possibly shields. They attacked and raided many neighboring tribes as British allies in the seventeenth century.

Contemporary Information

Government/Reservations Yuchis maintain three traditional ceremonial grounds in Oklahoma: Polecat, Sand Creek, and Duck Creek. The headquarters of the Yuchi Tribal Organization is in Sapulpa, Oklahoma.

Economy Yuchis are fully integrated into the local mixed-farming economy.

Legal Status The Yuchi Tribal Organization is presently unrecognized. The Yuchi Nation was provisionally denied federal recognition in 1998.

Daily Life Many Christian Yuchis belong to the Pickett Prairie Methodist Church. There is also a Yuchi chapter of the Native American Church. Yuchi is still spoken.

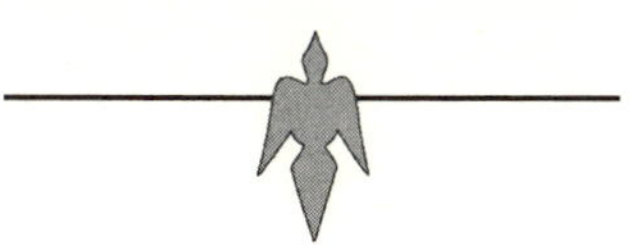

Chapter Eight

The Northeast Woodlands

Below: The Winnebago people lived in rectangular bark or mat-covered lodges. There was also a rectangular council house for meetings and ceremonies and similarly built sweat houses. *Below right:* A delegation of chiefs, photographed in 1866, wears headgear that includes a cloth turban and a fur turban with a shell-disk decoration.

Below: These Ojibwa pictographs depict the sequence for invocations, offerings, and songs for a particular ritual. *Far right:* Potawatomi women replaced porcupine quillwork in geometric designs with ribbon appliqués on their garments during the nineteenth century.

Northeast Woodlands

The area known as the Northeast Woodlands encompasses close to one million square miles. Bordered by the Atlantic Ocean on the east, its northern frontier is the start of the boreal forest. To the west, the trees themselves separate the woodlands from prairie and plains, although fringe tribes hunted buffalo and shared other characteristics of Plains Indians. The region shades almost imperceptibly into the Southeast cultural area, which tends to be characterized by increased social stratification, denser populations, and a greater reliance on agriculture.

Aboriginal populations are difficult to establish, since disease epidemics began so long ago, but probably some two million Indians lived in the Northeast Woodlands in the sixteenth century. Southern New England and the mid-Atlantic region had the highest population densities. Thick forest covers the hilly Northeast Woodlands except in the far western regions, where relatively flat forest and prairie predominate. The highest mountain is Mount Washington (6,288 feet). The Appalachian Mountain chain and the Great Lakes dominate the region geologically. The entire area is well watered by an abundance of rivers and lakes. Major rivers include the Hudson, Ohio, Susquehannah, and St. Lawrence.

The region's temperate climate is moderated along the coast by Gulf Stream influences. Winters in the northern parts are particularly severe; summers, although pleasantly warm, are also relatively short. Conifers mix with deciduous trees, replacing them in the more northern locations and the higher elevations.

All northeastern Indians but the Siouan Winnebagos spoke either Algonquian or Iroquoian

Native Americans of the Northeast Woodlands

languages. (Besides being a major northeastern language group, Algonquian was also spoken by former Woodlands and well-known Plains tribes such as the Arapaho, Blackfeet, and Cheyenne. Even the Californian Yuroks spoke an Algonquian language.) Most northeastern Indians cultivated corn and other aboriginal crops using slash-and-burn agriculture. They also hunted, fished, and gathered wild plant foods to varying degrees.

Non-natives arrived in this region before they came to any other place in the New World. Norse explorers from Scandinavia visited coastal areas from about Newfoundland to Cape Cod. However, the Norse apparently left little of permanent influence. It was the trade in beaver furs as well as disease epidemics, beginning around 1600, that transformed life in the northeast. By the mid–nineteenth century, many Indian groups had simply disappeared, and most of those who remained had been militarily defeated and largely resettled on reservations, some of which were located far from home. On the other hand, there are more Indians in the northeast today than many people realize. Although the Indians are largely acculturated, many proudly maintain an Indian identity. On both sides of the international border, Native Americans continue to struggle for recognition, land, economic development, and sovereignty.

People have lived in the Northeast Woodlands for at least 12,000 years. The first residents may have come from the Southwest and moved north and east as the glaciers receded. During the Paleo-Indian stage, small bands pursued ancient species of large game. Although the Archaic period begins with the disappearance of the last of the Canadian ice (as well as the ancient large game) about 6000 B.C.E., the environment was still changing dramatically during those years, and people did not become fully established in the northeast until around 3,000 years later. Hunter-fisher-gatherer subsistence patterns and material culture from that period lasted into the seventeenth century among some interior Algonquian people. The first Mesoamerican influences entered the region about 2000 B.C.E. in the form of pottery and polished stone items.

The great eastern prehistoric civilizations influenced northeastern people during the Woodland period (circa 1000 B.C.E.–1500 C.E.). The Adena culture flourished around Kentucky and Ohio between about 800 B.C.E. and 200 C.E. These people cultivated crops, produced pottery, and cremated their dead or buried them in a flexed position under mounds. They also used copper tools and evolved considerable artistic traditions. The use of red ocher in burial customs was also associated with Adena culture. It is important to note that all Woodland cultural influences manifested themselves in ways that were highly specific yet variable in terms of time and place.

Hopewell cultures (circa 300 B.C.E.–700 C.E.) extended from the Great Lakes to the Gulf Coast and west of the Appalachians to the Great Plains. They also focused on complex death rituals, including mounds, and are known for their stamped pottery and other types of fine art. Hopewell was marked by larger population centers and the establishment of vast trade networks that extended throughout most of the present-day United States east of the Rocky Mountains. These people were excellent metal workers as well as weavers and craftspeople.

Most influential in western parts of the region, Mississippian Culture (circa 700–1500) was characterized by intensive agriculture, fine pottery, distinctive art themes, stockaded villages, and flat-topped pyramid mounds. There was an important Mississippian center at Cahokia, near present-day St. Louis, whose influence extended north into Wisconsin. Other late prehistoric cultural complexes include Fort Ancient and Monongahela Woodland, both located in the Ohio Valley.

Aboriginal trade generally took place between local groups. Trade patterns favored the exchange of Iroquoian agricultural products and Algonquian animal products, especially in the north. Birch items also went to those groups south of the primary birch area. Other trade items included pottery, shell objects, and copper as well as foods. There was some limited specialization, such as Iroquois pipes and Nanticoke beads.

Algonquians tended to use swift and light birch-bark canoes, in contrast to slower Iroquoian elm-bark models. The Iroquois proper did much of their traveling over land. Men made small canoes for use on rivers and large ones (holding up to ten people or more) for lakes. Styles were based on expected wind

and water conditions. Canoes were often framed with cedar and trimmed with maple. Bark was sewn onto the frame with spruce roots and caulked with pine pitch or spruce resin. Some groups, particularly those who needed seaworthy crafts, hollowed out tree trunks for dugout canoes as well.

Other material items included grass, root, and bark baskets; cords and rope hand-spun and braided from plant fibers; woven hempen and basswood bags; and soapstone and carved wood bowls and utensils. Women made ceramic vessels for cooking, serving, and storage. Some Great Lakes groups made (and traded) tools of native copper. In addition to food and raw materials, wild plants provided hundreds of medicines. Wampum—strung shell beads—of native manufacture was originally used for tribal records and ceremonial purposes; its use was broadened into money and treaty confirmation in the historical period.

Artistic expression in the northeast ranged from baskets decorated with dyed fibers and woven in geometric patterns to painted and incised pottery to finely carved wooden bowls, spoons, and cups. The Iroquois carved wooden masks for use in certain curing ceremonials. Some women were expert at decorating clothing using softened porcupine quills.

Political organization varied across the region. Among most groups, chiefs (sachems, sagamores) led bands or groups of bands. Some chiefs were stronger than others; however, village councils acting in unanimity often decided important matters. Although among most groups political leadership had a hereditary component, social stratification in general was strongest in southern New England.

In the west, central Algonquians created parallel civil and military political organizations. Many of these tribes were divided into two distinct groupings that played important roles in games and celebrations. Most western tribes also had warrior organizations to perform policing activities. Women held formal political power in some western groups, such as the Miami, Shawnee, and Potawatomi.

In general, religious activities reinforced core values of generosity, bravery, and loyalty to the community. Iroquoian religion was based on the belief in a creator or creative life force balanced by the forces of evil and destruction. Algonquians, too, took notice of a host of evil spirits that might be used or abused by sorcerers. For these people, spirits were ubiquitous. They had human attributes and in fact could assume human form. The spirits included cannibal giants as well as the great creative spirit, Manitou, which was occasionally identified with the sky or the sun.

Among many groups, puberty was the time to undertake a vision quest, which included fasting and isolation, in order to attract the lifelong assistance of a spirit power. Dreaming was important for many Woodland Indians, because in dreams the human soul was thought to be able to leave the body and assume different shapes. Indians believed in life after death or the perpetual existence of the soul. Most cultures also recognized mythic culture heroes/transformers, such as Gluskap among the Micmac.

In addition to conducting ceremonies, religious specialists or shamans often had subspecialties, such as curing and divining. They performed their various feats with the help of their spirit powers. Shamans cured by sucking or blowing illness out of the body.

Important ceremonies among different groups included the Midewiwin, the feast of the dead, medicine dances, and the Green Corn festival. The Midewiwin may be aboriginal but most likely evolved in response to the unprecedented degree of disease and death endured by Indians beginning in about the sixteenth century.

Practitioners among the Ojibwa kept written records of proceedings on birch-bark scrolls. Some western groups had sacred bundles, whose medicines were associated with special powers. Especially among Great Lakes peoples, the pipe, or calumet—usually made of pipestone (catlinite)—was an especially sacred object and was associated with utmost solemnity and honesty. Religious significance also accrued to various games, such as lacrosse, especially among the Iroquois.

Algonquians typically lived in dome- or cone-shaped wigwams. These tended to be made of bark strips or woven mats or reeds attached to a frame of bent saplings tied together with spruce roots. Woven mats also covered interior walls and floors. Sleeping platforms were located around the perimeter; skins and furs were placed over the platforms as bedding. Smoke holes could be closed with a flap. There were usually two doors.

Summer and winter wigwams were of similar construction, but the latter tended to be smaller. Some Algonquian groups also used rectangular, multifamily houses with peaked roofs. Other buildings included menstrual huts, sweat houses, and temporary brush shelters at special hunting and fishing areas. Some Great Lakes groups built large wooden council houses in the center of their villages.

By the twelfth century, Iroquoians had developed longhouses. In the early historical period they were about 25 feet wide and up to 200 feet long, although most averaged less than 100 feet. Constructed of pieces of bark over a curved sapling frame, the longhouses were divided into six to eight two-room sections, each sharing a fire and housing one family. Storage bins divided the sections. Residents were generally members of the same maternal lineage. Inside the apartments were low platforms covered with skins or mats. Eastern longhouses tended to be covered with elm bark and western with cedar bark. Both had vaulted roofs.

The forests provided a home for a great variety of large and small creatures. Deer was generally the most important food animal, but people also hunted moose, caribou, bear, elk, beaver, muskrat, otter, wolf, fox, and rabbit. Fowl, especially turkey, were common in many areas.

Among some groups, saltwater and freshwater fish, turtles, shellfish, and marine mammals played an important dietary role. Fish was often smoked to preserve it for the winter. Depending on location, different groups used a variety of other food sources, such as maple sap (a sweetener), fresh greens, nuts, berries, honey, and roots.

After around 1000, or even as late as 1400 around parts of the Great Lakes, corn, followed by beans and squash, became an important food. In parts of the Great Lakes region, wild rice—really a grain—took the place of corn as a staple food source. Some groups also grew sunflowers, and most grew tobacco, although, unlike the other crops, doing so was considered the province of men. In general, people wintered in small groups, generally in hunting grounds, and summered in large ones, near their fields.

Women made most clothing from the hides of white-tailed deer. In general, clothing consisted of breechclouts, skirts, leggings, and moccasins. Additional clothing, such as fur robes, was worn in winter. Women decorated the clothing with softened and dyed porcupine quills and/or paint. Some groups also wore fringed garments. Shell and stone jewelry, tattoos, and body paint were common among most groups.

Warfare was endemic among most prehistoric Woodland Indians. The Iroquois revered war, although from about 1500 on, give or take 50 years or so, it was reserved for non-natives and tribes outside of the Iroquois League. The ritual torture of captives was common. Some groups also engaged in cannibalism. Both of these activities were associated with sun sacrifice and may show Mesoamerican influences. Among many groups, captives were frequently adopted to make up for population losses.

Coastal groups and the Iroquois developed gradually into the historic period. Cultural developments generally occurred in situ. Technological changes, such as ceramics, agriculture, and the use of shellfish, slowly advanced to their natural limits. The situation differed in the upper Great Lakes and in Illinois and the Ohio Valley, however, where ethnic continuity between prehistoric and historic peoples is speculative. Little-known residents of the Ohio Valley were gone by the mid–seventeenth century as a result of warfare and fast-moving epidemics. The region was later repopulated by historic tribes from other locations.

Half a millennium passed between the Norse visits and the arrival of other Europeans. Indians of coastal Maine were using items of non-native manufacture by 1602, and many Europeans arriving even in the early contact days met Indians already familiar with their goods and knowledgeable in sophisticated trade practices.

Profound changes in Indian life followed the arrival of non-natives. The rate of change was uneven, but the most rapid and common impact was the decimation of Indian populations owing to epidemics of smallpox, typhus, and other diseases. Some tribes experienced as much as 95 percent population loss in the initial rounds (early seventeenth century in the east) alone. Furthermore, with the growing European demand for furs from the mid–sixteenth century on, the New World became a new center of

competitiveness between France and Britain, and Native Americans soon became a part of both the trade and the rivalry.

The intrusion and eventual domination of fur trapping led to a dependence on alternate sources of food and technology. It even led to famine in some cases, as groups dependent on marine foods were cut off from the coast and spent more time trapping inland. Many groups eventually relocated to be near trade centers, even if the new locations were detrimental to their traditional subsistence activities. Time formerly spent making items was spent in trade-related activities, resulting in the decline of native arts and material culture. Early trade items of non-native manufacture included cloth, iron nails, knives, glass beads, and brass kettles, not to mention firearms.

Political and social structures were also affected. For their own convenience, non-natives promoted more centralized political authority among Indian groups. Some "trade chiefs" divided group land into distinct territories. This practice had several results, including an increase in individual ownership of subsistence areas, a breakdown in reciprocal arrangements and sharing, and increased social stratification. Indians also suffered further population decline, as well as a serious deterioration of traditional mores, from the introduction of alcohol and the accompanying sharp increase of venereal disease. They were as unprepared for liquor as they were for smallpox, and unscrupulous traders took full advantage of the fact.

Along the coast, once Indians taught non-natives how to survive in the New World, the latter quickly moved from friendliness to slave raiding, robbery, extortion, and demands for land and religious conversion. The Pequot war and King Philip's war stemmed at least in part from colonial opposition to acts of Indian self-determination, such as selling land and making independent alliances. Both involved the slaughter of hundreds of Indian women and children and the ensuing cession/capture of much Indian land.

Numerous other conflicts stemmed from non-native lust for land, outright brutality practiced against Indians (often justified with recourse to Christian values), trade-related issues, and simple fear and misunderstanding. All took place within the context of the wider international struggle between France and Great Britain. Warfare, both interracial and among Indians themselves, occasionally escalated into attempted genocide: More than once smallpox-infected blankets were intentionally traded to "troublesome" Indians, and some Indian groups, notably the Iroquois, succeeded in virtually annihilating other tribes. In short, ritual warfare was transformed slowly into economic and political warfare as a result of the fur trade and competition over land.

One important aspect of non-native influence was a steady pressure, almost from the beginning, to accept Christianity. Although relatively few Indians truly accepted Christian doctrine before the nineteenth century, a significant number did convert, mainly to Catholicism. Reasons for taking this action included not only genuine personal conviction but also the hope for trade and/or political advantage. Indians were well aware, for instance, that the French would trade firearms only to Christians.

Many Indians attempted to hold on to traditional beliefs and religious practice despite the breakdown of religious structures. Those in this camp often came to accept neotraditional beliefs such as the Handsome Lake (Longhouse) religion and, later, the Native American Church. With these new religions, Indians found a way to blend the old with the new without feeling that they had abandoned their heritage.

In general, Algonquians tended to favor the French whereas Iroquoians were pro-British. After the French defeat in 1763, many Algonquian tribes, recognizing the threat to their lands, fought with the British against the colonists. Most upper Great Lakes Indians supported the British in the American Revolution. Indians also acted on their own or in multitribal coalitions (Pontiac, 1763; Little Turtle, circa 1790; Tecumseh, 1810; and Black Hawk, 1832), in vain efforts to stem the tide of westward emigration.

The first half of the nineteenth century saw the cession of practically all remaining Indian land east of the Mississippi and the consolidation of tribes on reservations. After relocating several times, most western tribes ended up in Indian Territory, although some groups refused to leave their homes and were able to remain in scattered pockets. Some also accepted reserves in Canada (the word "Canada" is derived from an Iroquoian word meaning "settlement" or "village"). Many of these Indians carried on in a semitraditional way until the fur trade finally drew to an end around 1900.

Into the twentieth century, Indian life, especially in the west but even in the east, was characterized by an inadequacy of food, shelter, and employment and by continuing assaults on the people's land, culture, and self-determination. Indians resisted as best they could. Their fortunes tended to rise and fall along with the general state of the U.S. economy as well as the prevailing Indian policy. In the east, job opportunities off of the reservation or community tended to encourage cultural assimilation. Cultural preservation was generally less difficult in Canada than in the United States.

As is the case with most North American Indians, the goal of self-determination remains paramount. On Cape Cod, Wampanoag Indians battle non-native vacationers and developers for the right to control their land. Recognition is also an issue for these people, as it is for the Houlton Band of Maliseet, the Pokanoket, and other Northeast Indians. Many are still trying to settle land claims and obtain reservation status for communities both recognized and unrecognized.

Indians in the northeast as well as Woodland descendants in Oklahoma seek economic development as well as housing and adequate medical care. Craft traditions remain strong but are not generally sufficient to provide a decent standard of living. Many communities remain riven by factionalism: The Mohawk, for example, are deeply divided over the issues of gaming and the nature of their political leadership—"traditional" or "progressive." Many groups have initiated various programs and gatherings in order to focus or refocus on their traditions. Among those groups whose native traditions have long since been lost, pan-Indianism has become important.

In Canada, at least six different governmental agencies have controlled Indian affairs since 1867, with the result that a consistent and effective policy has yet to be developed. Canadian Indians, especially the thousands of Métis (or mixed Indian and Anglo-French descendants) in Canada's southeast, face continuing problems of recognition. In both countries, despite almost 500 years of contact with non-natives and extremely strong pressures during those centuries to abandon their traditions and culture, many descendants of the forest dwellers remain Indians. Far removed from the life of their ancestors, they insist upon their identity as they continue to adapt their deeply rooted traditions.

Abenaki

Abenaki (`Ä bə `nä kē), more properly Wabenaki, "Dawn Land People" or "easterners," were a group of Algonquian tribes. They are sometimes discussed as Eastern Abenaki (including Kennebec, Penobscot, Arosaguntícook, and Pigwacket) and Western Abenaki (including Penacook, Winnipesaukee, and Sokoki). There was also a seventeenth- and eighteenth-century Abenaki Confederacy consisting of these and other tribes, such as the Maliseet, Micmac, and Passamaquoddy. *See also* Maliseet; Micmac; Passamaquoddy; Penobscot.

Location Abenakis lived near major rivers of northern New England and southern Quebec in the early seventeenth century. Today, there are Micmac, Penobscot, and Passamaquoddy Reservations in northern and eastern Maine. Maliseets live in northern Maine and southeastern Quebec, and Abenakis live in northern Vermont and southern Quebec.

Population There were perhaps 10,000 Eastern and 5,000 Western Abenakis in the early seventeenth century. In 1990, around 1,700 Western Abenakis lived in northern Vermont, about 800 lived in New Hampshire, and roughly 1,800 lived in Quebec, Canada. There were about 2,000 Penobscots in the early 1990s.

Language Abenakis spoke dialects of Eastern Algonquian languages.

Historical Information

History Abenakis originally came from the Southwest, according to their legends. They may have met early explorers such as Giovanni da Verrazano in

the sixteenth century. They were definitely visited by Samuel de Champlain and others, including missionaries, early in the seventeenth century, shortly after which time the Abenakis became heavily involved in the fur trade. Western groups traded with the Dutch and entered the fur trade later than the eastern groups.

Almost immediately, many eastern villages disappeared as a result of war (mostly Micmac attacks) and disease. Among the survivors, material culture and subsistence economy changed rapidly with the availability of non-native items. Indians and French regularly intermarried. Western groups came in conflict with the Iroquois from the mid– to late seventeenth century. Abenakis first arrived in Quebec from Maine in the late seventeenth century. They lived on the banks of the Chaudière River before moving to their present territory in the early eighteenth century.

Abenakis were staunch allies of the French in the colonial wars, although eastern groups needed to cover their bases with the British in the interest of preserving trade. Fierce Abenaki fighters sacked many British settlements throughout New England in the late seventeenth century and early eighteenth century. The Western Abenakis, in particular, played a significant role in much of the history of New France, including fur trading, exploring, and fighting the Seneca and Mohawk.

The Indians steadily lost land during the late seventeenth and eighteenth centuries. The Penobscot slowly emerged as the strongest eastern tribe. When the town of Norridgewalk fell to the British in 1724, many Eastern Abenakis withdrew to Quebec. Although Penobscots urged Abenaki neutrality in the French and Indian War, other Eastern Abenakis, now living in Quebec, fought with the French. The Penobscots were eventually drawn in: The treaty of 1763 marked the British victory as well as the Penobscot defeat. Meanwhile, after the fighting ended in 1763, Western Abenakis returned to their territory to find British squatters. They abandoned most of these lands after 1783, settling near a reserve on the Ste. Francois River in Quebec.

In the nineteenth and early twentieth centuries, most Western Abenakis sought to avoid anti-Indian sentiment by speaking French, selling ash-splint baskets to tourists, and keeping to themselves. Some hunted in a large territory north of the St. Lawrence River, and some returned to northern New England for seasonal cash work and subsistence activities. Many Western Abenakis attended Dartmouth College in the nineteenth century.

In 1941, the establishment of a wildlife refuge by the state of Vermont ended the people's ancient hunting and fishing rights. A postwar resurgence of the western group was based on controversies over fishing and hunting rights and a lack of official recognition. These groups held fish-ins to dramatize their situation. State recognition in 1976 was withdrawn the following year.

Religion Western groups tended to believe in a supreme creator, and both Eastern and Western Abenakis enjoyed a rich mythology. Many ceremonies were based on crops or the hunt as well as on greeting visitors, weddings, and funerals. At least among the western group, boys might seek the help of supernatural beings by obtaining a guardian spirit through a vision quest around the time of puberty. Dances were often associated with the spirit power. Shamans, often employing drums, foretold the future, located game, and cured illness.

Government Authority was gained as a result of leadership qualities, although there was also an element of patrilineal descent. Eastern chiefs of extended families were also sometimes shamans and after the seventeenth century were known as sagamores. Western groups recognized lifelong civil and war chiefs as well as a council of elders. The chiefs' powers were relatively limited.

Customs Several related nuclear families living together made up a household, which was the basic social and economic unit. Descent was patrilineal. Social status was somewhat hierarchical, especially in the east, where chiefs might have more than one wife. Shamans or special healers were brought in when herbal or plant-based cures and sweats failed.

In general, men provided animal foods, fought, and made tools and houses; women grew crops, gathered foods, prepared and cooked food, made clothing, and took care of children. Men engaged in

Abenaki men engaged in frequent races and archery contests. They also played ball games, including lacrosse. This nineteenth-century drawing by Seth Eastman depicts men playing ball on the ice.

frequent races and archery contests. They also played ball games, including lacrosse. People kept dogs as pets and used them to track game.

The use of stories and gentle group pressure was sufficient to discipline children. Boys gave away their first big game animal kills (all men gave away their first kill of the season). Marriage, considered official after gifts were given to the bride's family, was celebrated by feasting and dancing (as were many occasions). The dead were buried as soon as possible with weapons and/or tools for use in the afterlife. The western group put bodies in bark coffins and placed east-facing triangular structures over the graves.

Dwellings Villages were located along streams and, among the western group, near meadows. Easterners lived in dome-shaped and square houses with pyramid roofs shingled with bark. There were smoke holes at the top, and deerskins covered two doors. At least in the early historical period villages were palisaded. Westerners tended to live in birch-bark longhouses with arched roofs. Several families lived in each house. They also built dome-shaped sweat lodges.

Diet A shorter growing season and poorer soil meant that Abenakis depended less on crops than did southern Algonquians. In small family groups they hunted caribou, deer, and bear and trapped beaver and other small game as well as birds. Western groups called and ran down moose.

Women gathered berries, nuts, potatoes, and wild cherries and other fruits. They also boiled maple and birch sap for syrup and sugar. In spring, the eastern group fished along the coast for salmon, shad,

eel, sturgeon, smelt, and other fish. They also gathered shellfish and other marine foods and hunted sea mammals. Fish were also important to the western group, who grew more corn, beans, squash, and tobacco.

Key Technology Men fished using hooks, nets, spears, and weirs and hunted using the bow and arrow, lance, and knife. Hunting bags, some made of woodchuck skin, included fire-making tools and pipe (clay and stone) and tobacco. Important tools included knives, awls, gouges, adzes, wooden and stone scrapers, and pounders. Some groups made carved wooden dishes and utensils as well as pottery.

Containers were made of folded bark, rushes, or grasses. Some were decorated with porcupine quills. From the early seventeenth century on, wampum beads were used to record treaties and major council decisions.

Trade Abenakis generally traded with neighboring groups until the beginning of the fur trade period, when they traded furs for corn from southern New England. At that time, wampum became a medium of exchange and political status.

Notable Arts Many items, including pottery, were carefully decorated. Bark containers, for example, were often decorated with incised, curved designs. Ash-splint baskets became popular after contact with non-natives, although the people may have woven some baskets aboriginally.

Transportation Men made birch-bark and dugout canoes, snowshoes, and toboggans.

Dress Women tanned skins to make most clothing. Men wore beaver-pelt breechclouts and belts. Western women wore skirts and blouses in addition to cold-weather gear. Both wore moccasins, leggings, moose hide coats, and fur robes and caps. Tunics were also common. Both sexes painted their faces and bodies and wore their hair long.

War and Weapons Before they joined the confederacy. Micmacs often fought eastern Abenakis. The western group often clashed with the Iroquois but were generally friendly with Algonquians. Weapons included the bow and arrow, knife, spear, and club. Among the western group, the question of war was discussed at a general council that all people attended and in which all could participate. If war was agreed upon, the war chief called for volunteers. Warriors painted their faces and bodies.

Contemporary Information

Government/Reservations There are Western Abenaki communities in Odanak (St. Francis; 607.02 hectares) and Wôlinak (Bécancour; 79 hectares), Quebec, Canada. The Odanak reserve had a 1994 population of 1,458, of whom 267 lived within the territory. The Wôlinak reserve had a 1994 population of 311, of whom 114 lived within the territory. There are communities in northern Vermont near Highgate and St. Albans (Traditional Abenaki of Mazipskwik). The community at St. Albans, also known as the St. Francis–Sokoki Band, is governed by a tribal council. The Quebec communities are governed by band councils and represented by the Grand Council of the Waban-Aki Nation. The Abenaki Indian Village is located in Lake George, New York.

Economy Most Abenakis work mainly in the local non-native economy. Canadian Abenakis have begun setting up an outfitting business by filing a claim for exclusive local hunting and fishing rights. Basketry also generates income for the two communities.

Legal Status The St. Francis–Sokoki Band of the Abenaki Nation of Vermont has petitioned for federal recognition. The Penobscot Nation and the Passamaquoddy tribe are federally recognized tribal entities. The Odanak and Wôlinak reserves are federally and provincially recognized.

Daily Life The Abenaki Self-Help Association attempts to meet people's health and housing needs. Many Western Abenakis maintain their family-based culture. Ongoing cultural events include a harvest dinner in October and traditional dances and ceremonies at late spring/early summer powwows. A few people still speak the native language in Quebec. Abenakis are working to have the language taught in local public schools. Two Canadian institutions, the

Société Historique (Odanak Historical Society) and the Musée des Abénaquis (Abenaki Museum) represent the culture of the people to the world. Penobscots, Maliseets, and Passamaquoddys have intermarried considerably. Penobscot children attend their own elementary school.

Algonquin

Algonquin (Al `gon kin or Al `gon kwin) or Algonkin, probably from a Micmac word meaning "at the place of spearing fish and eels from the bow of a canoe," is the name of a northeastern group of bands that also gave its name to an important language family. The original self-designation was *Anishinabeg,* or "true men." Principal Algonquin bands included the Weskarini (Algonquin proper), Abitibi, and Temiskaming. *See also* Anishinabe; Ottawa; Wyandotte.

Location In the early seventeenth century, Algonquins lived in the Ottawa Valley of Quebec and Ontario, particularly along the northern tributary rivers. Today they live on reserves in Ontario and Quebec and in regional cities and towns.

Population There were roughly 6,000 Algonquins in the early seventeenth century and about 8,000 in the mid-1990s. Of the roughly 7,300 Quebec Algonquins, about 4,300 live among nine communities.

Language Algonquins spoke an Algonquian language.

Historical Information

History Algonquins lived on the north shore of the St. Lawrence River from about 1550 to 1650. They began trading with the French in the early sixteenth century and later became important French allies. Trade frictions soon provoked a war with the Mohawk. The Algonquin won that skirmish with assistance provided by the French in order to maintain an important trade partner.

However, the French had made a powerful enemy in the Mohawk, and within a few decades the local military situation had been reversed, with the Iroquois now firmly in control. Meanwhile, the Huron had replaced the Algonquin as the key French trade partner. The Mohawk, needing to expand their trapping area, soon attacked again. The Algonquin were forced to abandon the upper St. Lawrence and, after about 1650, the Ottawa Valley. They returned in the 1660s when peace was reestablished. An epidemic in the 1670s left them further weakened.

During the late seventeenth century, some Algonquin bands merged with the Ottawa Indians. French trading posts were established, and missionaries became a permanent presence in their territory by the early eighteenth century. Some Algonquins traveled to the far west to trap for Canadian companies. After the final French defeat in 1763, the Algonquin became staunch British allies. Reserves for the group were created in the nineteenth century, when their lands were overrun by British settlers. The decline of the fur trade and of their hunting grounds (mainly owing to local logging operations) as well as a growing dependence on non-natives led many Algonquins to adopt a sedentary lifestyle.

Religion The people believed in a great creator spirit and a host of lesser spirits, both good and evil. Both shamans and hunters sought guardian spirits to help them with their work, which included interpreting dreams and healing the sick. After death, the spirits of hunters were thought to pursue the spirits of animals.

Government Small bands were composed of one or more clans with local chiefs. People smoked tobacco silently before council meetings.

Customs Algonquins entertained visitors with the annual Feast of the Dead, a dance with a war theme. When entertaining guests, the host did not eat. Clan descent as well as the inheritance of hunting territories may have been patrilineal. Bands tended to come together in summer and disperse in winter. People placed wooden rooflike structures with painted self-images at one end over the graves of high-status people. People were reluctant to mention their real names for fear of misuse by witches.

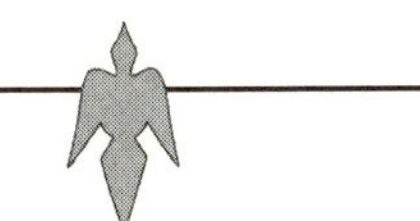

Dwellings People lived in cone-shaped, tipilike dwellings. They also built rectangular birch-bark hunting shelters.

Diet Men fished in both summer and winter (through holes cut in the ice). They hunted game such as moose, deer, caribou, and beaver. Agricultural crops played a small role in their diet. Some bands made maple sugar. Dog was eaten on occasion.

Key Technology Important material items included birch-bark containers sewn with spruce roots, basswood bags and mats, wooden cradleboards, bows and arrows, and double-headed drums.

Trade Algonquins imported fish nets and cornmeal from Hurons and also traded extensively with Iroquoian tribes. They traded animal pelts and porcupine quills to nearby groups in exchange for corn, tobacco, fishing gear, and wampum.

Notable Arts The people decorated many birch-bark items with the use of templates. Decorative styles included zigzag bands and floral motifs. Most designs were symmetrical. Southern bands decorated items with porcupine quillwork.

Transportation Men made birch-bark canoes, snowshoes, and toboggans.

Dress Dress varied according to location. Most clothing was made of buckskin or moose skin. Clothing included breechclouts, skirts, ponchos, leggings, robes, and moccasins; moccasins were often dyed black. Fur garments were added in cold weather. Both men and women tended to wear their hair long and braided.

War and Weapons Algonquins fought with bows and arrows, spears, and knives; they were early allies with the Huron. They dominated the Iroquois before the latter banded together in their great confederacy.

Contemporary Information

Government/Reservations The two Algonguin communities in Ontario are Golden Lake and Wahgoshig. Quebec communities include Abitibiwinni (90.5 hectares; 674 people in 1994, of whom 388 lived within the territory), Barrière Lake (28 hectares; 520 people in 1994, of whom 409 lived within the territory), Eagle Village–Kipewa (21.49 hectares; 494 people in 1994, of whom 170 lived within the territory), Kitcisakik (12.14 hectares; 302 people in 1994, of whom 272 lived within the territory), Kitigan Zibi Anishinabeg (11,165.14 hectares; 2,094 people in 1994, of whom 1,313 lived within the territory), Lac Simon (275.01 hectares; 1,104 people in 1994, of whom 874 lived within the territory), Long Point (37.84 hectares; 558 people in 1994, of whom 273 lived within the territory), Témiscamigue (2,428.08 hectares; 1,241 people in 1994, of whom 473 lived within the territory), and Wolf Lake (Hunter's Point; 4 hectares; 185 people in 1994, of whom 7 lived within the territory). Canadian communities are governed by band councils. Algonquin communities are also represented by the Anishinabe Algonquin Nation Council and the Algonquin Nation Programs and Services Secretariat.

Algonquins also live on Gibson Reserve, Ontario, primarily a home to Iroquois people.

Economy Some people raise gardens, and some serve as guides to visiting sportsmen. Some maintain a traditional hunting and trapping life. Important local industries include construction, forestry, and transportation. The Algonquin Development Association provides support for the initiation of economic projects.

Legal Status The Canadian communities listed under "Government/Reservations" are legally recognized tribal entities. Long Point and Kitcisakik do not have the status of a reserve. In 1994, a framework for negotiations was reached between the people of Golden Lake and provincial officials concerning a land claim for 3,400 square kilometers of land in Ontario.

Daily Life Many Algonquins have intermarried with non-natives and merged with non-native society. Still, at least 60 percent of Quebec Algonquins probably speak their ancestral language. The community of Kitigan Zibi Anishinabeg has a primary and secondary school, a women's shelter, a youth center, and other resources. The Matciteeia Society is an Algonquin cultural organization.

Anishinabe

Anishinabe (Ä nish i n`ä bā), "People," are also variously known by the band names Ojibwe/ Ojibwa/Ojibway/Chippewa, Mississauga, and Salteaux. The name Ojibwa means "puckered up," probably a reference to a style of sewn moccasin. With the Potawatomi and Ottawa, with whom they may once have been united, some groups were part of the Council of Three Fires in the nineteenth century. Northern groups had a Subarctic as well as a Woodlands cultural orientation (*see* Chapter 9, especially Cree). *See also* Ojibwa, Plains (Chapter 6); Ottawa.

Location Anishinabe groups lived north of Lake Huron and northeast of Lake Superior (present-day Ontario, Canada) in the early seventeenth century. In the eighteenth century, northern Ojibwas lived between the Great Lakes and Hudson Bay, and the Lake Winnipeg Salteaux lived just east and south of that body of water.

Today, there are Anishinabe communities and reservations in central and northern Michigan, including the Upper Peninsula; northern Wisconsin; northern and central Minnesota; northern North Dakota; northern Montana; and southern Ontario. Anishinabe also live in regional cities and towns.

Population The people numbered at least 35,000, but perhaps more than double that figure, in the early seventeenth century. There were roughly 125,000 enrolled Anishinabe in the United States in the mid-1990s, including about 48,000 in Minnesota, at least 30,000 in Michigan, 25,000 members of the Turtle Mountain Band in North Dakota, 16,500 in Wisconsin, and 3,100 at Rocky Boy Reservation in Montana, plus other communities in Montana and elsewhere in the United States. There were about 60,000 Anishinabe in Canada in the mid-1990s, excluding Métis.

Language The various Anishinabe groups spoke dialects of Algonquian languages.

Historical Information

History The Anishinabe probably came to their historical location from the northeast and had arrived by about 1200. They encountered Frenchmen in the early seventeenth century and soon became reliable French allies. From the later seventeenth century on, the people experienced great changes in their material and economic culture as they became dependent on guns, beads, cloth, metal items, and alcohol.

Pressures related to the fur trade, including Iroquois attacks, drove the Anishinabe to expand their territory by the late seventeenth century. With French firearms, they pressured the Dakota to move west toward the Great Plains. They also drove tribes such as the Sauk, Fox, and Kickapoo from Michigan and replaced the Huron in lower Michigan and extreme southeast Ontario. With the westward march of British and especially French trading posts, Ojibwa bands also moved into Minnesota and north-central Canada (Lake of the Woods and the Red River area), displacing Siouan and other Algonquian groups (such as the Cheyenne).

As early as the late seventeenth century, Anishinabe bands had moved west into the Lake Winnipeg/North Dakota region. Many people intermarried with Cree Indians and French trappers and became known as Métis, or Mitchif. By the eighteenth century, Anishinabe bands stretched from Lake Huron to the Missouri River.

The people were most deeply involved in the fur (especially beaver) trade during the eighteenth century. They fought the British in the French and Indian War and in Pontiac's rebellion. In 1769, in alliance with neighboring tribes, they utterly defeated the Illinois Indians. They fought with the British in the Revolutionary War. Following this loss, they kept up anti-American military pressure, engaging the non-natives in Little Turtle's war, Tecumseh's rebellion, and the War of 1812.

By the early nineteenth century, scattered, small hunter-fisher-gatherer bands of northern Ojibwa and Salteaux were located north and west of the Great Lakes. These people experienced significant changes from the early nineteenth century, such as a greater reliance on fish and hare products and on non-native material goods.

The Plains Ojibwe (Bungi) had moved west as far as southern Saskatchewan and Manitoba and North Dakota and Montana. They adopted much of Great Plains culture. The southeastern Ojibwe (Mississauga), living in northern and southern Michigan and nearby Ontario, were hunters, fishers, gatherers, and gardeners. They also made maple sugar and, on occasion, used wild rice. Their summer villages were relatively large. Finally, the southwestern Ojibwe had moved into northern Wisconsin and Minnesota following the departing Dakotas. They depended on wild rice as well as hunting, fishing, gathering, gardening. and maple sugaring.

Anishinabe living in the United States ceded much of their eastern land to that government in 1815 upon the final British defeat. Land cessions and the establishment of reservations in Wisconsin and Minnesota followed during the early to mid–nineteenth century. Two small bands went to Kansas in 1839. In the 1860s, some groups settled with the Ottawa, Munsee, and Potawatomi in the Indian Territory.

Michigan and Minnesota Anishinabe groups (with the exception of the Red Lake people) lost most of their land (90 percent or more in many cases) to allotment, fraud, and other irregularities in the mid– to late nineteenth century. They also suffered significant culture loss as a result of government policies encouraging forced assimilation. In the late nineteenth century, many southwestern Ojibwe worked as lumberjacks. Many in the southeast concentrated more on farming, although they continued other traditional subsistence activities when possible. Transition to non-native styles of housing, clothing, and political organization was confirmed during this period.

Plains Ojibwa took part in the Métis rebellion of Louis Riel in 1869–1870. These groups were finally settled on the Turtle Mountain Reservation in the late nineteenth century and on the Rocky Boy Reservation in the early twentieth century. Around the turn of the century, the Turtle Mountain Chippewa, led by Chief Little Shell, worked to regain land lost in 1884 and to reenroll thousands of Métis whom the United States had unilaterally excluded from the tribal rolls. In 1904, the tribe received $1 million for a 10-million-acre land claim, a settlement of 10 cents an acre. Soon thereafter, most of the Turtle Mountain land was allotted. One result of that action was that many people, denied adequate land, were forced to scatter across the Dakotas and Montana. Most of the allotments were later lost to tax foreclosure, after which the tribal members, now landless, drifted back to Turtle Mountain.

The growing poverty of Michigan bands was partially reversed after most accepted the Indian Reorganization Act (IRA) in the 1930s and the United States reassumed its trust relationship with them. Many of these people moved to the industrial cities of the Midwest, especially in Michigan and Wisconsin, after World War II, although most retained close ties with the reservation communities.

Among the northern Ojibwa, bands had made treaties with the Canadian government since the mid–nineteenth century. The Canadian Pacific Railway was completed in the 1880s and the Canadian National Railway around 1920. Supply operations changed again during the 1930s, when "bush planes" began flying. Many people began growing small gardens at that time as well.

Religion Some groups may have believed in the existence of an overarching supreme creative power. All animate and inanimate objects had spirits that could be good or evil (the latter, like the cannibalistic Windigo, were greatly feared). People attempted to keep the spirits happy through prayer and by the ritual use of tobacco and the intervention of shamans. Tobacco played a significant role in many rituals.

By fasting and dreaming in a remote place, young men sought a guardian spirit that would assist them throughout their lives. In general, dreams were considered of extreme importance. There was probably little religious ceremonialism before people began dying in unprecedented numbers as a result of hitherto unknown diseases of Old World origin. The Midewiwin or Medicine Dance was a graded curing society that probably arose, except among the northern Ojibwa, in response to this development.

Membership in the Midewiwin was gained by experiencing particular visions or dreams. Candidates received a period of instruction and paid certain fees. Once a year, a secret meeting lasting several days was held in a special long lodge to

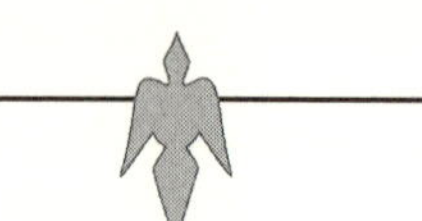

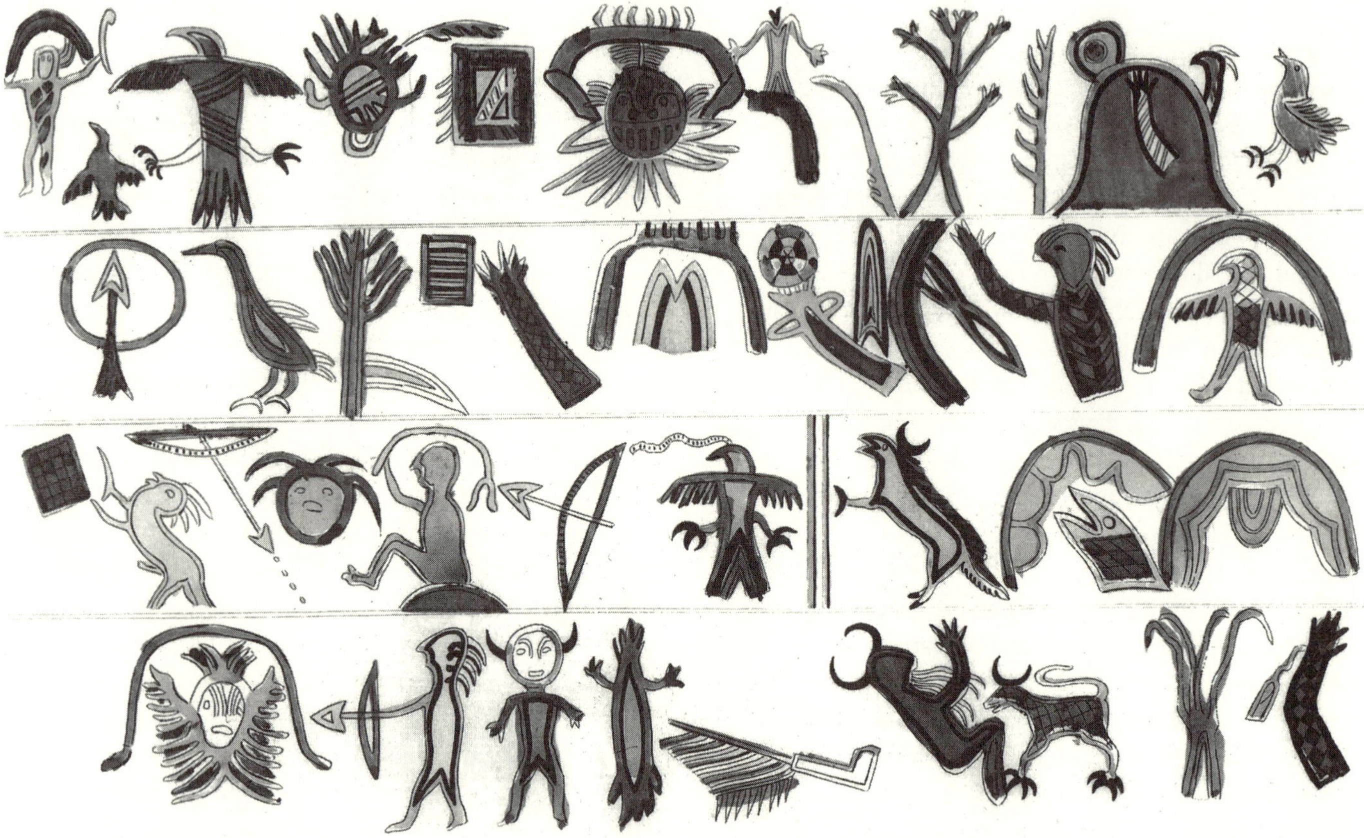

These Ojibwa pictographs depict the sequence for invocations, offerings, and songs for a particular ritual.

initiate new members, who could be men or women. Initiates were shot with a sacred white shell, through which supernatural power entered the body, and were then restored by a priest. One member recorded the proceedings by carving and painting bark scrolls. Members wore special medicine bags around their necks. Initiates did not become shamans, but many were cured through entering the society; members also achieved greater supernatural power as well as prestige.

Bears were revered and were the focus of a special ceremony. Shamans, usually older men, cured the sick with recourse to spiritual power, and herbalists offered effective cures using hundreds of local plants. Several degrees of shaman were recognized. Among the Lake Winnipeg Salteaux, shamans cured disease by using sucking tubes, sometimes after communicating with their spirit helpers in a special shaking tent. These shamans engaged in contests for authority by showing off their evil powers. People also observed special first-fruits ceremonies over wild rice and bear.

Government Men led autonomous bands of perhaps 300–400 people on the basis of both family and ability. Bands were related by marriage but never politically united. Band headman were often war captains but had little direct authority before the fur trade period; for their own advantage, traders worked to increase the power of the headman. These efforts ultimately led to the creation of a patrilineal line of chiefs.

Customs About 15–23 patrilineal clans were linked into the larger divisions. Bands came together in villages during summer and dispersed for the winter hunting season. Within the context of a social organization that was relatively egalitarian, there were people with higher status than others, such as chiefs, accomplished warriors, and shamans.

Infants spent most of their first year on a cradle board with a moss "mattress." Names were ultimately spirit derived. A close relationship existed between the namer and the named. Children were raised with little harsh discipline.

Although a special feast was held to celebrate a boy's first kill, the major male puberty rite was the vision quest, which entailed a four-day fast deep in the forest to await a propitious dream. At that time he received a guardian spirit power that could be used for good or evil; with the spirit came various names and songs. Contact with the spirit was maintained throughout the man's life by means of food offerings and tobacco. Girls might also have visions, but they were not generally required to undergo a quest.

Girls were chaperoned at all times. A man might play a flute to court a prospective wife, who was likely chosen by his parents. A man brought food to the future wife's family to formalize the engagement. Eventually they moved into their own lodge. Important men might have more than one wife. Divorce was easy to obtain on grounds as basic as incompatibility.

Corpses were washed and well presented. Wrapped in birch bark, they were removed from the wigwam, after a period of lying in state, through an opening in the west side. A priest gave a funeral ceremony, after which the body was buried with tools and equipment. The soul was said to travel for four days to a happy location in the west. The mourning period lasted one year.

The Anishinabe enjoyed regular visiting as well as social dancing (although on such occasions men often danced apart from women). They also enjoyed various sports, such as lacrosse and a game in which they threw a pole along frozen snow, and contests; gambling invariably played a part in these activities. Lacrosse was rough and carried religious overtones.

Dwellings The traditional Anishinabe dwelling was a domed wigwam of cattail mats or birch bark over a pole frame. There was a smoke hole in the center over the fire. The doorway was covered with bark, hide, or a blanket. Mats and furs were placed around the sides for sleeping and storage. Floors were covered with cedar inner bark, bullrush mats, or, in the north, boughs.

There were also larger, elliptical wigwams that housed several families. These had a fireplace at either end. Hunters also used temporary bark-covered A-frame lodges, and people built smaller sweat lodges, used for purification or curing, as well as menstrual huts and Midewiwin lodges.

Diet Women grew small gardens of corn, beans, and squash in the south. Men hunted and trapped a variety of large and small game, mostly in winter, as well as birds and fowl. Meat was roasted, stone boiled, or dried and stored. Some was dried and mixed with fat and chokecherries to make pemmican, an extremely nourishing, long-lasting food. Men fished year round, especially for sturgeon, sometimes at night by the light of flaming birch-bark torches. People also ate shellfish where available. Dog was often served at feasts.

In the fall, women in canoes gathered wild rice, which became a staple in the Anishinabe southwest and important as well around Lake Winnipeg. Wild rice was actually a grass with an edible seed that could be knocked into the canoe with sticks. It was stored and eaten after being dried, parched, and winnowed. They also gathered a variety of berries, fruits, and nuts, and some groups collected maple sap for sugar, which they used as a seasoning and in water. Northern Ojibwas had access neither to wild rice nor to maple sap.

Key Technology Most items were made of wood and birch bark, but people also used stone, bone, and possibly some pottery. Important material items included birch-bark containers and dishes; water drums, flutes, tambourines, and rattles; cattail, cedar, and bulrush mats; and basswood twine and bags. Fishing equipment included nets, spears, and wood or bone lures and hooks. Lake Winnipeg people made distinctive black steatite pipes as well as sturgeon-skin containers.

Trade Trade items included elm-bark bags and assorted birch-bark goods, carved wooden bowls, food, and maple sugar. As they expanded west, the people began to trade Woodland items for buffalo-derived products.

Notable Arts Clothing and medicine bags were decorated with quillwork. Men carved wooden utilitarian as well as religious items (figurines). Pattern designs were bitten into thin birch-bark sheets. The

The southeastern Ojibwe, living in northern and southern Michigan and nearby Ontario, were hunters, fishers, gatherers, and gardeners as well as makers of maple sugar and, on occasion, users of wild rice. This nineteenth-century drawing by Seth Eastman depicts the Ojibwa harvesting wild rice.

Anishinabe were also known for their soft elm-bark bags. Lake Winnipeg women made fine moose-hide mittens, richly decorated in beads. As with many native peoples, storytelling evolved to a fine art.

Transportation Men made birch-bark canoes and snowshoes. Horses were acquired in the late eighteenth century. Northern Ojibwas used toboggans and canoe-sleds, sometimes hauled by large dogs, from the nineteenth century on.

Dress Dress varied according to location. Most clothing was made of buckskin. Ojibways tended to color their clothing with red, yellow, blue, and green dyes. In the southwestern areas, women wore woven fiber shirts under a sleeveless dress. Other clothing included breechclouts, leggings, robes, and moccasins, the last often dyed and featuring a distinctive puckered seam. Fur garments were added in cold weather. Both men and women tended to wear their hair long and braided.

War and Weapons The Anishinabe were generally effective but unenthusiastic fighters. They were traditional allies of the Ottawa and Potawatomi; their enemies included the Iroquois and Dakota. Battles were fought on land as well as occasionally from canoes. Weapons included the knobbed wooden war club, bow and arrow, knife, and moose-hide shield. Enemies were generally killed in battle. Some were ritually eaten. Warriors sometimes exchanged their long hair for a scalp lock.

The Anishinabe ("Original People") are also variously known by the band names Ojibwe/Ojibwa/Ojibway/Chippewa, Mississauga, and Salteaux. This Chippewa man is shown mending his birch-bark canoe (1887). Men fished year-round, especially for sturgeon, sometimes at night by the light of flaming birch-bark torches.

Contemporary Information

Government/Reservations The following are Anishinabe reservations in Michigan:

L'Anse Reservation (Keweenaw Bay, L'Anse, and Otonagan Bands), Baraga County, established in 1854, consists of about 13,000 acres of land, almost two-thirds of which is allotted. There were about 3,100 enrolled members in the early 1990s. The 1990 Indian population was 724.

The Lac Vieux Desert Reservation, Gogebic County, consists of 104 acres of land. The 1990 Indian population was 119. This band had an enrollment of about 240 in the early 1990s. The reservation remains officially unrecognized.

The Bay Mills Indian Reservation (Bay Mills and Sault Ste. Marie Bands), Chippewa County, established in 1850, consists of 2,209 acres of land. The 1990 Indian population was 403. Enrolled membership was about 950 in the early 1990s.

The Sault Ste. Marie Reservation (Sault Ste. Marie Band), Alger, Chippewa, Mackinac, and Schoolcraft Counties, owns 293 acres of land. The 1990 Indian population was 554. There were about 20,630 enrolled band members in the early 1990s. The reservation remains officially unrecognized.

Isabella Reservation and Trust Lands, Isabella and Aranac Counties (Saginaw Chippewa Tribe), established in 1864, contains 1,184 acres, about half of which is tribally owned. A ten-member tribal council is elected at large. The 1990 Indian population was 790. This band had almost 2,200 enrolled members in the early 1990s.

The Grand Traverse Reservation (Ottawa and Chippewa), Leelanau County, consists of about 600 acres of land. The 1990 Indian population was 208. The tribe had about 2,300 members in the early 1990s. The reservation remains officially unrecognized.

The Burt Lake (State) Reservation (Ottawa and Chippewa), Brutus County, consists of about 20 acres. There were over 500 enrolled Chippewas and Ottawas in the early 1990s.

The Anishinabe communities in Minnesota, which are member reservations of the Minnesota Chippewa Tribe, are self-governed by an elected tribal council or business committee, in cooperation with local councils. Each community is also represented in an overall tribal executive committee, headquartered at Cass Lake community, Leech Lake. Red Lake Reservation is self-governing. The communities are as follows:

Nett Lake (Bois Forte) Reservation (Deer Creek Band), Koochiching and St. Louis Counties, established in 1854, consists of almost 42,000 acres. The 1990 Indian population was 345.

Fond du Lac Reservation, Carlton and St. Louis Counties, established in 1854, consists of almost 22,000 acres. The 1990 Indian population was 1,102.

Grand Portage Reservation, Cook County, established in 1854, consists of almost 45,000 acres. The 1990 Indian population was 206.

Leech Lake Reservation (Mississippi and Pilanger Bands), Beltrami, Cass, Hubbard, and Itasca Counties, established in 1855, consists of roughly 27,500 acres. The 1990 Indian population was 3,390.

Mille Lacs Reservation, Aitkin, Crow Wing, Kanabec, Mille Lacs, and Pine Counties, established in 1855, consists of almost 4,000 acres. The 1990 Indian population was 428.

White Earth Reservation, Blecker, Clearwater, and Mahnomen Counties, established in 1867, consists of roughly 56,000 acres. The 1990 Indian population was 2,759.

Red Lake Reservation, Beltrami, Clearwater, Koochiching, Lake of the Woods, Marshall, Pennington, Polk, Red Lake, and Roseau Counties, established in 1863, consists of roughly 564,000 acres of land. There were almost 8,000 enrolled members of this band in the early 1990s. The 1990 Indian population was 3,601.

The following are reservations of the Lake Superior Tribe (Wisconsin) of Chippewa Indians. Each is governed and administered by an IRA-style tribal council of from 5 to 12 members, headed by an executive officer. Tribal courts are also in the process of expanding their authority to cover welfare and environmental issues. The communities are also members of regional organizations such as the Great Lakes Inter-Tribal Council.

Bad River Reservation, Ashland and Iron Counties, established in 1854, consists of about 56,000 acres, less than half of which is tribally owned. The 1990 Indian population was 868. Tribal membership in the early 1990s was about 4,500 people.

Lac Courte Oreilles Reservation and Trust Lands, Sawyer, Burnett, and Washburn Counties, established in 1854, consists of about 48,000 acres, less than half of which is tribally owned. The 1990 Indian population was 1,769. Tribal membership in the early 1990s was about 4,000 people.

Lac du Flambeau Reservation, Iron, Oneida, and Vilas Counties, established in 1854, consists of almost 45,000 acres, about two-thirds of which is tribally owned. The 1990 Indian population was 1,431. Tribal membership in the early 1990s was about 2,700 people.

Red Cliff Reservation and Trust Lands, Bayfield County, established in 1854, consists of almost 75,000 acres, about three-quarters of which is tribally owned. The 1990 Indian population was 727. Tribal membership in the early 1990s was about 2,800 people.

The St. Croix Reservation and the Sokaogon Community and Trust Lands are also located in Wisconsin. St. Croix Reservation, Barron, Burnett, and Polk Counties, established in 1938, consists of about 2,200 acres, all of which is tribally owned. The 1990 Indian population was 459. Tribal membership in the early 1990s was about 750 people. The community is governed by a tribal council with officers.

Sokaogon Community and Trust Lands (Mole Lake Band), Forest County, established in 1938, consists of about 1,900 acres, all of which is tribally owned. The 1990 Indian population was 311. Tribal membership in the early 1990s was about 1,400 people. The community is governed by a tribal council with officers.

Other communities are in Montana and the Dakotas. The Rocky Boy Chippewa-Cree Reservation (1,485 resident Indians in 1990) and Trust Lands (397 resident Indians in 1990), located in Chouteau and Hill Counties, Montana, established in 1916, contains 108,015 acres. The tribe is governed by a written constitution delegating authority to the Chippewa-Cree Business Committee. There is also a tribal court. Roughly half of the population lives off of the reservation.

The Little Shell people, some of whom are of Cree descent, had a 1990 population of 3,300. They are governed by a tribal council under a constitution. Their main offices are in Havre and Helena, Montana. They are related to scattered groups of landless Chippewas living in and near Lewistown, Montana.

There is also a community of Chippewa, established during the process of allotting the Turtle Mountain Reservation, living in eastern Montana. The seat of their government is in Trenton, North Dakota.

The Turtle Mountain Reservation and Trust Lands, Rolette, Burke, Cavalier, Divide, McLean, Mountrail, and Williams Counties, North Dakota, and Perkins County, South Dakota, established in 1882, contains over 45,000 acres, of which about 30 percent is controlled by non-Indians. The 1990 resident Indian population was 6,770. The reservation is governed by an elected nine-member tribal council under a 1959 constitution and by-laws. Headquarters are located in Belcourt, North Dakota.

Canada recognizes over 130 Indian communities that are wholly or in part Anishinabe. They are located in Alberta, Manitoba, Ontario, and Saskatchewan and include Walpole Island (Ontario),

where Anishinabe Indians live with some Potawatomis and Ottawas.

Economy All of the acknowledged Michigan tribes operate successful casinos. Minnesota reservations operate at least one casino each. There is a women's cooperative that produces and sells wild rice and crafts at White Earth, Minnesota, and there is a fisheries cooperative at Red Lake, Minnesota. All Wisconsin reservations operate casinos. Forestry is an important industry. Many people are also part of local off-reservation economies. Unemployment is often around 50 percent.

The Rocky Boy Chippewa-Cree Development Company manages that tribe's economic resources. The tribe's beadwork is in high demand. The company organized a propane company and owns a casino as well as recreational facilities. The largest employers on the reservation are the tribal government, Stone Child Community College, and industry. Other activities include cattle grazing, wheat and barley farming, some logging and mining, and recreation/tourism. Unemployment regularly approaches 75 percent.

People in the Montana Allotment Community are integrated into the local economy. Turtle Mountain operates a casino, a manufacturing company, and a shopping center.

Many northern Ojibwas work at seasonal or part-time employment in industries such as construction, logging, and tourism. Fire fighting and tree planting offer some employment possibilities. There has also been an increase in government assistance.

Legal Status The following are federally recognized tribal entities in Michigan: the Bay Mills Indian Community of the Sault Ste. Marie Band of Chippewa Indians, Grand Traverse Band of Ottawa and Chippewa, Keweenaw Bay Indian Community of L'Anse of Chippewa Indians, Keweenaw Bay Indian Community of Lac Vieux Desert of Chippewa Indians, Keweenaw Bay Indian Community of Ontonagon Bands of Chippewa, Sault Ste. Marie Band of Chippewa Indians, and Saginaw Chippewa Indian Tribe.

In Minnesota, the federally recognized tribal entities are the Minnesota Chippewa Tribe (Bois Forte [Nett Lake] Band, Fond du Lac Band, Grand Portage Band, Leech Lake Band, Mille Lacs Band, and White Earth Band) and the Red Lake Band of Chippewa.

The Chippewa-Cree Indians of Rocky Boy Reservation is a federally recognized tribal entity in Montana.

The Turtle Mountain Band of Chippewa Indians is a federally recognized tribal entity in North Dakota.

The following are federally recognized tribal entities in Wisconsin: the Lake Superior Tribe of Chippewa (Bad River Band, Lac Courte Oreilles Band, Lac du Flambeau Band, and Red Cliff Band), the St. Croix Chippewa Indians, and the Sokaogon Band of Chippewa Community of the Mole Lake Band of Chippewa Indians.

The Burt Lake Band of Ottawa and Chippewa Indians is recognized by the state of Michigan and is pursuing federal acknowledgment. The Lake Superior Chippewa of Marquette Tribal Council (Michigan) has petitioned for federal recognition. The Consolidated Bahwetig Ojibwas and Mackinac Tribe (Michigan) has petitioned for federal recognition. The Kah-Bay Kah-Nong (Warroad) Chippewa (Minnesota) have petitioned for federal recognition.

The Little Shell Tribe of Chippewa Indians (North Dakota and Montana), as well as some of the "landless Chippewa" in Montana, have been seeking federal recognition since the 1920s. The Christian Pembina Chippewa Indians have also petitioned for federal recognition. Other officially unrecognized communities include the NI-MI-WIN Ojibweys (Minnesota), the Sandy Lake Band of Ojibwe (Minnesota), and the Swan Creek and Black River Chippewa (Montana).

The following are officially recognized northern Ojibwa bands in Ontario: Angling Lake, Bearskin Lake, Big Trout Lake, Caribou Lake, Cat Lake, Deer Lake, Fort Hope, Kasabonika lake, Kingfisher, Martin Falls, Muskrat Dam Lake, Osnaburgh, Sachigo Lake, and Wunnumin. Manitoba bands included Garden Hill, Red Sucker Lake, St. Theresa Point, and Wasagamack. Total population in 1980 was around 10,000.

Lake Winnipeg Salteaux bands in Ontario include Pikangikum, Islington, Grassy Narrows, Shoal Lake No. 39, Shoal Lake No. 40, Northwest Angle No. 33, Northwest Angle No. 37, Dalles, Rat

Portage, Whitefish Bay, Eagle Lake, Wabigoon, Wabauskang, Lac Seul, Big Island, Big Grassy, and Sabaskong. Manitoba bands include Little Black River, Bloodvein, Hole River, Brokenhead, Roseau River, Berens River, Fort Alexander, Peguis, Little Grand Rapids, Jackhead, Fairford, Lake St. Martin, and Poplar River. Total population in 1980 was around 19,000.

Daily Life The Michigan Anishinabe retain hunting and gathering rights on some ceded land. The Midewiwin society remains active in most communities, and most tribes maintain an active schedule of traditional or semitraditional events such as powwows, sweat lodges, and conferences. The Bay Mills Community operates its own community college. The Sault Ste. Marie tribe hosts two powwows and publishes a newspaper.

In Minnesota, most people retain their Indian identity in a number of important ways. A community college at Fond du Lac emphasizes tribal culture. People are pursuing several land reacquisition projects and subsistence rights cases. There are a number of powwows and other traditional and semitraditional activities throughout the state. The Ojibwa language, which roughly 30,000 people speak, is taught in schools and colleges. Authors continue a tradition of writing about their culture. Artists and craftspeople continue to produce moccasins, clothing, baskets, and other items. Leech Lake hosts five annual powwows, operates a school and a tribal college, and publishes a newsletter.

Although about half of Wisconsin Anishinabes live in mostly non-native cities and towns, most retain close ties to their home communities. The people maintain their Indian identity through events such as powwows, athletic contests, and traditional subsistence activities. Since a landmark court case in 1983 reaffirmed their subsistence rights on ceded land, the people have redoubled their efforts to defend those rights against a non-native backlash. Toward this end, they have established a number of environmental organizations, such as the Great Lakes Indian Fish and Wildlife Commission, to manage their natural resources and provide other related enforcement and public relations services.

Lac Courte Oreilles Community College provides crucial educational services to Wisconsin's Indians, including a radio station and courses on native language and cultures. Ongoing cultural traditions include Midewiwin lodges, the Drum Society (a late-nineteenth-century phenomenon), and subsistence activities. Although most are less than fluent, many people continue to speak the language.

Turtle Mountain Community College, which administers many tribal and federal social, health, and educational programs, is an important part of the Turtle Mountain, North Dakota, community. Ojibwe and Métis are still spoken. Most of these people are Catholic. Economic self-sufficiency remains a high priority.

In 1968, three Anishinabe founded the American Indian Movement (AIM), a self-help organization that proceeded to fight both quietly and openly for Indian rights. Important AIM actions have included the 1969 takeover of Alcatraz Island, the 1972 occupation of the Bureau of Indian Affairs in Washington, and the 1973 defense of Wounded Knee, South Dakota.

Northern Ojibwas in Canada have enjoyed decent health care facilities and educational opportunities since the 1950s. Trapping remains important but considerably less so than in the past. Many people live near their relatives. Many people are Christians.

Many Lake Winnipeg Salteaux people in Canada have intermarried with Cree Indians. The native religion has practically disappeared. Christianity, including some fundamentalist sects, has largely taken over, with one result being a high degree of factionalism. Roads have connected the people to the outside world only since the 1950s.

Brothertown

See Pequot

Cayuga

The Cayuga (Kī ` ū gä), from their word for "People of Oiogouen," were one of the five original tribes of the Iroquois League. The name Iroquois ("real adders") comes from the French adaptation of the

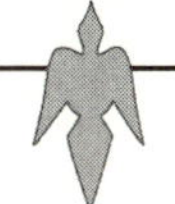

Algonquian name for these people. Their self-designation was *Kanonsionni,* "League of the United (Extended) Households." Iroquois today refer to themselves as *Haudenosaunee,* "People of the Longhouse." *See also* Seneca.

Location In the early historical period, the Cayuga lived in upstate New York, especially between Cayuga and Owasco Lakes, land between that of the Onondaga and the Seneca. At the height of their power, the Iroquois controlled land from the Hudson to the Illinois Rivers and the Ottawa to the Tennessee Rivers. Today, Cayugas live in Canada, western New York, Wisconsin, and Oklahoma.

Population There were about 1,500 Cayuga in 1660 and possibly as many as several thousand or more a century earlier, of perhaps 20,000 members of the Iroquois League. In the 1990s fewer than 500 Cayugas lived in New York, about 3,000 lived in Canada, and about 2,500 Seneca-Cayugas lived in Oklahoma. There were roughly 70,000 Iroquois Indians living in the United States and Canada in the mid-1990s.

Language Cayugas spoke a Northern Iroquois dialect.

Historical Information

History The Iroquois began cultivating crops shortly after the first phase of their culture in New York was established around 800. Deganawida, a Huron prophet, and Hiawatha, a Mohawk shaman living among the Onondaga, founded the Iroquois League or Confederacy some time between 1450 and 1600. It originally consisted of five tribes: Cayuga, Mohawk, Oneida, Onondaga, and Seneca; the Tuscarora joined in the early eighteenth century. The league's purpose was to end centuries of debilitating intertribal war and work for the common good. Both Deganawida and Hiawatha may have been actual or mythological people.

Iroquois first met non-natives in the sixteenth century. There were sporadic Jesuit missions in Cayuga country throughout the mid–seventeenth century. During those years, the Cayuga were more friendly toward the French than were some other Iroquois tribes. The people became heavily involved in the fur trade during the seventeenth and eighteenth centuries. Trading, fighting, and political intrigue characterized those years. Although they were good at playing the European powers off against each other, the Iroquois increasingly became British allies in trade and in the colonial wars and were instrumental in the ultimate British victory over the French.

Diplomatic success allowed the Iroquois to concentrate on expanding their trapping territory and increasing their trade advantages, mainly by fighting many tribes to their west and south. The Cayuga warpath led as far south as Virginia. Iroquois power blocked European westward expansion. Two Siouan tribes, the Tutelo and the Saponi, joined the Cayuga in 1753.

The British victory in 1763 meant that the Iroquois no longer controlled the regional balance of power. Despite their long-standing allegiance, some Indians joined anti-British rebellions in an effort to protect their land. One such rebellion took place in 1774 and was led by Logan, a Cayuga chief of the Iroquoian Mingos of Pennsylvania.

The confederacy split its allegiance in the Revolutionary War, with most Cayugas siding with the British. This split resulted in the council fire's being extinguished for the first time in some 200 years. The Iroquois suffered a major defeat in 1779. After the final U.S. victory, many Cayugas migrated to Ontario, Canada, where they established two villages on the Six Nations Reserve. Others settled with the Seneca in western New York. Still others remained for several more years in their homelands. However, by 1807 the Cayuga had sold all their land to the United States. After the Buffalo Creek and Tonawanda Reservations were sold in 1842, Indians who had been living there, including many Cayugas, relocated to the Cattaraugus and Allegany Reservations. Most Cayugas went to Cattaraugus.

The Iroquois Council officially split into two parts during that time. One branch was located at the Six Nations Reserve and the other at Buffalo Creek. Gradually, internal reservation affairs as well as relations with the United States and Canada assumed more significance than intraconfederacy matters. In the 1840s, when the Buffalo Creek Reservation was sold, the fire there was rekindled at Onondaga.

In Canada, the Cayugas, known with the Onondagas and Senecas as the "lower tribes," tended to retain more of their traditional beliefs than did the "upper" Iroquois tribes. Many subsequently adopted the Handsome Lake religion. Traditional structures were further weakened by the allotment of reservation lands in the 1840s; the requirement under Canadian law, from 1869 on, of patrilineal descent; and the transition of league councils and other political structures to a municipal government. In 1924, the Canadian government terminated confederacy rule entirely, mandating an (all male) elected system of government on the reserve.

The native economy gradually shifted from primarily hunting to farming, dependence on annuities received for the sale of land, and some wage labor. The people faced increasing pressure from non-natives to adopt Christianity and sell more land. The old religion declined during that time, although on some reservations the Handsome Lake religion grew in importance.

In 1817, some of the New York Cayuga, along with other Iroquois and Delaware Indians, moved west to near the Sandusky River in Ohio. They were removed to Indian Territory (Oklahoma) in 1831. Some other Cayugas moved to Wisconsin in 1832 with a group of Oneidas. The Cayuga maintained a separate tribal government in Oklahoma until 1937. Mainly because of fraud and outright theft, their 65,000-acre reservation had been reduced to 140 acres of tribal land by 1936. In 1937, the Seneca-Cayuga incorporated under Oklahoma law, adopting a constitution and by-laws and electing a business committee. Although their land base quickly grew, almost 300 acres were later taken away as a result of reservoir construction. The tribe successfully resisted termination in the 1950s. With other members of the confederacy, the Cayuga resisted the 1924 citizenship act, selective service, and all federal and state intrusions on their sovereignty.

Religion The Cayuga recognized *Orenda,* a supreme creator. Other animate and inanimate objects and natural forces were also considered of a spiritual nature. They held important festivals to celebrate maple sap and strawberries as well as corn planting, ripening (Green Corn ceremony), and harvest. These festivals often included singing, male dancing, game playing, gambling, feasting, and food distribution.

The eight-day new year's festival may have been most important of all. Held in midwinter, it was a time to give thanks, to forget past wrongs, and to kindle new fires, with much attention paid to new and old dreams. A condolence ceremony had quasi-religious components. Curing societies also conducted ceremonies, since illness was thought to be of supernatural origin.

In the early nineteenth century, many Iroquois embraced the teachings of Handsome Lake. This religion was born during the general religious ferment known as the Second Great Awakening and came directly out of the radical breakdown of Iroquois life. Beginning in 1799, the Seneca Handsome Lake spoke of Jesus and called upon Iroquois to give up alcohol and a host of negative behaviors, such as witchcraft and sexual promiscuity. He also exhorted them to maintain their traditional religious celebrations. A blend of traditional and Christian teachings, the Handsome Lake religion had the effect of facilitating the cultural transition occurring at the time.

Government The Iroquois League comprised 50 hereditary chiefs, or sachems, from the constituent tribes. Each position was named for the original holder and had specific responsibilities. Sachems were men, except where a woman acted as regent, but they were appointed by women. The Cayuga sent ten sachems to meetings of the Iroquois Great Council, which met in the fall and for emergencies. Their symbol at this gathering was the Great Pipe.

Tribes were divided into two divisions within the league, the Cayuga belonging to the "younger brothers." Debates within the great council were a matter of strict clan, division, and tribal protocols, in a complex system of checks and balances. Politically, individual league members often pursued their own best interests while maintaining an essential solidarity with the other members. The creators of the U.S. government used the Iroquois League as a model of democracy.

Locally, the village structure was governed by a headman and a council of elders (clan chiefs, elders, wise men). Matters before the local councils were handled according to a definite protocol based on the

clan and division memberships of the chiefs. Village chiefs were chosen from groups as small as a single household. Women nominated and recalled clan chiefs. Tribal chiefs represented the village and the nation at the general council of the league. The entire system was hierarchical and intertwined, from the family up to the great council. Decisions at all levels were reached by consensus.

There were also a number of nonhereditary chiefs ("pine tree" or "merit" chiefs), some of whom had no voting power. This may have been a postcontact phenomenon.

Customs The Cayuga recognized a dual division, each composed of two more matrilineal, animal-named clans. The clans in turn were composed of matrilineal lineages. The Cayuga probably had nine clans. Each owned a set number of personal names, some of which were linked with particular activities and responsibilities.

Women enjoyed a high degree of prestige, being largely equated with the "three sisters" (corn, beans, and squash), and they were in charge of most village activities, including marriage. Great intravillage lacrosse games included heavy gambling. Other games included snowsnake, or sliding a spear along a trench in the snow for distance. Food was shared so that everyone had roughly the same to eat.

Personal health and luck were maintained by performing various individual rituals, including singing and dancing, learned in dreams. Members of the False Face medicine society wore wooden masks carved from trees and used rattles and tobacco. Shamans also used up to 200 or more plant medicines to cure illness. People committed suicide on occasion for specific reasons (men who lost prestige; women who were abandoned; children who were treated harshly). Murder could be revenged or paid for with sufficient gifts.

The dead were buried in a sitting position, with food and tools for use on the way to the land of the dead. A ceremony was held after ten days. The condolence ceremony mourned dead league chiefs and installed successors. A modified version also applied to common people.

Dwellings In the early eighteenth century, Cayugas lived in at least three villages of 30 or more longhouses, each village with 500 or more people. The people built their villages near water and often on a hill after about 1300. Some villages were palisaded. Other Iroquois villages had up to 150 longhouses and 1,000 or more people. Villages were moved about twice in a generation, when firewood and soil were exhausted.

Iroquois Indians built elm-bark longhouses, 50–100 feet long, depending on how many people lived there, from about the twelfth century on. The longhouses held 2 or 3 or as many as 20 families, related maternally (lineage segments), as well as their dogs. There were smoke holes over each two-family fire. Beds were raised platforms; people slept on mats, their feet to the fire, covered by pelts. Upper platforms were used for food and gear storage. Roofs were shingled with elm bark. The people also built some single-family houses.

Diet Women grew corn, beans, squash, and gourds. Corn was the staple and was used in soups, stews, breads, and puddings. It was stored in bark-lined cellars. Women also gathered a variety of greens, nuts, seeds, roots, berries, fruits, and mushrooms. Tobacco was grown for ceremonial and social smoking.

After the harvest, men and some women took to the woods for several months to hunt and dry meat. Men hunted large game and trapped smaller game, mostly for the fur. Hunting was a source of potential prestige. They also caught waterfowl and other birds, and they fished. The people grew peaches, pears, and apples in orchards from the eighteenth century on.

Key Technology Iroquois used porcupine quills and wampum belts as a record of events. Wampum was also used as a gift connoting sincerity and, later, as trade money. These shell disks, strung or woven into belts, were probably a postcontact technological innovation.

Hunting equipment included snares, bow and arrow, stone knife, and bentwood pack frame. Fish were caught using traps, nets, bone hooks, and spears. Farming tools were made of stone, bone, wood (spades), and antler. Women wove tobacco trays, mats, and baskets.

Other important material items included elm-bark containers, cordage from inner tree bark and fibers, and levers to move timbers. Men steamed wood

or bent green wood to make many items, including lacrosse sticks.

Trade Cayugas obtained birch-bark products from the Huron. They imported copper and shells. They were extensively involved in the trade in beaver furs from the seventeenth century on.

Notable Arts Men carved wooden masks worn by the Society of Faces in their curing ceremonies. Women decorated clothing with dyed porcupine quills.

Transportation Unstable elm-bark canoes were roughly 25 feet long. The people were also great runners and preferred to travel on land. They used snowshoes in winter.

Dress Women made most clothing from deerskins. Men wore breechclouts and shirts; women wore skirts. Both wore leggings, moccasins, and corn-husk slippers in summer. Clothing was decorated with feathers and porcupine quills. Both men and women tattooed their bodies extensively.

War and Weapons Boys began developing war skills at a young age. Prestige and leadership were often gained through war, which was in many ways the most important activity. The title of Pine Tree Chief was a historical invention to honor especially brave warriors.

All aspects of warfare, from the initiation to the conclusion, were highly ritualized. War could be decided as a matter of policy or undertaken as a vendetta. Women had a large, sometimes decisive, say in the question of whether or not to fight. During war season, generally the fall, Iroquois war parties ranged over hundreds of miles. Their weapons included the bow and arrow, ball-headed club, shield, rod armor, and guns after 1640.

Male prisoners were often forced to run the gauntlet: Those who made it through were adopted, but those who did not might be tortured by widows. Women and children prisoners were regularly adopted. Some captives were eaten.

Contemporary Information

Government/Reservations The Cayuga have no reservation. Most live on the three Seneca reservations—Allegany, Oil Spring, and especially Cattaraugus—and on the Onondaga Reservation. The tribe is governed by a council of hereditary chiefs. Their headquarters is located in Versailles, New York.

Cayugas also live on the Six Nations/Grand River Reserve, Ontario, Canada. Established in 1784, it is governed by both an elected and a hereditary council, although only the first is federally recognized.

The Seneca-Cayuga Tribe is located in Ottawa County, Oklahoma. The tribe owned roughly 4,000 acres of trust and allotted land in 1993.

Economy There is generally high unemployment in New York and Canada. Many Cayugas are integrated into local economies, especially in construction, the trades, and the service industries. Oklahoma Cayugas work in ranching and in nearby cities.

Legal Status The Cayuga Nation of New York and the Seneca-Cayuga Tribe of Oklahoma are federally recognized tribal entities. There are ongoing negotiations with the federal government over land claims; in one such case, a federal court ruled against the state of New York in 1991.

Daily Life Traditional political and social (clan) structures remain intact, as does the language. One major exception is caused by Canada's requirement that band membership be reckoned patrilineally. The tribe generally meets annually in Versailles and in the Buffalo area. Cayugas and Senecas have yet to resolve issues of Cayuga land ownership on the Cattaraugus reservation. Cayugas may avail themselves of health, education, and other programs of the Seneca Nation.

Cayugas gather with other Iroquois Indians for various festivals, such as the Six Nations festival held on Labor Day weekend. They make some traditional foods, such as hulled corn soup, especially for special occasions. The political structure of the Iroquois League continues to be a source of controversy for many Iroquois (Haudensaunee). Some recognize two seats—at Onondaga and Six Nations—whereas others consider the government at Six Nations a reflection of or a corollary to the traditional seat at Onondaga. Important issues concerning the confederacy in the later twentieth century include Indian burial sites, sovereignty, gambling casinos, and land claims.

The Six Nations Reserve is still marked by the existence of "progressive" and "traditional" factions, with the former generally supporting the elected band council and following the Christian faith and the latter supporting the confederacy and the Longhouse religion. Traditional Iroquois Indians, many of whom are Cayugas, celebrate at least ten traditional or quasi-traditional ceremonies, including the Midwinter, Green Corn, and Strawberry. Oklahoma Cayugas maintain ties with their northeastern relatives. They celebrate the Green Corn and other ceremonies and maintain a longhouse.

Chippewa

See Anishinabe

Delaware

See Lenápe

Fox

Fox (Fäks), possibly from one of the tribe's clans. Their self-designation was *Mesquaki,* "Red Earth People." The Fox were culturally related to the Kickapoo. *See also* Sauk.

Location In the seventeenth century, the Fox were located in a wide area on the border between the Woodlands and the prairie, centered in eastern Wisconsin near Lake Winnebago. By the eighteenth century the Anishinabe had forced them into extreme southwest Wisconsin, extreme northwest Illinois, and northern Iowa. Today, most Fox Indians live in central Iowa. Headquarters for the Sac and Fox Nation is in Lincoln County, Oklahoma.

Population There were about 2,500 Fox in the mid–seventeenth century. The tribe had approximately 1,000 enrolled members in the early 1990s.

Language The Fox people speak an Algonquian language.

Historical Information

History The Fox may once have lived just west and/or south of Lake Erie and, before that, along the southern shore of Lake Superior. They were driven by Iroquois raids into the upper Fox River–Chicago River area, perhaps in the early seventeenth century.

After non-natives first appeared among them in the mid–seventeenth century, the Fox quickly joined the fur trade. Unlike most Algonquians, however, they refused to settle near trading posts or missions. They also made enemies by requiring a toll from French traders plying the Fox River and were even able to block French access to the Mississippi if and when they chose.

The Fox fought the French and their Indian allies in the early to mid–eighteenth century, armed primarily with British weapons. They were almost destroyed during that period by warfare and disease, which was in fact the goal of French forces. Survivors took refuge with the Sauk in 1733, beginning an alliance that lasted until the 1850s. Refusing to give up their Fox friends, in 1735 the Sauk held off French attackers, and both tribes escaped to Iowa. The French pardoned both tribes in 1737, and shortly thereafter they returned to Wisconsin.

In 1769, the Sauk, Fox, and other tribes dealt a permanent defeat to the Illinois tribes and moved south and west into some of their former territory and ultimately back into Iowa. By that time they had become highly capable buffalo hunters. Hunting parties traveled far west of the Mississippi in search of the herds, and they adopted many aspects of typical Great Plains buffalo-hunting culture.

The Fox took an active part in Little Turtle's war (1790–1794) and in Tecumseh's rebellion (1809–1811), two defensive actions in which the tribes of the old west made a last-ditch effort to hold onto their lands. Lead mines near Dubuque, Iowa, at which the Fox had been mining up to two tons of lead a year, were illegally seized by non-native interests in the early nineteenth century. In 1842, the Sauk and Fox ceded their remaining lands and were relocated to a reservation in Kansas.

Some Fox remained with the Sauk in Kansas and went with them in 1869 to the Indian Territory (Oklahoma). However, after a series of disputes with the Sauk, most Fox returned to Iowa in the late

1850s, settling near Tama and acquiring land there. Ownership of their own land prevented future allotment and enabled the people to maintain their physical boundaries and thus much of their traditional culture. The people generally refused to enroll their children when the Bureau of Indian Affairs opened a boarding school in the late nineteenth century, but they did accept a day school after 1912. They adopted an Indian Reorganization Act–based government in 1937.

Religion The Fox recognized an upper and a lower region. The former was ruled by the great or gentle manitou. There were also any number of other nature-related spirits, or manitous, the most important of which were connected with the four directions. People might gain the attention and assistance of the manitous by offering tobacco, blackening the face with charcoal, fasting, and wailing.

The vision quest, undertaken at puberty, was another way to attract spiritual power. Those who were especially successful assembled a medicine pack or bundle; certain packs represented power that affected and were the property of entire lineages. Two annual ceremonies were related to the medicine packs.

The Midewiwin was a key ceremony. Others included the Green Corn and Adoption ceremonies. As part of the latter, a person was formally adopted to take the place of someone who had died or been killed. The calumet, or sacred pipe, played a vital role in all sacred activities, including peace negotiations. A head shaman instructed others in curing, hunting, agricultural, and other ceremonies.

Government Fox society was divided into bands or villages, of fluid composition, that formed in summer but broke up in winter. There were dual political divisions of peace and war. Officers were the main chief, subchiefs, and criers.

A hereditary peace chief held authority over gatherings, treaties, peace councils, intertribal negotiations, and rituals. In return for access to his property, the people regularly gave him gifts. War chiefs were chosen by other warriors on the basis of merit, although there may have been a hereditary component. These people commanded the camp police and presided over councils during war when a stricter, more disciplined organization was needed.

Customs The Fox recognized about 14 patrilineal clans. Membership in one of the two tribal divisions was determined by birth order. Each summer house was an economic unit as well as a social one. The families of murder victims usually accepted compensation, but they were at liberty to require blood vengeance. Lacrosse was a popular game.

Birth took place in special lodges in the company of only women; the mother remained subject to special postpartum restrictions for up to a year or more. The baby was named by an elderly relative, who could choose from among the stock of clan names. As adults, people might acquire additional, nonclan names as a result of dreams or warfare. Parents rarely inflicted corporal punishment upon their children.

At the onset of puberty, girls were secluded for ten days and were subject to various restrictions. Both sexes marked puberty by undertaking a vision quest. Vermilion face paint indicated an adult status. Marriages were generally arranged by the couple in question and were formalized when the families exchanged gifts. The couple lived with the wife's family for a year before establishing their own household. Some men had more than one wife. Adultery was generally cause for divorce.

Burial took place after various rituals had been performed. Warriors might be buried in a sitting position. All people were buried in their finest clothing, wrapped in bark or mats with their feet toward the west. Sacred tobacco was placed on the graves. A dog might be killed as a companion on the way to the land of the dead. The mourning period lasted for at least six months, during which time mourners were subject to a variety of behavioral restrictions.

Dwellings Summer villages were located near crop fields in river bottoms. Extended families of some ten people lived in houses about 50 feet long by 20 feet wide and covered with elm bark. These houses were oriented in an east-west direction and were built in parallel rows, with an open game and ceremonial area in between. People moved the villages when firewood became scarce or when attacks forced them to move.

Extended families of roughly 10 people lived in houses about 50 feet long and 20 feet wide and covered with elm bark, as depicted in this photo. These houses were oriented in an east-west direction and were built in parallel rows, with an open game and ceremonial area in between.

When in their winter camps, people lived in small, dome-shaped wigwams covered with reed mats and located in sheltered river valleys. The camps ranged in size from just one or two families to an entire band.

Diet Fox women grew corn, beans, squash, and tobacco. They also gathered a number of wild plant foods, including nuts, honey, berries, fruits, and tubers. Men hunted a variety of large and small game, especially deer, as well as buffalo from at least the eighteenth century until about 1820.

Key Technology Pipes were made of carved pipestone (catlinite) and wooden or reed stems. Most tools and utensils were made of wood, grasses, stone, or bone. The people also made bark containers.

Trade The Fox exported deerskins and tallow as well as lead.

Notable Arts The people made silk appliqué from the mid–eighteenth century on.

Transportation Men made bark and dugout canoes.

Dress Clothing was generally light and consisted mainly of buckskin breechclouts, dresses or aprons, leggings, and moccasins. Hide or fur robes were added for extra warmth. The people also tattooed and painted their bodies.

War and Weapons Reasons for war included conflict over territory, retaliation, and the achievement of status. War parties had to be authorized by the war council. Leaders of war parties began by fasting to obtain a vision and undertook several more ritualistic activities before the party departed. The leader carried his sacred ark, which was said to provide the party with spiritual power. Warriors were subject to a number of rituals on their return as well.

Prisoners were often adopted. War calumets were decorated with red feathers and peace calumets with white feathers. Traditional enemies included the Anishinabe and occasionally the Dakota; allies were the Sauk from the early eighteenth century on and the Kickapoo.

Contemporary Information

Government/Reservations The Mesquaki Nation lives on or near their own settlement established in 1856 and located near Tama, Tama County, Iowa.

A delegation of Sauk, Fox, and Ioway chiefs, photographed in 1866, wears headgear that includes, from left to right, a cloth turban with roach, an otter-skin turban with beaded tail, a cloth turban, and a fur turban with a shell-disk decoration. Their moccasins and leggings are beaded with either geometric or floral designs.

The nation holds roughly 5,000 acres of land, none of which has been allotted. The 1990 Indian population was 563. Government is by a seven-member tribal council with officers, all of whom must be enrolled in the tribe and living in the community. Some members still recognize the authority of the hereditary chief.

Economy There is some corn and soybean farming, some farmwork or wage work in neighboring towns, and some income from land leased to non-natives. There is also bingo, and a casino and other tourist-related enterprises are planned.

Legal Status The Sac and Fox Tribe of the Mississippi in Iowa (Mesquaki Nation) is a federally recognized tribal entity.

Daily Life "Traditional" and "progressive" factions have struggled for control of the tribe for much of the twentieth century. Traditional kinship ties remain important, and the language remains vital. The Sac and Fox Settlement School, bilingual and bicultural, enrolls children from kindergarten through the eighth grade. Christian sects, the Native American Church, and the Drum religion are all active, as are elements of traditional Fox religion. The annual powwow is held in August.

Huron

See Wyandotte

Illinois

Illinois (I li `noy) were a group of bands, probably all Algonquians, that included but were not limited to the Cahokia, Kaskaskia, Michigamea, Moingwena, Peoria, and Tamaroa. The word "Illinois" is a French adaptation of their self-designation, *Inoca.* The Illinois were a borderline Eastern Woodlands group, with much of their territory consisting of prairie. They were culturally similar to the Miami.

Location The Illinois lived south of Lake Michigan in the early seventeenth century. Later in that century they were located in present-day Illinois, western Missouri, northern Arkansas, and eastern Iowa, especially along the Illinois River. Today, most surviving Peorias live in northeastern Oklahoma.

Population There were about 10,000 Illinois in 1650 and approximately 2,000 Peorias in the mid-1990s.

Language Illinois was an Algonquian language.

Historical Information

History The Illinois may have come to their historic territory from the northeast. They may have mixed with the Cahokian (Mississippian) people when they moved into Illinois in the mid–seventeenth century. The people fought two major wars with the Winnebago from about 1630 to 1645: They lost the first and won the second. In the mid–seventeenth century, the Illinois also attacked the Miamis and pushed them northward out of northern Illinois.

Iroquois attacks drove the people west of the Mississippi in about 1660. They did not return until pushed east by the Dakota after 1870. After this time they began slaving raids on Siouan and Pawnee tribes west of the Mississippi. The Illinois tribes first met French explorers in the 1670s and became French allies shortly thereafter. The Iroquois, aided by the Miami, kept up their attacks against the Illinois until at least the late seventeenth century.

Abandonment of the Illinois River region and a southward movement began around 1700, marking a general defeat at the hands of tribes such as the Kickapoo, Fox, and Sauk, who also sought French favor. With the exception of the Peoria, who held out in the north until the later eighteenth century, most Illinois tribes became associated with specific French agricultural settlements. By 1800, the Michigamea, Cahokia, and Tamaroa merged with the Kaskaskia and Peoria.

The Wisconsin tribes maintained more or less continuous pressure on the Illinois tribes during the eighteenth century. The final battle may have come after an Illinois Indian, said to be in the pay of Britain, killed Chief Pontiac in 1769. In any case, those Illinois still free of French protection were all but wiped out, suffering upward of 90 percent casualties. Meanwhile, the southern Illinois, through

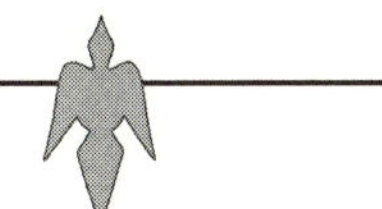

their contact with the French, had become missionized, poor, and alcoholic.

Survivors of the wars with the Great Lakes Algonquians, mainly members of the Kaskaskia and Peoria Bands, signed treaties in the early nineteenth century ceding their lands to the United States. Their culture practically gone, these people moved to eastern Kansas in 1833, where they lived with the Wea and Piankashaw (Miami) Bands until 1867, when they all bought land in northeastern Oklahoma. In 1873 they took the name United Peoria and Miami. Their lands were allotted in 1893, and any remaining tribal land was lost when Oklahoma became a state in 1907. The group reincorporated as the Peoria Tribe of Oklahoma in 1940. They were terminated in 1950 but restored in 1978.

Religion Manitou, a supreme being or creator, dwelled to the east and may have been identified with the sun. Men probably undertook a vision quest at adolescence, during which they hoped to attract a personal guardian spirit. At the onset of puberty, girls fasted in a special lodge until they received a personal guardian spirit. Shamans, or medicine people (they could be men or women and were usually older), conducted religious ceremonies. They acquired their powers from powerful animal spirits. Most ceremonies included dancing and smoking tobacco from a sacred pipe, or calumet. There were regular summer ceremonies involving the ritual death and revival of a patient.

Government Each tribe was an independent entity and lived either in a separate village or in a separate section of a multitribe village. There may have been peace and war chiefs as well as criers to make announcements. Camp police during the summer buffalo hunt enforced strict discipline.

Customs Illinois tribes recognized patrilineal clans. Hospitality was a primary value. A ritual feast followed a boy's first game kill. Boys who showed such an inclination might become berdaches, or men who dressed like women and assumed all of their roles. Berdaches were regarded as having a particularly sacred element: They attended all ceremonies, and their advice was sought at council meetings. Murderers were either killed or were allowed to pay retribution. Lacrosse was a popular game.

Men usually refrained from marriage until they had proven themselves as warriors and hunters. Marriage negotiations were held in clearly defined ways between the two families and revolved around gift exchange. Men often had more than one wife. Women could destroy the property of men who attempted to marry without the proper lineage controls. Female adultery was punished by death, mutilation, or mass rape. A man who killed his wife's lover was subject to blood retribution.

Each sex was responsible for burying its own dead. After their face and hair were painted, corpses were dressed in fine clothing, wrapped in skins, and buried in the ground or on scaffolds. Tools, pipes, and other goods were set by the grave, which was marked by two forked sticks with a cross-stick or, in the case of a chief, by a painted log. Various ceremonies were then performed that honored the dead by reenacting a favorite activity. Souls or spirits were said to travel to an afterlife. Property exchange also accompanied death. The official mourning period lasted about a year.

Dwellings The Illinois built semipermanent summer villages strung out for miles along river banks. The villages consisted of up to 300 or more lodges, each with one to four fireplaces and housing up to 12 families. There were also small menstrual/birth huts and possibly an additional structure used for political or ceremonial purposes.

Large, rectangular summer houses were built of woven mats over a pole frame. Mats were also placed on the ground as floors. The people also built temporary summer and winter hunting camps. Summer huts were bark-covered buildings, whereas winter lodges were covered with rush mats.

Diet Meat formed the most important part of the Illinois diet. Men hunted elk, bear, deer, mountain lion, turkey, beaver, and other animals. They also hunted buffalo on the nearby prairies. Communal hunts took place in summer. Before they acquired horses, Illinois men generally surrounded buffalo with a ring of fire and then shot them with a bow and arrow. Women and children went along on the hunt

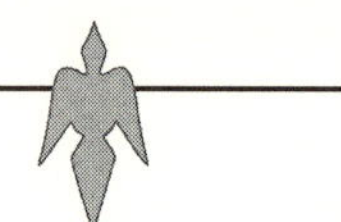

to dry the meat and pack it home. Women grew corn, beans, and squash. They also gathered a variety of wild fruits, nuts, berries, and roots.

Key Technology Wood was the basic material, but tools and other items were also made from bone, stone, and shell. Women made a variety of mats and bags with yarn spun of buffalo and bear hair.

Trade The people exported animal and wood products, crops, and some woven items.

Notable Arts Illinois found artistic expression in painting buffalo robes, weaving, woodcarving, and doing quillwork.

Transportation Men fashioned dugout canoes of up to 50 feet in length from butternut trees.

Dress Men wore breechclouts; women wore long dresses. Both sexes wore buffalo robes and blankets. They also tattooed and painted their bodies and wore various personal adornments of animal teeth, colored stones, feathers, and other items.

War and Weapons The Illinois were considered relatively poor fighters and were mainly unenthusiastic about war. Raiding parties were generally small, although there were large ones accompanied by women. Birds were the supernatural spirit related to war, and each warrior kept bird skins in a special reed mat. Raids were led by a person who sponsored a dog feast; the group then engaged in an all-night ceremony designed to propitiate the bird spirits. Personal bird cries accompanied the actual attack. Success was defined by the relative loss of warriors, and leaders had to compensate relatives for lost men.

Illinois enemies included the Iroquois, Dakota, Quapaw, Pawnee, and Osage in the seventeenth century and the Great Lakes Algonquians and the Chickasaw in the eighteenth century. Otoes were occasional allies. Weapons included bows and flint-tipped arrows, spears, clubs, flint knives, and long buffalo-hide shields. Berdaches fought with clubs rather than bows.

Capturing prisoners rated higher war honors than killing them. Male prisoners were usually burned and eaten, whereas women and children were distributed among the population. Some were ultimately adopted, but some maintained a slavelike identity.

Contemporary Information

Government/Reservations Peoria tribal headquarters is located in Miami (Ottawa County), Oklahoma. A 1981 constitution provides for an elected business council plus officers. The tribe includes descendants of the Miami bands as well as bands of the Illinois Confederacy. It owns almost 40 acres of land.

Economy Tribal members own local businesses. Some people work in Tulsa. The unemployment rate among tribal members regularly approaches 90 percent.

Legal Status The Peoria Tribe of Oklahoma is a federally recognized tribal entity.

Daily Life Peorias work with neighboring tribes (Seneca, Miami, Quapaw, and Ottawa) in areas of common interest. Most are assimilated into mainstream life. Tribal members participate in local and regional Indian celebrations, such as Indian Heritage Days, held in June. Although most traditional culture has disappeared, including the language, some members know some old songs and dances, and there is an effort to revive the Calumet Dance as well as traditional arts and crafts.

Iroquois

See Cayuga; Mohawk; Oneida; Onondaga; Seneca. *See also* Tuscarora (Chapter 7).

Kickapoo

Kickapoo (`Kik ə pū), possibly from *kiwegapaw,* "he moves about, standing now here, now there." The Kickapoo were culturally similar to the Sauk and Fox and may once have been united with the Shawnee.

Location The Kickapoo lived around the Fox and Wisconsin Rivers (present-day southern Wisconsin) in the mid–seventeenth century, although they inhabited present-day Michigan and Ohio earlier and Illinois and Kansas somewhat later. Today, Kickapoos live in northeast Kansas, central Oklahoma, and northern Mexico.

Population There were between 2,000 and 3,000 Kickapoos in the mid–seventeenth century and approximately 3,000 in the 1990s.

Language Kickapoos spoke an Algonquian language similar to Sauk and Fox.

Historical Information

History The Kickapoo may have originated in southeast Michigan. In the seventeenth century, pressure from the Iroquois drove them west to southern Wisconsin, where they encountered French missionaries. They may have shared villages with the Miami at that time.

Kickapoos entered the fur trade, but throughout the later seventeenth century and early eighteenth century resisted pressure to assimilate and cede their lands. They were often at war with the French during that period, although the two groups established an alliance in 1729. They also fought various Indian tribes.

In the early eighteenth century, the Kickapoo joined tribes such as the Ojibwa, Ottowa, Sauk, and Fox to defeat the Illinois Confederacy and occupy their territory. The Kickapoo moved south to the Illinois River, where the tribe soon divided. One group headed farther south to the Sangamon River. Known as the Prairie Band, they increased their buffalo hunting. The other group moved east toward the Vermillion Branch of the Wabash River. This band retained their forest hunting practices. The band also absorbed the Mascouten, or Prairie Potawatomi, tribe of Indians.

Part of the Prairie Band moved into southwest Missouri in the mid-1760s. Following the French defeat in 1763, the Kickapoo transferred their allegiance to the Spanish. They participated in Pontiac's rebellion and later accepted British aid against the United States, with whom they never had good relations.

The early nineteenth century saw greatly increased non-native settlement in the region. Most Kickapoos participated in Little Turtle's war. The Vermillion Band also supported Tecumseh's rebellion, which the Prairie Band opposed. Both groups, however, were drawn into the War of 1812. Some chiefs of each band ceded the people's Illinois land in 1819, a move that forced most Kickapoos to join the group already living in Missouri.

Some Kickapoos, however, under Chief Mecina and the prophet Kenakuk, continued to resist relocation by passive means as well as guerrilla tactics. They were finally forced to move to Kansas in the early 1830s following their defeat in Black Hawk's war (*see* Sauk). Most Missouri Kickapoos had accepted a reservation in Kansas in 1832. Some later fought with the United States against the Seminole in 1837.

From their base in Kansas, the tribe broke into several smaller groups, some remaining in Kansas and some migrating to Oklahoma; Texas, where they settled on the Sabine River with a group of Indians from several tribes; and Mexico. Horse-stealing raids, particularly in Texas, were an important activity throughout much of the nineteenth century. In 1862, some Kickapoo land was allotted and some was sold to a railroad company.

In the early to mid-1860s, fighting erupted between Mexican Kickapoos and Texas Rangers attempting to prevent some Kansas Kickapoos from crossing Texas to join their relatives. In the 1870s, the U.S. Army illegally crossed the Mexican border and destroyed the main Kickapoo village in Mexico. They also brought a group of women and children back to the Indian Territory as hostages; many men then agreed to leave Mexico and join them there.

In 1883, these people were granted a 100,000-acre reservation in Oklahoma. However, when that reservation was allotted ten years later, and pressure to assimilate increased, many people returned to Mexico, first to Nacimiento and then to northern Sonora. In 1908, the Kansas reservation was allotted to individuals. In 1937, the Kansas Kickapoos reorganized under the Indian Reorganization Act. They successfully resisted termination in the 1950s.

Religion All things, animate and inanimate, contained spirits, or manitou. Kicitiata, the supreme manitou, or creator, dwelled in the sky. Tobacco facilitated communication with the manitous. Young

people may have undertaken vision quests. Dreams, which may have been encouraged by fasts, also had spiritual significance.

The main ceremony was a weeklong renewal and thanksgiving in early spring, at which time sacred bundles were opened and repaired. The people also celebrated the Green Corn and Buffalo Dances. Priests were in charge of religious observances. There may have been a ritual office, held by a woman, that gave approval to hold certain ceremonies. In the 1830s, the prophet Kenakuk preached a Christian-influenced religion that emphasized acculturation and prohibited alcohol, polygyny, and warfare. His message attracted some Kickapoos and Potawatomis.

Government The Kickapoo were divided into constituent bands, which were probably led by chiefs. A council of clan heads took decisions by consensus.

Customs Kickapoo society was organized in patrilineal clans. Furthermore, a dual division formed the basis for various cultural features such as joking (informal enforcement of social norms), games, races, and ritual seating. People played dice and ball games (such as lacrosse), held archery contests, and danced socially. They may have eaten human flesh.

Personal names were tied to dreams or visions. Menstrual seclusion was particularly long and rigorous the first time, at which time the woman was advised by older women on how to behave as an adult. After killing their first game, boys were given a feast, which included songs and prayers.

Courting may have involved the use of a flute. Marriage was finalized by gift giving between the families. Funeral or death ceremonies included feasting, song, and prayer as well as quiet moments. The dead were dressed in travel clothing and buried with tobacco, wooden spoons, food, and water in stone slabs or log vaults. Their feet faced west, the direction of the land of the dead. Graveyards were in or near villages. People left the village for four days following a death, after which time ceremonial adoptions were often performed.

Dwellings Rectangular summer and round or oval winter houses were framed with green saplings. Summer houses were covered with elm bark and were often attached to an arbor. Sleeping platforms lay along the sides. Doors faced east, and there was a smoke hole in the roof. Temporary winter houses were covered with woven cattail or tule mats. The people also built separate cook and menstrual/birth huts.

Diet Kickapoos were heavily dependent on crops. Women grew corn, beans, and squash, and they gathered various wild foods. Men hunted deer, bear, and other game, including some buffalo, and they fished.

Key Technology Carved wooden prayer sticks recorded prayers and myths as well as events. Pottery containers could hold water. There were many wooden items, such as utensils, bowls, and cradle boards. Spoons held particular significance.

Trade Kickapoos served as intermediaries in the mid–nineteenth century Comanche horse trade.

Notable Arts Important art objects included pottery and carved and decorated (with porcupine quills) wooden items. Silk appliqué was popular from the mid–eighteenth century on as clothing decoration.

Transportation The people acquired the horse earlier than most Indians of the northeast, probably in the early eighteenth century.

Dress Kickapoo dress depended largely on their location. Basic items were breechclout, dress or apron, leggings, and moccasins, although they tended to borrow local customs, especially with regard to personal ornamentation.

War and Weapons Kickapoo warriors were known as extremely fierce, able, and enthusiastic fighters. Among their seventeenth- and early-eighteenth-century enemies were the Chickasaw, Osage, Dakota, Iroquois, Fox, and Illinois. They were periodically allied with the Sauk, Fox, and other tribes as well as with the French after 1730. Their warfare and raiding took them from New York and Pennsylvania into Georgia and Alabama, throughout the entire Great Lakes and prairie regions, and into Texas and Mexico.

Contemporary Information

Government/Reservations The Kickapoo Reservation in Brown County, Kansas, contains 19,200 acres of land, slightly more than a third of which are owned by Indians. Of this land, about half is held by individuals. The 1990 reservation Indian population was 368, although almost 200 Kickapoos lived nearby.

Oklahoma Kickapoos live in Lincoln, Potawatomi, and Oklahoma Counties. Tribal offices are located near the town of McCloud. The people are governed by a five-member business committee. Of the 22,000 acres originally allotted, individuals now own roughly 6,000 acres of land. There were about 1,900 tribal members in the early 1990s.

The Texas (Mexican) Kickapoos live in El Nacimiento Rancheria, Coahuilla, Mexico, on roughly 17,000 acres of land. Their village is located under the international bridge over the Rio Grande. A small group also lives in the state of Sonora. In 1984, the Kickapoo Trust Land Acquisition Committee purchased 125 acres of land along the Rio Grande in Texas, about eight miles south of Eagle Pass, but so far the people have preferred to remain in their old village. Band population in the mid-1980s was roughly 650.

Economy In Kansas, much of the allotted land is leased to non-natives. There is also a tribal farm and ranch, as well as a buffalo herd, on lands purchased with land claims settlement money. Some people work for the tribe or the Bureau of Indian Affairs. Unemployment remains around 40 percent, and more than a third of the people lived below the federal poverty level in the early 1990s. The tribe is attempting to build a gambling casino.

In Oklahoma, most land is leased to non-natives. Kickapoos in Mexico lived a traditional subsistence lifestyle until after World War II; now many work in the United States as migrant laborers. Unemployment is extremely high in Oklahoma, Texas, and Mexico.

Legal Status The Kickapoo Tribe in Kansas, the Kickapoo Tribe of Oklahoma, and the Texas Band of Kickapoo (Kickapoo Traditional Tribe in Texas) are federally recognized tribal entities. In 1983, the United States recognized the Texas Band as a self-governing entity within the Oklahoma tribe and extended to them federal benefits that included the right to move freely across the international border. About one-quarter of this group are U.S. citizens.

Daily Life The Kansas Kickapoo own a gymnasium, day care center, and housing and other facilities for seniors. There is also a Kickapoo Nation school serving grades K–12. Few people have college degrees. The language is no longer spoken. Many Kansas Kickapoos have married neighboring Prairie Band Potawatomis. Ongoing traditions include the Kenakuk religion, the Drum religion (Dream Dance), and the Native American Church.

The Oklahoma and Texas Kickapoo regard themselves as one people. Kickapoos in Mexico migrate to the United States to work as farm laborers from spring through fall and then return to their villages for the winter ceremonial season. In Mexico, they live in cardboard and cane houses. The native religion remains intact in Mexico, as does much else of traditional culture. It centers on a seasonal round of ceremonies that are attended by many Kickapoos from Oklahoma. Many Oklahoma Kickapoos speak only Kickapoo; only a small number of them, mostly young people, are fluent in English.

Lenápe

Lenápe (Le `nä pā), or Leni Lenápe, "Human Beings" or "Real People" in the Unami dialect, were part of a group of Algonquian speakers from North Carolina to New York. The Lenápe tribes who lived around the Delaware River are more commonly known as Delaware Indians (from Baron De La Warre, governor of Virginia). This central group of northeastern Algonquian Indians was referred to as "grandfather" by other Algonquian tribes, in recognition of its position as the group from which many local Algonquian tribes diverged.

Location In the sixteenth century, the Lenápe were located in the Delaware River area, both along the coast and inland. The Unami lived in southeastern Pennsylvania and northern Delaware; the Munsee lived in northern New Jersey, extreme southern New York, and southeastern Connecticut. A quasi-division known as Unalachtigo lived mainly in New Jersey.

Late-twentieth-century Lenápe communities were located in New Jersey, Pennsylvania, Wisconsin, Oklahoma, Kansas, and Ontario, Canada.

Population There were roughly 10,000 Lenápe in 1600. The present-day Lenápe population is hard to determine, but it is probably around 16,000 people.

Language Munsee and Unami are Algonquian languages.

Historical Information

History According to the Walum Olum (see "Key Technology"), the Lenápe may have originated to the northeast, possibly in Labrador, where they were united with the Shawnee and the Nanticoke. They may have passed through the eastern Great Lakes region and the Ohio Valley, where they met and possibly defeated Hopewell Mound Builder people. They likely encountered non-natives in the early to mid–sixteenth century.

Contact with Henry Hudson in 1609 was followed by the people's rapid involvement in the fur trade. In short order, their dependence on items of non-native manufacture, such as metal items, guns, and cloth, fundamentally altered their economy as well as their relations with neighboring peoples. Other changes in material culture included the introduction of new foods such as pigs, chickens, and melons. In 1626, the Manhattan Band of Lenápe traded the use of Manhattan Island to a Dutchman for about $24 worth of goods. This arrangement was quickly interpreted as a sale by the Dutch, who, unlike the Lenápe, valued property ownership.

Growing numbers of non-natives, Indian land cessions and pressure for more, and intertribal rivalries brought on by competition over furs led to conflict with the Dutch from the 1640s until the British took possession of the colony in 1663. In 1683, the Lenápe people, represented by Chief Tamanend (from whose name the designation of Tammany Hall was taken), signed a treaty of friendship with the Quaker William Penn (who gave his name to the state of Pennsylvania).

By the late seventeenth century, the Lenápe population had been decimated by disease and warfare. In the early eighteenth century, the Iroquois Confederacy dominated the Lenápe people, even going so far as to sell some of their land to the British. By the middle of that century, more and more Lenápes had moved into western Pennsylvania and the Ohio River Valley. A group of Lenápe established farms in eastern Ohio, but hostilities with non-natives increased as the frontier moved west. About 100 Lenápes were slaughtered by Kentucky frontiersmen at a Moravian mission in 1782.

Unami speakers living in the lower Allegheny and upper Ohio Valleys in the mid–eighteenth century formed the nucleus of the emerging Lenápe or Delaware tribe. These people were organized into three groups, or clans—Turkey, Turtle, and Wolf—each with a chief living in a main village. One of the chiefs acted as tribal spokesman. The Lenápe fought the British in the French and Indian War and were generally divided in the Revolutionary War. In 1762, a Lenápe medicine man called Delaware Prophet helped to unite the local Indians to fight in Pontiac's rebellion. Some Lenápe also participated in Little Turtle's war (1790–1794) and in Tecumseh's rebellion (1809–1811).

As the non-natives kept coming, groups of Lenápe continued west into Missouri and even Texas, where they remained until forced into western Oklahoma in 1859. These "absentee Delaware" began hunting buffalo and assumed some aspects of Plains life.

After the Lenápe remaining in Ohio were defeated, with their Indian allies, in the 1794 Battle of Fallen Timbers, they moved to Indiana, Missouri, and Kansas. From their base in Kansas they fought with the Pawnee, who claimed their land, as well as with other Plains tribes. Many also served as scouts in the U.S. Army. After living in Kansas for a couple of generations as farmers, trappers, and guides, they were forced to relocate to Oklahoma in the 1860s. Following a court battle, these Lenápe became citizens of the Cherokee Nation.

Meanwhile, groups of Munsee speakers had joined the Stockbridge Indians in Massachusetts and New York and moved with them to a reservation in Wisconsin. Others joined the Cayuga in New York and migrated with them to the Six Nations Reserve in Ontario in the late eighteenth century. Still others moved to Canada as well, one group founding a

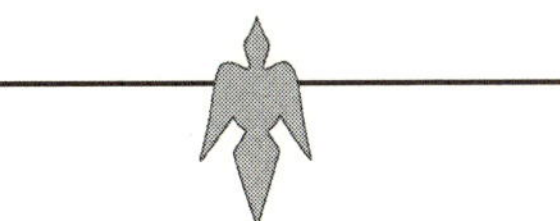

Moravian village in 1792 along the Thames River and another group living at Munceytown. Yet another group joined the Swan Lake and Black River Chippewa near Ottawa, Kansas.

Religion Like many Algonquins, the Lenápe believed in a great spirit (manitou) as well as the presence of other spirits in all living things. Personal guardian spirits were acquired in adolescence and were said to be connected with future success.

The fortnight-long bear sacrifice, held in midwinter, was the most important of at least five annual religious festivals. Others revolved around foods, such as maple sugar (early spring), corn (late spring and late summer), and strawberries (early summer), as well as curing. Many festivals were held in a long wooden structure that had 12 ceremonial masks carved on its posts. The festivals included singing and dancing as well as drumming on deerskin drums and shaking turtleshell rattles.

After death, spirits were said to travel to an afterlife. Names were given with the benefit of a personal vision by the name giver, which enhanced his or her status. Chiefs often served as religious as well as political leaders of the village. Shamans of both sexes were responsible for holding the curing ceremonies.

Government Each of the three autonomous divisions maintained its own territory; there was never any political unity. Each village group of several hundred people had its own hereditary chief (sachem or sagamore). The chief had no coercive powers, instead acting as mediator, adviser, and hunt leader. With the chief, other lineage leaders and elders formed a council.

Village groups were autonomous, but they often acted in concert for purposes of hunting drives and defense. There were also specific rules governing shared resource use areas and social contacts.

Customs There were traditionally three matrilineal clans. Women grew and prepared foods, took care of children, gathered firewood, and prepared skins. Men hunted, fished, traded, fought, cured, made houses and most tools, and served as chiefs. People from the coast tended to visit the interior in the spring, when they moved to fishing and hunting camps, whereas people from the interior visited the coast in summer. Murder was generally expiated by a payment.

Infants were kept on a cradle board, which mothers wore on their backs supported with tumplines, for most of the first year. Girls were secluded and observed strict behavioral taboos during their periods. Premarital sexual relations were condoned, but adultery was not, except where consent was given, such as in wife lending on the part of a polygynous chief. There was a yearlong betrothal period. Intermarriage was frequent between the village groups. Divorce was easily and frequently obtained. Corpses were buried in a sitting position with some possessions. Mourners blackened their faces and visited the grave annually. Widowers could marry again after making a payment to the former wife's family.

Dwellings Each of 30–40 villages, located on river and tributary meadows, was surrounded by fields and hunting grounds. Houses were circular, domed wigwams or 30- to 60-foot (but up to 100 foot) multifamily, grass or bark-covered, single doorway longhouses with both pitched and arched roofs. Both dwellings contained smoke holes. Interior longhouses may have been palisaded in times of war. Bark partitions did not meet the opposite wall, leaving room for a structure-long corridor. Multilevel wall platforms served as seats, beds, and storage areas. Woven reed mats were placed on floors and hung on walls for added insulation. Crops were strung on the ceiling to dry. Most interior people left the villages in winter, when they retired to the woods to live generally in small dwellings.

Diet From at least circa 1300, inland groups depended mostly on corn; beans and squash were also important. Corn was prepared to make soup, bread, dumplings, and many other dishes. Game hunted in seasonal trips included deer, elk, bear, raccoons, rabbit, wolves, squirrel, and fowl. Fire surrounds were used as part of a general practice of burning the undergrowth of certain lands. Men also trapped various small mammals, turkeys, and other birds. Fresh meat and fish were boiled or fire roasted. Coastal people depended mainly on fish and shellfish (generally dried and preserved), seaweed, birds,

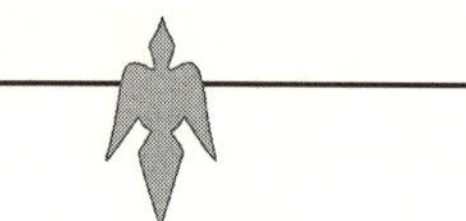

berries, and meat and oil from stranded whales. Women gathered various roots, greens, wild fruits, and nuts as well as maple sap. Tobacco was also grown.

Key Technology The Walum Olum ("red score") was a pictographic history, painted or engraved on wood or bark, of the people's legends and early migrations. A later manuscript, the only one that survives in any form, interpreted the pictographs in the Lenápe language.

Fishing equipment included various types of nets as well as spears, traps, bow and arrow, and weirs. Women made rush (coast) and corn-husk (interior) baskets. Along the coast, people used fish bones as needles and sharp mollusk shell edges as blades; sharp rocks served as blades in the interior. Old people generally made pottery, fishnets, and other items. Men hunted using bows and arrows, traps, fire surrounds, and drives.

People carved dishes and bowls from wood or simply used gourds. Hollowed stumps served as mortars, with wood or stone pestles. Plant fibers or the inner bark from particular trees supplied cordage material. Corn was stored in mat-lined pits. Most cutting tools were made of stone. Men affixed stone, bone, horn, or tooth arrowheads with fish glue or resin.

Trade The Lenápe traded in, among other items, rounded-bottom pots; grass mats, bags, and baskets; wampum (polished shell); and bark and skin containers. Summer was the main trade season.

Notable Arts Woven items, such as baskets, were decorated with painted spruce roots or porcupine quills.

Transportation Men made dugout and bark canoes.

Dress Women made clothing of deerskins and furs. People generally wore few clothes, such as breechclouts for men and skin kilts for women, in warm weather. Both added leggings, deerskin moccasins, and robes of bear or other skins in winter (women sometimes wore feather robes). Other items of clothing included turkey feather cloaks, leather belts, and temporary cornhusk footwear. Men also wore snakeskin or feather headbands.

Some clothing was painted or tasseled and fringed. People dressed their hair and bodies with bear or raccoon grease mixed with onion, in part as a protection against the sun and insects. Women tended to wear braids, whereas men roached their hair. Various personal adornments included earrings and necklaces, tattoos, and body paint.

War and Weapons There was some fighting between Lenápe villages. Most Lenápe warfare was limited in nature. Warriors painted their faces, wore special attire, and used a special jargon. Weapons included the bow and arrow, wooden helmet, wooden war club, and large wooden or moose-hide shield. Captives were generally adopted or tortured and killed. Special war dances were associated with wars and raids. Intertribal confederacies were occasionally formed in times of major wars.

Contemporary Information

Government/Reservations The Delaware Tribe of Indians, Washington, Nowata, Craig, and Delaware Counties, Oklahoma, is governed by the Delaware Tribal Business Committee. Tribal population was about 10,000 in the early 1990s.

The Delaware Tribe of Western Oklahoma, established in 1866, is located near Anadarko, Oklahoma. Their land area is roughly 63,600 acres, held with the Wichita and Caddo tribes. Fewer than 3,000 acres are tribally owned. Tribal enrollment was around 1,000 in 1990.

A small number of Citizen Delaware (Munsee and Ojibwa) live near Ottawa, Kansas.

The Stockbridge-Munsee Reservation, Shawano County, Wisconsin (established in 1856), consists of approximately 46,000 acres of land, roughly one-third of which is held in trust by the federal government. The 1990 Indian population was 447, with about an additional 1,000 people also enrolled. The tribe is governed by a seven-member elected tribal council.

Other U.S. communities include the Ramapough Mountain Indians in New Jersey (about 2,500 people), the Powhatan-Renápe Nation at Rancocas, New Jersey (about 600 people), the

Brotherton Indians (Wisconsin), and the Eastern Lenápe Nation (Pennsylvania).

The Six Nations Reserve, Ontario, was home to roughly 350 mixed Lenápe in the early 1990s. Delaware Indians also live on the following three Ontario reserves: Delaware of Grand River, Moravians of the Thames, and Muncey of the Thames.

The Moravians of the Thames Reserve, Kent County, Ontario, consists of roughly 1,200 hectares and is home to roughly 500 mixed Lenápe.

Roughly 200 Muncee Indians live on the Muncey of the Thames Reserve near London, Ontario, on about 2,700 acres.

Economy In Oklahoma, most Lenápe are integrated with the non-native population. Tribal enterprises include bingo and tobacco sales. The Oklahoma Delawares received a land claims settlement of about $15 million in the late 1970s.

Legal Status The Delaware Tribe of Indians, the Delaware Tribe of Western Oklahoma (Absentee), and the Stockbridge-Munsee Band of Mohican Indians of Wisconsin are federally recognized tribal entities.

Other tribal organizations include the Native Delaware Indians (New Jersey), the Nanticoke Lenni-Lenápe Indians (New Jersey), the Delaware-Munsee (Kansas), the Powhatan-Renápe Nation (New Jersey), the Munsee Thames River Delaware Tribal Council (Colorado), the Eastern Lenápe Nation (Pennsylvania), and the Nanticoke Indian Association (Delaware). The Ramapough Mountain Indians (New Jersey) have been denied federal recognition (1997).

Daily Life Most Lenápe are Christians, and some belong to the Native American Church, especially in Oklahoma. Each Oklahoma community hosts a powwow in summer. Some communities still hold "secular" naming ceremonies. The native language remains alive but not in common use, and there are programs in Oklahoma devoted to maintaining and building an awareness of some traditional culture. The Delaware Nation Grand Council of North America, incorporated in 1992, coordinates ongoing relations between the scattered groups of Lenápe.

Mahican

Mahican (Mu ˋhē kə n), from *Muh-he-con-ne-ok,* "People of the Waters That Are Never Still." This tribe is often confused with the Mohegans, a Connecticut tribe, in part because of the J. F. Cooper book *Last of the Mohicans,* a fictional story about a fictional tribe of Indians. There were originally several members of the Mahican confederacy, including, in the late seventeenth century, the Housatonic, Wyachtonoc, and Wappinger.

Location The Mahican proper lived on both sides of the northern Hudson (Mahicanituck) River, in present-day eastern New York and western Vermont. The confederacy was centered around Schodac, near present-day Albany, and included tribes living along the lower Hudson River as well as in western Massachusetts and Connecticut. Today, Mahican descendants live in north-central Wisconsin and Oklahoma.

Population There were between 4,000 and 5,000 Mahicans in 1600 and around 500 in 1700. There were approximately 1,500 Stockbridge-Munsees in the early 1990s.

Language Mahican was an Algonquian language.

Historical Information

History The Mahicans were drawn into the fur trade shortly after they encountered Henry Hudson in 1609. They soon began collecting tribute from the Mohawk for access to a Dutch trade post established in Mahican country in 1614. Shell beads, or wampum, came into use at that time as currency. For a time the Mahicans, trading with Algonquians to the north, monopolized the regional fur trade.

As nearby fur areas became trapped out, the European powers had some success encouraging their Indian partners to expand through intertribal conflict. With the help of French firearms, for instance, Mohawks drove the Mahicans east of the Hudson River Valley in 1628. The latter reestablished their council fire to the north, around Schaghticoke. Some defeated New England tribes joined this group in the 1670s.

Throughout the late seventeenth century, the Mahican fought the Munsee, Iroquois, and others in the Piedmont and the Ohio Valley in their quest for pelts. They even ranged as far west as Miami territory, where some of them remained. By 1700 or so, Mahican culture was in retreat, and the people began to sell or otherwise abandon traditional lands to non-natives. Traditional social and political structures, such as localized clan and lineage patterns (see "Government"), began to break down owing to the demands of the fur trade, as did traditional manufacture and economies. The people also underwent a general moral breakdown, due in part to the influence of alcohol and the general cultural disruption.

In the 1670s, some groups withdrew to live among the Housatonic Band of Mahicans, in Westenhunk, although Mahicans also remained in the Hudson River Valley. Some Mahicans also merged with the Saint Francis Abenaki in the Saint Lawrence Valley and joined other Indian communities as well. In the mid-1730s, a group migrated to Wyoming, Pennsylvania, and some resettled in the mission town of Stockbridge, Massachusetts. The so-called Stockbridge Indians fought with the British in the French and Indian War and with the patriots in the American Revolution. In the mid-1740s, Moravian missionaries persuaded local Indians to remove to the area of Bethlehem, Pennsylvania. This group ultimately settled in Ottawa, Canada.

By the mid– to late eighteenth century, the Indians had completely lost their subsistence economy. Most survived by selling splint baskets, other crafts, and their labor. Despite assisting the colonies in their various wars of this period, the Stockbridge Mahicans were soon dispossessed, and many joined their relatives in the Susquehanna River area in Pennsylvania, there to merge with other tribes, especially the Algonquian Delaware.

By the end of the American Revolution, most of the dispirited remnant of the Mahican Nation had left Stockbridge and nearby areas and settled near the Oneida Indians in New York, where they established a thriving non-native–style farm and craft community. Between 1818 and 1829, these Indians left the Oneida country and migrated west to Wisconsin, where missionaries had purchased land for them. They moved again several years later, after the Wisconsin Indians repudiated their land sales.

Some of this group dispersed to Kansas or died along the way after an abortive move to the Missouri River in 1839. In 1856, they were granted a reservation in Wisconsin, with the Munsee Band of Delaware Indians and, later, a group of Brothertown Indians (*see* Pequot). The community was marked by factionalism and various removals for years.

The tribe lost a significant amount of land in the post-1887 allotment process. It was officially terminated in 1910. In the 1930s, the Stockbridge-Munsee, landless and destitute, reorganized under the Indian Reorganization Act and acquired 2,250 acres of land.

Religion Manitou—the Great Spirit—was present in all things. Some families owned sacred dolls, which were feasted so that their spirit would protect the owners. The Mahican celebrated the Green Corn Dance at the beginning of harvest season as well as various first fruits and first game rituals. They believed that the soul did not die with the body.

Government Each autonomous village had its own chief and councilors. The positions of lineage leaders and clan chiefs (who may also have been village chiefs) were inherited matrilineally. The head chief, or sachem, kept the tribal bag of peace, which contained wampum, at least in the historical period. As Mahican local and regional power grew, the sachem acquired three assistants: owl, or orator and town crier; runner, or messenger; and hero, or war chief.

Customs The three matrilineal clans may have inhabited separate villages. Men helped women with the harvest after celebrating the Green Corn festival. Families scattered into the woods in late fall and remained through midwinter, when they returned to the villages. Old people remained in the villages all winter long, generally doing craft work. There may have been a recognized system of social status. People were buried in a sitting position and then covered with wood and stones. Graves were stocked with provisions such as food, dishes, and weapons for use in the afterlife.

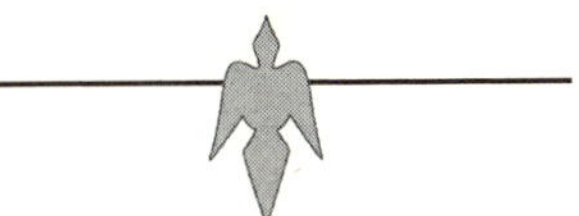

Dwellings Villages were often located on a hill near a river. At least from the seventeenth century on they were often palisaded. Roughly 200 people lived in a village. Each village contained from 3 to 16 long, rectangular bark lodges, as well as domed wigwams, framed with hickory saplings and covered with birch, elm, or basswood bark pressed flat. Longhouses averaged three fireplaces and as many nuclear families. Animal skins were hung on interior walls for insulation. Villages were moved every ten years or so owing to exhaustion of land and firewood.

Diet The Mahican practiced slash-and-burn field clearing and regular rotation of fields. They used fish and ash as fertilizer. Women grew beans, squash, probably sunflowers, and several varieties of corn. Corn was used in bread, soup, and other dishes. Cornmeal mixed with maple sap and water made a trail food for hunters and warriors. Crops were the most important food. Women also gathered waterlily roots, greens, mushrooms, nuts, and berries and made sassafras and wintergreen tea. Maple sap may have been boiled into sugar.

Men hunted game such as bear, deer, moose, beaver, rabbit, otter, squirrel, raccoon, turkey, passenger pigeons, and many other birds. Deer were hunted in fall, moose in spring. In summer, men gathered mussels and caught herring, shad, and other fish. Fish as well as meat was eaten fresh or dried and smoked.

Key Technology Corn was stored in bark containers or bark-lined pits. Men caught fish with bone hooks, weirs, and nets. They hunted with spears and traps in addition to the bow and arrow. Their bows were made of hickory or red cedar, and they used flint arrowheads. Most Mahican technology was wood based: Wooden or bark items included bowls, utensils, and containers. Mortars were fire-hollowed stumps. Women made pottery and wove baskets, bags, and mats.

Trade Mahicans acted as intermediaries in the shell bead trade from the coast to the Saint Lawrence Valley. Major trade partners included Algonquins to the east and south.

Notable Arts Containers and clothing were decorated with porcupine quills and paints.

Transportation Men made dugout and birch-bark canoes as well as snowshoes.

Dress Women made most clothing of finely tanned skins. Men wore breechclouts, and women wore skirts. Both wore shirts, blankets, high leggings, and moccasins. Both also wore long braids dressed with bear grease and tattooed their faces.

War and Weapons War season began after the harvest was in. Warriors sometimes burned or plucked out their hair except for a strip down the middle. Mahican enemies included Iroquois tribes, especially the Mohawk, although this relationship sometimes became an alliance in the mid–seventeenth century.

Contemporary Information

Government/Reservations The Stockbridge-Munsee Reservation, Shawano County, Wisconsin (established in 1856), consists of approximately 46,000 acres of land, roughly one-third of which is held in trust by the federal government. The 1990 Indian population was 447. The community is governed by a seven-member elected tribal council.

Economy The casino is a major employer on the Stockbridge-Munsee Reservation. Other tribal members have jobs associated with tribal facilities and programs as well as small tribal businesses. Some people work in the local non-native economy.

Legal Status The Stockbridge-Munsee Band of Mohican Indians is a federally recognized tribal entity.

Daily Life Longtime president of the tribe Arvid Miller helped establish the Great Lakes Intertribal Council in the 1960s. The tribe, along with Menominee Indians and neighboring non-natives, has been fighting a huge low-level radiation dump since the late 1970s. Tribal facilities include offices, a health center, residential and recreational facilities for the elderly, a library and museum, a campground, and a casino.

The people observe a traditional 12-day new year celebration. Most Stockbridge-Munsees are Christians, although some participate in sweat lodge ceremonies. Some people study the Munsee-Mahican

language and would like to teach it. Most traditional culture has been lost. The tribe hosts a large powwow in early August.

Maliseet

Maliseet (`Mal ə sēt), or Malicite, probably a Micmac word for "lazy speakers" or "broken talkers." The tribe may have derived from people of Passamaquoddy (maritime) and Natick (inland) extraction. Together with the Passamaquoddy they have also been known as the Etchemin tribe. *See also* Abenaki; Micmac; Passamaquoddy.

Location The Maliseet traditionally lived along the Saint John River drainage in present-day New Brunswick, Canada, as well as in northeastern Maine. Today, Maliseets live on and near reserves in extreme southeast Canada, including the Gaspé, as well as in nearby and regional cities and towns.

Population With the Passamaquoddy, the Maliseet numbered about 1,000 in the early seventeenth century. In the early 1990s, the Malecites of Viger (Malecite First Nation) (Quebec) had a population of 425 out of a total Maliseet population of around 3,000.

Language Maliseets and Passamaquoddys spoke dialects of the same Algonquian language.

Historical Information

History The Maliseet people may have come to their historical territory from the southwest, where they probably had contact with the Ohio Mound Builders in ancient times. They may also have been united with the Passamaquoddy in the distant past. Their first contact with non-natives probably occurred in the early seventeenth century when they met Samuel de Champlain, although they may have encountered fishermen from northern and western Europe as much as a century earlier.

A growing involvement in the French fur trade led to a parallel dependence on items of non-native manufacture. The people also accepted Catholic missionaries in the seventeenth century. Throughout the eighteenth century, the Maliseet population declined sharply as a result of disease, abuse of alcohol, and loss of land. They joined the pro-French Abenaki Confederacy in the mid–eighteenth century. They also sided with the French in the colonial wars and intermarried with them.

By the late eighteenth century, British settlers had pushed the Maliseet out of many of their best subsistence areas, and the traditional annual round of subsistence activities had been seriously disrupted. Reserves were established from 1876 on, although the Maliseet resisted a sedentary lifestyle for a long time. In the mid– to late nineteenth century, many Maliseets worked as loggers, stevedores, craftspeople, guides, and farm laborers. Logging and potato farming transformed the region in the 1870s. Local Maliseets, such as the several families who roamed around Houlton, Maine, also worked as house cleaners and in the mills, made baskets, and hunted, fished, and gathered foods where possible.

In the twentieth century, some old communities were abandoned, as many people congregated in a few reservations or moved off the reservations altogether. Along with other landless Indians, Maliseets formed the Association of Aroostook Indians in 1970.

Religion Guardian spirits gave people the ability to protect subsistence areas from trespass. They also gave shamans the power to cure, which they did by chanting, blowing, and possibly sucking. Sweat lodges and dances were associated with spiritual power.

Government Skilled hunters generally provided local leadership. In the seventeenth century there was a supreme hereditary chief who lived at the main village. In general, leadership was more formalized under the confederacy, with graduated civil offices and a war chief. The Maliseets were part of the Abenaki Confederacy from the mid–eighteenth century to the mid– to late nineteenth century, when the confederacy ceased to exist.

Customs The people came together in large villages in summer and dispersed into small hunting camps in winter. They preferred football, a kicking game, to lacrosse. They also played any number of dice gambling games. Herb doctors could be men or women.

Men served their prospective in-laws for at least a year before marriage. During this period, the woman

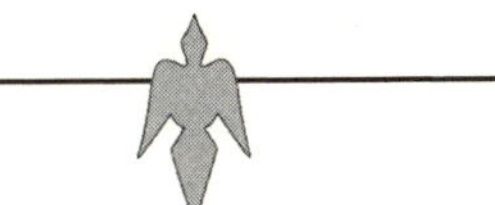

made the man's clothing and footgear. Weddings were marked by feasting, oratory, and the formal recognition of the groom's ancestry. At least in the historical period, sexual mores were strict, and divorce was rare. Children were generally treated gently and with a high degree of freedom, at least when compared with the early French in the area. Boys could sit in council with the older men after killing their first moose. When death was expected, it was sometimes hastened by pouring cold water on the victim, who may also have been buried alive.

Dwellings Some summer villages were palisaded. They included multi- and single-family dwellings. The former were conical, pole-frame wigwams covered with birch bark; the latter, as well as council houses, were rectangular log-frame structures with birch-bark roofs. Council houses could hold up to 100 people.

Diet Farming, especially corn, was the key economic activity. Harvested corn was either stored or taken on the winter hunts. Men hunted inland animals such as moose, bear, otter, and muskrat. They also fished for salmon, bass, and sturgeon. This, with wild grapes and roots gathered by the women, made up most of the summer diet. Women also gathered fiddlehead ferns in early spring.

Key Technology Corn was stored in bark-lined pits. Various birch-bark items included canoes, containers, baskets, dishes, and boxes, some of which were decorated with porcupine quills. Cordage came from spruce roots or cedar bark. The crooked knife was an important woodworking tool. Men summoned moose with a birch-bark calling instrument. Musical instruments included boards (for beating time), drums, rattles, flageolets, and flutes.

Trade Although part of a wide-ranging network, Maliseets traded mainly among local groups. They exported corn and birch-bark products, mainly to people living to the south.

Notable Arts Many items were decorated with porcupine-quill embroidery. Maliseets made excellent ash-splint baskets and beadwork in the historical era.

Transportation Men made lightweight canoes of birch bark, moose hide, or spruce bark. They also made snowshoes.

Dress The basic dress was breechclouts for men, dresses for women, and moccasins. Furs and heavy skins were used in cold weather. Beaverskin caps protected people's heads from the cold. There were also temporary raincoats made of birch bark.

War and Weapons War chiefs may have predated the historical era. This position was never inherited or elected. The war chief had responsibility for attracting followers for a raid. Weapons included the bow and arrow and the spear.

Contemporary Information

Government/Reservations The Houlton Band of Maliseet Indians, Houlton, Maine, had a population of around 550 in the early 1990s. At the same time, its land base was around 800 acres. It is governed by an elected tribal council.

Canadian Maliseets had a population in the early 1990s of about 2,500. New Brunswick communities include Oromocto, Devon (St. Mary's), Kingsclear (Pilick), Woodstock, Tobique, and St. Basile (Madawaska First Nation). Nobody lives on the Quebec reserves of Whitworth (173 hectares) and Cacouna (.17 hectares), but Quebec Maliseets are members of the Malecite First Nation (Viger). Canadian Maliseets are organized into a number of nonprofit corporations.

Economy Unemployment seldom dipped below 50 percent in the early to mid-1990s. The band provides some jobs, primarily in administration, economic development, and housing projects. There is seasonal work with potatoes and blueberries.

Legal Status The Houlton Band of Maliseet Indians is a federally recognized tribal entity. The Canadian bands listed under "Government/Reservations" are federally and provincially recognized.

Daily Life State of Maine services date from 1973. Although the Houlton Band receives numerous benefits as a party to the 1980 Maine Indian Land

Claims Settlement Act, such as cash, land, and access to federal services, many unaffiliated Maliseet families remain without services or recognition. Facilities in Houlton include a new tribal center. Maliseets and Passamaquoddys have long enjoyed close relations and continue to intermarry. Canadian Maliseets have largely assimilated into French society. Few people outside of New Brunswick speak the native language fluently. The Tobique Reservation operates its own school as well as shops selling locally made arts and crafts. The Wabanaki Aboriginal Music Festival is held there over Labor Day weekend. Saint-Anne Day is celebrated in July.

Menominee

Menominee (Me ˋno mə nē), from *Manomini,* Anishinabe for "Wild Rice People." The Menominee were culturally related to the Winnebago and Anishinabe.

Location The Menominee controlled nearly 10 million acres along the northwestern shore of Lake Michigan and west into central Wisconsin. Today, most live on a reservation on the Wolf River in northern Wisconsin.

Population From a population of perhaps 3,000 in the early seventeenth century, the Menominee have grown to around 7,000 people in the early 1990s.

Language Menominees speak an Algonquian language.

Historical Information

History Shortly after the first non-natives made contact with the Menominee people in the mid–seventeenth century, Iroquois warriors drove the Menominees into the Green Bay area, possibly from Michilimackinac. Jesuit missionaries arrived among them in 1671. The people maintained generally friendly relations with non-natives, especially the French, with whom they occasionally intermarried.

Participation in the fur trade from the late seventeenth century through the early nineteenth century broke the tribe into small, mobile bands of hunters-trappers. They avoided many of the colonial and other wars of the eighteenth and nineteenth centuries, although some sided with the British in the American Revolution and the War of 1812. With the fur-bearing animals depleted, and under pressure from non-natives, the Menominee in 1854 ceded all of their remaining lands except for a reservation on the Wolf River in north-central Wisconsin.

On the reservation, a split soon developed between pagans and Christians, traditionalists and progressives. Some people tried farming in the later nineteenth century, but as this was generally unsuccessful, many soon turned to lumbering. In the early twentieth century, with the help of the U.S. Forest Service, the Menominee began harvesting their prime timber resources for sustained yield. Their sawmill became the center of economic activity and the tribe's most important employer.

Despite the government's mismanagement of the tribe's timber resources (for which the tribe won a legal judgment and collected an award of over $7.5 million in 1951), the Menominee were among the country's most economically stable and prosperous tribes by the early 1950s. Suddenly, they learned that they were to experience the effects of a new government policy. The tribe was officially terminated, or removed from its special relationship with the federal government, in 1961. The reservation became a county and the tribe a corporation.

The Menominee are perhaps the classic termination disaster. Termination-related expenses

Governor Nelson of Wisconsin is shown signing a bill that created Menominee County, July 31, 1959. After the Menominee signed this agreement, their community fell upon hard times.

soon depleted their cash reserves. When the hospital was forced to close, the people experienced a sharp rise in tuberculosis and other health problems. The low tax base could not finance needed government services, and the tribe, once self-sufficient, sank into poverty. Faced with total financial collapse, it was forced in the late 1960s to sell off prime waterfront real estate to non-natives. Many people began to judge the intent of termination by its effects: the destruction of a relatively prosperous Indian group and the further transfer of its prime land to non-natives.

In reaction to these developments and to the related possibility that non-natives would make up a majority of the county's voters, a new organization, the Determination of Rights and Unity for Menominee Shareholders (DRUMS), called for a new federal trust relationship for the tribe as well as tribal self-determination. Although termination was reversed in 1973, and most of the former reservation was restored, the tribe has yet to recover from the devastating effects of the termination.

Religion Mecawetok, who may have been identified with the sun, was the Great Spirit and supreme creative force. There were many levels of deities and spirits, some friendly and some evil; the latter were assumed to reside below the earth. Most people sought to obtain spiritual power with the help of a guardian spirit, which one acquired in a vision through fasting and dreaming. Dreams were in some ways the entire basis of living: They determined an individual's sacred songs, dances, and ceremonies. One's power was said to increase with age.

Medicine bundles contained various personal sacred charms. There may have been several old religious cults made up of medicine men or people with outstanding power. People with particularly strong powers included witches and "jugglers." The latter were curers and diviners.

The Midewiwin (medicine lodge) Society was a secret society of shamans. Membership was by invitation or inheritance; initiation was highly ritualized. Each member possessed a medicine bag as well as strong and benevolent medicines.

The Dream Dance or Drum Dance contained some precontact elements. Membership was relatively unrestricted. Members petitioned the sacred spirits with drums and related rituals to obtain supernatural power. The ceremonies were highly ritualized, and codes of behavior were associated with what essentially was a religion.

Ernest Neconish, elder statesman of the Menominee Indians of Wisconsin, chats with Senator Gaylord Nelson of Wisconsin during a Washington, D.C., ceremony, April 22, 1975, in which the tribal land of the Menominee Indians was restored to reservation status.

Government Clan chiefs were probably hereditary. Chiefs of the Bear Clan served as tribal chiefs, and the various lineage chiefs made up the village council. Nonhereditary chiefs achieved status through their dreams or war exploits. These people might be war leaders, lead public celebrations, or enjoy other duties and responsibilities.

A band system replaced clans and villages during the late seventeenth century and early eighteenth century. Bands tended to follow clan lines but were mostly based on friendships. The hereditary system of leadership became less important, replaced by skills such as excellence in trapping and an ability to negotiate with non-natives. There was also a tribal council from this time on.

Customs The Menominee were divided into two divisions, Bear and Thunderbird. Each was in turn divided into patrilineal clans. Smoking tobacco accompanied nearly every important activity. Certain relatives were allowed or encouraged to joke with

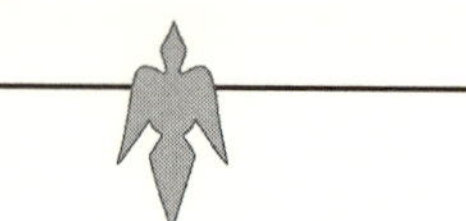

each other as a means of maintaining social mores and order.

The male sphere included ceremonies, tool and weapon manufacture, and war. Women saw to the home and children; grew, collected, and prepared all food; were responsible for firewood, water, and carrying goods; and made clothing and items associated with food and the home. Women could also participate in many male activities, such as fishing, hunting, dancing, and some power ceremonies.

Boys and girls undertook ten-day dream fasts at puberty; these were the culmination of short childhood fasts. There was also a feast following a boy's first game kill. Children were toughened by icy plunges and other such means. Women were isolated during their menstrual periods and after childbirth because they were thought to threaten the balance of spiritual power.

Marriages were generally arranged by elders, who took their lead from a couple to a greater or lesser degree. They were probably formalized by an exchange of gifts. Men might have more than one wife. Corpses were placed on scaffolds, but in the later historical period they were painted red and placed in birch-bark coffins, along with personal items. Mourners blackened their faces with charcoal, but funerals were accompanied by feasting and sport.

Dwellings Winter houses were domed wigwams, with cattail and reed mats placed over bent saplings. These structures were especially used after contact with non-natives in winter hunting camps. Rectangular summer houses were made of bark over a pole framework. Other hut-type buildings were used for sweat lodges, for women's seclusion, and for ceremonial purposes. Permanent villages usually contained a lacrosse field.

Diet Wild rice—which is not rice but a grass seed—gave this tribe its name and was a staple, along with fish. It was collected in summer by people, usually women, in canoes. The method entailed bending the plants over and knocking them with paddles; the seeds fell into the bottom of the canoes. They were then dried, pounded, and winnowed, with the grain boiled and served in a stew or with maple syrup.

Men hunted large game, such as deer and buffalo. They also hunted small game from canoes. They relied more on hunting once they became involved in the fur trade. Bundles or charms helped ensure cooperation from spirits. Men also fished for sturgeon and other fish in Green Bay and in nearby streams. They fished through the ice in winter. Women grew small gardens of corn, beans, squash, and tobacco. They also gathered berries and maple sap.

Key Technology Fish were caught using traps, hooks, spears, and woven bark-fiber gill nets. Women wove pouches of plant fibers and buffalo hair. These items served many purposes, such as food storage and protection of ceremonial items. They also wove and dyed cattail, rush, or cedar-bark mats and winnowing trays, and they made pottery. Hunting equipment and weapons of war included the bow and arrow, clubs, and knives made of a variety of materials such as bone, stone, and copper. The people also used stone axes.

Trade Wild rice was a major export, as were items made of stone and wood. The people imported buffalo hides and other prairie items, catlinite (pipestone), and copper.

Notable Arts Menominee women made especially fine pottery, pouches, and clothing decorated with porcupine quills and animal hair. Motifs included geometric figures and sacred beings.

Transportation Men made bark and dugout canoes as well as snowshoes.

Dress Men wore deerskin breechclouts, shirts, leggings, and moccasins. Women wore woven nettle shirts as well as deerskin robes, leggings, and moccasins. Both decorated their clothing with paint and porcupine quills. Both also wore copper jewelry and rubbed oil and grease on their hair and bodies.

War and Weapons The Menominee were not known for their aggressiveness. Nevertheless, they were often at war. They were generally friendly with

the Winnebago and occasionally enemies with the Sauk and Fox. Weapons were similar to hunting tools.

Contemporary Information

Government/Reservations The Menominee Reservation, Menominee and Shawano Counties, Wisconsin (established in 1848) consists of roughly 230,000 acres of land. The 1990 Indian population was nearly 3,200. A 1977 constitution and by-laws call for an elected nine-member legislature as well as a tribal chair, a judiciary, and a general council.

Economy Gaming operations are central to the new tribal economy; profits underwrite a host of social and health services.

Legal Status The Menominee Indian Tribe of Wisconsin is a federally recognized tribal entity.

Daily Life Most tribal members are Christians, although the Big Drum religion is also popular, as are the Ojibwa-based Warrior's Dance, the Native American Church, and Medicine Lodge ceremonies. A renewed clan structure exists among the people. The language is in use and taught in school. The College of the Menominee Nation is located in Keshena. The people host an annual powwow. Substance abuse remains a daunting challenge. The tribe is committed to maintaining its sovereignty and its Indian identity.

Miami

Miami (Mī `a mē), possibly from the Ojibwa word *Omaumeg,* "People of the Peninsula," or from their own word for pigeon. Their original name may have been *Twaatwaa,* in imitation of a crane. The traditional bands were Atchatchakangouen, Kilatika, Mengakonkia, Pepicokia, Wea, and Piankashaw. Miamis were culturally and linguistically related to the Illinois.

Location From a position possibly south of Lake Michigan, the Miami moved into northern Illinois and southern Wisconsin in the mid–seventeenth century. Within a few generations, they moved south of Lake Michigan, roughly between the Wabash and the Ohio Rivers, and especially along the St. Joseph River. Today Miamis live in Ottawa County, Oklahoma, and in Allen, Huntington, and Miami Counties, Indiana.

Population There were approximately 4,500 Miamis in the mid–seventeenth century. In the early 1990s, about 6,000 lived in Indiana. In the mid-1990s about 4,500 lived in Oklahoma.

Language Miami is an Algonquian language.

Historical Information

History Miami culture evolved at least in part from the prehistoric Ohio Mound Builders. In the mid–seventeenth century, the people effected a temporary retreat west of the Mississippi in the face of Iroquois war parties; Dakota pressure, including a huge military defeat, sent them back east (with French assistance). Peace was established between the Miami and the Iroquois in 1701.

Miamis traded with the French from the mid–seventeenth century on but tended to side with the British in the colonial wars. Some Miamis guided Jacques Marquette and Louis Joliet down the Mississippi in the 1670s. The tribe experienced early factionalism over the issue of Christianity. The Miami participated in Pontiac's rebellion (1763), after which they ceded most of their Ohio lands and concentrated in Indiana. They fought with the British against the Americans in the Revolutionary War.

The Miami war, also known as Little Turtle's war, was led by the great strategist Michikinikwa, or Little Turtle. The Indian coalition included Objibwas, Ottawas, Lenápes, Shawnees, Potawatomis, and Illinois as well as Miamis. The war was a defensive one, fought to contain non-native settlement of the Ohio Valley. The coalition enjoyed significant victories in the early years, thanks mainly to Michikinikwa's strategy of guerrilla warfare. In the end, however, sheer numbers of non-native soldiers wore the Indians down. Although Michikinikwa foresaw the inevitable defeat and advised a cessation of hostilities, the coalition replaced him with another leader and was decisively defeated at the Battle of Fallen Timbers in 1794. The ensuing Treaty of Greenville forced local

Indians to cede all of Ohio and most of Indiana to the United States.

The Miami underwent a dramatic population decline beginning in the late eighteenth century. Groups of Wea and Piankashaw began moving to Missouri as early as 1814. The United States forcibly removed a group of about 600 Miami to Kansas in 1846. In 1854, these groups came together to join the remnants of the Illinois tribe, forming the Confederated Peoria Tribe. They were later relocated to Oklahoma. There, in 1873, the Miami joined that confederacy, which changed its name to the United Peoria and Miami. The group that remained in Indiana consisted of about 1,500 people whose chiefs had been granted private land.

By the early twentieth century, Miami land in both Oklahoma and Indiana had largely been lost through allotment and tax foreclosure. Through the process of losing their lands, both communities, but especially that in Indiana, suffered significant population loss, as people moved away to try to survive. Forty years after the Indiana Miami lost federal recognition in 1897, they organized a nonprofit corporation in an effort to maintain their identity.

Religion The sun was the supreme deity, possibly the revered master of life central to Miami religion. There were also lesser manitou, or spirits, which were involved in a vision quest complex. Both sexes undertook a vision quest at puberty, for which they began training by fasting at a young age. Some men were directed by their guardian spirit to act and dress like women; this role was generally accepted, although if they engaged in warfare they did so as men.

Priests who cured with magic powers made up the Midewiwin or Grand Medicine Society. There were also shamans who cured with herbs and plant medicines. The most important ceremonies focused on the harvest and the return from the winter hunt. In both cases, celebrations included feasting, dancing, games, and music.

Government The six traditional bands had consolidated by the eighteenth century into four: the Miami proper, the Pepicokia, the Wea, and the Piankashaw. Of these, the second soon merged into the last two, which by the nineteenth century acted as separate tribes. Even in the nineteenth century, each of the three Miami tribes was divided into bands.

Each village had a council made up of clan chiefs; the council in turn confirmed a village chief, generally a patrilineally inherited position, who was responsible for civil functions and was in turn supported by the people. There was also a war chief who oversaw war rituals. This person generally inherited his position but might obtain it by merit (as was the case with Little Turtle). There were also parallel female peace and war chiefs: The former supervised feasts, and the latter provisioned war parties and could demand an end to various types of hostilities.

The village council also sent delegates to the band council, which in turn sent delegates to the tribal council. All leaders enjoyed respect and a great deal of authority. In fact, early tribal chiefs may have had a semidivine status, reflecting the influence of Mound Builder culture.

Customs The Miami recognized roughly five patrilineal clans and possibly a dual division. Elderly women may have named children based on dreams. Names were clan specific, although adults might change names to alter their luck or to avert bad luck. Children were rarely punished; parental instruction and discipline consisted mostly of lectures and behavior modeling. Adult status was indicated by face painting. Adults enjoyed athletic competitions, especially footraces.

Marriages were either arranged or initiated by couples. The formalities included a gift exchange. Newly married couples generally lived with the father's family. Killing an adulterous wife (or clipping off the end of her nose) or an abusive husband was condoned; however, other murders were either avenged by blood or by money or property.

Burial, either extended or seated, took place on scaffolds, in hollowed-out logs, and in small, sealed huts. Only food and water and perhaps some personal adornments went with the corpse. Postfuneral activities included a performance of the dead's favorite dance or activity and, if a parent, a ceremonial adoption of a new parent a year later.

Dwellings The people built small summer villages along river valleys. Private houses were made of an oval pole framework covered with woven cattail or rush mats. There were also village council houses. Structures in winter hunting camps tended to be covered with elm bark or hides.

Diet Miamis developed and grew a particularly fine variety of corn, in addition to beans, squash, and, later, melons. Men hunted buffalo on the open prairies, using fire surrounds and bow and arrow before they acquired horses. The whole village, except the old and infirm, would accompany the hunters, with the women and children helping to prepare and pack the meat for the trip home. Women also gathered wild roots and other plant food.

Key Technology Men made pipes of Minnesota pipestone (catlinite). Musical instruments included drums, rattles, flutes, and whistles. Women made bags from spun buffalo hair.

Trade Miamis exported agricultural products, pipes, and buffalo products. They imported shell beads, among other items.

Notable Arts Some items of clothing were decorated by quillwork with bands in a twining or geometric pattern. Buffalo robes were also painted with representational and geometric designs. The people made silk appliqué from the mid–eighteenth century on. Red was a favorite color for decoration.

Transportation Dugout canoes were often made of butternut trees, although the people traveled mainly on land.

Dress Except for soft-soled moccasins, men often went naked in summer; women wore a wraparound skirt, leggings, and a poncho. In winter, men wore deerskin shirts and breechclouts. Both occasionally wore painted animal robes, especially during ceremonies. Knife sheaths were attached to leather or woven belts. Men wore their hair in a roach and were extensively painted and tattooed.

War and Weapons With the help of the council, war chiefs decided the issue of whether or not to wage war. Traditional allies included the Kickapoo, whereas enemies included the Dakota (until the eighteenth century) as well as the Chickasaw and other southeastern tribes. The people held a ceremony to ensure the safe return of the war party. War rituals, such as the all-night war dance and the homecoming of a successful war party, were clan based, and leaders of war parties were not considered responsible for deaths or members of their own clan. Warriors carried large buffalo-hide shields.

Contemporary Information

Government/Reservations Headquarters for the Miami Tribe of Oklahoma is located in Miami, Oklahoma. The people own 38 acres of land. Their constitution provides for a principal chief, other officers, and a council. There is an annual meeting of all tribal members.

The Miami Nation of Indiana is located near Peru. A powerful principal chief and elders council are chosen by clans and serve for life. There is also a vice chief, a principal chiefress (female chief), and a spiritual leader. About 2,500 tribal members lived in Indiana in the early 1990s.

Economy In Indiana, bingo provides most tribal funds. Tribal resources in Oklahoma include a trucking company, gasoline reserves, a motel and supper club, bingo, and tourism.

Legal Status The Miami Tribe of Oklahoma is a federally recognized tribal entity. The Miami Nation of Indiana asked for summary action to overturn their 1897 termination and reinstate tribal recognition. Their recognition petition was rejected in 1992.

Daily Life The Indiana Miami meet twice annually and hold an annual picnic in August. Their agenda for years has focused on reinstating federal recognition, reacquiring land, and economic development. Facilities include three buildings, which house the tribal headquarters, a museum, a day care center, various social programs, and a gymnasium.

Facilities in Oklahoma include the tribal headquarters, a common room, a library, and a community kitchen and dining area for elders. There is also a brick longhouse, at which tribal meetings are held. Both Miami tribes helped found the Minnetrista Council for Great Lakes Native American Studies, in Muncie, Indiana, an organization dedicated to preserving and promoting Woodlands culture.

Micmac

Micmac (`Mik mak), or Mi'kmaq, "allies." The Micmac called their land Megumaage and may have called themselves *Souriquois.* They were members of the Abenaki Confederacy in the eighteenth and nineteenth centuries. Culturally similar to the Maliseet, Penobscot, and Passamaquoddy, they were known to the seventeenth-century British as Tarantines, possibly meaning "traders."

Location The people were traditionally located in southeast Quebec, the Maritime Provinces, and the Gaspé Peninsula of eastern Canada, a region of forests, lakes, rivers, and a rugged coast. They lived there and in northern Maine in the late twentieth century.

Population The Micmac population was between 3,000 and 5,000 in the sixteenth century. There were approximately 20,000 registered Canadian Micmacs in 1993, including about 15,000 in the Maritimes and 4,000 in Quebec, and several thousand more in the United States.

Language Micmac was an Algonquian language.

Historical Information

History The Micmac were originally from the Great Lakes area, where they probably had contact with the Ohio Mound Builders and were exposed to agriculture. They may have encountered Vikings around 1000. The Cabots, early explorers, captured three Micmacs at their first encounter. Friendly meetings with Jacques Cartier (1523) and Samuel de Champlain (1603) led to a long-term French alliance.

The Micmac were involved with the fur trade by the seventeenth century, becoming intermediaries between the French and Indian tribes to the south. A growing reliance on non-native manufactured metal goods and foods changed their cultural and economic patterns, and war, alcohol, and disease vastly diminished their population. In 1610, the grand chief Membertou converted to Catholicism after being cured by priests.

In the eighteenth century, the French armed Micmacs with flintlocks and encouraged them, with scalp bounties, to kill people from the neighboring Beothuk tribe. This they did to great effect, nearly annihilating those Indians, after which they occupied their former territory in Newfoundland. British attempts at genocide against the Indians included feeding them poisoned food, trading them disease-contaminated cloth, and indiscriminate individual and mass murder.

By the mid–eighteenth century, most Micmacs had become Catholics. They continued fighting the British until 1763. Much of this fighting took place at sea, where the people showed their excellent nautical skills. Following the American Revolution and the end of the fur trade, Micmacs remained in their much-diminished traditional area, which was increasingly invaded by non-natives.

In the nineteenth century, Micmacs were forced to accept non-Indian approval of their leadership as well as a general trimming of lands guaranteed by treaty. The people continued some traditional subsistence activities during the nineteenth century but also moved toward working in the lumber,

A late-nineteenth-century illustration of a Micmac delegation meeting with Lord Lorne, the governor general of Canada. In the nineteenth century, Micmacs were forced to accept non-native approval of their leadership as well as a general trimming of lands guaranteed by treaty.

construction, and shipping industries and as migrant farm labor. They were generally excluded from skilled or permanent (higher-paying) jobs. Starvation and disease also stalked the people during those years.

Micmacs had lost most of their Canadian reserves by the early 1900s. Schools were located on many of those that remained. Hockey and baseball became very popular before the Depression. Significant economic activities in the early to mid–twentieth century included logging, selling splint baskets, and local seasonal labor, such as blueberry raking and potato picking. An administrative centralization of reserves in the 1950s led to increased factionalism and population flight.

In the 1960s, many Micmac men began working in high-steel construction, on projects mainly in Boston. Women used vocational training to find work as nurses, teachers, and social workers. They also became increasingly active in band politics. Canadian Micmacs formed the Union of New Brunswick Indians and the Union of Nova Scotia Indians in 1969 to coordinate service programs and document land claims. They and other landless tribes formed the Association of Aroostook Indians in 1970 to try to raise their standard of living and fight discrimination. The tribe formed the Aroostook Micmac Council in 1982.

Religion Manitou, the ubiquitous creative spirit, was identified with the sun. Other deities in human form could be prevailed upon to assist mortals. All animals, but especially bears, were treated with respect, in part because it was believed that they could transform themselves into other species. The Micmacs' rich mythology included Gluscap, the culture hero, as well as several types and levels of magical beings, including cannibalistic giants. Shamans were generally men and could be quite powerful. They cured, predicted the future, and advised hunters.

Government Small winter hunting groups, composed of households, came together in summer as bands, within seven defined districts. They also joined forces for war. Bands were identified in part through the use of distinctive symbols. There were three levels of chiefs, all with relatively little authority. Local hunting groups of at least 30 to 40 people were led by a hereditary headman (sagamore), usually an eldest son of an important family. These groups were loosely defined and of flexible membership. Chiefs of local groups provided dogs for the hunt, canoes, and food reserves. Sagamores also kept all game killed by unmarried men, and some of the game killed by married men.

There were also chiefs of the traditional seven districts. These leaders called district council meetings, entertained visiting chiefs, and participated in the grand council. At the top of the pyramid, at least from the nineteenth century on, there was also a grand chief or sagamore. In summer, this leader conferred grand councils to consider treaties as well as issues of war and peace.

Customs The general Micmac worldview valued moderation, equality, generosity, bravery, and respect for all living things. When the people gathered together from spring through fall, each group camped at a traditional place along the coast. There was a recognized social ranking in which commoners came below three levels of chiefs but above slaves, who were taken in war.

Children were welcomed and treated indulgently. A newborn's first meal was bear or seal grease. Women resumed normal activities immediately after giving birth. They generally avoided new pregnancies for several years, until the child had been weaned. Children as well as the elderly were treated with respect and affection, although little or no effort was made to help ill or old people remain alive.

There were many occasions for feasting and dancing, especially as part of life-cycle events. The Micmac probably observed a woman's puberty ceremony; boys were considered men when they had killed their first large game. There were elaborate menstrual taboos, including seclusion. Women's tasks included gathering firewood, making clothing and bark containers, bringing game into camp, and setting up the wigwam. Older brothers and sisters generally avoided each other. Men used the sweat lodge for purification.

Marriages were generally arranged. A prospective husband, usually at least age 20, spent at least two years working for his future father-in-law as a hunter and general provider. After the probationary period,

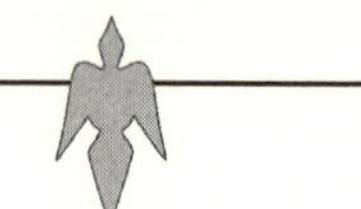

he provided game for a big wedding feast, including dancing (first marriages only). The birth of children formalized a marriage. Adultery was rare, although polygyny was practiced.

Longevity (life spans over 100 years) was not unusual before contact with Europeans. People gave their own funeral orations shortly before they died, if possible. Burial and a feast followed a three-day general mourning period. In some locations, corpses were wrapped in bark and buried with personal effects on an uninhabited island. There was also scaffold burial. Close relatives cut their hair and observed a yearlong mourning period.

Dwellings Micmacs built their inland winter camps near streams. Single extended families lived in conical wigwams of birch bark, skins or woven mats. Each had a central indoor fireplace. The inside was divided into several compartments for cooking, eating, sleeping, and other activities. Floors were covered with boughs, and fur-covered boughs served as beds. The people may have had rectangular, open, multifamily summer houses.

Diet In winter, small bands hunted game such as moose, bear, caribou, and porcupine. They also trapped smaller game such as beaver, otter, and rabbit and ate land and water birds (and their eggs). Moose were stalked with disguises and attracted with callers. Dogs helped in the hunt. Meat and fish were eaten fresh, roasted, broiled, boiled, or smoked. Pounded moose bones yielded a nutritious "butter."

People fished in spring and summer for eel, salmon, cod, herring, sturgeon, and smelt. They also collected shellfish and hunted seals and other marine animals. Salmon and fowl were sometimes speared at night with the light of birch-bark torches. The sea provided most of the summer diet.

They also gathered a number of wild berries, roots, and nuts. They occasionally ate dog, especially at funeral feasts, but they generally avoided snakes, amphibians, and skunks.

Key Technology Men made birch-bark moose calls and boxes. They also made double-edged moose-bone-blade spears and bows and stone-point arrows for hunting as well as snares and deadfalls for trapping. They fished with nets, bone hooks, weirs, and bone-tipped harpoons.

Meat was boiled with hot stones in hollowed wooden troughs. Women made reed and coiled spruce-root baskets, woven mats, and possibly pottery.

Trade Micmacs generally served as intermediaries between northern hunters and southern farmers.

Notable Arts Women decorated clothing and containers with dyed porcupine quillwork. Wigwams were sometimes carefully painted, especially with symbols distinctive to each band.

Transportation Men built 8- to 10-foot-long, seaworthy birch-bark and caribou-skin canoes. They made two types of square-toed snowshoes, one for powder and one for frozen surfaces. Women carried burdens using backpacks and tumplines.

Dress People dressed in skin robes fastened with one (men) or two (women) belts, moose-skin or deerskin leggings, and moccasins. Men also wore loincloths. Both sexes wore their hair long. People tattooed band symbols on their bodies.

War and Weapons Small population groups came together as bands for war. The people were allied with southern Algonquians as members of the Abenaki Confederacy. Their traditional enemies included the Beothuk, Labrador Eskimo, Maliseet (occasionally), Iroquois (especially Mohawk) around the St. Lawrence River, and New England Algonquians.

The Micmac adopted some Iroquois war customs, such as the torture of prisoners by women. Their weapons included bows, poisoned arrows, spears with moose-bone blades, and possibly stone tomahawks. There was some interband fighting (intraband disputes were generally resolved by individual fighting or wrestling). Captives were taken as slaves, tortured and killed, or, especially in the case of young women, adopted.

Contemporary Information

Government/Reservations The Aroostook Band of Micmacs is governed by an elected board of directors. Headquarters for the tribal council is in Presque Isle,

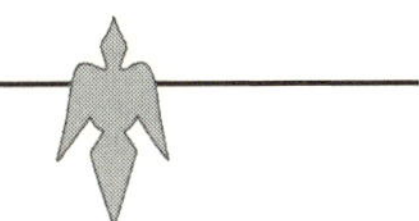

Maine. Band membership was slightly less than 500 in 1991.

The approximately 28 Canadian reserves include Pictou Landing, Eskasoni, and Shubenacadie in Nova Scotia and Burnt Church, Eel River Bar, Pabineau, Red Bank, Eel Ground, Indian Island, Bouctouche, Fort Folly, and Big Cove in New Brunswick. The three Micmac communities in Quebec are Listuguj (3,663.22 hectares; 2,621 people in 1994, of whom 1,641 live within the territory), Gesgapegiag (182.26 hectares; 936 people in 1994, of whom 432 live within the territory), and Gaspé (no area; 435 people in 1994).

Each is governed by a band council. Some are represented by captains of the Grand Council. The Grand Council, traditional government of the Micmac Nation, unites the six districts of Micmac territory (Quebec's Gaspé Peninsula, northern and eastern New Brunswick, Nova Scotia, Newfoundland, and Prince Edward Island).

Economy Fishing, especially for salmon, remains important. Maine Micmacs operate a mail-order crafts cooperative. There have been some land claims victories in Canada, particularly a $35 million settlement to the Micmac of the Pictou Landing reserve.

Legal Status The Aroostook Band of Micmacs is a federally recognized tribal entity. Excluded from the giant 1980 Maine Indian land claim settlement, the tribe persuaded the federal government in 1991 to pass the Aroostook Band of Micmacs Settlement Act, which provided it with land and a tax fund as well as federal benefits. Newfoundland Indians organized in 1973 and were recognized under the Indian Act in 1984.

Daily Life Many Micmacs still speak the native language. Most are Catholics. Micmacs tend to be active in various pan-Indian organizations. There have been some gains in Canadian Micmacs' quest to regain their hunting and fishing rights. Canadian Micmacs still face severe problems such as substance abuse, discrimination, and a high suicide rate. Roughly 40 percent of Canadian Micmacs speak their ancestral language.

Mohawk

Mohawk (`Mō häk), Algonquian for "eaters of men," one of the five original tribes of the Iroquois League. The Mohawk self-designation was *Kaniengehawa,* "People of the Place of Flint." They were the Keepers of the Eastern Door of the Iroquois League. The name Iroquois ("real adders") comes from the French adaptation of the Algonquian name for these people. Their self-designation was *Kanonsionni,* "League of the United (Extended) Households." Iroquois today refer to themselves as *Haudenosaunee,* "People of the Longhouse."

Location The Mohawk were located mainly along the middle Mohawk River Valley but also north into the Adirondack Mountains and south nearly to Oneonta. At the height of their power, the Iroquois controlled land from the Hudson to the Illinois Rivers and the Ottawa to the Tennessee Rivers. Today, Mohawks live in southern Quebec and Ontario, Canada, and extreme northern New York.

Population There were perhaps 15,000–20,000 members of the Iroquois League around 1500 and roughly 4,000 Mohawks in the mid–seventeenth century. About 70,000 Iroquois Indians were living in the United States and Canada in the mid-1990s. Of these, about 28,000 were Mohawks: about 13,000 in Canada and 15,000 in the United States.

Language Mohawks spoke a Northern Iroquois dialect.

Historical Information

History The Iroquois began cultivating crops shortly after the first phase of their culture in New York was established around 800. Deganawida, a Huron prophet, and Hiawatha, a Mohawk shaman living among the Onondaga, founded the Iroquois League or Confederacy some time between 1450 and 1600. It originally consisted of five tribes: Cayuga, Mohawk, Oneida, Onondaga, and Seneca; the Tuscarora joined in the early eighteenth century. The league's purpose was to end centuries of debilitating intertribal war and work for the common good. Both Deganawida and Hiawatha may have been actual or mythological people.

Iroquois first met non-natives in the sixteenth century. There were sporadic Jesuit missions in Mohawk country throughout the mid–seventeenth century. During these and subsequent years, the people became heavily involved in the fur trade. Trading, fighting, and political intrigue characterized that period. Although they were good at playing the European powers off against each other, the Iroquois increasingly became British allies in trade and in the colonial wars and were instrumental in the ultimate British victory over the French.

Shortly after 1667, a year in which peace was concluded with the French, a group of Mohawk and Oneida Indians migrated north to La Prairie, a Jesuit mission on the south side of the St. Lawrence River. This group eventually settled south of Montreal at Sault Saint Louis, or Kahnnawake (Caughnawaga). Although they were heavily influenced by the French, most even adopting Catholicism, and tended to split their military allegiance between France and Britain, they remained part of the Iroquois League. Some of this group and other Iroquois eventually moved to Ohio, where they became known as the Seneca of Sandusky. They ultimately settled in Indian Territory (Oklahoma).

At about the same time, a group of Iroquois settled on the island of Montreal and became known as Iroquois of the Mountain. Like the people at Caughnawaga, they drew increasingly close to the French. The community moved in 1721 to the Lake of Two Mountains and was joined by other Indians at that time. This community later became the Oka reserve. Other Mohawks traveled to the far west as trappers and guides and merged with Indian tribes there.

Early in the eighteenth century, the first big push of non-native settlers drove into Mohawk country. Mohawks at that time had two principal settlements and were relatively prosperous from their fur trade activities. The establishment of St. Regis in the mid–eighteenth century by some Iroquois from Caughnawaga all but completed the migration to the St. Lawrence area. Most of these people joined the French in the French and Indian War, and their allegiance was split during the American Revolution.

The British victory in 1763 meant that the Iroquois no longer controlled the balance of power in the region. Despite the long-standing British alliance, some Indians joined anti-British rebellions as a defensive gesture. The confederacy split its allegiance in the Revolutionary War, with most Mohawks, at the urging of Theyendanegea, or Joseph Brant, siding with the British. This split resulted in the council fire's being extinguished for the first time in roughly 200 years.

The British-educated Mohawk Joseph Brant proved an able military leader in the American Revolutionary War. Despite his leadership and that of others, however, the Mohawks suffered depredations throughout the war, and by war's end their villages had been permanently destroyed. When the 1783 Treaty of Paris divided Indian land between Britain and the United States, British Canadian officials established the Six Nations Reserve for their loyal allies, to which most Mohawks repaired. Others went to a reserve at the Bay of Quinté, which later became Tyendinaga (Deseronto) Reserve.

The Iroquois council officially split into two parts during that time. One branch was located at the Six Nations Reserve and the other at Buffalo Creek. Gradually, the reservations as well as relations with the United States and Canada assumed more significance than intraconfederacy matters. In the 1840s, when the Buffalo Creek Reservation was sold, the fire there was rekindled at Onondaga.

In Canada, traditional structures were further weakened by the allotment of reservation lands in the 1840s; the requirement under Canadian law, from 1869 on, of patrilineal descent; and the transition of league councils and other political structures to a municipal government. In 1924, the Canadian government terminated confederacy rule entirely, mandating an (all male) elected system of government on the reserve.

The native economy gradually shifted from primarily hunting to farming, dependence on annuities received for the sale of land, and some wage labor. The people faced increasing pressure from non-natives to adopt Christianity and sell more land. The old religion declined during that time, although on some reservations the Handsome Lake religion grew in importance. During the nineteenth century, Mohawks worked as oarsmen with shipping companies, at one point leading an expedition up the

Private Huron Eldon Brant, a Mohawk, served with the Hastings and Prince Edward Regiment during World War II. He is pictured here receiving the military medal for courage in action during the Sicilian campaign.

Nile in Egypt. They also began working in construction during that period, particularly on high scaffolding.

At Akwesasne (see "Government/Reservations"), most people farmed, fished, and trapped during the nineteenth century. Almost all resident Indians were Catholic. Government was provided by three U.S.-appointed trustees and, in Canada, by a mandated elected council. With other members of the confederacy, Mohawks resisted the 1924 citizenship act, selective service, and all federal and state intrusions on their sovereignty.

Religion The Mohawk recognized Orenda as the supreme creator. Other animate and inanimate objects and natural forces were also considered to be of a spiritual nature. The Mohawk held important festivals to celebrate maple sap and strawberries as well as corn planting, ripening (Green Corn ceremony), and harvest. These festivals often included singing, male dancing, game playing, gambling, feasting, and food distribution.

The eight-day new year's festival may have been most important of all. Held in midwinter, it was a time to give thanks, to forget past wrongs, and to kindle new fires, with much attention paid to new and old dreams. A condolence ceremony had quasi-religious components. Medicine groups such as the False Face Society, whose members wore carved wooden masks, and the Medicine, Dark Dance, and Death Feast Societies (the last two controlled by women) also conducted ceremonies, since most illness was thought to be of supernatural origin.

In the early nineteenth century, many Iroquois embraced the teachings of Handsome Lake. This religion was born during the general religious ferment known as the Second Great Awakening and came directly out of the radical breakdown of Iroquois life. Beginning in 1799, the Seneca Handsome Lake spoke of Jesus and called upon Iroquois to give up alcohol and a host of negative behaviors, such as witchcraft and sexual promiscuity. He also exhorted them to maintain their traditional religious celebrations. A blend of traditional and Christian teachings, the Handsome Lake religion had the effect of facilitating the cultural transition occurring at the time.

Government The Iroquois League comprised 50 hereditary chiefs, or sachems, from the constituent tribes. Each position was named for the original holder and had specific responsibilities. Sachems were men, except where a woman acted as regent, but they were appointed by women. The Mohawk sent nine sachems (three from each clan) to meetings of the Iroquois Great Council, which met in the fall and for emergencies. Their symbol at this gathering was the shield.

Debates within the great council were a matter of strict clan, division, and tribal protocols, in a complex system of checks and balances. Politically, individual league members often pursued their own best interests while maintaining an essential solidarity

with the other members. The creators of the U.S. government used the Iroquois League as a model of democracy.

Locally, the village structure was governed by a headman and a council of elders (clan chiefs, elders, wise men). Matters before the local councils were handled according to a definite protocol based on the clan and division memberships of the chiefs. Village chiefs were chosen from groups as small as a single household. Women nominated and recalled clan chiefs. Tribal chiefs represented the village and the nation at the general council of the league. The entire system was hierarchical and intertwined, from the family up to the great council. Decisions at all levels were reached by consensus.

There were also a number of nonhereditary chiefs ("pine tree" or "merit" chiefs), some of whom had no voting power. This may have been a postcontact phenomenon.

Customs The Mohawk recognized a dual division, each composed of three matrilineal, animal-named clans (Wolf, Bear, and Turtle). The clans in turn were composed of matrilineal lineages. Each owned a set number of personal names, some of which were linked with particular activities and responsibilities.

Women enjoyed a high degree of prestige, being largely equated with the "three sisters" (corn, beans, and squash), and they were in charge of most village activities, including marriage. Great intravillage lacrosse games included heavy gambling. Other games included snowsnake, or sliding a spear along a trench in the snow for distance. Food was shared so that everyone had roughly the same to eat.

Personal health and luck were maintained by performing various individual rituals, including singing and dancing, learned in dreams. Members of the False Face medicine society wore wooden masks carved from trees and used rattles and tobacco. Shamans also used up to 200 or more plant medicines to cure illness. People committed suicide on occasion for specific reasons (men who lost prestige; women who were abandoned; children who were treated harshly). Murder could be revenged or paid for with sufficient gifts.

Young men's mothers arranged marriages with a prospective bride's mother. Divorce was possible but not readily obtained because it was considered a discredit. The dead were buried in sitting position, with food and tools for use on the way to the land of the dead. A ceremony was held after ten days. The condolence ceremony mourned dead league chiefs and installed successors. A modified version also applied to common people.

Dwellings In the seventeenth century, Mohawks lived in three villages (Caughnawaga, Kanagaro, and Tionnontoguen) of 30 or more longhouses, each village with 500 or more people, as well as roughly five to eight smaller villages. The people built their villages near water and often on a hill after circa 1300. Some villages were palisaded. Other Iroquois villages had up to 150 longhouses and 1,000 or more people. Villages were moved about twice in a generation, when firewood and soil were exhausted.

Iroquois Indians built elm-bark longhouses, 50–100 feet long, depending on how many people lived there, from about the twelfth century on. They held around 2 or 3 but as many as 20 families, related maternally (lineage segments), as well as their dogs. There were smoke holes over each two-family fire. Beds were raised platforms; people slept on mats, their feet to the fire, covered by pelts. Upper platforms were used for food and gear storage. Roofs were shingled with elm bark. The people also built some single-family houses.

Diet Women grew corn, beans, squash, and gourds. Corn was the staple and was used in soups, stews, breads, and puddings. It was stored in bark-lined cellars. Women also gathered a variety of greens, nuts, seeds, roots, berries, fruits, and mushrooms. Tobacco was grown for ceremonial and social smoking.

After the harvest, men and some women took to the woods for several months to hunt and dry meat. Men hunted large game and trapped smaller game, mostly for the fur. Hunting was a source of potential prestige. They also caught waterfowl and other birds, and they fished. The people grew peaches, pears, and apples in orchards from the eighteenth century on.

Key Technology Iroquois used porcupine quills and wampum belts as a record of events. Wampum was also used as a gift connoting sincerity and, later, as trade money. These shell disks, strung or woven into belts, were probably a postcontact technological innovation.

Hunting equipment included snares, bow and arrow, stone knife, and bentwood pack frame. Fish were caught using traps, nets, bone hooks, and spears. Farming tools were made of stone, bone, wood (spades), and antler. Women wove corn-husk dolls, tobacco trays, mats, and baskets.

Other important material items included elm-bark containers, cordage from inner tree bark and fibers, and levers to move timbers. Men steamed wood or bent green wood to make many items, including lacrosse sticks.

Trade Mohawks obtained birch-bark products from the Huron. They imported copper and shells and exported carved wooden and stone pipes. They were extensively involved in the trade in beaver furs from the seventeenth century on.

Notable Arts Men carved wooden masks worn by the Society of Faces in their curing ceremonies. Women decorated clothing with dyed porcupine quills or moose-hair embroidery.

Transportation Unstable elm bark canoes were roughly 25 feet long. The people were also great runners and preferred to travel on land. Women used woven and decorated tumplines to support their burdens. They used snowshoes in winter.

Dress Women made most clothing from deerskins. Men wore shirts and short breechclouts and a tunic in cooler weather; women wore skirts. Both wore leggings, moccasins, and corn-husk slippers in summer. Robes were made of lighter or heavier skins or pelts, depending on the season. These were often painted. Clothing was decorated with feathers and porcupine quills. Both men and women tattooed their bodies extensively. Men often wore their hair in a roach, whereas women wore theirs in a single braid doubled up and fastened with a thong. Some men wore feather caps or, in winter, fur hoods.

War and Weapons Boys began developing war skills at a young age. Prestige and leadership were often gained through war, which was in many ways the most important activity. The title of Pine Tree Chief was a historical invention to honor especially brave warriors. Mohawks were known as particularly fierce fighters. Their enemies included Algonquins, Montagnais, Ojibwas, Crees, and tribes of the Abenaki Confederacy. In traditional warfare, at least among the Mohawk, large groups met face to face and fired a few arrows after a period of jeering, then engaged in another period of hand-to-hand combat using clubs and spears.

Weapons included the bow and arrow, ball-headed club, shield, rod armor, and guns after 1640. All aspects of warfare, from the initiation to the conclusion, were highly ritualized. War could be decided as a matter of policy or undertaken as a vendetta. Women had a large, sometimes decisive, say in the question of whether or not to fight. During war season, generally the fall, Iroquois war parties ranged up to 1,000 miles or more. Male prisoners were often forced to run the gauntlet: Those who made it through were adopted, but those who did not might be tortured by widows. Women and children prisoners were regularly adopted. Some captives were eaten.

Contemporary Information

Government/Reservations Kahnawake/Caughnawaga (5,0599.17 hectares) and Doncaster (7,896.2 hectares) Reserves, Quebec, Canada, were established in 1667 as a Jesuit mission for mostly Oneida and Mohawk Indians. The mid-1990s population was about 6,500, of a total population of almost 8,000. The reserves are administered by a band council.

Oka/Kanesatake/Lake of Two Mountains, Quebec, Canada, established in 1676 by residents of Kahnawake, is populated mainly by Algonquians and several Iroquois tribes. It is roughly 10 square kilometers in size and is governed by a band council. The mid-1990s Mohawk population was about 1,800.

Gibson Reserve (Watha Mohawk Nation), Ontario, Canada, was established in 1881 at Georgian Bay by people from Oka/Kanesatake who resented resistance offered by the Sulpician Catholics to their cutting timber from the home reserve. The mid-1990s population was about 800.

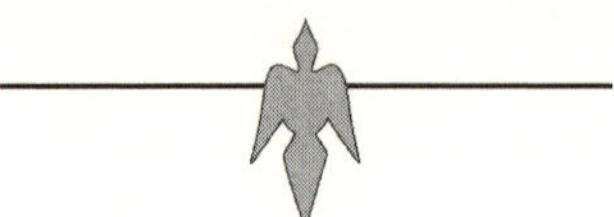

St. Regis Reservation/Akwesasne Reserve, Franklin County, New York, and Quebec and Ontario, Canada, was formerly a mission established on the St. Lawrence River in the mid–eighteenth century for Mohawks and other groups. The resident Indian population in 1990 was 1,923, but the enrolled population approached 13,000. A tribal council provides local self-government. The 14,600 acres of this community straddle the international border.

Six Nations/Grand River, Ontario, Canada, was established in 1784. It is governed by both an elected and a hereditary council, although only the first is officially recognized by Canada.

Tyendinega Reserve (Deseronto), Hastings County, Ontario, Canada, is mainly a Mohawk reserve. The mid-1990s population was around 3,000.

Ganienkeh Reservation, Altoona, New York, had a mid-1990s population of about 300.

There is a small population of Mohawk high-steel workers in Brooklyn, New York.

In 1993, a small group from Akwesasne reestablished a Mohawk presence in New York's Mohawk Valley, for the first time in 200 years. Known as Kanatsioharehe, the Mohawk population in the mid-1990s was about 50.

The Mohawk (Kahniakehaka) Nation does not recognize the U.S.-Canadian border, nor do they consider themselves U.S. or Canadian citizens. Their communities are governed under authority of the Grand Council of the Haudenosaunee Confederacy.

Economy At Kahnawake/Caughnawaga, most people engage in small-scale farming, high-steel work, factory work, and reservation government. There are also four schools on the reserve as well as a radio station, a newspaper, a hospital, and a credit union. At St. Regis/Akwesasne there is mainly high-steel work; small businesses, including bingo halls; and tribal government.

Legal Status The St. Regis Band of Mohawk Indians is a federally recognized tribal entity. The Canadian reserves listed under "Government/ Reservations" are provincially and federally recognized.

Daily Life Mohawks, particularly those from Kahnawake, have earned a first-rate reputation as high-steel workers throughout the United States since the late nineteenth century. People from Kahnawake have pursued self-determination particularly strongly. In 1990 there was a major incident, sparked by the expansion of a golf course, that resulted in an armed standoff involving local non-natives and the communities of Oka, Kahnawake, and Kanesatake. Akwesasne Mohawks have continued to battle the U.S. and Canadian governments over a number of issues. In 1968, by blocking the Cornwall International Bridge, they won concessions making it easier for them to cross the international border. The same year, a Mohawk school boycott brought attention to the failure of Indian education. In 1974, they and others established a territory called Ganienkeh on a parcel of disputed land. In 1977, New York established the Ganienkeh Reservation in Altoona.

The Akwesasne community has also been beset by fighting from within. In 1980, after the New York State Police averted a bloody showdown between traditionalists and "progressives," that body replaced the tribal police. In the late 1980s, violence was rampant over the issue of gambling. This situation had quieted but had not been resolved by the mid-1990s. Community leaders have had difficulty uniting around these and other divisive issues such as state sales and cigarette taxes, pollution, sovereignty, and land claims.

As a result of generations that have worked in high steel, Mohawk communities exist in some northeastern cities. Most of these people remain spiritually tied to their traditions, however, and frequently return to the reserves to participate in ceremonies, including Longhouse ceremonies, which have been active at least since the 1930s.

Akwesasne Mohawks publish an important journal, *Akwesasne Notes.* There is a museum and library at St. Regis. Many Mohawks still speak the native language, which remains the people's official language. Akwesasne Mohawks face a barrage of administrative barriers, owing to their location in two U.S. counties and two Canadian provinces. Since the 1968 boycott, dropout rates have plunged from about 80 percent to about 10 percent. Major educational

reforms have included the establishment of the Akwesasne Freedom School, the North American Indian Traveling College, language and culture courses, and an Indian library.

In general, traditional political and social (clan) structures remain intact. One major exception is caused by Canada's requirement that band membership be reckoned patrilineally. The political structure of the Iroquois League continues to be a source of controversy for many Iroquois (Haudenosaunee). Some recognize two seats—at Onondaga and Six Nations—whereas others consider the government at Six Nations a reflection of or a corollary to the traditional seat at Onondaga. Important issues concerning the confederacy in the later twentieth century include Indian burial sites, sovereignty, gambling casinos, and land claims.

The Six Nations Reserve is still marked by the existence of "progressive" and "traditional" factions, with the former generally supporting the elected band council and following the Christian faith and the latter supporting the confederacy and the Longhouse religion. Traditional Iroquois Indians celebrate at least ten traditional or quasi-traditional events, including the midwinter, green corn, and strawberry ceremonies. Iroquois still observe condolence ceremonies as one way to hold the league together after roughly 500 years of existence. The code of Handsome Lake, as well as the Longhouse religion, based on traditional thanksgiving ceremonies, is alive on the Six Nations Reserve and other Iroquois communities. Roughly 15 percent of Canadian Mohawks speak their native language.

Mohegan

See Mahican; Pequot

Nanticoke

Nanticoke (`Nan tə cōk), from *Nentego,* "Tidewater People," one of a group of similar Algonquian Indian tribes that also included the Choptank, Assateague, Pocomoke, Patuxent, Conoy, and Piscataway. *See also* Lenápe.

Location In the seventeenth century, Nanticokes lived on the peninsula between Delaware and Chesapeake Bays. Today, most live in Canada, Oklahoma, and Delaware.

Population The Nanticoke and neighboring tribes numbered around 12,000 people in 1600, although the Nanticoke proper made up only slightly more than 10 percent of this number. In the 1990s there were about 1,000 Nanticokes in Delaware.

Language Nanticokes and their neighbors spoke Algonquian languages.

Historical Information

History The Nanticoke may have originated to the northeast, possibly in Labrador, with the Shawnee and the Lenápe. They may also have passed through the eastern Great Lakes region and the Ohio Valley, where they met and possibly defeated Hopewell Mound Builder people.

Contact in 1608 with British Captain John Smith probably came a generation or two later than their neighbors' encounters with earlier British and Spanish explorers. In any case, the people soon became involved in the local beaver trade. Some groups allied themselves with the British as protection against Iroquois raids. In eastern Maryland, some groups, including the Nanticoke, continued to have problems with the British, based on the presence of alcohol and disease, throughout most of seventeenth century.

British settlers granted the Nanticokes a reservation in 1684 between Chicacoan Creek and the Nanticoke River. The British also reserved the right to confirm Nanticoke leaders and to collect a formal tribute. Other groups signed similar treaties during the later seventeenth century. Nanticokes and other neighboring tribes also became subordinate to the Iroquois Confederacy during that time.

After non-natives usurped their original reservation, in 1707 the people obtained a 3,000-acre tract on Delaware's Broad Creek, which was sold in 1768. In 1742, they were forced to eliminate the position of grand chief. In 1744, with Iroquois permission, they settled near Wyoming, Pennsylvania, and along the Juniata River, although ten years later

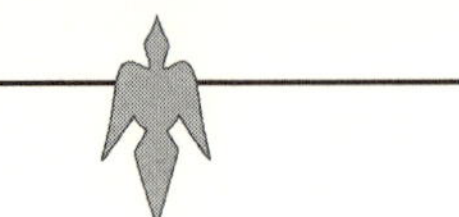

they were living farther up the Susquehanna in a former Onondaga town. At about that time they merged with the Piscataway and became administratively linked with the Iroquois Confederacy.

Nanticokes (and many Conoys who had joined them in the 1740s) remained neutral in the French and Indian War, but they did side with the British during the American Revolution. In 1778, about 200 Nanticokes moved to Fort Niagara and subsequently to the Six Nations Reserve in Canada. Some Nanticokes also remained at Buffalo Creek, New York, while another group of Nanticokes and Conoys went west with the Lenápe, ending up in Kansas and, after 1867, Oklahoma.

Throughout the later nineteenth century and into the twentieth century, the Nanticoke remaining in Delaware gradually lost their official tribal status and were in danger of losing their Indian identity completely. In 1922, Delaware Nanticokes incorporated the Nanticoke Indian Association. They elected a chief and assistant chief and began to recapture interest in some of their former traditions. The annual powwow dates from that time.

Religion The people recognized good and evil deities. There may have been a formal priesthood. First fruits ceremonies were directed at a benevolent deity.

Government A great chief or sachem was the overall leader. Each village may also have been ruled by a lesser chief, who might be a woman. The office of chief was probably inherited. The people also recognized war captains.

Customs Descent was matrilineal. There may have been a social hierarchy, with the chiefs and their councilors having more material worth and respect and better clothing. The people poisoned their enemies and even other tribal members; poisoners were often considered witches. Shell bead money could be used to compensate for crimes and to purchase trade goods. The people may have observed a male puberty ceremony as well as polygyny.

Corpses were buried or placed on scaffolds. In the historical period, their bones were stored temporarily in log houses, whose shelves also held pipes and other personal belongings. Bones of up to several hundred people were later buried to the accompaniment of a spirit dance, which was meant to send them off to the afterlife. Chiefs' bones were preserved in temples.

Dwellings There were at least five Nanticoke towns in the early seventeenth century. These were built along stream banks, and some were palisaded, especially those closest to the Iroquois. Houses may have been at least 20-foot rectangles with barrel roofs, covered with bark or mats. There was a smoke hole over the central fire and mat-covered shelves along the sides for beds.

Diet Women planted corn, beans, and pumpkins. They pounded corn in mortars to make meat, fish, or vegetable hominy. They also gathered nuts and other wild foods. Fishing and shellfishing took place in summer. The whole village removed to the woods for the fall hunt, which included deer, bear, turkey, squirrel, and other small game and fowl. Meat was roasted on a spit or stewed.

Key Technology Men glued bone, antler, or stone arrowheads to wooden shafts. They built springpole snares and set traps on trees felled across a river. Women used a hollowed log mortar and a wooden pestle. They made yucca and rush baskets as well as pottery. Bowls were made of wood.

Trade The Nanticoke were notable traders. Shell bead money could be used to purchase trade goods

Notable Arts Nanticoke art included pottery, woven baskets, and carved wood bowls. Baskets were decorated with spruce or porcupine quills. The people also made shell necklaces and similar items.

Transportation The people used mainly dugout canoes, although bark canoes were used for trips beyond the fall line.

Dress Skin clothing consisted of breechclouts and knee-length aprons fastened with a belt. Children generally remained naked. People wore fur cloaks in winter and cloaks without fur in summer. They

painted their faces and bodies and covered themselves with bear grease. Various personal ornaments included bird claws, animal teeth, and shells.

War and Weapons Weapons included bow and arrow, wooden war clubs, and poisoned arrows.

Contemporary Information

Government/Reservations The Nanticoke in Delaware (Nanticoke Indian Association) live in a community near Millsboro. There may also be other small communities of Nanticoke descendants scattered around the region.

Economy Nanticokes participate fully in the non-native economy.

Legal Status The Nanticoke Tribe has requested federal recognition. Other organizations include the Nanticoke Lenni-Lenápe Indians (recognized by the state of New Jersey) and the Eastern Lenápe Nation.

Daily Life The Nanticoke Indian Heritage Project, dating from 1977, established a tribal museum and encourages continued exploration of Indian traditions. The Nanticoke Lenni-Lenápe Indians maintain a museum and library, and they host an annual powwow.

Narragansett

Narragansett (Na rə `gan sit), "People of the Small Point," was the name both of a specific tribe and a group of tribes—such as Shawomet, Pawtuxet, Coweset (Nipmuc), and eastern Niantic—dominated by Narragansett sachems. *See also* Pequot.

Location In the sixteenth century, the Narragansett proper were located in south-central Rhode Island, although the greater Narragansett territory extended throughout all but northwest and extreme southwest Rhode Island. Today, most Narragansetts live in southern Rhode Island.

Population There may have been about 3,000 Narragansetts in 1600. There were at least 2,400 in the mid-1990s.

Language Narragansetts spoke an Eastern Algonquian language.

Historical Information

History This group may have originated well to the southwest of their historical territory. They were the most powerful New England tribe until 1675, dominating neighbors such as the Niantic and Nipmuc. They may have encountered non-natives in 1524, although there was no significant contact for another century or so afterward.

Trade with the British and Dutch was under way by 1623. Although the Narragansetts largely avoided the epidemics of 1617–1619, smallpox and other diseases dramatically weakened the people in 1633 and thereafter. As British allies, some Narragansetts fought against the Indians in the Pequot war of 1636–1637. In 1636, the grand sachem Canonicus sold land to Roger Williams, on which he established the future state of Rhode Island.

In an effort to protect themselves from non-native depredations, the tribe voluntarily submitted to Britain in 1644. Despite Williams's entreaties to treat the Indians fairly, many British remained extremely hostile. Eventually, they forced the Narragansett people to join the Nipmucs and Wampanoags in King Philip's war (1675–1676). A huge defeat in December 1675, in which more than 600 Narragansetts were killed and hundreds more captured and sold into slavery, signaled the beginning of the end of the war as well as the virtual destruction of the tribe itself.

After the war, survivors dispersed among the Mahican, Abenaki, and Niantic, the last group thenceforth assuming the name Narragansett. Some of the Mahicans joined the Brotherton Indians in 1788 (*see* Pequot) and later moved with them to Wisconsin. Those who remained in Rhode Island (probably fewer than 100) worked as servants or slaves of the non-native settlers, who moved quickly to occupy the vacated Narragansett lands.

The people underwent a general conversion to Christianity in the mid–eighteenth century, at which time a Christian reservation community was established in Charlestown. After the last hereditary sachem died during that period, government changed to an elected president and council. The last native speaker died in the early nineteenth century. A

constitution was adopted in 1849. All of the Narragansett Reservation, except for two acres, was sold in 1880, and the tribe was terminated by the state at that time. The Rhode Island Narragansett incorporated in 1934 under the terms of the Indian Reorganization Act.

Religion Cautantowwit, the supreme deity, lived to the southwest. There were also numerous other spirits or deities, who could and did communicate with people through dreams and visions. Priests or medicine men (powwows) were in charge of religious matters. They were usually men who realized their profession in a dream or a vision experience. Their main responsibilities included curing, bringing rain, and ensuring success in war. A harvest ritual was held in a longhouse near the sachem's house. At one important ceremony, possibly held in winter, participants burned their material possessions.

Government Narragansetts recognized a dual (junior and senior) chief or sagamore. Power was shared with a council of elders, sachems, powwows, and other leaders. Sachems were responsible for seeing to the public welfare and defense and for administering punishment. The office of sagamore may have been inheritable and was occasionally held by a woman. Within the larger administrative body there were smaller groups presided over by lesser sachems.

Customs People changed their names at various life-cycle ceremonies. They were generally monogamous. The dead were wrapped in skins or woven mats and then buried with tools and weapons to accompany them to an afterworld located to the southwest. Only good souls joined the creator there; bad souls wandered aimlessly forever.

Women mostly assumed agricultural duties, set up the houses, made carrying and cooking items, and gathered wild foods and shellfish. Men made house poles and canoes and also hunted, fished, and fought. Some men also made tools and wampum, and old men made turkey-feather mantles.

Dwellings Narragansetts lived in dome-shaped, circular wigwams about 10–20 feet in diameter, covered with birch and chestnut bark in summer and mats in winter. Smoke passed through an opening at the top. Winter hunting lodges were small and built of bark and rushes. People erected temporary field houses where they stayed when guarding the crops. Villages were often stockaded.

Diet Women grew corn, beans, squash, and sunflowers; men grew tobacco. The men also hunted moose, bear, deer, wolves, and other game and trapped beaver, squirrels, and other small animals and fowl. Deer were stalked and may have been hunted communally. People fished in freshwater and salt water. They gathered much marine life, including the occasional stranded whale, as well as strawberries and a number of other wild foods.

Key Technology Crops were dried and stored in underground pits. Fish weirs were often made of stone. Needles were made from bone; necklaces and wampum from shell. Women made twined baskets, pottery, and mats.

Trade The Narragansett were notable traders. They dealt in wampum, skins, clay pots, carved bowls, and chestnuts. They imported carved stone and wooden pipes from the Mohawk.

Notable Arts Clothing was decorated with quillwork and wampum beads.

Transportation Canoes were mainly of the dugout variety.

Dress People generally wore deerskin breechclouts, skirts, and leggings. They might also wear turkey-feather mantles and moccasins. In winter they donned bear- and rabbit-skin robes, caps, and mittens.

War and Weapons Enemies at times included the Pokanoket (Wampanoag) and Pequot, and allies included the Niantic. Surprise attacks were favored, as were small attacks, although large-scale fights did occur. The people built forts within their territory; as a last resort they withdrew into swamps. Weapons were generally identical with hunting tools.

Contemporary Information

Government/Reservations In Charleston, Rhode Island, the Narragansett have 1,800 acres held in federal trust. They also own several hundred acres, acquired in 1991 from a private donation, in Westerly. Under its by-laws, the tribe recognizes an elected tribal council, a chief sachem, a medicine man, and a Christian leader (or prophet). A number of committees deal with various matters. Major decisions require the approval of the entire community.

Economy A fishery and high-stakes gambling were under consideration in the late 1990s, the latter being especially controversial.

Legal Status The Narragansett Tribe is a federally recognized tribal entity.

Daily Life In 1985, the state of Rhode Island returned two pieces of land of about 900 acres each. The August annual meeting and powwow have been held for the last 250 or more years on the old meeting ground in Charlestown. Other ceremonies are both religious (such as the Fall Harvest Festival held in the longhouse) and secular (such as the commemoration of the 1675 battle) in nature. There are tribal programs for the elderly and for children. Tribal representatives are involved in local non-native cultural and educational programs.

Ojibwe

See Anishinabe

Oneida

Oneida (Ō `nī dä), "People of the Standing Stone," one of the five original tribes of the Iroquois League. Their name refers to a large boulder near their main village. The name Iroquois ("real adders") comes from the French adaptation of the Algonquian name for these people. Their self-designation was *Kanonsionni,* "League of the United (Extended) Households." Iroquois today refer to themselves as *Haudenosaunee,* "People of the Longhouse."

Location The Oneida were located between the Mohawk and the Onondaga, between Lake Ontario and the upper Susquehanna River, and especially around Oneida Creek. At the height of their power, the Iroquois controlled land from the Hudson to the Illinois Rivers and the Ottawa to the Tennessee Rivers. Today most Oneidas live around Green Bay, Wisconsin; in Ontario, Canada; and around Oneida and the Onondaga Reservation in New York.

Population There were perhaps 15,000–20,000 members of the Iroquois League around 1500, and roughly 1,000 Oneidas in the mid–seventeenth century. In the early 1990s, there were 11,000 members of the Wisconsin Oneida tribe, 4,600 Oneidas in Ontario, and about 700 in New York. The total number of Iroquois Indians approached 70,000.

Language The Oneida spoke a Northern Iroquois dialect.

Historical Information

History The Iroquois began cultivating crops shortly after the first phase of their culture in New York was established around 800. Deganawida, a Huron prophet, and Hiawatha, a Mohawk shaman living among the Onondaga, founded the Iroquois League or Confederacy some time between 1450 and 1600. It originally consisted of five tribes: Cayuga, Mohawk, Oneida, Onondaga, and Seneca; the Tuscarora joined in the early eighteenth century. The league's purpose was to end centuries of debilitating intertribal war and work for the common good. Both Deganawida and Hiawatha may have been actual or mythological people.

Iroquois first met non-natives in the sixteenth century. During these and subsequent years, the people became heavily involved in the fur trade. Trading, fighting, and political intrigue characterized the period. Although they were good at playing the European powers off against each other, the Iroquois increasingly became British allies in trade and in the colonial wars and were instrumental in the ultimate British victory over the French.

In the late seventeenth century, battles with the French and allied Indian tribes as well as disease epidemics severely reduced the Oneidas' already small

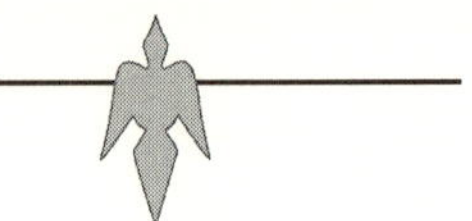

population. As much as two-thirds of the tribe in those years was made up of enemies such as Hurons and Algonquins. Following the Tuscarora wars in 1711–1713, people of that tribe began resettling on Oneida land. The Oneida sponsored the Tuscarora tribe as the sixth member of the Iroquois Confederacy in the early 1720s. Some Oneidas began to drift into the Ohio Valley as early as the mid–eighteenth century. By that time, longhouse living had seriously declined, with houses of nuclear families taking their places.

The British victory in 1763 meant that the Iroquois no longer controlled the balance of power in the region. Despite the long-standing British alliance, some Indians joined anti-British rebellions as a defensive gesture. From 1767 on, evangelical missionaries provided a theoretical/religious basis for the new Pine Tree Chiefs/warriors, such as the Susquehannock Shenendoah, to oppose the traditional chiefs. The missionaries attacked traditional religion and politics, and in this were aided by the warriors, who saw a way to topple control by the clan mothers and traditional chiefs. The 1760s were also a time of famine, increased pressure from non-natives for land, and growing alcohol abuse, all of which provided fertile ground for the missionaries and their new converts.

The confederacy split its allegiance in the Revolutionary War, with most Oneidas (and Tuscaroras), after a period of neutrality, siding with the patriots at the warriors' urging. This split resulted in the council fire's being extinguished for the first time in roughly 200 years. Oneidas participated in American attacks on Onondaga, Cayuga, and Seneca villages. The Iroquois suffered a defeat in 1779 that broke the power of the confederacy. The Oneida ended the war a scattered people, alienated from their fellow Iroquois, with little food and their traditional social, political, and economic systems in ruins.

The Oneidas welcomed two more groups of Indians in the late eighteenth century. Stockbridge Indians arrived to build the community of New Stockbridge, New York, in 1785. Three years later, a group of Mohegans, Mahicans, Narragansetts, Pequots, Montauks, and other Algonquian Indians, as well as some Oneidas, formed the Brothertown Community near New Stockbridge.

Following the Revolutionary War, New York state and the new U.S. government guaranteed the territorial integrity of nearly six million acres of Oneida land. However, the Oneida bowed to pressure and sold most of their lands in New York, gradually relocating westward. Under the influence of an Episcopal missionary and despite the objections of most Oneidas, about half of the tribe settled around Green Bay, Wisconsin, in the 1820s and 1830s, on land they purchased from the Menominee tribe. Following the Treaty of Buffalo Creek (1838), which called for the removal of all Iroquois from New York to Kansas, other Oneidas moved to the Six Nations Reserve in Ontario, Canada; the Thames River near London, Ontario; the Onondaga Reservation near Syracuse; and their original territory near Utica.

The Iroquois council officially split into two parts during that time. One branch was located at the new Six Nations Reserve and the other at Buffalo Creek. Gradually, the reservations as well as relations with the United States and Canada assumed more significance than intraconfederacy matters. In the 1840s, when the Buffalo Creek Reservation was sold, the fire there was rekindled at Onondaga.

In Wisconsin, most people practiced Christianity, with few elements of their traditional religion. Political leadership was based mainly on personal qualities and affiliations, although a hereditary council maintained considerable power. Most land had been allotted by 1908; as usual, the allotments were lost through tax default and foreclosure. At the same time, municipal governments began to replace the tribal structures. Although many people left the community permanently or seasonally to find work, Indian life remained centered on family, medicine societies, church, and several associations.

The Oneida community in Ontario reestablished the traditional tribal council shortly after they arrived in 1839 (although most power was exercised by a general assembly). Clan leaders also represented the tribe at the Council held at the Six Nations Reserve. Kinship ties and traditional medicine societies remained strong. Most people farmed throughout the nineteenth century, with perhaps seasonal lumbering in winter. In the twentieth century, the economic focus shifted to wage labor in white communities. This development led to increased factionalism and

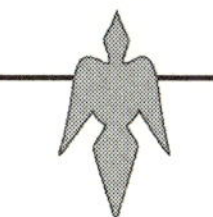

the eventual creation of a parallel tribal council supported by adherents of the Longhouse religion. After a third faction arose in the 1930s, the Canadian government unilaterally mandated an elective system. With other members of the confederacy, the Oneida have tried to resist governmental intrusions on their sovereignty.

Religion The Oneida recognized Orenda as the supreme creator. Other animate and inanimate objects and natural forces were also considered of a spiritual nature. They held important festivals to celebrate maple sap and strawberries as well as corn planting, ripening (Green Corn ceremony), and harvest. These festivals often included singing, male dancing, game playing, gambling, feasting, and food distribution.

The eight-day new year's festival may have been most important of all. Held in midwinter, it was a time to give thanks, to forget past wrongs, and to kindle new fires, with much attention paid to new and old dreams. A condolence ceremony had quasi-religious components. Medicine groups such as the False Face Society, which wore carved wooden masks, and the Medicine, Dark Dance, and Death Feast Societies (the last two controlled by women) also conducted ceremonies, since most illness was thought to be of supernatural origin.

In the early nineteenth century, many Iroquois embraced the teachings of Handsome Lake. This religion was born during the general religious ferment known as the Second Great Awakening and came directly out of the radical breakdown of Iroquois life. Beginning in 1799, the Seneca Handsome Lake spoke of Jesus and called upon Iroquois to give up alcohol and a host of negative behaviors, such as witchcraft and sexual promiscuity. He also exhorted them to maintain their traditional religious celebrations. A blend of traditional and Christian teachings, the Handsome Lake religion had the effect of facilitating the cultural transition occurring at the time. Among the Oneida, however, this movement lost out to a revitalization of traditional religious beliefs in the early nineteenth century.

Government The Iroquois League comprised 50 hereditary chiefs, or sachems, from the constituent tribes. Each position was named for the original holder and had specific responsibilities. Sachems were men, except where a woman acted as regent, but they were appointed by women. The Oneida sent nine sachems to meetings of the Iroquois Great Council, which met in the fall and for emergencies. Their symbol at this gathering was the great tree.

Debates within the great council were a matter of strict clan, division, and tribal protocols, in a complex system of checks and balances. Politically, individual league members often pursued their own best interests while maintaining an essential solidarity with the other members. The creators of the U.S. government used the Iroquois League as a model of democracy.

Locally, the village structure was governed by a headman and a council of elders (clan chiefs, elders, wise men). Matters before the local councils were handled according to a definite protocol based on the clan and division memberships of the chiefs. Village chiefs were chosen from groups as small as a single household. Women nominated and recalled clan chiefs. Tribal chiefs represented the village and the nation at the general council of the league. The entire system was hierarchical and intertwined, from the family up to the great council. Decisions at all levels were reached by consensus.

There were also a number of nonhereditary chiefs ("pine tree" or "merit" chiefs), some of whom had no voting power. This may have been a postcontact phenomenon.

Customs The Oneida recognized a dual division, each composed of probably three matrilineal, animal-named clans. The clans in turn were composed of matrilineal lineages. Each owned a set number of personal names, some of which were linked with particular activities and responsibilities.

Women enjoyed a high degree of prestige, being largely equated with the "three sisters" (corn, beans, and squash), and they were in charge of most village activities, including marriage. Great intravillage lacrosse games included heavy gambling. Other games included snowsnake, or sliding a spear along a trench in the snow for distance. Food was shared so that everyone had roughly the same to eat.

Personal health and luck were maintained by performing various individual rituals, including

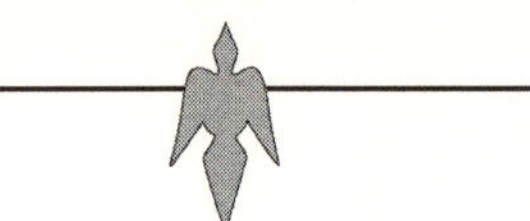

singing and dancing, learned in dreams. Members of the False Face medicine society wore wooden masks carved from trees and used rattles and tobacco. Shamans also used up to 200 or more plant medicines to cure illness. People committed suicide on occasion for specific reasons (men who lost prestige; women who were abandoned; children who were treated harshly). Murder could be revenged or paid for with sufficient gifts.

Young men's mothers arranged marriages with a prospective bride's mother. Divorce was possible but not readily obtained because it was considered a discredit. The dead were buried in a sitting position, with food and tools for use on the way to the land of the dead. A ceremony was held after ten days. The condolence ceremony mourned dead league chiefs and installed successors. A modified version also applied to common people.

Dwellings The main aboriginal village, Oneniote, had over 60 longhouses and was palisaded. The people built their villages near water and often on a hill after circa 1300. Some Iroquois villages had up to 150 longhouses and 1,000 or more people. Villages were moved about twice in a generation, when firewood and soil were exhausted.

Iroquois Indians built elm-bark longhouses, 50–100 feet long, depending on how many people lived there, from about the twelfth century on. They held around 2 or 3 but as many as 20 families, related maternally (lineage segments), as well as their dogs. There were smoke holes over each two-family fire. Beds were raised platforms; people slept on mats, their feet to the fire, covered by pelts. Upper platforms were used for food and gear storage. Roofs were shingled with elm bark. Painted animal figures marked the clan of the inhabitants. The people also built some single-family houses.

Diet Women grew corn, beans, squash, and gourds. Corn was the staple and was used in soups, stews, breads, and puddings. It was stored in bark-lined cellars. Women also gathered a variety of greens, nuts, seeds, roots, berries, fruits, and mushrooms. Tobacco was grown for ceremonial and social smoking.

After the harvest, men and some women took to the woods for several months to hunt and dry meat. Men hunted large game and trapped smaller game, mostly for the fur. Hunting was a source of potential prestige. They also caught waterfowl and other birds, and they fished. The people grew peaches, pears, and apples in orchards from the eighteenth century on.

Key Technology Iroquois used porcupine quills and wampum belts as a record of events. Wampum was also used as a gift connoting sincerity and, later, as trade money. These shell disks, strung or woven into belts, were probably a postcontact technological innovation.

Hunting equipment included snares, bow and arrow, stone knife, and bentwood pack frame. Fish were caught using traps, nets, bone hooks, and spears. Farming tools were made of stone, bone, wood (spades), and antler. Women wove corn-husk dolls, tobacco trays, mats, and baskets.

Other important material items included elm-bark containers, cordage from inner tree bark and fibers, and levers to move timbers. Men steamed wood or bent green wood to make many items, including lacrosse sticks.

Trade Oneidas obtained birch-bark products from the Huron. They imported copper and shells and exported carved wooden and stone pipes as well as dried salmon. They also raised and traded ginseng with other tribes. They were extensively involved in the trade in beaver furs from the seventeenth century on.

Notable Arts Men carved wooden masks worn by the Society of Faces in their curing ceremonies. Women decorated clothing with dyed porcupine quills or moose-hair embroidery.

Transportation Unstable elm bark canoes were roughly 25 feet long. The people were also great runners and preferred to travel on land. They used snowshoes in winter.

Dress Women made most clothing from deerskins. Men wore shirts and short breechclouts and a tunic in cooler weather; women wore skirts. Both wore leggings, moccasins, and corn-husk slippers in summer. Robes were made of lighter or heavier skins or pelts, depending on the season. These were often painted. Clothing was decorated with feathers and porcupine quills. Both men and women tattooed their bodies extensively. Men often wore their hair in a roach; women wore theirs in a single braid doubled up and fastened with a thong. Some men wore feather caps or, in winter, fur hoods.

War and Weapons Boys began developing war skills at a young age. Prestige and leadership were often gained through war, which was in many ways the most important activity. The title of Pine Tree Chief was a historical invention to honor especially brave warriors. Oneidas were known as particularly fierce fighters. In traditional warfare, large groups met face to face and fired a few arrows after a period of jeering, then engaged in another period of hand-to-hand combat using clubs and spears. Population losses were partially offset by the adoption of captives. Former enemies became Oneidas because they were brought in to fill specific roles in specific lineages; the clan mothers could order the death of anyone who did not do what was expected of him.

Weapons included the bow and arrow, ball-headed club, shield, rod armor, and guns after 1640. All aspects of warfare, from the initiation to the conclusion, were highly ritualized. War could be decided as a matter of policy or undertaken as a vendetta. Women had a large, sometimes decisive, say in the question of whether or not to fight. During war season, generally the fall, Iroquois war parties ranged up to 1,000 miles or more. Male prisoners were often forced to run the gauntlet: Those who made it through were adopted, but those who did not might be tortured by widows. Some captives were eaten.

Contemporary Information

Government/Reservations The checkerboard Oneida Reservation (established in 1838) is located in Brown and Outagamie Counties, Wisconsin. In the mid-1990s it contained roughly 2,500 acres, most of which had been repurchased since the 1930s by the federal government. The 1990 Indian population was 2,447. The community is governed under an Indian Reorganization Act constitution by an elected business committee, which itself is subject to the general assembly.

The New York Oneida community owns 32 acres of land in Madison County, near Oneida. The land, acquired in 1794, is not recognized as a reservation by either the state or federal governments. The 1990 Indian population was 37, but about 700 live in the community at large. Some Oneidas also live on the Onondaga Reservation, New York.

Ontario Oneidas live on the Six Nations/Grand River Reserve (1,800 Indian residents in the mid-1990s) and Oneida of the Thames, near London (2,800 Indian residents in the mid-1990s). The Six Nations/Grand River Reserve was established in 1784. It is governed by both an elected and a hereditary council, although only the first is federally recognized. In 1934, Canada mandated a political system consisting of elected councilors and an elected chief, although adherents of the Longhouse religion maintain their own hereditary council.

Economy The two U.S. communities have gaming establishments. The proceeds go in part to reacquiring land, building new facilities, and sponsoring activities. The Wisconsin tribe employs 2,000 tribal members in its various enterprises, including a hotel. The Canadian Oneidas are largely dependent on government funding.

Legal Status The Oneida Nation of New York and the Oneida Tribe of Wisconsin are federally recognized tribal entities. The Oneida people in all three communities are involved in an extended lawsuit over land against two New York counties.

Daily Life Descent is bilateral in Wisconsin, where most Oneidas are either Episcopalians or Methodists. Some follow the Longhouse religion. Few people speak Oneida, although the tribal school teaches classes in the native language. Important crafts include beadwork, wood carving, and silver work. There is an annual powwow.

Although most people are Christian, there are also many adherents of the Handsome Lake religion among the Ontario Oneida community. Descent is patrilineal by Canadian law, and clan identification has lost much of its significance.

In New York, leadership has been in dispute since at least the 1950s, when a newly organized

elective system was more or less successfully challenged by traditionalists. Sachems and clan mothers now hold the leadership positions. Most members are Christians, although many are also members of the Longhouse religion. The nation operates a health center, youth and elderly programs, and a housing development. Facilities include a pool and recreation center and a museum/cultural center. The community also publishes a newsletter. Some New York Oneidas still speak the language.

The political structure of the Iroquois League continues to be a source of controversy for many Iroquois (Haudenosaunee). Some recognize two seats—at Onondaga and Six Nations—whereas others consider the government at Six Nations a reflection of or a corollary to the traditional seat at Onondaga. Important issues concerning the confederacy in the later twentieth century include Indian burial sites, sovereignty, gambling casinos, and land claims. The Six Nations Reserve is still marked by the existence of "progressive" and "traditional" factions, with the former generally supporting the elected band council and following the Christian faith and the latter supporting the confederacy and the Longhouse religion.

Traditional Iroquois Indians also celebrate at least ten traditional or quasi-traditional ceremonies, including the midwinter, green corn, and strawberry. Iroquois still observe condolence ceremonies as one way to hold the league together after roughly 500 years of existence. Many Iroquois continue to see their relationship with the Canadian and U.S. governments as one between independent nations and allies, as opposed to one marked by paternalism and dependence.

Onondaga

Onondaga (`O nən `dä gä), "People of the Hill," were one of the five original tribes of the Iroquois League. As Keepers of the Council Fire, they hosted the annual great council. The name Iroquois ("real adders") comes from the French adaptation of the Algonquian name for these people. Their self-designation was *Kanonsionni,* "League of the United (Extended) Households." Iroquois today refer to themselves as *Haudenosaunee,* "People of the Longhouse."

Location The Onondaga were the geographically central tribe of the Iroquois confederacy, located near Onondaga Lake and the Oswego River, near present-day Syracuse. At the height of their power, the Iroquois controlled land from the Hudson to the Illinois Rivers and the Ottawa to the Tennessee Rivers. Most Onondagas today live on the Six Nations Reserve in Ontario, Canada, and in Onondaga County, New York.

Population There were perhaps 15,000–20,000 members of the Iroquois League around 1500, and approximately 1,000 Onondaga in the mid–seventeenth century. Of perhaps 70,000 Iroquois living in the United States and Canada in the mid-1990s, roughly 1,600 Onondagas lived in the United States and another 3,000 lived in Canada.

Language Onondagas spoke a Northern Iroquois dialect.

Historical Information

History There were Indians in upper New York at least 10,000 years ago. The Iroquois began cultivating crops shortly after the first phase of their culture in New York was established around 800. Deganawida, a Huron prophet, and Hiawatha, a Mohawk shaman living among the Onondaga, founded the Iroquois League or Confederacy some time between 1450 and 1600. It originally consisted of five tribes: Cayuga, Mohawk, Oneida, Onondaga, and Seneca; the Tuscarora joined in the early eighteenth century. The league's purpose was to end centuries of debilitating intertribal war and work for the common good. Both Deganawida and Hiawatha may have been actual or mythological people.

Iroquois first met non-natives in the sixteenth century. During those and subsequent years, the people became heavily involved in the fur trade. Trading, fighting, and political intrigue characterized the period. Although they were good at playing the European powers off against each other, the Iroquois increasingly became British allies in trade and in the

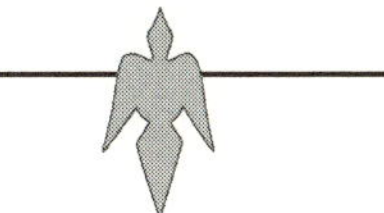

colonial wars and were instrumental in the ultimate British victory over the French.

Still, as a result of trade-motivated efforts to make peace with the French, a pro-French faction existed at Onondaga from the mid–seventeenth century on. The French also established a Catholic mission in their territory about that time. By the mid–seventeenth century, war with the Susquehannock was taking a heavy toll on the Onondaga and other Iroquois tribes. In fact, captive foreigners outnumbered Onondagas in the tribe by the time the war ended in 1675.

Fighting with the French at the end of the seventeenth century led to the torching and temporary abandonment of the main Onondaga village. In the mid–eighteenth century, a number of Onondagas and other Iroquois went to live at Oswegatchie, a mission on the upper Saint Lawrence River. These people became French allies in the French and Indian War, although they sided with the British in the American Revolutionary War.

The British victory in 1763 meant that the Iroquois no longer controlled the balance of power in the region. Despite the long-standing British alliance, some Indians joined anti-British rebellions as a defensive gesture. The Onondaga and the confederacy as a whole split their allegiance in the Revolutionary War. This split resulted in the council fire's being extinguished for the first time in roughly 200 years.

The Iroquois suffered a defeat in 1779 that broke the power of the confederacy. By war's end most of their villages had been destroyed. When the 1783 Treaty of Paris divided Indian land between Britain and the United States, British Canadian officials established the Six Nations Reserve for their loyal allies, to which over 200 Onondagas repaired. Several hundred others moved to Buffalo Creek, New York, where groups of Senecas and Cayugas were living. A 100-square-mile Onondaga Reservation was established in 1788, although most of it had been lost by the early nineteenth century. In 1806, the Oswegatchies were removed. They scattered to St. Regis, Onondaga, and elsewhere in New York.

The Iroquois council officially split into two parts during that time. One branch was located at the Six Nations Reserve and the other at Buffalo Creek. Gradually, the reservations as well as relations with the United States and Canada assumed more significance than intraconfederacy matters. In the 1840s, when the Buffalo Creek Reservation was sold, the fire there was rekindled at Onondaga.

In Canada, the Onondagas, referred to along with the Cayugas and Senecas as the "lower tribes," tended to retain more of their traditional beliefs than did the "upper" Iroquois tribes. Many subsequently adopted the Handsome Lake religion. Slowly, the general influence of non-natives increased, as tribal councils, consensus decision making, and other aspects of traditional culture fell by the wayside. Traditional structures were further weakened by the allotment of reservation lands in the 1840s. The council eventually came to resemble a municipal government. In 1924, the Canadian government terminated confederacy rule entirely, mandating an (all male) elected system of government on the reserve.

In the mid–nineteenth century there were significant Onondaga communities at Onondaga (Onondaga Reservation), on the Six Nations Reserve, and on Seneca and Tuscarora land, especially the Allegany Reservation. The native economy gradually shifted from primarily hunting to farming, dependence on annuities received for the sale of land, and some wage labor. There was also increasing pressure for Indians to sell more land and adopt Christianity, although the Onondaga remained fairly resistant to both. The old religion declined in importance during that time, although among some Iroquois, including many Onondaga, the Handsome Lake religion grew in importance.

In 1898, the wampum belts remaining among the Onondaga were placed in the keeping of the New York State Museum. With other members of the confederacy, the Onondaga resisted the 1924 citizenship act, selective service, the Indian Reorganization Act, and all federal and state intrusions on their sovereignty.

Religion The Onondaga recognized Ha-wah-ne-u as the supreme creator. Other animate and inanimate objects and natural forces were also considered of a spiritual nature. They held important festivals to celebrate maple sap and strawberries as well as corn planting, ripening (Green Corn ceremony), and harvest. These festivals often included singing, male

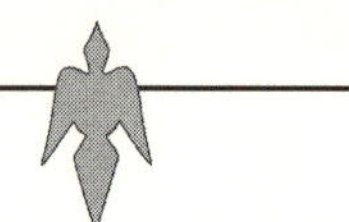

dancing, game playing, gambling, feasting, and food distribution.

The eight-day new year's festival may have been most important of all. Held in midwinter, it was a time to give thanks, to forget past wrongs, and to kindle new fires, with much attention paid to new and old dreams. A condolence ceremony had quasi-religious components. Medicine groups such as the False Face Society, which wore carved wooden masks, and the Medicine, Dark Dance and Death Feast Societies (the last two controlled by women) also conducted ceremonies, since most illness was thought to be of supernatural origin.

In the early nineteenth century, many Iroquois embraced the teachings of Handsome Lake. This religion was born during the general religious ferment known as the Second Great Awakening and came directly out of the radical breakdown of Iroquois life. Beginning in 1799, the Seneca Handsome Lake spoke of Jesus and called upon Iroquois to give up alcohol and a host of negative behaviors, such as witchcraft and sexual promiscuity. He also exhorted them to maintain their traditional religious celebrations. A blend of traditional (especially thanksgiving ceremonies) and Christian teachings, the Handsome Lake religion had the effect of facilitating the cultural transition occurring at the time.

Government The Iroquois League comprised 50 hereditary chiefs, or sachems, from the constituent tribes. Each position was named for the original holder and had specific responsibilities. Sachems were men, except where a woman acted as regent, but they were appointed by women. The head of the council was always an Onondaga. This person was assisted by a council of two other Onondagas, and a third Onondaga kept the council wampum. The Onondaga sent 14 sachems to meetings of the Iroquois Great Council, which met in the fall and for emergencies.

Debates within the great council were a matter of strict clan, division, and tribal protocols, in a complex system of checks and balances. Politically, individual league members often pursued their own best interests while maintaining an essential solidarity with the other members. The creators of the U.S. government used the Iroquois League as a model of democracy.

Locally, the village structure was governed by a headman and a council of elders (clan chiefs, elders, wise men). Matters before the local councils were handled according to a definite protocol based on the clan and division memberships of the chiefs. Village chiefs were chosen from groups as small as a single household. Women nominated and recalled clan chiefs. Tribal chiefs represented the village and the nation at the general council of the league. The entire system was hierarchical and intertwined, from the family up to the great council. Decisions at all levels were reached by consensus.

There were also a number of nonhereditary chiefs ("pine tree" or "merit" chiefs), some of whom had no voting power. This may have been a postcontact phenomenon.

Customs The Onondaga probably recognized a dual division, each composed of eight matrilineal, animal-named clans. The clans in turn were composed of matrilineal lineages. Each owned a set number of personal names, some of which were linked with particular activities and responsibilities.

Women enjoyed a high degree of prestige, being largely equated with the "three sisters" (corn, beans, and squash), and they were in charge of most village activities, including marriage. Great intravillage lacrosse games included heavy gambling. Other games included snowsnake, or sliding a spear along a trench in the snow for distance. Food was shared so that everyone had roughly the same to eat.

Personal health and luck were maintained by performing various individual rituals, including singing and dancing, learned in dreams. Members of the False Face medicine society wore wooden masks carved from trees and used rattles and tobacco. Shamans also used up to 200 or more plant medicines to cure illness. People committed suicide on occasion for specific reasons (men who lost prestige; women who were abandoned; children who were treated harshly). Murder could be revenged or paid for with sufficient gifts.

Dancing was popular; the Onondaga had up to 30 or more different types of dances. Young men's mothers arranged marriages with a prospective bride's mother. Divorce was possible but not readily obtained because it was considered a discredit. The dead were buried in a sitting position, with food and tools for

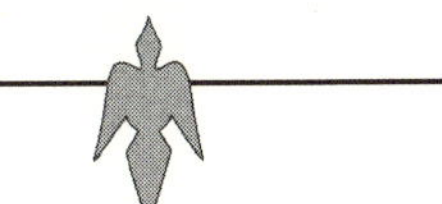

use on the way to the land of the dead. A ceremony was held after ten days. The condolence ceremony mourned dead league chiefs and installed successors. A modified version also applied to common people.

Dwellings In the seventeenth century, Onondagas probably lived in two villages, a large one (roughly 140 longhouses) and a small one (roughly 24 longhouses). The people built their villages near water and often on a hill after circa 1300. Some villages were palisaded. Other Iroquois villages had up to 150 longhouses and 1,000 or more people. Villages were moved about twice in a generation, when firewood and soil were exhausted.

Iroquois Indians built elm-bark longhouses, 50–100 feet long, depending on how many people lived there, from about the twelfth century on. They held around 2 or 3 but as many as 20 families, related maternally (lineage segments), as well as their dogs. There were smoke holes over each two-family fire. Beds were raised platforms; people slept on mats, their feet to the fire, covered by pelts. Upper platforms were used for food and gear storage. Roofs were shingled with elm bark. The people also built some single-family houses.

Diet Women grew corn, beans, squash, and gourds. Corn was the staple and was used in soups, stews, breads, and puddings. It was stored in bark-lined cellars. Women also gathered a variety of greens, nuts, seeds, roots, berries, fruits, and mushrooms. Tobacco was grown for ceremonial and social smoking.

After the harvest, men and some women took to the woods for several months to hunt and dry meat. Men hunted large game and trapped smaller game, mostly for the fur. Hunting was a source of potential prestige. They also caught waterfowl and other birds, and they fished. The people grew peaches, pears, and apples in orchards from the eighteenth century on.

Key Technology Iroquois used porcupine quills and wampum belts as a record of events. Wampum was also used as a gift connoting sincerity and, later, as trade money. These shell disks, strung or woven into belts, were probably a postcontact technological innovation.

Hunting equipment included snares, bow and arrow, stone knife, and bentwood pack frame. Fish were caught using traps, nets, bone hooks, and spears. Farming tools were made of stone, bone, wood (spades), and antler. Women wove corn-husk dolls, tobacco trays, mats, and baskets.

Other important material items included elm-bark containers, cordage from inner tree bark and fibers, and levers to move timbers. Men steamed wood or bent green wood to make many items, including lacrosse sticks.

Trade Onondagas obtained birch-bark products from the Huron. They imported copper and shells and exported carved wooden and stone pipes. They were extensively involved in the trade in beaver furs from the seventeenth century on.

Notable Arts Men carved wooden masks worn by the Society of Faces in their curing ceremonies. Women decorated clothing with dyed porcupine quills and moose-hair embroidery.

Transportation Unstable elm-bark canoes were roughly 25 feet long. The people were also great runners and preferred to travel on land. They used snowshoes in winter.

Dress Women made most clothing from deerskins. Men wore shirts and short breechclouts and a tunic in cooler weather; women wore skirts. Both wore leggings, moccasins, and corn-husk slippers in summer. Robes were made of lighter or heavier skins or pelts, depending on the season. These were often painted. Clothing was decorated with feathers and porcupine quills. Both men and women tattooed their bodies extensively. Men often wore their hair in a roach; women wore theirs in a single braid doubled up and fastened with a thong. Some men wore feather caps or, in winter, fur hoods.

War and Weapons Boys began developing war skills at a young age. Prestige and leadership were often gained through war, which was in many ways the most important activity. The title of Pine Tree Chief was a historical invention to honor especially brave warriors. Enemies included Algonquins, Montagnais,

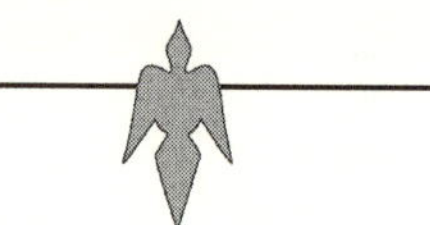

Ojibwas, Crees, and tribes of the Abenaki Confederacy. In traditional warfare, large groups met face to face and fired a few arrows after a period of jeering, then engaged in another period of hand-to-hand combat using clubs and spears.

Weapons included the bow and arrow, ball-headed club, shield, rod armor, and guns after 1640. All aspects of warfare, from the initiation to the conclusion, were highly ritualized. War could be decided as a matter of policy or undertaken as a vendetta. Women had a large, sometimes decisive, say in the question of whether or not to fight. During war season, generally the fall, Iroquois war parties ranged up to 1,000 miles or more. Male prisoners were often forced to run the gauntlet: Those who made it through were adopted, but those who did not might be tortured by widows. Women and children prisoners were regularly adopted. Some captives were eaten.

Contemporary Information

Government/Reservations The Onondaga Reservation, Onondaga County, New York, contains 7,300 acres, all of which is tribally owned. The Indian population was about 1,600 in the mid-1990s. Government is by a council of hereditary chiefs, selected by the clan mothers.

The Six Nations/Grand River Reserve, Ontario, Canada, was established in 1784. It is governed by both an elected and a hereditary council, although only the first is federally recognized.

Economy Like most Indians, the Onondaga face high unemployment. Many people work in Syracuse, especially in the construction (high-steel especially) and service industries.

Legal Status The Onondaga Nation of New York is a federally recognized tribal entity. The Six Nations/Grand River Reserve is provincially and federally recognized.

Daily Life Onondagas are considered to be the most conservative of the Six Nations. The Onondaga Reservation is again the capital of the Iroquois Confederacy. The leader of the Iroquois League, who alone can summon meetings of the Great Council, is always an Onondaga. Recent political activism has resulted in the return of wampum belts, education reforms, and the prevention of acquisition of reservation land for road widening by New York State. In 1994 the tribe ceased seeking or accepting federal grants.

There is a K–8 school on the reservation. Although most Onondagas are Christian, all chiefs must adhere to the Longhouse religion. This requirement ties them to other Iroquois Longhouse communities throughout the United States and Canada. A hereditary council heads both political and religious life. Many people speak Onondaga, although English is the official tribal language. The community is known for its artists and athletes, especially its lacrosse players. Mutual aid remains strong.

In general, traditional political and social (clan) structures remain intact. One major exception is caused by Canada's requirement that band membership be reckoned patrilineally. The political structure of the Iroquois League continues to be a source of contrversy for many Iroquois (Haudenosaunee). Some recognize two seats—at Onondaga and Six Nations—whereas others consider the government at Six Nations a reflection of or a corollary to the traditional seat at Onondaga. Important issues concerning the confederacy in the later twentieth century include Indian burial sites, sovereignty, gambling casinos, and land claims.

The Six Nations Reserve is still marked by the existence of "progressive" and "traditional" factions, with the former generally supporting the elected band council and following the Christian faith and the latter supporting the confederacy and the Longhouse religion. Traditional Iroquois Indians celebrate at least ten traditional or quasi-traditional events, including the midwinter, green corn, and strawberry ceremonies. Iroquois still observe condolence ceremonies as one way to hold the league together after roughly 500 years of existence.

Many Iroquois continue to see their relationship with the Canadian and U.S. governments as one between independent nations and allies, as opposed to one marked by paternalism and dependence. Occasionally, the frustrations inherent in this type of situation boil over into serious confrontation.

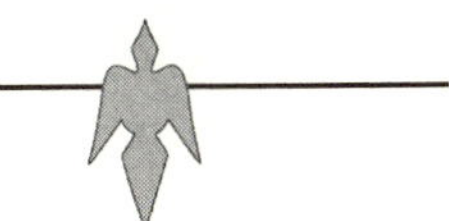

Ottawa

Ottawa (`Ä tu wu) or Odawa, from *adawe,* "to trade." Before about 1600, the name was loosely applied to several groups of upper Algonquians. Their self-designation was Anishinabe ("People"). *See also* Anishinabe.

Location Ottawas lived in the northern Lake Huron region, specifically Manitoulin Island, Georgian Bay, and the Bruce Peninsula, in the early seventeenth century. By the end of the century most were living in Michigan's lower peninsula. Today, most live in northern lower Michigan and southern Ontario. There are also scattered populations in Oklahoma and Wisconsin.

Population There were approximately 8,000 Ottawas in about 1600 and about 10,000 in the mid-1990s, of whom about 4,000 lived in Canada and perhaps 6,000 in Michigan.

Language Ottawas spoke a dialect of Anishinabe, an Algonquian language.

Historical Information

History According to legend, the Ottawa migrated from the Northwest as one people with the Anishinabe and the Potawatomi. They probably arrived on the east side of Lake Huron in about 1400. They first encountered non-natives in 1615, in the person of Samuel de Champlain. The people traded furs to Huron intermediaries, in exchange for European goods, until the 1649 Iroquois defeat of the Huron. At that point, the Ottawa took over direct trade with the French, taking their canoes up the St. Lawrence river to Montreal.

In 1660, the Ottawa suffered their own military defeat at the hands of the Dutch-armed Iroquois, at which time they moved west to the Green Bay area. Some groups continued even farther west, to around Lake Superior and the Mississippi River (these were soon driven back by Dakota warriors). With a guarantee of French protection, many returned to their old homes in 1670. By 1680, most had joined the Huron at Mackinaw. There were many Ottawa settlements around Lakes Michigan and Huron in the eighteenth century.

Like most Algonquins, the Ottawa took the French side in the colonial wars. The Ottawa chief Pontiac led a coalition of regional Indians in an anti-British rebellion in 1763, after the latter's decisive victory over French forces. Pontiac and Delaware Prophet convinced many Indians of the need for unity. The coalition at first enjoyed much success, forcing the British to abandon many of their posts and killing thousands of non-natives. However, it failed to take the two most important British forts, Pitt and Detroit, in part because the defenders of Fort Pitt spread smallpox among the Indians by using infected blankets. Other reasons for the ultimate Indian defeat were the lack of French support, factionalism, and the need of the warriors to provide for their families for the coming winter. Pontiac surrendered and obtained a British pardon in 1766, only to be killed three years later by an Illinois Indian, probably under British orders.

The people tried to remain neutral during the American Revolution, although some actively sided with the Americans; they were similarly divided in the War of 1812. Most Ottawas had converted to Catholicism by the early nineteenth century. By the terms of an 1833 treaty, Ottawas south and west of Lake Michigan, about 500 people, were relocated to Iowa and Kansas with some Chippewas and Potawatomis, with whom they had united in an alliance called the Three Fires.

Other groups, forced to move by the scarcity of game and pressure from non-natives, relocated to the Lake Huron islands or to Michigan reservations or allotments. In 1867, most Kansas Ottawa bought land on the Quapaw Reservation in Indian Territory (Oklahoma). This land was allotted in severalty in the 1890s. The tribe was officially terminated in 1956 but was reinstated in 1978. In 1965, the people received just over $400,000 in land claims settlements pertaining to their time in Kansas.

During the mid– and later nineteenth century, when many Ottawa groups merged or otherwise became associated with Ojibwa and Potawatomi Indians, the United States created an ersatz tribal entity called the Ottawa and Chippewa Bands. This bogus "tribe" was the basis on which the Michigan Ottawa were wrongly but effectively assumed to have been officially terminated. These people have been seeking redress for losses of various benefits and payments for over 100 years. The government has consistently refused to recognize them, even under the Indian Reorganization Act.

Northern Ottawas farmed or worked in lumbering throughout most of the twentieth century. After World War II, however, many moved from local communities to regional cities in search of employment. In 1948 the people created the Northern Michigan Ottawa Association (NMOA) to represent them in all litigation.

Religion The Ottawa recognized Manitou, the great spirit, along with many lesser spirits, both good and evil. Around puberty, boys and girls sought visions through dreams or in isolated areas. There were three religious cults, as well as the Midewiwin medicine society; the latter, open to both men and women initiates, was designed to channel spiritual power toward the well-being of members. Shamans cured through intercession with the spirits.

Government At least four, or possibly up to seven bands, had their own relatively weak chief or chiefs. These bands were composed of local villages, each with their own leadership.

Customs Small hunting groups left the villages during winter, returning to plant crops in spring. Men might have more than one wife. The dead were cremated, buried, or placed on scaffolds. A feast honoring the dead was held every year or so. Mourners blackened and scratched their faces.

Dwellings Permanent villages were sometimes palisaded. The Ottawa built longhouses of fir or cedar bark on pole frames with barrel roofs. They also used temporary mat-covered conical lodges while on trips.

Diet Men hunted and trapped large and small game and birds. Game was often taken in fire drives. Meat and fish were smoked, fried, roasted, and boiled. Fishing was of key importance, especially around the lake shores. Women gathered various berries and other plant food. They also grew corn, beans, and squash and collected maple sap. They baked cornmeal bread in ashes and hot sand.

Key Technology The people fished with nets and used wooden digging sticks in their fields. Women ground grain using log mortars and wooden pestles. They also wove and decorated rush mats. Other material items included birch-bark and hide containers and pouches.

Trade The Ottawa were heavily engaged in trade from precontact days on, mainly between the Huron and tribes hundreds of miles to the west. Among other items, they traded rush mats for shells, paints, and pottery. They also dealt in furs, cornmeal, herbs, copper, tobacco, and sunflower oil.

Notable Arts Men carved various wooden objects. The Ottawa were also known for their woven mats. The people decorated many birch-bark items with the use of templates. Decorative styles included zigzag bands and floral motifs. Most designs were symmetrical. Southern bands decorated items with porcupine quillwork. Robes were often painted.

Transportation People navigated lakes and rivers in birch-bark canoes. They wore two kinds of snowshoes—round for women and children and tailed for men—when traveling in snow.

Dress In summer, men went naked or wore a light robe; they added fitted, decorated breechclouts for special occasions. They added leggings and heavier robes made of skin or pelts in winter. They wore their hair short and brushed up in front. Women wore wraparound skirts, with added ponchos and robes in winter. They generally wore their hair in one braid wrapped with fur or snakeskin. Moccasins were of deer or moose skin, with attached retractable cuffs. Both sexes tattooed their bodies and faces and wore ornaments of copper, stone, and shell in pierced noses and ears.

War and Weapons Ottawa warriors fought with bows and arrows, war clubs, and large hide shields. Allies included the neighboring Algonquian tribes as well as the Wyandotte. Despite a close trade relationship, relations with the Huron were often strained. Other enemies included the Iroquois and the Dakota.

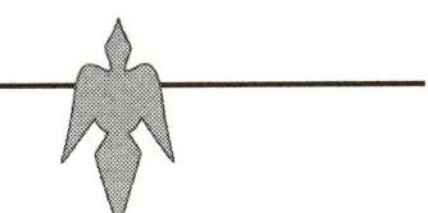

Contemporary Information

Government/Reservations The following bands live in Michigan: Burt Lake (Charlevoix, Cheboygan, and Emmet Counties), Grand River (Kent, Ottawa, and Muskegon Counties), Grand Traverse (Benzie, Grand Traverse, Kalkaska, Leelanau, and Manistee Counties), Little River (Manistee and Mason Counties), and Little Traverse Bay (Charlevoix, Delta, Emmet, Mackinac, and Schoolcraft Counties).

The Grand Traverse Band of Ottawa and Chippewa Indians owns 12.5 acres of land in Peshawbestown, Michigan; reservation status was achieved in 1982.

Most Canadian Ottawas (about 4,000 in the mid-1990s) live with the Ontario First Nations on Cockburn, Manitoulin, and Walpole Islands.

Most of the roughly 400 Oklahoma Ottawas live near Miami, Oklahoma. Their constitution provides for a chief and a tribal council.

Economy Many people are engaged making crafts for the tourist trade. In general, the people work in sawmills and as farmers and fishing guides. Poor economic opportunities and low wages characterize life in Michigan. Most Oklahoma Ottawa are engaged in business and agriculture.

Legal Status The Grand Traverse Band of Ottawa and Chippewa Indians has been a federally recognized tribal entity since 1980. The Ottawa Tribe of Oklahoma, the Little River Band of Ottawa Indians, and the Little Traverse Bay Band of Odawa Indians are federally recognized tribal entities.

The Burt Lake Band of Ottawa and Chippewa Indians is recognized by the state of Michigan and has petitioned for federal recognition. Other unrecognized Ottawa groups in the United States (there are over 20 in total) include the Grand River Band of the Ottawa National Council and the 9,000-member Northern Michigan Ottawa Association.

Daily Life Michigan Ottawas have regularly suffered arrest and other actions for asserting their treaty rights to hunt and fish. The language survives in Michigan mainly among elders, although the people have instituted various language and cultural preservation programs (many Ontario Ottawas speak their native Algonguian language). Most Michigan Ottawas are Christian, although some celebrate quasi-traditional feasts, naming ceremonies, and other festivals. Michigan Ottawas are active in producing quasi-traditional and contemporary crafts such as birch-bark containers, sweetgrass baskets, buckskin clothing, and maple sugar candy. Contemporary issues focus on the continuing fight for federal recognition and economic development.

The Oklahoma Ottawa are highly acculturated. Few people speak the native language. The annual powwow is held over Labor Day weekend.

Passamaquoddy

Passamaquoddy (Pa su mu `kwä dē), "those who pursue the pollack" or "pollack-spearing place." Together with the Maliseet, they have also been known as the Etchemin tribe. *See also* Abenaki; Maliseet; Penobscot.

Location The traditional location of the Passamaquoddy is in the vicinity of Passamaquoddy Bay and the St. Croix River. Many contemporary Passamaquoddys also live on the Penobscot Reservation at Old Town, Maine, as well as in industrial centers of New England.

Population With the Maliseet, their population reached about 1,000 in the early seventeenth century. There were approximately 2,500 tribal members in the early 1990s.

Language Maliseets and Passamaquoddys spoke dialects of the same Algonquian language.

Historical Information

History The Passamaquoddy may once have been united with the Maliseet. First contact with non-natives probably occurred with Samuel de Champlain in the early seventeenth century, although the people may have met fishermen from northern and western Europe as much as a century earlier.

With their growing involvement in the French fur trade, the people soon became dependent on items of non-native manufacture. They also accepted Catholic missionaries. Their population declined

With their growing involvement in the French fur trade, the Passamaquoddy soon became dependent on items of non-native manufacture. They also accepted Catholic missionaries. Pictured here are three Maine Indians with a Jesuit priest.

severely throughout the eighteenth century, owing to disease, abuse of alcohol, and loss of land.

They joined the pro-French Abenaki Confederacy in the mid–eighteenth century. Many Passamaquoddys married French men and women. By the late eighteenth century, British settlers had pushed them out of many of their best subsistence areas, and the traditional annual round of subsistence activites had been seriously disrupted. The state of Massachusetts set aside 23,000 acres of land for them in 1794 as part of a treaty never ratified by the federal government. The two reservations were founded around 1850 by competing political factions, the "progressive" one based at Sipayik and the conservatives at Motahkokmikuk.

In the mid– to late nineteenth century, many Passamaquoddys worked in sea-related industries and as farmers, loggers, and guides. They also worked as migrant laborers (potatoes, blueberries) and made baskets, paddles, moccasins, and other items for sale to the tourist trade. Both reservations became enclaves of poverty in a poor region, and by the 1960s many Indians had left to pursue economic opportunities elsewhere. During World War II, the government used part of Indian Township as a German prisoner of war camp; this land was later sold to non-natives. This and other such actions ignited the native rights struggle in Maine and led ultimately to the Maine Indian Claims Settlement Act.

Religion Guardian spirits, acquired through vision quests, gave shamans the power to cure and regular people the ability to protect subsistence areas from trespass. Shamans cured by chanting, blowing, and possibly sucking. Sweat lodges were also associated with spiritual power. Any number of supernatural beings included Kuloscap, the culture hero. Dances were mainly associated with spiritual power.

Government Skilled hunters provided local leadership. The people recognized a supreme hereditary chief in the seventeenth century who lived at the main village. The last such chief died in the 1870s. Leadership became more formalized under the confederacy, with graduated civil offices and a war chief. The people remained part of the Abenaki Confederacy from the mid–eighteenth century to the mid– to late nineteenth century, when the confederacy ceased to exist.

Customs The people came together in large villages in summer and dispersed into small hunting camps in winter. They preferred football, a kicking game, to lacrosse. They also enjoyed any number of dice gambling games.

Men served their prospective in-laws for at least a year before marriage. During that period, the woman made the man's clothing and footgear. Weddings were marked by feasting and oratory recognizing the groom's ancestry. At least after contact, sexual mores were strict, and divorce was rare. Children were generally treated gently and with a high degree of freedom, at least when compared with the region's early French. Boys could sit in council with the older men after killing their first moose. When death was expected, it was sometimes hastened by pouring cold water on the victim, who may also have been buried alive. Herb doctors could be men or women.

Dwellings Summer villages were sometimes palisaded. They included multi- and single-family dwellings. The former were conical pole-frame

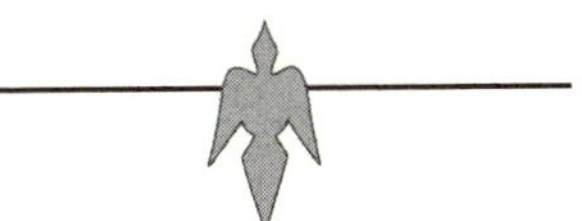

wigwams covered with birch bark; the latter as well as council houses were rectangular log-frame structures with birch-bark roofs. Council houses could hold up to 100 people.

Diet Farming, especially of corn, was the key economic activity. Harvested corn was stored and taken on the winter hunts. There was some hunting of inland animals such as moose, bear, otter, and muskrat. More important was the capture of marine animals such as seal and porpoise. The people also ate stranded whales as well as other marine foods, including lobster, shellfish, and sea birds and their eggs. Marine mammals were hunted in canoe teams. They also fished for salmon, bass, and sturgeon and gathered wild grapes, roots, and fiddlehead ferns. Maple sugaring may have predated contact with non-natives.

Key Technology Fish were generally speared. Corn was stored in bark-lined pits. Various birch-bark items included canoes, containers, baskets, dishes, and boxes. Some were decorated with porcupine quills. Cordage came from spruce roots or cedar bark. The crooked knife was an important woodworking tool. The people also made a birch-bark moose call.

Trade Locally traded goods included birch-bark items, corn, and shells. They also exported porpoise and seal oil and skins.

Notable Arts Clothing and other items were decorated with porcupine quill embroidery. The people made excellent ash-splint baskets and beadwork from the eighteenth century on.

Transportation Lightweight canoes were made of birch bark, moose hide, or spruce bark. Snowshoes were worn in winter.

Dress Clothing was made from skins. Beaverskin caps shielded people's heads from the cold. They also wore temporary birch-bark raincoats.

War and Weapons War chiefs existed at least from the eighteenth century on. This position was never inherited or elected. The war chief could attract followers for raids.

Contemporary Information

Government/Reservations The Pleasant Point State Reservation is home to Sipayik, the main Passamaquoddy village since 1770. Population in the early 1990s was about 560 people. The reservation consists of about 225 acres in Washington County, Maine.

Indian Township State Reservation is the site of the town of Motahkokmikuk, population about 550 in the early 1990s. The town has two distinct neighborhoods: Peter Dana Point and the Strip. The reservation contains about 23,000 acres on the Schoodic Lakes in Maine.

The tribe also owns over 130,000 acres of trust land in Maine. Each reservation elects a government that includes a six-member council. A joint tribal council is led by the governors of both reservations. In addition, each reservation alternately selects a representative to the state legislature.

Economy The tribe sold a cement plant for a $60 million profit in 1988. It has also invested in a blueberry farm and owns a high-stakes bingo establishment, media outlets, several small businesses, and a patent for a coal-emissions scrubber. The tribe itself is the largest employer of Passamaquoddy Indians. Tribal members receive quarterly per capita payments.

Legal Status The Passamaquoddys are a federally recognized tribal entity. In 1981, they and the Penobscots (and the Houlton Band of Maliseet Indians) settled a landmark federal and state land claims case against the state of Maine. The Indians won millions of dollars with which they purchased 150,000 acres as trust land. They also gained a unique status as both a federally recognized tribe and a municipality.

Daily Life Tribal facilities include many new buildings, such as offices, schools, homes, and a museum. The people enjoy free health care. The native language is falling into disuse, with most speakers among the older population. It is taught in school, as are traditional crafts and tribal history. Alcoholism, high unemployment, and anti-Indian prejudice are obstacles that remain to be fully

conquered. Most Passamaquoddys are Catholic. The tribe holds an annual festival.

Penobscot

Penobscot (Pə `nob scot), "where the rocks widen," refers to falls on the Penobscot River. The Penobscot were members of the Abenaki Confederacy and are sometimes referred to as being among the Eastern Abenaki people (others include the Kennebec, Arosaguntícook, and Pigwacket). They are culturally similar to the Micmac and Passamaquoddy. *See also* Abenaki.

Location Penobscots traditionally lived along the Penobscot River, from the headwaters to the mouth, including tributaries. Today, most Penobscots live in east-central Maine, although many live in various cities and towns throughout New England and elsewhere.

Population There were perhaps 10,000 Eastern Abenakis around 1600 and about 1,000 Penobscots in the early eighteenth century. The 1992 Penobscot population was approximately 2,000.

Language Penobscots spoke an Eastern Algonquian language.

Historical Information

History Tribal tradition has these people originating in the Southwest. Shortly after their first encounter with non-natives, in the sixteenth century, a story began to circulate in parts of Europe about Norumbega, a fantastic (and mythical) Penobscot town. This tale greatly encouraged British interest in the region.

Because early British visitors mistreated the Indians, the Penobscots showed a preference for contacts with French traders. Intertribal war with the Micmac ended in 1615, about the same time that devastating epidemics drastically reduced the local Indian population. Involvement in the fur trade from the seventeenth century on signaled the virtual end of many aspects of traditional material culture, as the Indians became dependent on cloth, glass beads, corn, metal items, guns, and items of non-native manufacture. Wampum became a currency as well as an important status symbol.

Winter dispersal into the forests and summer trips to the shore became less necessary, as village Indians could eat corn and other foods obtained in trade for furs. Some groups started growing their own corn at that time. Penobscots were often at war with the British, some of whom were pushing into Penobscot territory, during the later seventeenth and the eighteenth centuries. However, since they needed the British as trade partners, they refrained from establishing a full-blown alliance with the French until the mid–eighteenth century, when they joined the Abenaki Confederacy. By that time, many Penobscots had exchanged their traditional dwellings for log cabins. Much of western Maine was in British hands, and other Eastern Abenakis had left the area for residence in Quebec.

Although the Penobscots tried to remain neutral in the French and Indian War, British bounties on their scalps pushed them into the French camp. The British victory ended their access to the ocean, among other calamities. Around that time, the Penobscots joined a confederacy of former French allies whose center was at Caughnawaga, Quebec. They remained members until 1862, when regional intertribal affairs could no longer hold their interest sufficiently.

Although Penobscots fought with the patriots in the American Revolution, Massachusetts took possession of most of their land in the late eighteenth century in exchange for in-kind payments (food, blankets, ammunition, and so on). An Indian agent appointed by the state of Maine was responsible for conducting the tribe's business after 1820.

In 1833, the tribe sold all but about 5,000 acres to Maine. Their traditional economy in ruins, Penobscots became farmers, seasonal wage laborers (loggers, hunting guides), artisans (snowshoes, canoes, moccasins), and basket makers for the tourist trade. Traditional government was superseded by state-mandated elections in 1866, and the last sagamore (chief) died in 1870.

In the 1920s, the tribe actively sought to bring tourists to the reservation by means of pamphlets and pageants. They also benefited from increasing work in local industries (canoes, shoes, textiles). With other Maine Indians, the Penobscot in the 1960s pushed for

and won improved services through a new state Indian Affairs department.

Religion Summer was the time for religious ceremonies. Shamans were religious leaders. They led ceremonies and cured illness of spiritual origin by blowing and dancing. Common ailments (those without a spiritual component) were cured with herbs and plant medicines.

Government Tribal organization traditionally consisted of a loose grouping of villages, each with its own sagamore. These leaders, who might or might not be shamans, consolidated their power through multiple marriage and by supporting and making alliances with nonrelatives. Leaders were chosen by merit, although there was a weak hereditary component. Sagamores had various social obligations that included feasting the band.

The Eastern Abenaki were politically united, prior to and through the time of the first European contact, under one chief sagamore named Bashabes. Penobscots had a chief sagamore, sometimes in name only, from at least the early seventeenth century to 1870.

Customs Penobscots were divided into patrilineal lineages, each with its own winter hunting territory that became more strictly defined in the fur trade era. They may have recognized a dual division. The tribe broke into small hunting groups in winter but came together in summer villages along rivers.

Most socializing, such as playing the hoop and pole game, took place in summer gatherings. Women were secluded during their menstrual periods. The first kill of the season was given away, as was the first kill of any boy. Gifts to the bride's family formalized a marriage; the quantity and quality of the gifts reflected the desirability of the bride and the status of her family. Leading men might have more than one wife.

Common illness was treated by means of sweating, herbs, and plant medicines. An anticipated death might be hastened by starvation. Those material goods not given away before death were buried with the body.

Dwellings There were no permanent villages until at least the eighteenth century. Some villages were palisaded, at least in the historical period. People lived in both square houses with pyramid roofs and cone-shaped wigwams. Both were covered with birch-bark sheets and were about 12 feet in diameter. They featured two deerskin-covered doors and a top smoke hole.

Diet Men hunted and trapped deer, moose, bears, beaver, otter, and other animals, especially in winter. Hunters wore deerskin disguises. Most meat and fish were dried and stored for winter. Eaten fresh, they were either roasted or boiled.

The people boiled maple sap for syrup. They gathered wild tubers, fruits, and berries, and they fished. On spring and summer trips to the ocean, they gathered shellfish and hunted porpoise, seals, and fowl. There may have been a small amount of corn cultivation.

Key Technology Hunting equipment included bows and arrows, knives, deadfalls, clubs, snares, and spears. Fishermen used harpoons, nets, weirs, and basketry traps. Birch bark was a key material; in addition to houses and canoes, the people made it into folded containers, baskets, and other important items. They also made smaller containers of bark, sweetgrass, and hide.

Pipes might be made of clay or stone, but most vessels were of clay. Utensils were carved of wood. The fire kit consisted of iron pyrite and pieces of chert (silica). Items were sewn with basswood inner bark, split spruce, or cedar roots. Lashings were generally of rawhide.

Trade Penobscots were part of a trade network that reached past the Mississippi to the west, almost to the Gulf Coast to the south, and north into Labrador. Still, most trade was local and included items such as canoes, pipes, pottery, and birch-bark goods.

Notable Arts Clothing was decorated in curvilinear designs with dyed quills and braided moose hair.

Transportation Men built canoes of birch bark (and occasionally moose hide) "skin" over cedar ribs and keel. The sheets were sewn together with basswood inner bark; pitch caulking made the seams watertight.

They also made ash and moose-hide snowshoes and toboggans.

Dress Most clothing, such as tunics, breechclouts, long skirts, and moccasins, came from tanned skins. In winter people wore removable sleeves and leggings and moose-hide coats. Beaver pelts were sometimes used for breechclouts and robes. Sagamores might wear special headgear. Men and women also engaged in extensive face and body painting.

War and Weapons Penobscot enemies included the Mohawk and Micmac. From the eighteenth century on, the Penobscot were part of the Abenaki Confederacy, which also included the Abenaki, Maliseet, Passamaquoddy, and Micmac.

Contemporary Information

Government/Reservations The Penobscot Reservation, Penobscot County, Maine, established in 1820, consists of about 4,400 acres of land on about 200 islands in the Penobscot River. The only regularly inhabited one, Indian Island, is home to the main village of Old Town. The people elect tribal officers, a 12-member tribal council, and a nonvoting delegate to the Maine legislature. The 1990 Indian population was 417. The tribe also owns about 55,000 acres of trust land in Penobscot County and in western Maine as well as roughly 69,000 acres of other land.

Economy Tribal members receive per capita payments from their share (over $40 million) of a 1980 land claims settlement. The money was also used to reacquire land (the trust land described under "Government/Reservations"), to provide for the tribe's elderly, and to finance development projects. Other income comes from land leased to logging companies and an audiocassette manufacturing plant. Although unemployment is relatively low (for an Indian reservation), poverty is still a problem.

Legal Status The Penobscot Tribe is a federally recognized tribal entity.

Daily Life There is a tribal police force and court as well as a primary school. Recognition in 1980 brought a host of new projects and improvements in infrastructure and standards of living. Substance abuse remains a significant problem. There is some interest in traditional crafts and religious ideas, although most traditional culture was lost over 100 years ago. Although only a few elders still know the native language, the people are attempting to preserve that language. Most Penobscots are Catholic. The people regularly intermarry with Maliseets and Passamaquoddys as well as with people from other tribes and non-natives.

Peoria

See Illinois

Pequot

Pequot (`Pē kwot), "destroyers." The tribe known as Mohegan ("wolf") sprang from a Pequot faction in the early seventeenth century. *See also* Narragansett.

Location Pequots lived in eastern Connecticut and extreme northeastern Rhode Island in the early seventeenth century. Their main villages were situated on the Thames and Mystic Rivers. Today, most Pequots live in southern Connecticut. Brotherton Indians, who include Pequot descendants, live in Milwaukee, Racine, and Green Bay, Wisconsin. There are other descendants among the Schaghticoke tribe in northwestern Connecticut.

Population There were approximately 4,000 Pequots in 1600 and about 25 Mashantucket Pequots in 1907. In the mid-1990s there were a handful of families on the Schaghticoke Reservation; 1,650 Brotherton Indians; about 600 Paucatuck Pequots; about 300 Mashantucket Pequots; and about 1,000 Mohegans.

Language Pequots spoke an Eastern Algonquian language.

Historical Information

History The Pequot may have arrived in their historical territory from the Hudson River Valley–Lake Champlain area, wresting land from the Narragansett and the Niantic in the late sixteenth

century. In the early seventeenth century, the grand sachem Sassacus dominated 26 subordinate sagamores. However, the people were driven out of Rhode Island by the Narragansett in 1635. About that time Uncas, son-in-law of Sassacus, led a group of Pequot to establish another village on the Thames River; that group became known as Mohegans.

Soon after the Dutch arrived in the region, they began trade with the Pequots, who sold them land at the future site of Hartford. However, control of that land had been disputed, and the British favored more local Indians. As tensions worsened, the Mohegan saw a chance to end their subordinate status. In 1637, they and the Narragansett aided British forces in attacking a Pequot village, killing between 300 and 600 people. The rest of the tribe fled to the southwest. Many were captured, however, and sold into slavery or given to allied tribes as slaves. Some did escape to Long Island and Massachusetts, where they settled with other Algonquins.

Surviving Pequots were forced to pay tribute to the Massachusetts Bay Colony and were prohibited from using the name Pequot. Sassacus and a large group of followers were killed by Mohawks while trying to escape. Uncas then became chief of the Pequots and Mohegans, now all known as Mohegans. He remained firm in his friendship with the colonists, fighting the Narragansett in 1657 and Britain's enemies in King Philip's war.

Although the Pequot/Mohegan survived that conflict, they and other local Indians were severely diminished, and they ceased to have a significant independent role other than as servants or indigents. Some joined other Indian tribes, such as those who passed through Schaghticoke in upstate New York to join the western Abenaki. In 1655, freed Pequot slaves in New England resettled on the Mystic River. The people suffered a continuing decline until well into the twentieth century.

The tribe divided in the later seventeenth century, into an eastern group (Paucatucks) and a western group (Mashantuckets). The former received a reservation in 1683, and the latter were granted land in 1666. Most of their land was later leased to non-natives and lost to Indian control.

In the 1770s, some Mohegans joined a group of Narragansetts, Mahicans, Wappingers, and Montauks in creating the Brotherton (or Brothertown) tribe in Oneida territory (New York). The community was led by Samson Occom, an Indian minister. In the early nineteenth century, this community, joined by groups of Oneidas and Stockbridge (Mahican) Indians, was forced to migrate to Wisconsin, where they received a reservation on Lake Winnebago that they shared with the Munsee band of Delaware Indians. The reservation was later divided and sold.

By the early twentieth century, most Brotherton Indians had been dispossessed, but the community remained intact, mainly because members kept in close contact and returned regularly for gatherings and reunions. Mohegan Indians began a political revival in the early twentieth century, forming the Mohegan Indian Council and becoming involved with the Algonquin Indian Council of New England.

Religion The people recognized a supreme deity as well as lesser deities. Medicine men called powwows used herbs, sweats, plants, and songs to cure illness and banish evil spirits. The people also celebrated a variety of the Green Corn festival.

Government Village bands were led by sagamores, or chiefs, who maintained their influence through generosity and good judgment. A council of important men together took all major decisions. There may have been a hereditary component to the position of village sagamore. There may or may not have been a grand sachem who led the bands in precontact times. Certainly, that was the case in the early seventeenth century, when Sassacus dominated the Pequot as well as some Long Island bands.

Customs Unlike many northeastern tribes, the Pequot dispersed in summer to designated resource sites such as fishing weirs, shellfish gathering places, gardens, and marshlands and came together in winter villages. They also dispersed in early winter to hunting camps. Leading men might have more than one wife, in part so that they could entertain more frequently and more lavishly and in part to built alliances with other families. Corpses were wrapped in skins and woven mats and buried in the ground with weapons, tools, and food. The ultimate destination was the land of the dead. Houses were abandoned after a death.

Dwellings Villages were usually located on a hill and were often palisaded. Consisting of at least several houses, they were moved when the supply of firewood was exhausted. People lived in bark or woven mat houses, framed with saplings or poles bent and lashed together. Smaller houses (roughly 15 feet in diameter) held two families. Square openings in the roof provided barely adequate ventilation. Doorways were low and mat covered. Larger bark-covered longhouses (up to 100 feet long and 30 feet wide) with multiple fires held up to 50 people.

Bedding consisted of skins and mats laid directly on the floor or on platforms raised 12–18 inches off the ground. Cooking pots were placed on poles suspended on forked sticks driven into the ground. There was a central village plaza for games and meetings. Temporary villages were located along the coast in summer and in the woods in winter.

Diet Women grew corn, beans, and squash; men grew tobacco. Corn was used in stew; cornmeal was also made into cakes and baked in hot ashes. The people gathered shellfish along the coast in summer. They also ate an occasional beached whale. Although deer was the animal staple, men hunted an enormous variety of large and small game as well as fowl, the latter including turkey, quail, pigeon, and geese. Deer were stalked and may have been hunted in communal drives. Fish and wild vegetables, nuts, and berries complemented the diet.

Key Technology The Pequots used hickory or witch hazel bows and arrows tipped with flint, bone, shell, or eagle claws. Fish were caught with nets, spears, and bone hooks. Other key items included rush baskets, carved wood bowls and utensils, Indian hemp cordage and twined baskets, wooden mortars, pottery jars, and stone woodworking tools.

Trade The Pequot were part of long-standing ancient trade networks. They engaged in little long-distance trade. Trade items included clay pots, carved wood bowls, chestnuts, and wampum (whelk and quahog shells that were ground into beads using stone drills). Wampum had ceremonial and mnemonic uses before it became a symbol of status and a medium of exchange in the postcontact period.

Notable Arts Porcupine quills were soaked, softened, and dyed and then used to decorate clothing. Jewelry was made from shell, bone, and other material. Pottery was generally basic although often decorated by incision.

Transportation Canoes were of the birch bark and especially the dugout variety.

Dress Deer, especially the white-tailed deer, furnished most of the people's clothing. Men generally wore breechclouts, leggings (in winter), and moccasins; women wore skirts or dresses and moccasins. Both donned fur robes in cold weather. Clothing was often decorated with quillwork as well as feathers, paints, and shells.

War and Weapons The bow and arrow were the basic weapon, along with spears and clubs. Enemies included the Long Island Montauk, the Narragansett, and the Niantic. The people had few known allies.

Contemporary Information

Government/Reservations The Mashantucket (western) Pequots own about 1,800 acres of land in New London County (Ledyard), Connecticut, which they acquired in 1667. Their 1974 constitution calls for an elected tribal council with a chair. The 1990 Indian population was 55.

The Paucatuck (eastern) Pequots occupy the approximately 226-acre Lantern Hill State Reservation in New London County (North Stonington), Connecticut (established in 1623). The 1990 Indian population was 15.

The Golden Hill Reservation (Paugussett Tribe [Pequot and Mohegan]), New London and Fairfield Counties, Connecticut, was established in 1886. The people are governed by an elected tribal council and officers. The community has purchased roughly 700 acres on the Thames River and hopes to acquire Fort Shantok State Park. The 1990 resident Indian population was two.

Schaghticoke State Reservation, Litchfield County, Connecticut, was established in 1792. It consists of about 400 acres and is governed by a tribal council. About five families lived on the reservation in the mid-1990s.

The Brotherton Tribe maintains a headquarters in Fond du Lac, Wisconsin, and is governed by an elected, nine-member tribal council.

Economy The Mashantucket economy is dominated by an enormously successful bingo operation and casino. The Mohegans operate a casino as well.

Legal Status The Mashantucket Pequot Tribal Nation and the Mohegan Indian Tribe are federally recognized tribal entities. The Paucatuck Pequots are recognized by the state of Connecticut and have applied for federal recognition. The Schaghticoke Tribal Nation is recognized as a self-governing entity and has applied for full federal recognition. The Brotherton Indians of Wisconsin have petitioned for federal recognition. The Golden Hill Paugussett Tribe has been denied federal recognition.

Daily Life Paucatuck Pequots continue to fight for full federal recognition as well as full recognition by the state of Connecticut of their rights and land claims. They are also attempting to ease the factionalism that has troubled them for some time. The Mashantucket Pequots were recognized and their land claims settled by Congress in 1983. A museum and cultural center are planned. They publish the *Pequot Times.*

Elements of the Pequot language exist on paper and are known by some people, especially tribal elders. Various gatherings and family reunions continue among the Brotherton people of Wisconsin. The spiritual center of the tribe is in Gresham, Wisconsin. Traditional culture has disappeared, but these people remain proud of their heritage.

The Mohegan have a land claim pending against the state of Connecticut for roughly 600 acres of land alienated in the seventeenth century. The Tantaquidgeon museum is a central point of reference for the tribe, as is the Mohegan church (1831) and the Fort Shantok burial ground. The people celebrate the wigwam festival or powwow, which has its origins in the Green Corn festival of ancient times.

Pokanoket

See Wampanoag

Potawatomi

Potawatomi (Po tə `wä tə mē), a word of uncertain meaning. The commonly ascribed translation, "People of the Place of Fire" or "Keeper of the Fire" is probably apocryphal and refers to their traditional obligation to maintain a council fire uniting them with the Ottawa and Anishinabe. Their own self-designation was *Weshnabek,* "the People." *See also* Anishinabe; Ottawa.

Location In the early seventeenth century, the Potawatomi lived in southwest Michigan. The people were located west of Lake Michigan, near Green Bay, in the later seventeenth century. By 1800, they lived all around the lower part of Lake Michigan; from Green Bay south and west to the Mississippi River; east into northern Illinois, Indiana, and extreme northwestern Ohio; and north to the Grand River and Detroit. Today, most Potawatomis live in Kansas and Oklahoma, with other communities in Indiana, Michigan, Wisconsin, and Ontario, Canada.

Population There were about 8,000 Potawatomis in the early seventeenth century and at least 10,000 in the early nineteenth century. In the mid-1990s there were some 22,000 Potawatomis in the United States and Canada. This number included almost 1,100 on the Kansas reservation; 836 members of the Hannaville Community; almost 18,000 members of the Citizen Band; roughly 750 members of the Wisconsin Band; and several hundred living in southern Michigan.

Language Potawatomi is an Algonquian language.

Historical Information

History Tradition has the people, once united with the Anishinabe and the Ottawa, coming to their historical territory from the northeast. Driven from southwest Michigan around 1640 by the Iroquois, Huron, and others, the Potawatomi took refuge in upper Michigan and then the Green Bay area, where they met other refugee groups and built advantageous alliances and partnerships, notably with the French but also with other tribes. At this time they occupied a single village and became known to history as a single tribe with their present name.

By the late seventeenth century, however, having consolidated their position as French trade and political allies, the single village had collapsed, mainly under trade pressures. Forced by Dakota raiding parties, Potawatomi groups began moving southward to occupy former lands of the Illinois Confederacy and the Miami. By the early eighteenth century there were multiclan Potawatomi villages in northern Illinois and southern Michigan. By the mid–eighteenth century, southern groups had acquired enough horses to make buffalo hunting a significant activity.

The French alliance remained in effect until 1763. The Potawatomi fought the British in Pontiac's rebellion. They also joined the coalition of tribes to administer the final defeat to the Illinois about that time, evicting them from northern Illinois and moving into the region themselves. The Potawatomi fought on the side of the British, however, in the Revolutionary War and continued to fight the American invasion of their territory in a series of wars in the late eighteenth and early nineteenth centuries that included Little Turtle's war (1790–1794); Tecumseh's rebellion (1809–1811), and the Black Hawk war of 1832. By that time, many southern Potawatomis had intermarried with non-natives.

After all these Indian losses, the victorious non-natives demanded and won significant land cessions (the people ultimately signed at least 53 treaties with the United States). The Potawatomis were forced to remove west of the Mississippi. Bands from the Illinois-Wisconsin area went to southwest Iowa while Michigan and Indiana Potawatomis went to eastern Kansas. In 1846 both groups were placed on a reservation near Topeka, Kansas. Some remained in Michigan and Wisconsin, however, and some managed to return there from the west. Others joined the Kickapoo in Mexico, and still other went to Canada.

Some Potawatomi in Kansas became relatively successful merchants and farmers. In 1861, a group of these people formed the Citizen Band as a separate entity from the Prairie Band. They were moved to Indian Territory in the 1870s, and their land there was allotted by 1890. Since much of the land was of marginal quality, however, people tended to leave the community in the early to mid–twentieth century. Many Citizen Band Potawatomis were educated in Catholic boarding schools in the early twentieth century.

The Prairie Potawatomi remained in Kansas. Despite their strong resistance, lands along the Kaw River in Kansas were allotted by 1895. The tribal council disbanded by 1900, and all government annuities ended in 1909. By 1962, less than one-quarter of their former lands remained in their possession, and much of this was leased to non-natives. The tribe rejected the 1934 Indian Reorganization Act (IRA) and was able to avoid termination in the 1950s.

Among those who refused to leave their homelands, a large group of Potawatomi refugees was still in Wisconsin in the mid–nineteenth century. These people had been joined by several Ottawa and Anishinabe families. With the help of an Anishinabe man, they obtained land and money to build a community, called Hannaville, in the 1880s. The U.S. Congress purchased additional land for them in 1913. The community adopted an IRA constitution and by-laws in 1936. Most people were farmers, and many also worked seasonally in the lumber industry. By the early twentieth century, the land was exhausted, the lumber industry had declined, and the state refused them all services, contributing to the onset of widespread poverty and exacerbating anti-Indian prejudice.

In 1839, Huron Potawatomis who had escaped removal purchased land for a community. The state of Michigan added another 40 acres in 1848. The Methodist Episcopal church served as the focus of community life. Near Waterviliet, Michigan, members of the future Pokagon Band bought land near Catholic churches. They continued a subsistence economy based on small-game hunting; gathering berries, maple sap, and other resources; and small-scale farming. They also worked on nearby farms when necessary. They created a formal government as early as 1866, which later pursued land claims against the United States. They and the Huron Potawatomis were denied federal recognition in the 1940s based on an arbitrary administrative ruling.

Religion The people may have recognized a chief deity that corresponded with the sun. Religion was

based mainly on obtaining guardian spirits through fasting. Sacred bundles were probably part of religious practice from prehistoric times on; at some point they became associated with the supernatural power of clans. There were three types of shamans: doctors, diviners, and adviser-magicians. The people observed the calumet (peace pipe) ceremony. Other festivals included the Midewiwin Dance, the War Dance, and the Sacred Bundle ceremony.

Government There were clan chiefs, but the decision makers were generally the clan's warriors, elders, and shamans. Chiefs of semiautonomous villages, who were chosen from among several candidates of the appropriate clans, lacked authority, since the democratic impulse was strong among the Potawatomi. There was no overall tribal chief, although a village chief, through his personal prestige, might lead a large number of villages. The chief was aided by a council of men. Women occasionally served as village chiefs. There was also an intratribal warrior society that exercised police functions in the villages.

Customs At least 30 patrilineal clans owned certain supernatural powers, names, and ritual items. Over time, clans died out, and new ones were created. They were a source of a child's name as well as part of his or her personal spirit power. They also had important ceremonial functions. A dual division by birth order had significance in games and some rituals. Lacrosse was a popular game, as were the woman's double ball game and dice games.

After the harvest, people generally broke into small hunting camps for the winter. Polygyny was common. Marriages were formalized by gift exchange between clans and by the approval of senior clan members. After the wedding, a man lived with his wife's family for a year, after which time the couple established their own household.

Women gave birth assisted by other women in special huts. They remained secluded with the infant for a month. Babies were named after a year and weaned after several years. Both sexes were recognized as adults at puberty. Both were isolated around that time, women during their periods and men to fast and seek a vision. Young women might also have visions at this time.

Corpses were dressed in their best clothes and buried in an east-west alignment (one clan practiced cremation) with considerable grave goods that included food, tools, and weapons. Graves were marked with painted or incised posts. Souls were said to travel to an afterworld located to the west.

Dwellings Summer villages, numbering up to 1,500 people of several clans, were built along lakes and rivers and often contained members of Anishinabe and Ottawa groups. Small winter camps lay in sheltered valleys. Some villages may have been palisaded.

Summer houses were bark-covered rectangular structures with peaked roofs. The people built smaller, dome-shaped wigwams with mats covering a pole framework for their winter dwellings. They also built ramadas with roofs of bark or limbs for use as cooking shelters. Rush-mat menstrual huts were built away from the main part of the village. There was also a nearby playing field.

Diet Women grew corn, beans, squash, and tobacco. Squash and meat were smoked or sun dried. Women also gathered wild rice, maple sap for sugar, beechnuts (which were pounded into flour), berries, roots, and other wild plant foods. Cranberries were smoked, as were fowl, after first being pickled. Men fished and hunted buffalo (especially from the eighteenth century on), deer, bear, elk, beaver, and many other animals, including fowl. Dogs were eaten mainly at rituals.

Key Technology Men hunted mainly with bows and arrows. Fishing equipment included nets, weirs and traps, hooks, and harpoons. People also made bark food storage containers, pottery, and stone or fired-clay pipes with wooden or reed stems. Pictographs on birch-bark scrolls served as mnemonic devices.

Trade Potawatomis imported copper and Atlantic coast shells. Intervillage trade helped to keep the people's identity intact.

Notable Arts Clothing was decorated with quillwork and paint. Silk appliqué was an important art from the mid–eighteenth century on.

Transportation Potawatomis used both dugout and bark-frame canoes. The latter were up to 25 feet long; construction and ownership of these vessels were limited. Horses were acquired well before 1800. A litter slung between two horses could carry materials or ill people; woven rush-mat saddlebags also held goods.

Dress Clothing was made of skins and furs. Men were tattooed. Both sexes painted their bodies. They wore personal adornments made of native copper and shell.

War and Weapons Potawatomi warriors fought with bows and arrows, war clubs, and hide shields. Allies included the Ottawa and other neighboring Algonquian tribes. Enemies included the Iroquois and the Dakota.

Contemporary Information

Government/Reservations The Potawatomi Reservation (Prairie Band), located in Jackson County, Kansas, consists of 121 square miles of land. The 1976 constitution calls for a tribal council. The 1990 Indian population was 503 (less than half of the total enrolled population).

The Citizen Band of Potawatomis owns land south of Shawnee, Oklahoma. Tribal lands consist of roughly 300 acres held in trust. They are governed by a five-person tribal council and an elected business committee.

The Pine Creek Reservation, Huron (Nottawaseppi-huron) Band, Barry and Allegan Counties, Michigan (established in 1845), consists of 120 acres of land. The 1990 Indian population was 20. The community is governed by an elected band council.

The Pokagon (Potawatomi Indian Nation) Potawatomi live in Berrien, Cass, and Van Buren Counties, Michigan, and St. Joseph County, Indiana. They are governed by a band council.

Hannaville community and trust lands, Delta and Menominee Counties, Michigan (established in 1913), contain roughly 3,200 acres of trust land. The 1990 Indian population was 173. They are governed by an elected tribal council.

The Forest County Potawatomi, Wisconsin, have almost 12,000 acres of land, most of which is tribally owned. About 460 Indians live in the three towns of Stone Lake, Blackwell, and Wabeno/Carter (mid-1990s). The general council elects an executive council annually.

Potawatomi women replaced porcupine quillwork in geometric designs with ribbon appliqués on their garments during the nineteenth century, as shown in this circa 1870 photograph. They also used metal brooches to decorate their blouses.

There are numerous Potawatomi communities in Ontario, including Walpole Island, Sarnia, Saugeen, Kettle Point, Manitoulin Island, and Cape Croker. There are also other groups of Potawatomi living in the region.

Economy The Kansas Potawatomi own a bingo establishment and are seeking to build a casino. Unemployment is chronically high. Hannaville has important farm, wildlife, and forest resources. A casino provides regular employment. The Citizen

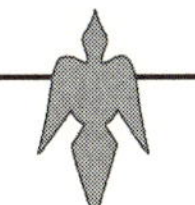

Band owns several businesses, including a bank, a museum and gift shop, a restaurant, and a golf course. It also owns a bingo establishment and is building a casino. The Wisconsin Potawatomi own two casinos and several small businesses. Tourism and lumbering are also important economic activities.

Legal Status The Prairie Band of Potawatomi, the Citizen Band Potawatomi, the Hannaville Indian Community, the Nottawaseppi-Huron Potawatomi Band, the Potawatomi Indian Nation (Pokagon Band), and the Forest County Potawatomi Community are federally recognized tribal entities. The Mash-she-pe-nash-she-wish Indian Tribe (Michigan) has been granted provisional federal recognition (1998).

Daily Life Income and educational levels among the Prairie Band remain low. The band is considered culturally conservative: Many people still speak the native language, and most belong either to the Drum religion, the Dream Dance, or the Native American Church.

The Hannaville Community maintains various social service programs. Grounded in traditional precepts and culture, they are expanding the number of native language speakers beyond a core of elders. People practice traditional or quasi-traditional religions as well as Christianity. They host the Great Lakes powwow.

The Methodist Episcopal Church still serves as a focus of the Huron Potawatomi. The band also hosts an annual powwow. Among the Pokagon band, the Catholic church has served as a similar focus. The band has worked hard for over 100 years to reestablish a government-to-government relationship with the United States. In addition to political considerations, both band councils emphasize economic development and social programs for their members.

In Oklahoma, the Citizen Band is noted for its entrepreneurial ethos. In addition to its many businesses, the tribe administers a variety of social and health services, including a summer program for young people. Most of the people are Christian and relatively assimilated. There are a tribal museum, a tribal newsletter, and an annual powwow held in June.

The Forest County Potawatomi retain a significant measure of their traditional culture. Many people speak the native language, and many traditional and semitraditional religions and ceremonies, such as the Medicine Drum Society, Native American Church, Dream Dance, War Dance, and naming feasts, remain vibrant.

Sauk

Sauk (Sok), or Sac, from *Osakiwugi,* "People of the Outlet," or "Yellow Earth People." The Sauk were culturally related to the Kickapoo and Potawatomi. *See also* Fox.

Location For much of their history, the Sauk straddled the area between the Northeast Woodlands and the Prairie. In the sixteenth century they lived around Saginaw Bay in eastern Michigan. In the mid–seventeenth century they lived in the vicinity of Green Bay, Wisconsin. Today they live in Lincoln County, Oklahoma, and on the Missouri-Nebraska line.

Population There were approximately 3,500 Sauk in the mid–seventeenth century and about 2,200 enrolled members of the Sac and Fox Tribe of Oklahoma in the early 1990s.

Language Sauk is an Algonquian language.

Historical Information

History The Sauk may once have been united with the Fox and the Kickapoo. The Anishinabe and/or the Iroquois pushed the Sauk out of eastern Michigan and toward the lower Fox River sometime in the late sixteenth or early seventeenth century. French explorers arrived around 1667.

The Sauk got along well with the British. The people also maintained good relations with the French until they began sheltering the Fox and other French enemies. Fox Indians fleeing the French took refuge with the Sauk in 1733, beginning an alliance that lasted until the 1850s. At that time, the Sauk and Fox moved away from the Green Bay area into eastern Iowa. They moved back to northern Illinois and southern Michigan after peace with the French was established in 1737.

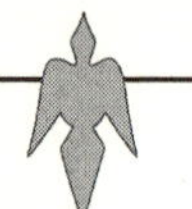

In the 1820s, the United States exercised an increasingly important role in Sauk internal politics, ultimately vesting as tribal chief Keokuk, pictured here, who had no hereditary claim to the position.

In 1769 the Sauk, Fox, and other tribes, under pressure from the French as well as the Menominee and Anishinabe, dealt a permanent defeat to the Illinois tribes. At that point the Sauk and Fox moved south and west into some of the Illinois tribes' former territory. Later they headed back into Iowa, where they adapted rapidly to a prairie/plains existence, becoming highly capable buffalo hunters. Their parties traveled far to the west of the Mississippi in search of the herds. They also continued to grow corn.

In 1804, one Sauk band (the Missouri Band) ceded all tribal lands, although they claimed they were only ceding a small parcel of land. The action was not binding, however, because the tribal council, in whom authority for land cessions was vested, refused to ratify the treaty. Anger at this treaty on the part of the rest of the Sauk people forced the Missouri Band to remain separate from the main group, ultimately settling on the eastern border of Kansas and Nebraska.

The Sauk took an active part in Little Turtle's war (1790–1794), but most remained neutral in Tecumseh's rebellion (1809–1811). They sided with the British in the War of 1812. After the war, the Sauk divided into two factions. Black Hawk headed the anti-U.S. band, which refused to accept the treaty of 1804, and Keokuk headed the accommodationist party. In the 1820s, the United States exercised an increasingly important role in Sauk internal politics, ultimately vesting Keokuk as tribal chief, a man with no hereditary claim to the position.

Black Hawk's war (1832) resulted directly from the controversy over the 1804 treaty. Black Hawk (Makataimeshekiakiak), a Saukenuk (Rock Island) Sauk leader, attempted to form a pan-Indian alliance to defend his homeland against illegal non-native usurpation. Despite the fact that Keokuk had agreed to relocate west of the Mississippi, Black Hawk and his people were determined to occupy their own lands. Some fighting ensued, after which the Sauk decided to retreat beyond the Mississippi. However, a U.S. steamer caught up with and shelled the Indians, many of whom were women and children, as they attempted to cross the river in rafts, slaughtering hundreds. Black Hawk himself surrendered several months later. Following his release from prison in 1833, he toured several cities and dictated his autobiography.

This Sauk and Fox delegation group went to Washington, D.C., in 1868 to complain about their agent, Albert Wiley. Wiley had the men arrested on their eastern journey on the grounds that they were an unofficial delegation.

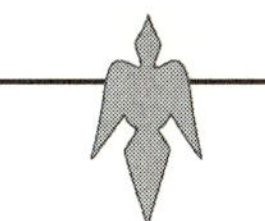

The Sauk and Fox soon defeated Dakota warriors in Iowa (who had themselves killed many of the survivors of the Mississippi shelling) and occupied their land. Over the next few years, the factions hardened, and relations became strained with the Fox, who resented the U.S.-backed Keokuk's control over the tribe. In 1842, the people were forced to cede their lands in Iowa and were relocated to a reservation in Kansas. They were joined by some members of the Missouri Band at that time. Most Fox returned to Iowa in the late 1850s. In 1867, the Sauk were forced into Indian Territory (Oklahoma). In 1890, most of the reservation was allotted in severalty, with the rest, almost 400,000 acres, opened to non-native settlement.

Religion The Sauk recognized any number of nature-related spirits, or manitous, the most important of which were Wisaka, founder of the Medicine Dance, and those connected with the four directions. People might gain the attention and assistance of the manitous by offering tobacco, blackening the face with charcoal, fasting, and wailing.

A vision quest at puberty was meant to attract manitous. Those who obtained especially powerful spirits assembled a medicine pack or bundle; certain packs represented spiritual power that affected and were the property of entire lineages. Two annual ceremonies were related to the vision packs.

The Midewiwin was a key ceremony. Others included green corn, naming, and adoption. In the last, there was a formal adoption to replace a family member who had died. The calumet, or sacred pipe, played a key role in all solemn activities, including peace negotiations. A head shaman instructed others in curing, hunting, and agricultural and other ceremonies.

Government The Sauk were divided into bands or villages, of fluid composition, that came together as one unit in summer. The chief of any one band was considered the tribal chief. Other officers were subchiefs and criers. A religious leader was in charge of ceremonies.

There was also a dual "peace and war" political division. A hereditary, clan-based village peace chief held authority over gatherings, treaties, peace councils, intertribal negotiations, and rituals. In return for access to his property, the people regularly gave him gifts. Two war chiefs were chosen by other warriors on the basis of merit, although there may have been a hereditary component. The war chief commanded the camp police and presided over war councils. He also assumed greater overall authority during war when a stricter, more disciplined organization was needed.

Customs Sauks recognized about 12 patrilineal clans. Membership in the dual division—peace/white and war/black—was determined by birth order. The families of murder victims usually accepted compensation, but they were at liberty to require blood vengeance. Lacrosse was a popular game.

Birth took place in special lodges in the company of only women; the mother remained subject to special postpartum restrictions for up to a year or more. An elderly relative named a baby from the stock of clan names. As adults, people might acquire additional, nonclan names as a result of dreams or warfare.

Parents rarely engaged in corporal punishment of their children. At the onset of puberty, girls were secluded for ten days and were subject to various other restrictions. Boys marked puberty by undertaking a vision quest. Girls also sought visions, although not in seclusion. Vermilion face paint indicated adult status.

Marriages were generally arranged by the couple and were formalized when the families exchanged gifts. The couple lived with the wife's family for a year before establishing their own household. Some men had more than one wife. Adultery usually led only to divorce.

Burial took place after various rituals had been performed. Warriors might be buried in a sitting position. All people were buried in their finest clothing and wrapped in bark or mats with their feet toward the west. Sacred tobacco was placed on the graves. A dog might be killed as a companion on the way to the land of the dead. The mourning period lasted for at least six months, during which time mourners were subject to a variety of behavioral restrictions.

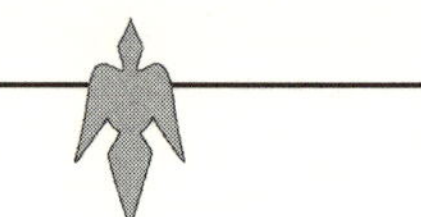

Dwellings Summer villages were located near fields in river bottoms. At least in the early nineteenth century, almost the entire tribe assembled at the summer villages. Each summer house was an economic unit as well. Extended families of some ten people lived in houses about 50 feet long and 20 feet wide and covered with elm bark. Houses were oriented in an east-west direction and were built in parallel rows, with an open game and ceremonial area in between. Villages were moved when firewood became scarce or when attacks forced the people to move.

In their winter camps, people lived in small, dome-shaped wigwams covered with reed mats and skins and located in sheltered river valleys. The camps ranged in size from one or two families to an entire band.

Diet Women grew corn, beans, squash, and tobacco. They also gathered a number of wild plant foods, including nuts, honey, berries, fruits, and tubers. Men hunted a variety of large and small game, especially deer, as well as buffalo until about 1820. There were fall, spring, and summer hunts.

Key Technology Men hunted mainly with bows and arrows and spears. They made carved pipes of pipestone (catlinite) attached to wooden or reed stems. Bark containers and bone needles were heavily used items.

Trade The Sauk mined and traded lead. They also exported corn. They imported deer tallow, feathers, and beeswax.

Notable Arts The people decorated their clothing with quillwork and paint. Art objects also included pottery and carved and quilled wooden items. Silk appliqué was an important art from the mid–eighteenth century on.

Transportation Water transportation was by bark and dugout canoe.

Dress Clothing was made of skin and furs and consisted mainly of breechcouts, dresses, leggings, and moccasins. Body tattooing and painting were common.

War and Weapons Reasons for war included conflict over territory, retaliation, and the achievement of status. Military adventures had to be authorized by the war council. Leaders of war parties began by fasting to obtain a vision and undertook several more ritualistic activities before they and their men departed. The leader carried his sacred ark, which was said to provide the party with spiritual power. Warriors were subject to a number of rituals on their return as well.

Weapons included the bow and arrow, spear, and war club. Most prisoners were adopted into the tribe. War calumets were decorated with red feathers, whereas peace calumets featured white feathers. Traditional enemies included the Anishinabe, Iroquois, Illinois, and later the Osage and Dakota. Allies included the Fox from the early eighteenth century on as well as the Kickapoo.

Contemporary Information

Government/Reservations The Sac and Fox Tribe of Oklahoma (Sac and Fox Nation) is located on over 16,000 acres of land in Lincoln County, Oklahoma, almost 1,000 of which is tribally owned. About 1,500 of the roughly 2,200 tribal members lived in the community in 1992. Under the 1987 constitution (successor to the original Indian Reorganization Act constitution of 1934), the tribe is governed by a governing council (every adult), which elects a five-member business committee and other committees. There are two main communities, one near Shawnee and a smaller one near Cushing.

The Sac and Fox Reservation (Sac and Fox of Missouri), Brown County, Kansas, and Richardson County, Nebraska, was established in 1842 and contains 354 acres. The 1990 Indian population was 48.

Economy Tribal members are generally assimilated into the regional economy. The oil industry has provided fluctuating benefits and advantages. There are also a bingo facility and tobacco shops in Oklahoma.

Legal Status The Sac and Fox Nation (so called since 1988) and the Sac and Fox Nation of Missouri in Kansas and Nebraska are federally recognized tribal entities.

Daily Life Eleven clans remain in existence. Classes will increase the number of people who speak the native language, now estimated at about 200. Many traditions continue, including seasonal ceremonies, adoptions, and naming. Crafts include appliqué, beadwork, basketry, and featherwork. Most people are Christians, but many adhere to the Native American Church.

Tribal facilities in Oklahoma include offices, a health center, a library and archives, and a community building. The tribe maintains its own police and court system. It publishes the *Sac and Fox News.* Local groundwater has been contaminated by oil. There is an annual all-Indian stampede and rodeo.

Most of the Kansas Sauks are acculturated and assimilated into the local economy.

Schaghticoke

See Pequot

Seneca

Seneca (`Se nə ku) were the largest, most powerful, and westernmost of the five original tribes of the Iroquois League. Their self-designation was *Onotowaka,* "Great Hill People." The name Iroquois ("real adders") comes from the French adaptation of the Algonquian name for these people. Their self-designation was *Kanonsionni,* "League of the United (Extended) Households." Iroquois today refer to themselves as *Haudenosaunee,* "People of the Longhouse." *See also* Cayuga.

Location The Seneca homeland stretched north to south from Lake Ontario to the upper Allegheny and Susquehanna Rivers and west to east from Lake Erie to Seneca Lake, but especially from Lake Canandaigua to the Genesee River. At the height of their power, the Iroquois controlled land from the Hudson to the Illinois Rivers and the Ottawa to the Tennessee Rivers. In the 1990s, most Senecas continue to live in upstate New York near their traditional land. Some live in Ontario, Canada, and northeastern Oklahoma.

Population There were perhaps 15,000–20,000 members of the Iroquois League around 1500 and about 5,000 Senecas in the mid–seventeenth century. In the mid-1990s, there were approximately 8,000 members of the Seneca Nation of Indians in the United States, including members of the Tonawanda Band; 2,500 Seneca-Cayugas; and some 1,000 Seneca in Canada. There were about 70,000 Iroquois Indians living in the United States and Canada in the mid-1990s.

Language The Seneca spoke a Northern Iroquois dialect.

Historical Information

History The Iroquois began cultivating crops shortly after the first phase of their culture in New York was established around 800. Deganawida, a Huron prophet, and Hiawatha, a Mohawk shaman living among the Onondaga, founded the Iroquois League or Confederacy some time between 1450 and 1600. It originally consisted of five tribes: Cayuga, Mohawk, Oneida, Onondaga, and Seneca; the Tuscarora joined in the early eighteenth century. The league's purpose was to end centuries of debilitating intertribal war and work for the common good. Both Deganawida and Hiawatha may have been actual or mythological people.

There were two Seneca groups in the sixteenth century and perhaps as early as the founding of the league, each of which had its own large village. The people first encountered Jesuit missionaries shortly before the latter established a mission in Seneca country in 1668. During the seventeenth and eighteenth centuries, the people became heavily involved in the fur trade. Trading, fighting, and political intrigue characterized this period.

In the course of their expansion to get more furs, especially beaver, the Iroquois, often led by the Seneca, wiped out tribes such as the Huron and Erie and fought many generally pro-French Algonquian tribes, such as the Algonquin, Ottawa, Miami, and Potawatomi. The Iroquois also fought and defeated the Iroquoian Susquehanna (or Conestoga) Indians during the early to mid–seventeenth century. Their power effectively blocked European westward expansion.

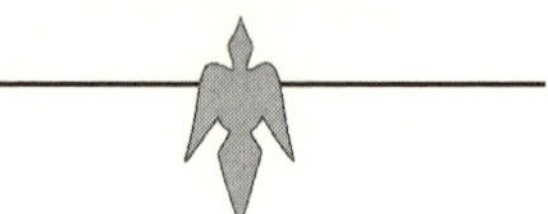

Although they were good at playing the European powers off against each other, the Iroquois increasingly became British allies in trade and in the colonial wars and were instrumental in the ultimate British victory over the French. The western Seneca (Chenussios) remained pro-French, however, even in the French and Indian War and Pontiac's uprising of 1763.

The British victory in 1763 meant that the Iroquois no longer controlled the balance of power in the region. Despite the long-standing British alliance, some Indians joined anti-British rebellions as a defensive gesture. The confederacy split its allegiance in the Revolutionary War, with most Seneca siding with the British. This split resulted in the council fire's being extinguished for the first time in roughly 200 years.

Despite the leadership of Cornplanter and others, however, the Seneca suffered depredations throughout the war, and by war's end their villages had been permanently destroyed. When the 1783 Treaty of Paris divided Indian land between Britain and the United States, British Canadian officials established the Six Nations Reserve for their loyal allies, to which many Seneca repaired.

Seneca lands were formally defined in the 1794 Canandaigua or Pickering Treaty. Most Seneca lands (except for 310 square miles) were sold in 1797. This action was the genesis of the Buffalo Creek, Tonawanda, Allegheny, Cattaraugus, and several other small reservations, most of which were soon sold. Chief Cornplanter also received a land grant from the Commonwealth of Pennsylvania around that time, in consideration of services rendered during the war. After the war, both Cornplanter and the Pine Tree Chief Red Jacket recognized the sovereignty of the United States. Cornplanter favored alliance with the new government, whereas Red Jacket urged his people to continue to live as traditionally as possible.

The Iroquois council officially split into two parts during that time. One branch was located at the Six Nations Reserve and the other at Buffalo Creek. Gradually, the reservations as well as relations with the United States and Canada assumed more significance than intraconfederacy matters. In the 1840s, when the Buffalo Creek Reservation was sold, the fire there was rekindled at Onondaga. Some Seneca who had settled with the Cayuga at Buffalo Creek traveled to Ohio and were removed from there to the Indian Territory (Oklahoma) in the early 1830s.

The Seneca Handsome Lake (half-brother of Cornplanter) founded the Longhouse religion in 1799 (see "Religion"). In 1838, the U.S. Seneca lost of their remaining land in a fraudulent procedure. Four years later, a new treaty replaced the fraudulent one. However, it still included the sale of the Buffalo Creek and Tonawanda Reservations.

In 1848, an internal dispute over the payment of annuities led to the formal creation of the Seneca Nation of Indians (Allegany and Cattaraugus) and the adoption of a U.S.-style constitution and government. With this action the people effectively withdrew from the Iroquois Confederacy and separated from the Tonawanda Reservation as well. In 1857, the Tonawanda Seneca won a long-standing fight to retain their reservation; part of it was bought back with the money that was originally intended to be used for their removal to Kansas. In the mid–nineteenth century, illegal land leases led to the formation of several non-native towns on the Allegany reservation, the largest being Salamanca.

In Canada, the Seneca, referred to along with the Onondaga and Cayuga as the "lower tribes," tended to retain more of their traditional beliefs than did the "upper" Iroquois tribes. Many subsequently adopted the Handsome Lake religion. Slowly, the general influence of non-natives increased, as tribal councils, consensus decision making, and other aspects of traditional culture fell by the wayside. Traditional structures were further weakened by the allotment of reservation lands in the 1840s; the requirement under Canadian law, from 1869 on, of patrilineal descent; and the transition of league councils and other political structures to a municipal government. In 1924, the Canadian government terminated confederacy rule entirely, mandating an (all male) elected system of government on the reserve.

In 1869, the Seneca Donehogawa (Ely Parker), a general in the U.S. Army, became the first Native American Commissioner of Indian Affairs. He stood for peace with the western tribes and fairness in general, shaking up the corrupt "Indian Ring." However, trumped-up charges, of which he was fully exonerated, led to a congressional investigation and ultimately to his resignation in 1871.

The native economy gradually shifted from primarily hunting to farming, dependence on annuities received for the sale of land, and some wage labor. By 1900 there were a number of missionary and state-supported schools on the reservations. Although there were also several churches, relatively few Seneca attended services. Instead, longhouses served as the place where the old ceremonies were maintained and continue to fill that role today. Most Seneca spoke English by that time. With other members of the confederacy, the Seneca resisted the 1924 citizenship act, selective service, and all federal and state intrusions on their sovereignty.

The Seneca in Oklahoma elected a tribal council from the 1870s to 1937. By that time their land base had shrunk, mostly through allotment and outright theft, from about 65,000 acres to 140 acres. At that time they incorporated under state law as the Seneca-Cayuga tribe, adopted a constitution and by-laws, and elected a business committee. The tribe resisted termination in the 1950s.

In the 1960s, despite massive protests, the army flooded over 9,000 acres of the Cornplanter tract and the Allegany Reservation to build the Kinzua Dam. Many important cultural and religious sites were lost. The tribe eventually received over $15 million in damages.

Religion The Seneca recognized an "earth holder" as well as other animate and inanimate objects and natural forces of a spiritual nature. They held important festivals to celebrate maple sap and strawberries as well as corn planting, ripening (Green Corn ceremony), and harvest. These festivals often included singing, male dancing, game playing, gambling, feasting, and food distribution.

The eight-day new year's festival may have been most important of all. Held in midwinter, it was a time to give thanks, to forget past wrongs, and to kindle new fires, with much attention paid to new and old dreams. A condolence ceremony had quasi-religious components. Medicine groups such as the False Face Society, which wore carved wooden masks, and the Medicine, Dark Dance and Death Feast Societies (the last two controlled by women) also conducted ceremonies, since most illness was thought to be of supernatural origin.

In the early nineteenth century, many Iroquois embraced the teachings of Handsome Lake. This religion was born during the general religious ferment known as the Second Great Awakening and came directly out of the radical breakdown of Iroquois life. Beginning in 1799, the Seneca Handsome Lake spoke of Jesus and called upon Iroquois to give up alcohol and a host of negative behaviors, such as witchcraft and sexual promiscuity. He also exhorted them to maintain their traditional religious celebrations. A blend of traditional and Christian teachings, the Handsome Lake religion had the effect of facilitating the cultural transition occurring at the time.

Government The Iroquois League comprised 50 hereditary chiefs, or sachems, from the constituent tribes. Each position was named for the original holder and had specific responsibilities. Sachems were men, except where a woman acted as regent, but they were appointed by women. The Seneca sent eight sachems to meetings of the Iroquois Great Council, which met in the fall and for emergencies.

Debates within the great council were a matter of strict clan, division, and tribal protocols, in a complex system of checks and balances. Politically, individual league members often pursued their own best interests while maintaining an essential solidarity with the other members. The creators of the U.S. government used the Iroquois League as a model of democracy.

Locally, the village structure was governed by a headman and a council of elders (clan chiefs, elders, wise men). Matters before the local councils were handled according to a definite protocol based on the clan and division memberships of the chiefs. Village chiefs were chosen from groups as small as a single household. Women nominated and recalled clan chiefs. Tribal chiefs represented the village and the nation at the general council of the league. The entire system was hierarchical and intertwined, from the family up to the great council. Decisions at all levels were reached by consensus.

There were also a number of nonhereditary chiefs ("pine tree" or "merit" chiefs), some of whom

had no voting power. This may have been a postcontact phenomenon.

Customs The Seneca recognized a dual division, each composed of eight matrilineal, animal-named clans. The clans in turn were composed of matrilineal lineages. Each owned a set number of personal names, some of which were linked with particular activities and responsibilities.

Women enjoyed a high degree of prestige, being largely equated with the "three sisters" (corn, beans, and squash), and they were in charge of most village activities, including marriage. Great intravillage lacrosse games included heavy gambling. Other games included snowsnake, or sliding a spear along a trench in the snow for distance. Food was shared so that everyone had roughly the same to eat.

Personal health and luck were maintained by performing various individual rituals, including singing and dancing, learned in dreams. Members of the False Face medicine society wore wooden masks carved from trees and used rattles and tobacco. Shamans also used up to 200 or more plant medicines to cure illness. People committed suicide on occasion for specific reasons (men who lost prestige; women who were abandoned; children who were treated harshly). Murder could be revenged or paid for with sufficient gifts.

Young men's mothers arranged marriages with a prospective bride's mother. Divorce was possible but not readily obtained because it was considered a discredit. The dead were buried in a sitting position, with food and tools for use on the way to the land of the dead. A ceremony was held after ten days. The condolence ceremony mourned dead league chiefs and installed successors. A modified version also applied to common people.

Dwellings From the early sixteenth century on, scattered Seneca villages were consolidated into two large (100 or more houses) villages (one eastern and one western) and one or two smaller (about 25 houses) ones. Gandagaro, the large eastern village, was also the main tribal village. The people built their villages near water and often on a hill after circa 1300. Some villages were palisaded. Other Iroquois villages had up to 150 longhouses and 1,000 or more people. Villages were moved about twice in a generation, when firewood and soil were exhausted.

Iroquois Indians built elm-bark longhouses, 50–100 feet long, depending on how many people lived there, from about the twelfth century on. They held around 2 or 3 but as many as 20 families, related maternally (lineage segments), as well as their dogs. There were smoke holes over each two-family fire. Beds were raised platforms; people slept on mats, their feet to the fire, covered by pelts. Upper platforms were used for food and gear storage. Roofs were shingled with elm bark. The people also built some single-family houses.

Diet Women grew corn, beans, squash, and gourds. Corn was the staple and was used in soups, stews, breads, and puddings. It was stored in bark-lined cellars. Women also gathered a variety of greens, nuts, seeds, roots, berries, fruits, and mushrooms. Tobacco was grown for ceremonial and social smoking.

After the harvest, men and some women took to the woods for several months to hunt and dry meat. Men hunted large game and trapped smaller game, mostly for the fur. Hunting was a source of potential prestige. They also caught waterfowl and other birds, and they fished. The people grew peaches, pears, and apples in orchards from the eighteenth century on.

Key Technology Iroquois used porcupine quills and wampum belts as a record of events. Wampum was also used as a gift connoting sincerity and, later, as trade money. These shell disks, strung or woven into belts, were probably a postcontact technological innovation.

Hunting equipment included snares, bow and arrow, stone knife, and bentwood pack frame. Fish were caught using traps, nets, bone hooks, and spears. Farming tools were made of stone, bone, wood (spades), and antler. Women wove corn-husk dolls, tobacco trays, mats, and baskets.

Other important material items included elm-bark containers, cordage from inner tree bark and fibers, and levers to move timbers. Men steamed wood or bent green wood to make many items, including lacrosse sticks.

Trade Summer was the main trading season. The people obtained birch-bark products from the Huron.

They imported copper and shells and exported carved wooden and stone pipes. They were extensively involved in the trade in beaver furs from the seventeenth century on.

Notable Arts Men carved wooden masks worn by the Society of Faces in their curing ceremonies. Women decorated clothing with dyed porcupine quills or moose-hair embroidery. The Seneca also made artistic baskets.

Transportation Unstable elm-bark canoes were roughly 25 feet long. The people were also great runners and preferred to travel on land. They used snowshoes in winter and wooden frame backpacks to carry heavy loads such as fresh meat.

Dress Women made most clothing from deerskins. Men wore shirts and short breechclouts and a tunic in cooler weather; women wore skirts. Both wore leggings, moccasins, and corn-husk slippers in summer. Robes were made of lighter or heavier skins or pelts, depending on the season. These were often painted. Clothing was decorated with feathers and porcupine quills. Both men and women tattooed their bodies extensively. Men often wore their hair in a roach; women wore theirs in a single braid doubled up and fastened with a thong. Some men wore feather caps or, in winter, fur hoods.

War and Weapons Boys began developing war skills at a young age. Prestige and leadership were often gained through war, which was in many ways the most important activity. The title of Pine Tree Chief was a historical invention to honor especially brave warriors. Weapons included the bow and arrow, ball-headed club, shield, rod armor, and guns after 1640. All aspects of warfare, from the initiation to the conclusion, were highly ritualized. War could be decided as a matter of policy or undertaken as a vendetta. Women had a large, sometimes decisive, say in the question of whether or not to fight. During war season, generally the fall, Iroquois war parties ranged up to 1,000 miles or more. Male prisoners were often forced to run the gauntlet: Those who made it through were adopted, but those who did not might be tortured by widows. Women and children prisoners were regularly adopted. Some captives were eaten.

Contemporary Information

Government/Reservations Allegany Reservation, Cattaraugus County, New York (Seneca Nation of Indians), established in 1794, consists of about 20,000 acres (excluding the area of the Kinzua Dam). The 1990 Indian population was 1,059.

Cattaraugus Reservation, Cattaraugus, Chatauqua, and Erie Counties, New York (Seneca Nation of Indians with Cayuga and Munsee), established in 1794, consists of about 21,600 acres. The 1990 Indian population was 2,051. The Seneca Nation of Indians (Allegany and Cattaraugus) is governed by a constitution with elected officials.

Oil Springs Reservation, Allegany and Cattaraugus Counties, New York (Seneca Nation of Indians), established in 1877, consists of 640 acres (a square mile). There were no residents in 1990.

Tonawanda Reservation, Erie, Genesee, and Niagara Counties, New York (Tonawanda Band), established in 1863, consists of 7,550 acres. The 1990 Indian population was 453. The community is governed by a tribal council of eight chiefs.

Six Nations/Grand River, Ontario, Canada, was established in 1784. It is governed by both an elected and a hereditary council, although only the first is federally recognized.

The Seneca-Cayuga Tribe is located in Ottawa County, Oklahoma. The reservation consists of about 4,000 acres, about one-quarter of which is tribally owned. Roughly 800 tribal members lived in northeastern Oklahoma in the mid-1990s.

There is also a small (roughly 100 of the original 9,000 acre) parcel of land located in Pennsylvania, near the Allegany Reservation, that belongs to the descendants of Cornplanter.

Economy The tribe received a federal settlement of $35 million in 1990 and a state settlement of $25 million in 1992. Many people work in Rochester and Buffalo. Tribal businesses include minimarts as well as bingo on the Allegany and Cattaraugus Reservations. Its natural resources include timber, sand and gravel, and natural gas. The tribe itself also provides a number of jobs. Many Seneca-Cayugas work in Tulsa

and Oklahoma City. Some also work in the ranching industry.

Legal Status The Seneca Nation of Indians, the Tonawanda Band of Seneca, and the Seneca-Cayuga Tribe of Oklahoma are federally recognized tribal entities.

Daily Life The Seneca have recently renegotiated thousands of leases in and around the town of Salamanca, New York, which is located on the Allegany Reservation. The possibility of casino gambling remains controversial. The Seneca Nation Health Department provides quality health care services. The Seneca Nation Education Department provides a number of quality educational programs. Children attend public schools, and the tribe offers scholarships to students interested in higher education.

Traditional political and social (clan) structures remain intact, as does the language, with the exception of Canada's requirement that band membership be reckoned patrilineally. The people participate in Longhouse and many other celebrations, such as the midwinter, maple, green corn, and harvest ceremonies. Not all are observed at all reservations, and of those that are, there are some local differences. A number of medicine ceremonies also continue to be performed.

There are a museum and library on the Allegany Reservation. The Cattaraugus Reservation features a museum, a library, and a sports arena. The community hosts a fall festival, an Indian fair, and two bazaars. Cayugas and Senecas have yet to resolve issues of Cayuga land ownership on the Cattaraugus Reservation. Few people there speak the native language, but the community does retain various traditional ceremonies.

The political structure of the Iroquois League continues to be a source of controversy for many Iroquois (Haudenosaunee). Some recognize two seats—at Onondaga and Six Nations—whereas others consider the government at Six Nations a reflection of or a corollary to the traditional seat at Onondaga. Important issues concerning the confederacy in the later twentieth century include Indian burial sites, sovereignty, gambling casinos, and land claims. The Six Nations Reserve is still marked by the existence of "progressive" and "traditional" factions, with the former generally supporting the elected band council and following the Christian faith and the latter supporting the confederacy and the Longhouse religion.

Many Iroquois continue to see their relationship with the Canadian and U.S. governments as one between independent nations and allies, as opposed to one marked by paternalism and dependence. Occasionally, the frustrations inherent in this type of situation boil over into serious confrontation.

Shawnee

Shawnee (Shä `nē), from *Shawanwa,* "southerner," their self-designation. These people acted in many ways as agents of cultural change and adaptation between the northeast Woodlands and the southeastern and prairie tribes. They were variously known to non-natives as Ouchaouanag, Chaouanons, Satanas, and Shawano. They were culturally related to the Sauk, Fox, and Kickapoo.

Location The Shawnee migrated often, but their territory in the late seventeenth century may have ranged from the Illinois River east to the Delaware, Susquehannah, and Savannah Rivers. Some scholars place them on the Cumberland River at or before that time. Shawnee villages have been located within an enormous area, ranging from the present states of New York and Illinois south to South Carolina, Georgia, and Alabama. Their aboriginal home may have been around the south shore of Lake Erie, and they lived in southern Ohio during the second half of the eighteenth century. Today, most Shawnees live in Oklahoma. There is also a significant community in and around Ohio.

Population There may have been as many as 50,000 or more Shawnee in the sixteenth century. Their population dropped to about 3,000 in 1650. In the mid-1990s, there were about 600 in Ohio and almost 12,000 in Oklahoma.

Language Shawnees spoke an Algonquian language.

Historical Information

History According to tradition, the Shawnee people were once united with the Lenápe and the Nanticoke, perhaps in Labrador. They may have originated north of or in the Ohio Valley. They were probably associated with the Fort Ancient cultural complex (1000–1700), which was characterized by a mixed subsistence economy, including agriculture, with fortified villages having central courtyards. Many tools were made of bone, and the people also made pottery. Town populations may have ranged up to 1,000 people.

The Iroquois may have begun pushing scattered Shawnee bands south into Ohio as early as the sixteenth century. Iroquois attacks on Shawnees in Ohio lasted until the mid– to late eighteenth century, when the Iroquois forced the last Shawnees out of that area. Shawnees pushed into Pennsylvania in the late seventeenth century, and a population center was established on the Savannah River by that time as well. In the early eighteenth century, bands began a general westward movement again, settling on the north bank of the Ohio River. By about 1750 most Shawnee had come to that location, with Iroquois permission. Some groups also joined the Creek Nation in Alabama about that time.

Heavy involvement in the fur trade from the early eighteenth century on soon left many Shawnee in the clutches of alcohol and debt. Most Shawnee bands were pro-French in the colonial wars, but some were steadfast British trade partners and military allies, especially those bands that came under the control of the Iroquois. Most Shawnees participated in Pontiac's rebellion of 1763–1764. Under Chief Cornstalk, they also fought the British later in 1764 over the issue of land. Pressured by the colonies to cede land, the Shawnee joined the British cause in the American Revolution, hoping that the country that promulgated the Proclamation Line of 1763 would defend their interests against the rapacious colonials. The loss in that war and in Little Turtle's war (1794) led to further land cessions in Ohio and Indiana. In the 1790s, a group of Shawnee and Lenápe moved to Missouri to occupy a Spanish land grant.

In the early nineteenth century, two Shawnees—twins by birth—achieved renown as among the last great military defenders of Indian land in the entire region. The shaman Tenskwatawa, or Shawnee Prophet, encouraged his people to return to their traditions and eschew all non-native elements, particularly Christianity and alcohol. He also claimed to have special medicine that would help repulse the whites. His brother was Tecumseh, a brilliant orator and military strategist. Envisioning an Indian country from Canada to the Gulf of Mexico, he encouraged pan-Indian solidarity and resistance to the domination of the United States. In particular, he believed that no single Native American had the moral right to sell or cede any Indian land.

Unlike many Indian military leaders, Tecumseh did not hate non-natives. He studied their history and admired aspects of their cultures. Furthermore, he insisted on fair treatment of prisoners of war. He traveled constantly throughout the Midwest and southeast in order to build his multitribal alliance. Slowly he began to win the support of even those groups whose strong feelings of tribal identity worked against pan-Indianism. Paradoxically, however, many Shawnee refused to join the coalition.

In 1812, Tenskwatawa foolishly moved against a non-native military expedition before the alliance was complete. The Indian forces were defeated, and Tenskwatawa's power proved to be ineffective. This action fatally disrupted the alliance before it had a chance to coalesce. Tecumseh quickly joined the British cause in the War of 1812, hoping that what remained of his alliance, in conjunction with British forces, could defeat the Americans. Although as a general in the British Army he led many successful campaigns, many Indians refused to join the war. Tecumseh was fatally shot in October 1833.

Their power broken, many Ohio tribes, including the Shawnee, became refugees, drifting in scattered bands throughout Kansas, Missouri, Arkansas, Oklahoma, and Texas. Meanwhile, the Missouri Shawnee living on Spanish land were slowly joined by other Shawnee groups. Resulting tensions forced the groups apart once again. About 1845, groups of Shawnees gathered near Oklahoma's Canadian River and later became known as the Absentee Shawnee (this tribe was composed mostly of the former divisions of Hathawekela, Kispokotha, and Piqua). Most members accepted allotments soon after the

Tecumseh, a brilliant orator and military strategist, joined the British cause in the War of 1812. Although he led many successful campaigns as a general in the British Army, many Indians refused to join the war. Tecumseh was fatally shot in October 1833, as depicted in this 1846 illustration.

reservation was officially established in 1872, and by 1900 most had assimilated into the dominant society. Factionalism between "progressives" and "traditionals" kept the two sides apart throughout the early twentieth century.

In 1825 the United States established a reservation in Kansas for those Indians still living on the Spanish land grant. Shawnees still in Ohio moved there in the early to mid–1830s, although they were forced into Oklahoma, where the groups split up. One part joined the Cherokee (known thereafter as the Cherokee [or Loyal, from their Unionist stance during the Civil War] Shawnee), and the other joined the Absentee Shawnee.

In 1831, a group of Shawnees and Senecas who had been living in Ohio settled in Ottawa County, Oklahoma. When the groups separated in 1867, the Shawnee became known as the Eastern Shawnee. They organized formally as the Eastern Shawnee Tribe of Oklahoma in 1937, when they officially broke apart from the Seneca. Despite their loyalty to the Union in the Civil War, most Shawnee were forced out of Kansas and into Oklahoma, where they merged with the Cherokee in 1869. During the nineteenth and twentieth centuries, scattered Shawnee communities in Ohio and Indiana retained their Indian identity and some of their traditions. These communities came together politically in 1971 as the United Remnant Band.

Religion A supreme deity, possibly female identified, controlled a large number of other deities, which in turn all had their places in Shawnee mythology. The people recognized 12 fundamental laws with religious/mythological origins. The Piqua division of the tribe was in charge of religious ceremonies. Each

division was conceived of as ritually discrete, and each held a sacred pack.

Important communal ceremonies included the Bread Dance, held at planting and harvest times and organized by women. The ceremony featured dancing and a feast of meat hunted by 12 men and cooked by 12 women. The people also celebrated the Green Corn Dance (a harvest/thanksgiving/renewal ceremony) and various other sacred ceremonies.

Prayer accompanied many life-cycle and cyclical events. Women might conduct ceremonies and often cured disease through their knowledge of medicinal plants. Young (less than age ten) boys and girls fasted to obtain spirit visions. Opposition in ceremonial activities, such as ball games, was based on gender.

Government The five Shawnee divisions were Chillikothe, Kispokotha, Piqua, Hathawekela, and Spitotha. They were linked through specific responsibilities, such as politics, ceremonialism, and war, and were associated both with specific territories and towns. Division membership was inherited patrilineally. This arrangement broke down with time.

Political functions fell under either the peace or war organization. Tribal, clan, and division chiefs were hereditary (clan chiefs may have been associated more with ritual than politics) prior to the nineteenth century, although the office of war chief also had a merit component. There was also a tribal council made up of the chiefs as well as elderly men. Town councils probably existed as well.

Women related to male leaders could be chiefs on the town level. Women were also associated with peace and war organizations. Among their prerogatives were the right to ask for the cancellation of a war party, the right to spare prisoners, and direction over feasts and planting crops.

Another type of tribal division was geographical in nature. These groups were fluid in number, size, and composition as the tribe shifted its territory. This system was eventually responsible for the three formal Shawnee divisions of the late nineteenth century.

Customs Up to 12 patrilineal clans controlled names; certain qualities associated with certain names also belonged to particular clans. Ritual and political appointments might follow from these qualities and were thus associated with clans. Women were in charge of the crops, of the game after it was killed, and of gathering wood and cooking. Murder could be redeemed by blood or by payment, with a women commanding more than twice the price of a man. The people enjoyed a number of social dances.

Birth occurred in a special, secluded hut, where mother and child remained for ten days, after which a naming ceremony was held. Marriage was probably arranged, at least in part, and was associated with gift giving. In a departure from tradition, divorce had become easy to obtain by the nineteenth century.

Only men buried Shawnee men, but both men and women buried women. The dead's possessions were divided among relatives, except for some that went to reward friends who played a prominent role in the funeral. Corpses were buried in their best clothing and usually prone, with the head facing west. Tobacco was sprinkled over the body. The mourning period of 12 days was bracketed with two feasts (spouses mourned for up to a year). Diverse death customs might include a condolence ceremony and, if a husband died, a replacement ceremony, when the widow chose a new husband about a year after the death.

Dwellings The Shawnee created various house styles, depending on period and location. Typical summer dwellings were bark-covered extended lodges. Town organization by division included ceremonial aspects as well, on the southeast "town" model. Each Shawnee town had a large, wooden council house used for a number of purposes, including sacred and secular group functions and ritual seclusion for warriors after fighting. In the eighteenth century such houses occasionally served as forts. Towns varied in size according to time and location, but the largest consisted of hundreds of houses and over 1,000 people.

Diet Women grew several varieties of corn. Household fields were grouped together. They also gathered a number of foods, including berries, cherries, and persimmon, and they tapped maple trees for their sap. Men hunted deer, bear, buffalo, and turkey. They also trapped a number of smaller mammals. The people left their summer towns in fall

to establish winter camps. From there, able-bodied men and women left on months-long hunting trips. There was also a summer deer hunt. The Shawnee diet also included fish.

Key Technology Musical instruments included drums and deer-hoof rattles. Pottery vessels held water and served other functions.

Trade Shawnees had many trade partners throughout their various locations. They exported items such as pottery, corn, and other foods and manufactured goods from plants and animals; they imported feathers and minerals. In the historical period they also traded in horses.

Notable Arts The wandering Shawnee did not develop much of an artistic tradition, with the exception of some pottery, carved wood containers, and quill-decorated clothing.

Transportation Although Shawnees did most of their traveling overland, they built dugout canoes to navigate local waterways.

Dress The people generally adopted the clothing of their neighbors, incorporating some styles of their former environs as well. In general, they wore little clothing. Items included buckskin breechclouts, aprons, and moccasins. Body painting and tattooing were extensively practiced. Personal ornamentation varied according to location.

War and Weapons Tribal and divisional war chiefs were selected by merit within certain clans and divisions. War chiefs announced the decision of the tribal council for war, subject to the possible review by a female chief. Female chiefs also had the power to spare prisoners.

War parties usually included a shaman/curer. The group held a dance before departing. There were also a feast and a dance upon arrival home, after which the warriors remained secluded for four days. Prisoners were either killed or distributed as slaves or for adoption. Generally, Shawnee enemies included the Chickasaw, Cherokee, Catawba, and Iroquois. Allies included the Lenápe from the late seventeenth century on and the Cherokee from the nineteenth century on. There was also an ancient association with the Creek.

Contemporary Information

Government/Reservations The Absentee Shawnee are located near Shawnee, Oklahoma. They are governed under a constitution that calls for an executive committee headed by a governor. Tribal membership was about 2,000 in the mid-1990s. The land base is roughly 13,500 acres.

The Eastern Shawnee live in West Seneca, Ottawa County, Oklahoma. The people adopted a constitution and by-laws in 1937. They are governed by a business committee. There were about 1,500 members in the mid-1990s. The tribe owns almost 100 acres of land on their reservation of almost 800 acres.

The Cherokee (or Loyal) Shawnee are located mainly in Whiteoak, Oklahoma, although members live throughout the United States. They are enrolled Cherokee citizens, although they maintain distinct rolls for their tribal membership of about 8,000. The tribe maintains a business committee consisting of officers and members. There is also a general council that passes judgment on membership eligibility.

The Shawnee Nation United Remnant Band (URB) live in and around Ohio. In the early 1990s, the tribe owned 117 acres of land at Shawandasse and another 63 acres at Chillicothe. The tribe recognizes a chief.

Economy The Absentee Shawnee gain income through farming, ranching, taxes on oil and gas contracts, small businesses, bingo, and tax-free sales. Among the Eastern Shawnee, some jobs are available with the tribe, in the bingo facility, and among the general population.

Legal Status The Absentee Shawnee and the Eastern Shawnee Tribe are federally recognized tribal entities. The Shawnee Nation United Remnant Band is recognized by the state of Ohio and has petitioned for federal recognition. The Piqua Sect of Ohio Shawnee Indians has petitioned for federal recognition. The Loyal Shawnee have received state recognition.

Daily Life The URB continues to purchase more land. Their main holdings now serve not as a

residence but as a ceremonial and cultural center, where the tribe conducts powwows, youth programs, and ceremonies. Most are well integrated into the surrounding non-native population. The Absentee Shawnee maintain a police force, a tribal court system, and a clinic. Most of the people are Christians, especially Baptists and Quakers. The native language is still spoken. The more traditional Big Jim Band holds quasi-traditional dances every year.

Facilities of the Eastern Shawnee include a tribal headquarters, a recreational park, and an eye clinic. The tribe also runs a nutrition clinic for the elderly, provides most of its own health care, and publishes a newsletter. Few speak their native language. The Loyal Shawnee maintain a cultural center and several traditions, such as the bread, green corn, and buffalo dances. The native language among these people is practically defunct.

Stockbridge-Munsee

See Mahican

Tuscarora

See Chapter 7.

Wampanoag

Wampanoag (Wäm pu ˋnō ag), "Eastern People." They were formerly known as Pokanoket, which originally was the name of Massasoit's village but came to be the designation of all territory and people under that great sachem. The Wampanoag or Pokanoket also included the Nauset of Cape Cod, the Sakonnet of Rhode Island, and various tribes of the offshore islands. *See also* Narragansett.

Location Traditionally, Wampanoags lived in southern New England from just north of Cape Cod, but including Nantucket and Martha's Vineyard, to Narragansett Bay. Today, there are Wampanoag communities in southeastern Massachusetts and around Bristol, Rhode Island.

Population There were approximately 6,500 Wampanoags in 1600, including tributary island tribes. The contemporary (mid-1990s) population is about 2,700.

Language Wampanoags spoke the Massachusett dialect of an Algonquian language.

Historical Information

History Wampanoag/Pokanoket culture developed steadily in their approximate historical location for about 8,000 years. The people have lived in their historic territory at least since the fifteenth century. They had already been weakened from disease and war with the Penobscot when they encountered non-natives in the early seventeenth century. They had also been forced by the Narragansett to accept tributary status.

The people greeted the Pilgrims in 1620, although there had been contact with the British some years earlier. The Grand Sachem Massasoit made a treaty of friendship with the British. His people helped the Europeans survive by showing them how to grow crops and otherwise survive in a land alien to them. Men named Squanto and Samoset are especially known in this regard. Largely as a result of Massasoit's influence, the Wampanoags remained neutral in the Pequot war of 1636. Many Indian residents of Cape Cod and the islands of Nantucket and Martha's Vineyard were Christianized during the mid–seventeenth century.

Massasoit died in 1662. At that time his second son, Metacomet, also known as Philip, renewed the peace. However, relations were strained by British abuses such as the illegal occupation of land; trickery, often involving the use of alcohol; and the destruction of resources, including forests and game. Diseases also continued to take a toll on the population.

Finally, local tribes reached the breaking point. The Pokanoket, now mainly relocated to the Bristol, Rhode Island, area and led by Metacomet, took the lead in uniting Indians from southern and central New England in King Philip's war (1675–1676). This was an attempt by the Wampanoag, Narragansett, and other tribes to drive the British out of their territory. However, the fighting began before all the preparations had been completed. In the end, hundreds of non-native settlers died, but the two

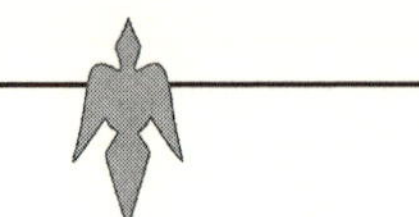

main Indian tribes were nearly exterminated. The tribal name of Pokanoket was also officially banned.

Most Wampanoags were either enslaved or killed. Survivors fled into the interior or onto the Cape and the islands, whose tribes had not participated in the war. Some also fled to the Great Lakes region and Canada. For centuries following this event, local Indians were cheated, discriminated against, used as servants, or, at best, ignored.

The Indian population on Nantucket Island declined from possibly 1,500 in 1600 to 358 in 1763 to 20 in 1792, mainly owing to disease. The last of the indigenous population died in 1855. Indians at Mashpee, on Cape Cod, were assigned 50 square miles of land in 1660. Self-government continued until 1788, when the state of Massachusetts placed the Indians under its control. Most of their lands were allotted in 1842. Trespass by non-natives was a large problem during the entire period. Near Mashpee, the 2,500-acre Herring Pond Reservation was allotted in 1850.

Indian land in Fall River was divided into lots in 1707, and a 160-acre reservation was created in 1709. The people's right of self-government was abrogated in the early nineteenth century. The reservation was eliminated entirely in 1907. Of the three reservations on Martha's Vineyard in the nineteenth century—Chappaquiddick, Christiantown, and Gay Head—only the latter remained by 1900. This group was never governed by non-native overseers, and its isolation allowed the people to retain their identity and cohesion to a far greater extent than other Wampanoag communities.

Other groups of Wampanoag descendants maintained a separate existence until the nineteenth century, when most became fully assimilated. The Wampanoag Nation was founded in 1928 in response to the pan-Indian movement of the times.

Religion The people recognized a supreme deity and many lesser deities. Priests, or medicine men (powwows), provided religious leadership. Their duties included mediating with the spirit world in order to cure, forecast the weather, and conduct ceremonies.

Government A hereditary chief sachem led the tribe. In theory his power was absolute, but in practice he was advised by a council of village and clan chiefs (sagamores). The village was the main political unit. Villages were led by chiefs with limited power; important decisions were made in consultation with influential men of the village. There was a hereditary element to village leadership. This factor may be responsible for the existence of women chiefs. Villages may have made their own temporary alliances. Overall political structure consolidated and became more hierarchical after the epidemics of 1616–1619.

Customs Wampanoags were organized into a number of clans. Their annual round of activities took them from winter villages to gathering sites at summer fields. Women had clearly defined and significant political rights. Social stratification was reflected in leadership and marriage arrangements. Leading men might have more than one wife. The dead were wrapped in mats and buried with various possessions. Mourners blackened their faces. The souls of the dead were said to travel west.

Dwellings There were at least 30 villages in the early seventeenth century, most of which were located by water. People lived in wigwams, both circular and rectangular. The largest measured up to 100 feet long; smaller ones were about 15 feet in diameter. The houses consisted of pole frames covered with birch bark, hickory bark, or woven mats. There were smoke holes in the roofs. The wigwams were often semiexcavated and lined with cattails, pine needles, or other such material.

Wigwams tended to have central fires, but longhouses featured rows of several fires. Some houses may have been palisaded. Their larger structures were probably built in winter villages. Mat beds stood on platforms against the walls or directly on the ground. Skins served as bedding. All towns featured a central open space used for ceremonies and meetings. The people also built sweat houses.

Diet Men hunted fowl and small and large game, with the white-tailed deer being the most important. They stalked, trapped, and snared deer and may have hunted them in communal drives. They also grew tobacco. The people ate seals and beached whales, and they gathered shellfish, often steaming them over hot

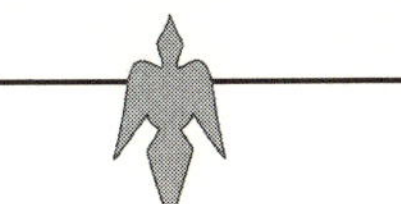

rocks. They fished for freshwater and saltwater species in winter (through the ice) and summer. Women gathered roots, wild fruits, berries, and nuts as well as maple sap for sugar. Women began growing corn, beans, and squash in the late prehistoric period. Fish may have been used as fertilizer. Dried corn was stored in underground caches.

Key Technology Hunting equipment included traps, snares, nets, witch hazel bows, and arrows. People caught fish with nets, bone hooks, and weirs. Cordage was made mainly of Indian hemp. Hoes were made of hardwood and clamshell. Women wove mats and baskets of rushes and grasses, including Indian hemp. Other material items included stone, bone, and shell tools; wooden bowls; and dishes and other items of stone and clay. Shell wampum was used for adornment and later for trade.

Trade Wampanoags were part of regional trade networks. There were few professional or long-distance traders; most trade was very local. Items traded included wampum, agricultural products, chestnuts, skins, pottery, and wooden bowls.

Notable Arts Carved wooden items, such as bowls, were especially fine.

Transportation Dugout canoes could hold up to 40 men, with the average being 10–15. There may have been some number of birch-bark canoes. Women carried burdens on their backs.

Dress Women wore skirts and poncho-style blouses as well as soft-soled moccasins. They donned rabbit and beaver robes in cold weather. Men wore skin leggings and breechclouts and soft-soled moccasins. They also wore turkey-feather cloaks and bone and shell necklaces. They tended to pull out all their hair except for a scalp lock.

War and Weapons Allies included the Massachusett; enemies included the Penobscot and Narragansett. The main weapons consisted of witch hazel bows; wooden arrows with stone, bone, eagle claw, and crab tail tips; and ball-headed war clubs. Men painted their faces for war.

Contemporary Information

Government/Reservations The Wampanoag Nation is divided into five groups: Gay Head, Mashpee, Assonet, Herring Pond, and Nemasket, each with a written constitution, a chief, and an elected tribal council. There is also a council of chiefs, and the mainland groups recognize a supreme medicine man.

The Wampanoag Reservation (Gay Head Wampanoags), also known as Aquinnah, is located at Gay Head on Martha's Vineyard, Massachusetts. Fewer than half of the roughly 600 members live on the island. The tribe owns several parcels of land—about 150 acres—in trust.

More than half of the approximately 1,000 Mashpee Wampanoag live in the town of Mashpee, Massachusetts. The Pokanoket Tribe of Wampanoag Nation is located in Bristol, Rhode Island.

Economy Most Wampanoags are integrated into local economies. At Gay Head, tourism and small Indian-owned businesses are important.

Legal Status The Gay Head Wampanoags are a federally recognized tribal entity. The Mashpee Wampanoags have petitioned for federal recognition. The Pokanoket Tribe of Wampanoag Nation plans to petition for federal recognition.

Daily Life Contemporary Wampanoag events, many of which have both sacred and secular/public components, include a powwow on the Fourth of July (Mashpee), Indian Day and Cranberry Day (Gay Head), and new year's ceremony and the Strawberry Festival (Assonet). Many Gay Head people have left the island, but many also plan to return. Recent construction on the island includes housing and a multipurpose building. The people hope to make remaining on the island a viable option.

In 1978, the Mashpee people lost a court case in which they sought the return to tribal ownership of the entire town of Mashpee. They continue to seek a land base and hope that federal recognition will advance their prospects. The community is in the process of working out a fair relationship with the increasingly non-native population of the town.

The Pokanoket tribe, led by descendants of Massasoit, seek federal recognition and as well as stewardship of 267 acres of land in Bristol, Rhode Island.

Winnebago

Winnebago (Wi nə `bā gō) is Algonquin for "People of the Filthy Water," referring to the lower Fox River and Lake Winnebago, which became clogged with dead fish every summer. This name was translated by the French into *Puants* and back into English as "Stinkards." The people's self-designation was *Hochungra,* "People of the Big (Real, or Parent) Speech (Voices)" or "Great Fish (Trout) Nation." Today they are known as the Ho-Chunk Nation.

The Winnebago shared cultural characteristics with Plains Siouans such as the Otoe, Ioway, and Missouria as well as with Woodland/prairie Algonquians such as the Sauk, Fox, and Menominee. Little is known of Winnebago culture prior to their brush with annihilation in the early seventeenth century.

Location In the early seventeenth century the people were located in Wisconsin on the Door Peninsula, Green Bay, just south of the Menominee. The Winnebago may also once have lived in west-central Wisconsin. By the early nineteenth century they lived in southwestern Wisconsin and northwestern Illinois. Today, there are communities in northeast Nebraska and central Wisconsin and in regional cities and towns.

Population From about 3,800 in the mid–seventeenth century or earlier, the Winnebago have grown to approximately 7,000 in 1990.

Language Winnebago belongs or is related to the Chiwere division of the Siouan language family.

Historical Information

History According to tradition, the Winnebago were united with the Chiwere Siouans in the distant past, perhaps in Kentucky. Their ancestors were in Wisconsin as early as around 700. As the groups moved north and west, and then south and west, the Winnebago may have remained in the forest while the other Chiwere speakers moved onto the prairie and plains in the early to mid–seventeenth century. They probably participated in the fifteenth-century Mound Builder culture. They were also probably allied with—and borrowed some cultural elements (perhaps including cannibalism) of—sixteenth-century Temple Mound people based at Cahokia, near present-day St. Louis. A colony of these people apparently lived near the Winnebago, at a settlement called Aztalan.

The Winnebago may have defeated the Illinois in the early seventeenth century. Shortly after the French arrival, around 1634, Michigan-area Algonquians fleeing from Iroquois attacks swarmed into Winnebago territory. Winnebago warfare against these people led to the defeat of most of these refugee groups. Despite their strength and military capability, by the mid–seventeenth century the Winnebago had been reduced to near extinction by disease and war with the Illinois, Ottawa, and other Algonquian tribes. At that point, the Winnebago were forced to sue for peace with their enemies, adopting and marrying many of them to make up for their losses and in the process incorporating many aspects of Algonquian culture.

They became involved in the fur trade from the mid– to late seventeenth century. That development tended to disperse the tribe west and south of Lake Winnebago. Material changes and technological dependence soon followed. They were French allies during the colonial wars, but pro-British in the American Revolution. They participated in Tecumseh's rebellion (1809–1811) and tentatively in Black Hawk's war (1832).

Unstable relations between the European and Euro-American powers had aided the Indian cause. The end of fighting between the United States and Britain in 1815 ushered in the era of land cessions and removals for the Winnebago. They were powerless to prevent the United States from pressuring the Menominee to cede land traditionally belonging to the Winnebago so that Indians from New York might have a home in the west.

Crowding by non-natives and pressure from the U.S. government led the Winnebago to cede their Wisconsin lands between 1825 and 1837 (at least the final treaty was blatantly fraudulent). By then two factions had developed within the tribe: those agreeing to removal and those determined not to

leave. The former group, determined to acculturate, soon moved onto several successive reservations in Iowa, Minnesota, South Dakota, and finally Nebraska. Up to one-third of the people died during the removals, particularly on the move to South Dakota. There was an especially severe smallpox epidemic in 1836.

In Nebraska, people continued to grow gardens and hunt. Most of the land was allotted by 1900. Allotments were generally leased to non-natives, who profited by the towns that grew up in the area, most notably the town of Winnebago. In the early twentieth century, most Winnebago land was sold to non-natives. At the same time, forced attendance at boarding schools had a particularly destructive effect on the Winnebago. Demoralization set in, and factionalism, based on religious differences (such as Christian sects and the Native American Church), rent the tribe. As was the case so often, educational and employment opportunities were closed to Indians.

The tribe reorganized in 1936 under the Indian Reorganization Act but was unable to stem the tide of despair, poverty, and growing social problems. Many aspects of traditional culture had vanished by that time. The government soon began a program of purchasing homes in scattered counties for tribal members. In the 1960s, the tribe benefited from both federal antipoverty programs and its own community development work.

Meanwhile, by the 1870s over half of the tribe had returned to Wisconsin, which some members had never left. In the 1880s, many members received scattered 40-acre parcels of land under the Homestead Act, most of which were later sold. The people lived in a semitraditional manner until well into the twentieth century, despite the growing presence of missionaries and missionary schools. In 1906, the people lost much of their land to tax foreclosure.

In 1908, many Wisconsin Winnebagos became involved with the Native American Church. As in Nebraska, the tribe soon developed bitter factions based at least in part on religious differences. The people continued to gather berries and harvest fruit and vegetables from non-native farms. Tourism—mainly craft sales (especially ash-splint baskets)—became increasingly important after World War I.

Religion The primary deity was the sun or earth maker. The people also recognized other deities, some sex identified, and many lesser spirits. Winnebago cosmology was intricate and complex, and although most people were unfamiliar with the details, most also observed the various rituals associated with aspects of traditional religious belief having to do with personal visions, clan membership, and life-cycle events.

Young people undertook vision quests in order to acquire guardian spirits. These were said to provide luck and success in hunting, war, or curing. The Midewiwin ceremony differed from the Algonquian version in that it dealt mainly with life and death as well as life after death. Clan feasts focused on making offerings to the clan animal. There was also a winter feast.

War bundle ceremonies, held under clan auspices, resulted from particular visions. They included ritual offerings and were meant to enhance the spiritual power of the military enterprise. There were several kinds of shamans: Those associated with war and curing were considered good, but those associated with hunting might be good or bad (witches). Certain older people used both medicinal plants and spiritual power to cure disease.

Government There was a hereditary head chief in former times. As the population dispersed during the eighteenth century, population centers became more autonomous. Dual chieftainships (peace and war chiefs) existed in villages and among head chiefs. The peace chief was always inclined toward peace and reconciliation. He was generous, strove for consensus in decision making, and tried to discourage most war parties. Civil chiefs came from a clan of the air division. War chiefs came from a clan of the earth division. They were concerned with rule breaking and punishment. Both civil and war chiefs were selected from hereditary candidates according to merit. One clan—the Bear—served as a tribal police force.

Customs Generosity may have been the people's highest value. The tribe was organized into two divisions, earth and air. There were also 12 patrilineal clans, 4 among the air division and 8 among the earth division. Clans were related to animals and were represented by mounds in the shape of animals. They governed marriage, leadership, and games such as lacrosse. Each clan also owned certain names, ceremonies, responsibilities, and restrictions. Descent may have been matrilineal in the distant past.

There may have been a social ranking, although the basis is unclear. Berdaches (transvestites), thought to be divinely inspired, were accorded respect. The mother's brother(s) played an important role in raising a boy. Although menstruating women were isolated, some degree of courtship may have taken place at those times. Marriages were often arranged by close male relatives of a woman. In-laws were generally avoided out of respect.

People enjoyed various sports, such as lacrosse, as well as gambling games such as the moccasin game. The Winnebago were cannibals. At four-night wakes held for the dead, people told stories and gambled for the souls of enemies, which would later assist the dead on their way to the afterlife. Corpses were buried on scaffolds.

Dwellings The few large late-seventeenth-century villages became 40 or so scattered settlements by the early nineteenth century. People lived in rectangular bark- or mat-covered lodges. There was also a rectangular council house for meetings and ceremonies and similarly built sweat houses. From the eighteenth century on, as populations became less concentrated, people began to build domed wigwams.

Diet Women grew gardens of corn, beans, and squash as well as tobacco. Corn was steamed in a pit layered with husks. It was also stored in pits or fiber bags. Men hunted buffalo communally on the nearby prairie and trapped small game. Other large game included deer and bear. Hunting parties probably included women. Runners traveled between winter hunting parties and the villages, exchanging fresh meat for dried vegetables. Fish was often taken at night by the light of pine-pitch torches. Women gathered fruit, berries, and tubers as well as wild rice from canoes.

Key Technology Fishing gear included spears, bow and arrow, and weirs. Carved hickory calendar sticks marked celestial occurrences. People also carved wooden bowls. Women made pottery jars and wove baskets and bags.

Trade Among other transactions, the Winnebago traded buffalo robes with the Menominee for wild rice. They also exported corn and pottery items.

Notable Arts Leather goods were decorated with dyed porcupine quills and feathers. Other arts included beadwork, woven baskets, and carved wooden bowls.

Transportation People traveled over water in birch-bark and dugout canoes. They used snowshoes in winter.

Dress Most clothing was made from tanned buckskin. Men wore deer-hair headdresses dyed red. They also wore breechclouts, leggings, and soft-soled moccasins, possibly fringed and/or decorated with quillwork. Women wore sleeveless dresses (consisting of two skins sewed together at the shoulder and belted) over a nettle-fiber undershirt, leggings, and moccasins with a distinctive flap over the toe. Both wore buckskin robes in cold weather.

The few large late-seventeenth-century Winnebago villages became 40 or so scattered settlements by the early nineteenth century. People lived in rectangular bark or mat-covered lodges. There was also a rectangular council house for meetings and ceremonies and similarly built sweat houses.

War and Weapons Winnebagos were known as enthusiastic fighters. Captured enemies were regularly eaten. Allies included the Menominee, Sauk, Fox, and Kickapoo; enemies included the Anishinabe, Dakota, and sometimes the Fox. Clans owned sacred war bundles, which contained items dictated in a vision by a particular war-related spirit. One clan—the Hawk—had the power of life and death over prisoners of war. War honors included counting coup. The people engaged in a celebratory dance when a war party returned.

Contemporary Information

Government/Reservations The Winnebago Reservation, Dixon and Thurston Counties, Nebraska, established in 1865, consists of over 27,000 acres. The 1990 Indian population was 1,151 of a total enrollment of roughly 4,000. Government consisted of a tribal council with officers.

The Winnebago Nation in Wisconsin includes the communities of Black River Falls, Wisconsin Dells, Tomah–La Crosse, Wittenberg, and Wisconsin Rapids. The community recognizes two types of government, a "progressive" business committee and a traditional chief-clan structure.

The Ho Chunk (Winnebago) Reservation, Dane, Jackson, Juneau, Monroe, Sauk, Shawana, and Wood Counties, Wisconsin, was established in 1875 on lands repurchased from aboriginal territory. The reservation consists of approximately 4,200 acres. The 1990 Indian population was 465, with an additional 101 Indians located on the trust lands (Adams, Clark, Crawford, Jackson, Juneau, La Crosse, Marathon, Monroe, Shawana, and Wood Counties). Total enrollment at that time was about 5,000.

Economy In Nebraska, a $4.6 million land claim settlement in 1975 was divided 65/35 between the tribe as a whole and per capita payments. Important programs that were developed with these funds include credit facilitation, land acquisition, and funerary programs. Other important economic activities include a casino and several small businesses. The tribe is seeking economic self-sufficiency. The Wisconsin Winnebago operate bingo establishments and casinos. The people also work in the general economy.

Legal Status The Winnebago Tribe of Nebraska and the Wisconsin Winnebago Indian Tribe are federally recognized tribal entities.

Daily Life The Nebraska Winnebago have a tribal court system. Community facilities include a hospital, tribal offices, and public schools. There is also a local campus of Nebraska Community College. The native language is spoken by relatively few people. Most Winnebagos are Christian. Diabetes is a serious health problem. The tribe hosts an annual powwow in July.

The Wisconsin Winnebago have retained their clan structure within the context of the two divisions, earth and air (or sky). Many people still observe traditional religious ceremonies such as the vision quest and various festivals. They celebrate a powwow around Labor Day. Gaming remains controversial, but even traditionalists defend it on grounds of sovereignty. Wisconsin Winnebagos are known in part for their dedicated service in the U.S. armed forces. The Native American Church remains popular in both locations.

Wyandotte

Wyandotte or Wyandot (`Wī un dot), from *Wendat,* "islanders," or "People of the Peninsula," the self-designation of the Huron people. The Wyandottes are a successor tribe to the Huron Confederacy, which was destroyed in 1650 and which consisted of four or five tribes: Attignaouantan (People of the Bear), Attigneenongnahac (Barking Dogs or People of the Cord), Arendahronon (People of the Rock), Tohontaenrat (People of the Deer), and possibly Ataronchronon (People of the Marshes). The name Huron is taken from a French word meaning "boarlike" or "boorish" and refers to the roached hair style. Contemporary Canadian Hurons are known as Hurons-Wendat.

Location In the sixteenth century, Hurons lived in the St. Lawrence River Valley. By 1600 at the latest, they inhabited an area known as Huronia, which included land between Georgian Bay (Lake Huron) and Lake Ontario. Today, most Wyandottes live in Wyandotte County, Kansas; Ottawa County, Oklahoma; and near Quebec City, Canada.

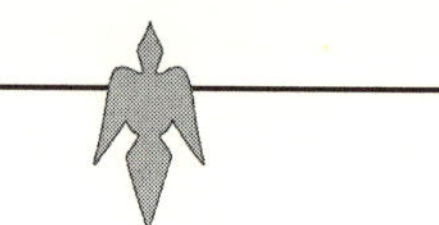

Population From between 16,000 and 30,000 people in the early seventeenth century, the Huron population dropped to about 10,000 in the mid–seventeenth century and to fewer than 200 in Canada in the early nineteenth century. There were around 500 Wyandottes in the Great Lakes region in the mid– to late seventeenth century. In the mid-1990s, about 2,000 tribal members lived in Oklahoma and Kansas. About 2,700 live in Quebec, Canada.

Language Huron/Wyandottes spoke mutually intelligible dialects of a Northern Iroquoian language.

Historical Information

History The Huron probably originated with other Iroquoians in the Mississippi Valley. They encountered Jacques Cartier in 1534 and Samuel de Champlain in 1609. The Iroquois wars probably began sometime in the sixteenth century, if not earlier, when those people drove the Huron tribes out of the St. Lawrence Valley, lands that they may originally have taken by warfare from the Iroquois. Thereafter the Huron sided with the Algonquians against the Iroquois.

The people entered the fur trade in the early seventeenth century, mainly as intermediaries between the French and other tribes. Catholic missionaries soon followed the traders, as did venereal disease and alcohol. Until the late 1640s, the Huron dominated the French beaver pelt trade. The French, however, were reluctant to sell arms to unconverted Hurons, a policy that was to have disastrous consequences. Severe epidemics in the late 1630s were followed by more Christian conversions and increased factionalism.

The Iroquois, armed with Dutch firearms, launched their final invasion in 1648. These tribes were allied with the British and sought to expand their trapping area and their control over neighboring tribes. Within two years they had destroyed the Huron. Some Hurons escaped to Lorette, near Quebec City, where they were granted land. They continued to grow crops, hunt, and trap until the end of the nineteenth century, when craft sales and factory work became the most important economic activities. They also intermarried regularly with the French.

Other Hurons settled among tribes such as the Erie, who were themselves later destroyed by the Iroquois. Many were adopted by the victorious Iroquois nations. Some Hurons escaped to the west, where they joined with the Tionotati (Petun, or Tobacco Nation), a related tribe. Under continuing pressure from the Iroquois, they began wandering around the Michilimackinac–Green Bay region, where they hunted and remained active in the fur trade. Although never a large tribe, membership in various alliances allowed them to play an important role in regional affairs.

Jesuits continued to minister to these people, who migrated to Detroit around 1700. They split into pro-British (at Sandusky) and pro-French groups in the mid–eighteenth century. The latter group became known as the Wyandotte and claimed territory north of the Ohio River, where they allowed Shawnee and Lenápe bands to settle. Wyandottes fought the British in Pontiac's rebellion (1763).

Land cessions to non-natives began in 1745 and continued into the nineteenth century. Wyandottes sold their lands on the Canadian side of the Detroit River in 1790 in exchange for reserves, most of which were ceded in the early nineteenth century; the rest were allotted in severalty later in the century. These people sided with the British in the Revolutionary War and split their allegiance in the War of 1812.

Their land in Ohio and Michigan was recognized by the United States after the War of 1812, but the tribe ceded most of it by 1819. With the decline of the fur trade, many Wyandottes began farming and acculturating to non-native society. More land was ceded in 1832, and in 1842 the people had ceded all Ohio and Michigan lands and moved to the Indian Territory (Kansas), on land purchased from the Lenápe and on individual sections. During this period, the question of slavery increased factionalism among tribal members; some were slaveholders, whereas others were adamant abolitionists.

An 1855 treaty provided for land allotment (most allotments were soon alienated) and divided the tribe into citizens and noncitizens. Three years later, roughly 200 Wyandottes settled on the Seneca Reservation. The more traditional group (noncitizen) relocated to the new Indian Territory (Oklahoma) in 1867, after the Seneca-Cayuga agreed to donate part

of their reservation there. This reservation was allotted in 1893. The Wyandotte Tribe of Oklahoma was created in 1937. It was terminated in the 1950s but was rerecognized in 1978. The "citizen" group remained in Kansas, incorporating as the Wyandot Nation of Kansas in 1959.

Religion The Huron recognized an almost unlimited number of spirits and deities, the most powerful of which were the sun and sky. Dreams were considered important as foreshadowing good or evil. There were four types of annual religious feasts: prewar singing, the departure of a dying man, thanksgiving, and healing. Of these, the last were related to medicine societies. Women participated in several formal dances.

Disease was caused by wounds and other obvious causes as well as by witches and soul loss (psychological disturbance). Dreams were important in curing problems of the latter type; otherwise, curers used magic, dancing, and other spiritual methods. Every winter, a three-day ceremony in which people feigned madness was held. There were also three types of shamans: conjurers, who were associated with the weather; diviners, who foretold the future and found lost objects; and healers.

The Dance of the Fire, which involved physical contact with boiling water and hot stones or coals, was meant to attract the assistance of a curing spirit. The most important celebration was the Feast of the Dead, held every ten years or so. Relatives cleaned, rewrapped, and buried bones in a common tribal grave. Then they feasted and honored their ancestors' lives in story. This ceremony was accompanied by games, contests, and gift giving.

Government The tribes of the Huron Confederacy were led by a council of chiefs from each tribe. This council had no jurisdiction in purely local matters. The position of chief was inherited matrilineally, but within that context it was subject to merit criteria and a confirmation process.

Large villages were governed by clan civil and war chiefs. The chiefs' male relatives acted as their councilors. Decisions were taken by consensus and were not, strictly speaking, binding on individuals or, if a tribal-level decision, on villages.

Customs Generosity was highly valued: Stinginess could leave one open to charges of witchcraft, a capital offense. Constituent clan families were led by the senior mother. These women also selected the chiefs from within the appropriate families. Certain lineages within clans were more important than others; holding feasts was a means to achieve status.

Crimes against the body politic, such as witchcraft or treason, were punishable by death, but serious crimes like murder were subject to settlement, including compensation. Popular diversions included lacrosse and gambling games.

Premarital sexual relations, beginning shortly after puberty, were common and accepted, within certain clan restrictions. A couple need not marry in the eyes of society, but if they chose to, marriages were apparently monogamous. Both the couple and their parents had to approve a marriage. Divorce was unusual after children had been born. In such cases, the children probably remained with the mother.

Corpses, wrapped in furs, lay in state for several days, during which time people gave speeches and feasted. The body was then laid on a scaffold and a small hut built over it. Gifts (food and tools) were placed near the body to help the spirit in the afterworld, which was regarded as similar to the world of the living. A mourning period lasted a year, during which time a surviving spouse could not remarry. Every ten years or so the tribe held a feast of the dead (see "Religion").

Dwellings There were at least 18 villages in the early seventeenth century. Villages were located on high ground near waterways and woods. The larger ones were often palisaded with up to five rows of sharpened stakes. Public spaces were located between the longhouses. Larger villages had up to 100 longhouses and 2,000 people or more; the average size was perhaps 800 people. Villages were moved every 10 to 20 years, after the soil and/or firewood was exhausted.

The people built pole-frame, bark (elm, cedar, or ash) houses, 25–30 feet wide and high and about 100–150 (even up to 240) feet long. Roofs were vaulted with closable smoke holes. A center passageway divided the house. Sleeping platforms ran along the sides, but people slept on the floor near the fire in winter. Rush mats served as doors and floors.

There were both large central hearths and smaller cooking fires.

Each longhouse was home to 8–24 families, with an average of about six people per family. The longhouses tended to be smoky, and fleas and mice were particular pests. The larger house of chiefs also served as council/ceremonial houses. Villages were economically self-sufficient.

Diet Women grew corn, beans, squash, and sunflowers. Men may have grown some tobacco. Corn, the staple food, was eaten mainly as soup with some added foods. Women also gathered blueberries, nuts, and fruits as well as acorns in times of famine.

Men hunted deer, bear, numerous other large and small game, and fowl. Deer were hunted in part by driving them into rivers or enclosures where they were shot with the bow and arrow. Bear were occasionally trapped and then fattened for a year or two before being eaten for special feasts. Dog was also eaten. The people fished throughout the year for whitefish, catfish, pike, and other species. Other aquatic foods included clams, crabs, and turtles.

Key Technology The digging stick and an antler or bone hoe were the primary agricultural tools. Men hunted with bows and arrows, snares, and spears. Fishing equipment included bone hooks and harpoons as well as large (up to 1,200 feet long) nets woven from nettles. Women wove mats, baskets, and nets of Indian hemp, reeds, bark, and corn husks. They also made leather bags; these and the baskets were painted or decorated with porcupine quills. Men made wooden items such as utensils, bowls, and shields as well as stone or clay pipes and heavy stone tools such as axes. Pottery and wooden mortars were related to food preparation.

Trade Most people traded to acquire goods to give away and thus acquire status. The Huron were important traders even before the French arrived. They had a monopoly on corn and tobacco. They also dealt in furs and chert, wampum beads, dried berries, mats, fish, and hemp. Important trading partners included the Petun (tobacco) and northern Algonquian people. The Nipissing were also important trade partners; they traded fish and furs for Huron corn. Extensive trade routes took the Huron all over much of the eastern Great Lakes and the St. Lawrence River region and kept their society rich and stable.

Trade routes were owned or controlled by the people who had made them as well as by other members of their lineage. Intratribal use of the trails entailed payment of a fee. Intertribal use was prohibited. June through September was the main trading season, during which time most men were away from the villages. The people also imported gourds.

Notable Arts Pottery and twined bags were two important arts. The people also wove belts and other items from native fibers. Designs were mostly geometric. Moccasins and other items were embroidered or appliquéd with moose hair.

Transportation Rivers were navigated via birch-bark canoe. Most intervillage communication was overland.

Dress Women made clothing from buckskin. It consisted generally of shirts, breechclouts, leggings, skirts, and moccasins. Fur capes were added in winter. Clothing was decorated with fringe and brightly painted designs. Face painting and tattooing were popular, especially among men.

War and Weapons Hurons never achieved the kind of unity of purpose and command essential for defeating or even realistically engaging an enemy as powerful as the Iroquois. People fought mainly for blood revenge as well as to gain personal status. War chiefs usually organized and led raiding parties, which might include up to 600 men.

Most fighting was practiced by surprise attacks on small groups. The main Huron enemies were the Iroquois, especially the Seneca. Hurons were allied with local Algonquian groups, especially the Ottawa, as well as the Susquehannock. Weapons included the bow and arrow, war clubs, wooden shield, and rod armor. Captives were often ritually tortured and sometimes eaten. Some, especially women and children, might be adopted.

Contemporary Information

Government/Reservations The Wyandotte Tribe, Ottawa County, Oklahoma, is governed under a constitution that calls for a chief, elected officers, and a tribal council. The land base consists of 192 acres of land in addition to individual allotments.

The Wyandot Nation of Kansas (1959), formerly the "citizen" or "absentee" Wyandottes, is located near Kansas City.

Huron Village (Wendake), Quebec, Canada, consists of 67 hectares. There were about 1,000 residents in the mid-1990s, of a total population of about 2,600. The community is governed by a band council.

Economy A casino is planned in Kansas. Many people are integrated into the local economy.

In Canada, many people still make and sell crafts such as snowshoes, moccasins, and canoes. One Huron group operates a bed-and-breakfast. A museum draws tourists in summer. The local economy is extensive and provides jobs for hundreds of non-natives.

Legal Status The Wyandotte Tribe of Oklahoma is a federally recognized tribal entity. The Wyandot Nation of Kansas is state recognized and has petitioned for federal recognition. Quebec Hurons-Wendats are provincially and federally recognized.

Daily Life The tribe in Oklahoma provides several important services, including student scholarships and meals for the elderly. Facilities include housing, a tribal center, and a preschool. A museum and cultural center are planned. The people are working on identifying and preserving aspects of their cultural traditions.

Hurons of Lorette (Quebec) are all Catholic and part French. The Canadian National Railway bisects the reserve. Most Indians own property. Children attend school on the reserve through grade four. The reserve is similar to neighboring towns in Quebec. There is some effort to revive the native language. The artistic custom of moose-hair appliqué persisted here longer than in the south.

Chapter Nine

The Subarctic

Above left: A Carrier Indian fishes for salmon from a platform in the Hagwelet Canyon.
Above right: This Cree man is imitating a moose call with an old-style birchbark device to amplify the sound.

Right: Mrs. Zulin and her three children.
Far right: Dogrib moccasins, moosehide coat, and moosehide leggings.

Subarctic

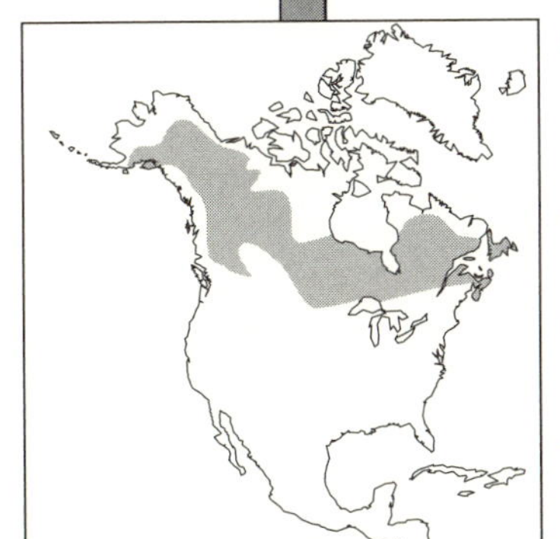

The vast Subarctic region stretches from the Atlantic Ocean in the east to the Rocky Mountains and the Alaska coast in the west and from the northern Great Lakes region and Great Plains to the tundra. Over two million square miles in area, the Subarctic is commonly divided into different geological zones, such as Canadian Shield (Hudson Bay and Mackenzie River lowlands), Cordillera (northern Rocky Mountain region), Alaska Plateau (central interior Alaska, including major river drainages), and Alaska Coast (primarily Cook Inlet and Copper River).

The boreal forest is the region's chief distinguishing physiographic feature. With the exceptions of birch and aspen, most trees, such as spruce, pine, fir, and tamarack, are conifers. There are thousands of streams and freshwater lakes, including Lake Winnipeg, Great Bear Lake, and Great Slave Lake, as well as Hudson Bay and coasts on two oceans. Low hills and rock outcroppings characterize much of the east. High mountains with glaciers, as well as plains, mark the far west. Major rivers include the Mackenzie, Peace, Churchill, Yukon, and Athabaska.

Despite its size and the variety of physical features, much of the region can be forbidding. Its continental climate is characterized by short, mild-to-hot summers (up to 38° Celsius/100° Fahrenheit) and long, bitterly cold winters (down to at least –38° Celsius/–100° Fahrenheit). Precipitation is generally low, except along the Alaska coast and in some mountain regions, and it falls mainly as snow. The short spring is marked by ice breakup and snow melt out as well as plagues of mosquitoes, black flies, and other insects. Travel is limited in spring and also during fall freeze up. Food, mainly in the form of game and fish, could be plentiful, but starvation was also a regular feature of life in the Subarctic.

Below: The Naskapi/Montagnais fashioned birch bark or animal skins into storage containers such as this one.

Native Americans of the Subarctic

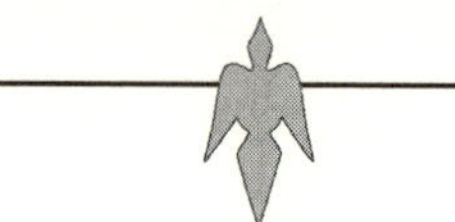

The sheer difficulty of living in the Subarctic accounts for its low aboriginal population. Probably no more than 100,000 people ever lived in the region at any one time. These hunter-gatherers spoke Athapaskan (mostly in the west) and Algonquian languages. Some southern groups blend almost imperceptibly into other cultural regions. For instance, the Anishinabe (Northern Ojibwa and Salteaux) are often discussed (as in this encyclopedia) with Northeast Indians, whereas Carrier and Chilcotin are sometimes grouped in the Plateau region. Alternatively, people such as the Shuswap, discussed in this book as Plateau Indians, are occasionally placed in the Subarctic region.

The arrival of non-natives—around 1500 in the extreme southeast and not until the nineteenth century in some western interior regions—affected Indian groups in different ways. Like Native Americans everywhere, however, all suffered sharp population losses. Most Subarctic Indians today mix Christianity, to different degrees, with significant elements of traditional belief and spirituality. Acculturation levels vary widely. Many people continue to hunt, fish, and trap, although giant hydroelectric and mining projects both claim and pollute the land. Contemporary Subarctic Indians still fight to regain their sovereignty. As people for whom traditions remain vital, they struggle to redefine their identities in the face of a global economy and culture that are increasingly part of their lives.

The first people entered the Subarctic region about the time that the frozen Bering Straits provided a land corridor between Asia and North America. This migration occurred at least 12,000 years ago but possibly as long as 25,000 or more years ago. Shallow lakes covered much of today's lowlands, and glacial ice persisted in some areas up to 7,000 years ago. On the other hand, southern grasslands and the boreal forest extended farther north than they do today, as did animal species like bison and caribou. Some of the earliest northwestern people used tools like stone microblades, which were straight-sided and flat. They probably had spears, snares, snowshoes, and canoes but not the bow and arrow.

Athapaskan speakers descend from a Northern Archaic culture that existed at least 6,000 years ago. About the same time, and over the next several thousand years, the Shield culture diverged in the east, as far as Labrador, from more ancient ones. Local technology changed only slowly until the first non-native influences arrived. People acquired the bow and arrow around 1,000 or perhaps 2,000 years ago. The Taltheilei tradition began about 2,600 years ago from Great Bear Lake to Lake Athabaska and the Churchill River.

The Laurel Culture of Manitoba and northern Ontario, characterized in part by a ceramic tradition acquired from the south, lasted from about 1000 B.C.E. to about 800 C.E. Laurel pots were coiled, impressed, incised, and then fired. Some were later painted red. Some people living in the extreme south built mounds over their dead. Later prehistoric cultures included the Selkirk and Blackduck Cree, who also made pottery, beginning about 1,500 years ago. Selkirk ceramics are fabric impressed.

Names of contemporary Indian tribes bear little relationship to aboriginal nomenclature or political organization. In general, the basic unit was the local group, which generally consisted of from 10 to 20 related people but could be up to 75 or so. Membership was fluid and nonbinding, in deference both to values of autonomy and the need for flexibility in a difficult environment. Leadership was extremely informal and nonauthoritarian, with the exception of those groups most influenced by Northwest Coast cultures. When conditions permitted, probably not quite every summer, local groups might come together as loosely constructed regional bands of several hundred people to socialize and renew family ties.

In parts of the Cordillera, the memorial potlatch was a major ceremonial event. Consisting of public celebration as well as ritual display of crests and distribution of wealth, it was used to enhance rank when the fur trade generated greater wealth. Even so, chiefs were recognized only among their own clan or lineage. Despite official opposition by non-natives in the nineteenth century, potlatches actually grew in importance.

Warfare was generally a local matter. Although some groups sought women, most people fought over revenge for trespass or a prior blood transgression. Warfare was better developed in the far west than in other regions. Weapons there included antler clubs

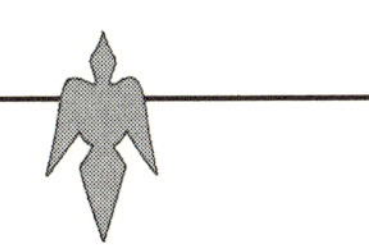

In this 1914 photo by Edward S. Curtis, strips of walrus and whale meat are shown hanging to dry after being smoked. Curtis's photographs often reflected his twin goals of documenting the aboriginal way of life and creating "art."

soaked in grease, armor, and spears as well as the bow and arrow. Nowhere did large, regional groups conduct full-scale wars.

Trade, which occurred at least as early as 10,000 years ago, provided a peaceful reason for travel and human interaction. Both goods and services, such as curing, were exchanged. Most material trade was in animal products. Northwest Coast peoples and Cordillerans exchanged animal products for marine products, including dentalium, salmon, and eulachon oil. Other trade goods included raw materials, such as birch bark, obsidian, copper, fused tuff, and manufactured goods, such as birch-bark containers, snowshoes, baskets, and clothing. Ancient trade also existed between Alaska and Asia. Except for the western Cordillera and Alaska Plateau, the existence of large, multitribal trade fairs remains a matter of speculation.

Religious conceptions and ceremonial innovation varied considerably throughout the Subarctic. Nearly everyone believed in the existence of various natural powers. In order to tap into those powers, they fasted, dreamed, and/or held vigils to attract guardian spirits, mainly animal related, that might provide individual assistance. Respect for all nature, especially animals and particularly food animals, was a key part of Subarctic religion and ceremonialism, as was a belief in reincarnation. Most groups had also formulated rich mythologies as well as conceptions of malevolent supernatural beings that were greatly to be feared.

Illness was generally associated with soul loss. Cures might be effected by shamans, men and/or women with particularly strong spirit powers. Shamans were also said to be able to find lost things, including game, and to foretell the future. Their

methods included scapulimancy, or looking at burn marks on an animal's shoulder blade, and communing with spirits in a shaking tent. Most people believed that shamans could also use their powers for ill.

Since the entire Subarctic is north of the limits of native agriculture, people fed themselves by hunting, fishing, and, to a variable extent, gathering berries and other plant foods. Unfortunately, many groups depended on a single species, such as moose or caribou, for the bulk of their diet. When game was plentiful this practice was not a problem, but since the population of key resources was subject to natural fluctuation, groups regularly suffered hunger and even starvation.

Caribou were often captured by means of large surrounds or corrals or were driven through fence systems into lakes, where they were shot. They were also stalked and snared, as were moose. In the extreme north, people brought firewood, tent stakes, and canoes out onto the Barren Grounds for the summer caribou hunt, thanks mainly to the strength and endurance of women. Fowl and smaller animals, such as hare, marmot, beaver, and muskrat, were also snared and shot. People caught fish with a variety of devices, depending on location, such as nets, traps, gaffs, hooks, and weirs. Coastal people relied also on sea mammals and shellfish. In the west, some groups, such as the Beaver, even hunted buffalo.

Subarctic natives generally used animal parts as well as wood, bark, roots, and stone (including, in some areas, native copper) as their raw materials. With a limited local tool kit, many groups borrowed liberally from neighbors, such as Northwest Coast Indians or Inuit. One key item, especially in the west, was babiche, or semisoftened rawhide. This material was used for everything from snares to netting to bowstrings. Although overland travel was preferred, the people did build bark canoes and, in some cases, moose-hide boats. They used bark, skin, or woven roots to make containers, including those that held water. In a successful effort to encourage certain microhabitats and environments, many Subarctic Indians also practiced controlled burning.

Shelter was remarkably homogeneous across the region. The most common type was the domed or conical lodge, consisting of poles covered with skins, boughs, or birch bark. Groups nearest Northwest Coast people built plank houses. Some northwestern groups built frame houses partially below the earth, using earth and moss as insulating materials, as well as bark-covered rectangular houses at fishing camps. Some groups used shelters with a double A-ridgepole framework and containing multiple fires. Drying racks, sweat houses, caches, menstrual huts, and other structures were also commonly built.

Women generally made the clothing, which came from moose, caribou, hare, or other skins, with trim of beaver or other fur. Winter items, such as parkas, hats, and mittens, were also made of fur. Hides were tanned, generally with brains or grease, and often dehaired. Many people wore leggings with attached moccasins. Clothing was variously decorated with fringe, paint, quills, claws, or down.

The general status of women varied according to local custom. Female infanticide was not unknown throughout much of the region. Women were generally subject to menstrual taboos, some quite rigorous. Some served essentially as pack animals while getting little to eat. On the other hand, benefiting from a general tradition of autonomy, some also attained both authority and power.

In this harsh climate, generosity and good humor were two key virtues. In most societies, newly married men were required to live with and serve their in-laws for a period of at least a year before establishing their own households. Descent was generally matrilineal, although this custom was neither important nor rigorously followed. Corpses were often cremated.

Indians living in the extreme east and southeast of the region may have encountered Vikings a thousand years ago. They certainly met Basques, Bretons, and other Europeans fishing in the Gulf of St. Lawrence around 1500. Indians of the interior Cordillera, however, did not actually encounter non-natives until the early to mid–nineteenth century, although items of non-native manufacture had reached them much earlier through aboriginal trade networks. The fur trade became the basis of interracial relations. The Hudson's Bay Company was chartered in 1670 and the Northwest Company in 1787. The two merged in 1821. Russian trade forts were founded in Alaska as early as the 1780s.

An Ahtna woman and her child. The most common type of subarctic shelter was the domed or conical lodge, consisting of poles covered with skins, boughs, or birch bark. The general status of women varied according to local custom. Some served essentially as pack animals while getting little to eat.

Throughout the region, the non-native presence profoundly affected Indians in several ways. Hitherto unknown diseases, such as smallpox, measles, scarlet fever, influenza, and syphilis, not to mention alcoholism and alcohol-related deaths, reduced populations by up to 90 percent or even 100 percent in some locations. Local economies slowly changed from subsistence to trade based, resulting in a decline in native manufacture and an accompanying loss of knowledge. A few more isolated groups rejected the attraction of trade, preferring to maintain their traditional patterns.

Another result of the non-native presence was increased hunger and poor nutrition, as big game dwindled in numbers and items such as white flour and refined sugar increasingly replaced healthy traditional foods. Social and political structures began to change as well in response to the demands of fur traders and, later, non-native governments. Especially in the nineteenth century, missionaries worked to eliminate native customs and beliefs and ultimately Christianized most Subarctic Indians, although, among many groups, traditional beliefs coexist with Christianity to varying degrees. Generosity, reciprocity, and autonomy were increasingly threatened by individualism and dependence.

Among the first actions of the Dominion of Canada (1867) was instituting federal control over

First Nations (as Indian bands are called in Canada). Under the various Indian Acts, the Canadian government required the election of band leaders; controlled Indian finances; undermined Indian religion and spirituality; and regulated Indians' movement, mobility, organizing abilities, and their very identity (for instance, Indian women who married non-natives officially lost their Indian "status"). The Indian departments were highly corrupt. Indian land was often alienated by methods that were quasi-legal at best.

The Canadian government signed 11 "numbered" treaties with Indian groups (with the general exception of those living in British Columbia and Yukon Territory) from 1871 to 1921. A common feature was the exchange of land rights for payments and other benefits. Informal groups of Indians accustomed to living near trading posts were officially recorded as fixed, legal bands with chiefs legitimized by the Canadian and U.S. governments. The treaties generally ignored the rights of Métis, or descendants of Indian–non-native unions. The federal and certain provincial governments fought over jurisdictional issues until 1927. Since the United States stopped treating with Indian groups after 1871, the question of land ownership in Alaska remained even nominally unresolved until well after the end of World War II.

By 1900, the numbers of missionaries, construction crews, miners, and other adventurers continued to grow. Railroads and steamboats reached isolated areas. Even groups that retained a nomadic lifestyle tended to congregate around the trading posts for Christian holidays. Indian groups began to use dog teams for winter transport. That development made trapping more efficient, but it also contributed to the sedentary lifestyle by increasing the need for fish (used as dog food). Although still few in number, there were growing job opportunities in industries such as transportation, mining, and forestry.

The 1940s were a watershed in Subarctic native history. The Alaska Highway was completed in 1943. It changed life dramatically for many natives, not least by ushering in a period of severe epidemics. Air service—for example, for medical treatment—to towns and even large cities became widely available. Educational opportunities as well as wide-ranging health and social services increased markedly. About the same time, fur prices collapsed. Seasonal trading post communities turned into permanent villages and towns. Native populations, after generally reaching their nadir in the 1920s, began to grow.

The post–World War II era has also been characterized by the creation of giant mining and hydroelectric projects. Inevitably, the interests of corporations and people have clashed, and the results have been ambiguous at best. For instance, the James Bay and Northern Quebec Agreement of the mid-1970s allowed the massive flooding of Cree lands. Although the people gained unprecedented (for the modern era) control over their internal affairs, they have had to cope with an equally unprecedented loss of territory, widespread pollution, and promises that remain unfulfilled.

Farther west, a proposed pipeline through Indian land spurred heightened consciousness and political unity. The Dene Nation successfully resisted that project and continues to fight for political sovereignty. In Alaska, the Alaska Federation of Natives was founded in 1966. That group was instrumental in passing the 1971 Alaska Native Claims Settlement Act, in which natives traded aboriginal rights for land and money. The people also agreed to subsume their political identities into local and regional corporations, the latter of which have tended to become enmired in legal entanglements. Some villages have Indian Reorganization Act–style governments, whereas others are incorporated or have reservation status. The eleven contemporary Alaskan Athapaskan groups are Ahtena, Han, Holikachuk, Ingalik (Deg Hit'an), Koyukon, Kutchin (Gwich'in), Tanacross, Tanaina (Dena'ina), Tanana, Upper Kuskokwim, and Upper Tanana.

The debates over Quebec independence and related constitutional issues have provided First Nations with an opportunity to press even more strongly for self-government. In fact, this goal has been achieved to a significant extent. Since the 1970s, for instance, schools, including curricula, have come increasingly under the control of local Indian organizations. In the 1980s, sections of the Indian Act dealing with federal control of band membership were repealed. At least in theory, native self-governance is now also the goal of the Canadian government.

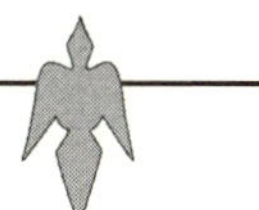

However, most federal policies are still taken without significant Indian input.

Today, some Subarctic Indians continue to trap, hunt, gather, and fish, although few remain long in the bush. Those who do often depend on snowmobiles and boats with outboard motors to get them where they need to go. Most live in towns and work for wages and/or receive government payments. Job opportunities remain limited. Many native languages survive, but despite efforts to slow or reverse the process, they are increasingly threatened. Electronic communication increasingly removes the younger generations from the world of their grandparents.

The statistical profile of Subarctic Indians shows high mortality rates, inadequate housing, health problems, and other ills. However, in many ways optimism and renewal are taking over. Native-owned businesses are on the rise. Substance-abuse programs are proliferating and are increasingly linked with successful and local social programs. Educational levels are rising sharply. On the crucial issue of sovereignty the people still have an uphill battle, but they are perhaps better prepared—and more willing—to wage that battle than they ever have been before.

Beaver

Beaver, from *Tsattine,* "dwellers among the beaver." Today the people refer to themselves as *Deneza* or *Dunne-za,* "Real People." They were culturally similar to the Chipewyan and Sekani.

Location Traditional Beaver territory (in the mid–eighteenth century) is the prairies south of the Peace River and east of the Rocky Mountains and on the upper Peace River (present-day Alberta and British Columbia). They may once also have lived in the Lake Claire area and the upper parts of the Athapaska River.

Population The Beaver population may have been between 1,000 and 1,500 in the seventeenth century. In 1990 there were approximately 800 officially recognized Beaver Indians.

Language The Beaver people speak a Northern Athapaskan language.

Historical Information

History Ancestors of the Beaver were in their historical territory 10,000 years ago. The Beaver and Sekani people may once have been united. By the mid–eighteenth century, Cree Indians, armed with guns, had confined the Beaver to the Peace River basin. At that time, eastern Beaver groups joined the Cree, adopting many of their customs and habits, while western groups moved farther up the Peace River, toward the eastern slopes of the Rocky Mountains. The Sarcee probably branched off from the Beaver about that time as well.

In 1799, the leader Makenunatane (Swan Chief) sought to attract both missionaries and a trading post. The people became more and more involved in the fur trade during the nineteenth century. Catholic missionaries arrived around 1845; most people had accepted Catholicism by about 1900, although many retained a core of their former religious ideas.

Although they had been obtaining arms and other items of non-native manufacture for years, direct contact between the people and non-native traders occurred only in 1876. New foods were introduced, and for the first time the subsistence activities of the people were fundamentally altered. Since some of the Peace River area was arable, non-native farmers began displacing the people as early as the 1890s. The Beaver signed Treaty 8 with Canada in 1899, under which the Indians accepted reserves but retained extensive subsistence rights. Canadian officials began appointing nominal chiefs after that.

In the early twentieth century, some Beaver were raising horses and trapping for a living. By 1930, non-native farmers had settled much of their territory. Construction of the Alaska Highway in the early 1940s disrupted the nomadic life of the last traditional Beaver bands. Oil and gas became major regional industries in the 1950s and 1960s.

Religion A well-defined cosmology and mythology were intimately connected with vision quests. Young people fasted to acquire guardian spirits, mainly in dreams. Various food and behavioral taboos, as well as songs and medicine bundles, were associated with a particular animal spirit. The people recognized a spiritual connection between people and animals, with the latter entitled to respect on an equal level with people.

The most important festival took place twice a year and involved the fire sacrifice of food to ensure continued bounty. Dreamers, or prophets—people in touch through dreams with the past and future—had special powers. Shamans were those who had acquired especially powerful guardian spirits. They cured by singing, blowing, and sucking illness-linked objects from the body.

Government Three or four independent bands had their own hunting areas and leaders. Leadership was based on skill and knowledge, which was in turn gained partly through experience and partly through dreaming. Bands were composed of hunting groups of roughly 30 people; the size and composition of the bands were variable. Groups grew in size during summer and broke into constituent parts in winter and early spring.

Customs Bands occasionally came together in summer to socialize. Festivities consisted in part of group singing and dancing around a fire, during which seating was ritually regulated. The people established a well-defined and close kinship system within which everyone was related on some level. Hunters fed the entire camp based on need. People slept facing east.

Men might have more than one wife. Newlyweds lived with the woman's family and served her parents for a period of time, but descent was patriarchal. Corpses were placed on birch-bark strips and buried in tree scaffolds or on platforms. Mourners gave away their possessions and grieved loudly and publicly. Men often cut their bodies and went to war; women cut their hair as well as part of a finger.

Dwellings The typical dwelling was a three-pole conical moose- or caribou-skin tipi. There were also winter lodges of logs covered with moss and earth. In summer, people mainly lived in conical brush shelters or simple lean-tos.

Diet The Beaver were basically nomadic hunters of moose, caribou, beaver, and other animals. Men drove buffalo into enclosures as late as the early nineteenth century. Fish were not an important part of the diet except in emergencies. People also snared smaller animals, such as rabbits, and women gathered berries and other plant food.

Key Technology Food was often hot-rock boiled in containers of spruce or birch bark or woven spruce roots. Bags were generally made of moose and caribou skins. Bark containers were important as well. Arrowheads were mostly flint, as were knife blades, although people also used moose horn or beaver teeth for this purpose. Fish were caught with rawhide (babiche) line and bone hook, nets, and stone weirs. Hunters used cone-shaped calls to summon moose. Food was served on birch-bark dishes. In order to encourage certain plants and animals, people regularly burned parts of the prairie.

Trade Favorite trade locations included Vermilion and the mouth of the Smoky River. Trade partners included the Chipewyan, Slavey, Sekani, and Cree. Buffalo products were a main trade item. In general, the Beaver did not particularly focus on acquiring material goods.

Notable Arts The relation of oral tradition was taken very seriously and considered a fine art. Clothing was decorated with porcupine-quill embroidery. The people also made fine bark containers.

Transportation Women drew toboggans before the advent of dog power in the twentieth century. People traveled in spruce-bark and birch-bark canoes as well as on snowshoes.

Dress Women made most clothing from moose skin. Clothing consisted of shirts, leggings, fur-lined moccasins, and a knee-length coat. Men added breechclouts after being influenced by the Cree. Women sometimes wore a short apron.

Items of personal adornment included horn and bone bracelets. Hunters wore grizzly bear claws around their necks. Both sexes painted their bodies and wore marmot or hare robes, caps, and mittens in winter.

War and Weapons Weapons were spears and the bow and arrow. The Sekani were occasional enemies, as were the Cree.

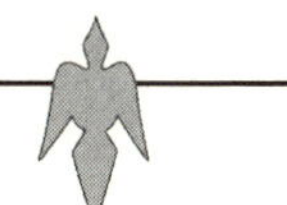

Contemporary Information

Government/Reservations The Blueberry River (formerly Fort St. John) Band owns two reserves with a total land area of 1,148 hectares. There were 263 members in the mid-1990s, of whom 151 lived on the reserves. The band is affiliated with the Treaty Eight Tribal Council. A chief and councilors are elected according to provisions of the Indian Act.

The Doig River (formerly Fort St. John) Band owns two reserves with a total land area of 1,348 hectares. There were 195 members in the mid-1990s, of whom 94 lived on the reserves. The band is affiliated with the Treaty Eight Tribal Council. A chief and councilors are elected according to provisions of the Indian Act.

The Halfway River Band owns one reserve with a total land area of 3,989 hectares. Band membership in the mid-1990s was 184, of whom 145 lived on the reserves. A chief and councilors are elected according to provisions of the Indian Act. The band is affiliated with the Treaty Eight Tribal Council.

The West Moberly First Nations (formerly part of Hudson Hope Band) own one reserve with a total land area of 2,034 hectares. Band membership in the mid-1990s was 116, of whom 69 lived on the reserves. A chief and councilors are elected according to custom. The band is affiliated with the Treaty Eight Tribal Council.

The Saulteau First Nation (Beaver and Cree) owns one reserve with a total land area of 3,026 hectares. Band membership in the mid-1990s was 628, of whom 325 lived on the reserve. A chief and councilors are elected according to custom. The band is affiliated with the Treaty Eight Tribal Council.

Other reserve communities include Clear Hills, Horse Lakes, Child Lake, and Boyer, all in Alberta. The local town is Fort St. John, British Columbia.

Economy There is minimal hunting and trapping, but some people work as guides and maintaining roads. At Doig River there is farming and cattle raising, fire fighting, trapping, and road maintenance. At Halfway River there is seasonal work, farming, trapping, guiding, forestry, and fire fighting. West Moberly offers logging, trapping, and a backhoe business, and at Saulteau there is a cattle ranch and farm, forestry, and a gravel operation.

Legal Status The bands listed under "Government/Reservations" are provincially and federally recognized. Legal action continues on Canada's attempt to remove a key parcel of land from Beaver control.

Daily Life The ancient prophet tradition has waned in recent years, although dreamers' songs remain the basis for much ceremonialism as well as an important part of the summer gatherings known as Treaty 8 Days. The Alaska and Mackenzie Highway has separated the Beavers of Alberta and British Columbia from one another. Most younger people are literate in English, although Beaver remains the first language for most.

Effective rule by Indian agents came to an end in the 1980s, when the people began to administer their own affairs through such organizations as the Treaty Eight Tribal Association. Children attend band and/or provincial and/or private schools. Most people have high school educations. In general, housing and social services are considered adequate.

Blueberry River Band facilities include a cultural center, a drop-in center, offices, and a school. Doig River facilities include offices, a community hall, a store, a kindergarten, and a garage. Halfway River facilities include offices, a community hall, a school, and a store. West Moberly facilities include offices and a community center. Saulteau's facilities include offices, a community hall, and a healing center.

Carrier

Carrier, from the French *Porteur,* originally from a Sekani word referring to the custom among certain bands for widows to carry their dead husbands' bones on their backs in a birch-bark container. They called themselves *Takulli* ("People Who Go upon the Water") in the nineteenth century, apparently a word given to them from without. The people usually refer to themselves by the subtribe or band name.

The Carrier were strongly influenced by Northwest Coast tribes and were culturally similar to the Sekani and the Chilcotin. They are sometimes located by anthropologists in the Plateau culture area (see Chapter 5).

Location Carrier territory is the region of Eutsuk, Francis, Babine, and Stuart Lakes and the upper Skeena and Fraser Rivers in north-central British Columbia.

Population From perhaps 8,500 in the late eighteenth century, the Carrier population in the mid-1990s stood at about 9,800.

Language Carriers spoke dialects (lower, central, and upper) of a northern Athapaskan language.

Historical Information

History The Carrier may have originated east of the Rocky Mountains and were probably in their historic location for at least several centuries before contact with non-natives. Major epidemics began in the late eighteenth century, about the time they met the Scotch trader and explorer Alexander Mackenzie (1793).

Beginning in the late eighteenth century, the Carrier began to acquire iron and other items of non-native manufacture, first through coastal intermediaries such as the Gitksan (north) and Bella Coola (south) and then directly. With the growing value of interior animal (beaver, marten, and lynx) pelts, Carrier wealth increased with their ability to export these products. Carrier control of some local trade networks in the early nineteenth century allowed some chiefs to amass wealth and power. Some high-ranking people began to intermarry with Bella Coola and Gitksan families around this time, as Northwest Coast cultural influences became much more pronounced.

The first local trade fort (James) was built in 1806 at Stuart Lake. A quasi-Christian prophet movement arose among the Carrier beginning in the 1830s. An entire band was exterminated by smallpox in 1837. Catholic missionaries arrived in the 1840s. Penetration by miners, farmers, and ranchers from the mid–nineteenth century on led to increased disease and general problems for the Indians.

Another ramification of increased contact was the decline of the potlatching complex. Retention of material goods became more important than status gained by giving them away. Also, there was a growing need to accumulate items of non-native manufacture just to survive, so giving them away became difficult. The Catholic church also worked to eliminate potlatching

Wage work, such as ranch, guide, cannery, sawmill, and construction work, began to take the place of traditional subsistence activities. The Carrier were prevented by law from preempting land after 1866. The Canadian Pacific Railway, completed in 1885, bisects Carrier territory. Most reserves were created in the later nineteenth century, although additional ones were established in the early twentieth century. Subsistence activities were increasingly government regulated by then.

Another railway line, completed in 1914, led to an influx of settlers and speculators. Commercial mining and lumbering began in the early twentieth century. Lumbering, including clear-cutting, expanded sharply after World War II. In the 1970s, the Carrier began organizing politically over the chronically unresolved issues of native land title and rights.

Religion Traditional religious belief may have included recognition of a supreme deity in the sky. Most important were a host of supernatural beings, mostly animal based, with whom the people tried to communicate through fasting and dreams. Through their rituals, the people sought to gain the favor and power of these spiritual beings. The people also believed in life after death, perhaps in a land to the west. Some especially Tsimshian-influenced groups adopted a secret cannibal society.

Young men fasted and dreamed in remote places in an effort to attract a guardian spirit protector (optional in southern regions). Those with special power became shamans. These people could cure illness, although they themselves might be killed if a patient died. Shamans could also retrieve lost souls and forecast the future. Their gear included carved wooden masks, wood rattles, grizzly bear claw and beaver tooth necklaces, and cloaks.

Government Each of roughly 15 independent subtribes/regional bands was composed of one or more villages/local bands. The subtribes were associated with specific subsistence areas. In the south, leaders were heads of extended families who acted as

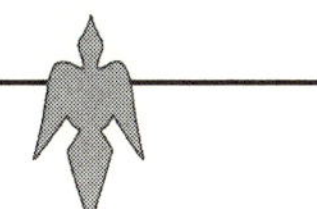

spokesmen and subsistence coordinators. Shamans were also politically important in the south.

Roughly 20 hereditary matrilineal clans were the most important political unit in central and northern areas. They were divided into houses, which had hereditary chiefs who supervised subsistence areas, provided for the poor, and represented clan interests in councils.

Hereditary chiefs of up to five larger divisions came from constituent clans. These people controlled the various subsistence areas within the division and settled disputes. Hereditary village chiefs were leaders of the most important divisions. They consulted other leaders, such as the clan leaders within their division and the other divisional chiefs, before making important decisions.

Customs Society was divided into ranked, hereditary social classes of nobles, commoners, and a few slaves. Depending on specific location, descent could be through the mother's or father's line. Except on the Tsimshian border, commoners had the possibility of obtaining sufficient goods to give potlatches and attain the noble rank. The nobility had crests and defined privileges, such as specific seating at dances or the right to recount certain stories. Crests were displayed on totem poles, houses, and regalia. Crests, titles, and honors were considered clan property and could usually be bought and sold. These customs varied according to geographical location and the customs of neighboring tribes.

Trespass was considered a serious offense, but chiefs could often work out an arrangement or decide on appropriate compensation. The extended family was the main social and economic unit. Several related families made up a band, which might have one or more villages.

Potlatching occurred in the north. Feasts were given and presents distributed at important life-cycle events. The installation of a new chief was considered the most important occasion of all, requiring numerous potlatches. The entire potlatch complex became especially important from the late eighteenth century through the late nineteenth century.

Women were responsible for most domestic tasks, such as carrying water and firewood, cooking, tanning skins, and sewing clothing. Men made houses, tools, and weapons; fought; and acquired animal foods. Women gave birth in a specially constructed hut assisted by their husbands and/or other women. Names were taken from a hereditary stock, if available, or from dreams if not.

At adolescence, boys were encouraged to increase their level of physical activity, whereas girls were secluded and their activity restricted for up to two years. They were subject to numerous food and behavioral taboos and were considered marriageable after the end of their seclusion. Young women selected a mate with their parents' assistance. The couple was engaged after the man gave valuable items to his prospective mother-in-law and married after the couple spent the night together at a later date. They lived with the woman's parents for up to a year while the new husband helped provide for his new in-laws.

Corpses were cremated. Widows were expected to hold their husband's burning body for as long as they could. In the east, women carried the charred bones of their husbands on their backs for several years.

Dwellings Semipermanent villages served as bases for hunting and fishing expeditions. Rectangular winter houses were built of pole frames covered with spruce bark. Gabled roofs extended to the ground. These houses held several families. Some southern groups built underground winter lodges similar to those of the Chilcotin and Shuswap.

Summer houses had low, plank walls and plank or bark gabled roofs. Some high-status men carved their crests into house pillars. Chiefs and their extended families lived in particularly large, semicommunal houses. There were also specialty menstrual, fishing, sweat, and smoking structures.

Diet Fish, especially salmon, was perhaps the most important item in the diet, although this was less true in the south. People fished through the ice for carp and other species. Fish was smoke dried and cached. Before the snow fell, men hunted caribou, mountain goats, and bear as well as smaller game such as beaver, marmot, and hare. Women gathered a number of roots, bulbs, greens, and berries.

Key Technology Cooking vessels were made of birch bark. To capture animals, men used bows with sinew

A Carrier Indian fishes for salmon from a platform in the Hagwelet Canyon in 1927. Salmon was a mainstay in the Carrier diet.

strings; babiche nets; several types of snares, some strong enough to capture big game; and deadfalls. Caribou were also driven along fences into corrals. People fished using weirs, traps, wooden rakes, willow and alder bark and nettle-fiber nets, hooks, and harpoons. Wood was an important raw material, as were bone and hide. Pestles and axes were among the few stone tools. Fire was made with the fire drill.

Trade Important trade partners included the Gitksan and Bella Coola. The Carrier imported woven baskets from the Bella Coola, Chilcotin, and Shuswap; Chilkat blankets, cedar boxes, and stone labrets from the Tsimshian; and wooden cooking boxes, eulachon oil, shell ornaments, and copper bracelets from other coast tribes. There was also some intratribal trade. The people mainly exported prepared hides and furs.

Notable Arts Crests were carved, painted, and tattooed on house posts, graves, clothing, and bodies. Some groups erected totem poles.

Transportation Men made spruce- and birch-bark canoes as well as cottonwood dugouts. Goods were carried overland with the help of tumpline and backpacks. Snowshoes and toboggans arrived with the non-natives.

Dress Skin clothing consisted of robes, leggings, and moccasins, with fur caps and mittens added in colder weather. In warm weather, men sometimes went naked; women wore a knee-length apron. High-status men wore Chilkat blankets for special occasions, and similarly ranked northern women wore wooden labrets in their mouths. Other ornaments were made of dentalium, bone, and haliotis shell.

War and Weapons Weapons included the bow and arrow, spear, club, and knife. Some groups had "armor" made of wooden slats or moose hide covered with small pebbles; others used oval shields and a bow "bayonet."

Contemporary Information

Government/Reservations The Broman Lake Band owns 11 reserves with a total land area of 620 hectares. There were 144 members in the mid-1990s, of whom 69 lived on the reserves. A chief and councilors are elected according to custom. The band is affiliated with the Carrier-Sekani Tribal Council.

The Burns Lake Band owns four reserves with a total land area of about 170 hectares. Band population was 72 in the mid-1990s, of whom 25 lived on the reserves. A chief and councilors are elected according to provisions of the Indian Act. The band is affiliated with the Carrier-Sekani Tribal Council.

The Cheslatta Carrier Nation owns eight reserves with a total land area of 1,403 hectares. Population was 218 in the mid-1990s, 89 of whom lived on the reserves. A chief and councilors are elected according to custom. The nation is affiliated with the Carrier-Sekani Tribal Council.

The Hagwilget Band owns two reserves with a total land area of 168.8 hectares. Population was 575 in the mid-1990s, of whom 207 lived on the reserves. A chief and councilors are elected according to provisions of the Indian Act. The band is affiliated with the Gitksan Wet'suwet'en Local Services Society.

The Kluskus Band owns 17 reserves with a total land area of 1,653 hectares. Population was 150 in the mid-1990s, of whom 68 lived on the reserves. A chief and councilors are elected according to custom. The band is affiliated with the Carrier-Chilcotin Tribal Council.

The Moricetown Band population was 1,437 in the mid-1990s, of whom 674 lived on the reserves. A chief and councilors are elected according to provisions of the Indian Act. The band is affiliated with the Gitksan Wet'suwet'en Local Services Society.

The Nadleh Whuten (formerly Fraser Lake) Band owns seven reserves with a total land area of 966 hectares. Population was 338 in the mid-1990s, of whom 197 lived on the reserves. A chief and councilors are elected according to provisions of the Indian Act. The band is affiliated with the Carrier-Sekani Tribal Council.

The Nak'azdli (formerly Necoslie) Band owns 16 reserves with a total land area of 1,460 hectares. Population was 1,333 in the mid-1990s, of whom 545 lived on the reserves. A chief and councilors are elected according to custom. The band is affiliated with the Carrier-Sekani Tribal Council.

The Nazko Band owns 18 reserves with a total land area of 1,844 hectares. Population was 261 in the mid-1990s, of whom 232 lived on the reserves. A chief and councilors are elected according to provisions of the Indian Act. The band is affiliated with the Carrier-Chilcotin Tribal Council.

The Nee-tahi-buhn (Moricetown) Band owns seven reserves with a total land area of 1,421 hectares. Population was 192 in the mid-1990s, of whom 66 lived on the reserves. A chief and councilors are elected according to custom. The band is affiliated with the Gitksan Wet'suwet'en Local Services Society.

The Red Bluff (formerly Quesnel) Band owns four reserves with a total land area of 683 hectares. Population was 109 in the mid-1990s, of whom 58 lived on the reserves. A chief and councilors are elected according to provisions of the Indian Act. The band is affiliated with the Carrier-Chilcotin Tribal Council.

The Stellat'en First Nation owns two reserves with a total land area of 834 hectares. Population was 297 in the mid-1990s, of whom 196 lived on the reserves. A chief and councilors are elected according to custom. The band is affiliated with the Carrier-Sekani Tribal Council.

The Stony Creek Band owns ten reserves with a total land area of 3,236 hectares. Population was 706 in the mid-1990s, of whom 433 lived on the reserves. A chief and councilors are elected according to provisions of the Indian Act. The band is affiliated with the Carrier-Sekani Tribal Council.

The Takla Lake Band owns 17 reserves with a total land area of 807 hectares. Population was 496 in the mid-1990s, of whom 254 lived on the reserves. A chief and councilors are elected according to custom.

The Tl'azt'en Nations owns 19 reserves with a total land area of 2,277 hectares. Population was 1,343 in the mid-1990s, of whom 922 lived on the reserves. A chief and councilors are elected according to custom. The band is affiliated with the Carrier-Sekani Tribal Council.

The Ulkatcho Band owns 20 reserves with a total land area of 3,213 hectares. Population was 683 in the mid-1990s, of whom 513 lived on the reserves. A chief and councilors are elected according to custom. The band is affiliated with the Carrier-Chilcotin Tribal Council.

Economy Although fish and game have become much scarcer in recent years, there is still some trapping, fishing, and hunting and also some small farming. Pollution has spawned some opposition to the lumbering industry in spite of employment possibilities. There is also some railroad work and spot and seasonal work in local industries such as ranching, fisheries, and tourism. There are some small businesses. People also avail themselves of government assistance.

Legal Status The bands listed under "Government/ Reservations" are federally recognized tribal entities.

Daily Life Most Carriers today live in individual houses. Many still speak Carrier. Clans exist today, especially among northern and central groups, although they are vastly less important than they used to be. Potlatch privileges and responsibilities are rarely observed except among those groups nearest the Tsimshian people. Most people are Christian, at least nominally, although ancient beliefs linger as well, including the power of dreams and the efficacy of shamans. Children attend band and/or provincial and/or private schools.

Local anti-Indian sentiment remains deeply entrenched. Carrier bands along the Nechako River have strongly opposed the completion of a hydroelectric project, the initial stages of which created forced relocations and other hardships for the people beginning in the 1950s. Struggles also continue over issues such as land title and rights. One example is the development of the so-called Mackenzie Grease Trail, which continues against Indian wishes and portrays them (when they are not ignored entirely) as little more than tourist attractions. Members of the Cheslatta Nation are negotiating with Alcan Aluminum for unflooded portions of their former reserves.

Band facilities include offices and a community center (Broman Lake); offices (Burns Lake); offices, workshops, and a recreation hall (Cheslatta); offices, a community hall, a clinic, a nursery school, and a fire station (Hagwilget); a school (Kluskus); offices, a maintenance yard, a community hall, a fire station, a recreation center, a clinic, a school, and a store (Moricetown); offices, a school, a store, and a

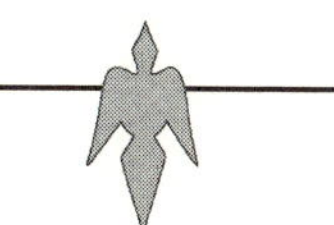

community hall (Nadleh Whuten); offices, a gymnasium, a school, a garage, and a crafts store (Nak'azdli); offices, a community hall, a workshop, a warehouse, and a nursery school (Nazko); offices, a community hall, a wood shop, and a fishery research station (Nee-tahi-buhn); offices, a barn, and a store (Red Bluff); offices and a community hall (Stallat'en); a store, a cultural center, a school, offices, a community hall, and elders' and adult centers (Stony Creek); offices, a community hall, a clinic, and an elders' center (Takla Lake); schools, clinics, offices, and a community hall (Tl'azt'en Nations); and offices, a store, a dormitory, and a school (Ulkatcho).

Chilcotin

Chilcotin (`Tsil kō tə n), "inhabitants of Young Man's River." The Chilcotin were culturally related to the Carrier, the interior Salish tribes, the Bella Coola, and the Kwakiutl. They are occasionally classified among Plateau groups.

Location The territory of the Chilcotin is along the headwaters of the Chilcotin River and the Anahim Lake district and from the Coast Range to near the Fraser River, British Columbia.

Population The Chilcotin population stood at approximately 1,500 in the seventeenth century. It increased to possibly 3,500 in the late eighteenth century. There were about 500 Chilcotins in the mid-1990s.

Language Chilcotin is an Northern Athapaskan language.

Historical Information

History Chilcotins first encountered non-natives in either 1793 or 1815. Fort Alexandria, a trading post, was established in 1821. A gold strike around the Fraser River around 1860 led to the large-scale invasion of Indian lands and widespread destruction of resources, with no compensation. Indian villages and even graves were looted by the newcomers.

There was a serious smallpox epidemic in about 1862. Chilcotins sent out war parties to attack road builders. Several warriors, including Chiefs Tellot, Elexis, and Klatsassin, were captured and hanged. After the epidemics and the fighting, many survivors worked on non-native–owned ranches, since Indians were explicitly excluded from preempting land, and much of their land was confiscated.

Missionaries helped established villages that became reserves. They also significantly influenced the selection of chiefs, or headmen. Some groups merged with the Shuswap and Carrier on the Fraser River at that time. Most were located on three reserves by 1900 and were largely acculturated. "Stonies," or Stone Chilcotin bands, remained semitraditional in the western mountains. In the early twentieth century, most people hayed and/or sold a few head of cattle or some furs for a living. There was little contact with the outside world until the 1960s.

Religion Boys, and girls to some extent, went into seclusion at adolescence to acquire a guardian spirit. Spirits could be any natural phenomenon and gave the person songs and dances as well as protective power. A person who acquired many spirits might become a shaman and engage in curing and seeing what most people could not.

Shamans could use their power for evil as well as good, although evil against an individual was generally considered to be practiced only for the general good. Illnesses that were not soul related were treated by medical specialists. Souls were said to be capable of leaving the body.

Government Three or four autonomous bands were each composed of camp groups. Bands were defined as people sharing a wintering territory. There was no overall leadership, and the people never came or acted together.

Customs Bands were divided into social classes of nobles, commoners, and slaves. Nobles and commoners were arranged into clans, the most powerful of which was Raven. Descent was bilateral.

Although sharing was highly valued, some people accumulated more material goods than did others. In those cases, the surplus was generally given away—effectively exchanged for prestige—in feasts. High rank was obtained by giving potlatches. When a

As with many Native American tribes, material goods became evenly distributed through potlatch ceremonies. Here, oxen meat is being prepared in anticipation of a potlatch in 1924.

member of the nobility died, clans gave large potlatches, at which they gave away most of his possessions.

Early adolescence was a time for adult training. Boys focused on endurance and survival skills. Girls were isolated during their first menstrual period, at which time they observed several behavioral restrictions and performed domestic tasks. Marriage occurred shortly after this adult training. Most marriages were arranged by parents with input from the children.

Women generally did all the camp work; men were responsible for getting animal foods, fighting, and making tools. The dead were buried in the ground, cremated, or simply left under a pile of rocks or branches. People amused themselves by playing bone and dice games, snowsnake (sliding a spear along a trench in the snow for distance), ring and arrow, and athletic contests. Social control was largely internalized. Extreme violators were ostracized or, rarely, killed.

Dwellings People generally lived in rectangular, pole-framed, earth-covered lodges with bark or brush walls and gable roofs. An open space at the top served as a smoke hole. There were also small, subterranean winter houses and dome-shaped sweat houses.

Diet Men hunted a variety of animals including caribou, elk, mountain goat, sheep, and sometimes bear. Smaller animals like marmots, beaver, and rabbits were trapped, as were fowl. Men and women caught fish such as trout, whitefish, and salmon. Women gathered camas and other roots as well a variety of berries.

Key Technology Baskets and water containers were made primarily of birch bark. Women wove rush mats

and learned from the Shuswap to make coiled baskets. Fish were taken using a variety of nets and spears. Hunting equipment included the bow and arrow and stone-tipped spear. A digging stick helped women to gather camas and other roots. Food-related equipment included horn spoons, bone knives, and wooden pestles. Other tools, such as scrapers, adzes, and awls, were made mainly of bone and stone. The people also had the fire drill and made drums and flutes.

Trade Chilcotins acquired salmon from the Shuswap and Bella Coola. They also imported shell ornaments, cedar-bark headbands, wooden containers, and stone pestles from the Bella Coola. They sent dried berries, paints, and furs to the Bella Coola and furs, dentalium shells, and goat-hair blankets woven by the Bella Coola to other tribes. Snowshoes were exported in the later historical period.

Notable Arts The people made fine coiled basketry with designs of humans and animals as well as geometric shapes.

Transportation Although most travel was overland, men carved spruce-bark and dugout canoes, some with pointed prows like those of the interior Salish. Snowshoes were used for winter travel. Goods were carried in skin sacks with tumplines.

Dress Dress generally consisted of moccasins, buckskin aprons, belts, and leggings. Cold-weather gear included caps; robes of marmot, hare, or beaver; and woven wool and fur blankets. Men's hair was generally no longer than shoulder length, although women grew their hair long and often wore it in two braids. The people used a number of personal ornaments of bone, shell, teeth, and claws. Both men and women painted or tattooed their faces and greased their bodies, face, and hair in cold, windy weather.

War and Weapons Weapons included clubs with stone heads, the bow and arrow, spears, and daggers. There was some use of hide or slat armor. Chilcotin enemies included the Carrier and Shuswap, although there was much friendly intercourse as well with these groups. Trespass was a reason to fight, as were murder and feuding. Fighters wore red and black face paint. Ritual purification, including vomiting, took place after a raid. Those who had killed lived apart from others for a time.

Contemporary Information

Government/Reservations The Alexandria Band owns 13 reserves with a total of 1,142 hectares of land. Band population in the mid-1990s was 135, with 59 living on reserves. The band is affiliated with the Ts'ilhqot'in Tribal Council. A chief and councilors are elected according to provisions of the Indian Act.

The Alexis Creek Tribal Government owns 37 reserves on almost 4,000 hectares of land. Band population in the mid-1990s was 496, with 345 living

Mrs. Sam Zulin and her three children, pictured in 1924 while visiting Bella Coola, British Columbia.

Westernmost Chilcotin Indians at breakfast at a temporary camp while visiting Bella Coola, British Columbia, in 1924.

on reserves. A chief and councilors are elected according to provisions of the Indian Act.

The Stone Band owns five reserves on 2,146 hectares of land. Band population in the mid-1990s was 304, with 189 living on reserves. A chief and councilors are elected according to provisions of the Indian Act. The band is affiliated with the Ts'ilhqot'in National Government.

The Tl'etinqox-t'in Government (formerly the Anaham Band) owns 19 reserves on 5,656 hectares of land. Band population in the mid-1990s was 1,111, with 599 living on reserves. A chief and councilors are elected according to provisions of the Indian Act. The band is affiliated with the Ts'ilhqot'in National Government.

The Toosey Band owns four reserves on 2,582 hectares of land. Band population in the mid-1990s was 201, with 95 living on reserves. A chief and councilors are elected according to provisions of the Indian Act. The band is affiliated with the Carrier-Chilcotin Tribal Council.

The Xeni Gwet'in First Nations Government (formerly the Neneiah Valley Band) owns eight reserves on 1,383 hectares of land. Band population in the mid-1990s was 350, with 259 living on reserves. A chief and councilors are elected according to custom. The band is affiliated with the Ts'ilhqot'in National Government.

Economy The following are important economic activities for the band members: Alexandria Band—farming and forestry; Alexis Creek and Stone Bands—farming, cattle, ranching, and forestry; Tl'etinqox-t'in Government and Xeni Gwet'in First Nations Government—farming, cattle ranching, and trapping; Toosey Band—individual farming and cattle ranching, a heavy equipment company, and trapping.

Legal Status The bands listed under "Government/Reservations" are recognized by Canada.

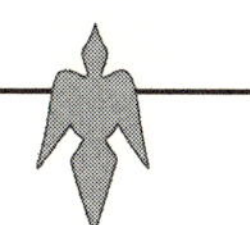

Daily Life The westernmost people still cross the mountains to visit the Bella Coola. Public lands containing natural resources from which Chilcotins traditionally derived subsistence have steadily decreased since the 1960s. Children attend various band and/or provincial and/or private schools. Band facilities include an office (Alexandria Band); offices, a community hall, warehouses, and schools (Alexis Creek Band); a community center, schools, offices, and a fire station (Stone Band); offices, a community hall, schools, a carpentry building, and the Native Law Center (Tl'etinqox-t'in Government); offices, a community hall, a fire station, and a machine shed (Toosey Band); and offices, a community hall, and a rodeo field (Xeni Gwet'in).

Chipewyan

Chipewyan (Chi pu `wī an), "pointed skins," from the Cree word *chipwayanewok,* referring to a style of drying beaver skins that left shirts pointed at the bottom. Their self-designation was *Dene,* "the People." Geographical divisions included the Athabaska (Chipewyan proper), Desnedekenade, Ethaneldi (Caribou Eaters), and Thilanottine. The Yellowknife (Tatsanottine) are sometimes considered to be a Chipewyan division. The people were known to the French as Montagnais, not to be confused with the people of eastern Canada.

Location In the early eighteenth century, Chipewyans occupied a huge expanse north of the Churchill River between the Great Slave Lake and Hudson Bay, in present-day Northwest Territories and northern Manitoba, Alberta, and Saskatchewan. In the later eighteenth century they filtered south and west to the Churchill River area and Lake Athabaska. Chipewyan land straddled the northernmost taiga and the southern tundra.

Population There were probably between 4,000–5,000 Chipewyans in the seventeenth century. The 1990 population was approximately 1,000.

Language The people spoke an Athapaskan language. The word "Athapascan" is taken from one of their divisions.

Historical Information

History The Chipewyan may have originated in the Rocky Mountains. The Hudson's Bay Company forced an uneasy truce between Chipewyans and Crees to their south in 1715, although fighting remained intermittent for another 45 years. In 1717, the Hudson's Bay Company established a post at Churchill in Chipewyan territory.

The Chipewyan soon acquired firearms, after which time they expanded north at the expense of the coast Inuit. They also harassed the Dogrib and the Yellowknife by excluding them from the fort, cheating them of goods, and kidnapping women. Chipewyans generally served as intermediaries in the fur trade between the British and the Yellowknife and Dogrib until their monopoly was ended in the late eighteenth century. Chipewyans such as the guides Thanadelther and Matonabbee helped non-natives explore the northland.

The people suffered a mortality rate of up to 90 percent in a 1781 smallpox epidemic. Survivors continued to trade at Fort Chipewyan, a closer North West Company fort, after 1788. Some groups moved into the boreal forest, where there were more fur-bearing animals, but in so doing they gave up their traditional dependence on the caribou.

Their subsequent lives were characterized by dependence on non-native goods and poor health caused by malnutrition and disease. Missionaries worked among them from the mid–nineteenth century. They accepted reserves and five-dollar per capita annuities in treaties signed from 1876 through 1906. Log cabin settlements were established in the 1920s. The post–World War II era saw increased school attendance, better health care, and the spread of social services among the people. In the 1960s, forcible relocation brought severe disruption to the most traditional group, the Caribou Eaters.

Religion Communication with the spirit world through dreams and visions provided success in hunting and other activities. Owing to the harsh environment there were no herbal curers: All illness was considered a function of witchcraft, and shamans, by virtue of their spirit powers, acted as curers. After death, only good souls were said to inhabit an island full of game.

Government There were many autonomous bands of various sizes within each division. Regional bands (at least 200–400 people) came together during caribou migration periods and broke into smaller local bands (perhaps 50 or so people) at other times. Bands were associated with particular subsistence areas. Leaders had little or no authority beyond an immediate activity such as hunting or war.

Customs When families met after the winter, they generally sat apart and listened to the old people tell about the recent deaths and problems. After the women wailed in mourning, the groups exchanged greetings. Men were named after seasons, animals, or places, but women's names always included the word for "marten."

In general, weaker men were at the mercy of the stronger, and women fared worst of all. They were separated from boys around late childhood, did most of the hardest work, and were the first to go without food in lean times. Women were segregated during their first menstrual periods and on subsequent occasions were subjected to behavioral taboos. Women were married at the onset of adolescence, often to considerably older men.

Good hunters had more than one wife. Old and/or sick people were often abandoned to starve to death. The dead were generally left on the ground. When someone died, their property was destroyed. Widows cut off their hair and observed a yearlong mourning period. Games of chance, such as ring and pin and the hand game, were popular.

Dwellings People lived in temporary encampments in open country in summer and in the woods in winter. Dwellings were conical caribou-skin tents with a smoke hole at the top. Spruce boughs and caribou skins served as floors. The tipis were semi-insulated with snow around the base in winter.

Diet The annual round of subsistence activities revolved around following the caribou, which was the main food for all Chipewyan groups. Caribou were driven into pounds, snared with ropes, and shot from canoes or by men on foot. Men also hunted buffalo, deer, bear, musk oxen, and moose. Some groups mixed dried meat with fat to make pemmican, which they stored in caribou intestines. Otherwise, meat was eaten boiled, roasted, smoked, and raw (the latter possibly learned from the Inuit).

The people also snared and trapped small game and fowl. They fished for trout, whitefish, and pike. Most fish were smoked or sun dried. There were also some plant foods, such as moss and lichen (the latter generally eaten fermented in an animal's stomach).

Key Technology Men hunted with spears and birch bows with arrows and babiche strings. Caribou were often hunted by means of a chute and pound up to a mile or more in circumference, within which snares were set. Fishing equipment included babiche nets, wooden and stone weirs, spears, clubs, and bone hooks.

Most tools were of stone and bone. The use of copper for tools such as hatchets, awls, knives, and arrow and spearheads probably came from the Yellowknife people. Water could be stone boiled in birch-bark and caribou-skin pots. The Chipewyan language contains counting systems. Moss was used for baby diapers. The people also made drums.

Trade Birch-bark items were acquired from the Cree. The people also imported shell, including dentalium, mainly for decorative purposes. There was some trade in copper in the late prehistoric period. Trade chiefs ("captains") emerged in the mid–eighteenth century.

Notable Arts The people made relatively crude wood paintings. They also used porcupine quills and moose hair to decorate clothing and bags, often with complex designs.

Transportation Birch-bark and spruce-bark canoes served as river transport. Snowshoes made from summer tent poles featured right and left sides. Women dragged heavy toboggans in winter and served as pack animals in summer, carrying goods, food, and skins on their backs. Dogs were not widely used as pack animals until the twentieth century.

Dress Well-tanned caribou-skin clothing consisted of shirts, leggings (sometimes joined to moccasins), breechclouts (men), dresses (women), caps, and

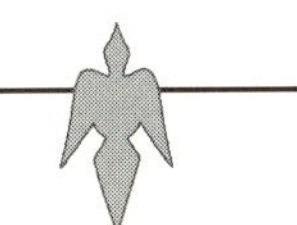

A small girl (Cree and Chipewyan) carries a birch-bark basket of blueberries (1914).

mittens. Caribou robes were hooded and trimmed with fur. The hair on the hides was shaved off in summer but left on and worn on the inside in winter. Children wore body suits of rabbit skin. People tattooed their faces with parallel lines on the cheek. Women wore their hair very long. Some men wore beards.

War and Weapons Enemies were often massacred, although afterward the murderers underwent numerous purification rites. Enemies included the Cree and Inuit. Weapons included shields painted with fighters' spirit symbols.

Contemporary Information

Government/Reservations There are currently five reserves in Alberta, six in Saskatchewan, two in Manitoba, and two in the Northwest Territories. The total reserve land base is about 337,000 acres. Bands include Barren Lands, Churchill, Cold Lake, English River, Fond du Lac, (Fort) Chipewyan, Fort McKay, Fort McMurray, Janvier, Lac le Hache, Peter Pond Lake, Portage, LaRoche, Resolution, Snowdrift, Stony Rapids, and Yellowknife.

Economy There is some commercial fishing and sporadic wage labor. Hunting and trapping are still important. Many people depend on government annuities and payments.

Legal Status The bands listed under "Government/Reservations" are federally and/or provincially recognized tribal entities.

Daily Life Hunting, fishing, and trapping remain important activities, although the bands live in permanent village of log or frame houses. Most people are at least nominal Christians. Most people still speak Chipewyan as their first language. Some groups have moved from the more settled communities they were forced to inhabit back to more traditional areas, mainly to be closer to caribou.

Cree

Cree (Krē), from *Kristeneaux,* a French word for the name (possibly Kenistenoag) of a small Cree band. The self-designation is *Ininiw,* "person," or, among the Woodland Cree, *Nehiyawak,* "those who speak the same language"; *Atheneuwuck,* "People"; or *Sackaweé-thinyoowuk,* "Bush People." Crees are commonly divided into Woodland (or Western Woods) Cree (west) and Muskegon (from *Omaskekow*), Swampy, or West Main Cree (east). Another division, the Plains Cree, is described in Chapter 6. (*See* Naskapi/Montagnais; *see also* Anishinabe [Chapter 8]). The East Cree, who live just east of James Bay, are generally regarded as being a division of the Naskapi/Montagnais (Innu). Cree speakers whose territory included land northwest of Quebec and Trois Rivières are known as Tête-de-Boule, or Attikamek. It

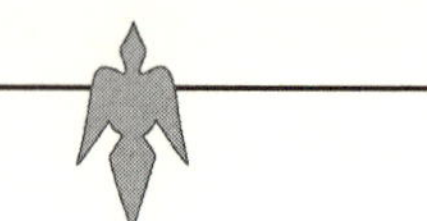

should be noted, however, that all such labels are spurious and that originally such groups consisted of autonomous groups or "nations."

Three divisions make up the Woodland Cree: Rocky Cree, Western Swampy Cree, and Strongwoods Cree. Information about the traditional lives of these people should be considered sketchy and incomplete. There may also have been a fourth group, the Athabaska-Cree. Traditional Swampy Cree bands include Abitibi, Albany, Attawapiskat, Monsoni, Moose River (Mousousipiou), Nipigon, Piscotagami, Severn, Winisk, and Winnipeg.

Location Around 1700, the Cree lived from south of James Bay westward into eastern Alberta, north to around Fort Churchill and Lake Athabaska, and south to a line running roughly from just north of Lake of the Woods to the Lesser Slave Lake. Swampy Cree land was roughly the easternmost 330 kilometers of this territory, including a considerable portion of coastline along James and Hudson Bays.

By about 1800, the people lived from Labrador in the east to Lubicon Lake in the west (includes the East Cree; *see* Naskapi/Montagnais), north almost to the Great Slave Lake, and south into North Dakota and Montana (includes Plains Cree; *see* Chapter 6).

Today, there are Cree reserves in practically all of this area. There are also Cree or Iroquois/Cree communities near Edmonton, Alberta, and in the Rocky Mountain foothills. These groups are descended from people who acted as guides for the fur companies.

Population There were at least 20,000 Crees in the sixteenth century and at least 120,000 in the mid-1990s. Most Crees live in Ontario and Quebec.

Language Crees spoke dialects of a Central Algonquian language.

Historical Information

History The Cree and Anishinabe probably share a common origin. Crees have been in their known aboriginal territory for at least 4,000 years. They first encountered non-natives when the Henry Hudson exploration arrived in 1610.

The first trade forts were founded among the Swampy Cree beginning around 1670 and in the west from the mid–eighteenth century on. Crees serving as guides and trappers increased their importance to local fur trade companies. French and Scottish trappers and traders regularly intermarried with Cree Indians. The mixed-race offspring, known as Métis, eventually developed their own culture. Some fought two wars with Canada in the mid– to late nineteenth century over the issues of land rights and sovereignty (*see* Cree, Plains entry in Chapter 6).

In the early trade days (seventeenth century in the east and mid–eighteenth to early nineteenth century in the west), the Indians prospered in part by playing the French and British off against each other. Their acquisition of firearms from the Hudson's Bay Company, as well as the completion of an alliance with the Assiniboine, precipitated a tremendous expansion almost to the Arctic Sea, the Rocky Mountains, and the Red River region. Groups of Crees arriving on the Great Plains, near the end of the seventeenth century, adopted many elements of classic Plains culture, especially including dependence on the buffalo.

Jesuit missionaries began working among the Swampy Cree for a short time in the late seventeenth century. The region was devoid of missionaries, however, from then until 1823, when the Church of England established a presence. By 1717, the Swampy Cree had become dependent on non-native traders for necessities such as cloth, blankets, and even food, in addition to trade goods. New foods included sugar and flour; alcohol and tobacco were also valued. Many traditional customs changed or disappeared during the trade period.

The people were devastated by smallpox in the early 1780s. Survivors succumbed to alcohol and were often attacked by enemies, including the Blackfeet Confederacy. Furthermore, the Cree's strong trade position led to overtrapping as well as depletion of the moose and caribou herds by the early nineteenth century. Although the effects were partially offset by the Indians' growing dependence on items of non-native manufacture, these trends combined to shrink the Indians' land base. Also about that time, western

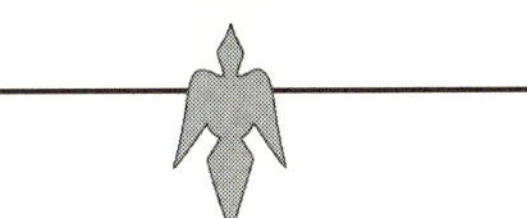

Crees, now using an iron chisel and moving on dogsleds, began taking more of an interest in fishing.

When the Hudson's Bay Company and the North West Company merged in 1821, many Cree began to abandon their traditional nomadic lives in favor of settlement at or near trade posts. Eventually, all-Indian communities arose in these areas. There was a second devastating smallpox epidemic in 1838. The people never fully recovered from this event. Severe tuberculosis and influenza epidemics struck in the early twentieth century as well.

Heavy missionary activity began in the mid–nineteenth century. Most Indians were at least nominally Christian by the mid–twentieth century, although many western groups retained a core of traditional beliefs and practices. In the mid–nineteenth century, northern and eastern groups adopted a missionary-devised syllabary that soon gained wide acceptance. Parallel to this development was the elimination of practically all traditional religion in favor of the Churches of Rome and England.

The treaty and reserve period began in the 1870s. People began slowly to settle into all-native log cabin communities, and the election of chiefs was made mandatory in the 1920s. Although their land and resources were being gradually but steadily whittled away, Crees were able to use their land in at least a semitraditional way well into the twentieth century.

After World War II, however, many Swampy Crees, their land essentially trapped out, began working in local cities and towns such as Moosonee and Churchill. Many Woodland Crees altered their lives fundamentally for the first time, attending school, using non-native medicine, accepting government financial assistance, and becoming connected to the outside world via road and air links. The advent of relatively extensive roads and rail lines in the 1950s and 1960s, as well as the expansion of the forestry industry, greatly increased pollution. At the same time there was a dramatic reduction in game animals. In 1975, the eastern Cree and Inuit ceded over 640,000 square kilometers of land to the James Bay Hydroelectric Project, in exchange for promises of hundreds of millions of dollars and various other provisions.

Religion Woodland Crees believed in the ubiquitous presence of Manitou, the great spirit power. Some coastal people also believed in a number of powerful creatures such as dwarfs and cannibalistic giants (Windigo). Some groups may have had the Midewiwin, which they probably borrowed from the Anishinabe.

Adolescents fasted and secluded themselves to obtain dream visions; the guardian spirits that they obtained in these visions were said to provide luck. Secret religious societies were dedicated to propitiating animal spirits. Special ceremonies followed the killing of a bear. Shamans, or conjurers, wielded much authority, in part because of the general fear that they would use their powers for evil purposes (sorcery). Several degrees of shaman were recognized. Their legitimate functions were to divine the future and cure illness. The latter activity was often associated with a "shaking tent" ritual. Both men and women could become shamans. (Herbalists also cured illness.)

Government Small local bands, consisting of several extended families, were the basic political units. Bands remained separated during all but the summer season, at which time they united on lake shores for ceremonies and councils. Band membership was fluid, and the bands probably had no clearly defined hunting territories. All groups were politically autonomous.

During the summer gatherings, temporary regional bands were led by chiefs. Band leaders had no explicit power; their authority was based on merit as well as the possession of spiritual power. In the contact period, specialty chiefs, who might have been band leaders, took charge of trade among their people.

Customs In the west, local band chiefs might have as many as seven wives. Parents had a great deal of influence regarding their childrens' mates. Girls were often married before they reached puberty. Newly married men worked for their wives' parents for a period of time. Among the eastern people, divorce was easily obtained. Men might temporarily exchange their wives with others and/or "lend" them to strangers as an act of hospitality, although adultery by the wife was severely punished.

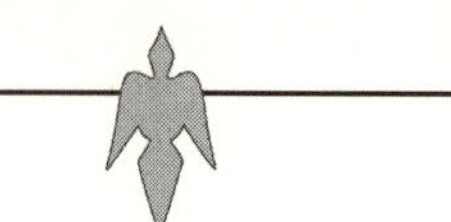

Babies kept on cradle boards used diapers of dried moss. Both twins were not permitted to live: If twins were of both sexes, the girl was killed (infant girls may have been killed under other circumstances as well). Children were generally raised with great affection and without physical punishment. Girls were subjected to isolation and a number of behavioral restrictions during and immediately following their first menstrual periods; a feast was held when a young man killed his first big game.

Widows and orphans were protected by the group. Death was not generally feared, and the very old or sick were often abandoned or killed. Corpses were wrapped in bark and buried in the ground or on a scaffold. Some weapons and tools were placed on the grave. The people held an annual feast of the dead.

Murder was avenged by relatives. Crees were forced into cannibalism during periods of starvation. They learned tobacco smoking from people of the St. Lawrence valley, and this custom became important among some groups. Eastern games included cup-and-pin, football, lacrosse, and string figures. All groups also held numerous athletic contests and games of skill. Singing and dancing occurred both socially and for luck (as in hunting).

Dwellings Toward the south, the people lived in conical or dome-shaped birch-bark wigwams with a three-pole foundation. Farther north and west, the lodges were covered with pine bark or caribou, elk, or moose skin. They sheltered extended families of ten or more people.

Floors were sometimes partially excavated. Doors faced south. Some groups also built rectangular bark- or skin-covered lodges with two fires inside. There were also sweat lodges, used in curing and for cleanliness, and menstrual lodges as well as various caches and ceremonial pavilions.

Diet Cree men were considered superb hunters. They targeted caribou, elk, moose, and beaver. They killed bear when they could get them, and hare when they could not. Some southern groups also hunted buffalo. There were many behavioral taboos and customs designed to mollify spirits related to the hunt. Every hunter carried his personal medicine pouch, and hides were often painted with red stripes and dots.

Meat was generally stone boiled. It was also dried and mixed with fat and berries to make pemmican. Fowl were plentiful, especially in certain areas. Woodland people fished only out of necessity, but Swampy Cree relied on fish such as lake trout, pike, whitefish, and pickerel. People on the coast occasionally ate seals and beluga whales, spearing them with harpoons. Seal fat was often added to meat and fish in the east.

Key Technology The primary hunting equipment included bows (strung with bark or babiche) and arrows and spears (fitted with stone, bone, or antler points). Animals were also trapped, snared (willow-bark hare snares were popular,) or caught in deadfalls. Fishing gear (in the east) included bone and spruce hooks, nets, and weirs. Other tools included bone awls and fleshers, stone axes, and beaver tooth chisels.

The people made birch-bark cooking vessels, except in the east, where woven spruce-root or soapstone (around James Bay) pots were used. Some vessels were also made of clay. Other food-related items included carved wood spoons, bowls, and trays.

Some groups used an Inuit-style curved knife for scraping hides, although farther west the women used a Plains-style tool shaped more like a chisel. A balancing stick was used while walking on snowshoes or pulling toboggans. People carved soapstone pipes and made birch-bark moose calls. Cordage came from spruce roots, hide, willow bark, and sinew. Fire was generally kept alive as coals in a birch-bark container.

Trade Most trade was local, with groups such as the Chipewyan. The Cree traded in elm-bark bags and assorted birch-bark goods, carved wooden bowls, and food items. As they expanded west, the people began to trade Woodland items for buffalo-derived products. They played an important role in the fur trade, and their acquisition through trade of firearms allowed them to expand their territory greatly.

Notable Arts Artistic expression took the forms of fine moose-hair and bird- and porcupine-quill embroidery, carved wood items, and face and body tattooing and painting. Clothing generally contained

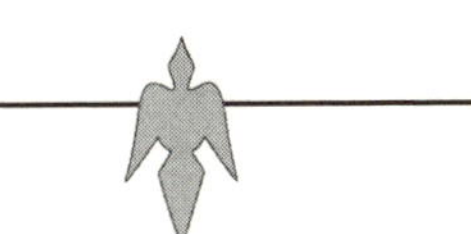

Cree men were considered superb hunters. They targeted caribou, elk, moose, and beaver. This man is imitating a moose call with an old-style birch-bark device to amplify the sound.

painted geometric patterns and, later, beaded floral designs. There was some rock painting of both realistic and stylized animals, people, and mythological personages.

Transportation People made birch-bark canoes, toboggans (of juniper in the west), and elongated birch-frame snowshoes. Many groups had horses by the mid–eighteenth century. The people adopted dogsleds beginning in the twentieth century.

Dress Moose-, caribou-, or elk-skin clothing was often fringed. Clothing generally consisted of breechclouts (belted in the east), shirts, dresses, belts, moccasins (extended in winter), and long leggings. Winter gear included beaver and caribou robes, socks, mittens, and hats as well as woven hare-skin coats and blankets and caribou coats. Women generally tattooed the corners of their mouths and men their entire bodies. Eastern men and women plucked facial hair. Hair was often braided. Cree men, especially, paid close attention to their various hairstyles. Ornaments were worn in pierced ears.

War and Weapons Allies included the Assiniboine (Stoney), the Blackfeet Confederacy before about 1800, and the Ojibwa. Enemies included the Blackfeet Confederacy after about 1800, the Gros Ventres, Iroquois, Dakota, and Inuit as well as western Athapaskan tribes.

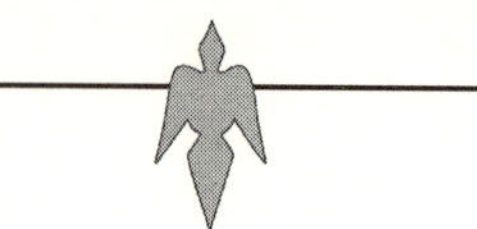

Contemporary Information

Government/Reservations Contemporary Swampy Cree bands include Albany, Attawapiskat, Churchill, Fort Severn, Fox Lake, Moose Factory, New Post, Shamattawa, Weenusk, and York Factory.

There were more than 60 official Western Woods Cree bands in 1980 with a total population of over 35,000. However, this information excludes Métis, and there are many "unofficial" bands or groups as well.

There are Cree reserves in Quebec, Ontario, Manitoba, Alberta, and Saskatchewan, Canada. Plains Crees live on the Rocky Boy Chippewa-Cree Reservation, Chouteau and Hill Counties, Montana.

The following are Attikamek reserves in Quebec: Manawan (771.36 hectares; 1,600 people in 1994, of whom 1,378 lived within the territory), Obedjiwan (926.76 hectares; 1,719 people in 1994, of whom 1,536 lived within the territory), and Weymontachie/Coucoucache (2,982.8 hectares; 1,056 people in 1994, of whom 866 lived within the territory). These communities are governed by band councils.

The following Cree communities fall under the aegis of the Grand Council of the Crees (established in 1974), the political voice of the James Bay Crees: Mistissini (1,380.43 square kilometers; 2,445 people in 1994, of whom 2,295 lived within the territory), Waswanipi (598.5 square kilometers; 1,249 people in 1994, of whom 864 lived within the territory), Eastmain (489.53 square kilometers; 483 people in 1994, of whom 432 lived within the territory), Wemindji (512.82 square kilometers; 1,048 people in 1994, of whom 925 lived within the territory), Waskaganish (784.76 square kilometers; 1,832 people in 1994, of whom 1,364 lived within the territory), Chisasibi (1,309.56 square kilometers; 2,715 people in 1994, of whom 2,634 lived within the territory), Nemaska (152.8 square kilometers; 306 people in 1994, of whom 292 lived within the territory), Whapmagootsui (316.2 square kilometers; 581 people in 1994, of whom 563 lived within the territory), and Oujé-Bougoumou (area still to be determined; 559 people in 1994, of whom 390 lived within the territory).

Economy Hunting and fishing are still important. A few people raise horses. Important industries include mining, transportation, logging, and commercial fishing. There is some employment with the James Bay Project. Craftwork, particularly bark baskets made by women, provides some income. People also work in administrative services and programs and receive government subsidies. Unemployment and underemployment are quite high throughout the region.

Legal Status Federally recognized Cree bands are listed in Appendix 1. The 1984 Cree-Naskapi Act provides for local self-government.

Daily Life In recent years, Crees have attained greater control over local services and resources and the ability to maintain legal pressure on non-native governments. The Cree school system in Quebec is under native control. Perhaps half of all Crees speak their native language. Yet the people face several crises, including the destruction of natural resources, the need for appropriate economic development, and the need to forge a viable relationship with provincial and national governments. Crees still face severe morale problems stemming from over a century of chronic disease, ill treatment at the hands of non-natives, and a diminished capability to pursue their traditional way of life. Clear- and overcutting of forests have also negatively affected Cree hunting and trapping lands.

The Lubicon Band of Treaty Eight area never received the reserve promised them in 1939. The region around Lubicon Lake, in northern Alberta, is rich in oil. In the 1970s, the band unsuccessfully fought to prevent road construction into the drilling site. By the early 1980s there were hundreds of oil wells in and near the community, creating dangerous levels of pollution.

The band is pressing for compensation for "irreparable damage to their way of life." Once a self-sustaining hunting community, its people now depend on welfare in order to survive. However, two subgroups have settled with the government. The newly created Woodland Cree Band (unrecognized by treaty chiefs) received a reserve of 142 square kilometers and a financial settlement of almost $50 million. The Loon Lake people are negotiating for a $30 million settlement.

The James Bay hydroelectric project was allowed to proceed in 1972 over the objections of the Grand Council of the Crees. A 1975 agreement called for an Indian cession of over 640,000 square kilometers of land. In exchange, the people were promised a cash settlement of over $230 million and special concessions, including land ownership of over 3,300 square kilometers, subsistence rights on over 20,000 square miles more, and a veto over mineral exploitation.

However, not all of the money was allocated, an epidemic of childhood diarrhea was caused by the pollution of vital water supplies, and Indians are often excluded from many of the better jobs. The final project—the completion of which the Cree still oppose—is expected to affect a land area of over 360,000 square kilometers.

Dogrib

Dogrib, from their self-designation, *Thlingchadinne,* "Dog Flank People," signifying their legendary descent from a dog. The people also call themselves *Done,* "men" or "People." They are culturally related to the Slavey.

Location In the nineteenth and twentieth centuries, Dogribs lived between Great Slave and Great Bear Lakes, Northwest Territories, an area that included both forest and tundra.

Population There were perhaps 1,250 Dogribs in the late seventeenth century. The mid-1990s population was about 3,000.

Language Dogrib is a Northeastern Athapaskan language.

Historical Information

History The people may have come to their historic location from the south and east. They first encountered non-natives in either 1744 or 1771. The first trade posts were built in the 1790s.

The fur trade and provisioning were the dominant economic activities throughout the nineteenth century, during which time the people gradually began settling around trade posts. Fort Rae (1852) marked the first permanent local post and the beginning of extensive contact for most Dogribs with non-natives. Fur trading became much more important at that time, especially after 1900 and the end of the Hudson's Bay Company monopoly. In addition to the usual fur-bearing animals, musk-ox robes were also in demand.

A Bear Lake Dogrib boy in 1924. The European style of dress illustrates the degree of acculturation even at this early date.

The people suffered severe epidemics from 1859 onward. Most Dogribs had been baptized Catholic by 1870. The first treaty with Canada was signed in 1900. In 1920, the Dogrib stopped accepting government payments as a protest against hunting and fishing restrictions. This issue was resolved when they accepted a special designation, but the signed agreement was later lost.

As part of a 1921 treaty, the leader Monphwi became a "government chief," and band leaders formed an official council. There was a brief local gold rush, at

Great Bear Lake, in 1930. The people were largely monolingual and semitraditional through the 1940s.

Religion People acquired guardian spirits in dreams. They also made offerings to spirits that inhabited bodies of water. Shamans caused and cured disease and foretold the future.

Government There were traditionally four autonomous bands, or divisions (Lintchanre, Takfwelottine, Tsantieottine, and Tseottine). Band leadership was informal; a chief hunter had helpful spiritual power but little authority. Bands were composed of local hunting groups. Membership in all groups was fluid.

Customs When a young man killed his first game, his peers would strip him and wish him continued good luck. Only indirect address was considered polite. The people enjoyed games and dancing; the latter was often accompanied by group male singing.

People's names often changed at the birth of their children. Brothers and sisters remained reserved with each other, as did a man with his brother-in-law and father-in-law. Men might have more than one wife, but they were required to serve their new in-laws for a period of time after the marriage. There may have been a practice of wrestling for wives as well as some female infanticide.

The elderly or ill were often abandoned. Streamers attached to burial scaffolds were meant to placate spirits of the dead. Mourners destroyed most of their property, and the women slashed their bodies. A memorial feast was held a year following the death.

Dwellings Dogribs lived in conical tipis covered with as many as 40 caribou skins sewn together with sinew or babiche. The sides were covered with snow in winter. There were also some rectangular pole-and-brush winter huts. In the coldest weather, people often slept outside in skin bags to avoid the interior drafts.

Diet Men hunted mainly caribou, which they snared in pounds and speared in lakes, in the forests, and on short trips onto the tundra. They also hunted musk ox, moose, hare and other small game, fowl, and birds. There was some fishing; later, with decreasing game in the nineteenth century, fish gradually assumed a greater importance in the diet. Fish and meat were roasted, stone boiled (in caribou stomach–lined holes), smoked, dried in strips, or mixed with marrow and perhaps berries and made into pemmican.

Women gathered some berries and other plant foods as well as poplar sap. Food taboos included the weasel, wolf, skunk, and dog.

Key Technology Fish were taken with the use of dams, weirs, and willow-bark fishnets. Men hunted with bows and arrows and snares. Food was wrapped in hide and cached on poles or platforms. The main raw materials were caribou parts and wood.

Trade The people exported native copper to the Slavey and Yellowknife, among other groups. They also traded in caribou skins, flint, chert, and pyrites as well as Inuit bone and ivory knives. They exported moose and fish products.

Notable Arts Women decorated a number of items, such as moccasins, shirts, and bags, with woven quillwork or moose hair. Musical instruments included drums and caribou-hoof rattles.

Transportation Most transportation was overland using sleds and snowshoes. Burdens were carried with a tumpline and chest strap. Birch-bark canoes were caulked with spruce gum.

Dress Typical clothing included a tailored skin shirt, breechclout, leggings, and moccasins. The latter two were separate. Winter items included moose-hide blankets, fur robes, hats, and mittens.

War and Weapons Enemies included the Yellowknife, Chipewyan, and Cree. A decisive military victory in 1823 destroyed the threat from the first group. War leaders were chosen on an ad-hoc basis. All enemies, except young women, were killed whenever possible.

Contemporary Information

Government/Reservations Contemporary bands include Follow the Shore People, Filth Lake People, Edge of the Woods People, People Next to Another

Dogrib moccasins, moosehide coat, and moosehide leggings such as these would have made up late traditional dress.

People, Bear Lake Dogrib, and Connie River People. Roughly 70 percent of the population lives at Rae. Other population centers include Yellowknife, Fort Franklin, and Edzo, Northwest Territories. A strong chief and council have been elected since the 1970s.

Economy Hunting, fishing, and trapping remain important. There is some wage labor as fishing guides and construction laborers. Women work at producing crafts.

Legal Status The bands listed under "Government/ Reservations" are federally recognized. The Treaty 11 Dogrib, formerly part of the larger Dene/Métis claim (*see* Kutchin), filed their own land claim in 1992. According to two interim agreements in 1994, the people will win the withdrawal of about 13,000 square kilometers of land from around four Dogrib communities as well as participation in the decision-making process concerning the North Slave region.

Daily Life Band membership is still recognized and considered important. Although the language is still in use, there is a high degree of acculturation among the people. Modern housing, non-native education, welfare eligibility, and medical services date from the 1960s. Most Dogribs are Catholic. Their lands are being rapidly developed, mainly by mineral extraction industries, without Dogrib input. This had led to a decision to negotiate a land claim settlement with the Canadian government in an effort to gain some control over development.

Han

See Ingalik; Kutchin

Hare

The name Hare comes from the people's reliance on the Arctic or snowshoe hare. Their self-designation was *Kawchottine,* "People of the Great Hares," or

Kasogotine, "Big Willow People." They were culturally similar to the Kutchin and Dogrib. This description of "aboriginal" culture includes some postcontact influences as well.

Location Hare Indians lived and continue to live west (to just past the Mackenzie River) and northwest of Great Bear Lake, present-day Northwest Territories. They ranged in parts of Alberta, Yukon, and Alaska. This territory includes tundra, taiga, mountains, and intermediary areas.

Population There were probably no more than 800 Hares in the early eighteenth century, and there are about the same number (or somewhat fewer) today.

Language Hare is a Northern Athapaskan language.

Historical Information

History Shortly after the people encountered Alexander Mackenzie in 1789, the North West Company built Fort Good Hope (1806) in the area. Rapid involvement in the fur trade brought dependence on items of non-native manufacture. Non-native traders created trade chiefs among the people, so that their political organization eventually became more hierarchical.

The people were decimated by epidemics throughout the nineteenth century. A local Catholic church was built around 1866. Gradually, nomadic band life was mitigated in favor of growing concentration around the trade posts. As the government created "bands" for administrative purposes and assigned subsistence areas for such groups, ethnic and group identity became stronger The people were largely acculturated, as Hare Indians, by 1900.

Treaties signed with the Canadian government in the early twentieth century provided for payments and services in exchange for land title, although the Indians retained the right to use land for subsistence activities. Children began attending Catholic boarding school in 1926. Tuberculosis was rampant between the 1930s and the 1960s, and the people suffered periodic outbreaks of other diseases as well.

During the 1920s, many people built log homes and left native manufacture further and further behind. The fur trade continued to flourish until World War II. People increasingly worked at seasonal wage labor after the war, mainly in the oil and construction industries. The more traditional Colville Lake community dates from around 1960.

Religion Guardian spirits formed the basis of Hare religious belief. Spirit helpers were not formally sought out but appeared in dreams. Shamans were able to attract particularly powerful guardians through dreams and visions. They were said to be able to summon game, defeat enemies, and cure illness. Cures were effected by using medicinal plants, singing, and sucking. Shamans sometimes hung by ropes from trees or tent poles when communicating with the spirits. Religious feasts included a memorial to the dead a year after death and on the occasion of a new moon. Singing and dancing formed a part of these ceremonies.

Government There were perhaps five to seven small, autonomous, nomadic bands of fluid size and composition. The bands had defined hunting territories but informal leaders with little authority other than respect for their hunting and/or curing abilities.

Customs Sharing and generosity were highly valued. The bands gathered together several times a year for ceremonies, socializing, and hunting and fishing during migration and spawning seasons. Girls entering puberty were isolated in special huts and required to observe food and behavior taboos. Certain of these taboos, such as those regarding fish and animals, were continued during every monthly period. A feast would be held for young men who killed their first big game.

Intermarriage was common with several peoples, such as Bearlake Mountain (Kaska and other tribes) and Kutchin Indians. Marriage occurred in the early teens and was generally arranged, although divorce was readily available. There was some period of bride service after marriage.

The elderly as well as some female babies were killed or left to die. Corpses were wrapped in blankets or moose skin and placed in above-ground enclosures. Relatives cut their hair and disposed of their property.

Ghosts were feared and provided with offerings to keep them at bay. Souls were said to be reborn at a later date.

Dwellings People lived in rectangular or A-frame winter pole-frame houses with gabled roofs, covered with spruce boughs, brush, and snow. Caribou-hide tipis date from the nineteenth century. Summer lean-tos were common as well.

Diet Caribou and musk ox were staples, although small animals (especially hare) and fish (such as trout and whitefish) contributed the bulk of the diet. Meat was generally roasted or stone boiled. Meat and fish were also pounded and mixed with grease and berries to make pemmican. Surpluses might be frozen or smoke dried. There was a severe lack of food every seven years or so when hares became scarce.

Women gathered a few plant foods, such as berries and material predigested by caribou and other animals. Mosses and lichens were used as beverages and medicines. Wolves and dogs were not eaten.

Key Technology Stone tools included adzes and knives, the latter having a beaver-tooth blade. The main hunting and fishing equipment included bows and arrows as well as babiche snares, willow-bark nets, hooks, weirs, and spears. People made caribou ice chisels and wood or bark dishes. Willow and spruce-root baskets served as cooking vessels.

Trade Trade partners probably included fellow Athapaskans such as Yellowknife, Dogrib, Beaver, and Slavey Indians. Items exchanged included animal skins, copper, and various minerals. There may have been some trade in Inuit knives.

Notable Arts Women decorated a number of items, such as moccasins, shirts, belts, and bags, with fringe and woven quillwork or moose hair. Musical instruments included drums and caribou-hoof rattles. Beads, dentalium shell, and then silk floral patterns and ribbon appliqué replaced more traditional decorative styles by the nineteenth century.

Transportation Most travel was overland. Snowshoes were used in winter. Women pulled wooden toboggans before dogs took over in the twentieth century. Men also made spruce, birch-bark, and occasionally moose-hide canoes.

As with many tribes in this area, Hare Indians relied on fish for part of their diet. A man lifts a herring net in a spring-run fishery, Great Bear Lake (1923).

Dress Most clothing came from hare pelts, supplemented by caribou and moose hides. The standard summer wardrobe was shirt, leggings, moccasins, and possibly a breechclout. In winter, the people wore robes, mittens, and hats and added hoods to their shirts. Clothing was often decorated with porcupine-quill embroidery. They wore caribou or hare hairbands. There was very little personal ornamentation except for facial tattooing and painting.

War and Weapons Hares fought the Inuit and Yellowknife, although the people generally took pains not to fight at all. They were allied with the Dogrib and Kutchin. Prisoners were staked to the ground and their hearts cut out for the women to eat.

Contemporary Information

Government/Reservations Contemporary bands are located at Fort Franklin, Colville Lake, and Fort Good Hope. Some local bands are ethnically mixed and consist of Slavey and Bearlake as well as Hare Indians.

Economy The Colville Lake people rely mainly on traditional subsistence activities. People at Good Hope live mostly on part-time, seasonal, and some full-time wage labor as well as government payments.

Legal Status The Colville Lake and Good Hope communities are federally recognized entities.

Daily Life Full access to western culture has led to increased levels of acculturation and a comparable decline of traditional knowledge and practice. The Colville Lake and Good Hope communities remain in close touch.

Ingalik

Ingalik (`Ēn gä lēk), from the Russian via an Inuit word for "Indian." The name has been loosely used to include such culturally related—but separate—tribes as Koyukon, Tanana, and Han. Their self-designation is *Deg Hit'an,* "People from Here." They were heavily influenced by their Yup'ik neighbors.

Location The Ingalik shared eastern parts of their traditional territory—the banks of the Anvik, Innoko, Kuskokwim, Holitna, and lower Yukon Rivers—with the Kuskowagamiut Inuit. The land consists of river valleys as well as forest and tundra. The Holikachuk, a related though distinct people, lived to their north.

Population There were between 1,000 and 1,500 Ingalik in the nineteenth century. Population in the early 1990s was roughly 650.

Language Ingaliks speak a northern Athapaskan language. However, by the later twentieth century most Kuskokwim Ingalik spoke the language of their Kuskowagamiut Inuit relatives.

Historical Information

History The people probably originated in Canada. They were driven west by the Cree to settle in present-day Alaska around 1200. They encountered Russian explorers in 1833. A trade post was constructed either around then or in 1867. There were Russian Orthodox missionaries in the region during that period. The major epidemics began in 1838–1839.

Steamboats began operating on the Yukon, expanding the fur trade, beginning in about 1867, the year the United States took possession of Alaska. Catholic and Anglican missionaries arrived in the 1880s and soon opened boarding schools. The caribou disappeared in the 1870s, leading to even more fishing and closer ties with the Kuskowagamiut Inuit. Non-natives flooded into the region during the Yukon gold rush of the late 1890s. Most Ingaliks had accepted Christianity by the mid–twentieth century.

Religion Everything, animate or inanimate, was thought to have had spirits. The Ingalik universe consisted of four levels, one higher and two lower than earth. Spirits of the dead might travel to any of the levels, depending on the method of death. A creator, spirits associated with nature, and various spiritual and superhuman beings, as well as people, inhabited the four worlds.

Most ceremonies were designed to maintain equilibrium with the spirit world. They included the two- to three-week Animals ceremony, the Bladder ceremony, the Doll ceremony, and four potlatch-type events with other villages. The single-village Bladder and Doll ceremonies involved paying respects to animal spirits and learning the future. Of the potlatch ceremonies, the Midwinter Death potlatch was the most solemn. The purpose was to honor a dead relative, usually a father, to gain status, and to maintain reciprocal giving arrangements with other families. Accompanying this ceremony was the so-called Hot Dance, a night of revelry.

The feast of the animals, involving songs, dances, costumes, and masks, was most important. Major roles were inherited. It involved a ritual enactment of hunting and fishing, with a clown providing comic relief. Other, more minor, ceremonies involved sharing food and occurred at life-cycle events and on occasions such as eclipses.

Songs, or spells, helped keep the human, animal, and spiritual worlds in harmony. They could be purchased from older people. Songs were also associated with amulets, which could be bought, inherited, or made. Male and female shamans were said to have more powerful souls than other people.

They acquired their powers through animal dream visions. Shamans' powerful songs, or spells, could be used for good or evil.

Government Each of four geographical groups contained at least one village that included a defined territory and a chief.

Customs Society was divided into ranked status groups or social classes known as wealthy, common people, and idlers. People in the first group were expected to be generous with their surpluses and did hold potlatches as a redistributive method. Members could lead ceremonies. The idlers were considered virtually unmarriageable; however, the classes tended to be fluid and were noninherited. Wealth consisted mostly of fish but also of items such as furs, meat, and any particularly well-wrought item, such as a carved bowl, a canoe, or a drum.

Ingaliks often intermarried with, and borrowed culturally from, the nearby Inuit. Marriage depended in part on the ability of the man to perform bride service. With a first wife's permission, a wealthy man might have two wives. Both parents observed food and behavioral restrictions for at least three weeks following a birth. Young women endured segregation for a year at the onset of adolescence, during which time they mastered all the traditionally female tasks.

Punishments for inappropriate social behavior, such as theft, included banishment or death. This was a group decision, on the part of the men and older women, whereas murder required individual blood revenge. Corpses were placed in wooden coffins and buried in the ground or in vaults. Cremation was practiced on rare occasions. Personal property was disposed of. Following funerals, the people observed a 20-day mourning period and often held memorial potlatches.

Dwellings Ingaliks maintained summer and winter villages as well as canoe or spring camps. The winter dwelling was dome shaped and covered with earth and grass. Partially underground, it housed from one to three nuclear families. Ten to 12 such houses made up a winter village. Men used a larger, rectangular, semisubterranean communal house for sleeping, eating, working, sweating, and conducting ceremonies. This "kashim" was adapted from their Yup'ik neighbors. Canoe and sled racks were placed in front of houses.

Canoe camps, containing cone-shaped spruce-pole and bough shelters, were built while people went in search of fresh fish. Summer houses were built of spruce plank, spruce bark, or cottonwood logs. There were also gabled-roof smoke houses and fish-drying racks. Temporary brush houses were located away from the village.

Diet Among most groups, fish were the most important part of the diet. Species included lamprey eels, caught under ice, as well as salmon, trout, whitefish, pike, and blackfish. The people also ate a variety of large and small animals. Caribou, hunted by communal surround, were the most important. Others included moose, bear, sheep, and numerous fur-bearing animals, especially hare.

Ingaliks also ate birds, mainly waterfowl, and their eggs, as well as berries and other plant foods. "Ice cream," a mixture of cottonwood pods, oil, snow, and berries, was eaten ceremonially and with some restrictions on who could receive it from whom. Food was generally cached in logs on posts.

Key Technology Hunting equipment included bows and arrows, spears, deadfalls, and snares. Fish were

These Ingalik men are ice-fishing with a woven willow trap, which has vertical poles to submerge the rig and meshwork to obstruct the fish and force them deeper into the funnel leading to the trap.

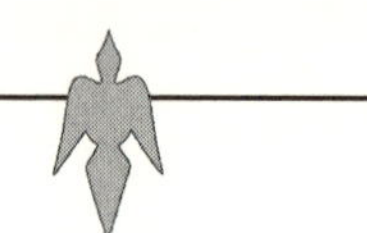

taken using a variety of nets, spears, traps, and hook (bone) and line (sinew). Stone tools included axes and wedges. The Ingalik made stone, horn, and wood knives, wooden bowls, and pottery as well as sewn birch-bark and twined grass and willow-bark baskets.

Trade The Ingalik did not trade extensively because they possessed rich natural resources. When they did exchange goods, it was mostly with Inuit groups, exporting wooden bowls, wolverine skins, and furs for seal products and caribou hides. They might also trade furs, wolverine skins, spruce gum, and birch-bark canoes for fish products and dentalia.

Notable Arts Hide and birch baskets were probably this group's most important material artistic achievement.

Transportation Ingaliks moved around in birch-bark canoes and on sleds and snowshoes.

Dress Most clothing was made from squirrel and other skins. Shirts and pants were common. as were parkas. Women's moccasins were attached to their pants; the men's were separate. Personal adornment included dentalium earrings and nose and neck decorations.

War and Weapons The Ingalik were a relatively peaceful people. When they did fight, their enemies included most neighboring tribes, especially the Koyukon and other Athapaskan tribes.

Contemporary Information

Government/Reservations Contemporary villages include Anvik, Holy Cross, and Shageluk.

Economy Most people still engage in traditional subsistence activities, supplemented with some wage work as fishing and hunting guides. There is also some government, seasonal, and utility work.

Legal Status Doyon, Inc., is the legal entity representing Ingalik villages in the ANCSA.

Daily Life For most people, life still revolves around the seasons. Frame or log houses have replaced traditional structures. Although many people struggle with a number of social problems related to high unemployment and cultural upheaval, and the people retain little aboriginal culture, traditional values remain palpable among the Ingalik.

Innu

See Naskapi/Montagnais

Kaska

Kaska (`Kas kə) is taken from the local name for McDame Creek. The Kaska were culturally related to the Sekani. They are also known, or included, with the Tahltan and others, among the people called Nahani (Nahane) or Mackenzie Mountain People.

Location Kaskas lived and continue to live in northern British Columbia and southern Yukon Territory, in a rough triangle from the Pelly River south to Dease Lake and east to the Fort Nelson River.

Population The Kaska probably numbered around 500 before contact with non-natives. Their official 1991 population was 705.

Language Kaska, along with Tahltan and Tagish, is a Northern Athapaskan language.

Historical Information

History The people traded with non-natives through Tlingit intermediaries until Fort Simpson, on the Laird and Mackenzie Rivers, was established in the early nineteenth century as the local trade center. Forts Laird and Nelson opened soon afterward. Fort Halkett, the first trade fort located directly in Kaska territory, was established soon after 1821. The people gradually came to rely on metal pots, nails, wire, and tools as well as items such as flour, soap, candles, guns and ammunition, and kerosene.

Kaska territory was invaded by gold seekers in the 1870s and again during the Klondike gold rush of

1897, seriously disrupting their traditional way of life. A Catholic mission was established in 1926. In the early 1940s the Alaskan Highway was built through their territory. Trapping remained important well into the contemporary period.

Religion Young men and women fasted in order to acquire animal guardian spirits in dreams and visions. Illness was said to be caused by breaking taboos. Shamans cured and foretold the future with recourse to their powerful spirit guides. Curing methods included blowing water onto the body or transferring the illness to another object.

Government There were at least four divisions. Each was composed of independent regional bands that had no fixed membership but generally consisted of local bands of extended families. Local band leadership was provided by the best hunters. Women occasionally served in important leadership positions.

Customs Two matrilineal clans, Wolf and Raven, were borrowed from coastal tribes, as was the institution of the memorial potlatch. Also from coastal cultures, women acquired the custom of attacking symbolic enemies while their husbands were away at war.

Birth took place apart from the community out of fear of spiritual contamination. From late childhood on, boys began training for the vision quest, as well building strength, with icy plunges and other physically demanding activities. Women were secluded and observed various taboos during their menstrual periods. Girls married in their mid-teens, boys slightly later or as soon as they could provide for a family. Men served their prospective in-laws for a year before the wedding; thereafter, they avoided speaking to one another. Though frowned upon, divorce was common. The dead were wrapped in skins and left under a pile of brush; later the tribe adopted cremation and underground burial.

The people enjoyed many games and contests. Most life-cycle events were marked by feasts. Names were inherited, as were some material items. Peer pressure usually sufficed as a means of social control; more serious offenses might be dealt with by exile, payments, or revenge.

Dwellings Two or more families lived in conical or A-frame lodges covered with sod, brush, or skin. Most people used simple brush lean-tos in summer.

Diet Men hunted mainly caribou, but also buffalo, mountain goat, bighorn sheep, and numerous smaller game. They drove large game into pounds, snared them, or caught them in deadfalls or pitfalls. Beaver were clubbed to death. Meat was generally boiled, often in a dried moose stomach, but could be sun dried and stored. It was rarely eaten raw. Salmon and other fish were caught in summer. Women gathered berries and a few other wild plant foods such as mushrooms, onions, lily bulbs, and rhubarb.

Key Technology From coastal groups, Kaskas learned to weave blankets and ropes of sheep wool and goat hair. Babies were carried in skin bags padded with moss and rabbit fur. Men hunted with the bow and arrow as well as with spears, clubs, and especially babiche snares. Some groups may have used the atlatl.

Other important items included fishing nets, weirs, and clubs; woven spruce baskets for cooking; horn or wood spoons; wood or birch-bark dishes; cordage of sinew, spruce root, and willow bark; and tools, such as axes, knives, and scrapers, made of stone, bone, antler, and horn. Skins were prepared and tanned in various ways.

Trade Kaskas traded with the Tahltan, Tlingit, and other groups along or near the coast.

Notable Arts Clothing was decorated with porcupine-quill and moose-hair embroidery. Some groups developed the custom of carving wooden animal masks for potlatches.

Transportation Men built dugouts and spruce-bark canoes; sewn caribou-skin toboggans; two different types of snowshoes, depending on the quality of the snow; and moose-skin boats. Gas-powered boats and dogsleds have been in wide use since the 1940s.

Two moose-skin boats sit on the bank, and the frame of an unfinished boat can be seen in the foreground (1918).

Dress Most clothing was made of sewn caribou skins. Both sexes wore belted breechclouts, skin shirt (hooded in winter), and leggings, belted and fastened to moccasins in winter. Other winter gear included mittens and hide robes. Clothing was often decorated with porcupine-quill embroidery, sewn fringe, and hard material obtained from moose stomach. People tattooed their bodies and wore ear and nose rings for personal ornamentation.

War and Weapons Wars were fought either to steal women or to avenge violent acts performed by strangers. War party leadership was selected on an ad hoc basis. Younger men carried the supplies while seasoned warriors did the fighting. There was some limited ceremonial cannibalism.

Contemporary Information

Government/Reservations Kaska bands include Laird River, Dease River, Lower Post, and Ross River. The Ross River Dena Council and the Laird First Nation are part of the Kaska Tribal Council.

Economy Important economic activities include fishing, trapping, and professional guiding and other wage labor.

Legal Status The bands listed under "Government/ Reservations" are federally recognized.

Daily Life Kaskas have spoken English for several generations. Most are Catholic.

Koyukon

See Ingalik

Kutchin

Kutchin (`Ku chin) or Gwich'in, "People." The Kutchin were a group of tribes or bands who called themselves by various names, each having the suffix "-kutchin." The name of one band—Tukkuth, or "People of the Slanting Eyes"—was translated by the French to *Loucheux,* a name now commonly used to designate the Kutchin people. Their self-designation is *Dindjie,* "person." They were culturally related to the Han, Tutchone, and Tanana and were culturally influenced by the Inuit as well as the Tlingit.

Location Kutchin territory is the Peel River Basin to its junction with the Mackenzie River as well as the Yukon River drainage (Alaska and Yukon).

Population The Kutchin population, between 3,000 and 5,000 in the eighteenth century, declined to around 1,300 in the mid–nineteenth century and around 700 in the mid-1970s. In the mid-1990s there were around 2,000 Gwich'in people in Canada and an additional 600 in Alaska.

Language Kutchin people spoke dialects of Kutchin, a Northern Athapaskan language.

Historical Information

History Kutchin people encountered the Mackenzie expedition in 1789. The North West Company founded Fort Good Hope in 1806; other trading posts followed in 1839 (Fort MacPherson) and 1847 (Fort Yukon). Fur trapping gained in importance among the people during the nineteenth century. Catholic and Protestant (Church of England) missions worked in Kutchin territory from the mid–nineteenth century on. Missionaries introduced a system of reading and writing (called Tukudh) in the 1870s.

Major epidemics stalked the people during the 1860s and 1870s, and again in 1897 and into the twentieth century. Many Kutchins left their immediate region to take advantage of the local whaling boom at the end of the nineteenth century.

The Klondike gold rush (1896) brought an influx of non-natives into the region, many of whom abused the Indians and stole their land. Religious residential schools existed from 1905.

Religion Shamans acquired spiritual power through fasting and dreaming. They could foretell the future, cure illness, and control the weather. They were quite powerful in the west but less so in the east. In general, most people seldom came in "official" contact with the shamans.

Spirits inhabiting nature were mollified with offerings of beads. Hunters prayed to moon-related deities, offering pieces of caribou fat thrown into the fire. Ceremonial feasts, including singing and dancing, were held on various occasion. The main ceremonies revolved around life-cycle events, lunar eclipses, and memorial potlatches. There was a general fear of giants and other monsters. Bear and caribou were considered to be especially deserving of respect, in part owing to a supposed physical connection (shared hearts) between people and caribou.

Government Kutchin bands included the Kutcha (Yukon Flats), Nakotcho (Mackenzie Flats or Arctic Red River), Natsit (Chandalor River), Tatlit (Peel River), Tennuth (Birch Creek), Tukkuth (Upper Porcupine River), Tranjik (Black River), Vunta (Crow Flats), and Dihai (Downriver People).

Tribal chiefs were chosen for their leadership qualities or wealth. In some cases the positions were hereditary, but leaders had no real power. Local groups (two or so extended families) lived in a defined area and used its resources.

Customs Animal-associated matrilineal clans declined in importance from west to east. The clans had marriage and ceremonial functions, playing significant roles in feasts and games. There were three social classes that may have been ranked: the "dark people" (Crow), "fair people" (Wolf), and "halfway people" (no crest). There were also some slaves, although they probably were not purchased. Among the distinct socioeconomic levels, the wealthy were considered better in every way.

Women carried babies in their coats or in birch-bark containers. They also performed most hard work (except for cooking, which men did) and ate only after the men had finished. Women generally selected husbands for their daughters. Female infants, as well as the elderly, were sometimes killed. From shortly before puberty until marriage, young men moved away from their parents to live in a lodge with other such young men. This was a period of self-denial and skill sharpening. Men without family might attach themselves to other families as servants.

Young women were segregated during their menstrual periods. At that time they observed many taboos, such as not looking at others, designed to prevent others being "contaminated" by their "condition." The dead were cremated. Their ashes were hung in bags from poles or, if the person were particularly influential, placed in coffins in trees until decayed and then burned. Relatives destroyed their property and cut their bodies.

Hospitality was a key value. The nuclear family was the basic unit, but grandparents might sleep in a lodge near the family and spend a lot of time with them. Items of value included dentalium shell beads, wolverine skins, and caribou products. Rich men of certain tribes gave potlatches but usually only at funerals. Everyone enjoyed singing, dancing, games, and contests. Games included stick and hand games, ball games, and athletic contests. Witches were greatly feared.

Dwellings Dome-shaped, caribou-skin tents were stretched over curved spruce poles painted red. These portable lodges were about 12 to 14 feet long and 6 to 8 feet high. There was a smoke hole at the top, fir boughs for flooring, and bough and snow insulation. Some groups covered the lodges with birch bark rather than caribou skin. Some groups built semisubterranean dwellings of moss blocks covering a wood frame, with gabled roofs. When traveling, men sometimes built dugout snow houses glazed with fire.

Diet Fishing took place mainly in summer. Pike and whitefish were important fish species. There were salmon along the Yukon River and moose along its banks. Men hunted mainly caribou but also moose, hare, beaver, muskrat, and other game. Dogs often assisted in the hunt. People also ate waterfowl and plant foods, such as berries, rhubarb, and roots.

Key Technology Many items were derived from the caribou. Bows, generally of birch, were made in several sections and bound with sinew or willow shoots. Men hunted with bows and arrows, deadfalls, and babiche snares. They also used caribou pounds or corrals. Fishing equipment included hooks, lures, spears, dip nets, and willow baskets.

Other important items included wooden and birch-bark trays, woven spruce and tamarack-root baskets and cooking vessels, and other containers made of bent wood and birch bark. There were any number of tools with which to work hides, bone, and wood. Blades were mostly of stone and bone. Musical instruments included wooden gongs, drums, and willow whistles.

Trade Trade partners included the Tanana, the Koyukon, the Inuvialuit, and the Inupiat as well as the Tlingit. Imported dentalium shell was used as a currency. The people also imported some copper blades. As intermediaries, they relayed Arctic coast oil, bon, and tusks to inland groups. They exported furs even before contact with non-natives.

Notable Arts Containers and clothing were decorated with porcupine quills. Skins were finely tanned.

Transportation Sleds were made with high-framed runners, which might be covered with bone or frozen sod coated with water or blood. Inuit-style birch-bark canoes had flat bottoms and nearly straight sides. The people also used moose-skin canoes, toboggans, and particularly well-made long, narrow snowshoes with babiche netting.

Dress Most clothing came from white caribou skin as well as furs. Shirts were pointed both front and rear. Wide (Inuit-style) leggings attached to moccasins were beaded or embroidered with porcupine-quill designs along the sides. Winter gear included long mittens, headbands, fur hats, and winter hoods. Most clothing was fringed and/or decorated with seeds or dentalium shell beads and/or painted and embroidered with porcupine quills.

Both sexes, but especially men, wore quill and dentalium shell personal ornamentation. Men also skewered their noses; women simply wore nose decorations. People took particular care with their hair. Men applied a large amount of grease and wore it in a ball at the neck, covered with bird down and feathers. They also painted their faces red and black. Women tattooed lines on their chins.

War and Weapons The Kutchin were a relatively aggressive people. Kutchin enemies included the Inuvialuit and Inupiat and sometimes the Tanana and the Koyukon Indians. Enemies, with the occasional exception of young women, were generally killed. There was some ritual cannibalism.

Contemporary Information

Government/Reservations Alaska Kutchins live in villages such as Arctic Village, Chalkyitsik, Circle, and Venetie. Some of these villages are shared with Inuits. Fort Yukon, Alaska, ranks as a town, the only Gwich'in population center to boast of the presence of roads. Villages corporations with elected boards of directors administer Alaska Native Claims Settlement Act (ANCSA) assets.

Economy Most people still rely on traditional subsistence activities as well as fur trapping and barter.

Legal Status According to the terms of the Dene/Métis Western Arctic Land Claim Agreement (1992), the Dene surrendered aboriginal and treaty rights in return for surface rights on about 24,000 square kilometers of land, some subsurface rights, and about $75 million in cash as well as hunting and fishing rights. The groups also participate in decision making about renewable resources, land use planning, and other environmental and development issues. In the early 1990s, the Mackenzie Delta Gwich'in broke away from the Dene Nation and Métis Association over this issue. They concluded a separate agreement with the Canadian government in 1991 for land and cash. Most Kutchin became members of the Doyon Corporation under the ANCSA.

The Vuntut Gwitch'in First Nation is included in an umbrella land claims settlement (1993) with the Council of Yukon First Nations. Its terms are similar to those of other Canadian/First Nation land claims settlements: land, a mixture of surface and subsurface

rights, cash, and participation in the overall decision-making process concerning development, land use, and other environmental issues.

Daily Life Some groups live in small wood-frame houses. Although some have access to modern inventions such as snowmobiles, televisions, and satellite dishes, more than most other Indians the Kutchin have been able to retain a semiaboriginal lifestyle and culture, including religious beliefs, to a considerable degree (although less so in Fort Yukon). Most are fluent in English, although there are efforts to retain the native language. The people are fighting to maintain the health and existence of the Porcupine caribou herd, which is threatened by development-related resource destruction.

Loucheux

See Kutchin

Mackenzie Mountain People

See Kaska

Nahani

See Kaska; Tahltan

Naskapi/Montagnais

Naskapi/Montagnais (`Nas ku pē/`Mon tun yā). Naskapi is a Montagnais word that may mean "rude or uncivilized people." Montagnais is French for "mountaineers." Their self-designation was *Nenenot,* "the People." Contemporary Naskapi and Montagnais refer to themselves as *Innu. See also* Cree (especially discussion of East Cree).

Location The territory of these groups, including the East Cree, ran from the Gulf of St. Lawrence to James Bay, along the northeastern coast of Hudson Bay to Ungava Bay, and east to the Labrador Sea. The division was more or less that the East Cree occupied the west of this region, the Naskapi the north, and the Montagnais the south and east. Much of this territory is extremely rugged and remote. Moose lived in the wooded Montagnais country, whereas Naskapi country, more open and grassy, was favored by caribou.

Population There were perhaps 4,000 Montagnais and 1,500 Naskapis in the fifteenth century. A centuries-long population decline began to reverse itself only after World War II. In the mid-1990s the Innu population stood at approximately 16,000, including a small percentage who had moved away from eastern Quebec and Labrador (known also as Nitassinan).

Language Montagnais and Naskapi are dialects of Cree, an Algonquian language.

Historical Information

History Humans—likely direct ancestors of the Naskapi/Montagnais—have lived on the Labrador Peninsula for at least 5,000 years. Indians may have lived peacefully alongside the Inuit in ancient times. These people were among the first North American groups to come in contact with non-natives, probably Basque and other European fishermen, in the early sixteenth century.

The Montagnais welcomed Champlain in 1603; his French muskets proved to be of some help against crippling Iroquois war parties. The people soon became heavily involved in the fur trade. They found it very competitive and profitable and soon began acquiring a large number of non-native goods. Europeans created Indian trade chiefs, or

A seventeenth-century European view of New France natives. The Huron warrior on the right wears a suit of wooden slats, while the one on the left is identified as a Montagnais.

"captains." Missionaries arrived among the Montagnais in 1615. Tadoussac remained a key trade town from the mid–sixteenth century until Quebec was founded in 1608.

However, both moose and caribou were soon overhunted. As food supplies became less certain, some starvation ensued. Problems with alcohol abuse exacerbated the situation. The people were able to trade furs for supplies until non-natives took over the best trapping grounds. Devastating disease epidemics reduced and weakened the Indian population. Further mass deaths resulted from relocating to the coast at the urging of missionaries.

The fur trade remained important during the eighteenth and early nineteenth centuries. The Naskapi became involved in the fur trade during that period. As they quickly increased their dependence on the trading posts and forsook the caribou hunt, they began to lose important elements of their traditional lives. By the mid–nineteenth century, traditional small local bands had generally become associated with a particular Hudson's Bay Company trading post. As forestry operations began replacing the fur trade, and non-natives continued to move into the St. Lawrence Valley, the people's hunting grounds became severely diminished. At that time the government created the first official Indian villages.

By the mid–twentieth century, the trading post communities were being replaced by larger, permanent settlements. Also, well-defined trapping areas of at least several hundred square miles had evolved. People generally remained around a settlement in summer, retiring to their territory in small groups (10–20 people) to hunt and trap during the other seasons.

Since 1940, Canada has built over 20 hydroelectric dams and plants in Labrador. The government created several new reserves in the 1950s. In 1975, the Eastern Cree and Inuit ceded over 640,000 square kilometers of land to the James Bay Hydroelectric Project, in exchange for promises of hundreds of millions of dollars and various other provisions.

Religion People may have believed in a great sky spirit to whom pipe smoke was occasionally offered. The people certainly believed in any number of spirits or supernatural beings. The key to Naskapi/Montagnais religion was to maintain a healthy and respectful relationship with the spirit world. This could be done both by observing the various taboos and by acquiring certain techniques.

They especially attempted not to offend the spirits or souls of the animals upon which they depended for food, mainly by being as respectful as possible toward them. Other primary concerns were good health and successful births. Ceremonies included the Mokosjan, in which people ate caribou bone marrow. Feasting was also considered a religious practice, as was drumming.

Prayer was always offered before beginning any important activity. Boys fasted to obtain spirit helpers. Male and female shamans cured and kept away evil spirits. Shamans sometimes demonstrated their magic powers. In the shaking tent rite, shamans communicated with their spirits in specially built lodges to learn of good hunting areas. People feared cannibalistic monsters called Windigo (Montagnais) or Atsan (Naskapi).

Government Society consisted of perhaps 25–30 small, independent hunting (winter) bands related by marriage. There were several lodge groups (families of 15–20 people) to a band. A named band, or division, probably consisted of two or three of these winter bands (up to 300 people or so) who shared a general area. Several named bands came together in summer on lake shores or river mouths for fishing, group hunting, and socializing. These gatherings might consist of between 1,000 and 2,000 people. In all cases, band affiliation was fluid. Traditional chiefs or headmen had little or no formal authority, and all decisions were taken by consensus.

Customs Within the context of group cooperation for survival, individuals answered to no one about their personal behavior. Most people were generous, patient, and good natured. Joking, or kidding, was effective in maintaining social mores, because real criticism was taken very seriously and avoided if possible. Montagnais had defined and patrilineally inherited family hunting grounds. Although groups were associated with specific subsistence areas, in lean times they readily gave permission to share.

Within the lodge groups there was no real dependence of one individual on another, since sexual relations were not limited to marriage, divorce was easy to obtain, and children were in many ways considered a group responsibility. These structures and relations encouraged a general egalitarianism.

Although gender roles were not especially rigid, men generally worked with wood and stone and women with leather. Men hunted big game while women set snares and gathered berries. Women were secluded during their menstrual periods. Parents generally arranged marriages. Men tended to marry in their early twenties, and women in their late teens. Some men had two wives, but a few had more. Men were obligated to perform bride service for a year or so. Joking, or familiar, relationships with cousins sometimes led to marriages.

Children were raised with tolerance and gentleness by both men and women, regardless of whether or not they were "legitimate." The old and sick were sometimes killed out of a sense of compassion. Dead Montagnais were wrapped in birch bark and buried in the ground. A memorial feast followed the funeral. Naskapis placed their dead on platforms or in trees.

Dwellings Conical dwellings were covered mainly in birch bark (Montagnais) and caribou skin (Naskapi). They held between 15–20 people and featured central fires with top smoke holes. The ground was covered with branches and then mats or skins. The people also used temporary lean-tos, some made of snow.

The Naskapi also built large A-frame or rectangular lodges to house several families and for winter dancing. This structure was covered with caribou skins and floored with boughs. There were several fires in these structures. Caribou-skin coverings of more traditional lodges were not sewn but rather overlapped.

Diet Men hunted primarily moose (Montagnais), caribou (Naskapi), and fowl as well as bear and other animals. The people used canoes to pursue big game after driving the animals into water and also wore snowshoes to run the game down. Meat was generally stone boiled or roasted. Small game, snared by women and sometimes men, included hares, porcupines, and beaver. The people also fished for salmon, eels, and trout. The Montagnais and Naskapi of Labrador also harpooned seals (among other things, seal oil repelled mosquitoes) and fished through the ice, both activities probably borrowed from the Inuit.

Some Montagnais had gardens and may have made maple syrup. Wild foods, such as berries, grapes, apples, and bulbs, played a small role in people's diet. Food was unsparingly shared when necessary. Meals were generally eaten silently. Before they were pushed north by non-natives, the Montagnais of the Saint Lawrence region had a greater variety of food resources than their more northerly kin.

Key Technology Babies were carried in moss-bag carriers and used moss diapers. Men hunted using the bow and arrow, deadfalls, nets, snares, and spears. Some groups attracted moose with a birch-bark call. The crooked knife was a basic tool from at least the early nineteenth century on. Most aboriginal tools were made from bone, antler, bark, wood, and stone. People fashioned birch bark or animal skins into storage containers and bone and sinew into needles and thread.

Trade The Montagnais traded meat and skins at Tadoussac and other places with Great Lakes people for tobacco, corn, and even some wild rice. This location became key during the fur trade period. Northern bands acquired cedar to use for canoe ribbing. Some groups also traded for birch bark.

The Naskapi/Montagnais fashioned birch bark or animal skins into storage containers such as this one.

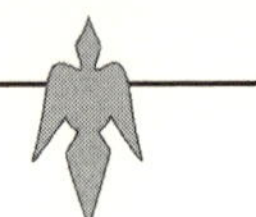

Notable Arts Red ochre and greasepaint were applied to clothing in geometrical patterns with bone or antler pens or stamps. Skin objects, including clothing and bags, were painted with groups of parallel lines, triangles, and leaf shapes.

Transportation The people made several varieties of snowshoes and birch-bark canoes as well as some log rafts. They used a canoe-sled with runners in spring. Toboggans were dragged with a cord across the chest. Dogsleds were used after around 1900.

Dress The Naskapi wore clothing of caribou skin that had been dressed, smoked, and sewn. Some southern groups wore breechclouts; leggings (sometimes attached with a belt); bear, moose, or beaver robes; and moccasins as well as attachable sleeves for winter wear. Clothing also included fur pants, sewn hare blankets, fur or hide headbands, and hide caps.

In the north, hooded winter coats had fur inside. Moccasins in the north were sometimes made of sealskin. Unlike many neighboring groups, who ran a charcoal-coated thread through the skin, the Naskapi tattooed themselves by simply rubbing charcoal or soot into a cut on the skin.

War and Weapons Warrior councils made military decisions. Weapons included bows and arrows, spears, and knives. The Montagnais also used clubs and shields, the latter custom probably borrowed from the Iroquois. They also adopted Iroquois methods of torture and cruelty.

Montagnais enemies included Micmac and Iroquois. They were allied with the Algonquin and the Maliseet. The Naskapi fought only with the Inuit to their east. They took few prisoners except that they might marry the women.

Contemporary Information

Government/Reservations Contemporary Innu communities in Quebec include Betsiamites (25,536.57 hectares; 2,752 people in 1994, of whom 2,352 lived within the territory), Kawawachikamach [Naskapi] (326.34 square kilometers; 526 people in 1994, of whom 456 lived within the territory), La Romaine (40.47 hectares; 832 people in 1994, of whom 812 lived within the territory), Essipit (formerly Les Escoumins; 38.5 hectares; 366 people in 1994, of whom 184 lived within the territory), Mashteuiatsh (3,150.99 hectares; 4,016 people in 1994, of whom 1,708 lived within the territory), Schefferville (Matimekosh [15.91 hectares] and Lac-John [23.5 hectares]; 660 people in 1994, of whom 608 lived within the territory), Mingan (3,887.82 hectares; 416 people in 1994, of whom 398 lived within the territory), Natashquan (20.63 hectares; 690 people in 1994, of whom 616 lived within the territory), Pakuashipi (Settlement of St. Augustin; 4.47 hectares; 217 people in 1994, of whom 216 lived within the territory), and Uashat (108.31 hectares) and Maliotenam (499.28 hectares) (total of 2,758 people in 1994, of whom 2,221 lived within the territory). Communities in Labrador include Sheshatshiu and Utshimassit (Davis Inlet; about 300 square miles; roughly 500 people in 1994). Government is generally by elected chief and councilors as well as an appointed band manager.

The Mushuau Innu (Davis Inlet), a community of around 535 people, are governed by a chief and the Mushuau Innu Band Council.

Sheshatshiu and Utshimassit (Davis Inlet) are represented politically by the Innu Nation. Other regional representational groups include Mamuitun, on the Quebec North Shore (Betsiamites, Essipit, Mashteuiatsh, Uashat-Maliotenam), and Mammit Innuat (La Romaine, Mingan, Natashquan, and Pakuashipi (St. Augustin).

Economy Among the East Cree, there are some jobs with the Hudson's Bay Company and oil and other companies. There is also some community-based service employment as well as some mainly short-term jobs in construction. Many people still hunt, fish, and trap. Some also work as guides, outfitters, and woodcutters. The salmon industry is important among some communities. The Naskapi Adventure Club is a northern travel agency. Government support is important.

Legal Status The communities listed under "Government/Reservations" are federally recognized, although Pakuashipi (St. Augustine) does not have reserve status. The Northeastern Quebec Agreement between the Innu of Schefferville, Hydro-Quebec, and provincial and federal governments (1978) pertained to the great regional dam projects. In exchange for payments of $9 million, confirmed land ownership, and land use rights, the people will see over 10,000 square kilometers of land flooded and tens of thousands more acres altered. A framework for negotiation was reached in 1995 between the Innu Nation and provincial officials concerning the former's claim of large portions of Labrador. Other land claims are under negotiation.

Daily Life Among the East Cree, many people retain elements of traditional religious belief either along with or instead of Christianity. Parts of these people's territory, such as north-central Labrador, has only recently been explored by non-natives. Most Innu, however, are Christian. In a marked departure from the precontact period, they have discarded former ideas about personal independence and duty to the group in favor of duty to individuals (women must obey men, children their parents, people their leaders). Few people remain self-sufficient.

Southeastern bands live in permanent frame-house villages. Hunting and trapping trips into the interior are far less important than they used to be, yet the cooperative ethic remains strong. Most people wear non-native dress, and most children go to non-native schools and are largely acculturated.

The Cree-Naskapi Act of Quebec (1984) replaced the Indian Act and provides for local self-government. The Labrador Innu (North West River) won an injunction in 1989, later overturned, preventing the military from continuing low-flying exercises of their region. The Naskapi-Montagnais Innu Association work for, among other issues, the sovereignty of the Davis Inlet Innu and the Sheshatshiu Montagnais. The Conseil Attikamek/Montagnais (12 bands in Quebec) is also negotiating for specific rights with the Canadian government.

In 1974, the people formed the Grand Council of the Crees (of Quebec) to deal with the ramifications of the James Bay hydroelectric project, which had been allowed to proceed over Indian opposition. The James Bay and Northern Quebec Agreement, ratified in 1975 but controversial ever since, called for cession of over 640,000 square kilometers of Indian land. In return, the people were promised a cash settlement of over $230 million and special concessions, including land ownership of over 3,300 square kilometers, subsistence rights on over 32,000 square kilometers more, and a veto over mineral exploitation.

However, not all of the money was allocated. An epidemic of childhood diarrhea was caused by the pollution of vital water supplies, and Indians are often excluded from many of the better jobs. The Cree still oppose the final stages of the project.

The people of Davis Inlet, led by the Mushuau Innu Band Council and the Mushuau Innu Renewal Committee (1993), have worked to address serious health and safety issues. They have constructed and renovated houses, instituted job training, and increased social services. Furthermore, in 1995 a multilateral agreement was signed calling for the return of the provincial court to Davis Inlet. This is part of the community's plan to assume greater responsibility in policing its own affairs.

Ojibwa, Northern

See Anishinabe (Chapter 8)

Salteaux

See Anishinabe (Chapter 8)

Sekani

Sekani (Se `kä nē), "People of the Rocks" (Rocky Mountains), from their own self-designation. They were culturally related to the Beaver and the Kaska.

Location Traditional Sekani territory is the Parsnip and Finlay River Basins, British Columbia. An eighteenth-century expansion to the south was largely checked by the Shuswap. In the nineteenth century, some groups had moved west into areas draining into the Pacific Ocean (Bear Lake and northern Takla Lake) to gain access to salmon. The people also gave up large parts of their eastern territory.

Population There were probably around 3,000 Sekani in the eighteenth century and around 200 in

the early nineteenth century, not counting 300 or so people in groups living west of the Arctic-Pacific divide. The 1991 Sekani population was 630, exclusive of Indians officially considered "non-status."

Language Sekanis spoke an Athapaskan language.

Historical Information

History The Sekani may have originated east of the mountains and been driven west by the Cree. They may once have been united with the Beaver. They probably first encountered non-natives in 1793. Around the same time, Shuswaps stopped the southward expansion of the people.

The North West Company established two posts in 1805, including Trout Lake (Fort McLeod). Trade forts continued to be established for the next several decades. The people began a decline shortly after the trade posts opened that was mainly linked with alcohol abuse and disease.

The Omineca gold rush occurred in 1861. By 1870, over 1,000 non-native trappers and miners had occupied the territory of the Senaki. Environmental degradation and the decline of natural resources, including game animals, were the result. In consequence of these trends, mal- and undernourishment were added to the people's woes, and their population declined even more sharply. Still armed mainly with traditional weapons, the people at that time were forced to give up their winter grounds east of the Rocky Mountains to the Beaver and Cree, who had access to firearms. Catholic missionaries were active in the area from about 1870 on.

Two new bands or groups created around the turn of the century were the T'lotona (Sasuchans intermarried with Gitksans) and Davie's Band (Otzane), people organized around the son of a French Canadian man and a Sasuchan woman. A large dam created in the 1960s displaced many bands and separated several traditionally linked Sekani groups.

Religion Young men fasted and dreamed alone in the wilderness to acquire supernatural guides, which were associated with animals or birds. These guides were only of help in emergencies. However, men might obtain other guides later in life, associated with either animals or natural forces, that might provide more regular assistance. These men became shamans, who were able to cause and cure disease, the latter for pay.

Women could not become curers but they could, through dreaming, acquire the power to foretell the future. Disease was considered to be caused by soul loss, taboo breaking, or malice. Some people were influenced by a quasi-Christian cult in the 1830s.

Government Several autonomous bands were led by a headman of little real authority. Sekani was the name of one such band. Regional bands in the nineteenth century were, from north to south, Tseloni, Sasuchan, Yutuwichan, and Tsekani. Other groups may have been Meadow Indians and Baucanne (Says-Thau-Dennehs). Bands owned hunting territories.

Customs Names were derived ultimately from guardian spirits. Most children were nursed for about three years. At puberty, girls were secluded and forced to observe special food and behavioral taboos, all designed to keep them apart from men and animals. Boys fasted and dreamed for spirit guides.

Men might have more than one wife, especially if the wives were sisters. Newly married men served their in-laws for a year or so but lived apart from them during that time. The dead may anciently have been buried in the ground or covered in brush huts; they were later cremated. Chiefs or other people of authority were placed in hollow-log coffins deposited in trees or on platforms. Daily mourning (wailing) could last for years after a death. The Sekani adopted matrilineal divisions and even quasi-potlatches for a short time in the nineteenth century, in imitation of the Carrier and Gitksan.

Dwellings Temporary conical lodges were covered with spruce bark or, later, moose hide. The people also built lean-tos covered with brush, bark, or skins as well as brush menstrual huts.

Diet Large game, such as moose, caribou, mountain sheep, and bear, constituted the bulk of the Sekani diet. Many other animals were also hunted, including porcupine, beaver, and marmot. There was some

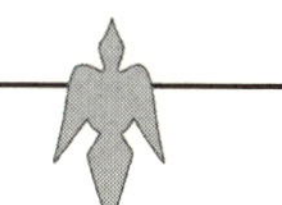

buffalo hunting, at least around 1800, in the eastern foothills and prairies. Some groups hunted in both summer and winter. Meat was boiled, roasted, or smoke dried.

Trout and whitefish were the most important fish species. Fish were occasionally taken at night, from canoes, in the light of pine torches. Other foods included fowl and berries. Surplus food was cached in trees.

Key Technology Hunting tools and war weapons included the bow and arrow, club (fashioned from a moose jawbone), and spear. The people also used deadfalls and babiche snares to take both large and small game. They caught fish with willow bark or nettle-fiber nets, bone hooks, spears, and some weirs. Most tools were made of bone, wood, and antler, with some stone for points and blades. They made spruce-bark or woven spruce-root containers and hide or netting bags. Babies were carried in bags lined with groundhog or rabbit fur.

Trade The Sekani traded with Carrier groups. They exported mainly products of the hunt.

Notable Arts Sekanis decorated their clothing with porcupine-quill and moose-hair embroidery.

Transportation Most people traveled overland, carrying their possessions on their backs. They used snowshoes in winter and, occasionally, some spruce-bark canoes.

Dress Men wore a sleeveless skin shirt, which they sometimes laced together between their legs, high skin leggings, and moccasins lined with fur. They added a breechclout after sustained contact with the Cree. Women wore similar clothing, although their leggings were shorter and their shirts were longer. Sometimes they wore a short apron as well.

Items of personal adornment included horn and bone bracelets. Hunters wore grizzly bear claws around their necks. Both sexes painted their bodies and wore marmot or hare robes, caps, and mittens in winter.

War and Weapons Enemies included the Cree, Beaver, and Shuswap. The Carrier were mostly friends, with notable exceptions. There was also some interband fighting. Bows were tipped with stone point "bayonets" for stabbing at close range.

Contemporary Information

Government/Reservations The Fort Ware Band owns three reserves with a total land area of 391 hectares. There were 328 band members in the mid-1990s, of whom 277 lived on the reserves. A chief and councilors are elected by custom. The band is affiliated with the Kaska Dene Tribal Council.

The Tsay Keh Dine Band (formerly known as Ingenika, a part [with Fort Ware] of the Finlay River Band [Tseloni and Sasuchan Bands]) owns five reserves with a total land area of 201 hectares. There were 282 band members in the mid-1990s, of whom 2 lived on the reserves (much of their land was flooded by BC Hydro) and a number on Crown lands. A chief and councilors are elected by custom. The band is affiliated with the Carrier Sekani Tribal Council.

The McLeod Lake Band is located in British Columbia.

Economy Important economic activities include freighting, trapping, guiding, logging, and construction.

Legal Status The above bands listed under "Government/Reservations" are federally recognized.

Daily Life Children attend federal and/or band and/or provincial schools. Fort Ware Band facilities include offices, a school, a community hall, a store, a clinic, and a motel. Tsay Keh Dine facilities include an airstrip, a school, offices, a fire station, and a community center.

Slavey

Slavey (`Slā vē), or Slave, is a translation of a name *(Awakanak)* given by the Cree enemies of these people. Their self-designation was *Dine'é,* "People." They were also known as *Etchareottine,* "People Dwelling in the Shelter." They are culturally related to the Dogrib and, like them, were not considered a "tribe" until relatively recently.

Location In the early eighteenth century, Slaveys lived between Lake Athabaska and Great Slave Lake. Their mid-nineteenth-century territory included the Mackenzie and Laird River Basins, from western Great Slave Lake south to around Hay Lake and north to Fort Norman, boreal forestland in present-day northeast British Columbia, northwest Alberta, and southwest Northwest Territories. The people live on reserves in this area today.

Population The Slavey population was possibly 1,250 in the late seventeenth century and was officially 5,120 in 1991.

Language Slaveys spoke dialects of a northeastern Athapaskan language.

Historical Information

History The Cree, carrying firearms, drove the people north from the Lake Athabaska area in the late eighteenth century. They encountered Alexander Mackenzie in 1789. The first trade post in the area was built in 1796, with additional posts following in the next 15 years. Anglican and Catholic missionaries arrived in 1858; Christianization was virtually complete by 1902.

Treaties signed with Canada in 1900, 1911, 1921, and 1922 generally called for land cessions in return for payments, services, and reserves. The high cost of trade items, as well as the relatively limited non-native presence in the area, kept the people from dramatically changing many aspects of their culture until well into the twentieth century. Slaveys adopted non-native material goods (such as metal items, firearms, flour, and tobacco) on a large scale after World War I, when many began trapping for income for the first time. At about the same time, groups began gathering for the summer at trade posts rather than at traditional lakeshore places, and gatherings were added for Christmas and Easter.

Permanent, significant governmental intrusion began only after World War II for some more remote groups, when the fur market collapsed. Oil and gas exploitation replaced furs as the region's most important commercial resource at about the same time. By the 1960s, most people had moved from the bush into towns and had enrolled their children in schools.

Religion People sought to acquire a guardian animal spirit in a dream, which would provide them with luck and assistance. Special songs usually accompanied powers provided by the guardian spirits. There were also malevolent spirits or supernatural beings, such as giants, who abducted young children. Quasi-medicine bundles, or collections of items inspired by the dream vision, were kept in a pouch or a box. With few herbal remedies, medicine men were primary curers through removing physical manifestations of illness from a patient. Souls were said to live again after death.

Government People with little real authority led several autonomous bands, each with perhaps 200 people, that came together only in summer, and even then only when conditions permitted. The bands were composed of local hunting groups of 10–15 people, within which food and other items were shared. Membership in all groups was fluid. An informal council of hunters settled disputes.

Customs Within the local group, all people fared roughly equally well or poorly in terms of subsistence. Most personal disputes were settled by compensation or, in extreme cases, banishment. Local groups often resolved differences by playing a game, such as the hand game, or through ritual competition by medicine men. The meeting of two local groups might be an occasion to feast and dance.

Individuals chose their own marriage partners, although parents also played a key role. A yearlong bride service for men followed a wedding. Men sometimes engaged in the custom of wrestling each other for their wives. Divorce was rare.

Women generally gave birth in a kneeling position attended only by women. There was some female infanticide. At her first menstrual period, a young woman left the camp and lived in a separate shelter for about ten days; she returned to the shelter every month. During this time she was subject to several food and behavioral taboos, such as avoiding eye contact with others and not traveling on an existing trail. Boys marked the passage into adulthood by making their first big game kill.

Unlike many groups, men did much of the hard work, such as obtaining firewood and preparing the lodge, in addition to hunting and fighting. Grandparents were important in the lives of children, often "joking" with them to teach proper behavior. The elderly and ill were rarely abandoned. Many people confessed wrongs on their deathbeds. The entire camp remained awake to witness a person's death. Death was greatly feared and was considered, with illness, to be the result of sorcery. Corpses were placed on scaffolds or covered with leaves and snow and placed with their property under a hut.

Dwellings The winter dwelling was a low pole-frame structure covered with moss, with a pitched spruce-bough roof and two doorways. There was an open smoke hole at the top. These structures might be 20 feet long and 10 feet wide and were inhabited by extended families. In summer, people built conical spruce, moose-hide, bark, or brush lodges.

Diet Men hunted mainly moose, but they also hunted woodland caribou, running them down and shooting them with bow and arrow in spring and snaring them with the help of dogs in summer and winter. Beaver were caught in wooden traps in fall and speared or clubbed in winter. Men also hunted numerous small animals as well as birds. Fish were also very important.

Meat and fish were either roasted, boiled, smoked, dried, or made into pemmican. Women gathered berries, roots, and some other plant foods. Food to be stored was cached in the ground (winter) or hung in a bag from a pole.

Key Technology Most animals were caught with babiche or sinew snares. Other hunting gear consisted of the bow and arrow, clubs, and spears. People fished with twisted willow bark or babiche nets and weirs as well as with hook and line. Other important items included stone adzes, beaver-tooth knives, bone or antler projectile points, woven spruce-root or -bark cooking vessels, and moose-hide, calf-skin, or hare-pelt diapers. Babies were carried in moose-hide bags lined with moss.

Trade Slaveys imported some native copper from the Yellowknife and Dogrib people. They also imported some caribou skins, flint, chert, and pyrites as well as Inuit bone and ivory knives. They exported moose and fish products.

Notable Arts There was some geometric-style painting and dyed porcupine-quill embroidery. The people made music from drums and caribou-hoof rattles.

Transportation The people used two types of snowshoes, beaver-hide or birch toboggans, birch or spruce-bark canoes, and some moose-hide rafts. Much travel took place overland, with goods carried on a person's back by means of a tumpline around the forehead.

Dress Clothing was mainly of moose skins and consisted of pointed shirts and coats, leggings joined to moccasins, tassels (men), dresses (women), robes, caps, and mittens. In some areas, women's clothing was made mostly of woven hare skins. Clothing was heavily fringed, with moose-hair and porcupine-quill decoration. People also wore moose-hide and rabbit-skin blankets.

Faces were tattooed with parallel lines on the cheek. Women wore woven spruce-root caps. Men plucked their facial hair and skewered their noses with wood or goose quills. Both sexes wore embroidered leather waist, wrist, and arm ornaments.

War and Weapons Despite their peaceful reputation, the Slavey were known to massacre Kaskas and other mountain Indian enemies. Neighboring tribes were reluctant to attack them for fear of witchcraft reprisals. The people also fought the Cree. War garments included bear-claw headdresses or feather caps. Weapons included willow-twig shields. War leaders were chosen on an ad hoc basis.

Contemporary Information

Government/Reservations Slavey communities include Hay River, Fort Laird, Fort Norman, Fort Providence, Fort Simpson, and Fort Wrigley in the Northwest Territories; Fort Nelson in British Columbia; and Hay Lakes Region in Alberta. The people own roughly 40,500 reserve hectares.

Fort Nelson (formerly the Slave Indian) Band owns four reserves with a total land area of 9,558

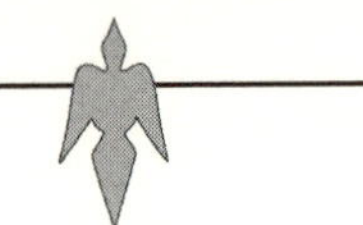

hectares. Total population was 575 in the mid-1990s, of whom 284 lived on the reserves. Local government is provided by an elected chief and councilors. The band is affiliated with the Treaty Eight Tribal Council.

Prophet River (formerly part of the Fort Nelson) Band owns one reserve with a total land area of 374 hectares. Total population was 151 in the mid-1990s, of whom 84 lived on the reserve. Local government is provided by a chief and councilors elected according to custom. The band is affiliated with the Treaty Eight Tribal Council.

Economy Government payments have largely taken the place of traditional strategies that provided long-term economic independence. There are seasonal jobs in oil and gas. At Fort Nelson, people engage in trapping, oil work, forestry, construction, guiding, road building, and freighting, and they collect gas royalties. Trapping, guiding, and work at a fur depot are the main activities at Prophet River.

Legal Status The Slavey are a federally recognized tribe.

Daily Life Traditional nomadic patterns have been replaced by a sedentary existence, especially since the 1960s. Since about the same time, the Slavey have become politically active to maintain control of their own affairs. The nature of local development, such as the proposed controversial oil and gas pipeline, may be the biggest issue of all.

Contemporary life is marked in part by a number of problems, including substance abuse and general ill health, substandard housing, limited educational and economic opportunities, crime, and racism. Most of these problems can be attributed to the tension between the loss of traditional culture and replacement by spiritually and materially inadequate non-native institutions, programs, and attitudes.

Facilities at Fort Nelson include offices, a community hall, a clinic, a school, and a garage. Facilities at Prophet River include offices and a store.

Tahltan

Tahltan (`Täl tan), from the Tlingit for "basin-shaped hollow," referring to a place at the mouth of the Tahltan River. There are also other possible origins and meanings of the name. Their self-designation was *Titcakhanotene,* "People of Titcakhan." They are sometimes classified, with the Kaska, as Nahani Indians and were culturally related to the Carrier.

Location The Tahltan lived, and continue to live, in northwest British Columbia, specifically the upper Stikine River drainage. They also shared the Stikine River Valley below Telegraph Creek with the Tlingit. The Tahltan hunted in the region in winter, whereas the Tlingit fished and gathered there in summer.

Population There were perhaps 2,000 Tahltans in the late eighteenth century and officially 1,330 in 1991.

Language Tahltan is a dialect of Tahltan-Kaska, an Athapsakan language.

Historical Information

History Tahltan history is in part a process of continuous adaptation of their native Athapaskan traditions to those of Pacific Coast cultures. Tahltans probably moved into their known territory in the seventeenth century. The rich natural resources of the region encouraged population growth, larger and more permanent habitations, acquisition of more material goods, increased social stratification, and a more complex culture in general.

Tlingit-Tahltan contact intensified after non-natives established a presence along the coast in the early nineteenth century. At that time, trade and the production of furs became increasingly important. As wealth grew, stratification became more pronounced. At the same time, with so many people dying, opportunities were rife for social mobility.

Major epidemics began in the early nineteenth century when coastal people brought germs into the interior. Up to 75 percent or more of Tahltans died from epidemics during the nineteenth century. Sustained contact with non-natives came when gold was discovered below Glenora in 1861 and especially after the 1874 gold strike at Cassiar. At that point, the Tahltan no longer controlled the Stikine River territory. In the late nineteenth century, survivors of various bands coalesced into one unit, or tribe, with a

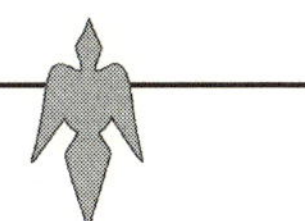

head chief. They built Tahltan village, a log house community.

The trend toward loss of land and control over their own destinies became even stronger following the Klondike gold rush of 1898, as thousands of non-native prospectors, missionaries, tourists, and entrepreneurs rushed into the region. Although many people were drawn into the wage economy as guides, wranglers, and government employees, most Indians remained engaged in traditional subsistence activities through the mid–twentieth century. Major employment opportunities during and after World War II included highway construction and asbestos mining.

Religion The people recognized a sky god and a sun god. Adolescent boys fasted in wilderness vision quests to obtain guardian animal or bird spirits and songs. Shamans dreamed powerful guardian animal spirits.

Government Six autonomous bands were each associated with a particular hunting territory. Leadership was relatively weak, and band membership was fluid. Eventually, under Tlingit influence, the bands became clans, which were led by a chief who inherited his office through his mother's line. (In the mid–eighteenth century a seventh clan was created, but it remained more of a Tlingit than a Tahltan entity.) Family and possibly clan leaders might be women. Clan leaders constituted an informal council. In about 1875, a single "tribal" leader emerged.

Customs Two matrilineal divisions, Raven and Wolf, each contained three of the clans. Eventually, the three clans in each division came to share hunting territories. People were socially ranked as either nobles, commoners, or slaves. The latter category was permanent, and the children of slaves were born slaves.

Commoners, however, could enter the nobility by accumulating wealth and giving potlatches and/or through marriage. Titles, which confirmed social status, could be inherited but also had to be earned, mainly by potlatching. Three kinds of potlatches existed among the Tahltans: those given by parents to acknowledge their childrens' rank, those given by rivals to increase their status, and memorial potlatches.

Men toughened themselves with icy plunges and by self-flagellation with willow switches. Girls reaching adolescence remained secluded for up to two years, receiving intensive training in the female tasks during that time and enduring a number of food and behavior taboos, such as keeping their faces covered. Young men served a prospective wife's family for a period of time before the wedding.

Widowers often married a sister of their late wife. Women were supported by—and often married—their nephews when their husbands died. The dead were cremated, after which the bones were placed on a post or within a small box raised off the ground. Death chants were sung for the dying and the dead. When a prominent person died, one of his slaves might be killed or, alternatively, freed.

Dwellings Tahltans lived in pole-frame lean-tos with bark roofs and earth-and-bough packing. Those who could covered the poles with moose hide. At semipermanent fishing villages, the people built bark-roofed huts with straight sapling walls and gabled roofs. In the main village, clans built structures up to 100 or more feet long that housed the clan's main families and served as a ceremonial hall. There were also special living and club houses for young, unmarried men.

Diet Tahltans ate mainly game, including caribou, moose, bear, buffalo, and a range of smaller animals, such as marmot and beaver. Dogs assisted in hunting. Fish, especially salmon, were an important part of the diet. Women gathered roots, berries, and other plant foods.

Key Technology Men hunted using bows and arrows, snares, deadfalls, spears, and traps. Caribou were caught in surrounds. People fished using weirs and a variety of nets. Women made various sized babiche net bags as well as bark cooking vessels. Babies were carried in leather bags.

Trade Tahltans had long-standing trade and other personal contacts with Tlingit, Kaska, and Sekani groups. They imported eulachon and salmon oil, dentalium and abalone shells and ornaments, stone

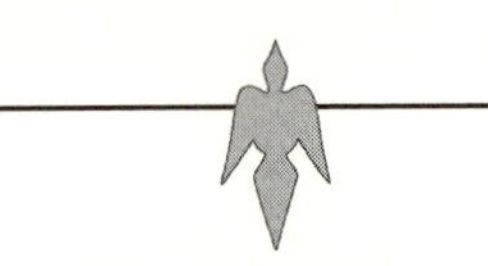

Fishing remains one of the Tahltan Indian's economic staples. These nets are hung out to dry along the Stikine River.

axes, woven blankets, and slaves (who originated among the Haida). Exports included moose and caribou products (such as cured hides and babiche) and furs.

Notable Arts Tahltans ornamented everyday objects, often with geometric designs.

Transportation The people made a few relatively poor quality spruce-bark canoes and temporary rafts. When people traveled overland, which they preferred to water travel, they might use snowshoes and carry baskets with tumplines. Women pulled a rough toboggan.

Dress Tanned skin and fur clothing included shirts and leggings, often with attached moccasins, for men and dresses (long shirts), leggings, and moccasins for women. Both sexes wore goat-skin and woven rabbit-fur robes as well as various personal adornments. Clothing was often decorated with quillwork.

War and Weapons Tahltans periodically fought the Inland Tlingit, Taku River Tlingit, and the Tsimshian (Ness River branch), mostly over trade and the use of subsistence areas. Weapons included bows and arrows, spears, and knives as well as antler bayonets. Warriors also used goat-skin helmets and armor. They took scalps and held women prisoners for ransom. There was also some ceremonial cannibalism. Allies included other Tlingit groups, the Dease River Kaska, and the Bear Lake Sekani.

Contemporary Information

Government/Reservations The Tahltan Band, located at Telegraph Creek, owns 11 reserves with a total land area of 3, 230 hectares. Band population in the mid-1990s was 1,309, of whom 238 lived on the reserves. A chief and councilors are elected according to provisions of the Indian Act. The band is unaffiliated.

The Iskut Band is of Sekani origin.

Economy Hunting, fishing, and trapping are still important. There is also some work as sport guides and miscellaneous seasonal and government wage work.

Legal Status The bands listed under "Government/ Reservations" are federally recognized.

Daily Life Children attend band and provincial schools. Tahltan band facilities include a community hall, an arts and crafts center, and stores.

Tanaina

Tanaina (Tu `nī nu), or Dena'ina, "the People." They were also known as *Knaiakhotana.* Designation as a tribe is a non-native convention, the people having consisted traditionally of various related tribes, or divisions, such as Kachemak, Kenai-tyonek, Upper Inlet, and Iliamna-susitna. They were culturally related to local Northwest Coast tribes such as the Tlingit.

Location Before contact with non-natives, Tanainas lived around the drainage of Cook Inlet, Alaska. Today, most Tanainas still live in cities, towns, and villages in the area as well as in other U.S. cities, particularly in the Northwest.

Population From perhaps 4,500 in the mid–eighteenth century, the Tanaina population dropped to around 3,000 in 1800. There were 400 Tanaina Indians in the United States in 1990.

Language Tanaina includes two major divisions—Upper Inlet and Lower Inlet—as well as many subdialects. It is an Athapaskan language.

Historical Information

History Captain James Cook entered the area in 1778, followed by more British traders. Local Indian groups already possessed iron and other items of non-native manufacture when Cook arrived. Although Indians welcomed the Europeans as traders, they strongly and, for some time, successfully opposed non-native settlement.

Russians built the first trading posts in the later eighteenth century. Relations between the Russians and Native Americans were difficult, even though the two groups regularly intermarried. Russians often attacked the native people and took them as hostages, ultimately turning many Indian and Inuit groups into forced labor. Russian control was generally brutal. As the violence subsided and more posts were built in the early to mid–nineteenth century, many native people became active in the fur trade.

A severe smallpox epidemic in 1838 took thousands of Indian lives. Other non-native diseases such as syphilis and tuberculosis also killed many Indians. The people had guns by the 1840s. Russian Orthodox missionaries arrived in force about 1845; the people were nominally converted within two generations, especially along the coast.

Although population decline and game shortages caused interior groups to consolidate their villages, the late nineteenth century was generally a time of increasing prosperity, owing mainly to the extension of credit and growing involvement in the fur trade. The peak years were between 1867 (when the United States purchased Alaska) and the fur market crash of 1897. As a consequence, traditional "rich men," or Indian trade leaders, became even wealthier and more powerful. One consequence of the U.S. purchase of Alaska was that the Tanaina lost legal rights as Russian citizens. U.S. citizenship was not granted until 1924.

The discovery of gold in the area around 1900 brought a flood of miners and other non-natives. Other factors, such as the growth of commercial fishing and canning industries (with their attendant pollution and resource monopolization), improved transportation, and continuing population declines

and game shortages, weakened social distinctions and contributed to the people's general decline.

These developments also hastened the transition from a subsistence to a wage economy. Canneries and commercial salmon fishing boomed by the mid–twentieth century. Schools, at least through the eighth grade, have been available to most Tanainas since the 1960s.

Religion Everything in nature was said to have a spirit. The people recognized three groups of beings in particular: mythological beings; supernatural beings, such as giants and tree people; and beings that interacted closely with people, such as loon, bear, and wolf spirits. There was also a fourth group of creatures known as Hairy Man and Big Fish. Ceremonies included memorial potlatches and first salmon rites.

Male and female shamans mediated between the human and spiritual worlds, using spirit powers acquired in dreams to cure illness and divine the future. To cure illness, shamans wore carved wooden masks and used dolls to locate and exorcise evil spirits. Shamanic power could be used for good or for evil. In addition to their spiritual power, many shamans enjoyed a great deal of political power, occasionally serving as the village leader ("rich man").

Government Tanainas traditionally organized into three distinct societies: Kenai, Susitna, and Interior. The three developed separately because of the difficulty of communicating across the hazardous Cook Inlet. The village was the main political unit. It was headed by one or more leaders ("rich men"), usually the wealthiest members of their clan lineage groups. Leadership functioned mainly as a redistributive mechanism, wherein goods flowed to the "rich man" and were redistributed by him according to need. The leader was also responsible for the moral upkeep of his people.

The power of these leaders was noncoercive, and their "followers" were bound to them only out of respect. Leadership qualities, in addition to wealth, included generosity, bravery, and hunting ability. A man who aspired to this position needed help and material support from his relatives.

Russians began appointing chiefs in the nineteenth century. These people were invested by the non-natives with the power to speak formally for their people. They acted as intermediaries between the non-natives and their people, especially in trade matters.

Customs Relatively stable winter villages gave rise to social hierarchy and other complex organizations. A dual societal division was further broken into matrilineal clans, approximately five in one division and ten in the other. Clans owned most property and controlled marriage as well as most hunting and fishing areas. Social control was maintained primarily by peer pressure, although revenge, physical retribution, and payments played a role also.

"Rich men" gave potlatches as an important means of economic redistribution and to increase or maintain their prestige. They were provided crucial support by their relatives. Potlatch occasions included life-cycle events as well as other opportunities to express generosity. Dentalium shells, certain furs, and, later, glass beads were the primary symbols of prestige. "Rich men" had several wives as well as slaves. The latter were generally well treated and not kept for more then several years. In general, women had a relatively high degree of prestige and honor and could become wealthy in their own right.

Men served their future in-laws for at least a year. Children were born in a separate house. Adoption was common. Puberty recognition was accorded to both sexes. Boys fasted, either in a room (Interior) or in the woods (Susitna), and ran in the morning. Girls were confined for the better part of a year, during which time they learned appropriate skills and proper behavior. They also endured various behavioral taboos during this time, including the prohibition against looking directly at anyone else.

People made loud noises around the sick and dying to keep malevolent spirits at bay. Corpses were cremated. Their ashes were placed either in boxes on posts or buried, and their possessions were destroyed or given away. Members of another clan were responsible for making all funeral arrangements. A mourning period of several weeks followed funerals. Memorial potlatches were held about a year after death.

Dwellings Winter villages consisted of from one to ten or more partially excavated houses with a tunnel

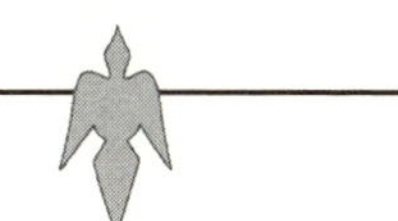

entry. Winter village population averaged between 50 and 200 people. These rectangular houses had log walls covered with grass and dirt. Spruce-bark or planked gabled roofs were also covered with dirt. There was a large main room with several side sleeping chambers. The total length ranged from 10 to 100 feet.

The houses featured rooms for several families, including a main room with a fire and sleeping platforms for adolescent boys. Compartments for married couples and their young children as well as adolescent girls were located underneath the platforms. Other chambers were for sweating, menstrual isolation, and sleeping for the elderly. Villages were often concealed or camouflaged against enemy attack.

Summer houses were similarly designed, but lighter. The people also built temporary houses, such as birch-bark or skin tents or log and sod structures, at fish and hunting camps. These houses held only nuclear or small extended families. House styles began to change in the nineteenth century with Russian influence.

Diet There was a wide dietary divergence between groups. Some, such as those in the extreme south, depended mainly on marine life, whereas the northern interior people were mainly hunters and fishers. Most groups depended on fish, especially all five kinds of salmon. Other important species included eulachon, halibut, and catfish.

Important sea animals included seals, otter, and beluga whale. Land animals included caribou, bear, moose, beaver, and rabbit. Caribou herds were driven into lakes and speared or shot, or they were channeled with fences into snares and surrounds. The people also ate birds and fowl as well as various roots and berries. Coastal people gathered shellfish.

Key Technology Fish were taken with nets, weirs, basket traps, and antler spears. Hunting equipment included spruce bows, deadfalls, traps, knives, clubs, and spears. Women wove spruce-root baskets. Babies rested in birch-bark cradles with moss diapers inside. There was some pottery.

Trade The Tanaina acquired kayaks and umiaks from the Alutiiq, serving also as intermediaries between those people and interior groups. The Tanaina participated in regional trade networks stretching across Alaska. Informally and at trade fairs, they traded with other Tanaina groups as well as with groups farther away. Wealthy men with established trade partners were especially successful. Traditional exports included wolverine skins, porcupine quills, and moose products. Imports included copper, dentalium shell, and cedar arrow shafts.

Notable Arts Men carved and decorated wooden bowls. Clothing was decorated with quills, shells, and ermine tails.

Transportation Water transportation included birch-bark canoes and moose-skin boats as well as Inuit-style sealskin kayaks and umiaks. People traveled overland in winter on foot (snowshoe); dogsleds dated from the mid–nineteenth century.

Dress Tailored clothing was made of tanned caribou or sheepskins. Both sexes wore a knee-length undergarment, a shirt, and boots. Fur coats and shirts were added in winter. Rain gear included a whale-membrane parka and waterproof salmon-skin boots. In winter, the long undergarment had knee-high bear or beluga whale–soled boots attached. Blankets were made of sewn rabbit skins. Skin shirts were worn in summer.

Clothing was often dyed brown or red, embroidered with porcupine quills, and decorated with fur trim and shells. Decoration often reflected social rank. Tattooing and face painting were common, especially among the wealthy. Women wore bone labrets in their lower lips. Both sexes pierced their ears and septa for shell decorations.

War and Weapons Enemies included the Alutiiq and occasionally the Ingalik. Villages were generally camouflaged to discourage attack. Captives on both sides were taken and sold as slaves.

Contemporary Information

Government/Reservations Tanaina population centers include Nondalton (roughly 160 native residents in 1990), which is governed by the seven-member elected Nondalton Tribal Council and a

seven-member elected city council); Pedro Bay (roughly 40 native residents in 1990), which is governed by the seven-member elected Pedro Bay Village Council); Anchorage; and Tyonek. The first two fall under the purview of the Bristol Bay Native Corporation and are members of the Lake and Peninsula Borough. Nondalton is located between Lake Clark and Lake Iliamna, and Pedro Bay is located on Lake Iliamna.

Moquawkie Reserve consists of 26,918 acres. Government is by village council, with elected officials such as mayor or president. The institution of "rich man" began to decline after about 1900. There have been no "rich men" in the traditional sense since the 1960s. Village corporations with elected boards of directors administer Alaska Native Claims Settlement Act (ANCSA) assets.

Economy Important economic activities include commercial fishing, including canning; construction; trapping; air transportation; and the oil industry. Tanainas also work as fishing and hunting guides. Tyonek village collects investments from oil revenues. Subsistence hunting and fishing also remain important.

Legal Status The Tanaina are represented by the Cook Inlet Region Corporation and the Bristol Bay Regional Corporation for the purposes of the ANCSA.

Daily Life Tanainas are generally acculturated, although many retain a strong pride in their heritage and traditions. The three traditional societies are no longer distinct. The clan system is still important in most areas. Most people are Russian Orthodox Christians, although some elements of traditional religion survive. Tyonek used revenue from oil leases in part to modernize village facilities. Local concerns include bridge construction and road improvement. A Tanaina Athapaskan Indian cultural facility has been proposed, perhaps to be built in Iliamna.

Tanana
See Ingalik

Tlingit, Inland
See Tlingit (Chapter 3)

Tutchone
See Kutchin

Yellowknife
See Chipewyan

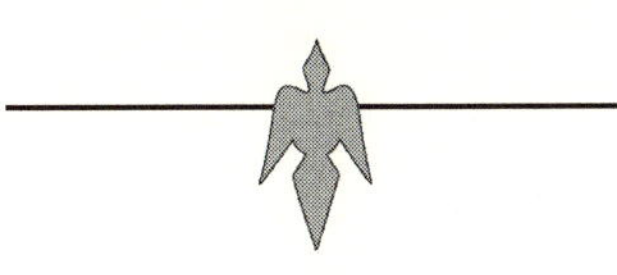

Chapter Ten

The Arctic

Above left: Yup'ik children arrive for school in reindeer-drawn sleds.
Above: This ivory carver uses a bow to cause his wooden drill to burn into and penetrate a walrus tusk.
Right: The Alutiiq hunted seals in part by the use of calls and decoys such as this wooden seal's-head helmet.

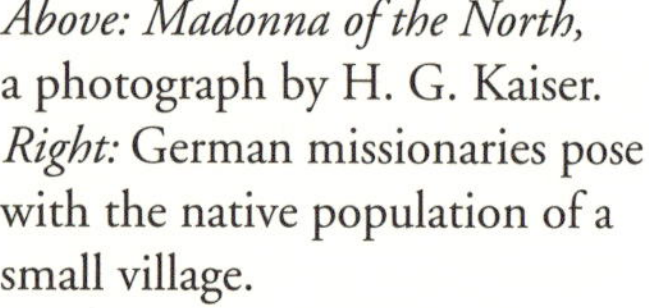

Above: Madonna of the North, a photograph by H. G. Kaiser.
Right: German missionaries pose with the native population of a small village.

Arctic

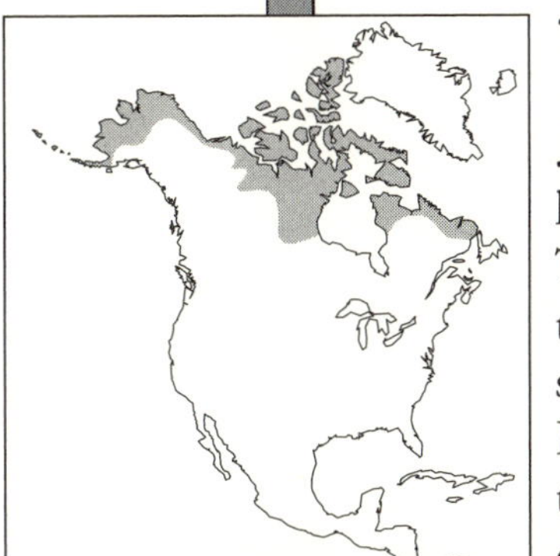

For people who have never lived there (and for some who have), the word "Arctic" conjures up a landscape almost incredibly forbidding. The Inuit, however, over the course of thousands of years, learned to live successfully in that cold, rugged country. Inuit (plural of Inuk) means "People" in the native language. In recent years, and especially in Canada and Greenland, it has replaced Eskimo, an Algonquian word meaning "eaters of raw meat" and one that many Inuit find offensive. The Unangan, or Aleut, are also generally considered to be Arctic, rather than Subarctic, residents.

The Arctic is a remarkable region in several ways. It stretches 5,000 miles from Asia (Siberia) to Greenland and 1,800 miles from southeast Labrador to the Queen Elizabeth Islands. It encompasses well over 2,000 miles of the Alaska coast and is generally considered to include the 1,000-mile-long Aleutian Island chain. Another way to think of the vastness of the Arctic region is that it is roughly 12,000 miles (20,000 kilometers) from the eastern Aleutian Islands and along the coast of northern Alaska and Canada to Greenland. The total aboriginal population—including perhaps 15,000 Unangans, 31,000 Yup'iks, and 35,000 Inuits—was probably in the vicinity of 80,000 people. Four modern nations claim Arctic lands: Canada, Denmark, Russia, and the United States.

Arctic winters are long, dark, and extremely cold, except less cold right along the Pacific Ocean and adjacent waters. Although the interior may be colder in winter, fierce winds blow relentlessly along the coast. The flat tundra is covered with ice and snow in winter, but owing to poor drainage and the presence of permafrost it becomes boggy in summer, a perfect environment for mosquitoes, black flies, and other such insects. Although there are few or no trees in most of the Arctic, there are, during the brief

Native Americans of the Arctic

Edward S. Curtis's photo of an Inuit hut and family. In the summer, the Inuit constructed summer tents of seal or caribou skin over bone or wood frames.

summer, dwarf flowers, mosses, and lichens. As little as four inches of precipitation may fall in a year, except for Labrador and especially southwest Alaska. It is fortunate that ocean ice tends to lose its salinity after a year or so; otherwise finding fresh water would have been a serious problem for many Arctic residents.

All native Arctic people speak languages belonging to the same family, known as Eskimo-Aleut, or Eskaleut. Aleut is considered a separate language with two main dialects. The Eskimo language is made up of Inuit-Inupiaq (Eastern Eskimo), or Inuktitut, and Yup'ik. Yup'ik is divided into five branch languages and several dialects, whereas Inuktitut is broken merely into mutually intelligible dialects. The Inuit also maintained a nonverbal language based on body expression and other cues.

Some Arctic peoples were forced to deal with non-natives in the 1780s, whereas others did not experience direct contact until almost the twentieth century. The initial results of contact were mixed: They included disease epidemics, the breakdown of traditional structures and morality, and growing economic dependence as well as a new and acceptable religion and helpful trade goods. In many cases, native people continued to live in at least a semitraditional way until after World War II. Since then they have experienced many changes but not, as in the south, genocidal wars and the wholesale confiscation of their land.

Anthropologists remain uncertain whether the various native Arctic people came directly from Siberia or adapted to their environment from the Subarctic. Many believe that ancestors of the Inuit arrived in North America far later than did ancestral American Indians—perhaps only about 4,000 years ago—and in fact were preceded by at least 10,000 years by paleo-Indians. Along the Alaskan Peninsula and parts of the Aleutians, two cultures—Kodiak (circa 2500 B.C.E.) and Aleutian (circa 2000 B.C.E.)—continued approximately unchanged until the Russians arrived in the eighteenth century. Both were characterized by the use of poisoned lances for whaling, detachable barbed-head harpoons, an emphasis on clothing and personal decoration, and the development of woodworking, painting, and weaving.

Meanwhile, a hunting tradition known as Arctic Small Tool (Denbigh) arose around the Bering Sea from the Paleo-Arctic peoples of the rest of Alaska and northern Canada around 5,000 years ago. After about 1,000 years it had diffused throughout much of Alaska and Canada. These people made small flint blades, skin-covered boats, bows and arrows, needles, semiexcavated houses, and stone lamps. In the east, this complex was further refined into the somewhat more sea-oriented Dorset Tradition by about 1000 B.C.E. Dorset people also adapted well to snow and ice, possibly originating the snow house.

Again beginning in the Bering Sea area, the Norton culture materialized about 2,000 years ago. It in turn gave way to the Thule culture, which gradually overtook all other cultural traditions save the Aleutian by about the twelfth century. Thule people had dogs and sleds, umiaks and kayaks, the bow and arrow, and the harpoon thrower (atlatl), and they hunted whales. Through increased specialization and adaptation to local environments, this culture led directly to those found by non-natives.

With the possible exception of Native Alaskans, Arctic peoples were not organized into tribes. Instead, they saw themselves as members of groups that were tied to the land but whose definition nevertheless depended on perspective. These groups carried the suffix *-miut,* "people of." The smallest and most basic unit was the nuclear family. The extended family generally formed a household. Camps, or settlements, were seasonal constructions comprising one or more households. The larger of these groups might be considered bands.

Whaling was a special occupation practiced mainly in northwest Alaska. The whaling umiaks were led by a captain and chief harpooner. This eighteenth-century drawing depicts whaling off the coast of Greenland.

Leadership was generally undeveloped in the Arctic. In certain temporary situations, such as whaling expeditions, strong leaders emerged, but there was little formal structure. Leaders were usually older, experienced men who might be heads of leading households and excellent hunters and who, in whaling cultures, probably owned an umiak. Authority was more formalized in southwest Alaska, owing partly to the influence of Northwest Coast cultures.

Hunting sea mammals—ringed and bearded seals, walrus, narwhal, and whales—was the main occupation of most Inuit men. Hunting walrus was considered inordinately dangerous, owing to the animals' size and aggressive nature. (Polar bears presented the same problem and were taken, if at all, mainly for their hides.) Most men hunted seals from

ice floes in winter. This was an extremely demanding task. Seals must come up for air, so men waited with their dogs and various equipment (see discussion of key technologies that applied to hunting) at breathing holes. In order to catch one seal, a man might have to guard a hole for hours, motionless in the dark and bitter cold. Breathing-hole sealing was done communally, so that a number of holes could be covered at once.

Whaling was a special occupation practiced mainly in northwest Alaska. The whaling umiaks were led by a captain and chief harpooner. Once the great animal was fatigued by the initial thrust and from the drags, it would slow down enough for other men to spear it to death. The whale was then either towed to shore or left to drift back. In the case of seals and whales, the kill was divided according to very precise and respected formulas.

In other seasons, a number of subsistence activities took place. Men stalked seals on the ice or harpooned them on open water from kayaks. Birds such as ptarmigan, ducks, and geese were taken, as were their eggs. In some areas, people gathered berries. Fishing was a three-season or in some areas a four-season activity.

Among the land animals, caribou were by far the most important source of food. Most groups took advantage of the great seasonal migrations, particularly those in late summer and fall. Men working together generally shot or speared the beasts from land or from kayaks as they crossed bodies of water or forced them, with corrals and/or stone cairns, into narrow places and shot them there. Other land animals used for meat and/or fur included musk ox, wolf, fox, wolverine, and squirrel.

In addition to food, caribou also provided the single most important source of raw material. From the caribou, and other animals as well, came clothing, shelter, bedding, boats, thread, and lines (sinew). The people made a variety of tools and weapons, such as harpoons, bow and arrow, needles, thimbles, knives, axes, adzes, drills, scrapers, and shovels, primarily from bone and antler. The defining women's tools, reflecting their main activities, were the ivory or bone needle, the semilunar, sinew-backed knife, and the stone skin scraper.

People used a number of chipped stone (flint, slate, or quartz) items, such as points, blades, pots, and scrapers. Some copper was also used around Coronation Gulf. Many people depended on soapstone (pottery in southwest Alaska) oil- or blubber-burning lamps with moss wicks for heat and cooking. Wood, mainly driftwood, might provide boat and house frames, boxes, tool and weapon handles, and dishes. Depending on location, baleen could also be worked into boxes or other items. Other key technologies included movement indicators (for breathing-hole sealing), various types of harpoons (especially with detachable heads), throwers (atlatls), seal nets, bird bolas, three-pronged spears, fishhooks, stone fish weirs, and small animal traps and snares. Most people started a fire either by striking two pieces of pyrite or by friction generated with a thong drill.

Chipped stone work was well developed among the Native Arctic people, but they were particularly

This ivory carver uses a bow to cause his wooden drill to burn into and penetrate a walrus tusk (1912).

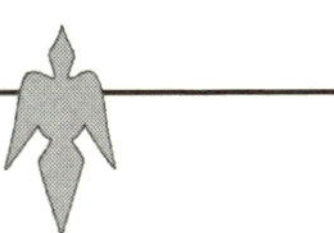

Although they varied somewhat from place to place, kayaks were basically one-man, closed-deck hunting canoes. A wooden frame was lashed with sinew and covered with sewn seal or caribou skin. Men propelled them with double-bladed paddles, as shown in this 1906 photograph, and used them mainly for hunting.

adept at carving figurines, amulets, toys, and other items out of bone, antler, and ivory. Tailored clothing was decorated with finely sewn furs. Some groups, mainly in Alaska, carved and painted wooden ceremonial and dance masks. Baskets were particularly fine among the Unangan, but people in southwest Alaska and in Labrador made them as well. In some areas, music and storytelling were considered high arts.

Although kayaks varied somewhat from place to place, they were basically one-man, closed-deck hunting canoes. They were made of a wooden frame lashed with sinew and covered with sewn seal or caribou skin. Men propelled them with double-bladed paddles and used them mainly for hunting. Skin-covered umiaks were larger, open boats, used either for whale hunting or simply for transportation, depending on the region. In the latter case they were rowed or paddled by women. Sleds, pulled by dogs and/or people, were used for winter travel. These were built of a wood frame lashed together with rawhide. The wood, hide, or bone runners were often covered with moss and then ice to ensure a smooth ride.

Inuit built two basic types of winter houses, depending on location. Primarily in the central region, snow houses were the rule. Two men could build one in a hour or so. Snow blocks were cut, placed on a circle about 10 to 15 feet in diameter, stacked in an inward-moving spiral, and knocked into place. Small porches were generally used for storage. Women chinked the gaps with snow. People entered through a passageway built underground to trap the cold air and keep it out. A sheet of clear ice or gut served as a window. Benches and tables were made of snow. Snow platforms, covered with willow twigs or baleen and then thick, warm skins and furs, served as beds. Women tended the lamp, over which was placed a cooking pot or drying rack. Snow houses often were attached to one another in the interests of sociability and added warmth. They were also used temporarily by travelers and hunters in other parts of the Arctic.

The other major winter house type was the semiexcavated nonsnow dwelling. This square or oblong house was constructed of a wood or whale bone frame covered by sod and snow. As with the snow house, entrance was generally gained through an underground or tunnel-like passageway. In some areas people entered these houses through the roof. Other structures included the *kashim,* or men's large ceremonial house, and summer tents of seal or caribou skin over bone or wood frames.

Dress, as might be imagined, was well constructed for warmth. Most clothing was made of tailored caribou skin, although polar bear, wolverine, squirrel, or even bird or fish skins were occasionally

An Arctic dwelling made of sod (right) and a storehouse (left) beside the Naknek River (1899). In this particular region of the Arctic, dwellings were mainly inhabited by related women and children. This photo also reveals the flatness of the tundra terrain. While there are few or no trees in the region, there are, during the brief summer, dwarf flowers, mosses, and lichens.

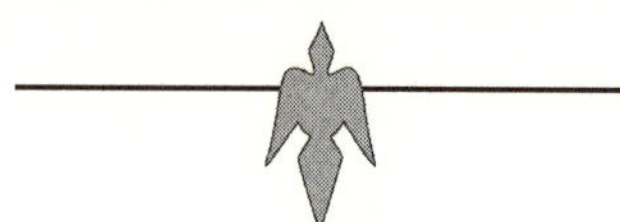

used by some groups. In general, people wore both inner and outer garments in winter, with the inner garment fur side in and the outer garment fur side out, although in summer only the inner garment was worn, fur side out. Outer shirts (parkas) were cut away at the sides and featured a long tail at the rear and a hood, which women wore extra large to shelter babies. Both sexes wore pants, stockings, insulated mittens, and sealskin boots or low shoes, depending on the season. Raincoats were carefully sewn of waterproof gut. Clothing was often decorated with colored furs or fringe. Items of personal adornment included labrets (lip plugs), ear pendants, nose rings, and tattoos.

Although regional variations must be acknowledged, some common threads concerning religious belief among native Arctic people may be discerned. Most people believed that all things, animate and inanimate, had souls, or spirits. These beings varied in appearance. In order to maintain a positive and respectful relationship with them, particularly with the spirits of game animals, people observed any number of taboos or behavioral proscriptions and rules. Observing the taboos was considered an essential aspect of health maintenance. In order to enlist the aid of helpful spirits or to ward off bad spirits, people also used magic or wore amulets (identified with specific spirits and functions). The loss of an individual's soul not only gave offense to other souls or spirits but might also cause illness or death.

Female and especially male shamans were in touch with and could control various beings of the spirit world. A long period of training was required before one could be considered a shaman. Shamans cured individual disease, and they saw to the overall health of the community, in part by ascertaining who broke which taboo when disaster befell the community. Performance was central to their method. They also exercised a degree of leadership in the community group. Their authority, however, was inspired more by fear than respect, as they were thought to be able to harm people through the agency of their supernatural powers.

In a more general sense, most native Arctic people recognized a dichotomy between the worlds of the land and the sea. There were various rules against using the same weapons to hunt land and sea animals, for example, and other taboos designed to maintain separation between the two realms. (This is one reason why the polar bear, which inhabited both land and sea, was considered so awesome.) There was also a general recognition (except in western Alaska and northwestern Hudson Bay) of an undersea female deity. Some western Alaska communities observed the Bladder and the Memorial Feasts. The Midwinter Feast was central to the ceremonial season in the central Arctic.

In terms of family and social customs, descent was generally bilateral. Kinship was of primary importance to these people, so much so that "strangers"—those who could not immediately document kin affiliations—were perceived as potentially hostile and might be summarily killed. Other groups of people subject to willful death were infants, especially females, and old people. Suicide was not uncommon, nor was cannibalism, but only in the most extreme cases of need. Prospective husbands often served a future bride's parents for a period of time (bride service). Wife stealing, committed in the overall competition for supremacy, might end in death, as might other conflicts, although murders were subject to revenge. Corpses were generally wrapped in skins and left on the ground. In southwest Alaska and the Aleutians, mummification was also practiced. Pastimes included kickball, acrobatics, string games, and storytelling.

Formal nonkin partnerships were a distinctive feature of most native societies in the Arctic. This custom stemmed from the need for nonkin members to work cooperatively. Partners might cooperate in a number of areas, including hunting, trade, and even death vengeance. Within certain male partnerships, wives might be exchanged for a more or less temporary period of time. Any children who resulted from such an arrangement were considered fully legitimate. Other types of formal nonkin relationships were formed between "joking partners" and people who shared the same name (though they might or might not be the same gender).

The direct encounter with non-natives began at widely divergent times in the Arctic; perhaps 500 years ago on Baffin Island and the Labrador coast to as little as 75 or so years ago east and north of the

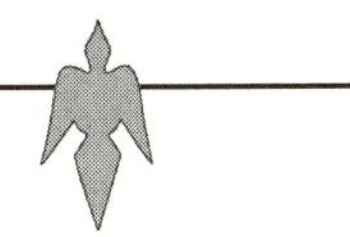

Mackenzie Delta. (Norse people may have met some northeastern Inuit as early as circa 1000.) Europeans came looking for the mythical northwest passage, a water route through the continent to Asia. Non-natives also came to exploit marine and land resources such as sea otter, whale, and walrus. In most cases, the initial period of contact was marked by some two-way trade, in which the natives received mainly metal products (and, later, rifles and ammunition), and the initiation of severe disease epidemics. Occasionally, natives served as guides and played other important roles in the exploration of the far north.

Traditional life began to change for most Arctic natives only with the introduction of fox fur trapping in the late nineteenth and early twentieth centuries. Trading posts sprang up in many native communities. Credit for food and other items extended in the fall was repaid with fox pelts in the spring. With more and more effort and resources going into trapping, and as opportunities for wage labor slowly increased, people began to drift away from their traditional lives. Residential areas around the posts grew in size, although most remained small until after World War II. Most included missionaries and, in Canada, a detachment of the Royal Canadian Mounted Police (RCMP). The former opened schools and clinics, and both worked to reduce violence among the Inuit.

Meanwhile, Russians had colonized southwestern Alaska and parts of the Aleutian Islands from the mid–eighteenth century on. The natives put up a fierce resistance to the Russians' general brutality. After becoming wealthy from sea otters and seals, and defeating the people into the bargain, the Russians "sold" Alaska to the United States in 1867. By then, Yankee whalers were plying the north Alaska coast, bringing alcohol, disease, and trade items as well as some jobs and a measure of cosmopolitanism to the natives.

The near extinction of the whale population by the early twentieth century coincided with the beginning of fox trapping, commercial fishing and canning, and various gold rushes. These activities all brought severe disruption to Native Alaskans, along with some employment. At about the same time, the U.S. government required all native children to be removed from their families and educated at remote boarding schools. It also attempted to force the people to "settle down" by pressuring them to maintain domestic reindeer herds—not to farm, as was the case with Native Americans to the south.

A nineteenth-century woodcut depicts an Arctic version of a ball game using a stuffed sealskin.

The market proved to be at least as mysterious and intractable a force as were the elements. When fox fur prices dropped sharply in the 1930s, many Arctic natives were devastated. Soon, however, military activity in response to World War II and the Cold War formed the basis for a recovery. Natives in both Canada and Alaska found jobs in construction and with government projects, although, at least in Alaska, many natives migrated to urban centers such as Anchorage and Fairbanks. In 1959, Alaska became the forty-ninth state of the United States.

At about the same time, the Canadian government, under the auspices of the Department of Northern Affairs and Natural Resources (DNANR; 1954), assumed responsibility for comprehensive public assistance as well as compulsory education and health care. As part of these programs, it encouraged natives to settle down in permanent communities. In theory, settlements were self-governing, but decisions were subject to review by Canadian officials. School curricula were culturally and practically inappropriate. Local jobs, where they existed, were generally unskilled and poorly paid. Progress with diseases such as tuberculosis was gradually offset by the rise of substance abuse and other health problems caused by a less healthy diet as well as a general moral breakdown.

Since the 1960s, native people of the Arctic have become increasing active politically. In Canada,

organizations like the Committee for Original People's Entitlement (COPE, 1970) and the Inuit Tapirisat of Canada (ITC, 1971) have taken the lead in advocating for land claims, appropriate resource management, language and educational rights, and other similar issues. In 1993, the Tungavik Federation of Nunavut (an outgrowth of the ITC) convinced the Canadian government to divide the Northwest Territories at the tree line and to establish in 1999 a new, mainly Inuit territory of roughly 350,000 square kilometers—roughly one-fifth of the land mass of Canada—to be known as Nunavut ("our land"). The settlement also includes over $1 billion in compensation as well as a strong Inuit role in decision making regarding land use and resource royalties. Other groups have claims pending as well.

Huge oil deposits were located on Alaska's North Slope in the 1960s, and plans for an 800-mile pipeline were begun. People began to organize around this and other issues, such as their exclusion from discussions about Alaska's native land claims as well as the low levels of opportunity for and the degree of poverty experienced by both rural and urban natives. In 1966, eight regional native organizations joined together to form the Alaska Federation of Natives (AFN) and proceeded to push a claim for almost 400 million acres of land.

In 1971, all sides resolved their interests with the signing of the landmark Alaska Native Claims Settlement Act (ANCSA). In brief, roughly 41,000 natives agreed to cede their aboriginal (including subsistence) rights in exchange for corporate ownership of 44 million acres and almost $1 billion in compensation for lands lost. Of the cash settlement, 10 percent went toward per capita payments and the rest toward the establishment of various capitalist ventures under the administration of 12 (later 13) regional and more than 200 village corporations. Corporate interests including mining, real estate, seafood processing, construction, and numerous other fields. There are also 12 nonprofit corporations, through which human service funding is channeled. The act has been amended several times, most notably in 1987.

The practical results of ANCSA have been mixed for the native population. Interpretation has given rise to seemingly endless legal and administrative entanglements. Stock ownership is subject to sale, a provision that recalls the 1887 Dawes Severalty Act. The issue of subsistence rights, in particular, has been very problematic, as have the issues of sovereignty and self-determination. Furthermore, not all corporations have been profitable. Native groups continue to act independently to advance what they perceive as their legitimate interests ignored by ANCSA.

Despite the growth of local cities and towns, most of the roughly 70,000 (1990) native Arctic people living on the Aleutian Islands and in Alaska (45,000) and Canada (25,000) still live in small communities in or near their traditional lands. Communities generally feature frame houses with all modern amenities. For reasons of survival as well as identity, many people still engage in subsistence activities, although guns, power boats, and snowmobiles have radically changed the hunting dynamic. Important economic activities in the far north also include commercial fishing, guiding, tourism, oil-related work, mining, construction, and government work and assistance. Various cooperative and traditionally organized businesses increase access to markets as well as goods and services. Arts and crafts, including sculpture, carvings, prints, and woven items, are a key part of the native economy.

In Canada, Inuktitut is spoken in all Inuit communities. Education is locally controlled, as it is in Alaska. Health problems, including substance abuse, death by accident and violence, malnutrition, and infectious disease, persist among Canadian Inuit. In general, Native Alaskans have access to good stores, transportation, and infrastructure. They face many of the same problems as do Canadian Inuit, however.

Building on a tradition of Inuit cooperation, and as part of a general pan-Inuit movement, the Inuit Circumpolar Conference (ICC) held its first assembly in Barrow, Alaska, in June 1977. The ICC holds NGO (nongovernmental organization) status within the United Nations. It represents the interests of native Arctic people of Greenland (Denmark), Scandinavia, Canada, Alaska, and Russia. Major issues facing Arctic natives include land claims, sustainable economic development, environmental pollution, climate change, and sovereignty. Pollution—mainly from oil spillage, industrial chemicals such as PCBs, nuclear waste, and other sources—remains a big

threat and a major issue in the Arctic. Despite the vast size of the Arctic, regional cooperation may offer the best hope for these people to make significant gains in the twin goals of political sovereignty and economic self-sufficiency.

Aleut

See Alutiiq; Unangan

Alutiiq

The word Alutiiq (A ˋlu tēk) means "a Pacific Eskimo person"; the plural form is Alutiit. The Alutiiq were a maritime people. The people are also known as Pacific Eskimos, Pacific Yup'ik, South Alaska Inuit, Yuit (with the Yup'ik), or Aleut; however, Aleut is easily confused with the culturally and linguistically separate native people of the Aleutian Islands. The word "Aleut" is of Russian origin.

The self-designation of the Alutiiq people is *Sugpiaq* ("real person"). The three traditional subgroups are Chugachmiut (Prince William Sound), Unegkurmiut (lower Kenai Peninsula), and Qikertarmiut, or Koniagmiut (Kodiak Island). There are many similarities to Unangan culture.

Location Alutiit lived and continue to live along coastal southern Alaska, between Prince William Sound and Bristol Bay. Kodiak Island was one of the most densely populated places north of Mexico.

Population The aboriginal (mid– to late eighteenth century) population was between 10,000 and 20,000 people. There were about 2,000 Alutiit in 1850 and roughly 5,000 in the 1990s.

Language Alutiit spoke the Sugcestun, or Suk, dialect of the Pacific Gulf Yup'ik branch of Eskimo, an Eskaleut language.

Historical Information

History The Alutiiq people had been living in their historic territory for at least 2,000 and perhaps as many as 7,000 years when the Dane Vitus Bering, working for Russia, arrived in 1741. Although he may not have actually encountered any people, contact became regular in the 1760s and 1770s. It was generally resisted by the Alutiiq. The first permanent Russian settlement was established in 1784, on Kodiak Island. By that time British and Spanish seamen had also visited the area.

In part by keeping their children as hostages, Russians soon forced the natives to hunt sea otter pelts and do other work for them. Disease and general oppression soon cut the Alutiiq population dramatically. Many people were acculturated to the Russian religion and customs when the United States gained political control of Alaska in 1867.

At that time there began a renewed push for acculturation in another direction. Children were soon sent to mission and Bureau of Indian Affairs boarding schools, where they were forced on pain of punishment to accommodate to the U.S. model. Economically, canneries and commercial fishing dominated the region from the late nineteenth century on.

Several Alutiiq villages suffered a devastating earthquake and tsunami in 1964. The Alaska Native Claims Settlement Act (ANCSA, 1971) had a profound influence on the people. The act established 12 formal culture areas, of which 3 fell in Alutiiq territory. In 1989 the *Exxon Valdez* ran aground and spilled nearly 11 million gallons of crude oil in Alutiiq territory, resulting in a tremendous loss of sea life, among other things.

Religion The people recognized one or several chief deities as well as numerous supernatural beings. Success in hunting required a positive relationship with the spirits of game animals. Human spirits were reincarnated through birth and naming. Trances, as well as certain masks and dolls, allowed contact with the supernatural.

A large variety of dances, ceremonies, and rituals, including masked performances, songs, and feasts, began in early winter. Specific ceremonies included a memorial feast, a ritual to increase the animal population, the Messenger's Feast (a potlatchlike affair that took place between two closely related villages), life-cycle events, the selection of chiefs, and preparation for the whale hunt. Wise men (Kodiak Island) were in charge of most religious ceremonies, although a dance leader

might direct ceremonies and instruct children in dances.

Male and female shamans forecast weather and other events, and they cured disease. Berdaches were often shamans as well. Women also acted as healers through bloodletting and herbal cures.

Government Despite the existence of 50 or more villages or local groups, there was no strong central government. Most important decisions were taken by consensus agreement of a council. Village leaders were chosen on the basis of merit, although there was a hereditary component. They were expected to earn respect and retained their offices by giving gifts and advice. Some controlled more than one village. Their primary responsibilities were to lead in war and guide subsistence activities. From the nineteenth century on, chiefs *(toyuq)* and secondary chiefs *(sukashiq)* were appointed by a consensus of elders.

Customs Descent was weakly matrilineal. Women generally had relatively high status, although they did not participate in formal governing structures such as councils. Society was divided into ranked classes: noble, commoner, and slave. Slaves might be acquired through trade or war, especially among the Chugach and the Koniag. High-stakes gambling was a favorite pastime.

Women were secluded in special huts during their menstrual periods and at the birth or death of a child. Seclusion during the initial menstrual period could extend for several months or more. Women's chins were tattooed when they reached puberty. Male transvestites were esteemed and performed the woman's role for life. Some girls were also raised as boys and performed male roles.

Marriage was formalized when gifts were accepted and the man went to live, temporarily, with his wife's family. A woman might have two husbands, although the second would have very low status. Men might also have multiple wives. Divorce and remarriage were possible. Babies' heads were flattened in the cradle, perhaps intentionally for aesthetic purposes. Children were generally raised gently, with no corporal punishment, but toughened with icy plunges.

Corpses were wrapped in seal or sea lion skin and kept in a special death house. High-status people were mummified. Slaves were sometimes killed and buried with a person of high rank. Mourners blackened their faces, cut their hair, and removed themselves from society. Graveside ceremonies went on for a month or more. Pieces of the corpse of a great whale hunter were sometimes cut up and rubbed on arrow points or used as talismans on hunting boats.

Dwellings Houses were semisubterranean, with planked walls and sod and straw-covered roofs. A common main room also served as kitchen and workshop. Side sleeping rooms, heated with hot rocks, were also used by both sexes for ritual and recreational sweats. Up to 20 people (several families) lived in each house. Winter villages were composed of up to ten or so houses. Some villages had large ceremonial halls *(kashims).* In fishing and other temporary camps, people lived in bark shelters or even under skin boats.

Diet Salmon was a staple, although other fish, such as herring, halibut, cod, and eulachon, were also important. Sea mammals, such as whales, porpoises, sea lions, sea otters, and seals, were also key. Seals were

Seals were hunted in part by the use of calls and decoys such as this wooden seal's-head helmet.

hunted in part by the use of decoys and calls. Dead whales were not pulled ashore but were allowed to drift in the hope that they would come back to camp. Whale darts may have been poisoned.

The people also ate sea birds. There was some gathering of shellfish and seaweed as well as greens, roots, and berries. Land mammals, such as caribou, moose, squirrel, mountain goat, and hare, also played a part in the diet.

Key Technology A foot-long slate dart on a five-foot-long shaft, possibly poisoned, was used for killing whales. A bow and arrow as well as several kinds of darts, spears, clubs, and harpoons sufficed to kill other marine and land mammals. Some land mammals were also snared or trapped. Seals and sea birds were also netted.

Fishing gear included hooks, weirs, harpoons, and rakes. Lines were made of certain algae and/or of sinew. Women wove spruce-root baskets and hats and sewed bags and clothing. Other tools were made of stone and wood. Some iron, probably acquired from shipwrecks, was also used. Lamps burned whale oil and grass. Bladders stretched over hoops served as drums.

Trade The Alutiiq acquired dentalia and slaves from the Northwest Coast. They exported caribou, mountain goats, and marmot parts. Messenger Feasts/potlatches also involved trade.

Notable Arts Woven spruce-root baskets were decorated with grass and fern embroidery. Men carved and painted wooden dance masks.

Transportation Two-hatch skin kayaks were the main vehicle for transportation, whaling, and sealing. They were made of sealskin stretched over branches. The people also used some dugout canoes, umiaks, and plank toboggans pulled by dogs.

Dress Alutiiq people wore long parkas of fur (squirrel or sea lion) and bird skin, sewn eagle-skin or -intestine rain parkas, and sea lion–, salmon-, or bear-skin boots in cold weather. Men's conical bentwood or woven spruce-root hats, worn at sea, may reflect a Tlingit influence. Men also wore Unangan-style wooden visors.

Women wore labrets and nose pins. Men also wore ornaments, such as sea lion whiskers, in their ears and noses. Other types of ornaments included coral, shell, and bone. Men braided their long hair, whereas women wore it tied up on their heads.

War and Weapons There was some fighting among Alutiiq groups and between Alutiit and nearby Indian tribes, particularly the Tlingit and Tanaina. Slave raiding was part of that activity. Men were generally killed or tortured, whereas women and children might be taken prisoner as slaves. Surprise attack was the preferred method of fighting. Weapons included slat armor, bow and arrow, and quivers.

Contemporary Information

Government/Reservations Five villages, all located on the south shore of the Alaskan Peninsula, fall under the purview of the Bristol Bay Native Corporation. Chignik Bay, 103 native residents, is governed by seven elected representatives to the Chignik Bay Village Council as well as seven elected members of the city council. Chignik Lagoon, 46 native residents, is governed by eight elected representative to the Chignik Lagoon Village Council. Chignik Lake, 122 native residents, is governed by seven elected representatives to the Chignik Lake Village Council. Ivanof Bay, 33 native residents, is governed by five elected representatives to the Ivanof Bay Village Council. Perryville, 114 native residents, is governed by five representatives to the native village of Perryville Village Tribal Council (Indian Reorganization Act [IRA]). The first four villages are also members of the Lake and Peninsula Borough. Some of these villages also have Unangan residents. Population figures are as of the early 1990s.

Other villages include Afognak, Akhiok, Kaguyak, Karluk, Larsen Bay, Old Harbor, Ouzinkie, and Port Lions (Kodiak Island) and English Bay, Port Graham, and Tatitlek (Kenai Peninsula). Villages are governed by elected tribal councils, some IRA-derived and some structured according to tradition. Towns, or communities within urban centers, are located in Anchorage, Cordova, Kodiak, Seward, and Valdez.

Economy The most important sources of income are commercial and subsistence salmon fishing and payments from the Alaska Native Land Fund.

Legal Status Under ANCSA, the Alutiiq people are represented by the Chugach Alaska Corporation, Koniag, Inc., and the Bristol Bay Native Corporation. The many village governments have government-to-government relationships with the United States. Tribal consortia representing village governments contract with the United States for health, education, and social services. These include the Bristol Bay Native Association, Chugachmiut (formerly North Pacific Rim), and the Kodiak Area Native Association.

Daily Life Many villages are only accessibly by air or water. Most people are Russian Orthodox, many older people speak Russian (along with English and Alutiiq), and there are considerable other Russian influences. Most village social activities are church related.

Some Alutiit are more identified with the ANCSA corporate entities than as Alutiit. Village concerns include protecting the local fisheries, road construction, and the construction of a boat harbor. Efforts to preserve the native culture include the formation of the Kodiak Alutiiq Dancers, language classes, oral histories, and craft (woodworking and kayak making) projects.

Eskimo, Bering Strait

See Inupiat

Eskimo, Kotzebue Sound

See Inupiat

Eskimo, Nunivak

See Yup'ik

Eskimo, Pacific

See Alutiiq

Eskimo, South Alaska

See Yup'ik

Eskimo, Southwest Alaska

See Yup'ik

Eskimo, St. Lawrence Island

See Yup'ik

Eskimo, West Alaska

See Yup'ik

Iglulik

Iglulik (I `glū lik), a name derived (with their main settlement, Igloolik) from the custom of living in snow houses, or igloos. *See also* Inuit, Baffinland.

Location Traditional Iglulik territory is north of Hudson Bay, including northern Baffin Island, the Melville Peninsula, Southhampton Island, and part of Roes Welcome Sound. It lies within the central Arctic, or Kitikmeot.

Population Estimated at 500 in the early nineteenth century, the 1990 Iglulik population was about 2,400.

Language Igluliks speak a dialect of Inuit-Inupiaq (Inuktitut), a member of the Eskaleut language family.

Historical Information

History The people encountered Scottish whalers early in the nineteenth century. Eventually, Scottish celebrations came to supplant traditional ones in part. By the time American whalers arrived in the 1860s, the Iglulik had acquired whaleboats, guns, iron items, tea, and tobacco. Later in the century, the people became involved with fox trapping and musk ox hunting. They also intermarried with non-natives and acquired high rates of alcoholism and venereal disease.

Regular contact with other Inuit, such as the Netsilik, was established at local trading posts and missions. These arrived in the early twentieth century, as did a permanent presence of the Royal Canadian

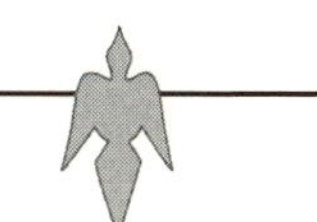

Mounted Police (RCMP). Improved medical care followed these inroads of non-native influence.

The far north took on strategic importance during the Cold War, about the same time that vast mineral reserves became known and technologically possible to exploit. These developments encouraged population movements. Also, as non-natives increased their influence, such aspects of traditional culture as shamanism, wife exchange, and murders began to disappear. In 1954 the federal Department of Northern Affairs and Natural Resources officially encouraged Inuit to abandon nomadic life. It built housing developments, schools, and clinics. Local political decisions were made by a community council subject to non-native approval and review.

The snowmobile, introduced in early 1960s, increased the potential trapping and hunting area and diminished the need for meat (fewer dogs to feed). Such employment as Inuit could obtain was generally unskilled and menial. With radical diet changes (including flour and sugar), the adoption of a sedentary life, and the appearance of drugs and alcohol, the people's health declined markedly.

Religion Religious belief and practice were based on the need to appease spirit entities found in nature. Hunting, and specifically the land-sea dichotomy, was the focus of most rituals and taboos, such as that prohibiting sewing caribou skin clothing in certain seasons. The people also recognized generative spirits, conceived of as female and identified with natural forces and cycles. A rich body of legends was related during the long, dark nights.

Male and female shamans *(angakok)* provided religious leadership by virtue of their connection with guardian spirits. They could also control the weather, improve conditions for hunting, cure disease, and divine the future. Illness was due to soul loss and/or violation of taboos and/or the anger of the dead. Curing methods included interrogation about taboo adherence, trancelike communication with spirit helpers, and performance.

Government There was no real political organization; nuclear families came together in the fall to form local groups, or settlements, that in turn were grouped into three divisions—Iglulingmiut, Aivilingmiut, and Tununermiut—associated with geographical areas *(-miuts)*. Local group leaders were usually older men, with little formal authority and no power. Leaders generally embodied Inuit values, such as generosity, and were also good hunters.

Customs Sharing was paramount in Inuit society. Descent was bilateral. People came together in larger group gatherings in late autumn; that was a time to sew and mend clothing and renew kinship ties. Spring was also a time for visiting and travel.

People married simply by announcing their intentions, although infants were regularly betrothed. Prospective husbands often served their future in-laws for a period of time. Men might have more than one wife, but most had only one. Divorce was easy to obtain. The people also recognized many other types of formal and informal partnerships and relationships. Some of these included wife exchanges.

A woman gave birth in a special shelter and lived in another special shelter, in which she observed various taboos, for some time after the birth. Because infant mortality was high, infanticide was rare, and usually practiced against females. Babies were generally named after a deceased relative. Children were highly valued and loved, especially males. They were generally given a high degree of freedom. After puberty, siblings of the opposite sex acted with reserve toward each other. This reached an extreme in the case of brothers- and sisters-in-law.

The sick or aged were sometimes abandoned, especially in times of scarcity, or the aged might commit suicide. Corpses lay in state for three days, after which they were wrapped in skins, taken out through the rear of the house, and buried in the snow. The tools of the deceased were left with him or her. No activities, including hunting, were permitted for six days following a death.

Feuds, with blood vendettas, were a regular feature of traditional life. Tensions were relieved through games; duels of drums and songs, in which the competing people tried to outdo each other in parody and song; some joking relationships; and athletic contests. Outdoor games included ball, hide-and-seek, and contests. There were many indoor games as well. These activities also took place on regular social occasions, such as visits. Ostracism and

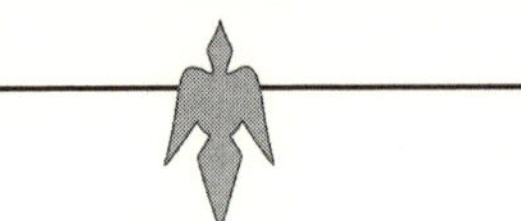

even death were reserved for the most serious cases of socially inappropriate behavior.

Dwellings The people lived in domed snow houses for part of the winter. They entered through an aboveground tunnel that trapped the warm air inside. Snow houses featured porches for storage and sometimes had more than one room. Ice or gut skin served as windows. Some groups lined the snow house with sealskins. Snow houses were often joined together at porches to form multifamily dwellings. People slept on raised packed snow platforms on caribou hide bedding. Some larger snow houses were built for social and ceremonial purposes. People generally lived in sealskin tents in summer. In spring and fall some groups used stone houses reinforced with whalebone and sod and roofed with skins.

Diet The Iglulik were nomadic hunters. The most important game animals were seals, whales, walrus, and narwhal. Men hunted seals at their breathing holes in winter and from boats in summer, as they did whales and walrus. In summer, the people traveled inland to hunt caribou, musk ox, and birds and to fish, especially for salmon and trout. Other foods included some berries and birds and their eggs. Meat, which might not be very fresh, was cooked in soapstone pots over soapstone blubber lamps or eaten raw or frozen. In summer, people burned oil-soaked bones for cooking fuel.

Key Technology Men used bone knives to cut blocks for snow houses. Other tools and equipment included harpoons, spears, snares, lances, bow and arrow, and bolas. They caught fox and wolf in stone or ice traps. Bows were made of spruce with sealskin and sinew backing. Some were also made of musk ox horn or antler. Many tools were made from caribou antlers as well as stone, bone, and driftwood. Blades were made of bone or copper. Fires were started with flint and pyrite or a wooden drill.

Fishing equipment included hooks, wooden or stone weirs and traps, and a variety of spears and harpoons. The people carved soapstone cooking pots and seal-oil lamps as well as wooden utensils, trays, dishes, spoons, and other objects. Women sewed with bone needles and sinew thread and used curved knives and scrapers to prepare skins.

Trade Material goods were exchanged with nearby neighbors, both Iglulik and non-Iglulik, mostly in summer.

Notable Arts The people carved wooden and ivory objects and made finely tanned skin clothing decorated with bands of color.

Transportation Men hunted in one- or two-person sealskin kayaks. Occasionally, several might be lashed together to form a raft. Umiaks were larger, skin-covered open boats. Dogs pulled wooden sleds, the whalebone or wood runners of which were covered with ice. Dogs also carried small packs during seasonal travel.

Dress Women sewed most clothing from caribou skins, although sealskins were commonly used on boots. Apparel included men's long, gut sealing coats and light swallowtail ceremonial coats. The people wore a double skin suit in winter and only the inner layer in summer. Most men's parkas had a long flap in the back; the woman's had two long, narrow flaps. Women's clothing featured large shoulders and hoods as well as one-piece, attached leggings and boots. They wore high caribou skin and sealskin boots containing square pouches. Men wore small loon-beak dancing caps with weasel-skin tassels. They sometimes shaved their foreheads. Both sexes wore tattoos and ivory or bone snow goggles.

War and Weapons There was some intragroup fighting and some fighting as well with the Netsilik. Hunting equipment generally doubled as weapons of war.

Contemporary Information

Government/Reservations Contemporary communities include: Ausuittuq (Grise Ford), Iglulik (Igloolik), Ikpiarjuk/Tununirusiq (Arctic Bay), Iqaluit, Mittimatalik/Tununiq (Pond Inlet), Qausuittuq (Resolute Bay), and Sanirajuk (Hall Beach). Government is by locally elected community council.

Translator Annie Iola, working with a specially designed word processor keyboard, translates English-language copy into Inuktitut at the *Nunatsiaq News,* a weekly publication in the northern Canadian town of Igaluit (1987).

Economy There is some employment in oil fields and mines. Government assistance is an important source of income for many Iglulik. The Iglulik economy today is mainly money based. Unemployment was officially pegged at 30 percent in 1994.

Native-owned and -operated cooperatives have been an important part of the Inuit economy for some time. Activities range from arts and crafts to retail to commercial fishing to construction. Woodcarving is particularly important among the Iglulik.

Legal Status Inuit are considered "nonstatus" native people. Most Inuit communities are incorporated as hamlets and are officially recognized. Baffin Island is slated to become a part of the new territory of Nunavut.

Daily Life The Baffin Regional Association was formed to press for political rights. In 1993, the Tungavik Federation of Nunavut (TFN), an outgrowth of the Inuit Tapirisat of Canada (ITC), signed an agreement with Canada providing for the establishment in 1999 of a new, mostly Inuit, territory on roughly 36,000 square kilometers of land, including Baffin Island.

The people never abandoned their land, which is still central to their identity. Traditional and modern coexist, sometimes uneasily, for many Inuit. Although people use television (there is even radio and television programming in Inuktitut), snowmobiles, and manufactured items, women also carry babies in the traditional hooded parkas, chew caribou skin to make it soft, and use the semilunar knives to cut seal meat. Full-time doctors are rare in the communities. Housing is often of poor quality. Most people are Christians. Culturally, although many stabilizing patterns of traditional culture have been destroyed, many remain. Many people live as part of extended families. Adoption is widely practiced. Decisions are often taken by consensus. However, with access to the world at large, social problems, including substance abuse and suicide among the young, have increased. Fewer than half of the people finish high school.

Politically, community councils have gained considerably more autonomy over the past decade or two. There is also a significant Inuit presence in the Northwest Territories Legislative Assembly and some presence at the federal level as well. The disastrous effects of government-run schools have been mitigated to some degree by local control of education, including more culturally relevant curricula in schools. Many people still speak Inuktitut, which is also taught in most schools, especially in the earlier grades. Children attend school in their community through grade nine; the high school is in Frobisher Bay. Adult education is also available.

Inuit, Baffinland

Baffinland Inuit (`I nyū it), "People." The people call themselves *Nunatsiaqmiut,* "People of the Beautiful Land." The Baffin region today, including Baffin Island, and the eastern High Arctic Islands, is known as Qikiqtaaluk.

Location The Baffinland Inuit live on mainly coastal parts of southern and central Baffin Island, eastern Northwest Territories. The land is rugged and includes mountains, plains, rolling hills, fjords, lakes, and rivers. The weather is also rugged and extreme, and the tides, especially in the east, are very high.

Population There were approximately 2,700 Baffinland Inuit in the mid–eighteenth century, most

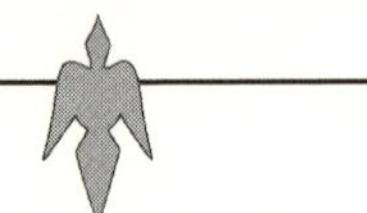

of whom lived on Cumberland Sound. The mid-1990s Qikiqtaaluk Inuit population was about 11,300.

Language The native language is Inuit-Inupiaq (Inuktitut), a member of the Eskaleut language family.

Historical Information

History Parts of Baffin Island were settled over 4,000 years ago. The Thule, or pre-Inuit culture, entered the region circa 1200. Norsemen may have visited Baffin Island around the year 1000, but definite contact with non-natives was not established until the people met early explorers in the late sixteenth century.

Non-native whaling began in the east (Davis Strait) in the eighteenth century. The Inuit people shortly began to experience high rates of tuberculosis and other diseases, such as measles. Whaling centers established in the nineteenth century employed Inuit and slowly changed their economy, marking the shift to dependency.

Anglican missionaries arrived in the early twentieth century and conducted the first baptisms. A missionary-derived syllabary was created and persisted well into the twentieth century. The Hudson's Bay Company built trading posts from 1911 on, signaling the end of whaling and the beginning of fur trapping as the most important economic activity. This period also saw the beginning of outside control of the people's lives by traders, missionaries, and police.

The far north took on strategic importance during the Cold War, about the same time that vast mineral reserves became known and technologically possible to exploit. The federal Department of Northern Affairs and Natural Resources (1954) encouraged the Inuit to abandon their nomadic life. It saw to the construction of housing developments, schools, and a general infrastructure. Local political decisions were made by a community council subject to non-native approval and review. Inuit found generally menial and poorly paying employment. With radical diet changes, the adoption of a sedentary life, and the appearance of drugs and alcohol, health declined markedly.

Religion Religious belief and practice were based on spirit entities found in nature and needing to be treated with respect. Rituals showing respect to an animal just killed focused on these beliefs, which were also the basis of most taboos and the use of amulets. People could acquire the spirits of objects as protectors. There were also more overarching, generative spirits identified with natural forces and cycles. These were largely female identified. Souls were said to be reincarnated.

Male and female shamans *(angakok)* provided religious leadership by virtue of their direct connection with guardian spirits. They led group religious activities. They could also cure disease and see into the future. Illness was perceived as having to do with soul loss and/or violation of taboos. Curing methods included interrogation about taboo adherence, trancelike communication with spirit helpers, and performance.

Government There was no formal political organization; instead, nuclear families combined to form villages in distinct geographical areas *(-miuts).* Villages occasionally came together as small, fluid, kinship-related bands. The bands were also geographically identified—their names carried the *-miut* suffix—although other groups were not specifically excluded. Larger but ill-defined population regions included Sikosuilarmiut, Akuliarmiut, Qaumauangmiut, Nugumiut, Oqomiut, Padlimiut, and Akudnirmiut.

Band leaders *(isumataq)* were usually older men with little formal authority and no power. Leaders embodied Inuit values, such as generosity, and were also good hunters.

Customs Sharing was paramount in Inuit society. All aspects of a person's life were controlled by kinship relationships. People married by announcing their intentions, although infants were regularly betrothed. Some men might have more than one wife. Divorce was easy to obtain. Wife exchange was practiced as part of formal male partnerships. Infanticide was rare and usually practiced against females. Names were taken from deceased people and given by elders. A person might have several names, each denoting a kinship relationship and particular behaviors. Names were not sex specific. Children were generally raised gently. Men hunted, made and repaired weapons and tools, and build kayaks, sleds, and shelter. Women prepared skins and made clothing, sewed hides for coverings, caught and prepared fish, raised children, and gathered moss, berries, and other items.

The sick or aged were sometimes abandoned, especially in times of scarcity. Corpses were wrapped in skins and covered with rocks. People brought weapons and food to the grave after four days. No work, including hunting, was performed during the days of mourning. Tensions were relieved through games, such as feats of strength, and duels of drums and songs, in which one person tried to outdo another in parody and song. Joking relationships also helped keep people's emotions in check. Games included ring-and-pin and cat's cradle. Children liked to play games, including tag and hide-and-seek. Ostracism and even death were reserved for the most serious cases of socially inappropriate behavior.

Dwellings Domed snow houses were used in winter, although people might also build stone houses covered with skin and plant material. Entrance through a tunnel kept the warm air inside. These houses sometimes had more than one room and had storage porches as well. Beds were raised snow platforms covered with branches and skins. The people also built some larger snow or sod and bone houses for ceremonial purposes. Skin tents were generally used in summer.

Diet Baffinland Inuit were nomadic hunters. The most important marine animals were seals and beluga whales, but they also hunted walrus, narwhal, and polar bear. Seals were hunted at their breathing holes and also on floe ice. In summer, the people traveled inland to hunt caribou and birds (and eggs) as well as some small game. They fished year-round and gathered some berries, roots, and shellfish.

Key Technology Men used bone knives to cut snow blocks for houses. Hunting equipment included harpoons, lances, spears, and the bow (driftwood or antler) and arrow. Wood and leather floats and drags were also used in whale hunting. Birds (their bones made excellent needles) were caught with wood and leather nets as well as whalebone snares; fish were caught with hooks and stone weirs. Most tools were made of caribou antlers as well as stone, bone, and driftwood. Sinew served nicely as thread. Other important items included carved soapstone cooking pots and lamps that burned seal oil/blubber and carved wooden trays, dishes, spoons, and other objects.

Trade Baffinland Inuit engaged in some trade and other intercourse with nearby neighbors; for instance, the people of Cumberland Sound were in contact with the Iglulik Inuit and those of southern Baffin Island with Inuit of Labrador (Ungava), where they obtained wood for their kayaks and umiaks. Other trade items included copper and ivory.

Notable Arts Some groups carved wooden and ivory figurines. Storytelling was also considered a high art. Drum dancing, a performance art, combined music, story, dance, and song. Some Inuit women also practiced a form of singing known as throat singing.

Transportation Men hunted using one- or two-person kayaks of driftwood frames and sealskin. Umiaks were larger, skin-covered open boats. Wooden sleds carried people and belongings to and from the interior. Dog traction dates generally from the early twentieth century to the 1960s.

Dress Most clothing consisted of caribou-skin and sealskin clothing and boots. Women's sealskin parkas

An Inuit woman splits a walrus hide (1928). Hunting walrus was considered inordinately dangerous, owing to the animals' size and aggressive nature.

had a larger hood for accommodating an infant. Some people were able to acquire polar bear–skin pants. Waterproof seal-intestine suits, partially lined with dog fur, were used for whale hunting. Women coiled or braided their hair.

War and Weapons Conflicts were local in nature. They generally took the form of raids. Hunting equipment such as spears and bows and arrows doubled as weapons of war.

Contemporary Information

Government/Reservations Population centers include Kangiqtugaapik (Clyde River), Broughton Island, Panniqtuuq (Pangnirtung), Frobisher Bay, Kimmirik (Lake Harbour), and Kinngait (Cape Dorset). There are also five small (fewer than 30 people) hunting villages. Government is by locally elected community councils.

Economy Subsistence hunting, trapping, and fishing are still important, as are various kinds of wage work and government assistance. Possible future developments include oil and gas exploration as well as tanker traffic. Cape Dorset artists are well known and relatively successful.

Native-owned and -operated cooperatives have been an important part of the Inuit economy for some time. Activities range from arts and crafts to retail to commercial fishing to construction.

Legal Status Inuit are considered "nonstatus" native people. Most Inuit communities are incorporated as hamlets and are officially recognized. Baffin Island is slated to become a part of the new territory of Nunavut.

Daily Life The Baffin Regional Association was formed to press for political rights. In 1993, the Tungavik Federation of Nunavut (TFN), an outgrowth of the Inuit Tapirisat of Canada (ITC), signed an agreement with Canada providing for the establishment in 1999 of a new, mostly Inuit, territory on roughly 36,000 square kilometers of land, including Baffin Island.

The people never abandoned their land, which is still central to their identity. Traditional and modern coexist, sometimes uneasily, for many Inuit. Although people use television (there is even radio and television programming in Inuktitut), snowmobiles, and manufactured items, women also carry babies in the traditional hooded parkas, chew caribou skin to make it soft, and use the semilunar knives to cut seal meat. Full-time doctors are rare in the communities. Housing is often of poor quality. Most people are Christians. Culturally, although many stabilizing patterns of traditional culture have been destroyed, many remain. Many people live as part of extended families. Adoption is widely practiced. Decisions are often taken by consensus.

Politically, community councils have gained considerably more autonomy over the past decade or two. There is also a significant Inuit presence in the Northwest Territories Legislative Assembly and some presence at the federal level as well. The disastrous effects of government-run schools have been mitigated to some degree by local control of education, including more culturally relevant curricula in schools. Many people still speak Inuktitut, which is also taught in most schools, especially in the earlier grades. Children attend school in their community through grade nine; the high school is in Frobisher Bay. Adult education is also available.

Inuit, Caribou

Caribou Inuit (`I nyū it) is a non-native term reflecting the people's reliance on caribou. The Inuit self-designation was *Nunamiut,* "inlanders."

Location The Caribou Inuit homeland is located on the southern Barren Grounds west of Hudson Bay (Keewatin District, Northwest Territories). The early population centered along the coast, near Whale Cove. As population grew during the nineteenth century, the trend was to expand to the north, south, and west (interior), especially as the Chipewyan Indians abandoned the latter region. This windy land consists mainly of gently rolling plains. It is very well watered, although little plant life exists there.

Population There were between 300 and 500 Caribou Inuit in the late eighteenth century. The population had grown to around 1,500 in 1915. In

the mid-1990s there were approximately 6,900 Inuit in the Keewatin District (Kivalliq).

Language The Caribou Inuit speak a dialect of Inuit-Inupiaq (Inuktitut), part of the Eskaleut language family.

Historical Information

History The historic Caribou Inuit descended directly from ancient Thule people, in local residence since about the twelfth century. The first non-native explorers arrived in the early seventeenth century, although there may not have been direct contact between the two peoples.

Regular trade with non-natives began shortly after the people were first visited by Hudson's Bay Company representatives in 1717. Ships brought foreign goods from Churchill, and the Inuit traded for items such as metal knives and axes, beads, tobacco, and, later, guns and powder. At that time they often acted as intermediaries between non-natives and the Iglulik, Netsilik, and Copper Inuit. Regular trade began at Churchill in 1790.

By the early nineteenth century, Caribou Inuit society had begun to reorient itself, with southerners focusing on the Churchill area and the non-native trade, and northerners making stronger ties with the Aivilik Iglulik Inuit. The two groups divided in about 1810. Shortly thereafter, the two societies became five.

The Hudson's Bay Company conducted commercial whaling from about 1860 to 1915. The Inuit people killed seals and whales each summer, trading most oil and other products, while shifting to almost total dependence on caribou as well as musk ox and fish to a lesser extent.

Canada established a formal presence in 1903. Trading posts and Catholic missionaries arrived in 1912, followed by various non-native settlements in the region. A severe famine from 1915 to around 1924 killed perhaps two-thirds of the people. After that event, the people turned to trapping (mainly fox fur) and the wage/trade economy as a means of survival. This marked the end of their essential independence.

Gradually, continuing hunger and epidemics began to fragment the societies, as the population continued to decline. The situation attracted governmental intervention in the 1950s. Administrative centers were established. Most people relocated by choice to one of five settlements, most of which contained a minority of Caribou Inuit (although a majority of Inuit).

The shift to towns was completed in the 1960s. The people lived in prefabricated housing, generally wore nontraditional clothing, and ate nontraditional foods. With the breakdown of the traditional economy, and nothing to take its place, many experienced for the first time problems of substance abuse. Children began learning English in school but little about their traditional culture. Acculturation quickly became established among the young. The arrival of television in the 1970s and then other electronic media accelerated these trends.

Religion The Caribou Inuit recognized a supreme creative force that took an interest in the affairs of people. This deity may have been associated with the female caribou. The souls of people who had lived well (observed all the taboos, of which there were many) were thought to rejoin this force when they died, thence to be reincarnated on earth. The souls of those who had not lived well were said to be eternally damned.

Religion was essentially hunting based. Respect was owed to all things in nature but especially game animals. People left offerings for the spirits of slain animals. A number of ceremonial danced reinforced these ideas. Shamans specialized in spiritual matters, acting as intermediary between the two worlds. They could find out, by communicating with the spirits, who had broken which taboo and how a problem situation could be rectified (curing).

Government Political leadership, such as it was, took place within the context of the family. The leader was generally an older man who sat atop the family kinship network. He was also likely to be strong, wise, highly skilled in hunting, and familiar with the spirit world. Other than this, informal, ad hoc leaders advised small groups on hunting matters and when to move camp.

There were five bands or societies in the mid–nineteenth century: Paatlirmiut, Qairnitmuit,

Ahiarmiut, Hauniqturmiut, and Harvaqturmiut. The societies were separate although related by marriage and descent.

Customs Betrothal took place as early as infancy. Cross cousins (children of a mother's brothers or a father's sisters) were regarded as highly desirable marriage partners. There was some regular intermarriage with other Inuit groups such as the Netsilik and Iglulik. There was little or no marriage ceremony. Newly married couples might live with either set of parents. Men might have more than one wife; widows, especially, tended to marry their brothers-in-law.

Occasional temporary partner swapping—considered a type of marriage—established further obligations and social ties. Other alternative relationships were known as dancing partners. This arrangement consisted of partners beating each other until one surrendered, after which time presents were bestowed. Later, they danced together to the sound of beating drums. These people generally lived apart but visited regularly.

Although children were highly valued and generally treated very well, and although childless couples often adopted children, there was some female infanticide. Corpses were wrapped in skins and placed within a circle of stones, along with various possessions. The mourning period was highly ritualized.

The extended family was the basic unit. The people displayed a distinct fondness for singing, feasting, and social drum dancing, sometimes in a large snow house or tent. They played several games, many of which included gambling, and took part in athletic contests. The art of making string figures was well developed.

Dwellings For most of their prehistory, coastal people used stone winter houses, chinked with moss and dirt and covered with snow. Around 1880 they learned, from the Iglulik, to build domed snow houses. These houses generally held ten people at most. A clear ice window was placed over the door. Storage was available on the sides of a long entryway, which itself was placed below ground level to keep the cold drafts out. Furniture consisted of snow platforms covered with skins and willow mats. Some people built a small connected kitchen with a smoke hole, although many cooked, when they cooked at all, outside on fires of moss and willow. There was generally no heat. Houses of family members might be linked by tunnels.

The people used conical skin (hair side out for waterproofing) tents as well as temporary brush windbreaks in other seasons. Most settlements were occupied by only one extended family, although groups might grow in size in spring and summer.

Diet Men engaged in extensive summer seal, walrus, and whale hunting before the early to mid–nineteenth century. A few coastal people continued these activities even after that time. Meat was sun dried and stored in sealskin bags and retained for winter use.

Especially from the mid–nineteenth century on, the people depended almost totally on migrating herds of caribou, which reached their peak numbers in autumn. People intercepted the animals at water crossings, drove them into lakes, and directed them down courseways where hunters waited. The men continued to hunt while women processed the meat and skins. Excess meat was covered with skins and hidden under rocks. Men also hunted musk ox when necessary, especially when the caribou meat began to run out. These were hunted to extinction by about 1900.

Most winter food was eaten frozen and raw. Fishing took place mostly in winter and spring. Other foods included birds and their eggs, some summer berries, and the plant foods inside of caribou stomachs. Winter food stores often ran quite low toward the end of the season. Sharing of food was well developed, to the point where hunters were not considered to own their own kills.

Key Technology Most material items, such as tools, scrapers, needles, hooks, and arrowheads, were derived from the caribou. Men used bone or antler snow knives to cut blocks of snow for winter houses. They hunted with bow and arrow, snares, pitfalls, lances, and harpoons. Stone weirs and hook and line were the most common fishing equipment. Other raw materials included wood and soapstone. Small, weak lamps burned caribou fat or fish oil. Cooking fires

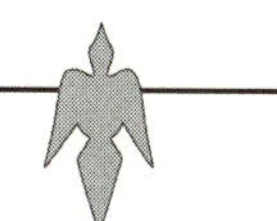

burned dwarf shrubbery. Musical instruments included drums, tambourine, and voice.

Trade All trade took place in summer. The people traded caribou skins and soapstone with the Chipewyan and Cree for snowshoes, moccasins, and pyrite. They also traded with the Aivilik Iglulik Inuit from about 1800 on. Exports included driftwood and seal dog traces and boot soles, among other items.

Notable Arts Caribou Inuit may have learned quill embroidery from the Chipewyan and/or Cree Indians.

Transportation Long, narrow, skin-covered kayaks were sometimes tied together to form rafts for crossing larger bodies of water. After around 1800, the people used dogsleds whose runners were coated with ice-covered peat. Most transportation was overland with the help of tumplines, the Caribou Inuit being particularly strong walkers.

Dress Six to eight caribou skins provided an adult suit of well-tailored clothing, including pants, boots, mittens, and outer and inner parkas. Furs and fur trim came from polar bears, wolves, wolverines, and foxes. Women wore bone or copper headbands. Women's parka hoods were extra large to accommodate babies carried high on the back. Wet clothing was dried only with great difficulty in winter.

War and Weapons Enemies of the Caribou Inuit included the Chipewyan (at least to the mid–eighteenth century) and Dogrib Athapaskans. Hunting implements doubled as weapons.

Contemporary Information

Government/Reservations Contemporary population centers include Arviat (Eskimo Point), Igluliagaarjuq (Chesterfield Inlet), Kangiqliniq (Rankin Inlet), Naujaat/Aivilik (Repulse Bay), Qamanittuaq (Baker Lake), Salliq (Coral Harbour), and Tikirarjuaq (Whale Cove). Government is based on elected councils.

The Caribou Inuit have pushed hard and successfully for the creation of an all-Inuit territory, Nunavut, which will include their territory. They are also active in the Inummarilirijikkut, or Inuit Central Institute.

Economy Hunting and fishing remain important subsistence activities. Wage labor includes trapping; some crafts, especially woodcarving; mining; working as support personnel; and government assistance.

Native-owned and -operated cooperatives have been an important part of the Inuit economy for some time. Activities range from arts and crafts to retail to commercial fishing to construction.

Legal Status Inuit are considered "nonstatus" native people. Most Inuit communities are incorporated as hamlets and are officially recognized. Baffin Island is slated to become a part of the new territory of Nunavut.

Daily Life The people never abandoned their land, which is still central to their identity. Traditional and modern coexist, sometimes uneasily, for many Inuit. Although people use television (there is even radio and television programming in Inuktitut), snowmobiles, and manufactured items, women also carry babies in the traditional hooded parkas, chew caribou skin to make it soft, and use the semilunar knives to cut seal meat. Full-time doctors are rare in the communities. Housing is often of poor quality. Most people are Christians. Culturally, although many stabilizing patterns of traditional culture have been destroyed, many remain. Many people live as part of extended families. Adoption is widely practiced. Decisions are often taken by consensus. Intermarriage between Inuit groups in the five population centers has blurred ethnic identity; people now tend to identify with their settlement.

Politically, community councils have gained considerably more autonomy over the past decade or two. There is also a significant Inuit presence in the Northwest Territories Legislative Assembly and some presence at the federal level as well. The disastrous effects of government-run schools have been mitigated to some degree by local control of education, including more culturally relevant curricula in schools. Many people still speak Inuktitut, which is also taught in most schools, especially in the earlier grades. Children attend school in their community through grade nine; the high school is in Frobisher Bay. Adult education is also available. Caribou overhunting has prompted increased government regulations, which are resisted by the Caribou Inuit, who still identify to a significant extent with the caribou.

Inuit, Copper

Copper Inuit (`I nyū it), "People." The people received this name from non-native explorers who found them using native copper in tools and weapons. *See also* Netsilik.

Location In the eighteenth century the Copper Inuit were living between Cape Parry and Queen Maude Gulf, especially on southern Victoria Island and along Coronation Gulf. The region is almost entirely tundra, except for some forest to the south and along the Coppermine River. Many Copper Inuit still live in this area of the central Arctic, known as Kitikmeot.

Population The native population was probably between 800 and 1,300 in the late eighteenth century. In 1990 there were around 2,000 Inuit in the local communities, most of whom were Copper Inuit. The mid-1990s population of the Kitikmeot Region (Copper and Netsilik Inuit) was roughly 4,000.

Language Copper Inuits speak a dialect of Inuit-Inupiaq (Inuktitut), a member of the Eskaleut language family.

Historical Information

History Historical Copper Inuit people are descended from ancient pre-Dorset, Dorset, and Thule cultures. They first encountered non-natives in the late eighteenth and early nineteenth centuries. Although they obtained some non-native trade goods, such as iron, and caught new diseases, traditional life remained relatively unchanged for some time thereafter.

Local trading posts were established in the 1920s, bringing items such as rifles, fish nets, and steel traps as well as cloth, tea and flour. These material changes had the result of extending the

In the 1920s, the establishment of local trading posts brought items such as rifles, fish nets, steel traps, cloth, tea, and flour into circulation. With the prevalence of rifles, the Inuit, for the most part, gave up their harpoons for hunting seals.

caribou season and generally reorienting the people away from the sea. This development, plus the regular presence of trade ships, began to undermine traditional self-sufficiency and social structures. The region's first missionaries arrived at about the same time, as did a permanent presence of the Royal Canadian Mounted Police (RCMP).

It was not until the 1950s, however, that the root aspects of traditional culture began to disappear. Some mixing with western Inuit newcomers occurred during that time. The far north took on strategic importance during the Cold War, about the same time that vast mineral reserves became known and technologically possible to exploit. These two industries offered some wage labor and contributed to the decline of nomadic life. Other factors contributed as well, such as the decline of the caribou herds.

The federal Department of Northern Affairs and Natural Resources (1954) began constructing wood-frame housing developments, clinics, and schools and encouraged resettlement in these permanent communities. Local political decisions were made by a community council subject to non-native approval and review. Population centralization was largely completed by the 1970s. Most job opportunities for Inuit were unskilled and menial, although hunting and trapping remained important. With radical diet changes, the adoption of a sedentary life, and the appearance of drugs and alcohol, health declined markedly.

Religion Religious belief and practice were based on the need to appease spirit entities found in nature. Hunting, and specifically the land-sea dichotomy, was the focus of most rituals and taboos, such as that prohibiting sewing caribou-skin clothing in certain seasons. The people also recognized generative spirits, conceived of as female and identified with natural forces and cycles.

Male and female shamans *(angakok)* provided religious leadership by virtue of their connection with guardian spirits. They could also control the weather, improve conditions for hunting, cure disease, and divine the future. Illness was due to soul loss and/or violation of taboos and/or the anger of the dead. Curing methods included interrogation about taboo adherence, trancelike communication with spirit helpers, and performance.

Government Nuclear families were the basic economic and political unit. Families were led by the oldest man. They were loosely organized into small local groups associated with geographical areas *(-miuts).* Local groups occasionally came together as perhaps six or seven small, fluid bands. The bands were also geographically identified, their names carrying the *-miut* suffix as well.

Customs Sharing was paramount in Inuit society. All aspects of a person's life were controlled by kinship relationships. The people recognized many types of formal and informal partnerships and relationships. Some of these included wife exchanges. People came together in larger group gatherings in late autumn; this was a time to sew and mend clothing and renew kinship ties. Men hunted, made and repaired weapons and tools, and build kayaks, sleds, and shelter. Women prepared skins and made clothing, sewed hides for coverings, caught and prepared fish, raised children, and gathered moss, berries, and other items.

Descent was bilateral. People married simply by announcing their intentions, although infants were regularly betrothed. Prospective husbands often served their future in-laws for a period of time. Men might have more than one wife, but most had only one. Divorce was easy to obtain. Names were taken from deceased people and given by elders. A person might have several names, each denoting a kinship relationship and particular behaviors. Names were not sex specific.

People often adopted orphans. Children were highly valued and loved, especially males. When a boy killed his first seal, the seal's body was ritually dragged over his. The sick or aged were sometimes abandoned, especially in times of scarcity. Corpses were wrapped in skins and buried in stone or snow vaults or, later, left outside within a ring of stones. The tools of the deceased were left with him or her. People brought weapons and food to the grave after four days. No work, including hunting, was performed during the days of mourning.

Tensions were relieved through games, such as feats of strength, and duels of drums and songs, in which one person tried to outdo another in parody and song. Joking relationships also helped keep people's emotions in check. Games included ring-and-pin and cat's cradle. Children liked to play games, including tag and hide-and-seek. Ostracism and even death were reserved for the most serious cases of socially inappropriate behavior.

Dwellings Men built domed snow houses in winter. Entrance through a straight-sided, flat-topped tunnel kept the warm air inside. Some houses had more than one room. Snow platforms covered with caribou, musk ox, or bearskins served as beds. The people used larger snow or sod and bone houses for ceremonial purposes. They also used caribou-skin and sealskin tents built over raised sod rings in summer and over pits in autumn.

Diet Copper Inuits were nomadic hunters. The most important game animals were seals and whales. Dogs helped roughly eight large bands of 50 to 200 people hunt seals at their breathing holes in winter. Some polar bears were caught in winter as well.

The people also hunted caribou, musk ox, small game, and fowl, mainly in small groups in summer and autumn. Women and children chased caribou through stone runways to where the men were waiting

with bows and lances. Caribou were also hunted from kayaks. The meat was sun dried or frozen and cached for the winter. Fishing was a year-round activity. Some berries were available in summer.

Key Technology Men used bone knives to cut blocks for snow houses. Other tools and equipment included harpoons, spears, snares, lances, bow and arrow, and bolas. Bows were made of spruce with sealskin and sinew backing. Some were also made of musk-ox horn or antler. Many tools were made from caribou antlers as well as stone, bone, and driftwood. Blades were made of bone or copper.

Fishing equipment included hooks, wooden or stone weirs and traps, and a variety of spears and harpoons. The people carved soapstone cooking pots and seal-oil lamps as well as wooden utensils, trays, dishes, spoons, and other objects. Women sewed with bone needles and sinew thread.

Trade Summer was trade season. The people exchanged goods, particularly copper and driftwood, with the Inuvialuit, the Caribou Inuit, and the Netsilik. There were occasional contacts with Athapaskan Indians to their south.

Notable Arts The most important artistic traditions were carved wooden and ivory figurines. Clothing decoration consisted mainly of bands of white fur or skin. There was some skin fringing.

Transportation One- or two-person kayaks, propelled with a double-bladed paddle, were generally used for hunting. Several men could hunt whales in umiaks, which were larger, skin-covered open boats. Dogs carried burdens in summer and pulled wooden sleds in winter. The sleds had wooden runners covered with whalebone, mud, or peat and then ice. Toboggans were occasionally made of skin.

Dress Women sewed most clothing from caribou skins, although sealskins were commonly used on boots. Apparel included men's long, gut sealing coats and light swallowtail ceremonial coats. The people wore a double skin suit in winter and only the inner layer in summer. Women's clothing featured large shoulders and hoods as well as one-piece, attached leggings and boots. Their coattails were long and narrow. Men wore small loon-beak dancing caps with weasel-skin tassels. They sometimes shaved their foreheads. Both sexes wore tattoos and ivory or bone snow goggles.

War and Weapons Spears and arrowheads were copper tipped. Most fighting was local and small-scale in nature.

Contemporary Information

Government/Reservations Contemporary Copper Inuit communities include Iqaluktuuttiaq (Cambridge Bay), Qingauq (Bathurst Inlet), Qurluqtuuq (Coppermine), Umingmaktuuq, and Taloyoak. Government is by locally elected council.

Economy Subsistence hunting, trapping, and fishing are still important, as are various types of wage work and government assistance. Possible future developments include oil and gas exploration as well as tanker traffic. Cape Dorset artists are well known and relatively successful.

Native-owned and -operated cooperatives have been an important part of the Inuit economy for some time. Activities range from arts and crafts to retail to commercial fishing to construction.

Legal Status Inuit are considered "nonstatus" native people. Most Inuit communities are incorporated as hamlets and are officially recognized. Kitikmeot is slated to become a part of the new territory of Nunavut.

Daily Life The people never abandoned their land, which is still central to their identity. Traditional and modern coexist, sometimes uneasily, for many Inuit. Although people use television (there is even radio and television programming in Inuktitut), snowmobiles, and manufactured items, women also carry babies in the traditional hooded parkas, chew caribou skin to make it soft, and use the semilunar knives to cut seal meat. Full-time doctors are rare in the communities. Housing is often of poor quality. Most people are Christians. Culturally, although many stabilizing patterns of traditional culture have been destroyed, many remain. Many people live as

part of extended families. Adoption is widely practiced. Decisions are often taken by consensus.

Politically, community councils have gained considerably more autonomy over the past decade or two. There is also a significant Inuit presence in the Northwest Territories Legislative Assembly and some presence at the federal level as well. In 1993, the Tungavik Federation of Nunavut (TFN), an outgrowth of the Inuit Tapirisat of Canada (ITC), signed an agreement with Canada providing for the establishment, in 1999, of a new, mostly Inuit, territory on roughly 36,000 square kilometers of land, including Kitikmeot.

The disastrous effects of government-run schools have been mitigated to some degree by local control of education, including more culturally relevant curricula in schools. Many people still speak Inuktitut, which is also taught in most schools, especially in the earlier grades. Children attend school in their community through grade nine; there is a high school in Frobisher Bay. Adult education is also available.

Inuit, Labrador or Ungava

Labrador or Ungava Inuit (`I nyū it), actually two groups of northeastern Inuit once differentiated by dialect and custom. Reflecting recent political developments, many people of the latter group now refer to themselves as *Inuit Kapaimiut,* "People of Quebec."

Location From the late sixteenth century on, these people have lived on the northern half of the Labrador peninsula, especially along the coasts and the offshore islands. There is some controversy as to whether or not Inuit groups ever occupied land bordering the Gulf of St. Lawrence. Contemporary communities are either located in Labrador or Nunavik (Quebec north of the 55th parallel).

Population The Labrador Inuit population in the mid–eighteenth century was between 3,000 and 4,200, about two-thirds of whom lived in the south. The mid-1990s Inuit population of Labrador and Nunavik was approximately 12,000 people.

Language The people speak dialects of Inuit-Inupiaq (Inuktitut), a member of the Eskaleut language family.

Historical Information

History This region has been occupied since about 2500 B.C.E., probably at first by people emigrating in waves from the Northwest. Norse explorers arrived circa 1000 C.E. The ancient Dorset culture lasted until around the fourteenth century, when it was displaced by Thule immigrants from Baffin Island. Around 1500, some Thule groups began a slow migration to the southern Labrador coast.

The people encountered Basque and other European whalers in the late fifteenth century. Inuit whaling technology was more advanced at that time. Contacts with non-native explorers, particularly those looking for the fabled northwest passage to Asia, continued throughout the sixteenth century. Early contacts between the Inuit and non-natives were generally hostile.

Whale and caribou overhunting, combined with the introduction of non-native diseases, led to population declines in the north by the late seventeenth century. The first trade centers were established in the north during the eighteenth century, although trade did not become regular there until close to the mid–nineteenth century.

In the eighteenth century, especially after the 1740s, sporadic trade began with the French fishery in the south. Moravian missions, schools, and trading posts, especially to the south, gradually became Inuit population centers after the mid– to late eighteenth century. Missionization began in Arctic Quebec in the 1860s. A mixed British-Inuit population (known as "settlers") also became established in the south from the mid–eighteenth century on. This influential group slowly grew in size and spread northward as well. Increased trade activity in the south in the mid–nineteenth century led to Inuit population declines as a result of alcohol use and disease epidemics. Fox trapping for the fur trade began in the early nineteenth century.

In the north, by later in the century, some families intermarried with non-native traders and otherwise established close relations with them. Fur trade posts became widespread in the north in the

In this eighteenth-century painting, a Moravian missionary speaks to Inuit at Nain, Labrador. Moravian missions, schools, and trading posts from the mid– to late eighteenth century gradually became Inuit population centers.

early twentieth century. Native technology began to change fundamentally and permanently during that period. Shamanism, too had all but disappeared, as most people had by then accepted Christianity, although not without much social convulsion.

In the south, the Moravians turned the Inuit trade over to the Hudson's Bay Company in 1926. There was an increasing government presence in the 1930s and 1940s. Few or no inland groups remained in Arctic Quebec after 1930, the people having moved to the coast. About the same time, the bottom dropped out of the fox fur market. Trade posts disappeared, and many people went back to a semitraditional mode of subsistence and technology.

The far north took on strategic importance during the Cold War, about the same time that vast mineral reserves became known and technologically possible to exploit. The federal Department of Northern Affairs and Natural Resources (1954) encouraged the Inuit to abandon their nomadic life. Extensive Canadian government services and payments date from that time. Local Moravian missions ceded authority to the government when Labrador and Newfoundland entered the Canadian confederation in 1949.

Some of Labrador's native communities were officially closed in the 1950s and their residents relocated. Most wage employment was of the unskilled and menial variety. By the 1960s, most people had abandoned the old ways. With radical diet changes, the adoption of a sedentary life, and the appearance of drugs and alcohol, their health declined markedly.

The entire region has experienced growing ethnopolitical awareness and activism since the 1970s. During that period, the Labrador Inuit Association (LIA) reached an accommodation with local biracial residents ("settlers") regarding representation and rights. The LIA is associated with the Inuit Tapirisat of Canada (ITC). This advocacy group works to settle land claims and to facilitate interracial cooperation. It also supports and funds local programs and services, including those relating to Inuit culture.

Religion Religious belief and practice were based on the need to appease spirit entities found in nature. Hunting, and specifically the land-sea dichotomy, was the focus of most rituals and taboos, such as that prohibiting sewing caribou-kin clothing in certain seasons. The people also recognized generative spirits, conceived of as female and identified with natural forces and cycles. Their rich cosmogony and mythology was filled with spirits and beings of various sizes, some superhuman and some subhuman.

Male and female shamans *(angakok)* provided religious leadership by virtue of their connection with guardian spirits. They could also control the weather, improve conditions for hunting, cure disease, and divine the future. Illness was perceived as stemming from soul loss and/or the violation of taboos and/or the anger of the dead. Curing methods included interrogation about taboo adherence, trancelike communication with spirit helpers, and performance.

Government Nuclear families were loosely organized into local groups of 20 to 30 people associated with geographical areas *(-miuts).* These groups occasionally came together as roughly 25 (perhaps 10 among the Ungava) small, fluid bands that were also geographically identified. The Ungava Inuit also recognized three regional bands (Siqinirmiut, Tarramiut, Itivimiut) that were identified by intermarriage and linguistic and cultural similarities.

The harpooner or boat owner provided leadership for whaling expeditions. The best hunters were often the de facto group leaders. Abuse of their authority was likely to get them killed. Still, competition for leadership positions was active, with people dueling through song and woman exchange. Women also competed with each other through singing. Local (settlement) councils helped resolve conflicts that arose in situations without a strong leader, especially in the south.

Customs Women were in charge of child rearing as well as skin and food preparation. They made the clothes, fished, hunted small animals, gathered plant material, and tended the oil lamps. Men hunted and had overall responsibility for all forms of transportation. They made and repaired utensils, weapons, and tools. They also built the houses.

Children were named for dead relatives regardless of sex; they were generally expected to take on the sex roles of their namesake, as opposed to those of their own sex. Children were occasionally brought up in the roles of the opposite gender for economic reasons. Adults occasionally married transvestites.

People married simply by announcing their intentions, although infants were regularly betrothed. Good hunters might have more than one wife (especially in the south), but most had only one. Divorce was easy to effect. Some wife exchanges were permitted within defined family partnerships; these relationships were considered as a kind of marriage.

Infanticide was rare and usually practiced against females; cannibalism, too, occasionally occurred during periods of starvation. Children were highly valued and loved, especially males. Adoption was common. The sick or aged were sometimes abandoned, especially in times of scarcity. Corpses were buried in stone graves covered by broken personal items.

Tensions were relieved through games; duels of drums and songs, in which the competing people tried to outdo each other in parody; and some "joking" relationships. Ostracism and even death were reserved for the most serious cases of socially inappropriate behavior. Murders led to ongoing blood feuds.

Dwellings The typical winter house was semiexcavated and made of stone, whalebone, and wood frames filled with sod and stone with a skin roof. Floors were also stone; windows were made of gut. Each house held up to 20 people; spaces were separated by skin partitions. The people also built mainly temporary domed snow houses. Conical and/or domed sealskin or caribou-skin tents served as summer housing. There were also large ceremonial and social structures *(kashim)* as well.

Diet Labrador Inuit were nomadic hunters, taking game both individually and collectively. Depending on location, they engaged in a number of subsistence activities, such as late summer and fall caribou hunting, whaling, and breathing-hole sealing in winter. They hunted seals from kayaks in spring and summer. Men and women fished year-round. People also ate birds and their eggs as well as walrus and bear (polar and black). Women gathered numerous berries and some roots as well as some shellfish and sea vegetables. Coastal hunters traveled into the interior in spring to hunt caribou, reemerging on the coast in the fall.

The results of a hunt were divided roughly equally, with those who played more important roles getting somewhat better (but not generally larger) shares. Food was eaten any number of ways, including frozen, raw, decayed, partially or fully boiled, and dried. Drinks included blood and water. There was some ritual division of "first fruits," particularly those obtained by adolescent boys or girls.

Key Technology Special harpoons, floats, and drags were used in whaling. Caribou were generally shot with bow and arrow or speared from kayaks. Birds were shot, snared, or brought down with bolas. Fish were caught with hooks, weirs, and spears.

Most tools were fashioned from caribou antlers as well as stone, bone, and driftwood. Specific tools included bone or ivory needles; thread of sinew, gut, or tendon; sealskin containers; whalebone and wooden utensils; wooden goggles with narrow eye slits; the bow drill; and soapstone (steatite) pots.

Soapstone lamps burned beluga oil (north) or caribou fat (south and interior). The latter provided light but not much heat. In the interior and more

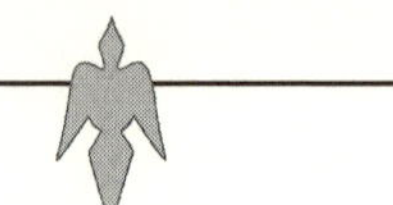

southern areas, people also molded caribou tallow candles in goose-leg skins. They started fires with pyrite, flint, and moss. Coiled baskets and woven willow mats were made around Hudson Bay.

Trade Southeastern groups imported wood for bows and arrows from the Beothuk Indians of Newfoundland. Inlanders and coastal residents exchanged dogs, ivory, caribou, and sealskins. The Inuit of present-day Quebec and those of modern Labrador engaged in regular trade. There was limited trade and contact between southern groups and the nearby Naskapi/Montagnais (Innu).

Notable Arts Art objects included woven grass baskets and carved ivory figures. There were also some petroglyphs in steatite quarries.

Transportation Travel was fairly well developed, allowing people to move with relative ease to exploit the various regions of their territory. Several types of kayaks were used generally for hunting sea mammals, birds, and caribou. Umiaks (larger, skin-covered open boats that might hold up to 30 people) were generally rowed by women on visits to offshore islands or during seasonal migrations. They were also used in the south for autumn whale hunting. Wooden sleds were pulled by dogs, who also carried some gear. Temporary boats might be made of caribou skin stuffed with branches. Long-distance walking, on snowshoes in winter, was common (snowshoes may not be native).

Dress Dress throughout Labrador was originally similar to that of the Baffinland Inuit. It consisted mainly of caribou-skin and sealskin clothing and boots. Skins of other animals were used as needed. Some island people made clothing of bird skins, especially those of ducks.

Coats probably had long flaps at the rear. Waterproof outerwear was made from gut. Other gear included sealskin boots (women of some groups wore theirs hip high) and mittens. In some areas, boots had corrugated soles made of looped leather strips.

Better hunters had newer and better clothing. Decoration was also age- and sex-appropriate. Ivory, wood, and other materials were used in clothing decoration. Some items were used as amulets or charms, whereas others were basically decorative. Women generally tattooed their faces, arms, and breasts after reaching puberty. Men occasionally tattooed noses or shoulders when they had killed a whale. Both men and women wore hair long, but women braided, rolled, and knotted theirs.

War and Weapons Inuit and Indians generally avoided each other out of mutual fear. The East Cree killed Inuit whenever possible. Intergroup and intragroup conflict regularly led to bloodshed. Hunting equipment doubled as weapons.

Contemporary Information

Government/Reservations Major Inuit communities in Labrador include Aqvituq (Hopedale), Nunainguk (Nain), Marruvik (Makkovik), Kikiak (Rigolet), Northwest River, Qipuqqaq (Postville), and Happy Valley/Goose Bay. Government is by locally elected community council, some dominated by "settlers."

Nunavik communities include Aupaluk, Chisasibi (also Cree), Ivujivik, Kangirsujuaq, Kangirsuk, Kangiqsualujjuaq, Kuujjuarapik, Kuujjuaq, Puvirnituq, Salluit, Tasiujaq, and Umiujaq. The Kativiq Regional Government is responsible for municipal services and various policies. There is also a local school board.

Economy Art, craft, food, and many other cooperatives date from the late 1950s. The Torngat Fish Producers Cooperative Society runs local fisheries operations. The Makivik Corporation, set up under the James Bay and Northern Quebec Agreement (JBNQA) (see "Daily Life"), manages tens of millions of dollars in development funds and represents the Inuit of northern Quebec on environmental, resource, and constitutional issues. Other JBNQA corporations manage interests in air transport, construction, communications, and cultural activities. Many people depend on government employment and assistance. Subsistence, especially fishing, is most important in northern Labrador. Associated cultural behaviors and traditions, such as sharing, remain correspondingly relatively strong.

Legal Status Inuit are considered "nonstatus" native people. Most Inuit communities are incorporated as hamlets and are officially recognized. The communities listed under "Government/Reservations" are provincially and federally recognized.

Daily Life The Northern Quebec Inuit Association (1971) approved the JBNQA in 1975. It provided for local and regional administrative power as well as some special rights in the areas of land use, education, and justice. There was also monetary compensation. This controversial agreement divided the Inuit on the issue of aboriginal land rights. The opposition, centered in the locally based cooperative movement, formed the Inuit Tungavingat Nunami (ITN). This group rejects the JBNQA, including the financial compensations, carrying on its opposition activities through local levies on carvings.

A cultural revival beginning in the 1980s led to the creation of museums, cultural centers, and various studies and programs. Newspapers, air communication, television, and telephone reach even remote villages. Education is locally controlled from grades 1–12, although the curriculum differs little from those in non-native communities. Issues there include mineral and other development versus protecting renewable resources. Many local committees and associations, such as the Labrador Women's Group (1978), provide needed social, recreational, and other services. Many Labrador Inuit still experience some ongoing racial conflict.

Traditional and modern coexist, sometimes uneasily, for many Inuit. Full-time doctors are rare in the communities. Housing is often of poor quality. Most people are Christians. Culturally, although many stabilizing patterns of traditional culture have been destroyed, many remain. Many people live as part of extended families. Adoption is widely practiced. Decisions are often taken by consensus.

Inuit, Mackenzie Delta

See Inuvialuit

Inuit, North Alaska

See Inupiat

Inupiat

Inupiat (In ˋū pē ut) "the People," an Inuit name covering the Eskimo or Inuit groups formerly known to anthropologists as Bering Strait, Kotzebue Sound, sometimes West Alaska, and North Alaska Eskimos. The last group has also been divided into two groups: coastal people, or Tareumiut, and the land-oriented Nuunamiut.

Location The Inupiat lived in northwest and northern Alaska, from about Norton Sound and the Seward Peninsula (with offshore islands) north and east to about the Canadian border, including the North Slope–Barrow region. This is considered to have been one of the world's most productive sea mammal regions. Many Inupiat still live in this area.

Population There were perhaps 9,500 Inupiat in the mid–nineteenth century. The population in the early 1990s was approximately 12,000.

Language Inupiat people spoke dialects of Inupiaq (Inuktitut), an Eskaleut language. Some Bering Strait Inuit spoke Yup'ik dialects.

Historical Information

History The historic Nuunamiut (interior North Alaska people) moved into their region from the south and west from circa 1400 through about 1800. Russian explorers and traders arrived in the early to mid–eighteenth century and remained for the next 100 years or so. Whalers and traders from other countries plied the local waters from about the 1840s on (1880s in the far north). Among other things, they introduced alcohol, tobacco, and non-native diseases. Traditional patterns began to break down as well after that time.

The Nuunamiut began a sharp decline from the mid–nineteenth century on, largely owing to disease and starvation (smaller caribou herds). Most families had left the interior by 1820, drawn to the coast, although a few families began moving back around 1840. There were severe epidemics throughout the region in the 1870s and 1880s. A severe famine struck the Kotzebue Sound region in 1880–1881.

Mining began in the Bering Strait area in the 1880s. Meanwhile, imported reindeer herding, fur

Madonna of the North, a 1912 photograph by H. G. Kaiser. Kaiser operated out of Nome, Alaska. By the time he took this photograph, the demand for gold rush photos had died down, but interest in the natives was climbing.

trapping, missionaries, and schools began to attract people to local settlements from the mid– to late nineteenth century on. Reindeer herding proved ultimately to be unsuccessful in the area. The Nome gold rush of 1898 saw the migration of many Inuit to the Nome area to sell crafts and, eventually, to work and to attend school. Anti-Inuit sentiment remained strong in Nome for some time thereafter.

Fur traders arrived around 1900, about the time of a severe measles epidemic and the near-depletion of the caribou herds. Another severe influenza epidemic struck in 1918. In the early twentieth century, the federal government assumed responsibility for Inuit education. To a greater extent even than the churches, the government increased the pressure to acculturate. For instance, government schools punished people severely for speaking their native language. The only high schools were located away from Inupiat-speaking centers.

The people experienced a general population growth after World War II, attributable to the return of the caribou, the introduction of moose into the region, and government efforts against disease. The far north took on strategic importance during the Cold War, about the same time that vast mineral reserves became known and technologically possible to exploit. Oil was discovered on the North Slope in 1968. Most jobs that Inuit were able to obtain were unskilled menial. Furthermore, with radical diet changes, the adoption of a sedentary life, and the appearance of drugs and alcohol, their health declined markedly.

In the late 1950s, Inupiat people began organizing politically over the U.S. government's threat to use nuclear weapons to build a deep-water port as well as over bird hunting restrictions. The Seward Peninsula Native Association, Alaska Federation of Natives, Inupiat Paitot, Northwest Alaska Native Association, and North Slope Native Association formed as a result of this activism. Land issues also gave rise to the Alaska Native Claims Settlement Act (ANCSA) in 1971. The settlement gave the people legal rights to millions of acres of land and shares in corporations worth millions of dollars in exchange for their cession of aboriginal title. Major land conservation laws were enacted in 1980.

Religion Religious belief was based on the existence of spirit entities found in nature. In particular, the spirits of game animals allowed themselves to be caught only if they were treated properly. Respect was expressed in behaviors such as maintaining a separation between land and sea hunting, opening the head of an animal just killed in order to allow its spirit to escape, speaking well of game animals, offering sea mammals a drink of cold water and land animals knives or needles, and many other taboos, rituals, and ceremonies as well as certain songs and charms.

Among whale hunters, personal spirit songs that were purchased or inherited were used to make the hunt more successful. Whale and caribou hunters and their wives were required to observe many rituals and taboos. Whaling ceremonies along the north coast and caribou ceremonies inland were the most important rituals, representing a sort of world renewal.

Male and older female shamans *(angakok)* provided religious leadership by virtue of their connection with the spirit world. They also participated in regular economic activities. They could cure disease and see into the future. Illness was seen as owing to soul loss and/or violation of taboos. Curing methods included interrogation about taboo adherence, trancelike communication with spirit helpers, and performance, including singing and sucking. (Nonspiritual ailments included infected eyes and respiratory problems, stomach diseases, boils, and lice.) Shamans might also be accused of and killed for causing a death.

Government Nuclear or small extended families were loosely organized into fluid local groups *(-miuts)* associated with geographical areas. These local groups occasionally came together as small, fluid, autonomous bands (family groups; tribes) of between 20 and 200 bilaterally related people. The bands were also geographically identified but were not political entities; their names carried the *-miut* suffix. People within them depended on each other for subsistence support and spoke the same subdialect. Several distinct societies of bands had formed in the interior north by the mid–nineteenth century.

Family heads (*umialik,* literally umiak captain, or whaling leader) were usually older men, with little formal authority and no power. Leaders generally embodied Inuit values, such as generosity, and were also good hunters. Within the context of a basically egalitarian society, they were relatively wealthier (owing to their following) and had more status than other men. Their main responsibilities included directing hunt, trade, and diplomatic activities. The *umialik* and his wife were also responsible for food redistribution.

Among the northern Inupiat, leaders might also impose their will on women as well. Potential leaders often competed with each other to hold their crews or hunters by such means as wife exchange and gift giving. Additional wives generally meant additional followers, wealth, and power. Leaders there might oversee not only the hunt but also religious ceremonies, festivals, and trade.

The northern Inupiat came together briefly for larger hunting (sea and land) forays, but mainly they remained in family groups. The Bering Strait and Kotzebue Sound tribes had principal winter villages. Each had one or more chiefs for each local group residing in the village. The chief(s) and a council oversaw local and intertribal affairs.

Customs Kinship networks were the most important social structure as well as the key to survival in terms of mutual aid and cooperative activity. This arrangement also led to ongoing blood feuds: An injury to one was perceived as an injury to the whole kin group and called for revenge.

Nonkin men teamed up for hunting or trade purposes. Such defined partnerships might include temporary wife exchanges, which were considered as a kind of marriage (interestingly, at least among the Bering Strait people, relations considered adulterous were harshly dealt with). Joking relationships between unrelated men also furthered mutual aid and support and served to reduce tension and conflict. Nonkin relationships also included adopted people and people who had the same name.

In some Bering Strait Inuit villages, family groups lived on patrilineally inherited plots of land. In larger groups, food was generally turned over to the *umialik* and his wife, who redistributed it according to various priorities. Generosity was highly valued. When hunters brought in a whale or caribou, no one went hungry. Hard work and individual freedom were other key values, the latter within the context of kinship associations.

Southerners especially celebrated fall and winter Messenger Feasts, in which a neighboring group was invited to feast and dance. Social status was related to largesse on these occasions, which were similar to potlatches. They brought some north Alaska Inuit together with some Athapaskan Indians.

People married simply by announcing their intentions, although infants were regularly betrothed. Marriage was considered to be mainly a kinship-building exercise. Successful hunters might have more than one wife, but most had only one. Divorce, or the end of cohabitation, was easy to obtain, especially before many children had been born. It was also the case that men might try to dominate women, including raping them, in their or another's household. In this endeavor the "bully" was usually

backed by members of his kinship group (as, in fact, older women might occasionally, by virtue of their supposed magical powers, capture a young man for a husband).

Infanticide was rare and usually practiced against females. Children were highly valued and loved, especially males. They were raised by the women with a great deal of liberty. Names, usually of dead relatives, were associated with specific food taboos. The sick or aged were sometimes abandoned, especially in times of scarcity. Death was attended by a minimum of ritual. Corpses were removed through skylights and left on the tundra. A mourning period of four or five days ensued, during which all activity ceased, and a feast was often held a year after a relative's death.

Tensions were relieved by playing games, joking, and competitive song duels, in which men took turns insulting each other in witty songs. Ostracism and even death were reserved for the most serious cases of socially inappropriate behavior, although punishment by death often led to blood feuds. Amusements included competitive gambling games, song contests, dancing, wrestling, and storytelling, especially in midwinter in the men's houses called *kashims.*

Dwellings The regular winter dwelling was a semiexcavated, domed, driftwood and sod house, roughly 12–15 feet long. Moss was placed between the interior walls and the sod for insulation. There was a separate kitchen with a smoke hole and storage niches off the entrance tunnel, which descended into a meat cellar and ended at a well that led up to the main room. The houses held from 8 to 12 people (two families). Inside were raised sleeping platforms and suspended drying racks. Stretched gut or ice served as windows.

Some groups also used a dome-shaped wooden structure covered with skins or bark and also temporary snow or ice houses. Interior groups also used willow-frame dome tents covered with caribou skin, bark, or grass. Some Bering Strait people built wood frame summer houses.

Larger men's houses *(kashim)* were present in communities with more than a few families. Reserved for men and boys by day, they became a family social center at night. They were also used for ceremonies and other activities and, along the coast, were associated with whaling crews.

Diet The Tareumiut and some Bering Strait and Kotzebue Sound people depended mainly on marine life such as seals, bowhead and beluga whales, and walrus, whereas the Nuunamiut hunted mainly caribou. Whale meat was stored in the permafrost and generally provided a reliable food source from season to season. Northern groups hunted whales from umiaks in spring and seal and walrus through the ice in winter.

The Kotzebue Sound and some Bering Strait people had a mixed land and marine hunting economy. Game animals included fowl, mountain sheep, bear, wolves, wolverines, hares, squirrels, and foxes. Men and women fished year-round.

Game was generally divided among the hunting party according to a precise set of rules. Food was often boiled, often with fat or blubber, although fish was also eaten frozen. Dogs were often fed walrus or human feces mixed with oil. The Bering Strait and Kotzebue Sound people also gathered a variety of greens, berries, and roots in summer.

Key Technology Stone-tipped, toggle-headed harpoons were attached to wooden floats and inflated sealskins to create drag on a submerging whale. Floats were also used to keep a slain whale from sinking before it could be towed to shore.

Hunting equipment included spears, bow and arrow, bolas (strings attached to stone balls to bring down birds), deadfalls, traps, and snares. The atlatl was used to throw sealing darts or harpoons. Fishing equipment included hooks, weirs, nets, traps, and spears. People used a variety of mainly stone and ivory butchering tools; some were fashioned of antler and driftwood as well. The key women's tool was a crescent-shaped knife. The Bering Strait people made some grass baskets and mats.

Boiling pots might be made of driftwood or pottery. Other important items included baleen seal nets; bone needles and sinew thread; carved wooden trays, dishes, spoons, and other objects; a bow drill to start fires and drill holes; sun goggles; and carved soapstone (north) or pottery (Bering Strait and Kotzebue Sound) cooking pots and lamps (the latter

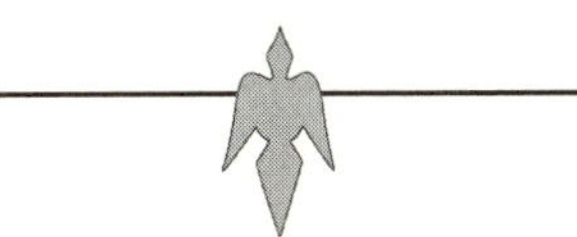

burned seal oil using moss wicks). Local stone around Kotzebue Sound included chert, slate, and jade. There was also some birch bark around Kotzebue Sound that the people made into containers.

Trade The two groups of northern Inupiat were mutually dependent, trading whale products, such as skin, oil, and blubber, for caribou skins on a regular basis. Other trade items included fish, driftwood, other skins, and ivory labrets.

Summer trade fairs were widely attended. The one at Sheshalik, on Kotzebue Sound, may have attracted 2,000 or more people. The other large northern Alaska trade fair was held in Nigalik (Colville River Delta) and was attended by Yup'ik people as well as Athapaskan Indians. In addition to trade, fairs included private contact between various partners, dancing, feasts, and competitions.

Kotzebue trade fairs were also attended by Siberians, who exchanged jade, pottery, reindeer skins, and beads for local products. Native Siberians (Chukchi) also provided Russian goods from the late seventeenth century on.

Notable Arts Most art objects were ceremonial in nature. They included carved wooden and ivory objects, such as labrets, masks, and marionettes.

Transportation The basic hunting vehicle was the one- or two-person closed skin kayak. Several men could hunt whales in umiaks (skin-covered open boats with a driftwood frame between 15 and 50 feet long). Umiaks might also hold 2,000 pounds of cargo. The people also used wooden sleds with iced runners. Dogs pulled (or helped pull) the sleds after about 1500. Some interior people used snowshoes.

Dress Women tanned skins and made sealskin and caribou-skin clothing, some with fur trim. In winter, people wore two suits of parkas and pants: The inner suit was worn with the fur turned in, whereas the outer had the fur turned out. Other winter clothing included mittens and hoods (women's were extra large for carrying babies). Clothing in the Kotzebue Sound area was sewn from untanned skins.

Other items of clothing included skin socks, boots of caribou skin and chewed seal-hide soles, and waterproof outer jackets of sewn sea mammal intestine. Men wore labrets, the lip being pierced around puberty. Many women had three lined tattoos down the chin. Babies wore moss and ptarmigan feather diapers. In general, clothing in this area exhibited considerable regional diversity.

War and Weapons Fighting was generally a matter of kin group involvement and remained limited in scope if not in time. Strangers outside of the kinship or alliance system were considered potential enemies and could be killed on sight, their goods and women taken. Blood feuds were the result of the lack of overall conflict-resolution structures. Fighting also took place among rival trade groups. Also, territory was defended against neighboring groups. The enemies of the Bering Strait people included Siberian Inuit and also nearby Athapaskan Indians. Some interior north Alaska groups were friendly with Athapaskan Koyukon and unfriendly with Athapaskan Kutchin. Hunting equipment generally doubled as weapons, except that some groups also wore armor.

Contemporary Information

Government/Reservations Regional political structures include the North Slope Borough (1972) and the Northwest Arctic Borough (1986). There are 11 permanent villages of the Kotzebue region, all of which have electricity and telephone service. Government is by elected mayors and city councils. There is also a northern interior village of Anaktuvuk Pass, which has been settled mainly since the early 1950s. Barrow and Kotzebue are far-northern cities.

Economy Important sources of income among Northwest Arctic Borough people include the Red Dog Mine, the school system, and the government. Among people in the North Slope Borough, sources of income are mainly local government and the oil industry. Employment opportunities also exist in the cities of Kotzebue and Barrow. Many people also count on government assistance. Chukchi Sea Trading Company is a cooperative of Inuit women from Point Hope who sell arts and crafts on the World Wide Web. In general, because most subsistence activities take place in winter, and most

wage work is available in summer, the Inupiat have made a relatively successful adaptation to new economic opportunities while maintaining traditional subsistence activities.

Legal Status The regional corporations under ANCSA are Arctic Slope, Bering Straits, and Nana. Other ANCSA entities include the Maniilaq and Inupiat Community Nonprofit Corporations of the Arctic Slope Regional Corporation.

Daily Life In response to severe problems with substance abuse, several communities have restricted or eliminated the sale of alcohol. Other efforts to remedy the problems are ongoing. Severe radioactive pollution exists around the Cape Thompson area. This is caused by the use by the Atomic Energy Commission (predecessor to the Nuclear Regulatory Commission) of the area as a nuclear dump and its conduct of nuclear experiments using local plant and animal life as well as by Soviet nuclear waste dumping. Negotiations over cleanup are ongoing.

Curricula and, in fact, control of education, shifted to local authorities beginning in the 1970s. Preservation and instruction of native culture are part of this effort. The native trade fair in Kotzebue follows the Fourth of July celebration, and the Messenger Feast is held in Barrow in January.

Most Inupiat people have access to all modern air and electronic transportation and communication. Most speak English as a first language, although most adults are bilingual. With the construction of roads from Anaktuvuk Pass to the North Slope oil fields, many people think that that town will some day be abandoned.

Inuvialuit

Inuvialuit (I `nū vē a `lū it) is the Inuit name for the people formerly known as Mackenzie Delta Eskimo or western (Canadian) Arctic Eskimo.

Location The homeland of this group is the Mackenzie Delta region, specifically from Herschel Island to the Baillie Islands, northwest Northwest Territories.

Population From between 2,000 and 2,500 people in the mid–eighteenth century, the Inuvialuit population was reduced to about 150 in 1910 and perhaps 10 in 1930. The mid-1990s Inuit population was about 5,000.

Language Inuvialuits speak a dialect of Inuit-Inupiaq (Inuktitut), a member of the Eskaleut language family.

Historical Information

History The people offered a generally friendly reception when they first met non-native traders in the late eighteenth and early nineteenth century. However, relations soon soured. Missionaries were active in the region by mid–nineteenth century, although few Inuvialuit accepted Christianity before 1900.

The heyday of the whaling period began in 1888, when some 1,000 non-native whalers wintered near the Mackenzie River; the region soon became a trade center as well as a haven for "frontier living" that included alcohol abuse, sexual promiscuity, and death from firearms. Traditional life declined sharply, as did the population, which was further beset by a host of hitherto unknown diseases such as scarlet fever, syphilis, smallpox, and influenza. By 1920 the Inuvialuit had all but disappeared from the Yukon. Most modern Inuvialuit are descended from Inupiat groups who moved east from Alaska about that time. Indians and non-natives moved in as well.

The far north took on strategic importance during the Cold War. In 1954, the federal Department of Northern Affairs and Natural Resources encouraged the Inuit to abandon their nomadic life. The department oversaw the construction of housing developments, schools, and clinics. Local political decisions were made by a community council subject to non-native approval and review. In 1959, the "government" town of Inuvik was founded as an administrative center.

Inuits generally found only unskilled and menial work. They also survived through dependence on government payments. With radical diet changes, the adoption of a sedentary life, and the appearance of drugs and alcohol, health declined markedly. The Committee for Original People's Entitlement (COPE), founded in 1969, soon became the political

German missionaries pose with the native population of a small village. The missionaries spread out all across the Arctic, trading with the Inuit and teaching Christianity.

voice of the Inuvialuit. Oil and gas deposits were found in the Beaufort Sea in the 1970s.

Religion Religious belief and practice were based on the need to appease spirit entities found in nature. Hunting, and specifically the land-sea dichotomy, was the focus of most rituals and taboos, such as that prohibiting sewing caribou skin clothing in certain seasons. The people also recognized generative spirits, conceived of as female and identified with natural forces and cycles.

Male and female shamans *(angakok)* provided religious leadership by virtue of their connection with guardian spirits. They could also control the weather, improve conditions for hunting, cure disease, and divine the future. Illness was perceived as stemming from soul loss and/or the violation of taboos and/or the anger of the dead. Curing methods included interrogation about taboo adherence, trancelike communication with spirit helpers, and performance.

Government Nuclear families were loosely organized into local groups associated with geographical areas *(-miuts).* These groups occasionally came together as perhaps five small, fluid bands or subgroups: Kittegaryumiut, Kupugmiut, Kigirktarugmiut, Nuvouigmiut, and Avvagmiut. The bands were also geographically identified. Informal or ad hoc village leaders *(isumataq)* were usually older men, with little formal authority and no power. They embodied Inuit values, such as generosity, and were also good hunters, perhaps especially good whalers.

Contact with neighboring Inuit groups may have influenced the development of a somewhat stronger village leadership structure, including inheritance in the male line, around the time of contact. The Inuvialuit population was generally less dispersed than that of other Inuit groups. Their largest summer village, for instance, contained up to 1,000 people.

Customs Descent was bilateral. Intermarriage was common between members of the five bands. People married simply by announcing their intentions, although infants were regularly betrothed. Men might have more than one wife, but most had only one. Divorce was easy to obtain. Some wife exchanges took place within defined partnerships between men; the relationship between a man and his partner's wife was considered as a kind of marriage.

Infanticide was rare and, when practiced, was usually directed against females. Children were highly valued and loved, especially males. Their names generally came from deceased relatives and were bestowed by shamans. Male adolescents had some teeth filed down and their cheeks and earlobes pierced. The sick or aged were sometimes abandoned, especially in times of scarcity. Corpses were not removed from houses through the door but rather through a specially made hole in the wall. They were then placed on the ground and covered with driftwood. Personal items were placed on top of the grave.

Tensions were relieved through games; duels of drums and songs, in which the competing people tried to outdo each other in parody; and some "joking" relationships. Ostracism and even death were reserved for the most serious cases of socially inappropriate behavior, such as murder, wife stealing, and theft. Relations between the Inuvialuit and their Indian neighbors were both cordial, including intermarriage, and hostile. Regular social gatherings might feature drum dances and bouncing on stretched walrus skins.

Dwellings The typical winter dwelling was a semiexcavated, rectangular, turf-covered, log framework house. Each one held about three families. Sleeping chambers were appended, giving the whole a cross shape. Each family had a separate cooking area as well. Entrance was via an underground tunnel. Houses were named. Windows or skylights were made of gut. Storage was located along the tunnel or in niches within.

The people occasionally used temporary domed snow houses in winter, mainly when traveling. Entrance was gained through a door. There were some larger open-roofed sod and wood houses as well for ceremonial purposes, although these may reflect a later Inupiat influence. Conical caribou-skin tents used in summer were strengthened by a hoop lashed to the frame about 6 feet from the ground. Also, each village had a men's house *(kashim)* up to 60 feet long.

Diet The Inuvialuit were nomadic hunters. The most important game animals were seals and baleen whales, especially beluga. Whales were hunted communally by driving up to 200 of them into shallow water with kayaks. Seals were netted on the edges of ice floes and hunted at their breathing holes in winter.

The people also hunted caribou (fall drives), moose, mountain sheep, hares, bears, musk ox, muskrat, beaver, and birds. Fishing took place especially in spring and summer, mainly for whitefish and herring. Most fish and meat were dried, frozen, or preserved in oil and stored for winter. Other than fish, which was often eaten raw, food was boiled or roasted and eaten with various oils and fats. Other foods included berries and some roots. People generally drank water or stock.

Key Technology Hunting equipment included several kinds of whale harpoons, lances, and spears as well as bow and arrow, knives, and bird bolas. Seals were also netted under the ice. Fishing equipment included hooks and weirs. Most tools were made from caribou antler tools as well as wood (including driftwood), ivory, and bone. There were some stone items as well, especially steatite (soapstone) ornaments and pots.

The people used some carved steatite lamps (that burned seal oil), although most cooking was done over an outdoor wood fire. They also carved wooden trays, dishes, spoons, and other objects. Bow drills were used to make fire. Wolves and foxes were killed when they ate sharpened baleen spring traps placed in fat.

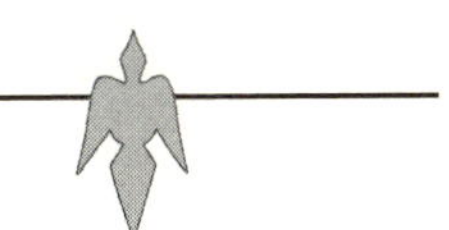

Trade Goods were exchanged with the Kutchin and Hare Indians as well as with the Inupiat to the west. Individual formal trade partnerships were a part of this process. The people exported wood, which they procured in the southern part of their territory.

Notable Arts Sewn clothing and carved wooden and ivory figurines were developed to artistic levels.

Transportation One- or two-person kayaks were used mostly for sea mammal hunting. Several men hunted whales in umiaks, or larger open boats covered with beluga skin. Overland travel was facilitated by the use of wooden dogsleds with iced-over runners of bone or antler.

Dress Clothing consisted mainly of sewn caribou skins. Men and women wore two layers, the under layer with the hair turned in and the outer layer with the hair turned out. Coats and pants were trimmed with fur, as were parka hoods. Men's hoods were made from caribou or wolf-head skin, the latter with the ears left on. Women's parkas were knee length and double flapped, as opposed to mens', which ended at the hip. Women's parka hoods were also made bigger to cover their double bun–shaped hairstyles. Other clothing included caribou-leg boots with beluga-skin soles and caribou mittens.

In summer, most people wore old inner garments with the hair turned out. Men who had killed a bear wore pieces of stone or ivory through their cheeks. Most men also wore polished stone or ivory labrets in their lips. Both sexes wore ornaments in pierced ears and nasal septa. Both men and women applied small tattoos on their faces and bodies. Children who had reached puberty had their teeth filed down; boys' cheeks and ears were pierced as well.

War and Weapons The Inuvialuit fought mainly with nearby Athapaskan Indians. Hunting equipment generally doubled as war weapons.

Contemporary Information

Government/Reservations Contemporary communities include Aklaavik, Ikaahuk (Sachs Harbour), Paulatuuq, Uluksartuuq (Homlan), and Tuktuujaqtuuq (Tuktoyaktuk). Government is provided by locally elected councils. These communities control the Inuvialuit Regional Corporation (IRC), formed in 1985 to administer the Inuvialuit Final Agreement (IFA) (see "Legal Status").

Economy The Inuvialuit Development Corporation (IDC) owns a multimillion-dollar transportation concern as well as air, energy, manufacturing, and real estate businesses. It also works to provide markets for musk ox meat and wool. The IDC also pays individuals annuities from corporate profits.

Subsistence hunting, trapping, and fishing are still important, as are various types of wage work and government assistance. Native-owned and -operated cooperatives have been an important part of the Inuit economy for some time. Activities range from arts and crafts to retail to commercial fishing to construction.

Legal Status The Western Arctic Claim Agreement (or IFA), signed in 1984, was the first comprehensive land claims settlement worked out by natives living in the Northwest Territories. It provides for the extinguishing of aboriginal title to the western Canadian Arctic in exchange for native ownership of approximately 91,000 square kilometers of land and payments of $45 million in benefits and $10 million for economic development, the latter to be administered by the IDC. However, federal and territorial laws apply in the region; the people have yet to work out a framework for self-government.

Daily Life The people never abandoned their land, which is still central to their identity. Traditional and modern coexist, sometimes uneasily, for many Inuit. Although people use television (there is even radio and television programming in Inuktitut), snowmobiles, and manufactured items, women also carry babies in the traditional hooded parkas, chew caribou skin to make it soft, and use the semilunar knives to cut seal meat. Full-time doctors are rare in the communities. Housing is often of poor quality. Most people are Christians. Culturally, although many stabilizing patterns of traditional culture have been destroyed, many remain. Many people live as part of extended families. Adoption is widely practiced. Decisions are often taken by consensus.

Politically, community councils have gained considerably more autonomy over the past decade or two. There is also a significant Inuit presence in the Northwest Territories Legislative Assembly and some presence at the federal level as well. The disastrous effects of government-run schools have been mitigated to some degree by local control of education, including more culturally relevant curricula in schools. Many people still speak Inuktitut, which is also taught in most schools, especially in the earlier grades. Children attend school in their community through grade nine; the high school is in Frobisher Bay. Adult education is also available.

Netsilik

Netsilik (`Net sil ik), "People of the Seal" or "there are seals." *See also* Inuit, Copper.

Location Netsilik territory is north of Hudson Bay, especially from Committee Bay in the east to Victoria Strait in the west, north to Bellot Strait, and south to Garry Lake. It is entirely within the Arctic Circle. The sea begins to freeze as early as September, and the thaw is generally not completed until the end of July. The summer tundra remains wet, since permafrost not far below the surface prevents drainage. Many Netsilik Inuit still live in this area of the central Arctic, known as Kitikmeot.

Population From about 500 in the late nineteenth century, the Netsilik population grew to around 1,300 in 1980, although this number included some non-Netsilik Inuit. The mid-1990s population of the Kitikmeot Region (Netsilik and Copper Inuit) was approximately 4,000.

Language The native language is a dialect of Inuit-Inupiaq (Inuktitut), a member of the Eskaleut language family.

Historical Information

History Netsiliks are descended from the ancient Thule culture. In about 1830 they encountered non-natives looking for the northwest passage. Still, contact with non-natives remained only sporadic until the early twentieth century. About that time, the people obtained firearms from the neighboring Iglulik. More productive hunting enabled them to keep more dogs, changing their migration and subsistence patterns.

The establishment of trading posts in their territory around 1920 heralded the economic switch to white fox fur trapping and trade for additional items of non-native manufacture, such as woolen clothing, tobacco, steel traps, fishing nets, canoes (which replaced kayaks), tea, and canvas tents. Game killed with rifles came to belong to the hunter, a practice that eroded and ultimately destroyed traditional exchange.

Missions established in the 1930s soon became permanent settlements. The Netsilik quickly accepted Christianity (Anglicanism and Catholicism), ending the taboo system and shamanic practices, not to mention infanticide and other social practices. The authority of traders, missionaries, and eventually the Royal Canadian Mounted Police (RCMP) undermined traditional leadership, such as it was.

The far north took on strategic importance during the Cold War, about the same time that vast mineral reserves became known and technologically possible to exploit. In 1954, the federal Department of Northern Affairs and Natural Resources began a program of population consolidation and acculturation. Coastal settlements were abandoned, and all people moved to one of three towns. The department oversaw the construction of housing developments, schools, and a general infrastructure. Local political decisions were made by a community council subject to non-native approval and review. The natives were offered generally unskilled employment. With radical diet changes, the adoption of a sedentary life, and the appearance of drugs and alcohol, their health declined markedly.

Religion Overarching, generative, female-identified deities or spirits were associated with natural forces and cycles. Another level of spirit entities were human and animal souls or spirits. Most religious activities were designed to propitiate the spirits of game animals specifically and potentially dangerous supernatural forces in general. Hunting and life-cycle events, particularly childbirth and death, were the basis of most taboos.

Magic spells, generally applicable to a single subject, were personal and secret and could be purchased or transmitted between generations. Souls were considered to be immortal. Those of people who died violently, including by their own hand, as well as those of good hunters and beautifully tattooed women were able to inhabit a paradise. The souls of lazy hunters and women without tattoos went to a sad and hungry place. Yet another type of supernatural being was numerous monsters and ghosts.

Male and female shamans (*angakok*) provided religious leadership by virtue of their connection with personal guardian spirits. They led group religious activities. They could also cure disease, see into the future (including such things as the location of game), and harm people. Training took place under the tutelage of an older shaman. Illness was said to be owing to soul loss and/or violation of taboos. Curing methods included interrogation about taboo adherence, trancelike communication with spirit helpers, and performance.

Government Nuclear families loosely combined into extended families or local groups associated with geographical areas *(-miuts).* Local group leaders *(isumataq)* were usually older men with little formal authority and no power. Leaders embodied Inuit values, such as generosity, and were also good hunters. Older women played a leadership role in food distribution.

Local groups occasionally traveled together as fluid hunting regional bands. The bands were also geographically identified and included Arvertormiut, Arviligjuarmiut, Ilivilermiut, Kitdlinermiut; Kungmiut, Netsilingmiut, and Qegertarmiut.

Customs Although the nuclear family was the basic social unit, survival required the regular association of extended families and, in fact, the existence of numerous complex relationships. For instance, although the people were generally monogamous, wives were exchanged within various defined male partnerships, such as song partnerships; these relationships were considered as a kind of marriage. The precise workings of wife (and husband) exchange were varied and ranged from short to long (or even permanent) and from willing to acrimonious.

Young women married around age 14 or 15, boys around age 20. People married simply by announcing their intentions, although infants and even fetuses were regularly betrothed. Women usually moved in with the husband's household. Men might have more than one wife, but most had only one. Divorce was easy to obtain. In general, the Netsilik enjoyed a high degree of sexual freedom. There was some in-law avoidance.

Infanticide was usually practiced against females, but the high rate of adult male mortality somewhat evened the gender balance. Children were highly valued and loved, especially males. Adoption was common. The sick or aged were sometimes abandoned, especially in times of scarcity. Suicide for those and other reasons, such as a general sense of insecurity or perceived weakness, was a regular occurrence as well. Corpses were abandoned, as the camp generally moved after a death. No work, including hunting, could be done within several days following a death.

Food was generally shared within the extended family or local group. In cases of collaborative hunting, such as winter sealing, food was shared according to precise rules. Tensions were relieved through games, duels of drums and songs (not the same as song partnerships, but contests of insulting songs sung by the wives), and some "joking" relationships. Tension was also occasionally resolved through physical separation, fights, and murder, although the latter inevitably brought on revenge. Ostracism and even execution were reserved for the most serious offenders of social norms. Strangers or people without direct relatives were feared and might be summarily killed.

Dwellings Villages of domed snow houses contained around 50 people but could hold up to 100. Entrance to the houses was gained through a tunnel that kept the warm air inside. Windows were made of freshwater ice. Two related nuclear families generally occupied a snow house, which had more than one room, and even a porch. The average house size was between 9 and 15 feet in diameter, although sizes varied widely. People slept on raised packed snow platforms covered with skins and furs.

Other structures included large ceremonial or dance snow houses, a platform for storing dog feed,

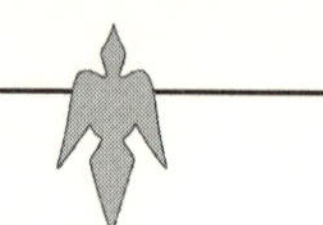

and a toilet room or outhouse. Some groups built ice houses in the fall. People used a combination snow house and skin tent in spring; these were snow houses with a skin roof. Summer dwellings were conical sealskin tents held down by stones.

Diet The Netsilik were nomadic hunters. The most important game animals were seals, which were hunted communally at their breathing holes in winter and stalked in spring. A hunter might have to stand motionless next to a breathing hole for hours in the dark and bitter cold. The people also hunted caribou, polar bear, and musk ox (in the east). The caribou were speared from kayaks as they crossed bodies of water during fall migrations or stalked and shot on land. Smaller animals included fox and squirrel. Meat was eaten raw, frozen, or, preferably, cooked. Large animals' stomach contents were eaten as well.

Fishing, particularly for salmon trout (Arctic char) and lake trout, occurred mainly in summer and autumn, individually or communally at inland weirs. Fish was mainly eaten raw, although it might be boiled or dried and cached for winter. Other food resources included fowl, gulls, and some berries. In winter, people drank melted old sea ice, which loses its salinity after a year or so. Blood was another common drink.

Key Technology Womens' semilunar knives were used mainly for skin preparation and fish cleaning. Men used antler knives to cut snow blocks for houses and to butcher caribou. Hunting equipment included various harpoons, spears, the bow and arrow, breathing-hole finders and protectors, down or horn seal motion indicators (also used for breathing-hole sealing), and other hunting equipment. Fish were caught with hooks, spears, prongs, weirs, and traps.

Most tools were made from caribou antlers as well as stone (including flint and soapstone) and bone. Wood was very scarce but when available was used for kayak frames, trays, handles, and other items. Other key tools included bone-tipped ice chisels, snow shovels made of sealskin lashed to antler, bone needles and caribou-sinew thread, the bow drill for tool manufacture and fire starting, and containers made of fowl skin, sealskin, and salmon skin. Sealskin thongs also provided cordage.

Men carved soapstone cooking pots and lamps (the latter burned seal oil or blubber and moss). Drying racks were placed above the lamps. Summer fires burned heather or mosses

Trade Netsiliks engaged in some trade with Iglulik bands. Western groups traded with their neighbors for items such as pots and lamps. Some groups imported copper and driftwood from the Copper Inuit and wood from the Caribou Inuit.

Notable Arts Some people carved fine wooden and ivory figurines. In the early postcontact period, women decorated clothing with beaded fringe and pieces of metal.

Transportation Men hunted seals and caribou from long, slender, one-person kayaks covered with sealskin. Umiaks were larger, skin-covered open boats. There were some wooden dogsleds, with runners covered with ice-coated peat or made of fish wrapped in sealskin. Polar bear skins were also used for sleds, especially in the east and in spring when the snow deteriorated. Winter travel was extremely difficult.

Dress Men skinned the caribou, and women did most of the hide preparation and sewed the clothing. They also prepared sealskins for summer clothing as well as boots and mittens. About 20 caribou skins were needed to outfit a family of four.

Mens' coats had short, fringed flaps, and womens' coats had long wide flaps. All were two-layered and had pointed hoods. The hair of the inner layer was turned in, and that of the outer layer was turned out. The outer coat had a sewn-in hood, although for women both layers had extra-large shoulders and sewn-in hoods to fit over babies, which were carried in a pouch at the back of a coat.

Four layers of caribou fur—socks, stockings, boots, and shoes—protected people's feet in winter. Men wore knee-length, two-layered pants; women made do with one layer. All outer coats (parkas) and womens' pants might be decorated with white fur. Women often braided their hair around two sticks. They also tattooed their faces and limbs. Childrens' clothing was often a one-piece suit.

The three lines on this woman's chin were tattooed at the onset of menstruation and are a mark of adulthood. Behind her are salmon split for drying (1905). Salmon fishing was a major Inuit industry.

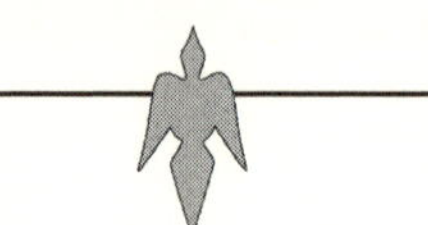

War and Weapons Neighbors tended to avoid the Netsilik in part because of their reputation for strength and magic.

Contemporary Information

Government/Reservations Netsilik communities include Arvilikjuak (Pelly Bay) and Uqsuqtuuq (Gjoa Haven). Government is provided by locally elected community councils.

Economy People still engage in some sealing and caribou hunting, although the caribou stock has been seriously overhunted. There is also government assistance and some wage work. Native-owned and -operated cooperatives have been an important part of the Inuit economy for some time. Activities range from arts and crafts to retail to commercial fishing to construction.

Legal Status Inuit are considered "nonstatus" native people. Most Inuit communities are incorporated as hamlets and are officially recognized. Baffin Island is slated to become a part of the new territory of Nunavut.

Daily Life In 1993, the Tungavik Federation of Nunavut (TFN), an outgrowth of the Inuit Tapirisat of Canada (ITC), signed an agreement with Canada providing for the establishment in 1999 of a new, mostly Inuit, territory on roughly 36,000 square kilometers of land, including Kitikmeot.

The people never abandoned their land, which is still central to their identity. Traditional and modern coexist, sometimes uneasily, for many Inuit. Although people use television (there is even radio and television programming in Inuktitut), snowmobiles, and manufactured items, women also carry babies in the traditional hooded parkas, chew caribou skin to make it soft, and use the semilunar knives to cut seal meat. Full-time doctors are rare in the communities. Housing is often of poor quality. Most people are Christians. Culturally, although many stabilizing patterns of traditional culture have been destroyed, many remain. Many people live as part of extended families. Adoption is widely practiced. Decisions are often taken by consensus.

Politically, community councils have gained considerably more autonomy over the past decade or two. There is also a significant Inuit presence in the Northwest Territories Legislative Assembly and some presence at the federal level as well. The disastrous effects of government-run schools have been mitigated to some degree by local control of education, including more culturally relevant curricula in schools. Many people still speak Inuktitut, which is also taught in most schools, especially in the earlier grades. Children attend school in their community through grade nine; the high school is in Frobisher Bay. Adult education is also available.

Unangan

Unangan (Ū ˋnän gə n), "People." The Unangan were formerly and are occasionally known as Aleut, possibly meaning "island" in a Siberian language. The Unangan consisted of perhaps nine named subdivisions, each of which spoke an eastern, a central, or a western dialect.

Location Unangan territory included the Pribilof, Shumagin, and Aleutian (west to the International Date Line) Islands and the extreme west of the Alaska Peninsula. Fog and wind, perhaps more than anything else, characterized the climate. In contrast to most of the Arctic region, the ocean remains ice free year-round.

Population The Unangan population was between 16,000 and 20,000 people, although there may have been fewer, in the early eighteenth century. There were about 4,000 Unangan in the early 1990s, of whom perhaps half lived away from their traditional lands. The Unangan people are known to have enjoyed relatively great longevity.

Language Unangans spoke three dialects of Aleut, a member of the Eskaleut language family.

Historical Information

History Ancestors of the Unangan probably moved east and then south across the Bering land bridge and then west from western Alaska to arrive in their historical location, where people have lived for at least

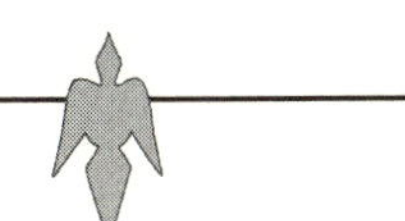

7,000 years. Direct cultural relationships have been established to people living in the region as long ago as 4,000 years.

The Russians, arriving in the 1740s, quickly recognized the value of sea otter and other animal pelts. For a period of about a generation, they tried to compel the Unangan to hunt for them, mainly by taking hostages and threatening death. The natives resisted, and there was much bloodshed during that time. However, after losing between a third and half of their total population they gave up the struggle and were made to do the Russians' bidding. Unangan men were forced to hunt sea mammals from Alaska to southern California for the Russian-American company. Large-scale population movements date from that period and lasted well into the twentieth century.

The strong influence of Russian culture dates from that period and includes conversion to the Russian Orthodox church by the early nineteenth century, when the worst of the Russian excesses ended. Other significant Russian influences include metal tools, steam baths, and larger kayaks, with sails. An Unangan orthography was created about that time, allowing the people to read and write in their own language.

Unangan hunters had come into increasing conflict with their Inuit and Indian neighbors as they were forced to go farther and farther afield for pelts. By the early nineteenth century, disease as well as warfare had diminished their population by about 80 percent. Survivors were consolidated onto 16 islands in 1831, but, by that time, Unangan culture had suffered a near-fatal blow.

The Russians left and the Americans took over around 1867, increasing fur hunting and driving the sea otter practically to extinction. The town of Unalaska had become an important commercial center by 1890. Fox trapping and canneries had become important to the local economy by the early twentieth century. Much of the Aleutian chain was designated as a national park in 1913. Some religious and government schools were opened in the early to mid–twentieth century. Still, the people endured high tuberculosis rates in the 1920s through the 1940s, and there were few, if any, village doctors.

The Japanese attacked the Aleutian Islands during World War II, capturing residents of Attu. The United States removed almost all Unangans west of Unimak Island, interning them in camps in southeast Alaska. Many people, especially elders who normally transmitted cultural beliefs and practices to the young, died during that period owing to the poor conditions in the camps. When the people returned home after the war, they found that many of their homes and possessions had been destroyed. As a result, many villages were abandoned.

The commercial fishing and cash economy grew sharply after the war. Most Unangan worked at the lowest levels of the economy. By then, Unangan children were attending high school in Sitka (Bureau of Indian Affairs) and Anchorage. Alaska received statehood in 1958. Nine years later, the native people founded the Alaska Federation of Natives (AFN) and the Aleut League. Unangan were included in the 1971 Alaska Native Claims Settlement Act (ANCSA), after initial rejection because of their high percentage of Russian blood.

Religion The people may have recognized a generative deity associated with the sun that had overall responsibility for souls as well as hunting success. They also recognized good and evil spirits, including animal spirits. These were the supernatural beings that influenced people's lives on a day-to-day basis. Adult men made offerings to the spirits at special sacred places and used a number of various charms, talismans, and amulets for protection. They also undertook spirit dances, although mainly to intimidate women and children into proper behavior

Souls were said to migrate between three worlds: earth, an upper sphere, and a lower sphere. Shamans mediated between the material and spiritual worlds. Their vocations were considered to be predetermined; that is, they did not seek a shamanic career. They had the usual responsibilities concerning hunting, weather, and curing.

Various winter masked dances and ceremonies were designed to propitiate the spirits. Perhaps the major ceremony was a memorial feast held 40 days following a death. Death was an important rite of passage. Some groups mummified dead bodies in order to preserve that person's spiritual power. A

whaler might even remove a piece of the mummy for assistance, but this custom was also considered potentially dangerous.

Government The eldest man usually led independent house groups, although all household leaders functioned as a council. One house group in a village was generally considered first among equals, the head of that group functioning as village chief if he merited the position. These leaders had little or no coercive power but mainly coordinated decision making over issues of war and peace and camp moves. They might become wealthy in part from receiving a share of subordinates' catch (wealth consisted not only of furs and skins but also of dentalium shells, amber, and slaves). This position could be inherited in the male line. In addition, there were also special leaders known as strong men. These people received special training but tended to die early.

Customs Among the Unangan, descent was probably matrilineal. Their class structure was probably derived from Northwest Coast cultures. The three hereditary classes were wealthy people (chiefs and nobles), commoners, and a small number of slaves, mainly women. The first two groups were usually related. Harmony, patience, and hard work were key values. Speech was judicious in nature, and silence was generally respected.

Villages claimed certain subsistence areas and evicted or attacked trespassers. Numerous formal partnerships between both men and women served to bind the community together. Berdaches were men who lived and worked as women. Women sewed and processed and prepared food. Truly incorrigible people might be put to death upon agreement by the village elders.

Boys moved from their mother's to their maternal uncle's home in mid-childhood. The uncle took over primary responsibility for raising the boy, with the father playing more of a supporting role. Boys were strengthened, toughened, and rigorously trained from a very early age for the life of a kayak hunter. When a girl began menstruating, she was confined for 40 days, during which time her joints were bound, in theory so they would not ache in her old age. She was also subject to a number of food and behavioral restrictions and admonishments and was allowed to cure minor illness, the people believing that she possessed special curative powers during these times.

Girls could marry even before they reached puberty, but boys were expected to wait until they were at least 18; that is, when they were capable providers. Most marriages were monogamous, except that particularly wealthy men might have more than one wife. Men performed a one- or two-year bride service. Cross cousins (children of a mother's brothers or a father's sisters) were considered potential, even preferred, spouses. Divorce was rare.

Winter was the time for ceremonies as well as social visits between communities. Village chiefs invited another community and extended great hospitality toward their guests. These visits featured wrestling, storytelling, and dance contests. Some dancers wore wooden masks to invoke spirits.

Some men paddled out to sea at the end of their lives, never to return. In fact, suicide tended to be seen in a positive light for a number of reasons. The insides of most corpses were removed and replaced with grass. Following this procedure, bodies would remain in the house, either in a corner or in a cradle over the bed, for up to several months. They were eventually buried in a flexed position in the house, either under the floor or within the walls. Central and eastern people also mummified some corpses, caching the mummies in warm, dry, volcanic caves. Widows and widowers were subject to a period of special behavioral restrictions, including some joint binding.

Dwellings Typical villages contained roughly 200 people, although up to 2,000 people may have populated some eastern communities. Rectangular, semiexcavated houses *(barabara)* were made of a driftwood and whalebone frame covered with matting and turf. Sizes varied widely. The average may have been about 35 to 60 feet long by about 15 to 30 feet wide. These houses held perhaps 40 people or several nuclear families related through the male line. The largest houses may have been up to 240 feet long by 40 feet wide, holding up to 150 people.

Sleeping compartments separated by grass mats ringed a large central room. Mats also served as flooring. Entrance was gained via a ladder placed

The interior of a habitation on Unalaska Island, 1778. These houses held approximately 40 people, or several nuclear families related through the male line. The largest may have been up to 240 feet long by 40 feet wide and held up to 150 people. Sleeping compartments separated by grass mats ringed a large central room. Mats also served as flooring.

through an opening in the roof. Cooking was generally outside the house. Large houses also served as dance halls.

Diet Depending on location, the people ate mainly sea lions, but also seals, sea otter, octopus, and some walrus. Most sea mammals were hunted by men in kayaks. Sea otters were hunted communally, in a surround, or clubbed on shore. Men who hunted sea otter avoided women for a month prior to the hunt.

There was also some whaling, especially in the west. Whaling was highly ritualized. For instance, men who had harpooned a whale retired to a special hut to feign illness, so that the whale would fall ill. Whaling privileges and powers could be inherited through the male line.

Other types of food included large and small game on the eastern islands and mainland. Important fish species included cod, flounder, halibut, herring, trout, and salmon. People ate birds, fowl, and their eggs, the latter gained mainly by climbing up or down steep cliffs. They also gathered seaweed, shellfish, roots, and berries, depending on location. Unangans tended to eat much of their food raw, although there was some pit cooking.

Key Technology Sea mammals were harpooned or clubbed. Atlatls helped give velocity to a harpoon throw. Eastern people hunted large game with the bow and arrow. Whale lances may have had poison tips. Fishing equipment included spears, nets, and wooden and tooth hooks. Birds were taken with bolas and darts, although puffins were snared and netted. Women used chipped stone semilunar knives for hide preparation and fish cleaning.

Most tools were made from stone and bone. Other important material items included sewn skin bags and pouches, some wooden buckets and bowls, sea lion stomach containers, tambourine drums, and spruce-root and grass baskets. Stone lamps burned sea lion blubber for light and heat. Cordage came from braided kelp or sea lion sinew. The people started fires with a wooden drill and flint sparks on sulphur and bird down. A highly developed counting system allowed them to reckon in five figures.

Trade Unagnan people traded both goods and ideas with Northwest Coast groups such as the Tlingit and Haida as well as with Yup'ik and Alutiiq peoples. Exports included baskets, sea products, and walrus ivory. The people imported items such as shells, slaves, blankets, and hides.

Notable Arts Art objects included carved wooden dancing masks and decorative bags. Women wove fine spruce-root and grass baskets and decorated mats with

A sixteenth-century illustration of the Inuit. Note that the hunter is holding an atlatl with a three-pronged spear. The atlatl was used to throw sealing darts or harpoons and helped give velocity to a harpoon throw.

geometric designs. Ivory carvings of the great creative spirit were hung from ceiling beams in houses, and other objects were decorated with ivory carvings as well. The Unangan were also known for their painted wooden hats. Storytelling was highly developed. Clothing decoration included feathers, whiskers, and fringe. Some items were painted, mainly with geometric patterns.

Transportation Men hunted in one- or possibly two-person kayaks. Larger skin-covered open boats were used for travel and trade but not for whaling.

Dress Women and men wore long parkas of sea otter or bird skin (men wore only the latter material). The women's version had no hood, only a collar. Men also wore waterproof slickers made of sewn sea lion gut, esophagus, or other such material. Particularly in the east, sealskin boots had soles of sea lion flipper. Boots were less common in the west. The people used grass for socks.

Men also wore wooden visors, painted and decorated with sea lion whiskers. They wore painted conical wooden hats on ceremonial occasions. Other ceremonial clothing was made of colorful puffin skins. Both sexes wore labrets of various materials. They tattooed their faces and hands and wore bone or ivory nose pins. Women wore sea otter capes.

Unangan men wore wooden visors, such as this one, painted and decorated with sea lion whiskers. They also wore painted conical wooden hats on ceremonial occasions.

War and Weapons The Unangan fought their Inuit neighbors, especially the Alutiiq, as well as themselves (especially those who spoke different dialects). Small parties often launched raids for women and children slaves or to avenge past wrongs. The people used stone and bone weapons, such as the bow and arrow, lances, wooden shields, and slat armor. Slain enemies were often dismembered, in the belief that an intact body, though dead, could still be dangerous. Prisoners might be tortured. On the other hand, high-status captives might be held for ransom or used as slaves.

Contemporary Information

Government/Reservations Unangan live on the Alaska coast, Aleutian Islands, Pribilof Islands, and Commander Islands. Communities include Atka, Akutan, Belkofski, Cold Bay, False Pass, Ivanof Bay (*see* Alutiiq), King Cove, Nelson Lagoon, Nikolski, Paulof Harbor, St. George Island, St. Paul Island, Sand Point, Squaw Harbor, and Unalaska. There are various forms of government, including traditional structures and those modeled on the Indian Reorganization Act. Elected village governments own no land.

Economy Economic development is recognized as key to survival. Many villages are in economic partnerships with seafood companies. Most jobs may be found with the fishing and military industries as well as other governmental bodies at lower levels.

Legal Status ANCSA granted some traditional lands to the Aleut Corporation and to village corporations but not to the tribes. The Aleut Corporation represents Unangans under ANCSA.

Daily Life Most Unangan are of the Russian Orthodox faith. Most also live in wood frame houses. There is a considerable degree of intermarriage with non-Unangans. The position of the corporations vis-à-vis the tribes has made for some bitter interfamily and intervillage divisions. Political sovereignty remains a major goal for most people. Some public schools feature courses in the Unangan language. A cultural facility on Bristol Bay is planned.

Yup'ik

Yup'ik (ˋYūp ik), "Real People." The Yup'ik people were formerly known as Nunivak Inuit (or Eskimo), St. Lawrence Island Eskimo, West Alaska Eskimo, South Alaska Eskimo, and Southwest Alaska Eskimo. They are also known as Bering Sea Yuit and, with the Alutiiq (Pacific Eskimo), simply as Yuit. The St. Lawrence Islanders were culturally similar to Siberian Eskimos. *See also* Alutiiq.

Location Yup'ik territory was located in southwestern Alaska, between Bristol Bay and Norton Sound, including Nunivak and St. Lawrence Islands.

Population The early-nineteenth-century Yup'ik population was between about 15,000 and 18,000. It was approximately 18,000 in the early 1990s.

Language The people spoke the Yuk or Central Alaskan Yup'ik (including St. Lawrence Island or Central Siberian Yup'ik) branch of Yup'ik. With Inuit-Inupiaq (Inuktitut), Yup'ik, or Western Eskimo, constitutes the Eskimo division of the Eskaleut language family.

Historical Information

History People have lived on Nunivak Island since at least 150 B.C.E. They made pottery and used mainly stone tools. The mainland has been inhabited for at least 4,000 years, with cultural continuity since circa 300 B.C.E.

Most groups avoided direct contact with non-natives until Russian traders established trading posts in Yup'ik territory, generally in the early nineteenth century. The Russians exchanged clothing, metal tools, and beads for beaver pelts. The Inuit began spending more time trapping beaver and less time on subsistence activities, eventually becoming dependent on the posts even for food. In general, Russian Orthodox missionaries followed the early traders. Most Inuit had accepted Christianity by the 1860s.

This process was uneven throughout the region. St. Lawrence Island people first met non-natives in the 1850s, whereas people on the Yukon Delta did not do so until the late nineteenth century. About 1,000 people (roughly two-thirds of the total population) of St. Lawrence Island died in 1878 from a combination of natural causes combined with a high incidence of alcohol abuse. Nunivak Island was similarly insulated (contact occurred in 1821 but perhaps not again until 1874), in part owing to the shallowness of the surrounding sea. The first trading post, which included a reindeer herd, was established there in 1920; missionaries and schools dated from about the 1930s. The people experienced various epidemics throughout the early to mid–twentieth century.

Little changed with the sale of Alaska to the United States until the advent of commercial fishing in Bristol Bay in the 1880s. Moravian missionaries appeared on the Kuskokwim River in 1885; those of other sects soon followed. Like most missionary schools, theirs forbade children to speak their native language. In an effort to undermine the traditional lifestyle, the U.S. government introduced reindeer to the region around 1900.

In addition to commercial fishing, fox hunting for the fur trade plus the manufacture of baleen and carved ivory objects formed the basis of a local cash economy from the late nineteenth century through the early twentieth century. Nunivak Islanders experienced the full cash economy only after World War II. By then the people had incorporated under the Indian Reorganization Act (IRA). The Bureau of Indian Affairs managed their reindeer herd.

The far north took on strategic importance during the Cold War, about the same time that mineral reserves became known and technologically possible to exploit. St. Lawrence Island became exposed to mainland life and tied to Alaska only after

Children arrive for school in reindeer-drawn sleds. In an effort to undermine the traditional lifestyle, the U.S. government introduced reindeer to the region around 1900.

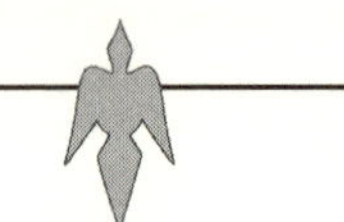

military installations were built there in the 1950s. Inuits generally found only unskilled menial labor. With radical diet changes, the adoption of a sedentary life, and the appearance of drugs and alcohol, health declined markedly. The Alaska Native Claims Settlement Act (ANCSA) was passed in 1971.

Religion Religious belief and practice were based on the conception of spirit entities found in nature and needing to be treated with respect. Most rituals focused on this belief, such as those that showed respect to an animal just killed. It was also the basis of most taboos as well as related objects and songs.

Souls were said to be reincarnated through naming. Spirits not yet reincarnated also needed to be treated with respect lest they cause harm. In some areas, secret, spirit-based knowledge, objects, and songs, all thought to bring success in hunting, were passed on from father to son. The people also believed in various nonhuman, nonanimal supernatural beings.

Male and female shamans *(angakok)* provided religious leadership by virtue of their connection with guardian spirits. They led group religious activities. They could also cure disease and see into the future. Illness was thought to be due to soul loss and/or the violation of taboos. Professional curing methods included interrogation about taboo adherence, trancelike communication with spirit helpers, extraction (such as sucking), and performance, including masked dances. Shamans were relatively powerful people, in part owing to their ability to use their spirit power to harm people.

The Messenger Feast, a major ceremony, included dancing and gift exchange between two villages. St. Lawrence Islanders held a spring whaling ceremony. When the successful crew returned, the umiak owner's wife offered the whale a drink of water as a token of respect. Then followed another feast and a thanksgiving ceremony. Some groups held memorial feasts about a year following a death.

In general, Yup'iks living along the Bering Sea had their main ceremonial season in the winter and early spring. The festivities featured spirit masks and dances. The Bladder Feast was another important ceremony dedicated to respect for animals, in this case, seals. This festival also underscored the ritual sexual division in society.

Government Nuclear families were loosely organized into extended families or local groups associated with geographical areas *(-miuts).* Local groups on the mainland occasionally came together as perhaps seven small, fluid subgroups or bands. From north to south, they were Kuigpagmiut, Maarmiut, Kayaligmiut, Kukquqvagmiut, Kiatagmiut, Tuyuryarmiut, and Aglurmiut. Older men, with little formal authority and no power, led *kashims* (men's houses) and kin groups (generally the same as villages on St. Lawrence Island). These leaders generally embodied Inuit values, such as generosity, and were also good hunters.

Customs The family was the most important economic and political unit. Descent was bilateral, except patrilineal on St. Lawrence Island. There, secret songs, ceremonies, house ownership, and hunting group membership were passed through patrilineal clans and lineages. Status was formally ranked within the *kashim* and depended on hunting and leadership skills.

People married simply by announcing their intentions, although infants were regularly betrothed. Men might have more than one wife, but most had only one. Divorce was easy to obtain. Both men and women remained respectful and distant toward their in-laws. Wife exchange was a part of certain defined male partnerships, such as mutual aid, "joking," and trade. Some of these relationships were inheritable. The alliance between the wife and the exchanged husband was considered as a kind of marriage. Formal female partnerships existed as well.

Infanticide was rare and usually practiced against females. Children were highly valued and loved, especially males. Adoption was common. Life-cycle events, such as berry picking and grass gathering by girls and seal killing by boys, were recognized by the community. Childbirth, girls' puberty, and death were the occasions for special taboos.

The sick or aged were sometimes abandoned, especially in times of scarcity. Corpses were generally removed through an alternate exit (not the door) and left on the ground with certain grave goods. Along the Bering Sea, some groups placed their dead in painted wooden coffins and erected carved wooden memorial poles to keep their spirits at bay. The mourning period generally lasted four or five days, during which time activities, including hunting, were severely restricted.

Work was fairly gender specific. Women made food and clothing and cared for children; men provided fish and land animals. Use of the real name was generally avoided, perhaps for religious reasons. Tensions were relieved through games; duels of drums and songs, in which the competing people tried to outdo each other in parody; and some "joking" relationships. Ostracism and even death were reserved for the most serious cases of socially inappropriate behavior.

Dwellings The people created larger settlements in winter to take advantage of group subsistence activities. Villages ranged in size from just two to more than a dozen houses, plus one or more *kashims* and storehouses.

There were several kinds of dwellings throughout the area, depending on location. Houses were generally of the semiexcavated variety, roughly 12 to 15 feet by 15 feet and made of sod, grass, and/or bark over wooden posts and beams. They were mainly inhabited by related women and children. Some might have plank walls with benches placed along them. Entrance was via an anteroom connected to the main room by an underground tunnel. A hearth and cooking area stood at one end of the open main room and raised sleeping platforms were at the other end. Windows were often made of sewn fish skins.

Except on St. Lawrence Island, men worked, bathed, slept, and ate in larger houses, or *kashims.* Women delivered the food. *Kashims* were also used as ceremonial houses. Political decisions were made there as well. Most villages contained at least one. Some groups built cut-sod spring camp houses, about 100 square feet in size. Skin tents were generally the norm in summer. Other structures included drying racks and food caches.

Diet Yup'ik people were nomadic hunters with either a land or a sea orientation, although most people also exploited the region opposite their own. The most important game animals were seals, walrus

The Yup'ik created larger settlements in winter to take advantage of group subsistence activities. Villages ranged in size from two to more than a dozen houses, plus storehouses, such as this storehouse in Togiak, Alaska (1909).

(especially St. Lawrence and Nunivak Island), and whales. Men hunted seals at their breathing holes in winter. On Nunivak, men hunted them from kayaks in spring and with nets under shore ice in fall. Some groups also hunted caribou (especially away from the coast and major rivers and on Nunivak Island until about 1900) and moose, especially in fall.

Fish, especially salmon, trout, smelt, and whitefish, were the most important dietary item in many locations and were generally taken in all seasons but winter. Fish were especially important inland, with marine mammals more important on the coasts and islands. Shellfish was gathered where possible. Birds and fowl, such as ptarmigan, were speared or netted and their eggs gathered. Some groups were able to obtain berries, roots, and greens.

Key Technology Hunting equipment consisted of various harpoons, spears, bows and arrows, and bone arrowheads. Caribou were snared or shot with the bow and arrow. Birds were netted, snared, speared, or captured with bolas. Fish were caught with hooks, spears, stone weirs, and caribou-skin or willow-bark nets.

Most tools were fashioned from caribou antlers as well as stone, bone, and driftwood (on St. Lawrence and Nunivak Islands, many items were made from walrus parts). Men and women had their own specialty stone knives. People cooked in pottery pots and burned seal or walrus oil in saucer-shaped pottery lamps. They carved wooden trays, boxes, dishes, spoons, and other objects.

Various kinds of containers were made out of gut, wood, and clay. St. Lawrence Islanders often used baleen as a raw material. Some groups made twined and coiled baskets of grasses and birch bark. In fact, grass was used extensively for items such as mats, baskets, socks, and rope, although some cordage also came from beluga sinew. The ceremonial tambourine drum was made of seal gut stretched over a wooden frame.

Trade The Yup'ik engaged in a general coastal-interior interregional trade, including trade with Unangan and Northwest Coast peoples. St. Lawrence Island people traditionally traded and otherwise interacted with those from Siberia.

Notable Arts The people made finely carved wooden and ivory figurines. Men painted designs, especially of animals, on wooden objects. Women decorated clothing borders, baskets, and pottery items.

Transportation Men hunted from one- or two-person sealskin-covered kayaks. Umiaks were larger, skin-covered open boats; several men could hunt whales or walrus in these. They were also used for trade voyages. Wooden sleds were used for overland winter travel. Some interior groups also used canoes.

Dress Women made most clothing of caribou and sealskin. Yup'ik clothing tended to fit relatively loosely. Some groups used skins of other animals, such as marmot and muskrat, as well as bird and even fish skins. Most people wore long hooded parkas and inner shirts and pants. Women's parkas were often shorter and featured front and rear flaps. Other items included sealskin (some groups used salmon skin) boots and mittens, skin or grass socks, fish-skin parkas and pants in summer, waterproof gut raincoats, and wooden snow goggles.

Men on St. Lawrence Island wore distinctive hairdos in which they shaved the tops of their heads but retained a circle of hair around the forehead. Women generally tattooed three lines on their chins. Personal ornaments included labrets and other items of walrus and bird parts.

War and Weapons The people regularly engaged in interregional raids. Victims were generally killed. Hunting equipment doubled as weapons of war.

Contemporary Information

Government/Reservations Villages represented by the Bristol Bay Native Corporation (BBNC) include Egegik (86 native residents; governed by the Egegik Village Council and a seven-member city council), Pilot Point (91 native residents; governed by the Pilot Point Village Council and a seven-member elected city council), Port Heiden (86 native residents; governed by the Port Heiden Village Council and a seven-member elected city council), and Ugashik (six native residents; governed by the Ugashik Traditional Village Council and a five-member elected city council). These villages are all

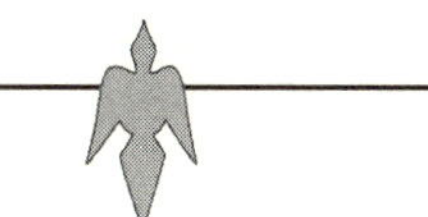

members of the Lake and Peninsula Borough and are located on the east side of Bristol Bay on the Alaska Peninsula (Chignik area).

BBNC villages located in the western portion of Bristol Bay (Togiak area) include Manokotak (368 native residents; governed by the seven-member Manokotak Traditional Council and an eight-member city council), Togiak (535 native residents; governed by the seven-member Togiak Traditional Council as well as six city councilors and a mayor), and Twin Hills (61 native residents; governed by the five-member Twin Hills Village Council as well as a traditional elders' council).

BBNC villages located in the Iliamna area include Igiugig (26 native residents; governed by the five-member elected Igiugig Tribal Council), Iliamna (62 native residents; governed by the five-member elected Iliamna Village Council), Kokhanok (137 native residents; governed by the five-member elected Kokhanok Village Council), Levelock (87 native residents; governed by the five-member elected Levelock Village Council), and Newhalen (151 native residents; governed by the seven-member elected Newhalen Tribal Council as well as a seven-member elected city council). All of these villages are also members of the Lake and Peninsula Borough. In addition, the villages of Nondalton and Pedro Bay are described in the Tanaina entry in Chapter 9.

BBNC villages in the Kvichak Bay area include King Salmon (108 native members; governed by the five-member elected King Salmon Village Council), Naknek (236 native residents; governed by the five-member Naknek Village Council), and South Naknek (108 native residents; governed by the five-member South Naknek Traditional Council). All of these villages are also members of the Bristol Bay Borough.

BBNC villages in the Nushagak Bay area include Aleknagik (154 native residents; governed by the seven-member Aleknagik Traditional Council and a seven-member city council), Clark's Point (53 native residents; governed by the five-member Clark's Point Traditional Council and a seven-member city council), Dillingham (1,125 native residents; governed by the five-member Dillingham Native Village Council and by an elected mayor and six city councilors), Ekuk (two native residents; governed by the three-member Ekuk Village Council), Ekwok (67 native residents; governed by the seven-member Ekwok Tribal Council and a seven-member city council), Koliganek (174 native residents; governed by the seven-member Koliganek Traditional Council), New Stuyahok (375 native residents; governed by the seven-member New Stuyahok Traditional Council and a seven-member city council), and Portage Creek (three native residents; governed by the three-member Portage Creek Village Council).

All BBNC village population figures are as of the early 1990s. Some villages have significant numbers of Alutiiq residents.

Regional population centers include Bethel, Dillingham, and St. Michael. The Association of Village Council Presidents (AVCP) is a regional nonprofit corporation representing 56 villages. Through it, some people hope to establish a regional tribal government.

On St. Lawrence Island there are three levels of local government: an IRA council, a state-mandated city council, and ANCSA village corporations.

Economy Commercial fishing is probably the most important single industry. Except in the Bristol Bay region, traditional subsistence activities remain very important. The people also do some muskrat and mink trapping in the Kuskokwim Delta region. Lake Iliamna has one of only two populations of freshwater seals in the world (the other is in Lake Baikal, Russia). Traditional crafts are an important industry on Nunivak Island. Many people depend on government payments. There is also some tourism, especially in the Nuchagak Bay area.

Legal Status Three ANCSA regional corporations serve Yup'ik territory: Bering Straits Corporation, Calista Corporation, and Bristol Bay Native Corporation. Nunivak Island is a national wildlife refuge in which local residents may carry out subsistence activities. Under ANCSA, St. Lawrence Island is owned by the native residents but managed by corporations.

Daily Life Bilingual education has been in force since the 1970s; most Yup'ik people still speak the native language. The Yukon Kuskokwim Health

Corporation serves the people's health needs with culturally appropriate programs and care.

Some communities have been more severely disrupted and are consequently less cohesive than others. Most St. Lawrence Islanders had been converted to Christianity by the mid–twentieth century, although many of the old ideas still resonate for the people.

The issue of subsistence hunting rights remains very important to the Yup'ik. Chignik area villages share certain concerns, such as the decline of the local caribou herd, possibly owing to excess sport hunting, and the threat to subsistence activities of industrial development. Togiak area villages are pressing for permission from the state of Alaska to conduct a permanent annual walrus hunt on Round Island and for funds to maintain their reindeer herd. They are also trying to prevent desecration of ancient burial sites.

Local concerns in the Iliamna area include road improvement, bridge construction, and air links. Concerns in the Kvichak Bay area include the maintenance of subsistence fishing rights, the use and contamination cleanup of the former air force base site, the construction and management of a visitor center at Katmai National Park, and the decline of the local caribou herd. Issues in the Nushagak Bay area include the possible formation of a Nuchagak and Togiak area borough, land allotments within Wood-Tikchik State Park, and proper management of the local caribou herd.

Glossary

Note: FR = French; SP = Spanish.

***Ak chin* farming:** Farming based on an irrigation method consisting of the collection and channeling of floodwaters from arroyo mouths.

Allotment: A term denoting the government action of carving up communally held tribal land and granting sections of it to individual Indians. This activity characterized the General Allotment Act of 1887 (the Dawes Act).

Annual round: The annual cycle of activities engaged in by traditional societies.

Arroyo (U `rō yō, SP): A dry, sandy wash, prone to flash flooding during storms.

Atlatl (Ät `lät l): A tool used to increase the leverage of the human arm in order for hunters to throw spears with greater velocity and accuracy.

Babiche (Bä `bēsh, FR): Semisoftened rawhide, used mainly in the far north for a number of purposes such as snares, nets, bowstrings, and line.

Baleen: A growth in the upper jaw of certain whales. Baleen is light, strong, and flexible. It serves the whales as a strainer and has been used by people to make tools and ceremonial objects.

Bent-corner boxes: An art form in which men steamed, bent, and then carved and/or painted pieces of red cedar. Bent-corner boxes were characteristic of Northwest Coast people.

Berdache (Bə r `də sh, FR): Literally "male prostitute," the term refers to any person participating in the cross-cultural practice of gender crossing. In general, females acting the male role were always considered women, whereas men were generally "reclassified."

Bola: A hunting weapon consisting of stone weights attached to thongs. When thrown, the bola entangles the feet of small animals and the wings of birds.

Breechclout: A piece of material, usually deerskin, used to cover the loins. It is also called a breechcloth or loincloth.

Bride service: The act of serving a new bride's parents, as a condition of marriage, for a period of time. Such service mainly consisted of obtaining food and other necessities.

Bureau of Indian Affairs (BIA): Founded in 1824 and referred to until the mid–twentieth century as the Office of Indian Affairs or the Indian Service, the BIA is the main bureaucratic arm of the U.S. government devoted to Indian affairs. In 1849 its jurisdiction was transferred from the War Department to the Interior Department. The Commissioner of Indian Affairs reports directly to the Secretary of the Interior.

Catlinite: *See* pipestone.

Clan: A group of families that traces descent through a common ancestor.

Coppers: Decorated, named plates of European copper that were important in later Northwest potlatching. A copper was worth the value of goods distributed at a potlatch and could only be bought at double that price. Coppers also played a role in rival potlatches: When one chief destroyed a copper, his rival was obliged to do the same or admit his social inferiority.

Coup (Kū, FR): Literally "blow," the term refers to a type of war honors common among early historical Plains cultures in which credit was earned (coup was counted) for acts of bravery and daring such as touching an enemy with a stick or knocking him off his horse.

Coureurs de bois (Cū `rūr de `bwä, FR): Independent, unlicensed fur traders and trappers who played an important role in early trade and exploration of later-seventeenth-century New France.

Datura: Also known as Jimsonweed, this tall, poisonous plant is sometimes used for ceremonial or medicinal purposes by certain Indians of California and the Southwest.

Deadfall: A type of trap in which a heavy object is rigged to fall upon prey.

Dentalium: A type of shell common to parts of the Pacific Northwest. With a natural hole that made threading easy, it was widely traded and highly valued for jewelry and exchange.

Enrollment: A category of tribal membership generally constituting formal acceptance by the U.S. or Canadian governments. Because of various laws and policies excluding certain groups of people, a given tribe might recognize as members far more people than a government recognizes as enrolled.

Exogamy: The custom of marrying outside a particular group (such as a clan).

Fiesta (Fē `es ta, SP): A celebration, usually religious in nature, featuring processions and dances.

Fire drill: A device for making fire in which a stick is twirled rapidly on another piece of wood. The resulting friction is sufficient to ignite bark or grass tinder.

First Nation: A term often used to refer to Canadian Indian bands.

Fiscales (Fēs `kä lās, SP): One of several officials of Spanish-mandated Pueblo governments, the *fiscales* were church assistants. Most Pueblo groups adopted these offices after 1620, when the Spanish began requiring them, but retained their own traditional and vastly more meaningful political and religious structures as well.

Games: An important part of most traditional Native American cultures, often having spiritual, ceremonial, and/or social implications. Games were often taken very seriously and were marked by intensive preparation, rigid codes of conduct, and wagering. Some of the most common and popular games were chunkey, the grass game, shinny, lacrosse (a running ball game played with web-pocketed sticks), and the hand game (a guessing game).

General Allotment Act of 1887 (Dawes Act): An act calling for the allotment of tribal land in severalty (a certain amount going to individual family heads), with the surplus to be opened for non-native settlement.

Grid plan of settlement: Houses laid out more or less evenly along ordered streets.

Hacienda (Hä cē `en dä, SP): A tract of land held by individual title; a plantation. Under the hacienda system,

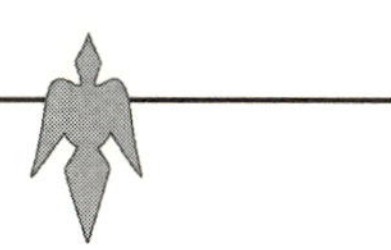

the dominant political, economic, and social system in nineteenth-century Mexico, the landowner maintained complete control over the land and the people on it. The system fostered peonage and the eradication of cultural differences.

Indian Act: The name applied to the body of Canadian federal laws pertaining to Indian affairs. The first Indian Act was passed in 1876. The act is regularly revised and updated.

Indian Reorganization Act (IRA): Legislation in 1934 that prohibited further allotment, which had been disastrous for most Indian groups, in favor of Indian self-government. Its provisions included the voluntary adoption of tribal councils within representative, constitutional governments.

Jerk (as meat): Jerking is the process of sun drying and/or smoking strips of meat.

Katsina (Kat `sē nä): Also known as kachinas, these are supernatural beings that figure prominently in the religion of Pueblo Indians. Katsina dolls and masks are used ceremonially to bestow blessings and teach proper behavior.

Kiva: An underground ceremonial chamber characteristic of Pueblo cultures.

L dialect: A dialect spoken by some bands/tribes in which the letter L was substituted for one letter of a word, commonly R or D. Thus Renápe becomes Lenápe and Dakota becomes Lakota in the L dialect (Dakota becomes Nakota in the Siouan N dialect).

Labret: A decorative plug worn in the lip.

Mano (`Mä nō, SP): The handheld upper millstone for grinding corn and other grains.

Matrilineal: Relating to descent through the maternal line.

Matrilocal: Relating to the residence of a wife's kin group.

Mesoamerica: Literally "middle America," the region between the continents of North and South America.

Mestiso/a: A man or woman of mixed European and American Indian ancestry.

Metate (Mə tä tä): A stone with a concave surface. Together with a mano, it is used for grinding corn and other grains.

Métis (Mā tē, FR): A people of mixed Cree-French or Cree-Scotch descent. By the nineteenth century, the Métis had developed a lifestyle with elements, including language and religion, drawn from both Indian and non-native traditions. The Métis were concentrated along the Red River of the North (Lake Winnipeg to the Minnesota River). Led by Louis Riel, they fought a series of unsuccessful wars in the mid–nineteenth century to defend their land rights.

Mother-in-law taboo: The custom in which a man avoided contact with his mother-in-law out of respect to her.

Olla (`Ō yä, SP): A container, usually a pot or a basket, for carrying or holding water.

Palisade: A high fence of pointed sticks enclosing an area for defensive purposes.

Parfleche (Pär `flesh, FR): Common mainly among Plains Indians, these were rawhide storage bags generally used to hold food.

Patrilineal: Relating to descent through the paternal line.

Patrilocal: Relating to the residence of a husband's kin group.

Pipestone: A type of clay, mainly found in Minnesota, widely used for making pipes. It is also referred to as catlinite after the painter George Catlin.

Polygamy: Having more than one wife or husband at a time.

Polygyny: Having more than one wife at a single time.

Powwow: Commonly used to describe a gathering at which native people dance, sing, tell stories, and exchange goods, the term also refers (in a mainly Algonquian context) to a healer or a healing ceremony.

Pueblo: Spanish for "village," the word refers to a style of architecture common among some southwestern Indian groups and characterized by multistory adobe or stone apartmentlike dwellings connected with ladders. The word

also refers to the people and culture associated with that style of architecture.

Quillwork: Decoration, often on clothing, bags, and other items, made from dyed porcupine quills.

Ramada (Rə `mä da, SP): A covered yard or plaza.

Rancheria (Ranch ə `rē ä, SP): A settlement composed of spatially separated dwellings of nuclear or extended family units. In the California context, a rancheria is a parcel of Indian land and may be as large as a settlement or as small as a small cemetery.

Rasp: An instrument resembling a notched stick, used as a musical instrument among certain Indian groups, especially in the upper Great Plains.

Sachem: The chief of an (Algonquin) tribe or confederacy.

Sagamore: An (Algonquin) chief or leader with somewhat lesser status than a sachem.

Sandpainting: An art form associated mainly with the Navajo and some other southwestern Indian groups, sandpainting, or dry painting—the creation of designs from sand, cornmeal, and pollen—carries with it rich and complex religious and spiritual implications. Sandpaintings were destroyed immediately after their ceremonial use.

Shaman (`Shā mə n): A traditional healer or holy man or woman.

Status Indians: Status is the term conferred by the Canadian government to those people who meet the official definition of Indian.

Taiga: The subarctic evergreen forest.

Termination: Federal Indian policy of the mid- to late 1950s that sought to end the relationship guaranteed by treaty between the government and Indian tribes.

Tipi (`Tē pē): A conical hide (usually buffalo) dwelling characteristic of Plains Indians. The tipi design had important cosmological implications.

Toloache: Any of several plants of the genus *Datura,* especially a narcotic annual herb used ceremonially by some California Indians.

Totem: A natural object or being serving as the emblem of a family or clan by virtue of a presumed shared ancestry with that object or being.

Travois (Trav `wä, FR): A transportation device common to Plains nomads. It consisted of two long poles (often lodgepole pines) connected by planks or hide webbing that supported goods and sometimes people. Dogs and, later, horses pulled the travois as the people migrated from place to place.

Tribe: A term, often misused, referring to the organization of a group of Indians. Tribes are generally composed of a number of constituent parts, such as bands or villages, and may share history, culture, and territory.

Tribelet: A single Indian group with a small territory, comprising a main settlement and one or more satellite villages. The tribelet's name was usually that of the principal town. The entire group often recognized a chief. Tribelets were autonomous but often acted as a unit in matters of land ownership, major ceremonies, and reaction to trespass and war. This form of political organization was most common in aboriginal California.

Tule (Tū lē): A type of reed used as a raw material by some southwestern and Californian Indians.

Tumpline: A strap across the forehead or chest that also supports a burden carried on the back.

Tundra: A treeless, Arctic region in which the ground is continually frozen no less than a few inches from the surface (permafrost). Various mosses and lichens will grow on tundra.

Voyageurs (Vō yä `jūr, FR): A group or class of Frenchmen who handled canoes and performed other trade-related tasks for the big fur companies in North America, primarily in the eighteenth and nineteenth centuries.

Wampum: An Algonquian word, wampum originally referred to strings or belts of shell (especially Quahog). They were used to record significant events as well as to communicate messages of peace or war between Indian groups. Shortly after non-natives arrived, wampum, now made increasingly of glass beads, was used as a medium of exchange and eventually as a form of money.

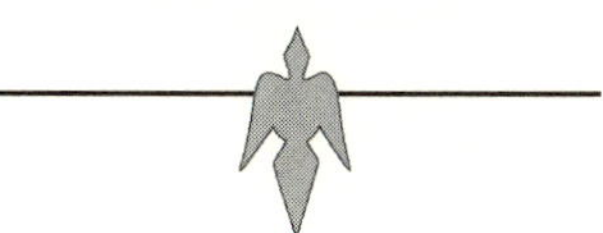

Wickiup (`Wi kē up): Dome-shaped, pole-framed dwellings covered with brush, grass, or reeds. Wickiups were often used by Apacheans.

Wigwam: A dwelling similar to a wickiup, although covered with products more reflective of their use among Algonquian people, such as skins, bark, or woven mats.

Bibliography

The following books are recommended for further study about native North Americans. I have omitted books on specific tribes or groups as well as the many helpful locations on the Internet. A growing number of tribes are also posting home pages on the World Wide Web.

General

Boxberger, Daniel. *Native North Americans: An Ethnohistorical Approach.* Dubuque, IA: Kendall/Hunt Publishing, 1990.

Champagne, Duane, ed. *The Native North American Almanac.* Detroit: Gale Research, 1994.

———. *Native America: Portrait of the Peoples.* Detroit: Visible Ink Press, 1994.

Confederated American Indians. *Indian Reservations.* Jefferson, NC: McFarland, 1986.

Davis, Mary. *Native America in the Twentieth Century.* New York: Garland Publishing, 1994.

Debo, Angie. *A History of Indians of the United States.* Norman: University of Oklahoma Press, 1970.

Dickason, Olive. *Canada's First Nations.* Norman: University of Oklahoma Press, 1992.

Dictionary of Indian Tribes of the Americas. Newport Beach, CA: American Indian Publishers, 1980.

Feest, Christian. *Native Arts of North America.* London: Thames and Hudson, 1992.

Frideres, James. *Native People in Canada.* Scarborough, Ontario: Prentice Hall Canada, 1983.

Gill, Sam, and Irene Sullivan. *Dictionary of Native American Mythology.* New York: Oxford University Press, 1992.

Hirschfelder, Arlene. *Native American Almanac.* New York: Prentice Hall, 1993.

Hoxie, Frederick, ed. *Encyclopedia of North American Indians.* Boston: Houghton Mifflin, 1996.

Jaimes, M. Annette. *The State of Native America.* Boston: South End Press, 1992.

Jenness, Diamond. *Indians of Canada.* 7th ed. Toronto: University of Toronto Press, 1977.

Johnson, Michael. *The Native Tribes of North America.* New York: Macmillan, 1995.

Jorgenson, Joseph J., ed. *Native America and Energy Development II.* Boston: Anthropological Research Center and Seventh Generation Fund, 1984.

Kehoe, Alice. *North American Indians.* Englewood Cliffs, NJ: Prentice Hall, 1981.

Klein, Barry. *Reference Encyclopedia of the American Indian.* 7th ed. West Nyack, NY: Todd Publications, 1995.

LePoer, Barbara Leitch. *Concise Dictionary of Indian Tribes of North America.* Algonac, MI: Reference Publications, 1979.

Markowitz, Harvey, ed. *American Indians.* Pasadena, CA: Salem Press, 1995.

Martin, Paul. *Indians before Columbus.* Chicago: University of Chicago Press, 1947.

Morrison, R. Bruce, and C. Roderick Wilson. *Native Peoples: The Canadian Experience.* 2d ed. Toronto: McClelland and Stewart, 1995.

O'Brien, Sharon. *American Indian Tribal Governments.* Norman: University of Oklahoma Press, 1989.

Paterek, Josephine. *Encyclopedia of American Indian Costume.* Santa Barbara, CA: ABC-CLIO, 1994.

Reddy, Marlita, ed. *Statistical Record of Native North Americans.* Detroit: Gale Research, 1993.

Spencer, Robert. *The Native Americans.* 2d ed. New York: Harper and Row, 1977.

Spicer, Eric. *A Short History of the Indians of the United States.* Malabar, FL: Robert E. Krieger Publishing, 1983.

Stewart, David E. *Glimpses of the Ancient Southwest.* Santa Fe, NM: Ancient City Press, 1985.

Sturtevant, William, ed. *Handbook of North American Indians.* Washington, DC: Smithsonian Institution, 1978.

Terrell, John W. *American Indian Almanac.* New York: World Publishing, 1971.

Thompson, William. *Native American Issues.* Santa Barbara, CA: ABC-CLIO, 1996.

Waldman, Carl. *Encyclopedia of Native American Tribes.* New York: Facts on File, 1988.

———. *Atlas of the North American Indian.* New York: Facts on File, 1985.

Wells, Robert, Jr. *Native American Resurgence and Renewal.* Metuchen, NJ: Scarecrow Press, 1994.

Wright, J. V. *A History of the Native People of Canada.* Hull, Quebec: Canadian Museum of Civilization, 1995.

Chapter 1: The Southwest

Beck, Peggy, and A. Walters. *The Sacred.* Tsaile, AZ: Navajo Community College Press, 1977.

Dutton, Bertha. *American Indians of the Southwest.* Albuquerque: University of New Mexico Press, 1983.

Ford, Richard I. *The Ethnographic American Southwest.* New York: Garland Publishing, 1985.

Gumerman, George, ed. *Themes in Southwest Prehistory.* Santa Fe, NM: School of American Research Press, 1994.

Minnis, Paul, and Charles Redman. *Perspectives on Southwestern Prehistory.* Boulder, CO: Westview Press, 1990.

Ortiz, Alfonso. *The Tewa World.* Chicago: University of Chicago Press, 1969.

Reid, J. Jefferson, and David Doyel. *Emil W. Haury's Prehistory of the American Southwest.* Tucson: University of Arizona Press, 1986.

Trimble, Stephen. *The People.* Santa Fe, NM: School of American Research Press, 1993.

Waters, Frank. *Book of the Hopi.* New York: Ballantine Books, 1963.

Chapter 2: California

Bean, Lowell, and Thomas Blakburn. *Native Californians.* Socorro, NM: Ballena Press, 1976.

Heizer, R., and M. Whipple. *California Indians.* Berkeley: University of California Press, 1951.

Kroeber, A. L. *Handbook of the Indians of California.* Washington, DC: Government Printing Office, 1925.

Thomas, David H. *Spanish Borderlands Sourcebooks.* New York: Garland Publishing, 1991.

Chapter 3: The Northwest Coast

Brown, Vincent. *Native Americans of the Pacific Coast.* Happy Camp, CA: Naturegraph, 1985.

Brugmann, M. *Indians of the Northwest Coast.* New York: Facts on File, 1989.

Drucker, Philip. *Cultures of the North Pacific Coast.* San Francisco: Chandler Publishing, 1965.

———. *Indians of the Northwest Coast.* New York: McGraw-Hill, 1955.

Gunther, Erna. *Indian Life of the Northwest Coast of North America.* Chicago: University of Chicago Press, 1972.

Lyman, R. Lee. *Prehistory of the Oregon Coast.* San Diego: Academic Press, 1991.

Ruby, Robert H., and John A. Brown. *A Guide to the Indian Tribes of the Pacific Northwest.* Rev. ed. Norman: University of Oklahoma Press, 1992.

Chapter 4: The Great Basin

Bennyhoff, James A. *Shell Beads and Ornament Exchange Networks between California and the Western Great Basin.* New York: American Museum of Natural History, 1987.

Hughes, J. Donald. *American Indians in Colorado.* Boulder, CO: Pruett Publishing, 1977.

Jennings, Jesse. *Prehistory of Utah and the Eastern Great Basin.* Salt Lake City: University of Utah Press, 1978.

Strong, Emory. *Stone Age in the Great Basin.* Portland, OR: Bimfords and Mort, 1969.

Sutton, Mark. *Insects as Food.* Menlo Park, CA: Ballena Press, 1988.

Thomas, David H. *A Great Basin Shoshonean Sourcebook.* New York: Garland Publishers, 1986.

Vander, Judith. *Shoshone Ghost Dance Religion: Poetry, Songs and Great Basin Context.* Urbana: University of Illinois Press, 1997.

Chapter 5: The Plateau

Ackerman, Lillian. *A Song to the Creator: Traditional Arts of Native American Women of the Plateau.* Norman: University of Oklahoma Press, 1996.

Schwartz, E. A. *The Rogue River War and Its Aftermath.* Norman: University of Oklahoma Press, 1997 [also applies to California and Northwest Coast].

Stern, Theodore. *Chiefs and Change in the Oregon Country.* Corvallis: Oregon State University Press, 1996.

———. *Chiefs and Chief Traders.* Corvallis: Oregon State University Press, 1993.

Tennant, Paul. *Aboriginal Peoples and Politics.* Vancouver: University of British Columbia Press, 1990.

Walker, Deward E. *Indians of Idaho.* Moscow: University of Idaho Press, 1978.

Chapter 6: The Great Plains

Bancroft-Hunt, Norman. *The Indians of the Great Plains.* Norman: University of Oklahoma Press, 1981.

Brown, Dee. *Bury My Heart at Wounded Knee.* New York: Holt, Rinehart & Winston, 1971.

Driben, Paul. *We Are Metis.* New York: AMS Press, 1985.

Dugan, Kathleen M. *The Vision Quest of the Plains Indians.* Lewiston, NY: The Edwin Mellen Press, 1985.

Ewers, John C. *Plains Indian History and Culture.* Norman: University of Oklahoma Press, 1997.

Haines, F. *The Plains Indians.* New York: Crowell, 1976.

Hassrick, Royal B. *The Sioux.* Norman: University of Oklahoma Press, 1964.

Iverson, Peter, ed. *The Plains Indians of the Twentieth Century.* Norman: University of Oklahoma Press, 1985.

Lowie, R. *Indians of the Plains.* New York: McGraw-Hill, 1954.

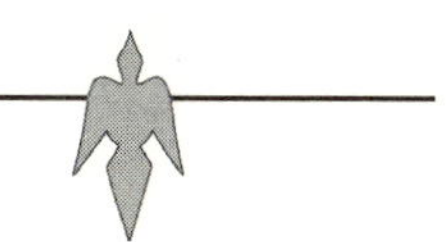

Matthiessen, Peter. *In the Spirit of Crazy Horse.* New York: Viking Press, 1980.

Schlesier, Karl. *Plains Indians.* Norman: University of Oklahoma Press, 1994.

Chapter 7: The Southeast

Binford, Lewis. *Cultural Diversity among Aboriginal Cultures of Coastal Virginia and North Carolina.* New York: Garland Publishing Company, 1991.

Burt, J., and R. Ferguson. *Indians of the Southeast.* Nashville: Abingdon Press, 1962.

Cotterrill, Robert Spencer. *The Southern Indians.* Norman: University of Oklahoma Press, 1954.

Debo, Angie. *And Still the Waters Run.* New York: Gordion Press, 1966.

Hudson, Charles. *The Southeastern Indians.* Knoxville: University of Tennessee Press, 1976.

———. *Four Centuries of Southern Indians.* Athens: University of Georgia Press, 1975.

Paredes, J. Anthony, ed. *Indians of the Southeastern United States in the Late Twentieth Century.* Tuscaloosa: University of Alabama Press, 1992.

Swanton, John. *The Indians of the Southeastern United States.* Washington, DC: U.S. Government Printing Office, 1946.

Williams, Walt. *Southeastern Indians since the Removal Era.* Athens: University of Georgia Press, 1979.

Chapter 8: The Northeast Woodlands

Bragdon, Kathleen. *Native People of Southern New England 1500–1650.* Norman: University of Oklahoma Press, 1996.

Custer, Jay. *Late Woodland Cultures of the Middle Atlantic Region.* Newark: University of Delaware Press, 1986.

Danziger, Edmund. *The Chippewas of Lake Superior.* Norman: University of Oklahoma Press, 1979.

Hyde, George. *Indians of the Woodlands.* Norman: University of Oklahoma Press, 1962.

Simmons, William. *Spirit of the New England Tribes.* Hanover, NH: University Press of New England, 1986.

Webb, William, and Charles Snow. *The Adena People.* Knoxville: University of Tennessee Press, 1974.

Chapters 9 and 10: The Subarctic and the Arctic

Balikci, Asen. *The Netsilik Eskimo.* Garden City, NY: Natural History Press, 1970.

Birket-Smith, Kaj. *Eskimos.* New York: Crown, 1971.

Clark, Donald. *Western Subarctic Prehistory.* Hull, Quebec: Canadian Museum of Civilization, 1991.

Crowe, Keith. *A History of the Original Peoples of Northern Canada.* Montreal: McGill-Queen's University Press for the Arctic Institute of North America, 1974.

Dumond, Donald. *The Eskimos and Aleuts.* London: Thames and Hudson, 1987.

Elias, Peter D. *Northern Aborginal Communities.* North York, Ontario: Captus Press, 1995.

Holmberg, H. *Holmberg's Ethnographic Sketches.* Translated by Fritz Jaensch. Fairbanks: University of Alaska Press, 1985.

Langdon, Steve. *The Native People of Alaska.* 3d ed., rev. Anchorage: Greenland Graphics, 1993.

Laughlin, William. *Aleuts, Survivors of the Bering Land Bridge.* New York: Holt, Rinehart & Winston, 1980.

Mitchell, Donald C. *Sold American: The Story of Alaska Natives and Their Land, 1867–1959.* Hanover, NH: University Press of New England, 1997.

Tuck, James. *Newfoundland and Labrador Prehistory.* Toronto: Van Nostrand Reinhold, 1976.

Vaudrin, Bill. *Tanaina Tales from Alaska.* Norman: University of Oklahoma Press, 1969.

Yerbury, J. C. *The Subarctic Indians and the Fur Trade.* Vancouver: University of British Columbia Press, 1986.

Appendix 1
Canada Reserves and Bands (1991)

Name	*Linguistic Group*	*Affiliation*[1]	*Elections*[2]	*Population*[3]	*No. of Reserves/Size*	*Key Economic Activities*
Alberta[4]						
Alexander	Cree Algonquian	Yellowhead Tribal Council	custom	1,334/740	1/17,990 acres	campground, cattle, golf, businesses
Alexis	Stoney Siouan	Yellowhead Tribal Council	custom	1,215/721	1/15,259 acres	store and gas station
Athabasca Chipewyan	Chipewyan Athapascan	Athapaska Tribal Corporation	custom	634/15	N/A[5]	fishery, store, heavy equipment
Beaver Lake	Cree Algonquian	Tribal Chiefs Ventures, Inc.	custom	725/265	N/A	agriculture, maintenance garage
Bigstone Cree Nation	Cree Algonquian	unaffiliated	custom	5,170/1,768	N/A	logging, social services, mall
Blood	Blood Algonquian	Treaty 7 Tribal Council	custom	8,473/6,774	N/A	art, farming, oil and gas, businesses
Boyer River	Beaver Athapaskan	N/A	N/A	N/A	N/A	
Chipewyan Prairie First Nation	Chipewyan Athapaskan	Athapaska Tribal Corporation	custom	530/206	N/A	
Cold Lake First Nations	Chipewyan Athapaskan	Tribal Chiefs Ventures, Inc.	custom	1,875/945	N/A	farming, logging, heavy equipment
Dene Tha' Tribe	Slavey Athapaskan	North Peace Tribal Council	custom	2,233/1,643	7/74,224 acres	retail and businesses, construction
Driftpile	Cree Algonquian	Lesser Slave Lake Reg. Council	Indian Act	1,742/598	1/15,688 acres	ranch, store, and service station
Duncan's	Cree Algonquian	Lesser Slave Lake Reg. Council	Indian Act	166/102	N/A	farm
Enoch Cree Nation #440	Cree Algonquian	Yellowhead Tribal Council	Indian Act	1,516/1,277	1/12,960 acres	ranch, golf, land development
Ermineskin	Cree Algonquian	Four Nations Administration	custom	2,683/1,942	2/30,191 acres	oil, strip mall
Fort McKay First Nation	Cree Algonquian	Athapaska Tribal Corporation	custom	462/211	N/A	transportation, store, contracting
Fort McMurray First Nation	Chipewyan Athapaskan	Athabaska Tribal Corporation	custom	491/153	N/A	pallet contract
Frog Lake	Cree Algonquian	Tribal Chiefs Ventures, Inc.	Indian Act	1,695/1,118	N/A	cattle, construction, transportation
Heart Lake	Chipewyan Athapaskan	Tribal Chiefs Ventures, Inc.	custom	222/135	N/A	oil
Horse Lake	Beaver Athapaskan	Lesser Slave Lake Reg. Council	custom	596/245	2/7,658 acres	
Kehewin	Cree Algonquian	Tribal Chiefs Ventures, Inc.	custom	1,408/805	N/A	sawmill, nursery, steel mfg.
Little Red River Cree Nation	Cree Algonquian	unaffiliated	custom	2,939/2,216	2/60,471 acres	sawmill, airline, businesses
Loon River	Cree Algonquian	Kee Tas Kee Now Tribal Council	custom	349/0	none	
Louis Bull	Cree Algonquian	Four Nations Administration	custom	1,301/1,044	2/13,122 acres	truck stop, ranch, land development
Lubicon Lake	Cree Algonquian	North Peace Tribal Council	custom	316/0	none	
Mikisew Cree First Nation	Cree Algonquian	Athapaskan Tribal Corporation	custom	1,980/3	N/A	air transport, businesses
Montana	Cree Algonquian	Four Nations Administration	custom	651/432	2/11,730 acres	ranch, lumber, businesses
O'Chiese	Ojibway Algonquian	North Peace Tribal Council	Indian Act	665/487	2/34,280 acres	logging
Paul	Stoney Siouan/Cree Alg.	unaffiliated	Indian Act	1,410/860	3/18,112 acres	golf, café
Piegan Nation	Piegan Algonquian	Treaty 7 Tribal Council	custom	2,941/2,056	2/112,656 acres	cattle, crafts, tourism
Saddle Lake	Cree Algonquian	Tribal Chiefs Ventures, Inc.	custom	7,070/5,114	N/A	construction, garage, farm
Samson	Cree Algonquian	Four Nations Administration	custom	5,252/4,337	2/38,569 acres	ranch, lumber, businesses
Sawridge	Cree Algonquian	Lesser Slave Lake Reg. Council	Indian Act	319/27	N/A	oil and gas, investments
Siksika Nation	Blackfeet Algonquian	Treaty 7 Tribal Council	Indian Act	4,833/3,031	1/175,406 acres	tourism, farm, ranch, mfg.
Stoney Tribal Administration (Chiniki, Bearspaw, Wesley)	Nakota Siouan	Treaty 7 Tribal Council	custom	3,527	N/A	transport, buffalo ranch, tourism
Sturgeon Lake	Cree Algonquian	Lesser Slave Lake Reg. Council	custom	1,843/972	N/A	trucking, campground, businesses
Sucker Creek	Cree Algonquian	Lesser Slave Lake Reg. Council	custom	1,763/436	N/A	ranch, diner, tourism
Sunchild First Nation	Cree Algonquian	Yellowhead Tribal Council	Indian Act	747/426	N/A	logging, businesses

(continues)

Name	*Linguistic Group*	*Affiliation*[1]	*Elections*[2]	*Population*[3]	*No. of Reserves/Size*	*Key Economic Activities*
Swan River First Nation	Cree Algonquian	Lesser Slave Lake Reg. Council	custom	872/272	N/A	forestry, fishery, campground
Tallcree	Cree Algonquian	unaffiliated	custom	859/351	2/9,206 acres	farming, businesses
Tsuu T'ina Nation	Sarcee Athapaskan	Treaty 7 Tribal Council	Indian Act	1,252/961	1/67,399 acres	trucking, golf, sports complex
Whitefish Lake	Cree Algonquian	Kee Tas Kee Now Tribal Council	custom	1,596/693	N/A	sawmill, oil service, school bus
Woodland Cree	Cree Algonquian	Kee Tas Kee Now Tribal Council	custom	773/595	N/A	
British Columbia[6]						
Adams Lake	Interior (Shuswap) Salishan	Shuswap Nation Tribal Council	U/R[7]	610/383	7/3,000 hectares	U/R
Ahousaht	Nootkan Wakashan	Nuu-chah-nulth Tribal Council		1,509/576	25/592 hectares	
Aitchelitz	Coast Salishan	Sto:lo Nation		21/19	N/A	
Alexandria	Chilcotin Athapaskan	Ts'inquot'in Nation Government		141/59	N/A	
Alexis Creek	Chilcotin Athapaskan	Ts'inquot'in Nation Government		522/381	N/A	
Alkali Lake/Esketemc	Interior (Shuswap) Salishan	unaffiliated		627/382	N/A	
Anaham	Chilcotin Athapaskan	Tsilhqot'in Nation Government		N/A	N/A	
Anderson Lake	Interior (Lillooet) Sal.	In-SHUCK-ch/N'Quatqua		246/161	1/804 hectares	
Ashcroft	Interior Salishan	Nlaka'pamux Nation Tribal Council		221/71	N/A	
Beecher Bay	Salishan	Te'Mexw Tribal Association		190/70	8/296 hectares	
Blueberry River	Beaver Athapaskan	Treaty 8 Tribal Council		288/191	N/A	
Bonaparte	Interior (Shuswap) Salishan	Shuswap Nation Tribal Council		668/201	6/1,332 hectares	
Boothroyd	Interior (Thompson) Sal.	Nlaka'pamux Nation Tribal Council		257/108	19/1,122 hectares	
Boston Bar	Interior (Thompson) Sal.	Nlaka'pamux Nation Tribal Council		200/69	12/609 hectares	
Bridge River	Interior (Lillooet) Salishan	Lillooet Tribal Council		349/163	3/3,940 hectares	
Broman Lake	Carrier Athapaskan	Carrier Sekani Tribal Council		149/65	11/620 hectares	
Burns Lake	Carrier Athapaskan	Carrier Sekani Tribal Council		72/28	4/164 hectares	
Canim Lake	Interior (Shuswap) Salishan	Cariboo Tribal Council		491/381	6/2,059 hectares	
Canoe Creek	Interior (Shuswap) Salishan	Cariboo Tribal Council		559/279	12/5,582 hectares	
Cayoose Creek	Interior (Lillooet) Salishan	Lillooet Tribal Council		155/103	3/687 acres	
Chaslattta Carrier Nation	Carrier Athapaskan	unaffiliated		221/93	8/1,403 hectares	
Chawathil	Coast Salishan	Sto:lo Nation		360/239	5/614 hectares	
Cheam	Coast Salishan	Sto:lo Nation		342/199	2/502 hectares	
Chehalis	Coast Salishan	unaffiliated		835/416	2/907 hectares	
Chemainus	Coast Salishan	Hul'qumi'num Treaty Group		911/745	4/1,225 hectares	
Coldwater	Interior (Thompson) Sal.	Nicola Valley Tribal Council		659/228	N/A	
Columbia Lake	Interior (Kootenayan) Sal.	Ktunaxa/Kinbasket Tribal Council		218/166	1/3,401 hectares	
Comox First Nation	Coast Salishan	unaffiliated		258/114	4/285 hectares	
Cook's Ferry	Interior (Thompson) Sal.	Nicola Valley Tribal Council		284/107	24/4,048 hectares	
Coquitlam	Coast Salishan	unaffiliated		52/3	2/89 hectares	
Cowichan	Coast Salishan	Hul'qumi'num Treaty Group		3,153/2,070	9/2,493 hectares	
Cowichan Lake	Coast Salishan	Hul'qumi'num Treaty Group		12/10	1/39 hectares	
Dease River	Kaska Athapaskan	Kaska Dena Council		N/A	N/A	
Ditidaht	Nootkan Wakashan	unaffiliated		523/207	7/727 hectares	
Doig River	Beaver Athapaskan	Treaty 8 Tribal Council		207/110	N/A	

Douglas	Interior (Lillooet) Salishan	In-SHUCK-ch/N'Quatqua	197/38	3/432 hectares
Ehattesaht	Nootkan Wakashan	Nuu-chah-nulth Tribal Council	196/107	9/136 hectares
Esquimalt	Coast Salishan	First Nations of South Island T.C.	751/166	N/A
Fort Nelson	Slavey Athapaskan	Treaty 8 Tribal Council	608/291	N/A
Fort Ware	Sekani Athapaskan	Kaska Dena Council	356/242	3/391
Gitanmaax	Tsimshian Penutian	Gitxsan	1,740/808	N/A
Gitanyow (Kitwancool)	Tsimshian Penutian	unaffiliated	615/380	N/A
Gitlakdamix	Tsimshian Penutian	Nisga'a Nation	1,511/745	30/~2,000 hectares
Gitsegukla	Tsimshian Penutian	Gitxsan	756/486	N/A
Gitwangak	Tsimshian Penutian	Gitxsan	939/456	N/A
Gitwinksihlkw	Tsimshian Penutian	Nisga'a Nation	326/224	6/655 hectares
Gwa'sala-'Nakwaxda'zw	Kwakiutl Wakashan	Winalagalis	571/422	26/752 hectares
Hagwilget	Carrier Athapaskan	Wet'suwet'en	594/227	2/119 hectares
Haisla Nation (Kitamaat)	Kwakiutl Wakashan	unaffiliated	1,364/624	17/665 hectares
Halalt	Coast Salishan	Hul'qumi'num Treaty Group	185/103	2/166 hectares
Halfway River	Beaver Athapaskan	Treaty 8 Tribal Council	190/138	N/A
Hartley Bay	Tsimshian Penutian	Tsimshian Tribal Council	593/174	14/520 hectares
Heiltsuk (Bella Bella)	Kwakiutl Wakashan	Heiltsuk Band Council	1,975/1,118	22/1,369 hectares
Hesquiaht	Nootkan Wakashan	Nuu-chah-nulth Tribal Council	554/151	5/320
High Bar	Interior (Shuswap) Salishan	unaffiliated	50/3	3/1,506 hectares
Homalco	Coast Salishan	unaffiliated	366/138	11/624
Huu-ay-aht (Ohiaht)	Nootkan Wakashan	Nuu-chah-nulth Tribal Council	490/95	13/816 hectares
Iskut	Tahltan/Sekani Ath.	unaffiliated	510/265	N/A
Ka;'K't'h'/Che:K'tles7et'h' (Kyuquot)	Nootkan Wakashan	Nuu-chah-nulth Tribal Council	416/146	26/382 hectares
Kamloops	Interior (Shuswap) Salishan	Shuswap Nation Tribal Council	883/576	5/13,249 hectares
Kanaka Bar	Interior (Thompson) Sal.	Fraser Canyon Indian Admin.	171/66	6/229 hectares
Katzie	Coast Salishan	unaffiliated	407/233	5/340 hectares
Kincolith	Tsimshian Penutian	Nisga'a Nation	1,750/370	N/A
Kispiox	Tsimshian Penutian	Gitxsan	1,237/577	N/A
Kitasoo	Kwakiutl Wakashan	Tsimshian Tribal Council	442/322	14/598 hectares
Kitkatla	Tsimshian Penutian	Tsimshian Tribal Council	1,391/422	21/1,885 hectares
Kitsumkalum	Tsimshian Penutian	Tsimshian Tribal Council	572/198	3/559 hectares
Kittselas	Tsimshian Penutian	Tsimshian Tribal Council	448/195	9/1,103 hectares
Klahoose	Coast Salishan	unaffiliated	270/56	10/1,357 hectares
Kluskus	Carrier Athapaskan	Carrier-Chilcotin Tribal Council	158/106	N/A
Kwakiutl	Kwakiutl Wakashan	Winalagalis	564/302	8/295 hectares
Kwa-Kwa-A-Pilt	Coast Salishan	Sto:lo Nation	38/25	1/63 hectares
Kwantlen (Langley)	Coast Salishan	Sto:lo Nation	147/67	6/557 hectares
Kwa-Wa-Aineuk	Kwakiutl Wakashan	Musgamagw Tsawataineuk T.C.	25/19	N/A
Kwiakah	Kwakiutl Wakashan	Kwakiutl Laich-kwil-Tach Nations Treaty Soc.	18/7	2/69 hectares
Kwicksutaineuk-Ah-Kwaw-Ah-Mish	Kwakiutl Wakashan	Musgamagw Tsawataineuk T.C.	244/50	N/A
Lakahahmen	Coast Salishan	Sto:lo Nation	286/110	10/490 hectares
Lakalzap	Tsimshian Penutian	Nisga'a Nation	1,492/589	3/1,836 hectares

(continues)

Name	*Linguistic Group*	*Affiliation*[1]	*Elections*[2]	*Population*[3]	*No. of Reserves/Size*	*Key Economic Activities*
Lake Babine	Carrier Athapaskan	unaffiliated		1,774/1,278	24/3,094 hectares	
Lax-Kw-Alaams	Tsimshian Penutian	Tsimshian Tribal Council		2,525/1,073	72/1,049 hectares	
Lheit-Lit'en (Fort George)	Carrier Athapaskan	unaffiliated		251/24	4/686 hectares	
Lillooet	Interior (Lillooet) Salishan	Lillooet Tribal Council		309/205	6/700 hectares	
Little Shuswap Lake	Interior (Shuswap) Salishan	unaffiliated		263/188	5/3,135 hectares	
Lower Kootenay	Interior (Kootenayan) Sal.	Ktunaxa Kinbasket Tribal Council		184/117	8/2,443 hectares	
Lower Nicola	Interior (Thompson) Sal.	Nicola Valley Tribal Council		856/505	9/7,096 hectares	
Lower Similkameen	Interior (Okanagan) Sal.	Similkameen Administration		398/293	11/15,276 hectares	
Lyackson	Coast Salishan	Hul'qumi'num Treaty Group		168/42	3/745 hectares	
Lytton	Interior (Thompson) Sal.	Nlaka'pamux Nation Tribal Council		1,576/706	54/5,980 hectares	
McLeod Lake	Sekani Athapaskan	unaffiliated		383/167	N/A	
Malahat	Coast Salishan	Te'Mexw Treaty Association		227/102	1/237 hectares	
Mamaleleleqala Que-qwa'sot'enox	Kwakiutl Wakashan	Kwakiutl Laich-kwil-Tach Nations Treaty Soc.		306/37	3/233 hectares	
Matsqui	Coast Salishan	Sto:lo Nation		183/88	4/419 hectares	
Metlaktla	Tsimshian Penutian	Tsimshian Tribal Council		598/126	16/162 hectares	
Moricetown	Carrier Athapaskan	Wet'suwet'en		1,524/679	N/A	
Mount Currie	Interior (Lillooet) Salishan	unaffiliated		1,607/1,058	10/2,929 hectares	
Mowachaht	Nootkan Wakashan	Nuu-chah-nulth Tribal Council		463/164	17/263 hectares	
Musqueam	Coast Salishan	unaffiliated		978/548	3/254 hectares	
Nadleh Whuten	Carrier Athapaskan	Carrier Sekani Tribal Council		355/273	7/966 hectares	
Nak'azdli	Carrier Athapaskan	Carrier Sekani Tribal Council		1,406/643	16/1,460 hectares	
Namgis First Nation	Kwakiutl Wakashan	Winalagalis		1,377/733	N/A	
Nanaimo	Coast Salishan	unaffiliated		1,197/479	6/26 hectares	
Nanoose First Nation	Coast Salishan	Te'Mexw Treaty Association		195/144	1/53 hectares	
Nazko	Chilcotin Athapaskan	unaffiliated		273/122	18/1,844 hectares	
Nee-Tahi-Buhn	Carrier Athapaskan	Wet'suwet'en		211/84	7/1,421 hectares	
Neskonlith	Int. (Shuswap/Thomp.) Sal.	Shuswap Nation Tribal Council		526/234	N/A	
Nicomen	Interior (Thompson) Sal.	Fraser Canyon Indian Administration		97/63	15/1,175 hectares	
Nooaitch	Interior (Thompson) Sal.	Nicola Valley Tribal Council		173/130	2/1,693 hectares	
North Thompson	Interior (Thompson) Sal.	Shuswap Nation Tribal Council		535/251	5/1,521 hectares	
Nuchatlaht	Nootkan Wakashan	Nuu-chah-nulth Tribal Council		122/38	11/92 hectares	
Nuxalt Nation	Coast (Bella Coola) Sal.	Oweekeno/Kitasoo Tribal Council		1,185/706	N/A	
Okanagan	Interior (Okanagan) Sal.	Okanagan Tribal Council		1,498/771	5/10,603 hectares	
Old Masset Village Council	Haida Athapaskan	Haida Central Council		2,301/726	1/907 hectares	
Opetchesaht	Coast Salishan	Nuu-chah-nulth Tribal Council		210/95	5/215 hectares	
Oregon Jack Creek	Interior (Thompson) Sal.	Nlaka'pamux Nation Tribal Council		45/12	6/823 hectares	
Osoyoos	Interior (Okanagon) Sal.	unaffiliated		338/250	2/13,052 hectares	
Oweekeno	Kwakiutl Wakashan	unaffiliated		207/92	3/713 hectares	
Pacheenaht	Nootkan Wakashan	unaffiliated		210/106	4/174 hectares	
Pauquachin	Coast Salishan	First Nations of South Island T.C.		279/179	2/319 hectares	
Penelakut	Coast Salishan	Hul'qumi'num Treaty Group		706/461	4/635 hectares	

Penticton	Interior (Okanagan) Sal.	unaffiliated	776/453	2/18,691 hectares
Peters	N/A	unaffiliated	107/46	N/A
Popkum	Coast Salishan	Sto:lo Nation	10/5	2/151 hectares
Prophet River	Slavey Athapaskan	Treaty 8 Tribal Council	164/107	N/A
Qualicum	Coast Salishan	unaffiliated	92/51	1/77 hectares
Quatsino	Kwakiutl Wakashan	Winalagalis	332/198	19/346 hectares
Red Bluff	Carrier Athapaskan	Carrier Sekani Tribal Council	118/72	N/A
St. Mary's	Kootenayan	Ktunaxa Kinbasket Tribal Council	257/213	4/7,446 hectares
Salteau	Beaver/Cree	Treaty 8 Tribal Council	649/324	N/A
Samahquam	Interior (Lillooet) Salishan	In-SHUCK-ch/N'Quatqua	249/23	5/183 hectares
Scowlitz	Coast Salishan	Sto:lo Nation	220/76	3/236 hectares
Seabird Island	Coast Salishan	Sto:lo Nation	641/411	1/2,140 hectares
Sechelt	Coast Salishan	unaffiliated	961/524	33/~1,000 hectares
Semiahmoo	Coast Salishan	unaffiliated	61/28	1/129 hectares
Seton Lake	Interior (Lillooet) Salishan	Lillooet Tribal Council	551/291	N/A
Shackan	Interior (Thompson) Sal.	Nicola Valley Tribal Council	113/72	2/3,874 hectares
Shuswap	Interior (Shuswap) Salishan	Ktunaxa Kinbasket Tribal Council	216/139	1/1,106 hectares
Shx'wow'hamel (Ohamil)	Coast Salishan	Sto:lo Nation	108/65	3/404 hectares
Sikokoak (Glen Vowell)	Tsimshian Penutian	Gitxsan	341/193	6/1,802 hectares
Siska	Interior (Thompson) Sal.	Nicola Valley Tribal Council	253/122	11/319 hectares
Skawahlook	Coast Salishan	Sto:lo Nation	71/21	2/75 hectares
Skeetchestn	Interior (Shuswap) Salishan	Shuswap Nation Tribal Council	420/155	1/7,908 hectares
Skidegate	Haida Athapaskan	Central Council of Haida Nation	1,122/580	11/670 hectares
Skookumchuk	Interior (Lillooet) Salishan	In-SHUCK-ch/N'Quatqua	333/53	10/676 hectares
Skowkale	Coast Salishan	Sto:lo Nation	172/131	2/68 hectares
Skuppah	Interior (Thompson) Sal.	Fraser Canyon Indian Administration	67/52	8/211 hectares
Skwah	Coast Salishan	unaffiliated	409/210	4/342 hectares
Skyway	Coast Salishan	unaffiliated	234/57	N/A
Sliammon	Coast Salishan	unaffiliated	811/593	6/1,907 hectares
Soda Creek	Interior (Shuswap) Salishan	Cariboo Tribal Council	292/186	2/2,093 hectares
Songhees	Coast Salishan	Te'Mexw Treaty Association	359/299	3/126 hectares
Soowahlie	Coast Salishan	Sto:lo Nation	266/169	1/461 hectares
Spallumcheen	Interior (Shuswap) Salishan	Shuswap Nation Tribal Council	638/314	3/3,095 hectares
Spuzzum	Interior (Thompson) Sal.	Fraser Canyon Indian Administration	175/32	16/636 hectares
Squamish	Coast Salishan	unaffiliated	2,875/1,767	8 villages
Squiala	Coast Salishan	Sto:lo Nation	108/72	2/128 hectares
Stellat'en/Stellaquo	Carrier Athapaskan	Carrier Sekani Tribal Council	327/224	2/834 hectares
Stone	Chilcotin Athapaskan	Ts'ilhqot'in National Government	330/233	N/A
Stony Creek	Carrier Athapaskan	Carrier Sekani Tribal Council	755/517	10/3,236 hectares
Sumas	Coast Salishan	Sto:lo Nation	235/147	1/234 hectares
Tahltan	Tahltan Athapaskan	unaffiliated	1,377/324	11/3,230 hectares
Takla Lake	Carrier Athapaskan	Carrier Sekani Tribal Council	537/282	17/807 hectares
Taku River Tlingit Council	Tlingit Athapaskan	unaffiliated	N/A	N/A
Tanakteuk	Kwakiutl Wakashan	Winalagalis	158/11	7/318 hectares
Tla-O-Qui-Aht First Nations	Nootkan Wakashan	Nuu-chah-nulth Tribal Council	675/271	10/220 hectares
Tlatlasikwala	Kwakiutl Wakashan	Winalagalis	39/8	6/3,474 hectares

(continues)

Name	*Linguistic Group*	*Affiliation*[1]	*Elections*[2]	*Population*[3]	*No. of Reserves/Size*	*Key Economic Activities*
Tl'azt'en Nation	Carrier Athapaskan	Carrier Sekani Tribal Council		1,281/692	19/2,277 hectares	
Tlowitsis-Mumtagila	Kwakiutl Wakashan	Kwakiutl Laich-kwil-Tach Nations Treaty Soc.		301/36	11/188 hectares	
Tobacco Plains	Interior (Kootenayan) Sal.	Ktunaxa Kinbasket Tribal Council		158/108	1/4,227 hectares	
Toosey	Chilcotin Athapaskan	Carrier-Chilcotin Tribal Council		224/127	N/A	
Toquaht	Nootkan Wakashan	Nuu-chah-nulth Tribal Council		111/14	7/196 hectares	
Tsartlip	Coast Salishan	First Nations of South Island T.C.		735/471	3/324 hectares	
Tsawataineuk	Kwakiutl Wakashan	Musgamagw Tsawataineuk Tribal Council		449/122	N/A	
Tsawout	Coast Salishan	First Nations of South Island T.C.		581/441	2/258 hectares	
Tsawwassen	Coast Salishan	unaffiliated		190/120	1/750 acres	
Tsay Keh Dene (Ingenika)	Carrier Athapaskan	unaffiliated		305/13	5/201 hectares	
Tseycum	Coast Salishan	First Nations of South Island T.C.		132/95	1/28 hectares	
Ts'kw'aylaxw (Pavilion)	Interior (Lillooet) Salishan	unaffiliated		422/145	7/2,112 hectares	
Tsleil-Waututh (Burrard)	Coast Salishan	unaffiliated		331/197	2/103 hectares	
T'sou-ke (Sooke)	Coast Salishan	Te'Mexw Treaty Association		186/98	2/67 hectares	
Tzeachten	Coast Salishan	Sto:lo Nation		287/129	1/282 hectares	
Uchucklesaht	Nootkan Wakashan	Nuu-chah-nulth Tribal Council		148/28	2/232 hectares	
Ucluelet	Nootkan Wakashan	Nuu-chah-nulth Tribal Council		581/195	9/199 hectares	
Ulkatcho	Carrier Athapaskan	Carrier-Chilcotin Tribal Council		747/575	N/A	
Union Bar	Coast Salishan	unaffiliated		82/12	N/A	
Upper Nicola	Interior (Thompson) Sal.	Nicola Valley Tribal Council		756/484	8/12,503 hectares	
Upper Similkameen	Interior (Okanagan) Sal.	Okanagan Tribal Council		48/47	7/2,602 hectares	
We Wai Kai (Cape Mudge)	Coast Salishan	Kwakiutl Laich-kwil-Tach Nations Treaty Soc.		796/351	5/1,648 hectares	
We Wai Kum (Campbell River)	Kwakiutl Wakashan	Kwakiutl Laich-kwil-Tach Nations Treaty Soc.		520/197	2/69 hectares	
West Moberly	Beaver Athapaskan	Treaty 8 Tribal Council		138/73	N/A	
Westbank First Nation	Interior (Okanagan) Sal.	unaffiliated		517/364	3/969 hectares	
Whispering Pines/Clinton	Interior (Shuswap) Salishan	Shuswap Nation Tribal Council		100/40	3/565 hectares	
Williams Lake	Interior (Shuswap) Salishan	Cariboo Tribal Council		424/255	1/1,927 hectares	
Xaxli'p (Fountain)	Interior (Lillooet) Salishan	unaffiliated		745/452	17/1,572 hectares	
Yakweakwioose	Coast Salishan	Sto:lo Nation		39/29	1/19 hectares	
Yale	Interior (Okanagan) Sal.	unaffiliated		128/57	16/255 hectares	
Manitoba[6]						
Barren Lands	Chipewyan Ath./Cree	Keewatin Tribal Council	custom	575/398	1/10,723 acres	comm. fish, trap, hunt
Berens River	Anishinabe Algonquian	S.E. Resource Dev. Council	N/A	2,004/1,296	2/6,907 acres	fish, trap, forestry
Birdtail Sioux	Dakota Siouan	Dakota Ojibway Tribal Council	N/A	538/411	3/7,124 acres	farming, development
Bloodvein	Anishinabe Algonquian	S.E. Resource Dev. Council	N/A	1,060/764	1/3,885 acres	comm. fish, trap
Brokenhead	Anishinabe Algonquian	S.E. Resource Dev. Council	N/A	1,231/423	1/13,375 acres	farming, businesses, gaming, ranch
Buffalo Point First Nation	Anishinabe Algonquian	S.E. Resource Dev. Council	N/A	80/34	2/9,877 acres	businesses, development
Canupawakpa Dakota (Oak Lake Sioux)	Dakota Siouan	Dakota Ojibway Tribal Council	N/A	516/382	3/2,689 acres	agriculture
Chemawawin First Nation	Cree Algonquian	Swampy Cree Tribal Council	custom	1,106/760	3/11,730 acres	fishing, logging, businesses

Cross Lake	Cree Algonquian	unaffiliated	N/A	5,003/3,333	6/N/A	businesses
Dakota Plains	Dakota Siouan	Dakota Ojibway Tribal Council	custom	249/205	1/1,310 acres	farming, greenhouse, store
Dakota Tipi	Dakota Siouan	unaffiliated	custom	225/116	N/A	
Dauphin River	Anishinabe Algonquian	Interlake Reserves Tribal Council	custom	173/95	1/805 acres	fish packing, store, tourism
Ebb and Flow	Anishinabe Algonquian	West Region Tribal Council	N/A	1,603/886	1/11,447 acres	farming, store, taxi, restaurant
Fairford	Anishinabe Algonquian	Interlake Reserves Tribal Council	N/A	2,058/1,141	1/11,315 acres	trap, hunt, fish, ranch, businesses
Fisher River	Cree Algonquian	unaffiliated	N/A	2,613/1,498	2/15,614 acres	comm. fish, farm, businesses
Fox Lake	Cree Algonquian	Keewatin Tribal Council	custom	839/150	3/4,300 acres	businesses
Gamblers	Cree Algonquian	West Region Tribal Council	custom	119/31	1/1,037 acres	farming
Garden Hill First Nation	Anishinabe/Cree	Island Lake Tribal Council	custom	2,968/2,698	2/17,829 acres	comm. fish, trap, businesses
God's Lake	Cree Algonquian	Keewatin Tribal Council	N/A	1,915/1,217	1/9,132 acres	fish, hunt, trap, guiding, businesses
God's River	Cree Algonquian	Keewatin Tribal Council	custom	503/427	2/700 acres	comm. fish, hunt, trap
Grand Rapids First Nation	Cree Algonquian	Swampy Cree Tribal Council	custom	1,097/461	1/4,577 acres	comm. fish, trap, hydro station
Hollow Water	Anishinabe Algonquian	S.E. Resource Dev. Council	N/A	1,083/593	1/4,000 acres	fish, hunt, trap, wild rice
Jackhead	Anishinabe Algonquian	Interlake Reserves Tribal Council	N/A	512/188	2/3,325 acres	comm. fish, trap
Keeseekoowenin	Anishinabe Algonquian	West Region Tribal Council	N/A	812/597	3/6,072 acres	farming, businesses
Lac Brochet/Northlands	Athapaskan	Keewatin Tribal Council	N/A	806/676	1/1,147 acres	trap, fish; businesses
Lake Manitoba	Anishinabe Algonquian	Interlake Reserves Tribal Council	N/A	1,280/900	1/9,317 acres	comm. fish; businesses
Lake St. Martin	Anishinabe Algonquian	Interlake Reserves Tribal Council	N/A	1,652/1,125	2/8,267 acres	farming, fishing
Little Black River	Anishinabe Algonquian	S.E. Resource Dev. Council	N/A	655/472	1/2,000 acres	trap, wild rice, hunt, comm. fish
Little Grand Rapids	Anishinabe Algonquian	S.E. Resource Dev. Council	N/A	1,108/939	1/4,956 acres	fish, trap, rice
Little Saskatchewan	Anishinabe Algonquian	Interlake Reserves Tribal Council	N/A	756/458	2/3,480 acres	comm. fish, hunt
Long Plain	Anishinabe/Dakota	Dakota Ojibway Tribal Council	custom	2,219/692	1/8,923 acres	land leases, rentals, businesses
Mosakahiken (Moose Lake)	Cree Algonquian	Swampy Cree Tribal Council	N/A	957/778	5/5,719 acres	fishing, hunting
Nelson House	Cree Algonquian	unaffiliated	N/A	3,682/1,962	4/14,450 acres	fish, hunt, trap, businesses
Norway House	Cree Algonquian	unaffiliated	N/A	4,906/3,570	3/19,435 acres	fish, hunt, trap, log, businesses
O-chi-chak-ko-sipi First Nation	Anishinabe Algonquian	West Region Tribal Council	N/A	628/288	1/8,705 acres	fishing, ranching, businesses
Opaskwayak Cree Nation	Cree Algonquian	Swampy Cree Tribal Council	N/A	3,584/2,293	17/14,641 acres	trap, hunt, fish, businesses
Oxford House	Cree Algonquian	Keewatin Tribal Council	N/A	1,895/1,585	1/12,049 acres	trap, fish, businesses
Pauingassi First Nation	Anishinabe Algonquian	S.E. Resource Dev. Council	custom	483/457	1/644 acres	trap, fish, rice
Peguis	Anishinabe/Cree	Interlake Reserves Tribal Council	N/A	6,244/2,766	9/75,665 acres	farming, businesses
Pine Creek	Anishinabe Algonquian	West Region Tribal Council	N/A	1,844/808	1/20,654 acres	hunt, fish, trap
Poplar River First Nation	Anishinabe Algonquian	S.E. Resource Dev. Council	N/A	1,054/911	1/3,800 acres	fish, trap, businesses
Pukatawagan (Mathias Colomb)	Cree Algonquian	Swampy Cree Tribal Council	N/A	2,682/1,690	2/29,058 acres	fish, trap
Red Sucker Lake	Anishinabe/Cree	Island Lake Tribal Council	custom	648/612	3/255 acres	trap, comm. fish, businesses
Rolling River	Anishinabe Algonquian	West Region Tribal Council	N/A	662/219	1/13,862 acres	farming, cattle, businesses
Roseau River	Anishinabe Algonquian	Dakota Ojibway Tribal Council	custom	1,717/847	2/7,576 acres	cattle, farming, development
Sagkeeng (Fort Alexander)	Anishinabe Algonquian	unaffiliated	N/A	5,249/2,971	1/21,674 acres	fish, trap, hunt, govt., businesses
St. Theresa Point	Anishinabe/Cree	Island Lake Tribal Council	custom	2,498/2,337	2/17,829 acres	fish, trap, businesses
Sandy Bay	Anishinabe Algonquian	Dakota Ojibway Tribal Council	custom	4,051/2,821	1/16,456 acres	comm. fish, trap, businesses
Sapotaweyak Cree Nation	Cree Algonquian	Swampy Cree Tribal Council	N/A	1,445/612	3/3,443 acres	fish, trap, cattle, logging
Sayisi Dene First Nation	Athapaskan	Keewatin Tribal Council	custom	515/300	1/524 acres	fish, hunt, trap
Shamattawa First Nation	Cree Algonquian	Keewatin Tribal Council	custom	594/841	1/5,725 acres	comm. fish, trap, sawmill
Sioux Valley	Dakota Siouan	Dakota Ojibway Tribal Council	custom	1,851/1,135	2/10,220 acres	farming, businesses
Split Lake	Cree Algonquian	Keewatin Tribal Council	N/A	2,385/1,517	3/11,333 acres	businesses
Swan Lake	Anishinabe Algonquian	Dakota Ojibway Tribal Council	N/A	1,002/524	4/14,409 acres	farming, bison, businesses

(continues)

Name	*Linguistic Group*	*Affiliation*[1]	*Elections*[2]	*Population*[3]	*No. of Reserves/Size*	*Key Economic Activities*
Tootinaowaziibeeng (Valley River)	Anishinabe Algonquian	unaffiliated	N/A	1,011/482	1/11,535 acres	farming, businesses
War Lake	Cree Algonquian	Keewatin Tribal Council	custom	197/56	N/A	comm. fish, trap, businesses
Wasagamak	Anishinabe/Cree	Island Lake Tribal Council	custom	1,195/1,006	2/17,829 acres	comm. fish, trap, businesses
Waterhen	Anishinabe Algonquian	West Region Tribal Council	N/A	927/330	1/4,585 acres	bison, businesses
Waywayseecapo First Nation	Anishinabe Algonquian	unaffiliated	N/A	1,717/1,197	1/24,856 acres	agriculture, businesses
Wuskwi Spihk (Indian Birch)	Cree Algonquian	Swampy Cree Tribal Council	N/A	385/230	1/1,940 acres	fish, trap
York Factory	Cree Algonquian	Keewatin Tribal Council	custom	828/341	1/2,390 acres	trap, hunt, businesses
New Brunswick[6]						
Big Cove	Micmac Algonquian	U/R	NYD[8]	2,207	1/1,667 hectares	U/R
Bouctouche Micmac	Micmac Algonguian			82	1/62 hectares	
Burnt Church	Micmac Algonquian			1,206	3/4,405 hectares	
Eel Ground	Micmac Algonquian			747	3/2,822 hectares	
Eel River	Micmac Algonquian			507	3/672 hectares	
Fort Folly	Micmac Algonquian			84	1/40 hectares	
Indian Island	Micmac Algonquian			140	1/26 hectares	
Kingsclear	Maliseet Algonquian			687	1/375 hectares	
Madawaska	Maliseet Algonquian			204	1/10 hectares	
Oromocto	Maliseet Algonquian			409	1/27 hectares	
Pabineau	Micmac Algonquian			189	1/429 hectares	
Red Bank	Micmac Algonquian			450	4/3,907 hectares	
St. Mary's	Maliseet Algonquian			1,062	2/132 hectares	
Tobique	Maliseet Algonquian			1,021	1/2,724 hectares	
Woodstock	Maliseet Algonquian			676	1/92 hectares	
Newfoundland						
First Nation Council of Davis Inlet[9, 10]	Innu Algonquian	U/R	U/R	~500	1/~300 sq. miles	U/R
First Nation Council of Northwest River[9]	Innu Algonquian			~1,000	1/~1,000 acres	
Maiwpukek[6]	Innu Algonquian			1,840	1/548 hectares	
Northwest Territories/Western Arctic[6]						
Aklavik	Kutchin Athapaskan	Gwich'in Tribal Council	U/R	727	U/R	hunt, fish, trap, businesses
Behdzi Adha'/Colville Lake	Hare/Slavey Athapaskan	Sahtu Dene Council		90		hunt, fish, trap
Dechi Laot'i (Snarelake) Dene	Dogrib Athapaskan	Dogrib Treaty F.N. Council		135		hunt, fish, trap
Dogrib Rae and Edzo	Dogrib Athapaskan	Dogrib Treaty F.N. Council		2,110		hunt, fish, arts and crafts
Fort Franklin/Deline	Hare/Slavey Athapaskan	Sahtu Dene Council		616		hunt, fish, trap, businesses
Fort Good Hope	Hare Athapaskan	Sahtu Dene Council		644		hunt, trap, businesses
Fort Laird/Acho Dene Koe	Slavey Athapaskan	Deh Cho First Nations		512		hunt, fish, trap, firefighting, businesses
Fort McPherson/Tetlit Gwich'in	Kutchin Athapaskin	Gwich'in Tribal Council		878		hunt, trap, oil, businesses
Fort Norman/Tulit'a	Slavey Athapaskan	Sahtu Dene Council		450		hunt, fish, trap, oil, businesses

Fort Providence/Deh Gah Gotie	Slavey Athapaskan	Dene Council		748		transportation, tourism, trap
Fort Resolution/Deninu K'ue	Chipewyan Athapaskan	NWT Treaty 8 Tribal Council		536		logging, trap, hunt, fish
Fort Simpson/Liidli Koe	Slavey Athapaskan	Deh Cho First Nations		1,257		govt., transportation, tourism
Fort Smith/Salt River F.N. #195	Chipewyan/Cree	NWT Treaty 8 Tribal Council		850		tourism, govt., hunt, trap
Gwicha Gwich'in/Arctic Red River	Kutchin Athapaskan	Tsiigehtchic		162		hunt, fish, trap
Hay River/West Point	Slavey/Chipewyan	Deh Cho First Nations		253		transport, communications, govt.
Holman/Uluqsaqtuuq	Inuvialuktun	N/A		361 in 1991		crafts, hunt, fish, oil, gas
Inuvik Native Band	Kutchin Athapaskan	Gwitch'in Tribal Council		328		college, communications, govt., oil
Jean Marie River Dene	Slavey Athapaskan	Deh Cho First Nations		109		crafts, hunt, fish, trap
Kakisa Lake/Ka'a'gee Tu	Slavey Athapaskan	Deh Cho First Nations		36		hunt, fish, trap
Nahanni Butte	Slavey Athapaskan	Deh Cho First Nations		75		trap
Norman Wells	Slavey Athapaskan	Sahtu Dene Council		627 in 1991		N/A
Paulatuk	Inuvialuktun	N/A		255 in 1991		hunt, fish, trap, crafts, oil, gas
Pehdzeh k'i (Wrigley) Dene	Slavey Athapaskan	Deh Cho First Nations		167		hunt, fish, trap, businesses
Rae Lakes/Gameti	Dogrib Athapaskan	Dogrib Treaty F.N. Council		256		hunt, fish, trap
Sachs Harbour/Ikaahuk	Inuvialuktun	N/A		125 in 1991		hunt, trap, oil, gas, tourism
Sambaa k'e (Trout Lake) Dene	Slavey Athapaskan	Deh Cho First Nations		68		hunt, fish, trap
Snowdrift/Lutsel K'e Dene	Chipewyan Athapaskan	NWT Treaty 8 Tribal Council		304		trap, fish, tourism
Tuktoyaktuk/Tuktujaartuk	Inuvialuktun	N/A		918 in 1991		transportation, oil, hunt, trap
Wha Ti (Lac La Martre)	Dogrib Athapaskan	Dogrib Treaty F.N. Council		418		hunt, fish
Whale Cove/Tikirarjuak	Inuktitut	N/A		235 in 1991		hunt, fish, trap, businesses
Yellowknives Dene	Chipewyan/Dogrib	NWT Treaty 8 Tribal Council		17,275		govt., mining
Nova Scotia[6]						
Acadia	Micmac Algonquian	U/R	U/R	823	5/750 hectares	U/R
Afton	Micmac Algonquian			424	3/430 hectares	
Annapolis Valley	Micmac Algonquian			184	2/145 hectares	
Bear River	Micmac Algonquian			250	3/690 hectares	
Chapel Island	Micmac Algonquian			454	2/1,254 hectares	
Eskasoni	Micmac Algonquian			3,062	3/4,195 hectares	
Horton	Micmac Algonquian			261	1/171 hectares	
Membertou	Micmac Algonquian			837	4/931 hectares	
Millbrook	Micmac Algonquian			1,037	7/443 hectares	
Pictou Landing	Micmac Algonquian			453	5/478 hectares	
Shubenacadie	Micmac Algonquian			1,874	4/2,098 hectares	
Wagmatcook	Micmac Algonquian			572	2/320 hectares	
Whycocomagh	Micmac Algonquian			647	2/1,490 hectares	
Ontario[11]						
Albany	Anishinabe/Cree	Mushkegowuk Tribal Council	custom	3,173/1,819	1/36,345 hectares	U/R
Alderville	Anishinabe Algonquian	Ogemawahj Tribal Council	Indian Act	886/275	1/1,216 hectares	
Aroland First Nation	Anishinabe Algonquian	Matawa F.N. Chief's Council	custom	420/16	none	

(continues)

Name	*Linguistic Group*	*Affiliation*[1]	*Elections*[2]	*Population*[3]	*No. of Reserves/Size*	*Key Economic Activities*
Attawapiskat First Nation	Cree Algonquian	Mushkegowuk Tribal Council	custom	2,339/1,553	2/27,144 hectares	
Batchewana First Nation	Anishinabe Algonquian	North Shore Tribal Council	Indian Act	1,901/679	4/2,224 hectares	
Bearskin Lake First Nation	Cree Algonquian	Windigo F.N. Council	custom	663/507	1/12,626 hectares	
Beausoleil	Anishinabe Algonquian	Ogemawahj Tribal Council	Indian Act	1,437/564	3/5,435 hectares	
Big Grassy	Anishinabe Algonquian	Pwi-di-goo-zing Ne-yaa-zhing Advisory Services	Indian Act	505/253	4/6,254 hectares	
Big Island	Anishinabe Algonquian	Pwi-di-goo-zing Ne-yaa-zhing Advisory Services	custom	301/119	6/4,330 hectares	
Brunswick House	Anishinabe/Cree	Wabun Tribal Council	Indian Act	527/116	2/9,314 hectares	
Caldwell	Potawatomi Algonquian	Southern F.N. Secretariat	custom	213/0	none	
Cat Lake	Anishinabe Algonquian	Windigo F.N. Council	custom	470/394	1/218 hectares	
Chapleau Cree	Cree Algonquian	unaffiliated	custom	317/58	1/108 hectares	
Chapleau Ojibway	Anishinabe Algonquian	Windigo F.N. Council	custom	29/19	2/1,020 hectares	
Chippewas of Kettle and Stony Point	Anishinabe Algonquian	Southern F.N. Secretariat	Indian Act	1,719/1,037	1/849 hectares	
Chippewas of Mnjikaning	Anishinabe Algonquian	Ogemawahj Tribal Council	Indian Act	1,146/458	3/908 hectares	
Chippewas of Nawash	Anishinabe Algonquian	unaffiliated	Indian Act	1,914/692	2/7,183 hectares	
Chippewas of Sarnia	Anishinabe Algonquian	Southern F.N. Secretariat	Indian Act	1,663/791	1/1,280 hectares	
Chippewas of the Thames	Anishinabe Algonquian	Southern F.N. Secretariat	Indian Act	1,945/781	1/3,333 hectares	
Cockburn Island	Anishinabe Algonquian	United Chiefs and Councils of Manitoulin	custom	105/23	2/958 hectares	
Constance Lake	Cree Algonquian	Matawa F.N. Chiefs Council	Indian Act	1,289/729	2/6,218 hectares	
Couchiching	Cree Algonquian	Pwi-di-goo-zing Ne-yaa-zhing Advisory Services	Indian Act	1,622/548	2/6,422 hectares	
Curve Lake	Anishinabe Algonquian	unaffiliated	Indian Act	1,541/761	3/957 hectares	
Deer Lake	Cree Algonquian	Keewaytinook/Okimakahac T.C.	custom	828/751	1/1,654 hectares	
Dokis	Anishinabe Algonquian	Waabnoong Bemjiwang Assoc. of F.N.	Indian Act	868/156	1/12,262 hectares	
Eabametoong	Anishinabe Algonquian	Matawa F.N. Chiefs Council	Indian Act	1,747/942	1/25,900 hectares	
Eagle River	Anishinabe Algonquian	Bimose Tribal Council	Indian Act	393/217	1/3,592 hectares	
Flying Post	Anishinabe/Cree	unaffiliated	custom	127/0	1/5,957 hectares	
Fort William	Anishinabe Algonquian	unaffiliated	Indian Act	1,400/635	1/5,815 hectares	
Fort Severn	Cree Algonquian	Keewaytinook/Okimakahac T.C.	custom	473/370	1/3,959 hectares	
Garden River	Anishinabe Algonquian	North Shore Tribal Council	Indian Act	1,827/848	1/14,901 hectares	
Georgina Island	Anishinabe Algonquian	Ogemawahj Tribal Council	Indian Act	602/155	3/1,353 hectares	
Ginoogaming	Anishinabe Algonquian	Matawa F.N. Chiefs Council	Indian Act	652/248	1/6,978 hectares	
Golden Lake	Algonquin Algonquian	unaffiliated	Indian Act	1,592/361	1/689 hectares	
Grassy Narrows	Anishinabe Algonquian	unaffiliated	Indian Act	1,018/653	1/4,145 hectares	
Gull Bay	Anishinabe Algonquian	unaffiliated	Indian Act	824/417	1/3,940 hectares	
Henvey Inlet	Anishinabe Algonquian	Waabnoong Bemjiwang Assoc. of F.N.	Indian Act	1,146/145	2/12,158 hectares	
Hiawatha	Anishinabe Algonquian	unaffiliated	Indian Act	412/168	2/790 hectares	
Iskatewizaagegan No. 39 Indep.	Anishinabe Algonquian	Bimose Tribal Council	Indian Act	475/322	3/3,997 hectares	
Kasabonika Lake	Cree Algonquian	Keewaytinook/Okimakahac T.C.	custom	684/657	1/10,806 hectares	

Kashechewan—see Albany					
Kee-Way-Win	Cree Algonquian	Keewaytinook/Okimakahac T.C.	custom	544/420	1/NYD
Kingfisher	Cree Algonquian	Shibogama F.N. Council	custom	373/361	5/6,963 hectares
Kitchenuhmaykoosib Inninuwug (Big Trout Lake)	Cree Algonquian	Independent F.N. Alliance	custom	1,103/781	1/29,938 hectares
Lac des Milles Lacs	Anishinabe Algonquian	Bimose Tribal Council	custom	448/6	2/4,948 hectares
Lac La Croix	Anishinabe Algonquian	Pwi-di-goo-zing Ne-yaa-zhing Advisory Services	Indian Act	333/290	1/6,214 hectares
Lac Seul	Anishinabe Algonquian	Independent F.N. Alliance	Indian Act	2,256/678	1/26,821 hectares
Lake Nipigon	Anishinabe Algonquian	Ojibway 1850 Treaty Council	custom	169/4	0
Lansdowne House	Anishinabe Algonquian	Matawa F.N. Chiefs Council	custom	312/30	1/0
Long Lake No. 58	Anishinabe Algonquian	Matawa F.N. Chiefs Council	Indian Act	1,035/388	1/217 hectares
McDowell Lake	Cree Algonquian	Keewaytinook/Okimakahac T.C.	custom	29/9	1/NYD
Magnetawan	Anishinabe Algonquian	Waabnoong Bemjiwang Assoc. of F.N.	Indian Act	192/66	1/4,715 hectares
Martin Falls	Anishinabe Algonquian	Matawa F.N. Chiefs Council	Indian Act	464/220	1/7,770 hectares
Matachewan	Anishinabe Algonquian	Wabun Tribal Council	Indian Act	419/64	1/4,159 hectares
Mattagami	Anishinabe Algonquian	Wabun Tribal Council	Indian Act	370/177	1/5,261 hectares
Michipicoten	Anishinabe Algonquian	Ojibway 1850 Treaty Council	Indian Act	602/61	2/3,630 hectares
Mishkeegogamang	Anishinabe Algonquian	unaffiliated	Indian Act	1,118/816	2/18,696 hectares
Missanabie Cree	Cree Algonquian	unaffiliated	custom	264/14	1/87 hectares
Mississauga	Anishinabe Algonquian	North Shore Tribal Council	Indian Act	871/431	1/1,977 hectares
Mississaugas of the Credit	Anishinabe Algonquian	unaffiliated	Indian Act	1,388/687	1/2,393 hectares
Mississaugas of Scugog Island	Anishinabe Algonquian	Ogemawahj Tribal Council	Indian Act	141/31	1/32 hectares
Mohawks of Akwesasne[12]	Mohawk Iroquoian	unaffiliated	custom	8,703/7,220	2/3,647 hectares
Mohawks of the Bay of Quinte/Tyendinaga	Mohawk Iroquoian	unaffiliated	Indian Act	6,569/1,750	1/7,362 hectares
Moose Cree	Cree Algonquian	Mushkegowuk Tribal Council	custom	3,021/1,391	2/17,393 hectares
Moose Deer Point	Anishinabe Algonquian	Ogemawahj Tribal Council	Indian Act	365/127	1/250 hectares
Moravian of the Thames	Delaware Algonquian	Southern F.N. Secretariat	custom	941/426	1/1,281 hectares
Munsee-Delaware Nation	Munsee-Delaware Alg.	Southern F.N. Secretariat	custom	449/173	1/1,054 hectares
Muskrat Dam	Cree Algonquian	Independent F.N. Alliance	custom	316/258	1/1,940 hectares
Naicatchewenin	Anishinabe Algonquian	Pwi-di-goo-zing Ne-yaa-zhing Advisory Services	Indian Act	295/228	3/2,489 hectares
Naotkamegwanning #158	Anishinabe Algonquian	Bimose Tribal Council	Indian Act	849/642	3/4,275 hectares
New Post	Cree Algonquian	Mushkegowuk Tribal Council	custom	185/73	2/2,188 hectares
Nibinamik	Anishinabe Algonquian	Mushkegowuk Tribal Council	custom	342/6	1/0 hectares
Nicickousemenecaning	Anishinabe Algonquian	Pwi-di-goo-zing Ne-yaa-zhing Advisory Services	Indian Act	199/125	4/4,086 hectares
Nippising First Nation	Anishinabe Algonquian	unaffiliated	Indian Act	1,781/768	1/21,007 hectares
North Caribou Lake	Cree Algonquian	Windigo First Nations Council	custom	749/664	1/9,172 hectares
North Spirit Lake	Cree Algonquian	Keewaytinook/Okimakahac T.C.	custom	388/299	1/1,816 hectares
Northwest Angle No. 33	Anishinabe Algonquian	Bimose Tribal Council	Indian Act	320/129	2/2,586 hectares
Northwest Angle No. 37	Anishinabe Algonquian	Bimose Tribal Council	Indian Act	252/116	5/5,310 hectares

(continues)

Name	*Linguistic Group*	*Affiliation*[1]	*Elections*[2]	*Population*[3]	*No. of Reserves/Size*	*Key Economic Activities*
Ochiichagwe'babigo'ining (Dalles)	Anishinabe Algonquian	unaffiliated	custom	266/118	1/3,257 hectares	
Ojibways of Onegaming	Anishinabe Algonquian	Pwi-di-goo-zing Ne-yaa-zhing Advisory Services	Indian Act	566/388	3/2,059 hectares	
Ojibways of Sucker Creek	Anishinabe Algonquian	United Chiefs and Councils of Manitoulin	custom	582/288	1/627 hectares	
Ojibways of the Pic River	Anishinabe Algonquian	unaffiliated	Indian Act	833/434	1/324 hectares	
Oneida Nation of the Thames	Oneida Iroquoian	Southern F.N. Secretariat	Indian Act	4,347/1,843	1/2,133 hectares	
Pays Plat	Anishinabe Algonquian	Ojibway 1850 Treaty Council	custom	176/90	1/225 hectares	
Pic Mobert	Anishinabe Algonquian	Ojibway 1850 Treaty Council	Indian Act	683/290	2/15 hectares	
Pikangikum	Anishinabe Algonquian	Independent F.N. Alliance	custom	1,664/1,568	1/906 hectares	
Poplar Hill	Anishinabe Algonquian	Keewaytinook/Okimakahac T.C.	custom	308/291	1/702 hectares	
Rainy River	Anishinabe Algonquian	Pwi-di-goo-zing Ne-yaa-zhing Advisory Services	Indian Act	726/275	2/2,464 hectares	
Red Rock	Anishinabe Algonquian	unaffiliated	custom	1,259/215	2/197 hectares	
Rocky Bay	Anishinabe Algonquian	Ojibway 1850 Treaty Council	custom	573/310	1/13 hectares	
Sachigo Lake	Cree Algonquian	Wabun Tribal Council	custom	582/377	3/8,145 hectares	
Sagamok Anishnawbek	Anishinabe Algonquian	North Shore Tribal Council	Indian Act	1,924/1,146	1/11,331 hectares	
Sand Point	Anishinabe Algonquian	unaffiliated	custom	136/20	0	
Sandy Lake	Cree Algonquian	Shibogama F.N. Council	custom	1,780/1,602	1/4,266 hectares	
Saugeen	Anishinabe Algonquian	unaffiliated	Indian Act	1,366/614	4/5,061 hectares	
Seine River	Anishinabe Algonquian	Pwi-di-goo-zing Ne-yaa-zhing Advisory Services	Indian Act	588/317	3/5,152 hectares	
Serpent River	Anishinabe Algonquian	North Shore Tribal Council	Indian Act	987/276	1/10,879 hectares	
Shawanaga	Anishinabe Algonquian	unaffiliated	custom	446/116	3/4,509 hectares	
Sheguiandah	Anishinabe/Ottawa	United Chiefs and Councils of Manitoulin	Indian Act	273/132	1/2,070 hectares	
Sheshegwaning	Anishinabe Algonquian	United Chiefs and Councils of Manitoulin	Indian Act	351/135	1/2,023 hectares	
Shoal Lake No. 40	Anishinabe Algonquian	unaffiliated	Indian Act	412/220	2/2,751 hectares	
Six Nations of the Grand River[13]	Iroquoian	unaffiliated	Indian Act	19,298/9,747	2/18,270 hectares	
Slate Falls Nation	Cree Algonquian	Windigo F.N. Council	custom	171/33	1/NYD	
Stanjikoming	Anishinabe Algonquian	Pwi-di-goo-zing Ne-yaa-zhing Advisory Services	custom	88/53	2/1,563 hectares	
Temagami	Anishinabe/Cree	unaffiliated	custom	500/196	1/293 hectares	
Thessalon	Anishinabe Algonquian	North Shore Tribal Council	Indian Act	460/68	1/942 hectares	
Wabaseemoong Indep. Nations (Islington)	Anishinabe Algonquian	Bimose Tribal Council	Indian Act	1,401/867	3/11,834 hectares	
Wabauskang	Anishinabe Algonquian	Bimose Tribal Council	custom	188/59	1/3,254 hectares	
Wabigoon Lake Ojibway Nation	Anishinabe Algonquian	Bimose Tribal Council	Indian Act	409/155	1/5,209 hectares	
Wahgoshig	Cree/Anishinabe	Wabun Tribal Council	custom	213/98	1/7,770 hectares	
Wahnapitae	Anishinabe Algonquian	Waabnoong Bemjiwang Assoc. of F.N.	custom	270/28	1/1,036 hectares	

Wahta Mohawk	Mohawk Iroquoian	unaffiliated	custom	620/128	2/5,992 hectares	
Walpole Island	Anishinabe/Potawatomi	unaffiliated	Indian Act	3,332/1,924	1/15,891 hectares	
Wapekeka	Cree Algonquian	Shibogama F.N. Council	custom	289/286	2/5,631 hectares	
Wasauksing (Parry Island)	Anishinabe Algonquian	Waabnoong Bemjiwang Assoc. of F.N.	Indian Act	886/370	1/7,487 hectares	
Washagmis Bay (Rat Portage)	Anishinabe Algonquian	unaffiliated	Indian Act	210/146	1/3,237 hectares	
Wauzhushik Onigum	Anishinabe Algonquian	Bimose Tribal Council	custom	434/273	1/2,207 hectares	
Wawakapewin	Cree Algonquian	Shibogama F.N. Council	custom	34/21	1/NYD	
Webequie	Anishinabe Algonquian	Matawa F.N. Chiefs Council	custom	596/10	1/N/A	
Weenusk	Anishinabe/Cree	Mushkegowuk Tribal Council	custom	415/10	2/5,310 hectares	
West Bay	Anishinabe Algonquian	United Chiefs and Councils of Manitoulin	Indian Act	1,892/874	1/3,095 hectares	
Whitefish Lake	Anishinabe/Ottawa	North Shore Tribal Council	Indian Act	668/249	1/17,704 hectares	
Whitefish River	Anishinabe Algonquian	United Chiefs and Councils of Manitoulin	Indian Act	908/306	1/5,673 hectares	
Whitesand	Anishinabe Algonquian	Ojibway 1850 Treaty Council	custom	813/18	1/249 hectares	
Wikwemikong	Anishinabe/Ottawa	unaffiliated	Indian Act	5,969/2,659	2/46,702 hectares	
Wunnumin	Cree Algonquian	Southern F.N. Secretariat	custom	455/426	2/9,649 hectares	
Prince Edward Island						
Abegweit	Micmac Algonquian	N/A	N/A	296/209	3/140 hectares	U/R
Lennox Island	Micmac Algonquian	N/A	N/A	645/298	1/534 hectares	
Quebec[9]						
Abenakis de Wolinak	Abenaki Algonquian	U/R	Indian Act	311	79 hectares	crafts, businesses, tourism
Abitibiwinni Algonquin	Algonquin Algonquian		custom	672	90 hectares	crafts, businesses, forestry, trapping
Barrière Lake Algonquin	Algonquin Algonquian		custom	520	28 hectares	crafts, trapping
Betsiamites	Innu Algonquian		custom	2,752	25,536 hectares	businesses, fishing, forest, trapping
Chisasibi	Cree Algonquian		custom	2,715	1,309 square km.	construction, tourism, trapping
Eastman	Cree Algonquian		custom	483	489 square km.	crafts, businesses, tourism, trapping
Gaspé	Micmac Algonquian		custom	436	none	crafts, businesses
Gesgapegiag Mingan	Micmac Algonquian		Indian Act	936	182 hectares	crafts, businesses, tourism
Grande Lac Victoria/Kitcisakik	Algonquin Algonquian		custom	302	12 hectares	businesses, trapping
Huronne-Wendat	Huronne-Wendat Iroquoian		Indian Act	2,642	112 hectares	businesses
Kanawake/Doncaster	Mohawk Iroquoian		custom	7,924	5,059/7,896 hectares	businesses
Kenesatake/Doncaster	Mohawk Iroquoian		N/A	2,642	958/7,896 hectares	agriculture, crafts, businesses
Kipawa	Algonquin Algonquian		Indian Act	494	21 hectares	crafts, businesses, forestry, trapping
Kitigan Zibi	Anishinabe Algonquian		Indian Act	2,094	11,165 hectares	crafts, businesses, forestry, trapping
La Romaine	Innu Algonquian		custom	823	40 hectares	crafts, business, tourism, trapping
Lac St. Jean/Mashteuiatch	Innu Algonquian		custom	4,016	3,151 hectares	crafts, business, tourism
Lac Simon	Algonquin Algonquian		custom	1,104	275 hectares	crafts, businesses, forestry, trapping
Les Escoumins/Essipit	Innu Algonquian		custom	366	38 hectares	crafts, business, forestry, tourism
Listuguj	Micmac Algonquian		Indian Act	2,621	3,663 hectares	crafts, business, forestry, tourism
Long Point/Winneway	Algonquin Algonquian		custom	558	38 hectares	businesses, forestry, trapping
Manouane	Attikamek/Cree Algonquian		Indian Act	1,600	771 hectares	businesses, forestry, trapping

(continues)

Name	*Linguistic Group*	*Affiliation*[1]	*Elections*[2]	*Population*[3]	*No. of Reserves/Size*	*Key Economic Activities*
Mingan	Innu Algonquian		custom	416	3,888 hectares	crafts, businesses, tourism, trapping
Mistissini	Cree Algonquian		custom	2,445	1,380 square km.	business, logging, tourism, trapping
Montagnais de Schefferville/ Kawawachikamach	Innu Naskapi		custom	526	326 square km.	tourism, trapping
Natashquan	Innu Algonquian		custom	690	21 hectares	crafts, business, tourism, trapping
Nemaska	Cree Algonquian		custom	306	153 square km.	businesses, trapping
Obedjiwan	Attikamek/Cree Algonquian		custom	1,719	927 hectares	crafts, business, forest, trapping
Odanak	Abenaki Algonquian		Indian Act	1,458	607 hectares	crafts, businesses
Oujé-Bougoumou	Cree Algonquian		custom	559	land pending	minerals, tourism, trapping
Pakua Shipi	Innu Algonquian		custom	217	25 hectares	crafts, business, trapping
Schefferville/Matimekosh/ Lac-John	Innu Montagnais		custom	660	39 hectares	crafts, construction, trapping
Temiskaming	Algonquin Algonquian		Indian Act	1,241	2,428 hectares	farming, forest, business, trapping
Uashat/Maliotenam	Innu Algonquian		custom	2,758	108/499 hectares	crafts, businesses, forest, trapping
Viger/Whitworth/Cacouna	Malicite Algonquian		custom	425	173 hectares	N/A
Waskaganish	Cree Algonquian		custom	1,832	785 square km.	crafts, businesses, trapping
Waswanipi	Cree Algonquian		custom	1,249	598 square km.	crafts, fishing, forestry, trapping
Wemindji	Cree Algonquian		custom	1,048	513 square km.	crafts, business, tourism, trapping
Weymonatchie/Coucouache	Attikamek/Cree Algonquian		custom	1,056	2,983 hectares	crafts, business, forestry, trapping
Whapmagoostui	Cree Algonquian		custom	581	316 square km.	crafts, businesses, trapping
Wolf Lake/Hunter's Point	Algonquin Algonquian		custom	185	4 hectares	paper, businesses, trapping
Saskatchewan[14]						
Antahkakoop	Cree Algonquian	U/R	U/R	2,113	43,025 acres	farming, trapping, forestry
Beardy's/Okemasis	Cree Algonquian			2,123	28,012 acres	agriculture
Big River	Cree Algonquian			1,980	29,581 acres	farming, forestry, trapping, fishing
Birch Narrows FNB/Turnor Lake/Churchill Lake	Chipewyan Athapaskan			368	6,670 acres	trapping, fishing
Black Lake/Chicken	Chipewyan Athapaskan			1,299	81,344 acres	fishing, trapping
Buffalo River Dene Nation/ Peter Pond	Chipewyan Athapaskan			833	26,456 acres	trapping, fishing, forestry
Canoe Lake/Eagle Lake	Cree Algonquian			1,211	18,130 acres	hunting, fishing, trapping, crafts
Carry the Kettle/Assiniboine	Stoney/Dakota Siouan			1,615	40,695 acres	agriculture
Clearwater River Dene/ La Loche	Chipewyan Athapaskan			765	23,390 acres	trapping, fishing
Cote First Nation Band	Anishinabe Algonquian			2,105	22,920 acres	agriculture
Cowessess	Cree Algonquian			2,544	28,422 acres	agriculture, tourism
Cumberland House Cree Nation/Pine Bluff/Muskeg River/Budd's Point	Cree Algonquian			693	4,639 acres	forestry, trapping
Day Star	Cree Algonquian			363	15,360 acres	agriculture
English River/La Plonge/ Elak Dase/Knee Lake/ Dipper Rapids/	Chipewyan Athapaskan			969	22,924 acres	fishing, trapping

Wapachewunak/Ile-a-la-Crosse/Primeau Lake				
Fishing Lake First Nation Band	Anishinabe Algonquian	1,064	7,706 acres	agriculture
Flying Dust/Meadow Lake	Cree Algonquian	732	9,269 acres	agriculture, investments
Fond du Lac	Chipewyan Athapaskan	1,279	91,667 acres	trapping, commercial fishing
Gordon	Cree/Anishinabe Algonquian	2,210	31,325 acres	agriculture
Hatchet Lake/Lac la Hache	Chipewyan Athapaskan	984	27,228 acres	trapping, commercial fishing
Island Lake FNB/Ministikwan	Cree Algonquian	797	17,163 acres	farming, trapping, fishing
James Smith/Cumberland	Cree Algonquian	2,101	37,187 acres	land leases
Joseph Bighead	Cree Algonquian	606	11,572 acres	farming, gas, oil
Kahkewistahaw	Cree Algonquian	1,074	19,457 acres	agriculture, recreation
Kawacatoose	Cree Algonquian	1,837	19,016 acres	agriculture
Keeseekoose	Anishinabe Algonquian	1,419	11,011 acres	agriculture
Key	Anishinabe Algonquian	823	14,933 acres	agriculture
Kinistin	Anishinabe Algonquian	637	11,199 acres	agriculture
Lac La Ronge	Cree Algonquian	5,714	13/102,748 acres	ag. leases, tourism, comm. fishing
Little Black Bear	Cree Algonquian	343	17,006 acres	agriculture
Little Pine	Cree Algonquian	1,167	17,267 acres	agriculture
Lucky Man	Cree Algonquian	79	7,869 acres	N/A
Makwa Mahgaiehcan	Cree Algonquian	916	14,792 acres	agriculture, tourism
Mistawasis	Cree Algonquian	1,555	31,110 acres	agriculture
Montreal Lake	Cree Algonquian	2,238	20,443 acres	trap, construction, forestry, fishing
Moosomin	Cree Algonquian	1,012	17,261 acres	agriculture
Mosquito/Grizzly Bear's Head/Lean Man	Stoney Siouan	925	31,499 acres	agriculture
Muscowpetung/Hay Grounds	Anishinabe/Cree Algonquian	936	20,634 acres	agriculture
Muskeg Lake	Cree Algonquian	1,170	17,708 acres	agriculture
Muskoday First Nation Band	Cree Algonquian	1,034	23,832 acres	agriculture
Muskowekwan	Anishinabe Algonquian	1,080	16,479 acres	agriculture
Nekaneet	Cree Algonquian	294	3,037 acres	agriculture
Ocean Man	Stoney Siouan/Cree Alg.	287	10,201 acres	agriculture
Ochapowace	Cree Algonquian	995	34,624 acres	agriculture, construction
Okanese	Cree/Anishinabe Algonquian	398	14,744 acres	agriculture
One Arrow	Cree Algonquian	937	10,209 acres	agriculture
Onion Lake/Seekaskootch/Makaoo	Cree Algonquian	2,836	43,306 acres	agriculture
Pasqua First Nation Band	Anishinabe/Cree Algonquian	1,297	22,141 acres	agriculture
Peepeekisis	Cree Algonquian	1,732	27,180 acres	agriculture
Pelican Lake/Chitek Lake	Cree Algonquian	803	8,705 acres	forest, tourism, farming, trapping
Peter Ballantyne Cree Nation Band	Cree Algonquian	5,306	9/33,000 acres	fishing, forestry, trapping
Pheasant Rump Nakota	Nakota/Stoney Siouan/Anishinabe/Cree	255	19,684 acres	agriculture
Piapot	Cree Algonquian	1,489	20,536 acres	agriculture
Poundmaker	Cree Algonquian	976	19,205 acres	agriculture
Red Earth	Cree Algonquian	867	5,637 acres	trapping, construction, forestry

(continues)

Name	*Linguistic Group*	*Affiliation*[1]	*Elections*[2]	*Population*[3]	*No. of Reserves/Size*	*Key Economic Activities*
Red Pheasant	Cree Algonquian			1,473	24,320 acres	agriculture
Sakimay	Anishinabe Algonquian (Plains Ojibway)			1,076	21,683 acres	agriculture, recreation
Saulteaux	Anishinabe Algonquian			742	14,387 acres	agriculture
Shoal Lake of the Cree Nation	Cree Algonquian			557	3,632 acres	forestry
Standing Buffalo	Lakota Siouan			869	5,566 acres	agriculture
Star Blanket/ Wa-Pii-Moos-Toosis	Cree Algonquian			411	13,759 acres	agriculture
Sturgeon Lake	Cree Algonquian			1,686	22,654 acres	land leasing, gravel
Sweetgrass	Cree Algonquian			1,244	42,078 acres	agriculture
Thunderchild	Cree Algonquian			1,621	16,791 acres	agriculture
Wahpeton Dakota Nation Band	Dakota Siouan			236	3,822 acres	agriculture
Waterhen Lake	Cree Algonquian			1,250	19,699 acres	trapping, forestry, tourism
White Bear	Cree/Anishinabe Alg./Stoney Siouan			1,524	42,539 acres	agriculture, recreation
Whitecap Dakota/Sioux FNB	Dakota Siouan			316	4,286 acres	agriculture
Witchekan Lake	Cree Algonquian			411	4,225 acres	farming, trapping, fishing, forestry
Wood Mountain	Lakota Siouan			158	5,811 acres	agriculture
Yellowquill/Nutt Lake	Anishinabe Algonquian			1,903	14,476 acres	agriculture
Yukon Territory[15]						
Carcross/Tagish	Tlingit/Tagish Athapaskan	Tlingit Tribal Council	custom	483/127	325 hectares	N/A
Champagne/Aishihik	S. Tutchone Athapaskan	Southern Tutchone Tribal Council	custom	678/12	none	N/A
Dease River First Nation	Kaska/Tahtan Athapaskan	Kaska Tribal Council	custom	146/61	4/80 hectares	garage, grocery store
Kluane First Nation	Tutchone Athapaskan	Southern Tutchone Tribal Council	custom	148/1	334 hectares	general store, jam mfg.
Kwanlin Dun First Nation	Tutchone Athapaskan	N/A	custom	1,130/46	1/129 hectares plus 348 hectares	N/A
Laird River	Kaska Athapaskan	Kaska Tribal Council	custom	891/143	9/1,432 hectares plus 328 hectares	N/A
Little Salmon-Carmacks	N. Tutchone Athapaskan	Northern Tutchone Council	custom	484/0	none	trading post, crafts
Lower Post First Nation	Kaska Athapaskan	Kaska Tribal Council	N/A	160/160	N/A	N/A
Na-Cho-Ny'a'k-Dun	N. Tutchone Athapaskan	Northern Tutchone Council	custom	434/156	129 hectares	N/A
Ross River Band	Kaska/Slavey Athapaskan	Kaska Tribal Council	custom	400/9	60 hectares	general store, land development
Selkirk First Nation	N. Tutchone Athapaskan	Northern Tutchone Council	N/A	469/275	none	N/A
Ta'an Kwach'an Council	Tutchone Athapaskan	Southern Tutchone Tribal Council	not yet officially recognized			
Taku River Tlingits	Tlingit Athapaskan	Tlingit Tribal Council	none	351/93	10/1,278 hectares	sawmill, construction, fishing
Teslin Tlingit Council	Tlingit Athapaskan	Tlingit Tribal Council	custom	512/185	3/187 hectares	N/A
Tr'on dek Hwech'in	Han Athapaskan	N/A	custom	570/3	406 hectares plus 366 hectares	mining, fishing, mushrooms
Vuntut Gwitchin (Old Crow)	Kutchin Athapaskan	N/A	custom	432	none	N/A
White River First Nation	S. Tutchone/Upper Tanana Athapaskan	N/A	custom	124/0	0 reserves plus 35 hectares	tourism, crafts

Nunavut Territory[16] (1999)[17]

Arviat/Eskimo Pt.	Inuktitut	U/R	U/R	1,323	U/R	crafts, businesses, hunt, trap
Baker Lake/Qamanittuaq	Inuktitut			1,186		hunt, trap, fish, crafts, businesses
Bathurst Inlet/Kinggauk	Inuinnaqtun			53		
Broughton Island/ Qikiqtarjvaq	Inuktitut			461		whaling, sealing, tourism
Cambridge Bay/Ikaluktutiak	Inuinnaqtun			1,118		communications, fishing, trap
Cape Dorset/Kingniat	Inuktitut			961		crafts, tourism, sealing
Chesterfield Inlet/ Igluligaarjuk	Inuktitut			316		hunt, trap, tourism, businesses
Clyde River/Kangiqlugaapik	Inuktitut			565		crafts, tourism, whaling, sealing
Coral Harbour/Salliq	Inuktitut			578		whaling, sealing, tourism
Gjoa Haven/Uqsuqtuq	Inuktitut			783		hunting, fishing, tourism
Grise Fjord/Aujuittuq	Inuktitut			130		hunting, trapping, fishing, tourism
Hall Beach/Sanivajak	Inuktitut			526		tourism, businesses
Igloolik/Iglulik	Inuktitut			936		hunting, fishing, trapping, tourism
Iqaluit/Frobisher Bay	Inuktitut			3,552		govt., tourism, hunting
Kugluktuk/Coppermine	Inuinnaqtun			1,069		oil, gas, crafts, hunt, sealing, fish
Lake Harbour/Kimmirut	Inuktitut			366		whaling, sealing, tourism
Nanisivik	Inuktitut			193		mining, govt. services
Pangnirtung/Panniqtuug	Inuktitut			1,135		whaling, sealing, crafts coop
Pelly Bay/Arviliqjuat	Inuktitut			409		sealing, crafts, tourism
Pond Inlet/Mittimatalik	Inuktitut			974		hunt, fish, seal, trap, tourism
Rankin Inlet/Kangiqting	Inuktitut			1,706		cannery, tsp, comm, govt., hunt
Repulse Bay/Naujat	Inuktitut			488		sealing, whaling, hunt, trap, crafts
Resolute/Qausuittuq	Inuktitut			171		oil, gas, mining, businesses
Sanikiluaq/Belcher Islands	Inuktitut			526		fish, hunt, trap, businesses
Taloyoak/Spence Bay	Inuktitut			580		comm. fish, hunt, trap, crafts

1. British Columbia affiliations for the purposes of the British Columbia Treaty Commission
2. Band political structure includes a chief and one or more councilors. Many bands also have a subchief as well as officers.
3. Total population/population living on reserve(s) (total only if one figure)
4. Population figures as of September 1997
5. N/A: Not available or unknown
6. Population figures as of 1996
7. U/R: Unavailable or not relevant for this province
8. NYD: Not yet designated
9. Population as of 1994
10. Relocation planned
11. Populations as of June 1997; reserve data as of 1990
12. Political authority includes grand chiefs, councilors, and district chiefs.
13. Bay of Quinte Mohawk, Bearfoot Onondaga, Delaware, Konadaha Seneca, Lower Cayuga, Lower Mohawk, Niharondasa Seneca, Oneida, Onondaga Clear Sky, Tuscarora, Upper Cayuga, Upper Mohawk, Walker Mohawk
14. Membership as of 1994
15. Population as of 1997, status Indians only
16. Population as of 1991
17. April 1, 1999, is the date of the official existence of the Nunavut territory.

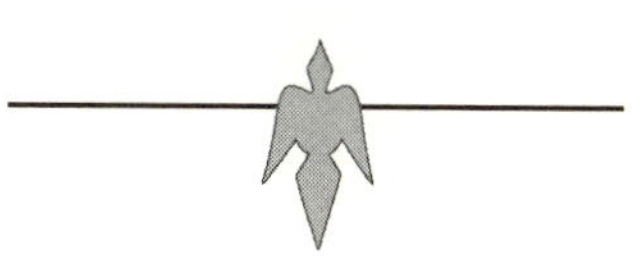

Appendix 2
Alaska Native Villages, by Language

Village	*Regional Corporation*	*Native Population (as of 1990)*	*Tribal Status*
Inupiaq			
Atqusuk	Arctic Slope	201	Traditional
Barrow	Arctic Slope	2,217	Traditional
Kaktovik	Arctic Slope	189	Traditional
Nuiqsut	Arctic Slope	328	Traditional
Point Hope	Arctic Slope	587	IRA[1]
Point Lay	Arctic Slope	113	IRA
Wainright	Arctic Slope	464	Traditional
Ambler	Nana	279	Traditional
Buckland	Nana	302	IRA
Deering	Nana	148	IRA
Kiana	Nana	360	Traditional
Kivalina	Nana	309	IRA
Kobuk	Nana	62	Traditional
Kotzebue	Nana	2,067	IRA
Noatak	Nana	322	IRA
Noorvik	Nana	498	IRA
Selawik	Nana	569	IRA
Shungnak	Nana	211	IRA
Elim	Bering Straits	242	IRA
Brevig Mission	Bering Straits	183	Traditional
Golovin (Chinik)	Bering Straits	118	Traditional
Inalik	Bering Straits	136	N/A[2]
Koyuk	Bering Straits	219	IRA
Shaktoolik[3]	Bering Straits	168	IRA
Shishmaref	Bering Straits	431	IRA
Solomon	Bering Straits	4	Traditional
Teller	Bering Straits	131	Traditional
Wales	Bering Straits	143	IRA
White Mountain	Bering Straits	158	IRA
Yup'ik			
St. Michael	Bering Straits	269	IRA
Stebbins	Bering Straits	379	IRA
Unalakleet	Bering Straits	534	IRA
Akiachak	Calista	457	IRA
Akiak	Calista	277	IRA

(continues)

Village	Regional Corporation	Native Population (as of 1990)	Tribal Status
Alakanuk	Calista	521	Traditional
Andreafsky	Calista	93	Traditional
Aniak	Calista	382	Traditional
Atmautluak	Calista	250	Traditional
Bethel/Orutsararmiut	Calista	2,986	Traditional
Bill Moore's Slough	Calista	N/A	Traditional
Chefornak	Calista	312	Traditional
Chevak	Calista	556	Traditional
Crooked Creek	Calista	96	Traditional
Eek	Calista	243	Traditional
Emmonak	Calista	591	Traditional
Georgetown	Calista	2	Traditional
Goodnews Bay	Calista	231	Traditional
Hamilton	Calista	N/A	Traditional
Hooper Bay	Calista	811	Traditional
Kalskag	Calista	146	Traditional
Kasigluk	Calista	405	Traditional
Kipnuk	Calista	458	Traditional
Kongiganak	Calista	286	Traditional
Kotlik	Calista	447	Traditional
Kwethluk	Calista	586	IRA
Kwigillingok	Calista	264	IRA
Lime Village	Calista	40	Traditional
Lower Kalskag	Calista	286	Traditional
Marshall	Calista	253	Traditional
Mekoryuk	Calista	176	IRA
Mountain Village/ Asa'carsarmiut	Calista	611	Traditional
Napaimute	Calista	4	Traditional
Napakiak	Calista	300	IRA
Napaskiak	Calista	211	Traditional
Newtok	Calista	193	Traditional
Nightmute	Calista	146	Traditional
Nunapitchuk	Calista	367	IRA
Ohogamiut	Calista	N/A	Traditional
Oscarville	Calista	52	Traditional
Paimiut	Calista	1	Traditional
Pilot Station	Calista	440	Traditional
Pitka's Point	Calista	129	Traditional
Platinum	Calista	59	Traditional
Quinhagak	Calista	401	IRA
Red Devil	Calista	27	Traditional
Russian Mission KU	Calista	233	Traditional
Russian Mission YU	Calista	159	Traditional
St.Mary's/Algaaciq	Calista	366	Traditional
Scammon Bay	Calista	331	Traditional

(continues)

Village	*Regional Corporation*	*Native Population (as of 1990)*	*Tribal Status*
Sheldon's Point	Calista	101	Traditional
Sleetmute	Calista	92	Traditional
Stony River	Calista	45	Traditional
Toksook Bay	Calista	401	Traditional
Tuluksak	Calista	342	IRA
Tuntutuliak	Calista	290	Traditional
Tununak	Calista	304	IRA
Aleknagik	Bristol Bay	154	Traditional
Clark's Point	Bristol Bay	53	Traditional
Dillingham	Bristol Bay	1,125	Traditional
Egegik[3]	Bristol Bay	86	Traditional
Ekuk	Bristol Bay	6	Traditional
Ekwok	Bristol Bay	67	Traditional
Igiugig	Bristol Bay	26	Traditional
Iliamna	Bristol Bay	62	Traditional
Ivanof Bay	Bristol Bay	33	Traditional
Kokhanok	Bristol Bay	137	Traditional
Koliganek	Bristol Bay	174	Traditional
Levelock	Bristol Bay	87	Traditional
Manokotak	Bristol Bay	368	Traditional
Naknek	Bristol Bay	236	Traditional
Newhalen	Bristol Bay	151	Traditional
New Stuyahok	Bristol Bay	375	Traditional
Nondalton	Bristol Bay	159	Traditional
Pedro Bay	Bristol Bay	38	Traditional
Pilot Point[3]	Bristol Bay	45	Traditional
Portage Creek	Bristol Bay	44	Traditional
South Naknek	Bristol Bay	108	Traditional
Togiak	Bristol Bay	535	Traditional
Twin Hills	Bristol Bay	61	Traditional
Ugashik[3]	Bristol Bay	11	Traditional
Alutiiq			
Chignik	Bristol Bay	85	Traditional
Chignik Lagoon	Bristol Bay	30	Traditional
Chignik Lake	Bristol Bay	122	Traditional
Perryville	Bristol Bay	102	IRA
Port Heiden/Meshick	Bristol Bay	86	Traditional
Afognak	Koniag	3	Traditional
Akhiok	Koniag	72	Traditional
Kaguyak	Koniag	N/A	Traditional
Karluk	Koniag	65	IRA
Larsen Bay	Koniag	124	Traditional
Old Harbor	Koniag	252	Traditional
Ouzinkie	Koniag	178	Traditional

(continues)

Village	Regional Corporation	Native Population (as of 1990)	Tribal Status
Port Lions	Koniag	150	Traditional
Uyak	Koniag	N/A	N/A
Woody Island/Lesnoi	Koniag	3	Traditional
English Bay/Nanwalek	Chugach	144	Traditional
Port Graham	Chugash	150	Traditional
Tatitlek	Chugash	103	IRA
Unangan/Aleut (excluding western islands)			
Akutan	Aleut	80	Traditional
Atka	Aleut	67	IRA
Belkofski	Aleut	10	Traditional
False Pass	Aleut	52	Traditional
King Cove/Agdaagux	Aleut	177	Traditional
Nelson Lagoon	Aleut	167	Traditional
Nikolski	Aleut	29	IRA
Pauloff Harbor	Aleut	N/A	Traditional
St. George	Aleut	131	IRA
St. Paul	Aleut	504	IRA
Sand Point/ Qagan Tayagungin	Aleut	433	Traditional
Unalaska/Qawalangin	Aleut	259	Traditional
Unga	Aleut	N/A	Traditional
Tlingit			
Angoon	Sealaska	525	IRA
Chilkat	Sealaska	113	IRA
Hoonah	Sealaska	534	IRA
Kake	Sealaska	514	IRA
Yakutat	Sealaska	294	Traditional
Haida			
Craig	Sealaska	288	IRA
Hydaburg	Sealaska	342	IRA
Kasaan	Sealaska	29	IRA
Klawock	Sealaska	392	IRA
Tsimshian			
Saxman	Sealaska	284	IRA
Ahtna			
Chistochina	Ahtna	37	Traditional
Chitina	Ahtna	23	Traditional
Copper Ctr/Kluti-kaah	Ahtna	155	Traditional
Gakona	Ahtna	0	Traditional

(continues)

Village	Regional Corporation	Native Population (as of 1990)	Tribal Status
Gulkana	Ahtna	61	Traditional
Mentasta Lake	Ahtna	70	Traditional
Slana	Ahtna	4	N/A
Tazlina	Ahtna	4	Traditional
Tanaina			
Alexander	Cook Inlet	2	
Eklutna	Cook Inlet	42	Traditional
Knik	Cook Inlet	31	Traditional
Ninilchik	Cook Inlet	58	Traditional
Salamatof	Cook Inlet	104	Traditional
Seldovia	Cook Inlet	48	IRA
Tyonek	Cook Inlet	142	IRA
Tanana			
Cantwell[3]	Ahtna	33	Traditional
Dot Lake	Doyon	38	Traditional
Healy Lake	Doyon	40	Traditional
Manley Hot Springs	Doyon	14	Traditional
Minto	Doyon	212	IRA
Nenana	Doyon	188	Traditional
Northway	Doyon	79	Traditional
Rampart	Doyon	64	Traditional
Tanacross	Doyon	100	IRA
Tanana	Doyon	270	IRA
Tetlin	Doyon	83	IRA
Han			
Circle	Doyon	63	IRA
Eagle	Doyon	5	IRA
Kutchin (Gwich'in)			
Anaktuvuk Pass	Arctic Slope	220	Traditional
Arctic Village	Doyon	90	Traditional
Beaver	Doyon	98	Traditional
Birch Creek	Doyon	38	Traditional
Chalkyitsik	Doyon	83	Traditional
Evansville	Doyon	19	Traditional
Fort Yukon	Doyon	493	IRA
Stevens Village	Doyon	93	IRA
Venetie	Doyon	171	Traditional
Koyukon			
Alatna[3]	Doyon	29	Traditional

(continues)

Village	*Regional Corporation*	*Native Population (as of 1990)*	*Tribal Status*
Allakaket[3]	Doyon	160	Traditional
Galena/Louden	Doyon	377	Traditional
Hughes	Doyon	50	Traditional
Huslia	Doyon	188	Traditional
Kaltag	Doyon	222	Traditional
Koyukuk	Doyon	123	Traditional
Nulato	Doyon	348	Traditional
Ruby	Doyon	126	Traditional
Holikachuk			
Grayling/Holikachuk	Doyon	194	IRA
Takotna[3]	Doyon	17	Traditional
Kolchan (Upper Kuskokwim)			
Nikolai[3]	Doyon	97	Traditional
Telida[3]	Doyon	32	Traditional
Ingalik			
Anvik	Doyon	75	Traditional
Holy Cross	Doyon	259	Traditional
McGrath[3]	Doyon	248	Traditional
Shageluk	Doyon	132	IRA

1. Indian Reorganization Act
2. Unavailable or not relevant
3. Status uncertain

Appendix 3
ANCSA Village Corporations
(data are as of 1980)

Ahtna Region
Atna, Incorporated
Chitina Native Corporation

Aleut Region
Akutan Corporation
Atxam Corporation
Belkofski Corporation
Cahluka Corporation
Isanotski Corporation
King Cove Corporation
Nelson Lagoon Corporation
Ounalashka Corporation
Sanak Corporation
Shumagin Corporation
St. George Tanaq Corporation
Tanadgusix Corporation
Unga Corporation

Arctic Slope Region
Atqusuk Corporation
Cully Corporation
Kaktovik Inpiat Corporation
Kuukpik Corporation
Nunamiut Corporation
Olgoonik Corporation
Tigara Corporation
Ukpeagvik Inupiat Corporation

Bering Straits Region
Brevig Mission Native Corporation
Council Native Corporation
Elim Native Corporation
Golovin Native Corporation
King Island Native Corporation
Koyuk Native Corporation
Mary's Igloo Native Corporation
Savoonga Native Corporation
Shaktoolik Native Corporation
Shishmaref Native Corporation
Sitnasuak Native Corporation
Sivuqaq Incorporated
Solomon Native Corporation
Stebbins Native Corporation
St. Michael Native Corporation
Teller Native Corporation
Unalakleet Native Corporation
Wales Native Corporation
White Mountain Native Corporation

Bristol Bay Region
Alaska Peninsula Corporation
Aleknagik Natives, Ltd.
Bay View Incorporated
Becharof Corporation
Chignik Lagoon Corporation
Chignik River, Ltd.
Choggiung, Ltd.
Ekwok Natives, Ltd.
Far West Incorporated
Igiugig Native Corporation
Iliamna Natives Limited
Kijik Corporation
Koliganek Natives, Ltd.
Levelock Natives, Ltd.
Manokotak Natives, Ltd.
Oceanside Corporation
Olsonville, Incorporated
Paug-vik Incorporated, Ltd.
Pedro Bay Native Corporation
Pilot Point Native Corporation
Saguyak Incorporated
Stuyahok, Ltd.
Tanalian, Inc.
Togiak Natives, Ltd.
Twin Hills Native Corporation

Calista Region
Akiachak, Limited
Alakanuk Native Corporation
Arviq Incorporated
Askinuk Corporation
Atmautluak, Limited
Azachorok, Incorporated
Bethel Native Corporation
Chefarnmute, Incorporated
Chevak Company Corporation
Chinuruk, Incorporated
Chuloonawick Corporation
Emmonak Corporation
Iqfijouaq Company
Kasigluk, Incorporated
Kokarmuit Corporation
Kongniglnilkomuit Yuita Corporation
Kotlik Yupik Corporation
Kugkaktlik, Incorporated
Kuitsarak, Incorporated
Kuskokwim Corporation
Kwethluk Incorporated
Kwik, Incorporated
Lime Village Company
Maserculiq, Incorporated
Napakiak Corporation
Napaskiak Corporation
Nerkilikmute Native Corporation
Newtok Corporation
Nima Corporation
Nunakauiak Yupik Corporation
Nunapiglluraq Corporation
Nunapitchuk, Limited
Oscarville Native Corporation
Paimuit Corporation
Pilot Station, Incorporated
Pitka's Point Native Corporation
Qanirtuuq, Incorporated
Qemirtalek Coast Corporation

Russian Mission Native Corporation
Sea Lion Corporation
St. Mary's Native Corporation
Swan Lake Corporation
Tulkisarmute, Incorporated
Tuntunrmiut Rinit Corporation
Tuntutuliak Land, Limited

Chugach Region
Chenega Corporation
English Bay Corporation
Eyak Corporation
Port Graham Corporation
Tatitlek Corporation
Grouse Creek Corporation (regional group)
Mt. Marathon Native Association (regional group)
Valdez Native Association (regional group)

Cook Inlet Region
Chickalook-Moose Creek Native Association, Inc.
Eklutna, Incorporated
Knikatnu, Incorporated
Ninilchik Native Association, Inc.
Salamatof Native Association, Inc.
Seldovia Native Association, Inc.
Tyonek Native Corporation
Alexander Creek, Incorporated (regional group)
Caswell Native Association (regional group)
Gold Creek-Susitna (regional group)
Montana Creek Native Association (regional group)
Point Possession, Inc. (regional group)
Kenai Native Association (historic village)

Doyon Region
Baan-O-Yeel Kon Corporation
Bean Ridge Corporation
Beaver Kwit'chin Corporation
Chalkyitsik Native Corporation
Danzhit Hanlaii Corporation
Deloycheet, Inc.
Dineega Corporation
Dinyea Corporation
Dot Lake Native Corporation
Evansville, Inc.
Gana-a 'Yoo, Ltd.
Gungwitchin Corporation
Gwitchyaa Zhee Corporation
Hee-Yea Lindge Corporation
Ingalik, Inc.
K'oyitl'ots'ina, Ltd.
Mendas Chaag Native Corporation
MTNT, Ltd.
Northway Natives, Inc.
Seth-de-ya-ah Corporation
Tanacross, Inc.
Tihteet'aii, Inc.
Toghotthele Corporation
Tozitna, Ltd.
Zho-Tse, Inc.

Koniag Region
Afognak Native Corporation
Akhiok-Kaguyak, Inc.
Anton Larsen, Inc.
Ayakulik, Inc.
Bells Flats Natives, Inc.
Leisnoi, Inc.
Litnik, Inc.
Natives of Kiodiak, Inc.
Old Harbor Native Corporation
Ouzinkie Native Corporation
Shuyak, Inc.
Uganik Natives, Inc.
Uyak, Inc.

Nana Region
Kikiktagruk Inupiat Corporation
Nana Corporation

Sealaska Region
Cape Fox Corporation
Goldbelt, Incorporated
Haida Corporation
Huna Totem Corporation
Kake Tribal Corporation
Kavilco, Incorporated
Klawock Heenya Corporation
Klukwan, Incorporated
Kootznoowoo, Incorporated
Shaan Seet, Incorporated
Shee Atika, Incorporated
Yak-tat-kwaan, Incorporated

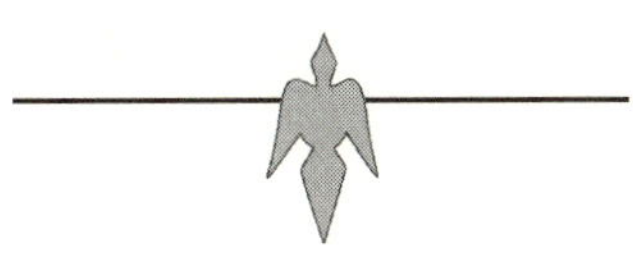

Illustration Credits

Chapter 1—The Southwest

4 [Banning swastika] UPI/Corbis-Bettmann
11 [Acoma Pueblo woman] Smithsonian Institute National Anthropological Archives #75–11253
12 [Geronimo] UPI/Corbis-Bettmann
28 [wickiups] Library of Congress USZ62–101255
30 [measuring cloth] Smithsonian Institute National Anthropological Archives #2575-I
40 [Havasupai students] Smithsonian Institute National Anthropological Archives #53,413-C
44 [katsina dolls] Courtesy Dept. of Library Services, American Museum of Natural History. Neg. no. 322167, Photo by Rota
45 [Hopi women] Library of Congress USZ62–94089
46 [adobe houses] Smithsonian Institute National Anthropological Archives #1846
53 [peaches] Smithsonian Institute National Anthropological Archives #56955
62 [Laguna men and women] Photo by Ben Wittick, Courtesy Museum of New Mexico, Neg. No. 15978 [Laguna]
64 [Mojave women] Library of Congress USZ62–101179
73 [weaving] Union Pacific Railroad
74 [Navajo couple] Photo by Ben Wittick, Courtesy Museum of New Mexico, Neg. No. 15713 [Navajo]
84 [Pima women] Smithsonian Institute National Anthropological Archives #2629
85 [Pima structures] Library of Congress USZ62–101173
124 [Two Tesuques] Smithsonian Institute National Anthropological Archives #2064
132 [Papago kitchen] Smithsonian Institute National Anthropological Archives #4548
136 [Yavapai scout] Smithsonian Institute National Anthropological Archives #56,889
146 [Zuñi pueblos] Smithsonian Institute National Anthropological Archives #2267-J

Chapter 2—California

150 [California baskets] Courtesy of California State Parks
160 [acorns] Courtesy of California State Parks
167 [Cupeño tribe] Courtesy of The Southwest Museum, Los Angeles. Photo #N.22962
169 [White Deerskin Dance] Field Museum
178 [Nisenan youth] Smithsonian Institute National Anthropological Archives #56,770
182 [conical houses] Courtesy of (California State Parks
189 [Pomo woman] Courtesy Dept. of Library Services, American Museum of Natural History. Neg. no. 32706B
190 [Pomo armor] National Anthropological Archives T11799, Smithsonian Institution
209 [Wiyot woman] Courtesy of (California State Parks
213 [Yokuts shaman] Courtesy of (California State Parks
217 [Yurok dwellings] Courtesy of (California State Parks
218 [Yurok men] Smithsonian Institute National Anthropological Archives #56,749
218 [Yurok headdress] Denver Art Museum 1944.50

Chapter 3—The Northwest Coast

225 [potlatch costume] Library of Congress USZ62–101170
226 [woman and child] Alaska State Library/Winter and Pond Collection/PCA 87–297
227 [dance robe] Courtesy of the Burke Museum of Natural History & Culture, cat.#117A, photo by Eduardo Calderon.
242 [Haida brass band] Smithsonian Institute National Anthropological Archives #72–496
243 [funeral of Chief Somihat] Smithsonian Institute National Anthropological Archives #72–514
245 [Haida chief] Royal British Columbia Museum, neg.#PN 701
246 [Haida clubs] Courtesy Dept. of Library Services, American Museum of Natural History. Neg. no. 323337, Photo by Lee Boltin
250 [winter initiation ceremony] Smithsonian Institute National Anthropological Archives #42,977-A

251 [thunderbird] Smithsonian Institute National Anthropological Archives #49,486
252 [cedar mask] Denver Art Museum 1948.229
258 [Maquinna] Smithsonian Institute National Anthropological Archives #43,219
266 [children] Smithsonian Institute National Anthropological Archives #53,502
276 [Southern Coast Salish performers] Smithsonian Institute National Anthropological Archives #56,752
291 [Klukwan] Alaska State Library/Winter and Pond Collection/PCA 87–0001
292 [totem poles] Smithsonian Institute National Anthropological Archives #14,838-C
293 [Tlingit blanket] Denver Art Museum 1926.26
295 [Mission Sunday School] Smithsonian Institute National Anthropological Archives #38,583-C

Chapter 4—The Great Basin

312 [Jack Wilson] SINNA #55,752
314 [Bannock family] SINNA #1713
316 [Bannock prisoners] SINNA #1712-A
319 [ramadas] Courtesy of (California State Parks
321 [Paiute men] Courtesy of The Southwest Museum, Los Angeles. Photo #PO.4879
324 [brush shelters] Smithsonian Institute National Anthropological Archives, #1633
327 [Chief Washakie's village] Smithsonian Institute National Anthropological Archives #1668
331 [Sacajawea] Courtesy Amon Carter Museum, Fort Worth, Texas
339 [Chief Ouray] Smithsonian Institute National Anthropological Archives, #1563
341 [Ute camp] Smithsonian Institute National Anthropological Archives, #1506
343 [Utes] Union Pacific Railroad
347 [Washoe man] Courtesy of (California State Parks

Chapter 5—The Plateau

352 [Secretary Ickes] UPI/Corbis-Bettmann
357 [Cayuse finery] Photograph by Lee Moorhouse; National Anthropological Archives 2899 B 2, Smithsonian Institution
361 [woman wearing Hudson's Bay blanket] Smithsonian Institute National Anthropological Archives #56,803
375 [Captain Jack, Wheum, and Buckskin Doctor] Smithsonian Institute National Anthropological Archives #86–4130
377 [Chief Joseph] Library of Congress
380 [Nez Percé warriors] Smithsonian Institute National Anthropological Archives #2987-B-12
384 [women on horseback] Montana Historical Society, Helena
385 [Chief Charlot] Montana Historical Society, Helena
402 [women hanging fish] Smithsonian Institute National Anthropological Archives #2890-B-34
405 [Wishram bride] Photograph by Edward S. Curtis; *The North American Indian,* Vol. VII: *Nez Perces, Wallawalla, Umatilla, Cayuse, Chinookan Tribes,* plate 281. Edward S. Curtis Norwood, MA: Plimpton Press, 1911

Chapter 6—The Great Plains

414 [buffalo hunt] Library of Congress
415 [buffalo hides] Kansas State Historical Society
423 [buffalo-skin tipis] Smithsonian Institute National Anthropological Archives #215-A
425 [Arikara men] Library of Congress USZ62–101186
425 [Arikara medicine man] Library of Congress USZ62–101188
428 [Assiniboine and Gros Ventre chiefs] Milwaukee Public Museum
432 [Blackfeet blow eagle-bone whistles] Smithsonian Institute National Anthropological Archives #56–814
434 [tipis] Library of Congress USZ62–101262
436 [Cheyenne dance] Library of Congress USZ62–101168
437 [meeting in Camp Weld] Colorado Historical Society
440 [White Antelope, Alights on a Cloud, and Little Chief] Smithsonian Institute National Anthropological Archives #240-A
441 [Comanche warrior] Smithsonian Institute National Anthropological Archives #55,490
448 [Indians on horseback] Union Pacific Railroad
449 [Indians near lodges] Union Pacific Railroad
451 [Crow home] Smithsonian Institute National Anthropological Archives #4644
453 [food rations] Smithsonian Institute National Anthropological Archives #56,630
454 [mass hanging of Santee Dakota Indians] Smithsonian Institute National Anthropological Archives #3485-D
455 [men in sweat lodge] Smithsonian Institute National Anthropological Archives #53,401-A

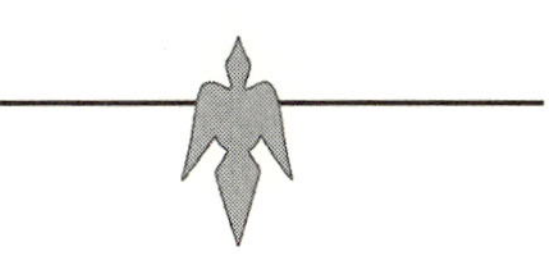

457 [Sam Kills Two] Nebraska State Historical Society
458 [cache pit] Courtesy Dept. of Library Services, American Museum of Natural History. Neg. no. 2A3100, Photo by Lee Boltin
458 [George Gillette] AP/Wide World Photos
468 [Kea-Boat] Smithsonian Institute National Anthropological Archives #1426-A
471 [beadwork] Smithsonian Institute National Anthropological Archives #56,388
473 [Red Cloud] Library of Congress
474 [Sitting Bull] Library of Congress
475 [Wounded Knee] Library of Congress
475 [Indians stand guard] UPI/Corbis-Bettmann
480 [Lakota Sioux Indians] Nebraska State Historical Society
481 [Girls in the sewing room] Smithsonian Institute National Anthropological Archives #53,372-B
482 [census] Smithsonian Institute National Anthropological Archives #2860-V8
484 [men's buffalo dance] *Bison-Dance of the Mandan Indians.* After Karl Bodmer; Joslyn Art Museum, Omaha. Gift of the Enron Art Foundation
489 [Struck by the Ree] Smithsonian Institute National Anthropological Archives #3545-A
497 [Omaha group] Smithsonian Institute National Anthropological Archives #47,704-K
506 [roach] Detroit Institute of Arts 81.94; [roach spreader] Detroit Institute of Arts 18–351
507 [Ponca Indians] Library of Congress USZ62–10128
514 [calumet and beaded pouch] Courtesy Dept. of Library Services, American Museum of Natural History. Neg. no. 332741, Photo by Logan
515 [Wichita shelters] Smithsonian Institute National Anthropological Archives #55,928

Chapter 7—The Southeast

531 [Sequoyah] Courtesy Dept. of Library Services, American Museum of Natural History. Neg. no. 319770, Photo by Lee Boltin
532 [Cherokee translation of Lincoln's pardon] From the Collection of Gilcrease Museum, Tulsa, acc. #3726.49
533 [Ayyuini] Smithsonian Institute National Anthropological Archives #1008
534 [Cherokee Ballplayers' Dance] Smithsonian Institute National Anthropological Archives #1044-B
541 [Sam Folsom] Smithsonian Institute National Anthropological Archives #1079
544 [cane blowgun] Smithsonian Institute National Anthropological Archives #1102-B-26
553 [Ku Klux Klan banner] AP/Wide World Photos
557 [Pocahontas] Library of Congress
559 [William Terrill Bradby] Smithsonian Institute National Anthropological Archives #893
560 [Powhatan family] Smithsonian Institute National Anthropological Archives #858
562 [Chief Osceola] Courtesy Dept. of Library Services, American Museum of Natural History. Neg. no. 33771, Photo by J. Kirschner
565 [Seminole family] Denver Art Museum
567 [Tunicas] Peabody Museum, Harvard University
571 [William Rickard and Wallace "Mad Bear" Anderson] Buffalo and Erie County Historical Society

Chapter 8—The Northeast Woodlands

584 [Abenaki men] Photo courtesy of The Newberry Library, Chicago
590 [Ojibwa pictographs] Photo courtesy of The Newberry Library, Chicago
592 [Ojibwa harvesting rice] Photo courtesy of The Newberry Library, Chicago
593 [Chippewa man] Library of Congress, LC-USZ62–101333
603 [house] Smithsonian Institute National Anthropological Archives #720-C
603 [delegation of Sauk, Fox, and Ioway chiefs] Photograph by Alexander Gardner; National Anthropological Archives 692, Smithsonian Institution
618 [Governor Nelson] State Historical Society of Wisconsin #WHi (X3) 14973
619 [Ernest Neconish with Senator Gaylord Nelson] AP/Wide World Photos
624 [Micmac delegation with Lord Lorne] National Archives of Canada, C-2295
629 [Private Huron Eldon Brant] National Archives of Canada, PA 130065
650 [three Maine Indians with Jesuit priest] Smithsonian Institute National Anthropological Archives #836
660 [Potawatomi women] Denver Art Museum 1701
662 [Keokuk] Smithsonian Institute National Anthropological Archives #617
662 [Sauk and Fox delegation] Smithsonian Institute National Anthropological Archives #691-B

672 [Tecumseh] Library of Congress
680 [Winnebago lodges] Smithsonian Institute National Anthropological Archives #45,479-F

Chapter 9—The Subarctic

691 [walrus and whale meat] Library of Congress USZ62–101258
693 [Ahtna woman and child] Smithsonian Institute National Anthropological Archives #75–5659
700 [Carrier Indian fishing] Canadian Museum of Civilization
704 [oxen meat] Canadian Museum of Civilization
705 [Mrs. Sam Zulin and children] Canadian Museum of Civilization
706 [Chilcotin Indians] Canadian Museum of Civilization
709 [small girl] Smithsonian Institute National Anthropological Archives #47,736
713 [Cree man imitating moose call] Smithsonian Institute National Anthropological Archives #56,963
715 [Bear Lake Dogrib boy] Canadian Museum of Civilization
717 [Dogrib moccasins, coat, and leggings] Canadian Museum of Civilization
719 [man with herring net] Canadian Museum of Civilization
721 [Ingalik men ice-fishing] Smithsonian Institute National Anthropological Archives #10,455-L-I
724 [moose-skin boats] Museum of Canadian Civilization
727 [New France natives] Photo courtesy of The Newberry Library, Chicago
729 [storage container] Courtesy Dept. of Library Services, American Museum of Natural History. Neg. no. 123954, Photo by Rota
738 [fishing nets] Canadian Museum of Civilization

Chapter 10—The Arctic

746 [Inuit hut and family] Library of Congress USZ62–101338
747 [whaling] Photo courtesy of The Newberry Library, Chicago
748 [ivory carver] Library of Congress USZ62–101243
749 [kayak] Smithsonian Institute National Anthropological Archives #34,358-B
749 [Arctic dwelling and storehouse] Smithsonian Institute National Anthropological Archives #33,370
751 [ball game using stuffed sealskin] Photo courtesy of The Newberry Library, Chicago
754 [seal's-head helmet] Peabody Museum, Harvard University
759 [Annie Iola] AP/Wide World Photos
761 [Inuit woman splits walrus hide] Alaska and Polar Regions Archives, Rasmuson Library, University of Alaska, Fairbanks, Geist Collection, Acc# 64–98–649N
766 [rifles] Alaska and Polar Regions Archives, Rasmuson Library, University of Alaska, Fairbanks, Lomen Family, Acc# 72–71–826N
770 [Moravian missionary] National Archives of Canada, C-124432
774 [*Madonna of the North*] Library of Congress USZ62–101165
779 [German missionaries with native population] Alaska and Polar Regions Archives, Rasmuson Library, University of Alaska, Fairbanks, Romig Collection, Acc# 90–43–200N
785 [tattooed woman] Smithsonian Institute National Anthropological Archives #46,736-H
789 [habitation on Unalaska Island] Peabody Museum, Harvard University
789 [illustration of the Inuit] National Archives of Canada, C-99320
790 [wooden visor] Smithsonian Institute National Anthropological Archives #36,727
791 [children in reindeer-drawn sleds] Alaska and Polar Regions Archives, Rasmuson Library, University of Alaska, Fairbanks, Van Valin Collection, Acc# 62–2036–195N
793 [Yup'ik storehouse] Smithsonian Institute National Anthropological Archives #56,720

About the Author

Barry Pritzker is currently working on a book about contemporary Native American communities for ABC-CLIO. He has contributed to the *Atlas of Native American History* and has written about Native Americans for the *Cambridge University Press Dictionary of American Biography.* A teacher of history and writing for seven years, he first taught at the Taos Pueblo Day School in New Mexico. He is also a former Fellow at the Newberry Library's D'Arcy McNickle Center for the History of the American Indian Summer Institute. His other written work includes books on Ansel Adams, Mathew Brady, and Edward Curtis as well as various articles and reviews in printed and electronic media. He lives with his wife and their two children in Tallahassee, Florida.

Index

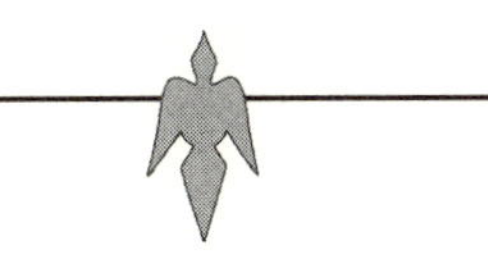

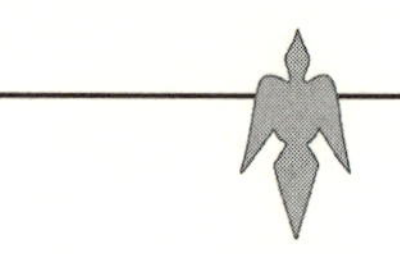

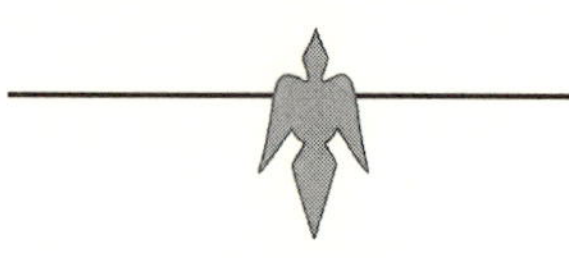

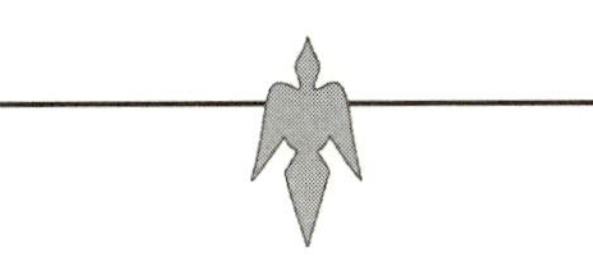

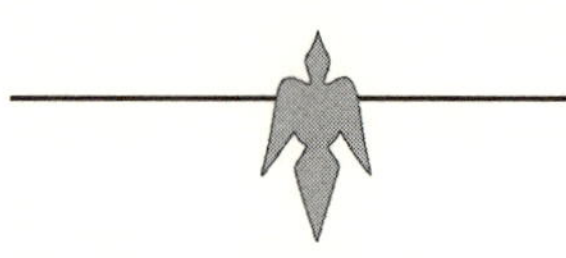

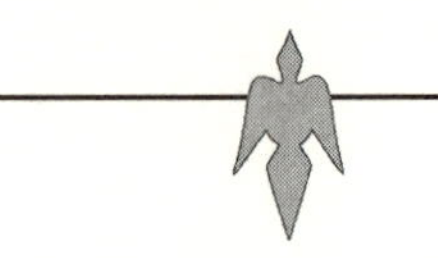

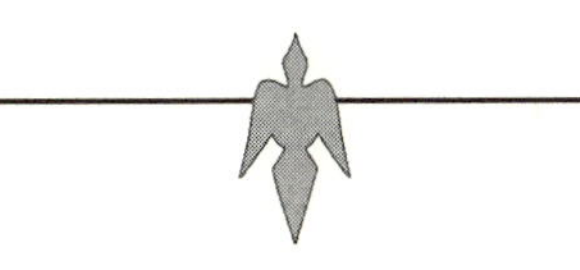

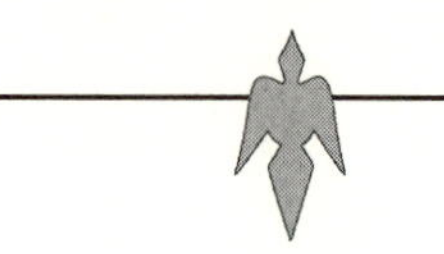

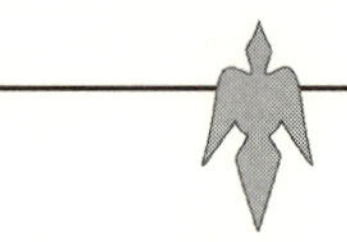

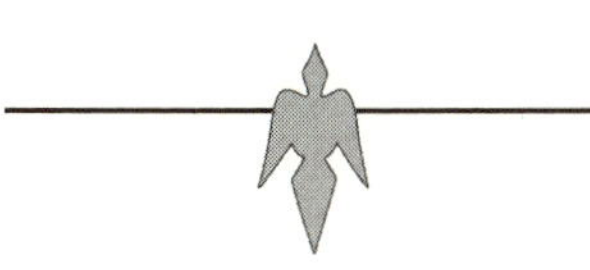

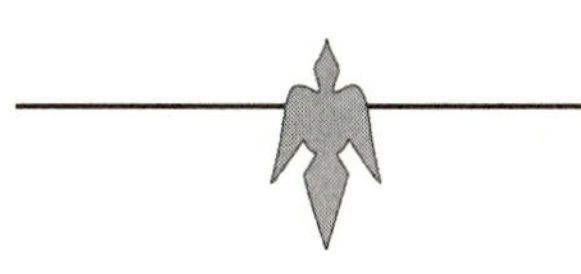

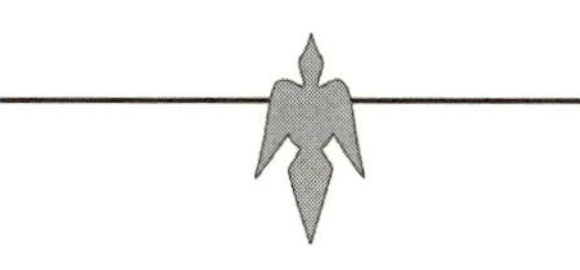

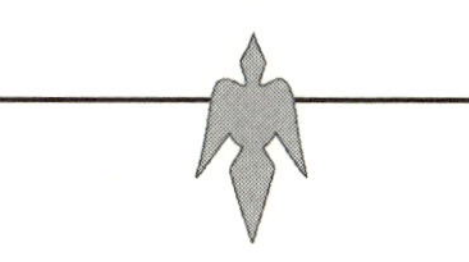

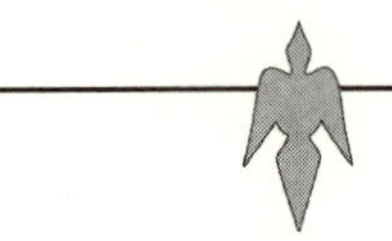